A BIBLIOGRAPHY OF THE WRITINGS OF
JONATHAN SWIFT

Sturter. Sheppard. Sc.

Captain Lemuel Gulliver, of
Redriff Ætat. suæ 58.

The frontispiece portrait of Capt. Lemuel Gulliver in the original state
without the legend around the oval frame. It was used only in the first
issue of the first edition of *Travels Into Several Remote Nations* (no. 289A).
(The University of Texas)

A BIBLIOGRAPHY OF THE WRITINGS OF
JONATHAN SWIFT

Second Edition, Revised and Corrected by
DR. H. TEERINK

Edited by
ARTHUR H. SCOUTEN

PHILADELPHIA
UNIVERSITY OF PENNSYLVANIA PRESS

© 1963 by the Trustees of the University of Pennsylvania

Published in Great Britain, India, and Pakistan
by the Oxford University Press
London, Bombay, and Karachi

Library of Congress Catalog Card Number: 62-11270

7373
Printed and bound in Great Britain
by William Clowes and Sons, Limited, London and Beccles

PUBLISHER'S PREFACE

After it was decided to publish Dr. Teerink's revision of his Swift bibliography, two major problems had to be resolved. First, the physical state of the manuscript: Dr. Teerink's additions had expanded it to where it could no longer be included in a single volume, and much of this new material was in longhand and required editing. Second, the completion of Dr. Teerink's work: he had not finished making certain projected changes, particularly his intended task of renumbering all the entries. Moreover, Dr. Teerink was ill at the time, and, since the University of Pennsylvania Library had acquired his Swift collection, he no longer had the books at hand with which to verify his material. At this point, A. H. Scouten, professor of English in the College, was requested to prepare the bibliography for the press.

Professor Scouten's first step was to seek advice from eighteenth-century scholars and bibliographers regarding Dr. Teerink's plan for renumbering the entries. Without exception, everyone he consulted advised him against discarding the old numbers, in view of the way the present Teerink numbering is embedded in books and articles on Swift and in dealers' catalogues. Dr. Teerink's reason for wishing to change the numbers requires an explanation of his policy in compiling this new edition.

The original printing, in 1937, was greeted with rather sharp criticism by the reviewers, who did not impugn the accuracy of the contents but complained of the absence of full bibliographical descriptions, disputed the attribution to Swift of several works which did not belong in the canon, and questioned the organization of the material. Furthermore, although the book was divided into overlapping categories, *e.g.*, "Collected Works," "A Tale of a Tub," "Gulliver's Travels," and "Separate Works," some critics argued that the writings of a major author should be listed in chronological order. Finally, there were objections to Dr. Teerink's inclusion under "Collected Works" of any book or pamphlet which happened to contain more than a single piece by Swift. When he began to transfer such entries from "Collected Works," the initial section of his opus, he observed of course that such a transfer immediately disarranged his old numbering system. Accordingly, he had a real reason for wishing to renumber, as all entries whose position had been changed would be difficult for the reader to find by number. Our resolution of this problem has been to retain the original numbers but to list in a table at the beginning the pages on which all Teerink numbers are located.

Admitting the logic of arranging all the entries in chronological order, one can still see some advantages in Dr. Teerink's organization for the present volume. It is useful to have all of the Faulkner editions placed together. It is convenient for the reader to have all of the printings of *Gulliver's Travels* in one section (where they are arranged chronologically, by country) rather than having to search through the entire book for them.

The revisions and additions which Dr. Teerink has made in the present work are as follows: (1) He has provided full physical descriptions for all important books and pamphlets. (2) He has brought the work up to date by including the bibliographical findings of Swift scholarship during the past twenty-five years and by listing books and pamphlets which he had not seen or known about in 1937. (3) He has removed a considerable number of pieces attributed to Swift, either by dropping them or by relegating them to the section entitled "Doubtful." (4) He has detached books or pamphlets containing several pieces from "Collected Works" and placed them in other sections. (5) He has transferred entries of works containing some contemporary comment on a work by Swift from the end of the book to where the work by Swift has been entered. These are indeed substantial contributions and would seem to justify a second verdict from Prince Posterity.

A statement needs to be made concerning the nature and extent of the editorial work done by Professor Scouten. He has verified all of the physical descriptions of the books and pamphlets that were contained in the Teerink Collection, now in the Library of the University of Pennsylvania, and has made minor reforms in using bibliographical symbols where Dr. Teerink gave a lengthier verbal account. In order to hold the work to one volume, he has arbitrarily cut off all entries after Sir Walter Scott's edition of 1814 (except under "Biography and Criticism," where the entries extended to 1895). He has completed the replacement of contemporary criticism begun by Dr. Teerink. He has assigned numbers to new entries established by Dr. Teerink, has provided a table showing the location of all entries, and has made an index. He has silently omitted entries of some works not belonging in the Swift canon, particularly the John Bull pamphlets. In only one place has he revised any entries; in the light of new information, he has rearranged those for "Verses on the Death of Dr. Swift."

Some of the items in Dr. Teerink's personal collection were destroyed during the allied attack on Arnheim during World War II. For this reason many of the copies described in the revision no longer exist and were not in the Teerink Collection when it was acquired by the University of Pennsylvania. The present editor Dr. Scouten, following Dr. Teerink's notes towards a revision, adheres to the practice of locating the destroyed items in Teerink's "own" collection. For a full account of the circumstances, see A. H. Scouten, "Materials for the Study of Swift at the University of Pennsylvania," *The Library Chronicle*, XXIII (1957), 47–52. Many of the new items catalogued by Dr. Teerink are descriptions of copies he saw at the home of J. Barry Brown, Esq., Naas, Co. Kildare, Ireland, on his last trip abroad. All the books and pamphlets pertaining to Swift in Brown's excellent collection are now in the possession of the Huntington Library.

The editorial work was long in completion because Professor Scouten was also preparing a history of the London theatres, and I wish to thank the University Committee for the Advancement of Research for two generous grants, and the English Department and the Library for funds enabling Douglas Wilson to assist Professor Scouten in verifying the entries and preparing the text for the press during the past two years. Acknowledgment is due to a number of scholars for providing advice or data on various cruxes, particularly Maurice Johnson and M. A. Shaaber, of the University of Pennsylvania, D. F. Foxon, of the British Museum, and G. W. Cottrell, Jr., of the Widener Library at Harvard.

THOMAS YOSELOFF
Director, University of Pennsylvania Press

TABLE OF SYMBOLS AND ABBREVIATIONS

Descriptive   adv(s)., advertisement(s); bl., blank; frontisp., frontispiece; f.t., full title; h.t., half title; i.a., *inter alia*; L.P., large paper; n.d., no date; Sm.P., small paper; t.p., title page.

Armagh   Public Library at Armagh, Ireland.

Barry Brown   Collection of J. Barry Brown, Esq., Naas, Co. Kildare, Ireland, now in the Huntington Library, San Marino, California.

Bodl.   Bodleian Library, Oxford.

Case   Arthur E. Case. *A Bibliography of English Poetical Miscellanies, 1521–1750.* Oxford, 1935.

Chapin   Chapin Library, Williams College, Williamstown, Massachusetts.

Clark   Clark Memorial Library, Los Angeles, California.

Corresp.   F. Elrington Ball, ed. *Correspondence of Jonathan Swift, D.D.* 6 vols. London, 1910–1914.

Danielson   Henry Danielson. *Bibliographies of Modern Authors.* London, 1921.

Dobell   Percy J. Dobell. *A Catalogue of Works by Dr. Jonathan Swift....* (cat. no. 105). London, [1933].

Dyce   Dyce Collection, Victoria and Albert Museum, London.

Elr. Ball   F. Elrington Ball. *Swift's Verse; An Essay....* London, [1929].

Eton   Eton College Library.

Evans   Charles Evans. *American Bibliography.* 14 vols. Chicago, 1903–1959.

Folger   Folger Shakespeare Library, Washington, D.C.

Forster   Forster Collection, Victoria and Albert Museum, London.

Freiburg   University Library, Freiburg im Bresgau.

Goldsmith's   Goldsmith's Library, Imperial Institute, London.

Griffith   Reginald Harvey Griffith. *Alexander Pope; A Bibliography.* Austin, 1922–27.

Guildhall   Guildhall Library, London.

Heidelberg   University Library, Heidelberg.

Hubbard   Lucius L. Hubbard. *Contributions Towards a Bibliography of Gulliver's Travels....* Chicago, 1922.

Huntington   Huntington Library, San Marino, California. SEE ALSO Barry Brown.

K.I.   King's Inn, Dublin.

Kon. Bibl.   Koninklijke Bibliotheek, The Hague.

Lambeth   Lambeth Palace Library, London.

Marsh   Archbishop Marsh's Library, Dublin.

Mazarine   Mazarine, Paris.

Mich.   University of Michigan Library, Ann Arbor.

Monck Mason   William Monck Mason. *Hibernia Antiqua et Moderna....* Dublin, 1819

Nic. Smith   D. Nichol Smith, ed. *The Letters of Jonathan Swift to Charles Ford.* Oxford, 1935.

NYPL   New York Public Library.

Penn   University of Pennsylvania Library, Philadelphia.

Poems   Harold Williams, ed. *The Poems of Jonathan Swift*. 3 vols. Oxford, 1958.

Powell Stewart Powell Stewart. *British Newspapers and Periodicals, 1632–1800*. Austin, 1950.

Preuszische   Preuszische Staatsbibliothek, Berlin. Holdings are now subject
  Staatsbibl.   to a disputed division between the Öffentliche Wissenschaftliche Bibliothek, East Berlin, and the Westdeutsche Bibliothek, Marburg.

P.R.O.   Public Record Office, London.

Prose Works   Herbert Davis, ed. *The Prose Works of Jonathan Swift*. 14 vols. Oxford, 1939, *et seq.*

R.I.A.   Royal Irish Academy, Dublin.

Rothschild   Lord Rothschild. *The Rothschild Library. A Catalogue of the Collection of Eighteenth-Century Printed Books and Manuscripts.* . . . 2 vols. Cambridge, 1954.

Sion   Sion College Library, London.

Smith Coll.   Smith College Library, Northampton, Massachusetts.

T.C.D.   Trinity College Library, Dublin.

Texas   University of Texas Library, Austin.

T.Sc.   Temple Scott, ed. *The Prose Works of Jonathan Swift, D.D.* 12 vols. London, 1897–1908.

U.L.C.   University Library, Cambridge.

Wagner   Henry R. Wagner. *Irish Economics 1700–1783: A Bibliography with Notes*. London, 1907.

Williams   Collection of Sir Harold Williams, 43 Albert Court, Kensington Gore, London.

TABLE OF LOCATION OF TEERINK NUMBERS

Numbers not included in the list are those which have been omitted
from this revised edition.

CONTENTS

LIST OF CHARTS

A BIBLIOGRAPHY OF THE WRITINGS OF
JONATHAN SWIFT

SECTION I

COLLECTED WORKS

✠✠✠

2. (1) Miscellanies / in / Prose / and / Verse. / [ornament] / *London:* / Printed for John Morphew, / near *Statio- | ners Hall.* MDCCXI.

(a) First edition, first state. 8vo; A–Dd⁸; A 1ʳ Title, verso blank; A 2ʳ–4ᵛ 'The Publisher to the Reader'; A 5ʳ–7ᵛ contents; A 7ᵛ blank; A 8ʳ (used for cancelling G 6 & 7), verso blank; B 1ʳ–Dd 8ᵛ Text. Copies: British Museum 838 g 1 and Rothschild 2015.

(b) Second state. 8vo; A⁷, B–F⁸, G 1–5, A 8, G 8, H–Dd⁸; 2 pp. (t. + bl.), 6 pp. (The Publisher to the Reader), 5 pp. (Contents) + bl., 1–91 + bl., 95–416. B 4 signed C 4. Published Feb. 27, 1711 (adv. in *The Post Boy*, Feb. 24–27; see also *Journal to Stella* under Feb. 28).

Copy: Penn.

Some 'Large Paper' copies were issued.

The original leaves G 6–7 (pp. 91–4), bearing the last paragraph of 'A Discourse Of The Contests And Dissentions In Athens And Rome' as printed in the original pamphlet, 1701, were cancelled and replaced by one new leaf (pp. 91 + bl.) omitting that paragraph, for which A 8 was used [cf. *Prose Works* (1939), I, 301]. The B.M. copy 838 g 1 has preserved the original leaves, and has the cancel before B 1.

Another state:

In all the copies I have seen, the last two lines of p. 64 (verso of E 8) are the same as the first two of p. 65 (recto of F 1); but Tregaskis, cat. 970, item 296, mentions a copy "with 66 and 67 cancelled and one leaf substituted", which is almost certainly wrong for 65 and 66, because 66 and 67 belong to different leaves. Apparently the new leaf F 1 corrects the mistake referred to.

(2) *Second edition:*

Miscellanies / In / Prose / And / Verse. / — / The Second Edition. / — / [ornament] / — / *London:* / Printed for John Morphew, near *Sta- | tioner's-Hall*, MDCCXIII.

8vo; A–Dd⁸ — π¹, 2 pp. (t. + bl.), 6 pp. (The Publisher to The Reader), 5 pp. (Contents) + bl., 1–414.

Published end Feb. 1714 (*The London Gazette*, Feb. 23–27, 1714). This is a page-for-page reprint of the first edition, but the numbering of the pages now being consecutive, the pagination comes to 414 instead of 416. Curiously enough, as in the first edition, the last two lines of p. 64 are again the same as the first two of p. 65. Query: Was this again corrected by a cancel?

(3) *Another second edition, also 1713:*

The same size, title, and collation as those of the other Second Edition, 1713, yet a different printing, as appears from the following points:

1. On p. 91 the word *Finis* in italics in one, in roman in the other.

2. Pp. 363, 365, 367, 381, 383 misprinted 163, 165, 167, 181, 183 in one, correct in the other.

3. On p. 261 the name of the astrologer spelt *Partridg's* in one, *Partridge's* in the other; on p. 268 *Parteridge* in one, *Partridge* in the other; on pp. 390–6 *Patrige* in one, *Partrige* in the other [cf. W. A. Eddy, "The Wits vs. John Partridge, Astrologer", in *Studies in Philology*, XXIX, Jan. 1932, 30 n.].

4. On p. 405, l. 7, *a-thwart* in one, *athwart* in the other.

In this printing the last two lines of p. 64 are again the same as the first two of p. 65.

Poems, I, 136 says that one of the 1713 editions has, on p. 404, the year 1720, a printer's error for 1710. The four copies which I have owned, three of the one printing and one of the other, have all correct 1710.

17. Miscellaneous / Works, / Comical & Diverting: / By / T.R.D.J.S.D.O.P.I.I. / In Two Parts. / I. The Tale *of a* Tub; with the *Frag-* / *ment*, & the Battel *of the* Books; / with considerable *Additions*, & explanatory / *Notes*, never before printed. / II. Miscellanies in Prose / & Verse, by the supposed Author of the / first part. / [ornament] / London, / Printed by Order of the Society / *de propagando, &c.* / — / M.DCC.XX.

The second title (p. 281) is:

Miscellanies / In Prose & Verse. / *A Second Part,* / *By a certain paultry Scribler,* / commonly called, / *The Author of the first.*

Sm. 8vo; *⁸, A–N⁸, O⁶, P⁸, Q⁶, R⁸, S⁴; T–X⁸, Y⁶, Z⁴; Aa–Cc⁸ — 2 pp. (t. + bl.), III–IX ('The Booksellers Advertisement On this new Edition' + 'Errata'.), X–XII, misnumbered XIII (Table of Contents), XIII misnumbered VIII–XIV (Catalogue of Treatises, and Mr. Wotton's Remark), [XV] (title: A Tale, &c.), [XVI] (quotation from Lucret.), 1–268, 2 pp. blank; 280–348; 369–416. There are several misnumbered pages: XII, XIII, 141, 168, 219–36 (219–20 repeated in numbering), 347, 348 misnumbered XIII, VIII, 14, 167, 119–36, 343, 368. The text was set up in three sections; hence the two gaps in the pagination; but nothing is wanting.

Contains: *Tale, Discourse* (called: A Fragment of The Tale of a Tub), *Battle, Table* (containing: The History of Martin), *Meditation Broomstick, Various Thoughts, Tritical Essay, Argument Abolishing Christianity, Bickerstaff Pamphlets, Verses.*

As this edition includes the *Tale*, it may claim to be a first attempt at a complete edition.

This book has been called a Dutch edition and a pirated one, while on account of *The History Of Martin*, for the first time printed in it (pp. 253–66), it has also been held spurious.

A Dutch edition it certainly is. I possess a copy of "The Works Of The Right Honourable Joseph Addison, Esq; 2 vols.; London, Printed for T. Johnson. M.DCC.XXII". Though the imprint says 'London', Johnson carried on business at The Hague, as appears from the three pages of advertisements, after p. 517 in Vol. II, headed: "English Books, Neatly printed in pocket volumes, and sold by T. Johnson Bookseller in the Hague"; and one of the books mentioned there is the one in question: "Miscellaneous Works comical and diverting, by D. S – – – ft. containing I. The Tale of a

Tub, with Notes and Additions. II. Miscellanys in Prose and Verse, by the Author of the first part (priced in Dutch currency: 1 gild. 10 stiv.)". For separate editions of *The History Of Martin*, see Nos. 783–4, *post*.

18. Miscellanies / In / Prose / And / Verse. / — / *The Fourth Edition, with the following Additions.* / — / *Viz.* / The Seventh Epistle of the first Book of *Horace* / Imitated, and Address'd to a Noble Lord. / A Letter from a Lay-Patron to a Gentleman / designing for Holy Orders. *These said to be / done by the same* Author. / The Battel of the Pygmies and Cranes. / The Puppet-Show. *These by Mr.* Addison. / A Friendly Conference between a Preacher / and a Family of his Flock, upon the 30*th* / of *January. By Mr.* S. B—r. / — / *Dublin:* / Printed by *S. Fairbrother*, Book-Seller, and are / to be Sold at his Shop in *Skinner-Row*, over / against the *Tholsel*, 2721. [*sic*]

[Title within double-lined frame.]
Sm.8vo; A⁴, B–R ⁸, * 1, S⁸, T⁴ — 8 pp., 1–256, 2 pp., 257–79. — A 3 verso signed S 3; L 3 and N 3 are unsigned; L 4 and R 4 are misprinted L 3 and Q 4. Pp. 53, 159, 171, 185, 206, 207, 218, 219 are misnumbered 33, 259, 150, 158, 06, 107, 118, 119. Contains the same pieces as the *Miscellanies*, 1711 and 1713 (see No. 2, *ante*) with two added (see the title-page).

This is undoubtedly a pirated edition; on Swift's opinion of Fairbrother, see No. 33.

Miscellanies, 1727 &c. (8vo)

Publication: The *Preface* before Vol. I tells us that the original plan consisted of a volume of Swift's prose pieces "printed about sixteen Years ago", a second ("and perhaps a third") volume containing "several small Treatises in Prose, wherein a Friend or two are concerned", while "the Verses are transferred into a Volume apart". Consequently on June 24, 1727 (*The Evening Post*, June 15–22; *The Craftsman*, June 24) appeared *The First Volume* and *The Second Volume*; and on March 7, 1727–8 (*The Daily Post*, March 8) the "Volume apart", called *The Last Volume*. There had been some delay, for though "quite printed" as early as Feb. 1727 (see Pope's letter to Swift, *Corresp.*, III, 380), the first two volumes had been waiting for Swift's arrival from Dublin, when the *Preface* was composed (dated: Twickenham, May 27, 1727). There was even more delay in the case of *The Last Volume* which appeared just in time to allow the year 1727 still to be printed on the title-page. [A *Fourth Volume Of Miscellanies* came out in 1728, but it is spurious; see No. 32, *post*.]

Apparently the first two volumes had had a quick sale, so that early in 1728, when another edition proved necessary, Motte could at once print a double number of *The Last Volume*. Part of them (with the year 1727 on the t. p.) went with the two 1727 volumes, the rest (with the year MDCCXXVIII on the t. p.) with the two 1728 volumes. At the same time the *Preface*, slightly altered in the opening paragraph, was lifted out of Vol. I and transferred to *The Last Volume*, 1728. *The Last Volume* was reprinted in 1732.

It was not until Oct. 4, 1732 (*The Daily Post*, Oct. 2) that *The Third Volume*, half promised in the *Preface*, 1727 ("and perhaps a third"), appeared. It is especially remarkable for the intricate question of copyright it involved, the story of which can be traced in *Corresp.*, IV, 307 to the end, *passim*; VI, 245; also in *Poems*, pp. xxiii–xxviii. The result was not only the name of Motte, but also that of Gilliver, in the imprint.

In Jan.–Feb. 1732 (*The Grub-Street Journal*, Jan. 30) *Volume the Fifth* (two issues) was added by another publisher, Charles Davis, who also published, in 1738, two volumes entitled *Political Tracts*, which, as well as *A Complete Collection Of Genteel And Ingenious Conversation*, published by Motte and Bathurst in 1738 (No. 761, *post*), may be considered as supplementary to the five volumes of *Miscellanies*.

Contents: As to the contents of the several volumes it is to be remarked that there is but little by Pope in them (admitted by Pope himself in the preface to the second volume of his *Works*, 1735, where he expressly mentions the few pieces in the *Miscellanies* for which he can be held responsible — cf. *Corresp.*, V, 216–17), and even less by Arbuthnot and Gay.

The First Volume consists entirely of pieces by Swift, namely the prose pieces of the *Miscellanies* of 1711, and two others of a later date. Three-fifths of *The Second Volume* is taken up by *The History Of John Bull*; the rest is partly by Swift. *The Last Volume* consists of *The Bathos* (hints by Arbuthnot or Swift or both, but Pope is responsible for its final shape — see *Corresp.*, IV, 4), and the verse of the *Miscellanies* of 1711 together with some that had since been written, of which total Swift says that at least five-sixths are his (*Corresp.*, III, 440).

So that the author (supposed to be Dean Jonathan Smedley) of the spurious *Gulliveriana: or, a Fourth Volume of Miscellanies*, 1728 (No. 32, *post*), cannot have been far wrong, when in his *Postscript* (pp. 333–6) severely criticizing the three volumes, he said: "Upon the whole, this plural Number, We, is ridiculous, P–e having writ so small a Share in these Three Volumes; and as for what A–t and G– can boast of therein, I own I can hardly find it out; so that all the Vanity of this sort amounts to no more, than that Swift had a mind, in order to support his Three insupportable Volumes, to hale in Three other Names, which, for the Reasons given, are, really, neither an Ornament or Defence to his Work, however these three Authors may excel and shine in their own Works".

For the rest it is curious to read in this same *Postscript* that Smedley charges Swift with having made Pope his "Skreen", imposing on Pope's weakness "to lend his Name, to help to blazon out Three Volumes, in which, truly, he has little or no Share"; whereas the case is rather the other way about, Pope, for love of money or of fame, having drawn Swift into the joint enterprise.

The Third Volume contains only "the ludicrous and little things; none of the political, or any things of consequence". (*Corresp.*, IV, 342, 484–6.) After its appearance, early in Oct. 1732, Swift expressed his displeasure at its contents, maintaining that the poetry (of which he admits six-sevenths or seven-eighths to be his) was too insignificant to be printed, and that the greater part of the prose was written by other hands (*Corresp.*, IV, 359–60, 367).

Volume the Fifth (consisting of poetry and prose relating to Ireland) and the two volumes of *Political Tracts* (containing principally the political pieces belonging to Swift's English period, 1710–14) were derived from Faulkner's edition, the former from Faulkner's second and fourth volumes, 1735 (admitted in the *Advertisement*, before the title in *Volume the Fifth*), the latter from Faulkner's fifth and sixth volumes, 1738 (admitted in the *Preface* in Vol. I).

25. (1a) Miscellanies / In / *Prose* and *Verse*. / — / The / First Volume. / — / [monogram] / = / *London:* / Printed for Benjamin Motte, at the *Middle-* / *Temple Gate* in *Fleet-Street*. M.DCC.XXVII.

8vo; A⁸, π², B–Cc⁸, Dd⁴ — 2 pp. (t. + bl.), 3–16 (Preface), 3 pp. (Contents), 1 p. (Errata), [1] — 408.
Copy: Penn.

(1b) *Another state:*
In later copies K 7–8 (pp. 141–4) and L 6–7 (pp. 347–50) were cancelled, and replaced by corrected leaves.
Copy: Penn.
The corrections in the first group concern the headlines; those in the second group imply the omission of 'J. Swift' on p. 348, and of 'By a Person of Quality' on p. 349. Moreover, on the latter page, 'Dated *January* 9. 1719/ 20.' has been altered into 'Dublin, January 9.'
Penn possesses a third copy once the property of Swift's friend Orrery and bearing his signature on inside of front cover, which has the original leaves in their proper places, and the reprinted and corrected ones bound in at the end of the book between pp. 402–3, and pp. 406–7.

(1c) *Second edition:*
Miscellanies / In / *Prose* and *Verse*. / — / The / First Volume. / — / [monogram] / = / *London:* / Printed for Benjamin Motte, at the *Middle-* / *Temple Gate* in *Fleet-Street*. / — / MDCCXXVIII.

8vo; π¹, B–Cc⁸, Dd⁴ — 2 pp. (t. + bl.), [I]–II (Contents), [1]–408 (351, 352 omitted in numbering). The *Preface* has been removed from this volume, and placed, in a slightly different text, in *The Last Volume*, 1728 (cf. 3e).

(2a) Miscellanies. / — / The / Second Volume. / — / [monogram, or entirely blank space] / = / *London:* / Printed for Benjamin Motte at the *Middle-* / *Temple-Gate* in *Fleet-Street*. MDCCXXVII.

8vo; π², A–L⁸ — 2 pp. (t. + bl.), 2 pp. (Contents + bl.), 2 pp. (title: John Bull + bl.), 7 pp. (Preface), 1 p. (blank), 1–358.
Copy: Penn.

(2b) *Another state:*
In all copies I have seen or heard of P 3 (pp. 219–20), bearing bastard-title: *A Key To The Lock*, &c. + blank, is a cancellar. Moreover, some copies have a leaf of advertisements before the title (not recorded above); others have not. It is not certain that this leaf is essential to the book; in other words, whether, when cancellation of the original T 3 took place (apparently before publication, no copies having turned up containing it), at first only a single leaf (new bastard-title) was substituted, and later a double-leaf (advs., and new bastard-title). Griffith, p. 572, mentions a copy in which the new bastard-title is in its appropriate place between pp. 218 and 221, while the double-leaf (advs., and new bastard-title) was used as a wrapper for the volume title-leaf and the Contents-leaf, so that this copy has the new bastard-title twice.

(2c) *Another state:*
There are copies in which the space for the monogram on the title-page is entirely left blank.

(2d) *Another state:*
P. 292, l. 8 has the misprint 'post' for 'port' in some copies; in others it has been corrected.

(2e) *Second edition*(?):
I have not seen a copy. But from advertisements in early and later catalogues it would seem there is a second edition, 1728.

(3a) Miscellanies. / — / The / Last Volume. / — / [monogram] / = / *London:* / Printed for B. Motte, at the *Middle* / *Temple Gate* *Fleet-Street*. 1727.

8vo; B–G⁸; A⁸, a–c⁸; B–T⁸, U³, K⁸, Y⁴ — 2 pp. (t. + bl.), 2 pp. (title: Bathos + bl.), [5]–g², 2 pp. (Contents 'Bathos'), 2 pp. (h.t.: Miscellanies in Verse + bl.); 2 pp. (f.t.: Miscellanies in Verse + bl.), 4 pp. (Contents of the 'Verse'), 2 pp. (title: Cadenus and Vanessa + bl.), 1–8, 17–64 (no break in the text between pp. 8 and 17); 1–313 (advs. on verso), 4 pp. (Contents of the whole volume).

The page-numbers and the headlines of pp. 270–1 are: '271 Lemuel Gulliver', and 'Mary Gulliver *to* 270', which should have been reversed. In the 1728 issue (see below) the page-numbers are correct, but the headlines have remained uncorrected. Case, No. 344, (3) (a) says: "Gathering U originally had four leaves, U 4 being the last leaf of the book: it was cancelled, because it had the word 'Finis' at the foot of p. 296, in order that the volume might be extended. The material on U 4 was reprinted on H 1. The copy in the British Museum (12269 gdd 2) has both leaves", the original U 4 (295–6) slit as for cancellation. There is no break in the pagination; U 3 (293–4) is followed by X 1 (295–6).

The first leaf B 3 and (in some copies) the first leaf G 3 are wrongly signed B and G 2; M 4, O 2, Q 2 and Y 2 are unsigned.
Copy: Penn.

(3b) *Another state:*
The same as above, but three leaves (A 1–3) have been removed (the stubs are clearly visible), namely the 2 pp. bearing f.t. *Miscellanies in Verse* + bl., and the 4 pp. *Contents* of the 'Verse'.
Copy: own.

(3c) *Another state:*
The same as the preceding copy, but with a leaf entitled 'Advertisement To The Reader' + bl. inserted after the general title-page (turn-over between pp. 14–15), reading:

[=] / Advertisement / To The / Reader. / What has been said in the Preface to / the first Volume in relation to these / Miscellanies in general, we think fit to re- / peat here of the Verses in particular, That / all which we have written of this kind are / contain'd in it; and that all others, printed / in our Names, are Impositions both on us and / on the Publick. / Jonath. Swift. / Alex. Pope.

This is Griffith, No. 196, but sometimes this leaf precedes the general title. See also (3e). Griffith says that "the first two groups of pages, 1–96 ["Bathos"] and 1–64 ["Cadenus"], were apparently inserted into this volume as an afterthought; though 'Cadenus' was in type as early as June, 1727".

(3d) *Another state:*
The same as the preceding copy, but at the end of the volume there is a leaf of *Errata*, referring to *The Second Volume* (pp. 292 and 296) and *The Last Volume* (p. 45). This is Griffith, No. 197.

(3e) *Another issue* (dated 1728):
Miscellanies. / — / The / Last Volume. / — / [monogram] / — / *London:* / Printed for Benjamin Motte, at / the *Middle-Temple Gate* in *Fleetstreet.* / MDCCXXVIII.

This is the Penn copy; it is the same printing as the second state above (i.e., three leaves, A 1–3, removed), but the title-leaf has been replaced by a whole sheet A (pp. [I]–XVI), bearing new title + blank, and *Preface* ([III]–XVI), slightly altered in the first paragraph (see I (2)), which made the extra-leaf (see (3c)) superfluous. Forster (8573) has this *Preface* in *The First Volume* 1728, but this is wrong, for the wording of the first paragraph clearly shows that in its altered shape it belongs to *The Last Volume.* The Bodleian copy, by mistake called 12 θ 1062, has wrongly preserved the extra-leaf.

(3f) *Second edition:*
Miscellanies. / — / The / Last Volume. / — / [monogram] / = / *London:* / Printed for B. Motte, at the *Middle* / *Temple Gate Fleet-Street.* 1732.

8vo; B–Ee⁸, Ff⁴ — 2 pp. (t. + bl.), 2 pp. (title: Bathos + bl.), [5]–434, 4 pp. (Contents), 2 pp. (advs.). — There is no Preface.
Copy: Forster 8573–34C37.
Case, No. 344 (3) (b) says: "The first leaf of gathering O, and of every succeeding gathering except Bb, has the volume-signature 'Vol. III.': Bb 1 is erroneously signed 'Vol. II.'"

(4a) Miscellanies. / — / The / Third Volume. / — / [monogram] / = / *London:* / Printed for Benj. Motte at the *Middle* / *Temple-Gate,* and Lawton Gilliver / at *Homer's Head,* against St. *Dunstan's* / Church in *Fleetstreet,* 1732.

8vo; π², A–F⁸, G²; [A]⁴, A–R⁸, S⁴ — 2 pp. advs., 2 pp. (t. + bl.), 1–100; 2 pp. (extra title, namely: 'Miscellanies. / — / The / Third volume. / — / [space for the monogram left blank] / = / *London:* / Printed for Ben. Motte, and Lawton / Gilliver in *Fleetstreet,* 1732.' + blank), [I]–II (The Booksellers Advertisement), [I]–4, 1–254, one leaf advs., 255–76, 2 pp. (Errata + bl.). The pages 1–4, 1–254 constitute a faulty numbering; there is no break in the text.
R 2–4 wrongly signed A 2–4. — In some copies p. 64 of the second part is misnumbered 62.

As there is *Finis.* on p. 254 (Q 7), followed by a leaf of advs. (Q 8), *A True and Faithful Narrative*, pp. 255–76 (R⁸, S 1–3), followed by a leaf Errata + blank (S 4), looks like an afterthought.

This is the B.M. copy 12269 dd 2 (p. 64 misnumbered 62); it has the extra title-leaf [A 1] slit as for cancellation (see next state).

(4b) *Another state:*

The same as above, but another arrangement, the prose part (1–276) preceding the verse part (1–100), which caused cancellation of the extra title-leaf [A 1], so that such a copy collates:

8vo; π², A 2–4, A–R⁸, S⁴; A–F⁸, G² — 2 pp. advs., 2 pp. (t. + bl.), [I]–II (The Booksellers Advertisement), [1]–4, 1–254, one leaf advs., 255–76, 2 pp. (Errata + bl.); 1–100.

Copies: Worcester Coll. Libr., Oxford (P.P. 1.21), U.L.C. (8 p. * 2. 288 (D)), and Penn.

The Booksellers Advertisement (pp. I–II) says: "The Verses are paged separately, that they may be added to that Volume which wholly consists of Verse, and the Treatise of the Bathos placed in their stead in This."; and consequently copies of *The Last Volume* are found containing only *Verse*, and copies of *The Third Volume* consisting of *Prose* only.

(5a) Miscellanies, / In Prose and Verse. / Volume the Fifth. / — / Which with the other Volumes already pub- / lished in *England*, compleats this Author's / Works. / — / [ornament] / = / *London:* / Printed for Charles Davis, in *Pater-noster* / *Row.* MDCCXXXV.

8vo; π², A², B–N⁸, O 1–4, [O] 3–4, O 5–8, P–Ee⁸ — 2 pp. (bl. + *Advertisement*), 2 pp. (t. + bl.), 4 pp. (Contents), 1–200, *197, *198, *199, *200, 201–432 (*Finis.* at foot). P. 422 is misnumbered 322. The Advertisement on verso of title reads: As most of this Author's Writings have been already published in the *Drapier*'s Letters, *Gulliver*'s Travels, and the four Volumes of *Miscellanies* printed for Messieurs *Motte* and *Gulliver*, it would have been injurious to the *English* Buyer, as well as Proprietor, to have reprinted here the *Dublin* Edition of his Works. We are therefore only to assure Both, that this Volume consists of such Pieces as are Not in the forementioned Volumes, but contain every thing in the *Dublin* Edition besides.

The following cancels occur:

E 3, 4 (pp. 53–6), replaced by one double-leaf signed E 3 and E 4; F 2 (pp. 67–8), replaced by a new leaf signed F 2; I 2, 3, 4, 5 (pp. 115–22), re- placed by two double-leaves signed I 2, I 3, I 4, and unsigned; K 8 (pp. 143–4), replaced by a new leaf unsigned; R 2 (pp. 243–4), replaced by a new leaf signed R 2; Y 2 (pp. 323–4), replaced by a new leaf signed Y 2; Ee 8 (pp. 431–2), replaced by a new leaf unsigned.

(5b) *A later addition to this volume:*

A / Collection / Of / Poems, *&c.* / Omitted in the Fifth Volume of Miscel- / lanies in Prose and Verse. / — / [ornament] / = / *Lon-* don: / Printed for Charles Davis, in *Pater-noster* / *Row.* MDCCXXXV. / Price 6 d.

8vo; π¹, Ff–Hh⁸ — 2 pp. (t. + Advertisement on verso, apologizing for the publication of this later addition), 433–80.

Copy: Bodl. G. Pamph. 57.

Dobell's cat. 39, item 565 is a copy with 432 pp., with *Contents* for 432 pp.

B.M. 12269 dd 2*, and Dobell cat. 39, item 566 are copies with 480 pp., with (reprinted) *Contents* for 480 pp. The title-leaf 'A Collection Of Poems, &c.' has been cancelled. U.L.C. Pp. *2.289 (D) is the same, but pp. *197–*200 are lacking, and the leaf bearing *Advertisement* follows the title.

Davis derived the pieces for this volume from Faulkner's Vol. II (verse) and Vol. IV (prose and verse), 8vo, 1735. As the cancels in Davis are the same as those in Faulkner (see above, and No. 41, *post*), Davis must first have acquired Faulkner's uncancelled sheets, next a copy with the cancels and the additional pieces, and lastly another verse piece: *Upon the Horrid Plot Discover'd By Harlequin* (*197–*200, above), which must have been a very late addition, as it is not listed in the reprinted *Contents*.

Prometheus, a very late addition in Faulkner's Vol. IV (see No. 41), is absent here.

(6) Political / Tracts. / — / Vol. I. / — / By the Author of / *Gulliver*'s Travels. / — / [ornament] / — / *London*, / Printed for C. Davis in *Pater-Noster-Row*. / MDCCXXXVIII.

8vo; A⁴, B–Y⁸, Z³, Aa⁸, Bb⁴ — 2 pp. (t. + bl.), 4 pp. (Preface), 1 p. (Contents), 1 p. (Errata), [1]–342, 24 pp. (Index).

(7) Political / Tracts. / — / Vol. II. / — / [rest as in Vol. I].

8vo; π², B–U⁸, X² — 2 pp. (t. + bl.), 2 pp. (Contents), [1]–288, 19 pp. (Index) + bl.

(8) A Complete Collection Of Genteel and Ingenious Conversation, 1738.

See No. 761, *post*.

Miscellanies, 1731, &c. (12mo)

In 1730 the *Miscellanies* were reprinted in 12mo, namely: *The First Volume, The Second Volume,* and *The Last Volume*.

Towards the beginning of 1733 these three volumes were reprinted and a fourth was added. But owing to the peculiar manner of naming the volumes (*First, Second, Last, Third*) errors were committed. *Vols. Last* and *III* were interchanged, i.e., *Vol. Last* was provided with a Vol. *III* title and the reverse. A certain number of these volumes were published and sold, till the errors were detected and rectified, i.e., the wrong titles were cancelled and replaced by correct ones. The result was:

(1) *Vol. I*, 1733 (correct);
(2) *Vol. II*, 2nd ed., 1733 (correct);
(3a) pieces of *Vol. Last*, but wrong title (1732) of *Vol. III*;
(3b) = (3a) correct title (1733) *Vol. Last*;
(3c) reprint: pieces of *Vol. Last*, but wrong title (1733) of *Vol. III* — In 1736 provided with correct title *Vol. Last*;
(4a) pieces of *Vol. III*, but wrong title (1733) of *Vol. Last*;
(4b) = (4a) correct title (1732) *Vol. III*;
(4c) reprint: pieces of *Vol. III*, correct title (1733) of *Vol. III*.

In 1735 *Volume the Fifth* and *Volume the Sixth* were added, containing the same pieces as *Volume the Fifth*, 8vo, 1735 (see No. 25).

In 1736 *The First Volume* and *The Second Volume* were reprinted twice: once with head- and tail-pieces and decorated initials, and once with printer's rules only. In these volumes Swift's pieces were for the first time marked: in the former by ☞ ☞, in the latter by ☞ ✳ .

The Last Volume, 1736, is the wrong *The Third Volume*, 1733 (see 3c above). It has head- and tail-pieces and decorated initials, and therefore suits the former set. Whether the latter set had also an appropriate *The Last Volume*, 1736 (with printer's rules only), I cannot say. *The Last Volume* was reprinted in 1738 (with ☞ ☞).

The Third Volume was reprinted in two varieties in 1736; of the second (printer's rules) I even possess two copies which show a slight difference in the imprint only. Remainder copies of *The Third Volume*, 1736 (second variety, i.e. printer's rules), turn up in 1744 with a new title-page.

Moreover, in 1736 *Vol. V* and *Vol. VI* were reprinted; again in 1738.

In 1742 were added *Vol. VII*, *Volume VIII*, and *Vol. IX* (a reprint of the two volumes of *Political Tracts*, 8vo, 1738).

And lastly, in 1743, was added *The Tenth Volume*, containing 'A Complete Collection Of Genteel And Ingenious Conversation'.

26. (1) Miscellanies. / — / The / First Volume. / — / [monogram] / — / *London:* / Printed for Benjamin Motte, at the *Middle-* / *Temple-Gate*, *Fleetstreet*, and sold by Weaver / Bickerton, at the Lord *Bacon*'s Head without / *Temple Bar*, and Lawton Gilliver, at *Homer*'s / Head over against St. *Dunstan*'s Church, *Fleetstreet*. / MDCCXXXI.

12mo; π^1, B–O^{12} — 2 pp. (t. + bl.), [1]–310, 2 pp. advs.

(2) The second volume has the same title, except: — / The / Second Volume. / —.

12mo; π^1, A–M^{12} — 2 pp. (t. + bl.), [1]–288.

(3) The third volume has the same title, except: — / The / Last Volume. / —.

12mo; A–O^{12} — 2 pp. (t. + bl.), 10 pp. (Preface), 2 pp. (title: Bathos + bl.), 15–333, 3 pp. (Contents).

These three volumes were published Oct. 1730 (adv. in *The Grub Street Journal*, Oct. 29).

Copies: Penn.

Contemporary criticism

(See "A List of Books, Papers, and Verses, in which our Author was abused, printed before the Publication of the Dunciad: With the true Names of the Authors", p. 185, etc., in the second edition of the *Dunciad*, London, Lawton Gilliver, 1729.)

32. *Gulliveriana:* / Or, A / Fourth Volume / Of / Miscellanies. / Being A / Sequel of the Three Volumes, / published by Pope and Swift. / To which is added, / Alexanderiana; or, A Comparison / between the *Ecclesiastical* and *Poetical* Pope. / And many Things, in Verse and Prose, / relating to the latter. / — / With an ample Preface; and a Critique / on the Third Volume of *Miscellanies* lately / publish'd by those two facetious Writers. / — / *Sequitur pede, poena, claudo*. Hor. / — / [ornament] / — / *London :* / Printed for J. Roberts, at the *Oxford Arms* in / *Warwick-lane*. M.DCC.XXVIII.

8vo; frontisp., A⁸, b⁸, c⁴, d², B–Y⁸, L⁴ — frontisp., 2 pp. (t. + bl.), 4 pp. (Dedication), [VII]–XXI (Preface), [XXII]–XXXIX (A Critique), [XL]–XLIV (Contents), [1]–344.
Copies: B.M., Dyce (9612), and Penn.
Wagstaff's New Catalogue of Rare Old Books, For 1780, item 1975, mentions a copy dated 1727, with a portrait whole length. I have not met with such a copy.
Contains only two genuine pieces by Swift: 'Elegy on Demar', 'The Journal'. — The author was Jonathan Smedley. Cf. Case, No. 351, and *Poems*, 1100.
Gulliveriana Secunda, Being a collection of many of the Libels in the Newspapers [by Smedley]. — Advertised in *The Craftsman*, Nov. 9, 1728. — No copy seen.

1284. A Compleat Collection Of all the Verses, Essays, Letters and Advertisements Which Have been occasioned by the Publication of Three Volumes of Miscellanies, by Pope and Company. &c. London, A. Moore, M.DCC.XXVIII. — 8vo; frontisp., I–XV + bl., 1–52.

8vo (in fours); [A]⁴, a⁴, B–G⁴, H² — 2 pp. (t. + bl.); III–XV + bl., 1–52. — Frontisp.
Copy: B.M. C 116 b2 (8).
This is a collection of the pieces which had appeared in the 'public Prints' (see Pope's *List*, where the newspapers and the authors are mentioned). It may be a Curll publication; the Preface is by Concannen.

1285. The Metamorphosis: A Poem. Shewing The Change of Scriblerus into Snarlerus: Or, The Canine Appetite: Demonstrated In the Persons of P—p—e and Sw—t. &c. London, A. Moore, MDCCXXVIII. [Title in double-lined frame] — Folio; [A]–B² — 2 pp. (t. + bl.), 3–8. — The B.M. copy 12273 m 1 (11) has this MS. note on title: This was writ by Dean Smedley.

1286. The Twickenham Hotch-Potch, For the Use of the Rev. Dr. Swift, Alexander Pope, Esq; and Company. &c. – – – – Written by Caleb D'Anvers. &c. London, J. Roberts, 1728. —

8vo (in fours); π¹, B–H⁴, I², K 1 — 2 pp. (t. + bl.), [I]–VII (Introduction) + bl., [I]–53 + bl.
Copy: B.M. 1415 f 63. — Though the last page says "The End of the First Part", no more was ever published.

1287. A Supplement To The Profund. &c. London, J. Roberts, M.DCC. XXVIII. —

8vo (in fours); [A]³, B–E⁴, F 1 — 2 pp. (t. + bl.), [III]–VI (Preface), [I]–34.
Copies: B.M. C116 b 2 (4), and 1077 h 60 (1).

1288. Characters Of The Times; Or, An Impartial Account Of The Writings, Characters, Education, &c. of several Noblemen and Gentlemen, libell'd in a

Preface to a late Miscellany Publish'd By P – – – – – pe and S – – – – – – ft. &c. London, A. Dodd &c., M.DCC.XXVIII.

8vo (in fours); [A]–F⁴ — 2 pp. (t. + bl.), III–VI (Preface), VII–VIII (List of Names), 9–46, 2 pp. blank.
Copies: B.M. C116 b 2 (3), and 1421 g 7 (3).

1289. An Essay Upon The Taste and Writings Of The Present Times, But with A more particular View to Political and Dramatick Writings. Occasion'd by a late Volume of Miscellanies By A. Pope, Esq; and Dr. Swift. &c. London, J. Roberts, 1728.

8vo (in fours); [A]–G⁴, H² — 2 pp. (t. + bl.), 6 pp. (Dedication), [1]–S 2.
Copy: B.M. 11826 b 7.

1291. The Arts of Logick And Rhetorick, &c. London, John Clark &c., M.DCC.XXVIII. — 8vo; I–XXXII, 1–418, 16 pp. (*Index*), 2 pp. (*advs.*) — Pp. 416–18 contain a criticism on Swift. [By J. Oldmixon.]

1292. A Discourse Concerning Ridicule and Irony In Writing, In A Letter To the Reverend Dr. Nathanael Marshall. &c. London, J. Brotherton &c., 1729. — 8vo; 1–77 + bl. — There are references to Swift on pp. 39–40. [By Anthony Collins.]

∗

27. (1) Miscellanies. / — / The / First Volume. / — / [monogram] / — / *London:* / Printed for Benjamin Motte, at the / *Middle-Temple-Gate, Fleet-street.* / — / M.DCC.XXXIII.

12mo; [A]–N¹² — 2 pp. (t. and bl.), 2 pp. (Contents), 1–308.

(2) Miscellanies / — / The / Second Volume. / — / The Second Edition. / — / [monogram] / — / *London,* / Printed for Benjamin Motte, at the / *Middle-Temple-Gate, Fleetstreet.* / MDCCXXXIII.

12mo; A–M¹² — 2 pp. (t. + bl.), [3]–288.

(3a) Pieces of *Last Vol.* ('Bathos' and 'Cadenus and Vanessa'), but wrong title:
Miscellanies. / — / The / Third Volume. / — / [monogram] / = / *London:* / Printed for Benj. Motte, at the *Middle* / *Temple-Gate,* and Lawton Gilliver / at *Homer's Head* in *Fleetstreet,* 1732.

12mo; π¹, [A] 1–11, B–O¹² — 2 pp. (advs.), 2 pp. (t. + bl.), 8 pp. (Preface), 2 pp. (title: Bathos + bl.), 13–22, 25–90 (Bathos), 2 pp. (Contents 'Bathos'), 2 pp. (title: Miscellanies in Verse + bl.), 95–333, 3 pp. (Contents). — No break in the text.
As leaf G 11 (pp. 165–6) had a confusing misprint in the first line of text on p. 166 ('Perse' for 'Peruse'), it was resolved to cancel it, and replace it by a corrected one. To that purpose the text of sheet A (pp. 1–24), apparently not yet printed off, was compressed into pp. 1–22, which gave a free leaf (A 12), and on it pp. 165–6 were reprinted. The Bodl. copy (12 θ 855) has preserved both the faulty leaf G 11 and the corrected leaf A 12 in their

original places, i.e. between pp. 164 and 167 and between pp. 22 and 25 respectively.

(3b) Same printing as (3a), correct title:
Miscellanies. / — / The / Last Volume. / — / [monogram] / — / *London*: / Printed for Benjamin Motte, at / the *Middle-Temple-Gate, Fleetstreet*. / MDCCXXXIII.

12mo; [A] 1–11, B–O¹² — 2 pp. (t. + bl.), 8 pp. (Preface), 2 pp. (title: Bathos + bl.), 13–22, 25–90 (Bathos), 2 pp. (Contents 'Bathos'), 2 pp. (title: Miscellanies in Verse + bl.), 95–333, 3 pp. (Contents). — No break in the text.
Copies: Bodl. 12 θ 1152, T.C.D. Fag. Gg–47, and own.
Like copy (3a), my own of this *correct* volume has preserved both the faulty leaf G 11 and the corrected leaf A 12 in their original places, i.e. between pp. 164 and 167 and between pp. 22 and 25 respectively.
Griffith, No. 287, mentions a copy of *The Last Volume*, 1733, in which the printer or binder, wishing to bring together poetry only (cf. No. 25 (4) *ante*, note), blundered.

(3c) Reprint: pieces of *Last Vol.* ('Bathos' and 'Cadenus'), but wrong title:
Miscellanies. / — / The / Third Volume. / — / [monogram] / — / *London*: / Printed for Benjamin Motte, at the / *Middle-Temple-Gate, Fleetstreet*, and Law- / ton Gilliver, at *Homer*'s Head over- / against St. *Dunstan*'s Church, *Fleetstreet*. / MDCCXXXIII.

12mo; [A]–N¹² — 2 pp. (bl. + advs.), 2 pp. (t. + bl.), 8 pp. (Preface), 2 pp. (title: Bathos + bl.), 15–90 (Bathos), 2 pp. (Contents 'Bathos'), 2 pp. (title: Miscellanies in Verse + bl.), 95–309, 3 pp. (Contents).
Copy: Bodl. 12 θ 1066.
In 1736 the title was cancelled and replaced by correct title: *The Last Volume*, 1736 (see No. 28 (3)).

(4a) Pieces of *Third Vol.* ('Narrative Robert Norris', and 'Journal Modern Lady'), but wrong title:
Miscellanies. / — / The / Last Volume. / — / [monogram] / — / *London*: / Printed for Benjamin Motte, at / the *Middle-Temple-Gate, Fleetstreet*. / MDCCXXXIII.

12mo; [A]–M¹², A–C¹², D¹⁰ — 2 pp. (t. + bl.), 2 pp. (Booksellers Advertisement), [5]–24, [1]–238, 2 pp. (advs.), [239]–260, 2 pp. (Errata + bl.), [1]–92.
Copy: Bodl. 12 θ 856.

(4b) Same printing as (4a), correct title:
Miscellanies. / — / The / Third Volume. / — / [monogram] / = / *London*: / Printed for Benj. Motte, at the *Middle* / *Temple-Gate*, and Lawton Gilliver / at *Homer*'s *Head* in *Fleetstreet*, 1732.

2—J.S.

12mo; π^2, A 2–12, B–M^{12}, A–C^{12}, D^{10} — 2 pp. (t. + bl.) 2 pp. (advs.), 2 pp. (Booksellers Advertisement), [5]–24, [1]–238, 2 pp. (advs.), [239]–260, 2 pp. (Errata + bl.), [1]–92. The wrong title (see 4a) evidently replaced by a double-leaf (correct title + advs.).
Copy: T.C.D. Fag. G.9.46.

(4c) Reprint: pieces of *Third Vol.* ('Norris' + 'Journal'), correct title:
Miscellanies. / — / The / Third Volume. / — / [monogram] / — / *London:* / Printed for Benjamin Motte, at the / *Middle-Temple-Gate, Fleetstreet,* and Law- / ton Gilliver, at *Homer*'s Head over- / against St. *Dunstan*'s Church, *Fleetstreet.* / MDCCXXXIII.

12mo; [A]–I^{12}, A–C^{12} — 2 pp. (t. + bl.), 2 pp. (The Booksellers Advertisement), [5]–216, 1–67 (misprinted 97), 5 pp. advs.
In the first group of pages, p. 72 is misnumbered 62, in the second A 3, A 5, A 6 are wrongly signed K 3, A 6, A 5.
Copies: Bodl. 12 θ 1155, and Penn.

(5a) Miscellanies, / In Prose and Verse. / Volume the Fifth. / Which with the other Volumes already pub- / lished in *England,* compleats this Author's / Works. / — / [ornament] / = / *London:* / Printed for Charles Davis, in *Pater-noster* / *Row.* MDCCXXXV.

12mo; π^2, a^2, B–I^{12}, K^4, K 3–4, L^{12}, M^4 — 2 pp. (bl. + *Advertisement,* the same as recorded in No. 25 (V)), 2 pp. (t. + bl.), 4 pp. (Contents), [1]–200, *197–*200, *201–*232.
(5b) The title of the sixth volume is the same, except:
– – – – – / Volume the Sixth. / – – – – –.
12mo; π^1, K 5–12, L–T^{12}, U^8, π^1 — 2 pp. (t. + bl.), 201–432 (*Finis.* at the end), 433–48, 2 pp. (advs.).
In these two volumes the following cancels occur (the same as in No. 25 (V)): D 3–4 (pp. 53–6), replaced by one double-leaf; D 10 (pp. 67–8); F 10–12, G 1 (pp. 115–22), replaced by two double leaves; G 12 (pp. 143–4); M 2 (pp. 243–4); P 6 (pp. 323–4); T 12 (pp. 431–2).
These two volumes were printed from the same type-setting as the 8vo volume (No. 25), after compression of the lines vertically, on a smaller-size paper (chain lines horizontal; in the 8vo vertical), and with different signatures and pagination, while some headings and several printer's ornaments were removed and replaced by others; all this to suit the 12mo size.
That the original plan was one volume, not two, appears from the fact that the signatures are consecutive, as well as from the *Advertisement* before the title and the title itself, which speak of one volume only. Evidently the one-volume idea was abandoned, when the new pieces were to be added, which would have made one volume too bulky. When eventually the new pieces (which in the 8vo were kept together and placed at the end of the book) were added to the 12mo, the new verse pieces were added to the verse part in *Volume the Fifth,* and the new prose pieces to the prose part in *Volume the Sixth.* Then the original 4 pp. 'Contents' for 432 pp. were cancelled (stubs visible), and replaced by 4 pp. reprinted 'Contents' (extended and rearranged).
The pagination of the last two pieces in the 'Contents', 465 and 474, which is correct for the 8vo, but wrong for the 12mo, proves that the 'Contents' in the 12mo were reprinted from the reprinted 'Contents' in the 8vo.

And lastly, just as in the 8vo, *Upon The Horrid Plot Discover'd By Harlequin* was added. As it was a verse piece, it was to be placed at the end of the verse part (paged *197–*200, signed [K 3] and [K 4], catchword at the end 'A Pro-', the same as on p. 200, and corresponding with p. 201). It is not listed in the 'Contents'.

Just as in the 8vo edition (see No. 25, (V)), *Prometheus*, a very late addition in Faulkner's Vol. IV (see No. 41), is absent here.

I doubt whether the book was ever published in a one-volume shape. Copies of Vols. V and VI: own, and Bodl., see below.

Copies:
(1) *The First Vol.* (1733): Bodl. 12 θ 853; T.C.D. G.9.44; Dyce 9611; and Penn.
(2) *The Second Vol.* (1733): Bodl. 12 θ 854; T.C.D. G.9.45; Dyce 9611; and Penn.
(3a) *The Last Vol.* (but wrong title: *Third Vol.*, 1732): Bodl. 12 θ 855.
(3b) *The Last Vol.* (1733): Bodl. 12 θ 1152; T.C.D. G.9.47; Dyce 9611; and Penn.
(3c) *The Last Vol.* (but wrong title: *Third Vol.*, 1733): Bodl. 12 θ 1066.
(4a) *The Third Vol.* (but wrong title: *Last Vol.*, 1733): Bodl. 12 θ 856.
(4b) *The Third Vol.* (1732): T.C.D. G.9.46.
(4c) *The Third Vol.* (1733): Bodl. 12 θ 1155; and Penn.
(5) *Vol. the Fifth* (1735): Penn; Bodl. 12 θ 1917.
(6) *Vol. the Sixth* (1735): Penn; Bodl. 12 θ 1249.

Further reprints:

28. (1) Miscellanies. / — / The / First Volume. / — / [monogram] / — / *London:* / Printed for Benjamin Motte, and / Charles Bathurst, at the *Middle-* / *Temple Gate, Fleetstreet.* MDCCXXXVI.

12mo; π^2, B–N^{12}, O^4 — 2 pp. (t. + bl.), 2 pp. (Contents), [1]–295 + bl.
The second volume has the same title, except:

(2) — / The Second Volume. / —.

12mo; A–M^{12} — 2 pp. (t. + bl.), 3–288.
Head- and tail-pieces and decorated capitals in both volumes; Swift's pieces indicated by ☞ ☞.
Copy: Penn.

(3) Miscellanies. / — / The / Last Volume. / — / [monogram] / — / *London:* / Printed for B. Motte and C. Bathurst, / at the *Middle-Temple-Gate, Fleetstreet.* / MDCCXXXVI.

Head- and tail-pieces (mostly stencils) and decorated capitals. This is the same printing as No. 27 (3c); only the title-page has been renewed.

Griffith, No. 439, mentions a copy of *The Last Volume*, 1736, wrongly containing 'Norris' and 'Journal'. Here, apparently, the binder blundered by placing the new title before a copy of the correct *The Third Volume*, 1733 (No. 27, 4c), instead of before one of the wrong *The Third Volume*, 1733 (No. 27, 3c).

(4) Query: Was there a *Third Volume*, 1736, with head- and tail-pieces and decorated titles, suiting this set?

(5) Miscellanies, / In / Prose and Verse. / The Fifth and Sixth Volumes. / Which with the other four already printed, / the *Drapier*'s Letters, *Gulliver*'s Travels, / and three *Tatler*'s, compleat this Author's / Works. / — / Vol. V. / — / [ornament] / = / *London:* / Printed for T. Woodward at the half Moon / between the *Temple* Gates, and Charles / Davis, in *Pater-noster-Row*. 1736.

12mo; A–K¹², L⁶ — 2 pp. (bl. + Advertisement), 2 pp. (t. + bl.), 4 pp. (Contents), 1–239, 5 pp. advs.
The *Advertisement* says that "these two Volumes" are complementary of the four already printed, and have been taken from the Dublin edition.

(6) Miscellanies, / In / Prose and Verse. / — / Vol. VI. / — / [ornament] / = / *London:* / Printed for T. Woodward at the half Moon / between the *Temple* Gates, and Charles / Davis, in *Pater-noster-Row*. MDCCXXXVI.

12mo; A–K¹², L⁶ — 2 pp. (t. + bl.), 2 pp. (Contents), 5–252.

29. (1) Miscellanies. / — / The / First Volume. / — / [monogram] / — / *London:* / Printed for Benjamin Motte and / Charles Bathurst, at the *Middle-* / *Temple-Gate, Fleetstreet*.

12mo; π², B–N¹² — 2 pp. (t. + bl.), 2 pp. (Contents).

(2) Miscellanies. / — / The / Second Volume. / — / [monogram] / — / *London:* / Printed for Benjamin Motte, and / Charles Bathurst, at the *Middle-* / *Temple-Gate, Fleetstreet*. MDCCXXXVI.

12mo; A–M¹² — 2 pp. (t. + bl.), [3]–288.
In these two volumes printer's rules only. Swift's pieces indicated by ☞ ✱.
(3) Query: Was there a *Last Volume*, 1736, with printer's rules, suiting this set?

(4a) Miscellanies. / — / The / Third Volume. / — / [monogram] / — / *London:* / Printed for Benjamin Motte, at the *Mid-* / *dle-Temple-Gate, Fleetstreet*, and Lawton / Gilliver, at *Homer*'s Head over-against / St. *Dunstan*'s Church, *Fleetstreet*. / MDCCXXXVI.

12mo; [A]–I¹², A–C¹² — 2 pp. (t. + bl.), 2 pp. (The Booksellers Advertisement), [5]–216, [1]–71 (advs. on verso).
Copy: Forster 8574.

(4b) *Another issue* (different imprint only):
– – – / *London:* / Printed for Benjamin Motte and Charles / Bathurst, at the *Middle-Temple-Gate,* / *Fleetstreet*, and Lawton Gilliver and / John Clarke, at *Homer*'s Head over- / against St. *Dunstan*'s Church, *Fleetstreet*. / MDCCXXXVI.

(4c) *Another issue* (different imprint only):

London: | Printed for Benjamin Motte and Charles | Bathurst, at the *Middle-Temple-Gate,* | *Fleetstreet*; Lawton Gilliver and John | Clarke, at *Homer*'s Head over-against | St. *Dunstan*'s Church, *Fleetstreet.* | MDCCXXXVI.

(4d) *Another issue* (new title only):

Miscellanies | In | Verse and Prose. | By | Alexander Pope, Esq; and Dean Swift. | — | In One Volume. | — | *Viz.* | [*First column:*] The strange and deplorable | Frensy of Mr. *John Dennis.* | A full and true Account of a | horrid and barbarous Re- | venge, by Poison, on the | Body of Mr. *Edmund Curll.* | With his Last Will and | Testament. | A strange, but true Relation | how *Edmund Curll* was con- | verted from the Christian | Religion, by certain *Jews,* | and how he was circumcised. | God's Revenge against Pun- | ning. | The wonderful Wonder of | Wonders. | The Wonder of all the Won- | ders, that ever the World | wonder'd at. | The humble Petition of the | Colliers, Cook Maids, | Blacksmiths, Jack-Makers, | Brasiers, and others. | Annus Mirabilis. | Origin of Sciences. | It cannot Rain, but it Pours; | [*Second column:*] or, *London* strew'd with Ra- | rities. | An infallible Scheme to pay | the Publick Debt of *Ire-* | *land,* in Six Months. | A modest Proposal. | A Vindication of my Lord | *Carteret* Lord Lieutenant | of *Ireland.* | On the Fates of Clergymen. | On modern Education. | A true and faithful Narra- | tive of what pass'd in *Lon-* | *don.* | Journal of a modern Lady. | Country Life. | Cutting down the old Thorn | at *Market-hill.* | A Pastoral Dialogue. | *Mary* the Cook Maid's Let- | ter to Dr. *Sheridan.* | A Dialogue between Mad | *Mullineux* and *Timothy.* | Epitaph on *Francis Ch—is.* | Soldier and Scholar. | With several more Epigrams, | Epitaphs, and Poems. | — | *London:* | Printed for John Thomas, near *St. Paul's.* | — | M.DCC.XLIV.

Copy: Bodl. 12 *θ* 1259.

30. (1) Miscellanies. | — | The | Last Volume. | — | [monogram] | — | *London:* | Printed for B. Motte, and C. Bathurst, at the | *Middle-Temple-Gate, Fleetstreet.* | MDCCXXXVIII.

12mo; A–M¹² — 2 pp. (t. + bl.), 6 pp. (Preface), [9]–285, 3 pp. (Contents). Swift's pieces indicated by ☞ ☞.
Copy: Forster 8574.

(2) Miscellanies. | In | Prose and Verse. | The Fifth and Sixth Volumes. | Which with the other four already printed, | the *Drapier*'s Letters, *Gulliver*'s Travels, | and three *Tatlers,* compleat this Author's | Works. | — | Vol. V. | — | [ornament] | = |

London, / Printed for T. Woodward at the *Half-Moon* / between the *Temple* Gates, and Charles / Davis in *Pater-Noster-Row*. 1738.

12mo; A–K¹², L⁶ — 2 pp. (advs.), 2 pp. (t. + bl.), 4 pp. (Contents), [1]–239, 5 pp. advs.

(3) Miscellanies, / In / Prose and Verse. / — / Vol. VI. / — / [ornament] / = / *London*, / Printed for T. Woodward at the *Half Moon* / between the *Temple-Gates*, and Charles / Davis, in *Pater-Noster-Row*. MDCCXXXVIII.

12mo; A–K¹², L⁶ — 2 pp. (t. + bl.), 2 pp. (Contents), 5–252.

31. (1) Miscellanies / In / Prose *and* Verse, / By Dr. *Swift*. / — / Vol. VII. / — / [ornament] / *London:* / Printed for T. Cooper, at the *Globe* in / *Pater-Noster-Row*. / — / MDCCXLII.

12mo; A⁴, B–N¹², O⁸ — 2 pp. (t. + bl.), III–VIII (The Bookseller To The Reader), [1]–301 + bl., 2 pp. (Contents).

(2) Miscellanies / In / Prose and Verse. / — / Volume VIII. / — / [ornament] / — / *London:* / Printed for T. Cooper, at the *Globe* in *Pater-* / *noster* Row. MDCCXLII.

12mo; π², B–P¹², Q⁴ — 2 pp. (t. + bl.), 2 pp. (Contents), [1]–344.

(3) Miscellanies / In / Prose. / = / Vol. IX. / = / [ornament] / = / *London*, / Printed for T. Cooper at the *Globe* in *Pater-* / *noster* Row. MDCCXLII.

12mo; π², B–Q¹², R³ — 2 pp. (t. + bl.), 2 pp. (title: Miscellanies in Prose + bl.), [1]–363 + bl., 2 pp. (Contents).

(4) Miscellanies. / — / The / Tenth Volume. / — / Containing / A Complete Collection / Of / Genteel and Ingenious Conversation, / In / Three Dialogues. / With an / Introduction. / And / Some Pieces in Verse. / — / *London:* / Printed for Charles Bathurst, at the / *Cross Keys*, opposite St. *Dustan*'s [*sic*] Church, / *Fleet-street*, 1743.

12mo; π⁴, B–L¹² — 2 pp. (advs.), 2 pp. (t. + bl.), 2 pp. (Advertisement + bl.), 2 pp. (title: A Complete Collection, &c. + bl.), I–LIV, 2 pp., 1–182, 2 pp. advs.
The leaf following the title bears this *Advertisement:*
It is thought proper to acquaint the Reader, that this Volume, with the Four Volumes of Miscellanies in Prose and Verse, publish'd by the Author, and the five subsequent Volumes of Miscellanies, together with a Tale of a Tub, *and* The Travels of *Captain* Lemuel Gulliver, *makes a compleat Edition in this Size, of all the Author is suppos'd to have written and publish'd.*

This volume has not got 'Vol. X.' at the foot of the first page of each new sheet, which makes me suppose that this volume was also issued separately, with another title-page not mentioning 'Miscellanies. The Tenth Volume.'.

***

Miscellanies (Dublin reprints), *1728, &c.*

In 1721 Sam. Fairbrother had already reprinted the *Miscellanies* of 1711, 1713 (see No. 1), which he had called *The Fourth Edition* (see No. 18). In 1728 he reprinted Motte's *First, Second,* and *Last* volumes of 1727, in two volumes, and called them *The Second Edition.*

In 1732 these two volumes were reprinted (called *The Third Edition*); and in 1733 a third was added (called *The Second Edition*) containing the same pieces as Motte's *Third* volume 1732, with some added, i.a. Pope's *Rape Of The Lock.* In 1735 a fourth volume was published, containing the same pieces as Davis's Vol. V, 8vo, 1735, with some added. [Swift had an unfavorable opinion of Fairbrother; he called him "a fellow I have never been able to endure", and "an arrant rascal in every circumstance" (*Corresp.*, V, 322, 332).]

33. (1a) Miscellanies / In Prose / And / Verse. / In Two Volumes. / — / By Jonathan Swift, D.D. / And / Alexander Pope, Esq; / — / To which is added, / A Poem written on the *North-* / Window of the Deanary-House of / St. *Patrick*'s, *Dublin*. / — / The Second Edition. / — / *London* Printed, and Re-printed in *Dublin*, / By and for Sam. Fairbrother, Bookseller in / *Skinner-Row*, opposite the *Tholsel*, 1728.

[Title within double-lined frame.]
12mo; π¹, A⁴, B–Q¹², R⁶ — 2 pp. (t. + advs. on verso), [III]–VIII (Preface), 2 pp. (Contents), 1–372.
(b) The second volume has the same title, except that instead of 'In Two Volumes.' there is: The Second Volume.
12mo; π¹, A–N¹², O⁴, P² — 2 pp. (t. + adv. on verso), 2 pp. (title: A Key To The Lock + bl.), 2 pp. (The Epistle Dedicatory To Mr. Pope), 1–140, 2 pp. (Contents To The Bathos), 2 pp. (title: Miscellanies In Verse + bl.), 1–172, 3 pp. (Contents), 1 p. advs.
Copy: Penn.

Third edition:
(2a) Miscellanies / In / Prose / And / Verse. / In Two Volumes. / — / By Jonathan Swift, D.D. / And / Alexander Pope, Esq; / — / To which are added / Several Poems, and other Curious / *Tracts* not in any former Impression. / — / The Third Edition. / London Printed, / And Re-printed in Dublin, by and for *Sam.* / *Fairbrother*, Bookseller in *Skinner-Row*, op- / posite to the *Tholsel*, MDCCXXXII.

[Title within double-lined frame.]
12mo; A–Q¹² — 2 pp. (t. + bl.), [III]–VIII (Preface), 2 pp. (Contents), [1]–372, 2 pp. advs.

Copies: T.C.D. (T m m 36), and Penn.
(b) The second volume has the same title, except that instead of 'In Two Volumes.' there is: The Second Volume.
[Title within double-lined frame.]
12mo; A–P^{12} — 2 pp. (f.t. + bl.), 2 pp. (title: 'A Key To The Lock' + bl.), 2 pp. (The Epistle Dedicatory to Mr. Pope), [1]–140, 2 pp. (Contents 'Bathos'); 2 pp. (title: 'Miscellanies In Verse' + bl.), 1–207, 3 pp. (Contents).
Copy: T.C.D. (T m m 36).

(3) Miscellanies / In / Prose / And / Verse. / — / The / Third Volume. / — / To which are added / Several Poems, and other Curious / *Tracts* not in the *English* Edition. / — / The Second Edition. / — / London Printed, / And Re-printed in Dublin, by and for *Sam.* / *Fairbrother*, at the *King's-Arms* in *Skinner-* / *Row*, opposite to the *Tholsel*, 1733.

[Title within double-lined frame.]
12mo; A–O^{12} — 2 pp. (t. + bl.), I–II (The Booksellers Advertisement), 1–199 + bl., 2 pp. (title *Miscellanies In Verse* + bl.), 1–128, 2 pp. *Contents* (unnumbered).
Copies: T.C.D. (T m m 36), and Penn.

(4) Vol. IV. / Of The / Miscellanies / Begun by / *Jonathan Swift*, D.D. / And / *Alexander Pope*, Esq. / Containing / All the Tracts in Prose and Verse / that have been since done by J.S. / D.D.D. S.P.D. to Compleat the / Three Former Volumes. / — / To which are added / Several other Poems by the same / Author, many of which are Print- / ed from Original Manuscripts, not / in any former Edition. / — / Dublin, / Printed by and for Samuel Fairbrother, / Bookseller, at the *King's-Arms* in *Skinner-* / *Row*, opposite to the *Tholsel*, 1735.

[Title within double-lined frame.]
12mo (in sixes); A–Ff^6 — 2 pp. (t. + bl.), 3 pp. (Publisher's Preface), 4 pp. (Contents), [I]–III (A History of Poetry), [1]–119 + bl., 2 pp. (title: Verse + bl.), 1–214.
Copy: Nat. Libr. of Ireland.
This volume contains one genuine piece here first printed: Ode to the King. On his Irish Expedition &c. 1691. Cf. *Poems*, XXXVII, 4–13, & No. 115.

Faulkner's 8vo Editions, 1735, &c.

Towards the end of 1734, when advertising his edition of the *Works*, Faulkner announced that "a few copies are printed on Royal Paper". This practice of printing copies on small and thin paper as well as on large and thick paper he continued for the later volumes. The order of their first publication (both L. P. and Sm. P.) is as follows: In 1735 Vols. I–IV were published; in 1738 Vols. V and VI (slightly different for L. P. and Sm. P.); in 1741 a volume of 'Letters', which later become Vol. VII; in 1746 Vol. VIII (two issues, the first partly on thick, partly on thin paper, the second on thin paper only — see No. 44) in 1752 for L. P.; in 1758 Vol. IX (slightly different for L. P. and Sm. P.); in 1762 Vol. X; in 1763 Vol. XI; in 1765 Vols. XII–XIII; in 1767 Vols. XIV–XVI; in 1768 Vols. XVII–XIX; in 1769 Vol. XX.

In 1759 Vol. III was reprinted (both L. P. and Sm. P.). Penn has a set of Vols. I–VIII, 1735–35–35–35, 38, 38, 41, 52 on very large and thick paper.

Penn also owns an L. P. set of 20 volumes; there is another in U.L.C. The title-page of Vol. I, dated 1768, says 'In Nineteen Volumes', but in 1769 Vol. XX was added. A look at the diagram on p. 47 shows the years; also how L. P. and Sm. P. copies from 1763 onwards are related. However, it is not clear when some of them were printed. Vols. III, V, VIII–XX present no difficulties; what happened with them can easily be read from the diagram. Vol. IV, dated 1769, has several special titles dated 1767. Vol. VII, dated 1770, has the special title of *Some Free Thoughts* also dated 1770. In these two cases we clearly have to do with volumes printed in 1767 and 1770 respectively, so that the Sm. P. copies of these two volumes dated 1763, which are exactly the same printing, must be cases of ante-dating. With the remaining volumes, I, II, VI, however, the case lies differently. Though their special titles are undated, and therefore do not betray any secret, it would seem that they were printed in 1763. At least, what happened with Vol. I points in this direction. The Vol. I, 1763, in the Gilbert Collection (see No. 45A (8a)) was soon exhausted, and had to be reprinted. The type having been distributed, it had to be reset. The body of the new book appears to be of the same printing in the 1763 Sm. P. (45 A (8b)), the 1768 L. P. (47) and the 1772 Sm. P. copies (48), but the prefatory matter is different. In the first 'To The Reader' is dated 'Dublin, October, 1762' at the end; there are no 'Contents' (apparently an oversight). In the other two 'To The Reader' is undated; there are 3 pages 'Contents'. From this it may be concluded that in 1762–3 both Sm. P. and L. P. copies were printed, that some of the Sm. P. copies were then published as just described, but that the rest of the Sm. P. copies and all the L. P. copies were preserved for future publication (in 1772 and 1768 respectively). Probably the same story holds for Vols. II and VI.

The growth of Faulkner's 8vo editions into sets (see the diagram after No. 48, *post*) is as follows:

I. *Works – – – In Four Volumes* (1735):

Though promised to appear towards the end of May 1734 at the farthest, these four volumes did not come out till Nov. 1734 and Jan. 1735 (see *Poems*, XXX, n.2). This delay was owing to Swift, who ordered certain things to be struck out that did not please him (*Corresp.*, V, 85).

II. *Works – – – In Six Volumes* (1738):

The first four volumes were reprinted, and Vols. V and VI were added. In this case the delay was even greater: promised towards the middle of May 1736, "or perhaps sooner", they did not appear until 1738.

III. *Works – – – In Six Volumes* (1742):

Vol. I was reprinted in 1742; hence a new title.

IV. *Works – – – In Eight Volumes* (1746):

Vols. V and VI had been reprinted in 1741, Vols. I and IV in 1742, Vol. III in 1743, and Vol. II in 1744. Moreover, in 1741, a volume of *Letters* had been published, but it had not been designated on the title-page as Vol. VII of the set. Yet it is generally found as such in this function. In 1746, however, when a new volume was added to the collection, this volume of *Letters*, 1741, was provided with a new title and called Vol. VII; and the new volume was then designated as Vol. VIII. In accordance with the new state of things Vol. I,

1742 (not yet exhausted), was then provided with a new title: *In Eight Volumes*, 1746. — Vol. III also appeared with the year 1746 on the title-page (information kindly supplied by Messrs. Heffer & Sons concerning a set in their cat. 321, item 870). However, as I have not seen this copy, I cannot say whether this is simply Vol. III, 1743, with a new title, or a reprint.

V. *Works – – – In Eight Volumes* (1751):

Some of the volumes being reprinted in this year, Vol. I, 1746 (not yet exhausted), was again provided with a new title: *In Eight Volumes*, 1751. The catalogue of the 'Bibliotheca Fageliana' mentions a copy Vol. V, 1751, but I have not seen it. Vol. VII was reprinted in 1751 (5th ed.), Vol. VIII in 1752, Vol. III in 1759.

VI. *Works – – – In Eleven Volumes* (1763):

To the existing eight volumes three new ones had been added, namely: Vol. IX in 1758, Vol. X in 1762 (*Prose Works* XII, 179) mentions a Vol. X, 1758, but I have not seen it, Vol. XI in 1763; so that there were now eleven volumes in all. As to their dates, however, they presented a very irregular appearance; and as Vol. I and Vol. V wanted reprinting, Faulkner resolved to create some order by providing all the eleven volumes with titles 1763. This enabled him to use up remainder volumes. If, for instance, we examine Vols. I–VI in the Gilbert Coll., Dublin, and Vols. VII–XI in Marsh, we find that Vol. I is new (1763), Vol. II is a 1735 copy, Vol. III 1759, Vol. IV 1735, Vol. V 1738, Vol. VI 1738, Vol. VII 1751, Vol. VIII 1752, Vol. IX 1758, Vol. X 1762, Vol. XI 1763 (new), all with new titles 1763. And it is of course possible that other early volumes were utilized in the same way (in fact, Vol. VII in the Gilbert Coll. is a 1741 copy, with title 1763, lacking, however, the last 4 + 32 pages). But at Penn is an eleven vol. set, all 1763, of which Vols. III, VIII, IX, X, XI are the same as above, while the rest are all different, Vols. I and V newly printed in 1763, and others printed later, and then provided with earlier titles 1763 (see Nos. 46 and 47, *post*, and the diagram after No. 48, *post*).

VII. *Works – – – In Nineteen Volumes* (1768):

Further volumes had been added to the collection: in 1765 Vols. XII and XIII, in 1767 three volumes of *Letters* (Vols. XIV, XV and XVI), in 1768 again three volumes of *Letters* (Vols. XVII, XVIII and XIX). Then Faulker resolved to an L. P. set 'In Nineteen Volumes' (see above; No. 47; and diagram). In 1769 the *Tale* was added to the set, with the appropriate title: 'Volume XX Of The Author's Works'. It was also issued separately.

VIII. *Works – – – In Twenty Volumes* (1772):

All the volumes in this set are earlier volumes, provided with new titles (see the diagram after No. 48, *post*).

Notes:

1. Faulkner's four volumes, 1735, constitute the first authoritative edition of Swift's works by themselves, i.e. not together with those of others as in the *Miscellanies*, 1727. As to the extent of Swift's co-operation in them opinions differ. See Orrery's *Remarks*, 1752, Letter VII; *Corresp.* IV, 318, 360, 390, 431, 444; V, 37, 81, 85, 145, 179–80, 224, 257, 338, 449; VI, 224 note 2; *Poems*, XXIX–XXXV; and especially A. E. Case, *Four Essays*. For Vol. II, see Elr. Ball, *Swift's Verse*, 271–2; for Vol. III, see No. 302, *post*, and Harold Williams, *Gulliver's Travels*, 1926, LXXXI–II; for Vol. IV see Herbert Davis, *The Drapier's Letters*, 1935, pp. LXXI, &c.

From this time dates a keen rivalry between Faulkner and the London publishers of Swift's works. In this bloodless strife Faulkner had for a long time the advantage on his side, he constantly adding, his rivals being frequently obliged to derive from him. It was not till 1765, when the first volumes of *Letters* were published in London, that this state of things became altered.

Another thing worth studying is the way in which Faulkner's volumes often came into existence. There is sometimes a considerable interval between the announcement of his promises to publish and the fulfilment of them. He frequently started printing as soon as he had got the disposal of new materials, even if they were insufficient for the formation of a complete volume, or though — as in the case of the earlier volumes — Swift placed obstacles in his way, often causing cancellation, especially in Vol. II, 1735. Hence often a difference of some years between the dates of his special titles and those of his volume-titles; and hence also his practice, apparent from his book advertisements, of "issuing separately" larger or smaller sections, or even complete volumes, before their inclusion into sets, or sometimes after it, with or without preservation of volume indications at the foot of the first page of each new sheet. Noteworthy also is Faulkner's practice of providing remainder copies of earlier volumes with later titles, sometimes even though new editions had appeared in the meantime. In some cases this was the result of his love of economy, in others of his desire for order.

2. In March 1754 Faulkner had great plans. In an *Advertisement* covering the last two pages of his edition of *Brotherly Love. A Sermon.* (see No. 808, *post*), he announced i.a. the publication of "the Works of the said Dr. *Swift*, in seven Volumes in large Quarto, fine Paper, and in a Beautiful New Type of this Size, With a Set of Cuts designed by the celebrated Hayman, of *London*". Has anyone ever seen such a 4to ed.?

3. The diagram clearly shows that Faulkner sometimes wished for order; witness the years 1763 and 1772. But equally clear is the fact that for the rest all kinds of combinations may occur. And yet, the 8 vol. set 1746, and the 19 vol. set 1768, are usually found in fixed shapes, namely in the combinations of volumes as given in the following pages under Nos. 44 and 47 respectively.

4. The various Faulkner editions, 8vo, 12mo, and 18mo, have plates in Vols. I–IV, in the *Tale* (those in the 8vo and 12mo editions are the same off-prints as those in the 1741 ed., No. 237, *post*; those in the 18mo ed. are different), and in Vols. XIV and XVII (the same off-prints in all three, 8vo, 12mo, and 18mo). The plates in Vols. I–IV give rise to the following observations:

There is a frontisp. portrait of Swift in Vol. I of all the editions, but they are from three different plates, for the 8vo, 12mo, and 18mo respectively.

There is a frontisp. in Vol. II, but not in the 18mo ed., nor in the later 8vo and 12mo editions. It is always from the same plate; but the 1735 8vo off-print is large, whereas all the others have been narrowed in on all four sides.

The frontisp. portrait of Gulliver, the 4 maps and 2 plans, in Vol. III, in the 18mo ed., are different from those in the others. In the 8vo and 12mo editions they are all from the same plates, with the exception of the frontisp. It is a good plate in the 1735 8vo ed. (inscribed: Capt. Lemuel Gulliver Splendide Mendax. Hor.), a much poorer one in all the others (inscribed: Capt. Lemiuel [*sic*]. Gulliver Splendide Mendax Hor.).

There is a frontisp. in Vol. IV, but not in the 18mo ed., nor in the later 8vo and 12mo editions. It is from two different plates, for the 8vo and 12mo editions respectively.

5. Some volumes, or parts of volumes, were published separately. They are: the *Tale*, Nos. 244 (47), 245 (52); *Gulliver's Travels*, Nos. 302 (49), 309 (53); *Poems*, Nos. 42, 51, 51A; *Letter Sacramental Test*, No. 512A; *Polite Conversation*, No. 763; *Directions To Servants*, Nos. 787, 788.

41. *Series-title:*

The / Works / Of / *J.S*, D.D, D.S.P.D. / In / Four Volumes. / Containing, / I. The Author's Miscellanies in Prose. / II. His Poetical Writings. / III. The Travels of Captain *Lemuel Gulliver* / IV. His Papers relating to *Ireland*, consisting of / several Treatises; among which are, The / Drapier's Letters to the People of *Ireland* / against receiving *Wood*'s Half-pence: Also, / two Original Drapier's Letters, never be- / fore published. / — / In this Edition are great Alterations and Addi- / tions; and likewise many Pieces in each Vo- / lume, never before published / — / *Dublin:* / Printed by and for George Faulkner, Printer / and Bookseller, in Essex-Street, opposite to / the Bridge. MDCCXXXV.

Miscellanies / In / Prose. / — / Vol. I. / — / [monogram] / = / *Dublin:* / Printed by and for George Faulkner, Printer / and Bookseller, in *Essex-Street*, opposite to the / Bridge. MDCCXXXV.

Volume II. / Containing the Author's / Poetical Works. / = / [monogram] / = / *Dublin:* / Printed by and for George Faulkner, Printer / and Bookseller, in *Essex-Street*, opposite to the / Bridge. MDCCXXXV.

Volume III. / Of the Author's / Works. / Containing, / Travels / Into Several / Remote Nations of the World. / In Four Parts, *viz.* / [*First column:*] I. A Voyage to Lil- / liput. / II. A Voyage to Brob- / dingnag. / III. A Voyage to La- / [*Second column:*] puta, Balnibarbi, / Luggnagg, Glubb- / dubdrib and Japan. / IV. A Voyage to the / Country of the / Houyhnhnms. / — / By *Lemuel Gulliver*, first a Surgeon, / and then a Captain of several Ships. / — / — — *Retroq*; / *Vulgus abhorret ab his.* / — / In this Impression several Errors in the *London* and *Dublin* / Editions are corrected. / — / *Dublin:* / Printed by and for George Faulkner, Printer / and Bookseller, in *Essex-Street*, opposite to the / Bridge. MDCCXXXV.

Volume IV. / Of the Author's / Works. / Containing, / A Collection of Tracts relating to / *Ireland;* among which are, The / *Drapier*'s *Letters* to the People of / *Ireland*, against receiving *Wood*'s / Half-pence: Also, two Original / *Drapier*'s *Letters*, never before / published. / = / [ornament] / = / *Dublin:* / Printed by and for George Faulkner, Printer / and Bookseller, in *Essex-Street*, opposite to the / Bridge. MDCCXXXV.

π^8, a^4, B–Y^8 — frontisp. (portrait of Swift), 2 pp. (t. + bl.), 2 pp. (title: 'Miscellanies In Prose' + bl.), 13 pp. (Subscribers' Names) + bl., 2 pp. (Contents), 4 pp. (The Publisher's Preface), [1]–323, 334–45 + bl. (no break in text; pages 324–35 are misnumbered 334–45).

π^4, B–Gg^8, Hh^7, Ii 1 — frontisp. (Swift in medallion), 2 pp. (t. + bl.), 2 pp. (Advertisement), 4 pp. (Contents), [1]–480.

π^2, $*_*{}^{*4}$, A^4, B–Cc^8, Dd^2 — frontisp. (L. Gulliver), 2 pp. (t. + bl.), 2 pp. (Advertisement + bl.), [I]–VI (Letter Gulliver to Sympson), VII–VIII (The Publisher to the Reader), 8 pp. (Contents), [1]–404 — 4 maps and 2 plans.

π^4, B–Bb^8, Cc^2 — frontisp. (Swift in arm-chair), 2 pp. (t. + bl.), 2 pp. (Advertisement), 4 pp. (Contents), 2 pp. (title: 'A Letter From A Member, &c.' + bl.), [I]–II (The Publisher's Advertisement To The Reader), [1]–58, 2 pp. (title: 1st Drapier Letter + bl.), 65–388. Pp. 61–4 omitted in the numbering. There are both Sm. P. and L. P. copies of these four volumes. In Vol. I pages 321 to the end are an afterthought.

In Vol. II several leaves have been cancelled, owing to Swift's wish to have certain things struck out after they had been printed (*Corresp.*, V, 85), to have introductions and footnotes inserted (*Corresp.*, VI, 224 n 2), and to the fact that several pieces came late to the editor's hands (cf. *Corresp.*, V, 449–52). They are: O^8 (pp. 207–8, replaced by *O; P 1–6 (pp. 209–20), replaced by three double-leaves, the first and second signed P and P 2; T 5–8 (pp. 281–8), replaced by two double-leaves, the first signed *J; U 1–6 (pp. 289–300), replaced by three double-leaves, the first and second signed U and U 2; Z 4–5 (pp. 343–6), replaced by one double-leaf, signed *Z; Aa 3 (pp. 357–8), replaced by one leaf, signed *Aa; Bb 2–6 (pp. 371–80), replaced by two double-leaves and one single leaf; Bb 2 signed *Bb 2; Ee 1–4 (pp. 417–424), replaced by two double-leaves, the first signed Ee; Hh 8 is absent, but replaced by Ii (pp. 479–80). Pp. 160 and 263 are misnumbered 148 and 236.

Another state:

In the Rothschild copy, No. 2151, P 1–6 and Ee 1–4 are not described as cancels; cancellans are inserted after U 3. Harvard has two copies of Vol. II; in one pp. 357–8 are the original leaf Aa 3, in the other the cancel *Aa, which enables us to see the alterations made, especially a softening of the introductory note on p. 358.

Cf. Davis's 8vo and 12mo, 1735 (Nos. 25^5 and 27A, *ante*), and Faulkner's Vol. II, 12mo, 1735 (No. 49, *post*) which has no cancels; it has a new chronological arrangement.

In Vol. III the page-numbers 250 and 251 have been interchanged; 285, 330, 331, 334, 335 have been misprinted 283, 310, 311, 314, 315. B 2 is signed A 2. In Vol. IV, pp. 112, 255, 346 are misprinted 12, 155, 349, while in L. P. copies p. 270 is misprinted 70. For a separate issue of the first tract of Vol. IV, see No. 512a.

Prometheus (pp. 385–8) is an afterthought; it is not listed in the *Contents*.

I 8 (pp. 127–8) is a cancel; Both Pickering and Chatto, cat. 357, item 822, and Rothschild, No. 2151, are copies in which I 8 is in its first state (*Prose Works*, X, 2U) signed *I.

In some copies (B.M., and two at Penn, Sm. P. and L. P.) the headpiece of p. 65 shows the Dean between two female figures, and an appropriate legend ("Detur Indigenti") at the top; in others (Forster, and Bibl. Nat. Paris) it is a neutral one representing a sheet of water with ducks, an angler, a bridge, etc.

Sheet N (pp. 177–92) others in three states:
(1) p. 184, l. 5 *pleat, I have printed*, &c.;
    p. 187, l. 8 received;
    p. 189, l. 11 another;
    p. 190, l. 26 was;
    p. 192, ll. 30–1 Parsimony, runs
(2) The second and fourth readings corrected into 'seen' and 'were'.

(3) All five corrected, the first, third, and fifth into '*pleat, I procured a Copy of the following Letter from one of the Author's Friends, with whom it was left, while the Author was in England; and I have printed* &c.', 'any other' and 'that runs'.

Harvard has a copy of (1) and another of (2); Penn's two copies, Sm. P. and L. P., are (3). As the second and fourth misprints occur in the inner forme, and the other three in the outer forme, it appears that during the presswork correction in this sheet took place twice, one at a later stage than the other.

Contemporary criticism

1313. Momus Mistaken: A Fable. Occasioned by the Publication of the Works of the Revd. Dr. Swift, D. S. P. D. in Dublin. By Mr. James Arbuckle, A. M. Dublin: Printed in the Year 1735. — Folio; 1 page.

Copy: B.M. 839g m 23 (192).

*

42. *Series title:*

The / Works / Of / *J.S*, D.D, D.S.P.D. / In / Six Volumes. / Containing, / I. The Author's Miscellanies in Prose. / II. His Poetical Writings. / III. The Travels of Captain Lemuel / Gulliver. / IV. His Papers relating to *Ireland*, consisting of / several Treatises; among which are, The / Drapier's Letters to the People of *Ireland* / against receiving *Wood*'s Half-pence. / V. The Conduct of the Allies, and the / Examiners. / VI. The Publick Spirit of the Whigs; and / other Pieces of Political Writings, / With Polite Conversation, *&c.* / = / *Dublin:* / Printed by George Faulkner, in / *Essex-street.* / — / M,DCC,XXXVIII.

Volume I. / Of The / Author's Works. / Containing / Miscellanies / In / Prose. / = / [monogram] / = / *Dublin:* / Printed by and for George Faulkner. / — / M,DCC,XXX,VIII.

Frontisp., π^1, $*_*{}^{*4}$, $2\pi^4$, $2*_*{}^{*4}$, B–U^8, X^6 — frontisp. (portrait of Swift), 2 pp. (series-title + bl.), 2 pp. (volume-title + bl.), 4 pp. (Preface), 2 pp. (Contents), 15 pp. Subscribers' Names + bl., [1]–318.

This order is not quite correct; according to the catchwords it should be: frontisp., series-title, volume-title, Subscribers' Names, Contents, The Publisher's Preface, text.

The numbering of O 5–8 is totally wrong; it is 201, 204, 205, 204, 205, 208, 209, 208, and should have been 201–8; after this, sheet P starts with 211.

Volume II. / Containing the Author's / Poetical Works. / = / [monogram] / = / *Dublin:* / Printed by and for George Faulkner, Book- / seller, in *Essex-street*, opposite to the Bridge. / — / M,DCC,XXXVIII.

Frontisp., A^4, B–Bb^8, Cc^4 — frontisp. (Swift in medallion), 2 pp. (t. + bl.), 2 pp. (Advertisement), 4 pp. (Contents), [1]–392.

Volume III. / Of The / Author's Works. / Containing / Travels / Into Several / Remote Nations of the World. / In Four Parts, *viz.* / [*First column:*] I. A Voyage to Lil- / liput. / II. A Voyage to Brob- / dingnag. / III. A Voyage to La- / [*Second column:*] puta, Balnibarbi, / Luggnagg, Glubb- / dubdrib and Japan. / IV. A Voyage to the / Country of the / Houyhnhnms. / — / By *Lemuel Gulliver*, first a Surgeon, / and then a Captain of several Ships. / — / — — *Retroq*; / *Vulgus abhorret ab his.* / = / *Dublin:* / Printed by and for George Faulkner. / — / M,DCC,XXX,VIII.

Frontisp., π^2, $_*{}^*_*{}^4$, A^4, B–Bb^8 — frontisp. (L. Gulliver), 2 pp. (t. + bl.), 2 pp. (Advertisement + bl.), I–VI (Letter Gulliver to Sympson), VII–VIII (The Publisher to the Reader), 8 pp. (Contents), [1]–382, 2 pp. blank — 4 maps and 2 plans.

Volume IV. / Of the Author's / Works, / Containing, A / Collection of Tracts, / Relating To / *Ireland*; / Among which are, / The Drapier's Letters / To The / People of Ireland, / Against / Receiving Wood's Half-pence: / Also, / Two Original Drapier's Letters. / = / *Dublin:* / Printed by and for George Faulkner, / in *Essex-street*, opposite to the Bridge. / — / MDCCXXXVIII.

Frontisp., A^4, B–Aa^8, Bb^4 — frontisp. (Swift in arm-chair), 2 pp. (t. + bl.), [III]–IV (Advertisement), V–VIII (Contents), 2 pp. (title: Letter, &c. + bl), I–II (The Publisher's Advertisement To The Reader), [1]–372.

Volume V. / Of The / Author's Works. / Containing / The Conduct of the Allies, / and the Examiners. / = / [monogram] / = / *Dublin:* / Printed by and for George Faulkner. / — / M,DCC,XXX,VIII.

A^2, B–Z^8 — 2 pp. (t. + bl.), 2 pp. (The Publisher's Preface), 2 pp. (title: Conduct + bl.), 2 pp. (Preface), [1]–338, 10 pp. Index. Pp. 336, 338 misnumbered 306, 328.

Volume VI. / Of The / Author's Works. / Containing / The Publick Spirit of the / Whigs; and other Pieces of Politi- / cal Writings, &c. With Polite / Conversation, &c. / = / [monogram] / = / *Dublin:* / Printed by and for George Faulkner. / — / M,DCC,XXX,VIII.

[A]^2, B–O^8, P^2, Q–Cc^8 — 2 pp. (t. + bl.), 1 p. (The Publisher's Preface), 1 p. (Contents), [1]–386, 2 pp. blank.
Copies: U.L.C. and Penn.
Vol. I, 1738 of the Bodleian set at the foot of the 1st page of the 15 pp. Subscribers' Names 'Vol. I. *Rt.', and at the foot of the 9th page 'Vol. V$*_*{}^*$ Rt.'; The Penn copy has 'Vol. I. *Rt.' and 'Vol. I. $*_*{}^*$ Rt.'

Vol. II, 1737, was also issued separately.

Vol. V, 1738, appears in two states or issues, differing only in the prefatory matter:

(x) The title-page has *Conduct*, and a thin monogram; the catch-word on the second page of 'The Publisher's Preface' is 'Subscriber's'.

(y) The title-page has CONDUCT, and a thick monogram; the catch-word is 'The'.

There are more differences in these four pages, i.a. in the head- and tail-pieces on the third and fourth pages. It would seem that (x) being soon detected to be susceptible to improvement was replaced by (y). The second state was then given with all L. P. copies and some Sm. P. ones; the first state with some Sm. P. copies only.

The 'Subscribers Names' occurs in various shapes:

(A) 13 pages + blank (at foot of 13th page: Vol. I. a The).

(B) 15 pages + blank.

(a) at foot of 1st page: Vol. VI ∗ Rt.
    at foot of 9th page: Vol. V ∗∗∗ Rt.

(b) at foot of 1st page: Vol. V ∗ Rt.
    at foot of 9th page: Vol. V ∗∗∗ Rt.

(c) at foot of 1st page: Vol. I ∗ Rt.
    at foot of 9th page: Vol. I ∗∗∗ Rt.

Copies: U.L.C. and Penn.

It seems that in 1738, when Vols. V and VI were added, the following happened:

(1) *Old* buyers (those who had bought Vols. I–IV in 1735):

L. P. (Vols. I–IV, 1735): Vol. I has (A); Vol. V (state y) has nothing. — Copy: Penn.

Sm. P. (Vols. I–IV, 1735): Vol. I has (A); Vol. V (state y) has nothing. — Copy: Penn.

(2) *New* buyers (those who did not buy till 1738):

L. P. (Vols. I–IV, 1735; not yet exhausted): Vol. I has (A); Vol. V (state y) has (B)(b). — Copy: P. S. O'Hegarty.

Sm. P. (Vols. I–IV, 1735; not yet exhausted): Vol. I has (A); Vol. V (state y) has (B)(b) — Copy: Harvard.

Sm. P. (Vols. I–IV, 1735 all sold; new volumes I–IV, 1738): Vol. I has (B)(c); Vol. V (state x) has nothing. Copy: Penn. (B)(a), with the misprint 'Vol. VI', apparently afterwards corrected in the type-setting, occurs in a copy of Vol. V (state y) in the Bibl. Nationale, Paris.

Harvard has another set (besides the one mentioned above) in which Vol. V showing (B)(b) is state x.

See 'Some Bibliographical Notes On Dublin Editions Of Swift', by P. S. O'Hegarty, in *The Dublin Magazine*, XIV, No. 1, Jan.–March 1939, 67–70.

Copies of Vol. VI are the same, except for sheets Q–Z^8, Aa 1–2 (pp. [213]–344), containing *A Treatise On Polite Conversation*. Besides several minor variations, some copies (L. P. and Sm. P. ones) have pictorial scenes as head-pieces on pp. 252, 302, 334; the D of the word 'Dialogues' on the second title-page, p. [249], is in upper case, the other letters of that word are in lower case; the imprint of that title has 'by and for'. Other (Sm. P. ones) have stencil-shaped headpieces; the word 'Dialogues' is entirely in upper case; the imprint has 'by' only.

On the verso (p.[214]) of the title there is:— | *Errata*, | *In the following Treatise.* | P. 231, l. 12, *for* Direction, *read* Discretion. | P. 234, l. 11, *for* I have therefore, by the | chief Patterns, *read* wherein I follow the chief | Patterns. | —.

Both L. P. and Sm. P. copies have these *Errata* printed on the verso of the title. But Penn has a Sm. P. copy with the two *Errata* correctly printed in the text, though the verso of the title preserves them.

For separate issue(s) see No. 763.

43. *Series-title:*

The / Works / Of / *J.S.* D.D.D.S.P.D. / In / Six Volumes. / Containing / I. The Author's Miscellanies in Prose. / II. His Poetical Writings. / III. The Travels of Captain Lemuel / Gulliver. / IV. His Papers relating to *Ireland*, consisting of / several Treatises; among which are, The / Drapier's Letters to the People of *Ireland* / against receiving *Wood*'s Half-pence. / V. The Conduct of the Allies, and the / Examiners. / VI. The Publick Spirit of the Whigs; and / other Pieces of Political Writings, / With Polite Conversation, *&c.* / = / *Dublin:* / Printed by and for George Faulkner, in / *Essex-street.* / — / MDCCXLII.

Volume I. / Of The / Author's Works. / Containing / Miscellanies / In / Prose. / = / [monogram] / = / *Dublin:* / Printed by and for George Faulkner, / — / M,DCC,XLII.

π^2, $*_*^{*2}$, $2\pi^1$, B–U^8, X^6 — 2 pp. (series-title + bl.), 2 pp. (volume-title + bl.), 4 pp. (The Publisher's Preface), 2 pp. (Contents), [1]–318. After p. 206 there are two unnumbered pages; then follows p. 211 — no break in text.

Copy: T.C.D. (C.5.43). No frontisp. portrait of Swift. Penn and Smith Coll. Libr. copies have neither frontisp. nor series-title.

Query: Is a frontisp. essential to this copy, or not?

Another state: π^2, B–U^8, X^6 $*_*^{*2}$ [inserted after X 3]; 2 pp. (t. + bl.), 2 pp. (Contents (Catchword 'The')), [1]–312 (text), 4 pp. (The Publisher's Preface), 313–18 (text).

Copy: Penn.

44. *Series-title:*

The / Works / Of / Jonathan Swift, D.D, D.S.P.D. / In / Eight Volumes. / Containing, / I. His Miscellanies in Prose. / II. His Poetical Writings. / III. The Travels of Capt. Lemuel Gulliver. / IV. Papers relating to Ireland, and the / Drapier's Letters. / V. The Conduct of the Allies, and the / Examiners. / VI. The Publick Spirit of the Whiggs, *&c.* / with Polite Conversation. / VII. Letters to and from Dr. Swift. / VIII. Directions to Servants, Sermons, / Poems, *&c.* / = / *Dublin:* / Printed by George Faulkner, in *Essex-Street,* / M,D,CC,XLVI.

Volume I. / Of The / Author's Works. / Containing / Miscellanies / In / Prose. / = / [monogram] / = / *Dublin:* / Printed by and for George Faulkner, / — / M,DCC,XLII.

π^2, $*_*^{*3}$, B–U^8, X^6. Except for the series title-page, this is the same printing as the 1742 copy (No. 43). This volume has a frontisp. portrait of Swift. After the two titles there are sometimes 3 pp. *Dedication to Lord Chesterfield* + bl., which properly belong to Vol. VIII.

Volume II. / Containing the Author's / Poetical Works. / = / [monogram] / = / *Dublin:* / Printed by and for George Faulkner, in / *Essex-Street.* / — / MDCCXLIV.

Frontisp., π^4, B–Bb^8, Cc^4 — frontisp. (Swift in medallion), 2 pp. (t. + bl.), 2 pp. (Advertisement), 4 pp. (contents), [1]–392 (page 86 misnumbered 66).

Volume III. / Of The / Author's Works. / Containing / Travels / Into Several / Remote Nations of the World. / In Four Parts, *viz.* / [*First column:*] I. A Voyage to Lil- / liput. / II. A Voyage to Brob- / dingnag. / III. A Voyage to La- / [*Second column:*] puta, Balnibarbi, / Luggnagg, Glubb- / dubdrib and Japan. / IV. A Voyage to the / Country of the / Houyhnhnms. / — / By *Lemuel Gulliver,* first a Surgeon, / and then a Captain of several Ships. / — / — — *Retroq;* / *Vulgus abhorret ab his.* / = / *Dublin:* / Printed by and for George Faulkner, in / *Essex-street,* opposite to the Bridge. / — / MDCCXLII.

Frontisp., π^2, A–Bb^8 — frontisp. (L. Gulliver), 2 pp. (t. + bl.), 2 pp. (Advertisement + bl.), I–VI (Letter Gulliver to Sympson), VII–VIII (The Publisher to the Reader), 8 pp. (Contents), [1]–382, 2 pp. blank — 4 maps and 2 plans (pp. 239 and 315 in some copies misnumbered 232 and 351).
III. (1746):
There is a Volume III, dated 1746 (Heffer, cat. 321, item 870), but I have not seen it.

Volume IV. / Of the Author's / Works, / Containing, A / Collection of Tracts, / Relating To / *Ireland;* / Among which are, / The Drapier's Letters / To The / People of Ireland, / Against / Receiving Wood's Half-pence: / Also, / Two Original Drapier's Letters. / = / *Dublin:* / Printed by and for George Faulkner, / in / *Essex-street,* opposite to the Bridge. / — / MDCCXLII.

Frontisp., A^4, B–Aa^8, Bb^4 — frontisp. (Swift in arm-chair), 2 pp. (t. + bl.), [III]–IV (Advertisement), V–VIII (Contents), 2 pp. (title: Letter, &c. + bl.), I–II (The Publisher's Advertisement To The Reader), [1]–372 (p. 241 misnumbered 141 in some copies).

Volume V. / Of The / Author's Works. / Containing / The Conduct of the Allies, / and the Examiners, *&c.* / = / [monogram] / = / *Dublin:* / Printed by and for George Faulkner. / — / M,DCC,XLI.

A^2, B–Z^8 — 2 pp. (t. + bl.), 2 pp. (The Publisher's Preface), 2 pp. (title: Conduct + bl.), 2 pp. (Preface), [5]–338, 10 pp. Index (pp. 13–16 repeated in numbering).

Volume VI. / Of The / Author's Works. / Containing / The Publick Spirit of the / Whigs; and other Pieces of Political / Writings; with Polite Con- / versation, &c. / = / [monogram] / = / *Dublin:* / Printed by and for George Faulkner, / — / M,DCC,XLI.

π^2, B–O^8, P^2, Q–Cc^8 — 2pp. (t. + bl.), 1 p. (The Publisher's Preface), 1 p. (Contents), [1]–386, 2 pp. blank.

Letters / To and From / Dr. J. Swift, D.S.P.D. / From The / Year 1714, to 1738. / To which are added, / Several Notes and Translations / not in the *London* Edition. / = / *Dublin:* / Printed by and for George Faulkner, / MDCCXLI.

π^1, B–S^8, T^4, U^8, X^2; 2 U–X^8, 2 C^2 — 2 pp. (advs.), 2 pp. (t. + bl.), 11 pp. Contents + bl., [1]–280 (*Finis.* at foot); 281–300 (Supplement — *Finis.* at foot); 2 pp. (title: Some Free Thoughts + bl.), 2 pp. (Advertisement to the Reader + bl.), 1–32 (*Finis.* at foot). There are both L. P. and Sm. P. copies of this volume. For a fuller description of this volume, see No. 64, *post.*

The [4 pp., 1–32] containing *Some Free Thoughts Upon The Present State Of Affairs*, were also issued separately (see No. 778, *post*).

Second issue:
Volume VII. / Of The / Author's Works, / Containing / Letters / To and From / Jonathan Swift, D.D, D.S.P.D. / = / *Dublin:* / Printed by and for George Faulkner, / M,DCC,XLVI.

π^7, B–S^8, T^4; U^8, X^2, *T 1; U–X^8, C^2 — 2 pp. (t. + bl.), 11 pp. Contents + bl., [1]–280 (*Finis.* at foot), 281–300 (Supplement — *Finis.* at foot), 301–302 (one more letter); 2 pp. (title: Some Free Thoughts + bl.), 2 pp. (Advertisement to the Reader + bl.), 1–32 (*Finis.* at foot).

This book is the same printing as the preceding one, but the first two leaves (bearing advertisements and title 'Letters – – – 1741') have been removed, and replaced by one leaf bearing title 'Volume VII – – – 1746'. Moreover, one leaf (pp. 301–2) bearing one more letter, has been inserted after page 300.

Volume VIII. / Of The / Author's Works, / Containing / Directions to Servants; / And / Other Pieces in Prose and Verse, / published in his Life-time; with several / Poems, Letters, and other Pieces never be- / fore printed. / — / [monogram] / — / *Dublin:* / Printed by and for George Faulkner, / M,DCC,XLVI.

π^{18}, B–E^8, F–I^4, K–Kk^8, Ll^3, π^2 — 2 pp. (t. + 'Advertisement To the London Edition' on verso), 3 pp. 'Dedication to Chesterfield' + bl., 7 pp. 'The Preface By The Dublin Bookseller' + bl., 4 pp. (Contents), I–XIV (Dr. Swift's Will), 2 pp. (title: 'Directions To Servants', dated 1745 + bl.), [I]–II (The Publisher's Preface), 1–21 + bl., 1–74, 77–9 + bl.; [81] (title: Reasons Humbly offered &c.), [82] (Advertisement), 83–466 (pp. 324, 362, 466 misnumbered 224, 162, 366), 4 pp. (music).

Second issue:

Volume VIII. / Of The / Author's Works, / Containing / Directions to Servants; / And / Other Pieces in Prose and Verse, / published in his Life-time; with several / Poems, Letters, and other Pieces never be- / fore printed. / — / [monogram] / — / *Dublin:* / Printed by and for George Faulkner, / M,DCC,XLVI.

π^9, *⁴, A–F⁸, G⁴, [K] 3–8, L–Kk⁸, Ll³, π^2 — 2 pp. (t. + 'Advertisement To the London Edition' on verso), 3 pp. 'Dedication to Chesterfield' + bl., 7 pp. 'The Preface By The Dublin Bookseller', 1 p. (advs.), 4 pp. (Contents), [I]–VIII (The Last Will and Testament of Swift), 2 pp. (title: 'Directions to Servants', dated 1746 + bl.), [I]–II (The Publisher's Preface), 1–12, 17–25 + bl., 1–6, 33–48, 23–77 + bl.; [81] (title: Reasons Humbly offered, &c.), [82] (Advertisement), 83–466 (pp. 324, 362, 466 misnumbered 224, 162, 366), 4 pp. (music). A 2 not signed.

In these two issues pages [81] to the end are the same printing; the rest is different. The full title of the first issue has the year M,DCC,XLVI., of the second M,DCC,XLVI. The *Preface by the Dublin Bookseller* is followed by a blank page in the first, by a page bearing two advertisements in the second issue. But the main difference lies in *Swift's Will* (in the first issue 14 pp., in the second 8 pp.), and in *Directions to Servants* (both printings also issued separately — cf. Nos. 787–8).

Reasons Humbly offered, &c. (already printed in 1743) starts on K 3 = p. [81]. In the first issue K is a complete sheet 1–8; in the second K has 6 leaves only (sewing-thread between K 4 and K 5), K 1 and K 2 having been cut away.

In both issues R 4 (pp. 195–6) is a cancel. In the first issue the new leaf is signed '****' only, in the second 'Vol. VIII. ****'. It replaces a leaf bearing 'Verses', as appears from the catchword of p. 194. Instead of them was printed 'The Elephant; or The Parliament — Man. Written many years since. Taken from Coke's Institutes', but apparently not by Swift (cf. *Swift's Verse*, 219; *Poems*, 1106).

It is curious to note that the first issue is printed partly on thick, partly on thin paper. Possibly it was intended at first to be added as Vol. VIII to the other L. P. volumes, but giving no satisfaction on account of the haphazard printing and pagination of the *Directions to Servants*, a far superior copy (both L. P. and Sm. P.) was printed in 1752 (see 45, and diagram).

Variants occur. The Nat. Libr. Dublin has a copy of the first issue with *Swift's Will* in the shorter form (pp. [I]–VIII). The Bodl. (Ratcl. E 231) has a copy of the second issue with *Swift's Will* in both shapes ([I]–VIII, and I–XIV).

45. *Series-title:*

The / Works / Of / Jonathan Swift, D.D.D.S.P.D. / In / Eight Volumes. / Containing, / I. His Miscellanies in Prose. / II. His Poetical Writings. / III. The Travels of Captain Lemuel / Gulliver. / IV. Papers relating to Ireland, and the / Drapier's Letters. / V. The Conduct of the Allies, and the / Examiners. / VI. The Publick Spirit of the Whiggs, / &c. with Polite Conversation. / VII. Letters to and from Dr. Swift. / VIII. Directions to Servants, Sermons, / Poems, &c. / = / *Dublin:* / Printed by George Faulkner, in *Essex-Street,* / M,DCC,LI.

Volume I. / Of The / Author's Works. / Containing / Miscellanies / In / Prose. / = / [monogram] / = / *Dublin:* / Printed by and for George Faulkner, / — / M,DCC,XLII.

Except for the series title-page, this is the same printing as the 1742 and 1746 copies (Nos. 43 and 44, *ante*). This volume has a frontisp. portrait of Swift.

Copies: Worcester Coll. Libr., Oxford, and Bibl. Nat. Paris.

45A. *Reprinted and new volumes:*
(1) Vol. V, 1751 is mentioned in the catalogue of the books in the 'Bibliotheca Fageliana', sold at auction, by Christie, in March 1802 (item 3380), but I have not seen a copy.

(2) Volume VII. / Of The / Author's Works: / Containing / Letters / To and From / Dr. J. Swift, D.S.P.D. / From The / Year 1714, to 1738. / As Also, / Some Free Thoughts upon the Present / State of Affairs. / = / The Fifth Edition. / = / *Dublin:* / Printed by and for George Faulkner. / MDCCLI.

A⁴, a², B–T⁸, U⁸ (two leaves, the first of them signed T 5, inserted in the middle of this sheet), X⁸, Y⁶ — 2 pp. (t. + bl.), 10 pp. (Contents), [1]–296, 297–9 + bl., 2 pp. (title: Some Free Thoughts + bl.), 2 pp. (Advertisement to the Reader + bl.), 301 [misprinted 300]–332. It seems as if two leaves, bearing two letters, have been inserted in the middle of sheet U. The catchword 'Some' on U 4 verso (p. 296) corresponds with the first word on U 5 recto (p. [297]).

Copies: K.I., Nat. Libr. Dublin, Worcester Coll. Libr. Oxford, Univ. of Mich. (Hubbard Coll.), and own.

(3) Volume VIII. / Of The / Author's Works, / Containing / Directions to Servants; / And / Other Pieces in Prose / and Verse. / — / [monogram] / = / Dublin: / Printed by George Faulkner. / — / MDCCLII.

π⁴, B–Ii⁸, Kk 1, π² (music) — 2 pp. (t. + bl.), 5 pp. (Contents), 1 p. (Advertisement), 1–497 + bl., 4 pp. (music).

Copies: Bodl. Z 518 Th, U.L.C., and Penn. There are both Sm. P. and L. P. copies of this volume; the former were used in 1763 (Nos. 46 and 46a) and in 1772 (No. 48).

(4a) Volume IX. / Of The / Author's Works, / Containing / Letters to Governor Hunter. / The History of the last Session of / Parliament, and the Peace of / Utrecht. Written at Windsor in / the Year 1713. / The Craftsman of December 12, 1730. / And the Answer thereto. / A Treatise on Good Manners and / Good Breeding. / — / By the Rev. Dr. J. Swift, D.S.P.D. / — / [monogram] / = / Dublin: / Printed by George Faulkner in Essex-street, / — / M,DCC,LVIII.

A–U⁸, X³; Y–Aa⁸ — 2 pp. (t. + bl.), 2 pp. (To the Reader), [5]–14, 2 pp. (title: The History Of The Last Session Of Parliament + bl.), [1]–310; [1]–44, 1 p. unnumbered, 3 pp. advs. — K 3 (133–4) is a cancel. There are only Sm. P. copies of this volume.

Copies: Smith Coll. Libr., and Penn.

(4b) *Another issue* (same title):

The difference between the two issues lies in the last 48 pp. In the second issue p. [34] has been left blank, and the *Treatise On Good Manners And Good Breeding* has been given a separate title [35–6], after which there was no room left for the 3 pp. advs., so that the last section collates: Y–Aa⁸ — [1]–47, 1 p. blank. There are both Sm. P. and L. P. copies of this volume; the former were used in 1763 (see Nos. 46 and 46a) and in 1772 (see No. 48).

Copies: U.L.C., and own.

There is also a separate issue of the *History* (see No. 810, *post*).

(5) Volume III. / Of The / Author's Works. / Containing / Travels / Into Several / Remote Nations of the World. / In Four Parts. / [*First column:*] I. A Voyage to Lilli- / put. / II. A Voyage to Brob- / dingnag. / III. A Voyage to Lapu- / [*Second column:*] ta, Balnibarbi, / Luggnagg, Glubb- / dubdrib, and Japan. / IV. A Voyage to the / Country of the / Houyhnhnms. / — / By *Lemuel Gulliver*, first a Surgeon, / and then a Captain of several Ships. / — / — — *Retroq*; *Vulgus abhorret ab his.* / = / Dublin: / Printed by George Faulkner, in Essex-street. / MDCCLIX.

π¹ frontisp., A⁸, b⁶, B–Cc⁸, Dd⁶ — frontisp. (L. Gulliver), 2 pp. (t. + bl.), 2 pp. (Advertisement + bl.), V–XI (Letter Gulliver to Sympson), XII–XIV (The Publisher To The Reader), 13 pp. Contents + bl., [1]–412 — 4 maps and 2 plans. There are both L. P. and Sm. P. copies of this volume; the latter were used in 1763 (see Nos. 46 and 46a) and in 1772 (see No. 48).

Copies: U.L.C., and own.

(6a) Volume X. / Of The / Author's Works. / Containing, / Sermons on several Subjects; / And / Other Pieces on Different / Occasions. / — / [monogram] / = / Dublin: / Printed by George Faulkner. / — / M,DCC.LXII.

π³, B–Ee⁸, Ff 1 — 2 pp. (t. + bl.), [III]–V (Contents), 1 p. blank, [3]–436. There are only Sm. P. copies of this volume.

Copies: U.L.C., and Penn.

(6b) *Another issue:*

Volume X. / Of The / Author's Works. / Containing, / Sermons on Several Subjects; / And / Other Pieces. / = / Dublin: / Printed by George Faulkner, / — / MD,CCLX,III.

Except for the title-page this is the same printing as (6a).

There are both Sm. P. and L. P. copies of this volume; the former were used in 1763 (see Nos. 46 and 46a) and in 1772 (see No. 48).

(7) Volume XI. / Of The / Author's Works. / Containing, / Letters on different Subjects; / And / Poems on several Occasions. / = / *Dublin:* / Printed by George Faulkner. / — / M,DCC,LXIII.

A⁷, B–Oo⁸, Pp² — 2 pp. (t. + bl.), 11 pp. Contents + bl., [1]–441 + bl. (423–4 repeated in numbering). There are both Sm. P. and L. P. copies of this volume; the former were used in 1763 (see Nos. 46 and 46a) and in 1772 (see No. 48).

(8a) *Series-title:*
The / Works / Of / Dr. J. Swift, D.S.P.D. / In / Eleven Volumes. / Containing, / [*First column:*] I. His Miscellanies in Prose. / II. His Poetical Writings. / III. The Travels of Captain / Lemuel Gulliver. / IV. Papers relating to Ireland, / and the Drapier's Letters. / V. The Conduct of the Al- / lies, and the Examiners. / VI. The Publick Spirit of the / Whigs, &c. with Polite / Conversation. / VII. Letters to and from Dr. / Swift. / VIII. Directions to Servants, / Sermons, Poems, &c. / [*Second column:*] IX. Letters to Governor Hun- / ter. The History of the / last Session of Parliament, / and the Peace of Utrecht. / Written at Windsor in the / Year 1713, &c. / X. Sermons on several Sub- / jects, and other Pieces on / different Occasions. / XI. Letters on different Sub- / jects. The Author's Life; / and Poems on several Oc- / casions. / = / *Dublin:* / Printed by George Faulkner. / — / M,DCC,LXIII.

Volume I. / Of The / Author's Works. / Containing, / Miscellanies / In / Prose. / — / [monogram] / = / *Dublin:* / Printed by George Faulkner. / — / M,DCC,LXIII.

π¹ frontisp., π², a⁴, b², [π⁶, a²], B–X⁸ — frontisp. (portrait of Swift), 2 pp. (series-title + bl.), 2 pp. (volume-title + bl.), [I]–XII (To The Reader, dated at the end: '*Dublin, October,* 1762.'), [13 pp. (Subscribers' Names) + bl., 2 pp. (Contents)], [1]–319 + bl.
There are only Sm. P. copies of this volume.
Copy: Gilbert Coll., Dublin.
The six leaves, a² (= 13 pp. Subscribers' Names + bl., 2 pp. Contents), which I have placed between square brackets, are old leaves of 1735, not properly belonging to this volume.

(8b) *Another reprint of Vol. I* (same titles):
π¹ frontisp., π², c², a⁴, b², B–Ee⁸ — frontisp. (portrait of Swift), 2 pp. (series-title + bl.), 2 pp. (volume-title + bl.), 3 pp. (Dedication to Chesterfield + bl.), [I]–XII ('To The Reader', dated at the end: '*Dublin, October,* 1762.'), [1]–431 + bl.
There are only Sm. P. copies of this volume.
Copy: Penn.
C² and B–Ee⁸ (Dedication and text) are new; the rest is the same; there are no 'Contents'.
(8c) A variant of (8b), differing from it in the prefatory matter only, printed on both L. P. and Sm. P., the former used in 1768 (see No. 47), the latter in

1772 (see No. 48): π^1 frontisp., A^8, b^2, C^2, B–Ee^8 — frontisp. (portrait of Swift), 2 pp. (series-title + bl.), 2 pp. (volume-title + bl.), [V]–XVII ('To The Reader', not dated at the end), 3 pp. (Contents), 3 pp. (Dedication to Chesterfield), 1 p. blank, [1]–431 + bl.

Only [A]^8, b^2 (the two titles, 'To The Reader', and the 'Contents') are new; the rest is the same.

(9) Volume II. / Of The / Author's Works. / Containing, / Poems / On / Several Occasions. / — / [monogram] / = / *Dublin:* / Printed by George Faulkner / — / M,DCC,LXIII.

A^3, b^3, B–Dd^8, Ee 1 — 2 pp. (t. + bl.), [III]–V (Advertisement), 1 p. blank, 5 pp. Contents + bl., [1]–417 + bl. There are both Sm. P. and L. P. copies of this volume.

(10) Volume V. / Of The / Author's Works. / Containing, / The Conduct of the Allies, / and the Examiners, *&c.* / = / [monogram] / = / Dublin: / Printed by George Faulkner, / — / MDCCLXIII.

A^2, B–Hh^8, Ii 1, Kk^4 — 2 pp. (t. + bl.), [I]–VI, [7]–481 + bl., 1–8 (Index). There are both Sm. P. and L. P. copies of this volume.

(11) Volume VI. / Of The / Author's Works. / Containing, / The Publick Spirit of the Whigs; / and other Pieces of Political Writings; / with Polite Conversation, / &c. / — / [monogram] / = / *Dublin:* / Printed by George Faulkner. / — / M,DCC,LXIII.

π^2, B–Ii^8, Kk^6 — 2 pp. (t. + bl.), 1 p. (The Publisher's Preface), 1 p. (Contents), [1]–508. There are both Sm. P. and L. P. copies of this volume.

46. *Series-title:*
The / Works / Of / Dr. J. Swift, D.S.P.D. / In / Eleven Volumes. / Containing, / [*First column:*] I. His Miscellanies in Prose. / II. His Poetical Writings. / III. The Travels of Captain / Lemuel Gulliver. / IV. Papers relating to Ireland, / and the Drapier's Letters. / V. The Conduct of the Al- / lies, and the Examiners. / VI. The Publick Spirit of the / Whigs, &c. with Polite / Conversation. / VII. Letters to and from Dr. / Swift. / VIII. Directions to Servants, / Sermons, Poems, &c. / [*Second column:*] IX. Letters to Governor Hun- / ter. The History of the / last Session of Parliament, / and the Peace of Utrecht. / Written at Windsor in the / Year 1713, &c. / X. Sermons on several Sub- / jects, and other Pieces on / different Occasions. / XI. Letters on different Sub- / jects. The Author's Life; / and Poems on several Oc- / casions. / = / *Dublin:* / Printed by George Faulkner. / — / M,DCC,LXIII.

Volume I. / Of The / Author's Works. / Containing, / Miscellanies / In / Prose. / — / [monogram] / = / *Dublin:* / Printed by George Faulkner. / — / M,DCC,LXIII.

This is a new, reprinted volume 1763 (see 45A (8a)).

Volume II. / Of The / Author's Works. / Containing, / Poems / On / Several Occasions. / — / [monogram] / = / *Dublin:* / Printed by George Faulkner / — / M,DCC,LXIII.

This is a copy 1735 (No. 41) with renewed title 1763, as above.

Volume III. / Of The / Author's Works. / Containing, / Travels / Into Several / Remote Nations of the World. / In Four Parts, viz. / [*First column:*] I. A Voyage to Lilliput. / II. A Voyage to Brobding- / nag. / III. A Voyage to Laputa, / [*Second column:*] Balnibarbi, Luggnagg, / Glubdubdrig, and Japan. / IV. A Voyage to the Country / of the Hoyhnhnms. [*sic*] / — / By *Lemuel Gulliver*, first a Surgeon, / and then a Captain of several Ships. / — / — — *Retroq;* / *Vulgus abhorret ab his.* / = / *Dublin:* / Printed by George Faulkner. / — / M,DCC,LXIII.

This is a copy 1759 (No. 45A (5)) with renewed title 1763, as above.

Volume IV. / Of The / Author's Works. / Containing, A / Collection of Tracts, / Relating To / *Ireland:* / Among which are, / The Drapier's Letters / Against / Receiving Wood's Half-pence: / Also, / Two Original Drapier's Letters. / = / Dublin: / Printed by George Faulkner, / — / MDCCLXIII.

This is a copy 1735 (No. 41) with renewed title 1763, as above. — The head-piece on p. 65 has the Dean between two female figures; p. [184] has the extra four lines.

Volume V. / Of The / Author's Works. / Containing, / The Conduct of the Allies, / and the Examiners, *&c.* / = / [monogram] / = / Dublin: / Printed by George Faulkner, / — / MDCCLXIII.

This is a copy 1738 (No. 42) with renewed title 1763, as above. — It is the issue with the catchword 'The'.

Volume VI. / Of The / Author's Works. / Containing, / The Publick Spirit of the Whigs; / and other Pieces of Political Writings; / with Polite Conversation, / *&c.* / — / [monogram] / = / *Dublin:* / Printed by George Faulkner. / — / M,DCC,LXIII.

This is a copy 1738 (No. 42) with renewed title 1763, as above. — It is the issue with the pictorial scenes.

Volume VII. / Of The / Author's Works. / Containing, / Letters / To and From / Dr. J. Swift, D.S.P.D. / From The / Year 1714, to 1738. / As Also, / Some Free Thoughts upon the / Present State of Affairs. / = / *Dublin:* / Printed by George Faulkner, / — / M,DCCL,XIII.

This is a copy 1751, 5th ed. (No. 45A (2)) with renewed title 1763, as above.

Volume VIII. / Of The / Author's Works. / Containing, / Directions to Servants; / And / Other Pieces in Prose / and Verse. / — / [monogram] / = / *Dublin:* / Printed by George Faulkner. / — / M,DCC,LXIII.

This is a copy 1752 (No. 45A (3)) with renewed title 1763, as above.

Volume IX. / Of The / Author's Works. / Containing, / Letters to Governor Hunter. / The History of the last Session of Parliament, / and the Peace of Utrecht. Written at Wind- / sor in the Year 1713. / The Craftsman of December 12, 1730, and / the Answer thereto. / A Treatise on Good Manners and Good Breed- / ing. / — / [monogram] / = / *Dublin:* / Printed by George Faulkner. / — / M,DCC,LXIII.

This is a copy 1758 (No. 45A (4b)) with renewed title 1763, as above.

Volume X. / Of The / Author's Works. / Containing, / Sermons on several Subjects; / And / Other Pieces. / = / *Dublin:* / Printed by George Faulkner, / — / MD,CCLX,III.

This is a copy 1762 (No. 45A (6a)) with renewed title 1763 as above.

Volume XI. / Of The / Author's Works. / Containing, / Letters on different Subjects; / And / Poems on several Occasions. / = / *Dublin:* / Printed by George Faulkner. / — / M,DCC,LXII.

This is a new volume 1763 — see No. 45A (7).
Only Vols. I and XI are new; the rest are remainders.
Copies of Vols. I–VI in the Gilbert Coll., of Vols. VII–XI in Marsh.
Vol. VII in the Gilbert Coll. is even a Vol. [VII], 1741 (14 pp., 1–300, the rest is lacking) with renewed title 1763, as above (cf. No. 44).

46A. Another set of 'Eleven Volumes' 1763, with the same titles as those of No. 46. Vols. III, VIII, IX, X, XI are entirely the same as those of No. 46; Vol. I was reprinted in 1763 ('To The Reader' has 'Dublin, October, 1762' at the end); Vols. V, and probably II and VI, were also reprinted in 1763; Vols. IV and VII are later printings provided with ante-dated titles 1763 (see note before No. 41). This is my own set. In 1765, 1767, 1768, 1769 new volumes were added (see the diagram).

8vo:

I: This is No. 45A (8b).
II: This is 45A (9).
III: This is No. 45A (5), with renewed title 1763.
IV: This is Vol. IV, 1769 (No. 47), with ante-dated title 1763.
V: This is No. 45A (10).
VI: This is 45A (11).
VII: This is Vol. VII, 1770 (No. 47), with ante-dated title 1763.
VIII: This is No. 45A (3), with renewed title 1763.
IX: This is No. 45A (4a), with renewed title 1763.
X: This is No. 45A (6b).
XI: This is No. 45A (7).

These eleven volumes, as well as the additional Vols. XII–XX (No. 47), all Sm. and thin Paper, were re-issued in 1772 (see No. 48, and the diagram).

47. *Series-title:*

The / Works / Of the Reverend / Dr. Jonathan Swift, / Dean of *St. Patrick*'s, Dublin. / In / Nineteen Volumes. / Containing / [*First column:*] I. His Miscellanies in Prose. / II. His Poetical Writings. / III. Gulliver's Travels. / IV. Papers relating to Ireland, / and the Drapier's Letters. / V. The Conduct of the Allies, / and the Examiners. / VI. The Publick Spirit of the / Whigs, &c. and Polite Con- / versation. / VII. Letters to and from Dr. / Swift. / VIII. Directions to Servants, / Sermons, Poems, &c. / IX. Letters; the History of / the last Session of Parliament, / and the Peace of Utrecht, / &c. / X. Sermons, and other Pieces. / XI. Letters, &c. the Author's / Life, and Poems. / [*Second column:*] XII. History of the four last / Years of Queen Anne's / Reign; Letters; and Ser- / mons, &c. Collected by / Deane Swift, Esq. / XIII. Letters to and from se- / veral very eminent Persons; / Poems on various Occa- sions. / Collected by Deane Swift, / Esq. / XIV. XV. and XVI. Letters to / and from Dr. Swift. With / Notes by the Rev. Thomas / Birch, D.D.F.R.S. John / Hawkesworth, L.L.D. / and Mr. Thomas Wilkes. / With many Original Pieces. / XVII. XVIII. and XIX. Let- / ters to and from Dr. Swift. / Collected by Deane Swift, / Esq. With several Originals. / = / *Dublin:* / Printed by George Faulkner. / MDCCLXVIII.

8vo (L. P.):

Volume I. / Of The / Author's Works. / Containing, / Miscel- lanies / In / Prose. / = / [monogram] / = / *Dublin:* / Printed by George Faulkner. / — / MDCCLXVIII. [This is No. 45A (8c).]

Volume II. / Of The / Author's Works. / Containing, / Poems / On / Several Occasions. / [monogram] / Dublin: / Printed by George Faulkner. / MDCCLXX. [This is No. 45A (9).]

Volume III. [This is No. 45A (5), 1759.]

Volume IV. / Of the Author's / Works, / Containing, A / Collection of Tracts / Relating To / *Ireland;* / Among which are, / The Drapier's Letters / To The / People of *Ireland*, / Against / Receiving Wood's Halfpence. / = / Dublin: / Printed by George Faulkner. / — / MDCCLXIX.

π^1 frontisp., π^1, A⁴, B–Hh⁸ — frontisp. (Swift in arm-chair), 2 pp. (t. + bl.), [I]–III (Advertisement), 1 p. blank, 4 pp. (Contents), [1]–480. Frontispiece and A gathering missing from Penn copy.

Volume V. [This is No. 45A (10).]

Volume VI. / Of The / Author's Works. / Containing / The Publick Spirit of the / Whigs; and other Pieces of Politi- / cal Writings, &c. With Polite / Conversation, &c. / [monogram] / *Dublin:* / Printed by George Faulkner. / MDCCLXXI. This is No. 45A (11).

Volume VII. / Of The / Author's Works. / Containing, / Letters / To And From / Dr. J. Swift, D.S.P.D. / From The / Year 1714, to 1738. / To which are added, / Several Notes and Translations / not in the *London* Edition. / = / *Dublin:* / Printed by and for George Faulkner. / M,DCC,LXX.

A–Cc⁸, Dd⁴, Ee² — 2 pp. (t. + bl.), 12 pp. (Contents), [1]–2 (advs.), [1]–372, 2 pp. (title: Some Free Thoughts + bl.), 2 pp. (Advertisement to the Reader + bl.), 1–36.

Volume VIII. [This is Vol. VIII, 1752.] This is No. 45A (3).

Volume IX. [This is Vol. IX, 1758, 2nd issue—see No. 45A, (4b) *ante*.] This is No. 45A (4a).

Volume X. [This is No. 45A (6b).]

Volume XI. [This is No. 45A (7).]

Volume XII. / Of The / Author's Works. / Collected And Revised / By Deane Swift, Esq. / of Goodrich in Herefordshire. / *Hæ tibi erunt artes*. Virgil. / [monogram] / Dublin: / Printed by George Faulkner, / — / MDCCLXV.

A⁴, B–Ee⁸ — 2 pp. (t. + bl.), III–V (Contents), 1 p. blank, VII–VIII (The Editors To The Reader), [1]–429, [1]–3 (advs.).

The / Works / Of / Dr. Jonathan Swift, / Dean of St. Patrick's, Dublin. / Volume XIII. / Collected And Revised / By Dean [*sic*] Swift, Esq; / Of Goodrich, in Herefordshire. / *Hæ tibi erunt artes.* Virgil. / = / Dublin: / Printed by George Faulkner. / — / MDCCLXV.

A⁴, B–Aa⁸, Bb 1 — 2 pp. (t. + bl.), 6 pp. (Contents), [1]–370.

Volume XIV. / Containing / Letters / To And From / Dr. Jonathan Swift, / Dean of St. Patrick's, Dublin, / From / The Year 1703, to 1743. / With / Notes Explanatory and Historical, / By / The Rev. Thomas Birch, D.D.F.R.S. / John Hawkesworth, L.L.D. / And / The Editor, Mr. Thomas Wilkes. / = / Dublin: / Printed by George Faulkner, / — / MDCCLXVII.

Frontisp., a⁴, b², a–e⁴, f 1, B–Gg⁸, Hh⁷ — frontisp. (bust of Swift), 2 pp. (t. + bl.), 2 pp. (Dedication to Temple + bl.), [V]–VI (The Publisher To The Reader), [VII]–XII (Preface), I–XLI (Contents), 1 p. blank, [1]–477 + bl.

Volume XV. / [same title as Vol. XIV, except:] / = / Dublin: / Printed by George Faulkner, 1767.

π², a³, b–e⁴, f², B–Z⁸, Aa² — 2 pp. (t. + bl.), 2 pp. (advs.), I–XLI (Contents), 1 p. blank, [1]–355 + bl.

Volume XVI. / [same title as Vol. XIV, except:] / — / With An / Appendix, / Containing many original Pieces. / = / Dublin: / Printed by George Faulkner, 1767.

π¹, a², b–d⁴, e², B–R⁸, S², A⁸, B⁴, C², D–E⁴, F² — 2 pp. (t. + bl.), I–XXXI (Contents), 1 p. blank, [1]–260, [6]–28 (Appendix), 29–48 (Index).

Volume XVII. / Of The / Author's Works. / Containing / Letters / Written By The Late / Dr. Jonathan Swift, / Dean of St. Patrick's, Dublin, / And / Several Of His Friends. / From the Year 1700 to 1742. / Published From The Originals; / Collected And Revised / By Deane Swift, Esq. / Of Goodrich In Herefordshire. / — / To which are added, / Some Originals, never before published; / And / Illustrated with Historical and Explanatory Notes, / by the Publisher. / = / *Dublin:* / Printed by and for George Faulkner, / MDCCLXVIII.

Frontisp., A–Cc⁸ — frontisp. (Stella), 2 pp. (t. + bl.), [III]–VII (Momus Mistaken), 1 p. blank, [1]–VII (Contents), 1 p. blank, [1]–376, 377–90 (Index), 2 pp. advs.

Volume XVIII. / [same title as Vol. XVII].

A⁶, Bb⁸, Cc² — 2 pp. (t. + bl.), [I]–X (Contents), [1]–378, 379–88 (Index).

Volume XIX. / [same title as Vol. XVII].

π^1, A⁶, B–Ff⁸ — 2 pp. (t. + bl.), I–XII (Contents), [1]–438, [439]–448 (Index).

Volume XX. / Of The / Author's Works. / Containing, The / Tale of a Tub. / — / [monogram] / = / *Dublin:* / Printed by George Faulkner. / — / MDCCLXIX.

> Frontisp., π^1, A⁸, b–d⁸, e³, B–T⁸ — frontisp., 2 pp. (t. + bl.), 2 pp. (title: Tale + bl.), III–XXVI (Apology), XXVII (Postscript), 1 p. blank, 1 p. (Treatises written), 1 p. blank, XXXI–XXXVII (Dedication to Sommers), 1 p. blank, XXXIX–XL (The Bookseller To The Reader), XLI–LI (Dedication to Prince Posterity), 1 p. blank. LIII–LXIX (The Preface), 1 p. blank, 1–286, 2 pp. advs. — 7 plates.
>
> Copies: U.L.C. and Penn.
>
> Vol. XX also issued separately, with the omission of the volume-title-leaf (see No. 244).

48. *Series-title:*

The / Works / Of the Reverend / Dr. Jonathan Swift, / Dean of *St. Patrick's*, Dublin. / In / Twenty Volumes. / Containing, / [*First column:*] I. His Miscellanies in Prose. / II. His Poetical Writings. / III. Gulliver's Travels. / IV. Papers relating to Ire- / land, and the Drapier's / Letters. / V. The Conduct of the Allies, / and the Examiners. / VI. The Publick Spirit of the / Whigs, &c. and Polite Con- / versation. / VII. Letters to and from Dr. / Swift. / VIII. Directions to Servants, / Sermons, Poems, &c. / IX. Letters; the History of / the Last Session of Parliament, / and the Peace of Utrecht, / &c. / X. Sermons and other Pieces. / XI. Letters, &c. the Author's / Life and Poems. / [*Second column:*] XII. History of the four last / Years of Queen Anne's / Reign; Letters; and Ser- / mons &c. Collected by / Deane Swift, Esq. / XIII. Letters to and from / several very eminent Per- / sons; Poems on various / Occasions. Collected by / Deane Swift, Esq. / XIV. XV. and XVI. Letters / to and from Dr. Swift. / With Notes by the Rev. T. / Birch, D.D. F. R. S. John / Hawkesworth, L.L.D. / and others. With many / Original Pieces. / XVII. XVIII. and XIX. Let- / ters to & from Dr. Swift. / Collected by D. Swift, Esq. / With several Originals. / XX. Tale of a Tub. / = / Dublin: / Printed by George Faulkner. / MDCCLXXII.

Volume-titles:

They are after the following pattern, with only the contents and the volume-number differing:

The / Works / Of the Reverend / Dr. Jonathan Swift, / Dean of *St. Patrick's*, Dublin. / Containing, / Miscellanies / In / Prose. / — / Volume I. / — / [monogram] / — / Dublin: / Printed by George Faulkner, / MDCCLXXII.

– – – / Poems / On / Several Occasions. / — / Volume II. / — / – – –

– – – / The Travels of / Lemuel Gulliver, first a Surgeon, / and then a Captain of several Ships. / Into Several / Remote Nations of the World. / In Four Parts. / [*First column:*] I. A Voyage to Lilliput. / II. A Voyage to Brobding- / nag. / III. A Voyage to Lapu- / ta, Balnibarbi, Lugg- / [*Second column:*] nagg, Glubb-dubdrib, / and Japan. / IV. A Voyage to the Coun- / try of the Houyhn- / hnms. / —— Retroq; / Vulgus abhorret ab his. / — / Volume III. / — / – – –

– – – / Tracts / relating to / Ireland. / Among which, are / The Drapier's Letters. / — / Volume IV. / — / – – –

– – – / The Conduct of the Allies, / and the Examiners. / — / Volume V. / — / – – –

– – – / The Publick Spirit of the / Whigs; and other Pieces of / Political Writings; with Polite / Conversation, &c. / — / Volume VI. / — / – – –

– – – / Letters to and from Several / Eminent Persons from the Year / 1714, to 1738. / As also some Free Thoughts / upon the Present State of / Affairs. / Volume VII. / — / – – –

– – – / Directions to Servants; / and / Other Pieces / in / Prose and Verse / Volume VIII. / — / – – –

– – – / Letters to Governor Hunter. / The History of the last Session of Parliament, / and the Peace of Utrecht. Written at Windsor in / the Year 1713. / The Craftsman of December 12, 1730. And the An- / swer thereto. / A Treatise on Good-Manners and Good-Breeding. / — / Volume IX. / — / – – –

– – – / Sermons on several Subjects; / and / Other Pieces on different / Occasions. / — / Volume X. / — / – – –

– – – / More of his Literary Correspondence, particularly / with Dr. King, Archbishop of *Dublin*, &c. / Original Poems on Several Occasions. / An Account of the Life and Writings of Dr. / *Jonathan Swift*. / — / Volume XI. / — / – – –

– – – / Memoirs of the four last Years of / Queen Anne's Reign. / Sermons on several Occasions, &c. &c. / Collected and revised / By Deane Swift, Esq. / of Goodrich, in Herefordshire. / Hæ tibi erunt artes. Virgil. / — / Volume XII. / — / – – –

– – – / Letters to and from many eminent / Persons. / And Poems on several Occasions. / Collected and revised / By Deane

Swift, Esq. / of Goodrich, in Herefordshire. / Hæ tibi erunt artes. Virgil. / — / Volume XIII. / — / – – –

– – – / Letters / to and from / Several Eminent Persons, / from / The Year 1703, to 1743. / With / Notes Explanatory and Historical, / By / The Rev. Thomas Birch, D.D.F.R.S. / John Hawkesworth, L.L.D. and others. / — / Volume XIV. / — / – – –

– – – / [same as preceding vol.] / — / Volume XV. / — / – – –

– – – / [same as preceding vol.] / — / With an / Appendix, / Containing many original Pieces. / — / Volume XVI. / — / – – –

– – – / Letters / To and From Several Persons, / From the Year 1700 to 1742. / Published from the Originals; / Collected and revised / By Deane Swift, Esq; / of Goodrich in Herefordshire. / — / And Illustrated with Historical and Explanatory Notes, by the Pub- / lisher. / — / Volume XVII. / — / – – –

– – – / [same as preceding vol.] / — / Volume XVIII. / — / – – –

– – – / [same as preceding vol.] / — / Volume XIX. / — / – – –

– – – / The / Tale of a Tub. / — / Volume XX. / — / – – –

All these twenty volumes are earlier ones (Sm. P.), provided with new titles as above (see the diagram); but the renewal has not always been effected with proper care. In some cases plates have been inserted into the wrong volumes, or titles have been preserved which should have been cancelled; while sometimes — and this is much worse — leaves in front bearing 'Advertisement' or 'Contents', special titles, or advertisement-leaves have been thrown away without any reason. However, the collations should be as those given in No. 47, *ante*.

*
* *

Faulkner's 12mo Editions, 1735, &c.

As the diagram after No. 52, *post* sufficiently shows the progress of Faulkner's 12mo editions, it is not necessary to enter into detail here. There is, however, room for the following remarks:

The 1738 set of six volumes has *In Four Volumes* on the title-page. Was this a mistake, or was the appearance of Vols. V and VI (in the same year) not yet foreseen, when Vols. I–IV were reprinted? In 1741 there were two editions of the *Letters*, one "for Edward Exshaw", the other "by and for George Faulkner". The former was in 1746 re-issued with a new title and Faulkner's name in the imprint. None of these three has 'Volume VII' on the title-page (see Nos. 51 and 64, *post*). The *Letters* were reprinted in 1748 (then for the first time called 'Volume VII' on title-page); again in 1753 ('Volume VII' and 'Sixth Edition' on title-page).

The *Preface* in Vol. I, 1747 (dated Oct. 1734) has a P.S., dated Nov. 1747, in which we are told that since the appearance of the first four volumes,

Faulkner Editions (8vo)

	In Four Vols.	In Six Vols.	In Six Vols.	In Eight Vols.	In Eight Vols.	In Eleven Vols.	In Nineteen Vols.	In Twenty Vols.
I	**1735**	1738	1742		1746 . = 1751	1763	1768	1772
II	**1735**	1737	= 1744	1746		1763 1763[1]	1770. =	1772
III	**1735**	1738	1743. . ?	1746	**1759**. =	1763	=	1772
IV	**1735**	1738	1742			1763[1] 1763[2]	**1769**. =	1772
V		**1738** (2) 1741			1751	1763 1763[2]	=	1772
VI		**1738** (2) 1741			(1738 =)	1763 1763[2]	**1771** =	1772
VII		[1741]	=	1746	1751 (5th ed.)	1763	**1770**. =	1772
VIII				**1746** (2)	**1752**. =	1763	=	1772
IX					**1758** (2)	1763	=	1772
X					1762 :=	**1763**	=	1772
XI						**1763**	=	1772
XII							=	1772
XIII						**1765**	=	1772
XIV						**1765**	1767	1772
XV							1767	1772
XVI							1767	1772
XVII							1768	1772
XVIII						1768	=	1772
XIX						1768	=	1772
XX							1769	1772

The years in bold type represent both L. P. and Sm. P. copies; the others Sm. P. copies only. Dates indicate editions or reissues; figures in parentheses represent slightly different printings for L. P. and Sm. P.

[1] Reprints of 1735.
[2] Reprints of 1738.

Vols. V and VI were added in 1735 (which, of course, is wrong; the *Preface* itself in Vol. V, 1738, is dated: April 18, 1738), Vol. VII in 1741, and Vol. VIII in 1745. This makes me think there may be a Vol. VIII, 1745.

The 1747 set is the only Faulkner edition that mentions the 'edition' on the title-page of Vol. I, namely: The Sixth Edition, revised and corrected.

As to the plates, see note 5, before No. 41, *ante*.

49. *Series-title:*
The / Works / Of / *J.S*, D.D, D.S.P.D. / In / Four Volumes. / Containing, / I. The Author's Miscellanies in Prose. / II. His Poetical Writings. / III. The Travels of Capt. *Lemuel Gulliver*. / IV. His Papers relating to *Ireland*, consisting / of several Treatises; among which are, / The Drapier's Letters to the People / of *Ireland*, against receiving *Wood*'s Half- / pence: Also, two Original Drapier's / Letters, never before published. / — / In this Edition are great Alterations and / Additions; and likewise many Pieces in / each Volume, never before published. / — / *Dublin:* / Printed by and for George Faulkner, / Printer and Bookseller, in *Essex street*, op- / posite to the Bridge. M,DCC,XXXV.

Miscellanies / In / Prose. / — / Vol. I. / — / [monogram] / — / *Dublin:* / Printed by and for George Faulkner, / Printer and Bookseller, in *Essex-street*, op- / posite to the Bridge. MDCCXXXV.

Frontisp., π^5, B–Bb^6 — frontisp. (portrait of Swift), 2 pp. (series-title + bl.), 2 pp. (volume-title + bl.), 2 pp. (Contents), 4 pp. (The Publisher's Preface), 1–288. [Aa 3 signed Aa 2].

Volume II. / Containing the Author's / Poetical Works. / = / [monogram] / = / *Dublin:* / Printed by and for George Faulkner, / Printer and Bookseller, in *Essex-street*, / opposite to the Bridge, M,DCC,XXXV.

Frontisp., π^4, B–Hh^6, Ii^2 — frontisp. (Swift in medallion), 2 pp. (t. + bl.), 2 pp. (Advertisement), 4 pp. (Contents), 1–363 + bl.

Volume III. / Of the Author's / Works / Containing, / Travels / Into Several / Remote Nations of the *World*. / In Four Parts, *viz.* / [*First column:*] I. A Voyage to Lil- / liput. / II. A Voyage to Brob- / dingnag. / III. A Voyage to La- / [*Second column:*] puta, Balnibarbi, / Luggnagg, Glubb- / dubdrib and Japan. / IV. A Voyage to the / Country of the / Houyhnhnms. / — / By *Lemuel Gulliver*, first a Sur- / geon, and then a Captain of several Ships. / — / — — *Retroq;* / *Vulgus abhorret ab his.* / — / In this Impression several Errors in the *London* and / *Dublin* Editions are corrected. / — / *Dublin:* / Printed by and for George Faulkner, / Printer and Bookseller, in *Essex-street*, / opposite to the Bridge. MDCCXXXV.

Frontisp., π^6, A^4, B–Dd^6, Ee^2, Ff 1 — frontisp. (L. Gulliver), 2 pp. (t. + bl.), 1 p. (Advertisement), 1 p. blank, [I]–VI (Letter Gulliver to Sympson), VII–VIII (The Publisher to the Reader), 8 pp. (Contents), [1]–312, 332–6 + bl. (no break in text) — 4 maps and 2 plans.

Second leaves not signed; except for signatures A, F, O, S, X, Cc, third leaves are signed 2.

Volume IV. / Of the Author's / Works. / Containing, / A Collection of Tracts rela- / ting to *Ireland;* among which / are, The *Drapier's Letters* to / the People of *Ireland*, against / receiving *Wood's* Half-pence: / Also, two Original *Drapier's* / *Letters*, never before pub- / lished. / = / = / *Dublin:* / Printed by and for George Faulkner, / Printer and Bookseller, in *Essex-Street*, / opposite to the Bridge. MDCCXXXV.

Frontisp., π^4, A^6, B^5, [π]^1, C–Z^6, Aa–Dd^6 [Cancel after [π] 4; A 5, 6 signed A 3, 4; C 5, 6 cancelled, inserts with vertical chain-lines; L 3 signed L 2, R 3 signed R 5, Z 2 signed Z 3; M 1, 2 are cancels, fail to pick up catch-words from L 6v] — frontisp. (Swift in arm-chair), 2 pp. (t + bl.), 2 pp. (Advertisement), 4 pp. (Contents), 2 pp. (title: A Letter + bl.), [I]–II (The Publisher's Advertisement To The Reader), 1–18, 2 pp. (title: A Proposal + bl.), 19–318.

Copies: T.C.D. (R. 11. 35–8), Univ. of Mich. (Hubbard Coll.), and Penn.

Compared with the four volumes 8vo, 1735 (No. 41), these four volumes 12mo show a chronological re-arrangement of the pieces in Vols. I and II. *Prometheus*, a verse-piece, has been removed from Vol. IV 8vo to Vol. II 12mo, where it belongs.

50. *Series-title:*
The / Works / Of / *J.S*, D.D, D.S.P.D. / In / Four Volumes. / Containing, / I. The Author's Miscellanies in / Prose. / II. His Poetical Writings. / III. The Travels of Capt. Lemuel Gulliver. / IV. His Papers relating to *Ireland,* / consisting of several Treatises; / among which are, The Drapier's / Letters to the People of *Ireland,* / against receiving *Wood's* Half- / pence: Also, two Original Dra- / pier's Letters, never before pub- / lished. / — / *Dublin:* / Printed by and for George Faulkner, Printer and / Bookseller, in *Essex-street*, opposite to the Bridge. / — / M,DCC,XXXVIII.

Miscellanies / In / Prose. / = / Volume I. / = / [monogram] / = / *Dublin:* / Printed by and for George Faulkner, Printer and / Bookseller, in *Essex-street*, opposite to the Bridge. / — / M,DCC,XXXVIII.

Frontisp., π^5, B–M^{12}, N^4, π^2 — frontisp. (portrait of Swift), 2 pp. (series-title + bl.), 2 pp. (volume-title + bl.), 2 pp. (Contents), 4 pp. (The Publisher's Preface), 1–272, 4 pp. advs.

Volume II. / Containing the Author's / Poetical Works. / = / [monogram] / = / *Dublin:* / Printed by and for George Faulkner,

Printer and / Bookseller, in *Essex-street*, opposite to the Bridge. / — / M,DCC,XXXVII.

> Frontisp., π^4, B–P^{12}, Q^6 — frontisp. (Swift in medallion), 2 pp. (t. + bl.), 2 pp. (Advertisement), 4 pp. (Contents), 1–348.

Volume III. / Of the Author's / Works. / Containing / Travels / Into Several / Remote Nations of the World. / In Four Parts, *viz.* / [*First column:*] I. A Voyage to Lilli- / put. / II. A Voyage to Brob- / dingnag. / III. A Voyage to La- / [*Second column:*] puta, Balni- barbi, / Luggnagg, Glubb- / dubdrib and Japan. / IV. A Voyage to the / Country of the / Houyhnhnms. / — / By Lemuel Gulliver; first a Surge- / on, and then a Captain of several Ships. / — / — — *Retroq;* / *Vulgus abhorret ab his.* / — / In this Impression several Errors in the *London* and / *Dublin* Editions are corrected. / — / *Dublin:* / Printed by and for George Faulkner, in *Fssex-street.* [*sic*] / M,DCC,XXXVIII.

> Frontisp., π^2, *$_*$*^{4}, A^4, B–N^{12}, O^8 — frontisp. (L. Gulliver), 2 pp. (t. + bl.), 2 pp. (Advertisement + bl.), [I]–V (Letter Gulliver to Sympson), VI–VII (The Publisher to the Reader), 1 p. advs., 8 pp. (Contents), [1]–302, 2 pp. blank — 4 maps and 2 plans.

Volume IV. / Of the Author's / Works. / Containing, A / Collection of Tracts, / Relating to / *Ireland;* / Among which are, / The Drapier's Letters / To The / People of Ireland: / Against / Receiving Wood's Half-Pence: / Also, / Two Original Drapier's Letters. / = / *Dublin:* / Printed by and for George Faulkner, Printer and / Bookseller, in *Essex-Street*, opposite to the Bridge. / — / MDCCXXXVIII.

> Frontisp., π^4, B–O^{12}, P^2 — frontisp. (Swift in arm-chair), 2 pp. (t. + bl.), 2 pp. (Advertisement), 4 pp. (Contents), 2 pp. (title: A Letter + bl.), [I]–II (The Publisher's Advertisement To The Reader), 1–17 + bl., 2 pp. (title: A Proposal + bl.), 25–316.

Volume V. / Of The / Author's Works. / Containing / The Conduct of the Allies, / and the Examiners. / = / [monogram] / = / *Dublin:* / Printed by and for George Faulkner. / — / M,DCC,XXX,VIII.

> π^2, B–N^{12}, O^6 — 2 pp. (t. + bl.), 2 pp. (The Publisher's Preface), 1 p. (title: The Conduct), 2 pp. (The Preface), [1]–289, 8 pp. (Index) — P. [1] begins on a verso!

Volume VI. / Of The / Author's Works. / Containing / The Publick Spirit of the Whigs; / and other Pieces of Political Writings; / with Polite Conversation, *&c.* / = / [monogram] / = / *Dublin:* / Printed by and for George Faulkner. / — / M,DCC,XXXVIII.

π^2, B–P^{12} — 2 pp. (t. + bl.), 2 pp. (The Publisher's Preface), [1]–333 (Contents on verso), 2 pp. blank.

I possess another set (the same as above), completed by Vol. [VII, 1746], Vol. VIII (1751), and *Supplement* (1739); see Nos. 51 and 58, *post*.

51. *Series-title:*

The / Works / Of / Jonathan Swift, D.D, D.S.P.D. / In / Eight Volumes. / Containing / I. His Miscellanies in Prose. / II. His Poetical Writings. / III. The Travels of Captain Lemuel / Gulliver. / IV. Papers relating to Ireland, and the / Drapier's Letters. / V. The Conduct of the Allies, and the / Examiners. / VI. The Publick Spirit of the Whigs, / &c. with Polite Conversation. / VII. Letters to and from Dr. Swift. / VIII. Directions to Servants, Sermons, / Poems, &c. / = / The Sixth Edition, revised and corrected. / = / Dublin: / Printed by George Faulkner, in Essex-Street. / — / MDCCXLVII.

Volume I. / Of The / Author's Works. / Containing / Miscellanies / In / Prose. / = / [monogram] / = / Dublin: / Printed by and for George Faulkner in Essex-street. / — / MDCCXLVII.

Frontisp., π^6, B–N^{12} — frontisp. (portrait of Swift), 2 pp. (series-title + bl.), 2 pp. (volume-title + bl.), 6 pp. (The Publisher's Preface), 2 pp. (Contents), 1–287 + bl.

Volume II. / Containing the Author's / Poetical Works. / = / [monogram] / = / *Dublin:* / Printed by George Faulkner, in *Essex-Street.* / — / M,DCC,XLVII.

Frontisp., π^4, B–P^{12}, Q^6 — frontisp. (Swift in medallion), 2 pp. (t. + bl.), 2 pp. (Advertisement), 4 pp. (Contents), 1–348.

Volume III. / Of the Author's / Works, / Containing / Travels / Into Several / Remote Nations of the World. / In Four Parts, *viz.* / [*First column:*] I. A Voyage to Lil- / liput. / II. A Voyage to Brob- / dingnag. / III. A Voyage to La- / puta, Balnibar- / [*Second column:*] bi, Luggnagg, / Glubbdubdrib, / and Japan. / IV. A Voyage to the / Country of the / Houyhnhnms. / — / By Lemuel Gulliver, first a Surgeon, / and then a Captain, of several Ships. / — / —— *Retroq; / Vulgus abhorret ab his.* / — / In this Impression several Errors in the *London* and / *Dublin* Editions are corrected. / — / *Dublin:* / Printed by and for Geo. Faulkner, in *Essex-street.* / M,DCC,XLIV.

Frontisp., π^2, $*_*{}^{*4}$, A^4, B–N^{12}, O^8 — frontisp. (L. Gulliver), 2 pp. (t. + bl.), 2 pp. (Advertisement + bl.), [I]–V (Letter Gulliver to Sympson), VI–VII (The Publisher to the Reader), 1 p. advs., 8 pp. (Contents), [1]–306 (145–8 omitted in numbering), 2 pp. blank — 4 maps and 2 plans.

Volume IV. / Of the Author's / Works. / Containing, A / Collection of Tracts, / Relating to / *Ireland;* / Among which are, / The Drapier's Letters / To The / People of Ireland: / Against / Receiving Wood's Half-Pence: / Also, / Two Original Drapier's Letters. / = / *Dublin:* / Printed by and for George Faulkner. / — / MDCCXLVIII.

Frontisp., π^4, B–O^{12}, P^2 — frontisp. (Swift in arm-chair), 2 pp. (t. + bl.), 2 pp. (Advertisement), 4 pp. (Contents), 2 pp. (title: A Letter + bl.), [I]–II (The Publisher's Advertisement To The Reader), 1–316.

Volume V. / Of The / Author's Works. / Containing / The Conduct of the Allies, / and the Examiners. / = / [monogram] / = / *Dublin:* / Printed by and for George Faulkner in *Essex-street*. / — / MDCCXLVII.

π^2, B–N^{12}, O^6 — 2 pp. (t. + bl.), 2 pp. (The Publisher's Preface), [1]–292, 8 pp. Index.

Volume VI. / Of The / Author's Works. / Containing / The Publick Spirit of the / Whigs; and other Pieces / of Political Writings; with / Polite Conversation, *&c.* / = / [monogram] / = / *Dublin:* / Printed by and for George Faulkner in *Essex-street*. / — / MDCCXLVII.

π^2, B–P^{12} — 2 pp. (t. + bl.), 2 pp. (The Publisher's Preface), [1]–334, 1 p. Contents + bl.

Letters / To and From / Dr. J. Swift, D.S.P.D. / From The / . Year 1714, to 1738. / = / [monogram] / = / *Dublin:* / Printed by and for George Faulkner, / — / MDCCXLI.

Letters / To and From / Dr. J. Swift, D.S.P.D. / From The / Year 1714, to 1738. / To which are added, / Several Notes and Transla- / tions not in the *London* Edition. / = / *Dublin:* / Printed by and for George Faulkner, / M,DCC,XLVI.

Volume VII. / Of The / Author's Works. / Containing / Letters / To and From / Jonathan Swift, D.D, D.S.P.D. / From The / Year 1714, to 1738. / = / Dublin: / Printed by and for George Faulkner in Essex-street. / — / MDCCXLVIII.

VII (1741): π^6, B–L^{12}; M^{12}, N 1–2; N 3–6, O^6, P^4 — 2 pp. (advs.), 2 pp. (t. + bl.), 8 pp. (Contents), [1]–240 (*Finis.* at foot); 241–56 (*Supplement — Finis.* at foot); 2 pp. (title *Some Free Thoughts* + bl.), 2 pp. (*Advertisement to the Reader* + bl.), 1–22 (*Finis.* at foot), 2 pp. blank.
For a fuller description of this volume see No. 64, *post*.
The last section (4 pp., 1–22, 2 pp. blank) also published separately (see No. 779, *post*).
VII (1746): A^4, B–T^6, U^2 — 2 pp. (t. + bl.), 6 pp. (Contents), [1]–182, 183–97, 198–220.

This is the 'Exshaw' volume (1741), provided with a new title-page. Cf. Nos. 62 and 64.

VII (1748): A⁶, B–M¹², N⁶ — one leaf blank, 2 pp. (t. + bl.), 8 pp. (Contents), [1]–248 (Letters), [249]–275 + bl. (Some Free Thoughts).

Volume VIII. / Of The / Author's Works. / Containing / Directions to Servants; / And / Other Pieces in Prose and Verse, / published in his Life-time; with several / Poems and Letters never before printed. / — / [monogram] / — / *Dublin:* / Printed by George Faulkner, in *Essex Street*, / — / M,D,CC,XLVI.

12mo (in sixes): π¹, a⁶, a², [*]⁶, B–Aa⁶, Bb⁴, Cc⁸, *A–*F⁶, G 1, π¹ — 2 pp. (title + Advertisement, on verso), 3 pp. + bl. (Dedication to Chesterfield), 8 pp. (Preface), I–IV (Contents), [I]–VIII (Swift's Last Will), 2 pp. (title: Directions, + bl.), [III]–IV (Publisher's Preface, dated: Dublin, Nov. 8, 1745.), 1–312, [1]–73 + bl., 2 pp. (music).

This is Penn's set, with Vol. VII, 1748 and Vol. VIII, 1751 (see below). The Kon. Bibl. has a set (188 H 7), in which Vol. VII is 1753 (see No. 51A).

Vol. II was also issued separately.

51A. *Reissued, reprinted, and new volumes:*

(1) Volume II. / Containing the Author's / Poetical Works. / = / [monogram] / = / Dublin: / Printed by George Faulkner in *Essex-street*, / — / M.DCC.LIX.

There is a separate title (following the f.t.), which reads:

Poems / On Several / Occasions. / By / J. Swift, D.D, D.S.P.D. / = / [monogram] / = / *Dublin:* / Printed by George Faulkner, in *Essex-Street.* / — / M,DCC,XLVII.

This is a re-issue of Vol. II, 1747 (see No. 51). The preservation of the 'Poems' title 1747 in the recorded copy (Univ. of Michigan, Hubbard Coll.) shows that for this purpose the separate issue of Vol. II, 1747 (see No. 51) was used.

(2) Volume III. / Of the Author's / Works, / Containing / Travels / Into Several / Remote Nations of the World. / In Four Parts, *viz.* / [*First column:*] I. A Voyage to Lil- / liput. / II. A Voyage to Brob- / dingnag. / III. A Voyage to La- / puta, Balnibar- / [*Second column:*] bi, Luggnagg, Glubbdubdrib, / and Japan. / IV. A Voyage to the / Country of the / Houyhnhnms. / — / By Lemuel Gulliver, first a Surgeon, / and then a Captain, of several Ships. / — / — — *Retroq;* / *Vulgus abhorret ab his.* / — / In this Impression several Errors in the former *London* / and *Dublin* Editions are corrected. / — / Dublin: / Printed by and for Geo. Faulkner, in *Essex-street.* / MDCCLII.

12mo; frontisp., π², *ₓ*⁴, 2π¹, A⁴, B–N¹², O⁸ — frontisp. (L. Gulliver), 2 pp. (t. + bl.), 2 pp. (Advertisement + bl.), [I]–V (Letter Gulliver to

Sympson), VI–VII (The Publisher to the Reader), 3 pp. advs., 8 pp. (Contents), [1]–302, 2 pp. blank. — 4 maps and 2 plans.
Copy: Univ. of Mich. (Hubbard Coll.).

(3) Volume III. / Of the Author's / Works, / Containing / Travels / Into Several / Remote Nations of the World. / In Four Parts, *viz.* / [*First column:*] I. A Voyage to Lil- / liput. / II. A Voyage to Brob- / dingnag. / III. A Voyage to La- / puta, Balnibarbi, / [*Second column:*] Luggnagg, Glubb- / dubdrib, and Ja- / pan. / IV. A Voyage to the / Country of the / Houyhnhnms. / — / By Lemuel Gulliver, first a Surgeon, / and then a Captain, of several Ships. / — / — — *Retroq;* / *Vulgus abhorret ab his.* / = / *Dublin:* / Printed by George Faulkner in *Essex-street,* / — / M.DCC.LIX.

The same collation and probably the same printing as No. 51A (2) with renewed title-leaf.
Copy: own.
In my copy the leaf bearing the last two pages of the advs. has been cut away; the same is the case in the re-issue 1763 (see No. 52).

(4) Volume IV. / Of the Author's / Works. / Containing, A / Collection of Tracts / Relating To / Ireland; / Among which are, / The Drapier's Letters / To The / People of Ireland, / Against / Receiving Wood's Halfpence. / = / Dublin: / Printed by George Faulkner in Essex Street. / — / MDCCLX.

12mo; π^4, B–O^{12}, P^2 — 2 pp. (t. + bl.), 2 pp. (Advertisement), 4 pp. (Contents), 2 pp. (title: A Letter + bl.), [I]–II (The Publisher's Advertisement To The Reader), 1–17 + bl., 2 pp. (title: A Proposal + bl.), [25]–316 (73–4 omitted, 97–8 repeated in numbering).

(5) Volume V. / Of The / Author's Works, / Containing, / The Conduct of the Allies, / and the Examiners, &c. / = / [monogram] / = / *Dublin:* / Printed by George Faulkner, M.DCC.LX.

12mo; π^2, B–O^{12}, P^6 — 2 pp. (t. + bl.), 2 pp. (The Publisher's Preface), [1]–316, 8 pp. Index (sheet O wrongly numbered 285–308, which should be 289–312).
Copy: Univ. of Mich. (Hubbard Coll.).

(6) Volume VII. / Of The / Author's Works. / Containing / Letters / To And From / Dr. J. Swift, D.S.P.D. / From The / Year 1714, to 1738. / As Also, / Some Free Thoughts upon the / Present State of Affairs. / The Sixth Edition. / Dublin: / Printed by George Faulkner, in Essex-street. / MDCCLIII.

12mo; π^5 (the second signed A 3), B–M^{12}, N^6 — 2 pp. (t. + bl.), [III]–X (Contents), [1]–275 (advs. on verso).
Copies: Univ. of Michigan (Hubbard Coll.), Kon. Bibl., and Penn.

(7) Volume VIII. / Of The / Author's Works. / Containing / Directions to Servants; / And / Other Pieces in Prose and Verse, / published in his Life-time, with several / Poems and Letters never before printed. / [monogram] / *Dublin:* / Printed by Gforge [*sic*] Faulkner, in *Essex-street,* / M,D,CC,LI.

12mo; π^4, A^6, B–P^{12}, Q^8, π^2 — 2 pp. (t. + bl.), 2 pp. (Advertisement + bl.), 4 pp. (Contents), I–X (Dr. Swift's Will), 1 p. (title: Directions), 1 p. (The Publisher's Preface), 1–352 (287–8 repeated, 335–6 omitted in numbering), 4 pp. music.

(8) Volume IX. / Of The / Author's Works, / Containing / Letters to Governor Hunter. / The History of the last Session of Par- / liament, and the Peace of Utrecht. Writ- / ten at Windsor in the Year 1713. / The Craftsman of December 12, 1730. And / the Answer thereto. / A Treatise on Good-Manners and Good- / Breeding. / — / By the Rev. Dr. J. Swift, D.S.P.D. / — / [monogram] / = / Dublin: / Printed by George Faulkner in / Essex-Street, M,DCC,LVIII.

12mo; A^8, B–M^{12}, N^4 — 2 pp. (t. + bl.), 2 pp. (To The Reader), [5]–14 (two letters), 2 pp. (title: The History + bl.), [1]–271 + bl.
Copies: Univ. of Mich. (Hubbard Coll.), and own. — There is also a separate issue of the *History* (see No. 811, *post*).

(9) Volume XI / Of The / Author's Works. / Containing, / More of his Litterary [*sic*] Correspondence, / particularly with Dr. King, Archbishop / of *Dublin, &c.* / To which are added, / An Account / Of The / Life and Writings / Of / Dr. *Jonathan Swift* / And / Original Poems on Several Occasions. / = / Dublin: / Printed by George Faulkner. M.DCC.LXII.

12mo; A^6, B–P^{12}, Q^{10} — 2 pp. (t + bl.), III–XI (Contents), 1 p. blank, [1]–356 (231–40 omitted in numbering).
Copy: Penn.

52. *Series-title:*
The / Works / Of the Reverend / Dr. J. Swift, D.S.P.D. / In / Eleven Volumes. / Containing, / [*First column:*] I. His Miscellanies in Prose. / II. His Poetical Writings. / III. The Travels of Capt. / Lemuel Gulliver. / IV. Papers relating to Ire- / land, and the Drapier's / Letters. / V. The Conduct of the / Allies, and the Ex- / aminers. / VI. The Publick Spirit of / the Whigs, &c. with / Polite Conversation. / VII. Letters to and from / Dr. Swift. / [*Second column:*] VIII. Directions to Ser- / vants, Sermons, Poems, / &c. / IX. Letters to Governor / Hunter. The History / of the last Session of / Parliament, and the / Peace of Utrecht, &c. / X. Sermons on several Sub- / jects, and other Pieces / on different

Occasions. / XI. Letters on different / Subjects. The Author's / Life; and Poems on se- / veral Occasions. / = / Dublin: / Printed by George Faulkner. / — / M,DCC,LXIII.

[No special title to Volume I.]

Frontisp., π^1, A^{11}, $B–N^{12}$, O^2 — frontisp. (portrait of Swift), 2 pp. (t. + bl.), [I]–XIII (To The Reader), 1 p. blank, 6 pp. (Preface), 2 pp. (Contents), 1–291 + bl.

Volume II. / Of The / Author's Works. / Containing, / Poems / On / Several Occasions. / — / [monogram] / — / *Dublin:* / Printed by George Faulkner, MDCCLXIII.

π^1, A^2, b^3, $B–P^{12}$, Q^2 — 2 pp. (t. + bl.), [I]–III (Advertisement), 1 p. blank, 5 pp. (Contents + bl.), 1–340.

Volume III. / Of The / Author's Works. / Containing, / Travels / Into Several / Remote Nations of the World. / In Four Parts, *viz.* / I. A Voyage to Lilliput. / II. A Voyage to Brobdingnag. / III. A Voyage to Laputa, Balnibarbi, / Luggnagg, Glubbdubdrib, and / Japan. / IV. A Voyage to the Country of the / Houyhnhnms. / — / By Lemuel Gulliver, first a Surgeon, / and then a Captain, of several Ships. / — / — — *Retroq; / Vulgus abhorret ab his.* / = / *Dublin:* / Printed by George Faulkner, MDCCLXIII.

This is the 1759 copy (No. 51A (3)), re-issued with new title-leaf 1763.

Volume IV. / Of The / Author's Works. / Containing, / A Collection of Tracts relative to / *Ireland;* / Among which are, / The Drapier's Letters / Against receiving / *Wood's* Half-Pence. / Also, / Two Original Drapier's Letters. / = / *Dublin:* / Printed by George Faulkner, MDCCLXIII.

This is the 1759 copy (No. 51A (4)), re-issued with new title-leaf 1763.

Volume V. / Of The / Author's Works. / Containing, / The Conduct of the Allies, and / the Examiners, &c. / — / [monogram] / = / *Dublin:* / Printed by George Faulkner, MDCCLXIII.

This is the 1760 copy (No. 51A (5)), re-issued with new title-leaf 1763.

Volume VI. / Of The / Author's Works. / Containing, / The Publick Spirit of the / Whigs; and other Pieces of / Political Writings; with Polite / Conversation, *&c.* / — / [monogram] / = / *Dublin:* / Printed by George Faulkner, MDCCLXIII.

π^3, $B–P^{12}$, Q^6 — 2 pp. (t. + bl.), 2 pp. (Contents + bl.), 2 pp. (The Publisher's Preface), [1]–347 + bl. (125–44 repeated, 149–68 omitted in numbering).

Volume VII. (1753 — see No. 51A (6), *ante.*)

This is 1753 copy, No. 51A (6).

Volume VIII. / Of The / Author's Works. / Containing, / Directions to Servants; / And / Other Pieces / In / Prose and Verse. / = / *Dublin:* / Printed by George Faulkner, MDCCLXIII.

This is the 1751 copy (No. 51A (7)), re-issued with new title-leaf 1763.

Volume IX. (1758 — see No. 51A (8), *ante.*)

This is the 1758 copy, No. 51A (8).

Volume X. / Of The / Author's Works. / Containing, / Sermons on several Subjects; / And / Other Pieces on different / Occasions. / — / [monogram] / = / *Dublin:* / Printed by George Faulkner. / M,DCC,LXIII.

π^2, B–O^{12} — 2 pp. (t. + bl.), [I]–II (Contents), [1]–312.

Volume XI. / Of The / Author's Works. / Containing, / Letters on different Subjects; / And, / Poems on several Occasions. / = / Dublin: / Printed by George Faulkner. / — / MDCCLXIII.

This is the 1762 copy (No. 51A (9)), re-issued with new title-leaf 1763.

Volume XII. / Of The / Author's Works. / Collected And Revised / By Deane Swift, Esq. / of Goodrich, in Herefordshiere. [*sic*] / *Hæ tibi erunt artes.* Virgil. / [monogram] / = / Dublin: / Printed by George Faulkner. / — / MDCCLXV.

π^1, A^2, B–O^{12}, P^4 — 2 pp. (t. + 'Errata' on verso), III–IV (The Editors To The Reader), V–VI (Contents), [1]–349 + bl. (313–42 omitted in numbering).

The / Works / Of / Dr. Jonathan Swift, / Dean of St. Patrick's, Dublin, / Volume XIII. / Collected And Revised / By Deane Swift, Esq; / of Goodrich, in Herefordshire. / *Hæ tibi erunt artes.* Virgil. / = / Dublin: / Printed by George Faulkner. / — / MDCCLXV.

A^4, B–L^{12}, M^8 — 2 pp. (t. + bl.), 6 pp. (Contents), [1]–253, 3 pp. blank.

Volume XIV. / Containing / Letters / To And From / Dr. Jonathan Swift, / Dean of St. Patrick's, Dublin, / From / The Year 1703, to 1743. / With / Notes Explanatory and Historical / By / The Rev. Thomas Birch, D.D. F.R.S. / John Hawkesworth, L.L.D. / And / The Editor, Mr. Thomas Wilkes. / = / *Dublin:* / Printed by George Faulkner, 1767.

Frontisp., a⁶, a–b⁶, c², B–N¹², O⁶, P² — frontisp. (bust of Swift), 2 pp. (t. + bl.), 2 pp. (Dedication to Temple + bl.), [V]–VI (The Publisher To The Reader), [VII]–X (Preface), 2 pp. blank, I–XXVII (Contents), 1 p. blank, [1]–304.

Volume XV. / Containing / Letters / To And From / Dr. Jonathan Swift, / Dean of St. Patrick's, Dublin, / From / The Year 1703, to 1743. / With / Notes Explanatory and Historical / By / The Rev. Thomas Birch, D.D. F.R.S. / John Hawkesworth, L.L.D. / And / The Editor, Mr. Thomas Wilkes. / = / Dublin: / Printed by George Faulkner, 1767.

π¹, a⁴, b⁶, c⁴, B–L¹² — 2 pp. (t. + bl.), I–XXVII (Contents), 1 p. blank, [1]–235, 3 pp. advs., 2 pp. blank.

Volume XVI. / Containing / Letters / To And From / Dr. Jonathan Swift, / Dean of St. Patrick's, Dublin, / From / The Year 1703, to 1743. / With / Notes Explanatory and Historical, / By / The Rev. Thomas Birch, D.D. F.R.S. / John Hawkesworth, L.L.D. / And / The Editor, Mr. Thomas Wilkes. / — / With An / Appendix, / Containing many original Pieces. / = / Dublin: / Printed by George Faulkner, 1767.

π¹, a², b⁶, c², d 1, B–H¹², I²; A¹², B⁶, C⁸ — 2 pp. (t. + bl.), I–XXII (Contents), [1]–195 + bl. (49–72 omitted in numbering); [1]–21 (Appendix), 3 pp. blank, [23]–48 (index).

Volume XVII. / Of The / Author's Works. / Containing / Letters, / Written By The Late / Dr. Jonathan Swift, / Dean Of St. Patrick's, Dublin, / And / Several Of His Friends. / From The Year 1700 To 1742. / Published From The Originals; / Collected And Revised / By Deane Swift, Esq; / Of Goodrich In Herefordshire. / — / To which is added, / Some Originals, never before published; / And / Illustrated with Historical and Explanatory Notes, by / the Publisher. / = / Dublin: / Printed by and for George Faulkner. / — / M,DCC,LXVIII.

Frontisp., A⁶, B–K¹², L⁶, M 1 — frontisp. (Stella), 2 pp. (t. + bl.), [III]–V (Momus Mistaken), [VI]–XII (Contents), [1]–214, 2 pp. blank, 215–28.

Volume XVIII. / Of The / Author's Works. / Containing / Letters, / Written By The Late / Dr. Jonathan Swift, / Dean Of St. Patrick's, Dublin, / And / Several Of His Friends. / From The Year 1700 To 1742. / Published From The Originals; / Collected And Revised / By Deane Swift, Esq; / Of Goodrich In Herefordshire. / — / To which is added, / Some Originals, never before published;

/ And / Illustrated with Historical and Explanatory Notes, by / the Publisher. / = / Dublin: / Printed by and for George Faulkner. / — / M,DCC,LXVIII.

A⁶, B–L¹² — 2 pp. (t. + bl.), [I]–X (Contents), [1]–240.

Volume XIX. / Of The / Author's Works. / Containing / Letters, / Written By The Late / Dr. Jonathan Swift, / Dean Of St. Patrick's, Dublin, / And / Several Of His Friends. / From The Year 1700 To 1742. / Published From The Originals; / Collected And Revised / By Deane Swift, Esq; / Of Goodrich In Herefordshire. / — / To which is added, / Some Originals, never before published; / And / Illustrated with Historical and Explanatory Notes, by / the Publisher. / = / Dublin: / Printed by and for George Faulkner. / —/ M,DCC,LXVIII.

π¹, a⁶, b 1, B–N¹², O²; A¹² — 2 pp. (t. + bl.), I–XIV (Contents), [1]–279 + bl., [281]–291 + bl. (Index); [1]–24 (Appendix).

Volume XX. / Of The / Author's Works. / Containing, The / Tale of a Tub. / — / [monogram] / — / *Dublin:* / Printed by George Faulkner, MDCCLXXI.

π¹ (frontisp.), A–M¹² — frontisp., 2 pp. (t. + bl.), 2 pp. (title: Tale + bl.), [V]–XXII (The Author's Apology), 2 pp. (Postscript + bl.), 2 pp. (Treatises written + bl.),[XXVII]–XXXII(Dedication to Sommers),[XXXIII]–XXXIV (The Bookseller To The Reader), [XXXV]–XLIII + bl. (Epistle Dedicatory), [XLVI]–LVIII (The Preface), [1]–225 + bl., 4 pp. advs. — 7 plates. (The same printing as those in the Faulkner ed. (eighth), 1741 (No. 237), with page-number erasures).
12mo; π¹, a¹, A–Q¹², R⁸, S 1 — 2 pp. (t. + bl.), [I]–IV (Contents), 2 pp. (Advertisement + bl.), 5–402.
Copy: Penn.

Faulkner's 18mo Edition, 1762, &c.

This edition is complete, not, as the 8vo and 12mo editions, in twenty volumes, but in nineteen, the *Tale Of A Tub* forming Vol. XI, which caused a different distribution of the pieces over the later volumes.
As early as 1754 Faulkner considered the publication of a 18mo edition of Swift's Works. In an *Advertisement* covering the last two pages of his edition of *Brotherly Love. A Sermon*, 1754 (see No. 808, *post*), he announced the publication of "a compleat, genuine, and correct Edition of the Tale of a Tub, free from the Errors of all former Editions, which will make the first, or eleventh Volume of Swift's Works, as the Purchaser shall please to bind them". This volume (in 18mo) was published in 1756. It had "Vol. XI." at the foot of several pages, and appeared both as Vol. XI of the set (with title 'Vol. XI', 1756, in front), and as a separate issue (No. 242, *post*).
Gulliver's Travels also appeared in 1756 in 18mo, both as Vol. III of the set and as a separate issue (see No. 309, *post*).

Faulkner Editions (12mo)

	In Four Vols.	In Four Vols.	In Eight Vols.	In Eleven Vols.
I	1735	1738	1747 (6th ed.)	1763
II	1735	1737	1747	1763
III	1735	1738	1744 ... = ? ... 1759	1763
IV	1735	1738	1752 ... =? ... 1759 =	1763
V		1738	1748 ... 1747 ... 1760=	1763
VI		1738	1747 ... 1760=	1763
VII		[1741]	1747	1763
VIII		[1746]	1748	1763
IX		1746	1748 ... 1751	1763
X			= ... 1758	1768
XI			1753 (6th ed.)	1763
XII			1762=	1763
XIII				1765
XIV				1765
XV				1767
XVI				1767
XVII				1767
XVIII				1768
XIX				1768
XX				1768 ... 1771

It was not until 1762, however, that the other volumes of this eleven vol. set were added. Vol. XI was then provided with a new title, dated 1762; whether this was also the case with Vol. III, I cannot say, as I have not met with a copy dated 1762. As to the plates, see note 5, before No. 41, *ante*.

53. *Series-title:*

The / Works / Of the Reverend / Dr. Jonathan Swift, / Dean of *St. Patrick*'s, Dublin. / With an Account of his / Life and Writings. / As Also, / Historical and explanatory Notes, and / a great Number of original Pieces, / in Verse and Prose. / The Whole properly digested. / — / In Eleven neat Pocket Volumes, printed in a new / beautiful Silver Type. / = / Dublin: / Printed by George Faulkner. MDCCLXII.

18mo (in sixes):

Volume I. / Of The / Author's Works. / Containing / Miscellanies / In / Prose. / = / [monogram] / = / Dublin: / Printed by George Faulkner. MDCCLXII.

Frontisp., A⁶, b⁶, c–d⁴, e², B–Dd⁶ — frontisp. (portrait of Swift), 2 pp. (series-title + bl.), 2 pp. (volume-title + bl.), [III]–XIX (To The Reader), 1 p. blank, 2 pp. (Contents), 19 pp. Subscribers Names + bl., [1]–312.

Volume II. / Of The / Author's Works. / Containing, / Poems / On / Several Occasions. / = / [monogram] / = / Dublin: / Printed by George Faulkner. / — / MDCCLXII.

A⁴, B–Ii⁶ — 2 pp. (t. + bl.), [III]–VII (Contents), 1 p. blank, 1–108, 119–381 + bl. (no break in text).

Volume III. / Of the Author's / Works, / Containing / Travels / Into Several / Remote Nations of the World. / In Four Parts. / [*First column:*] I. A Voyage to Lil- / liput. / II. A Voyage to Brob- / dingnag. / III. A Voyage to / Laputa, Balni- / [*Second column:*] barbi, Luggnagg, / Glubbdubdrib, / and Japan. / IV. A Voyage to the / Country of the / Houyhnhnms. / — / By Lemuel Gulliver, first a Surgeon, / and then a Captain, of several Ships. / — / — *Retroq;* / *Vulgus abhorret ab his.* / = / Dublin: / Printed by George Faulkner, in Essex-Street, / — / MDCCLVI.

Frontisp., Aa⁶, A–Dd⁶ — frontisp. (L. Gulliver), 2 pp. (t. + bl.), 2 pp. (Advertisement + bl.), I–V (Letter Gulliver to Sympson), 1 p. blank, VII–VIII (The Publisher to the Reader), 12 pp. (Contents), 1–312. — 4 maps and 2 plans.

Also published separately (No. 309); I have not seen a copy with title-page 1762.

Volume IV. / Of The / Author's Works. / Containing / Tracts / Relating to / Ireland. / Among which are, The / Drapier's Letters.

/ = / [monogram] / = / Dublin: / Printed by George Faulkner. / — / MDCCLXII.

π^3, B–Hh^6, Ii^2 — 2 pp. (t. + bl.), [III]–V (Contents), 1 p. blank, 2 pp. (title: A Letter + bl.), 2 pp. (The Publisher to the Reader + bl.), 1–357 + bl. (211–12 repeated in numbering).

Volume V. / Of The / Author's Works. / Containing / The Examiners. / The Conduct of the Allies. / Remarks on the Barrier Treaty. / And The / Public Spirit of the Whigs. / = / [monogram] / = / Dublin: / Printed by George Faulkner. / — / MDCCLXII.

π^2, B–Oo^6, P^2 — 2 pp. (t. + bl.), 2 pp. (Contents + bl.), [1]–436.

Volume VI. / Of The / Author's Works. / Containing, A / Preface to the Bishop of Sarum's / Introduction. / Polite Conversation. / Directions to Servants, / &c. &c. &c. / = / [monogram] / = / Dublin: / Printed by George Faulkner. / — / MDCCLXII.

π^2, B^4, C–Hh^6 — 2 pp. (t. + bl.), 2 pp. (Contents), [1]–355 + bl.

Volume VII. / Of The / Author's Works. / Containing, / Letters / To and From / Dr. J. Swift, D.S.P.D. / On / Several Occasions. / = / *Dublin:* / Printed by George Faulkner. / — / MDCCLXII.

π^3, B^4, C–Ff^6 — 2 pp. (t. + bl.), [I]–IV (Contents), [1]–331 + bl.

Volume VIII. / Of The / Author's Works. / Containing, / Letters / To and From / Archbishop King, Dr. Swift, &c. / And / Poems on several Occasions. / = / Dublin: / Printed by George Faulkner. / — / MDCCLXII.

π^3, B^4, C–Y^6, Z^4 — 2 pp. (t. + bl.), [III]–VI (Contents), [1]–256.

Volume IX. / Of The / Author's Works. / Containing, / The History of the last Session of / Queen Anne. / The / Craftsman and Answer. / Also, Memoirs of / Capt. John Creichton. / And / The Guardian, No. 96. / = / Dublin: / Printed by George Faulkner. / — / MDCCLXII.

π^2, B–Gg^6 — 2 pp. (t. + bl.), 2 pp. (Contents + bl.), [1]–348.

Volume X. / Of The / Author's Works. / Containing, / Sermons / On / Several Subjects; / And / Other Pieces / In / Prose and Verse. / = / *Dublin:* / Printed by George Faulkner. / — / MDCCLXII.

π^3, B–I^6, K^4, L–Ee^6, Ff^2 — 2 pp. (t. + bl.), [III]–V (Contents), 1 p. blank, 2 pp. (title 'Eight Sermons' + bl.), 3–323 + bl.

Volume XI. / Of The / Author's Works. / Containing, The / Tale of a Tub. / To which is added, The / Life / Of the Reverend / Dr. Jonathan Swift, / Dean of *St. Patrick*'s, Dublin. / = / Dublin: / Printed by George Faulkner. MDCCLXII.

Frontisp., π^2, A^6, b–d^6, B–Q^6, R^4, S–Ff^6, Gg^2 — frontisp., 2 pp. (t. + bl.), 2 pp. (Contents + bl.), 2 pp. (title: Tale, dated 1756 + bl.), III–XVIII (Apology), XIX–XXIII (Dedication to Sommers), 1 p. blank, XXV–XXVI (The Bookseller To The Reader), XXVII–XXXIII (Epistle Dedicatory), 1 p. blank, XXXV–XLVII (Preface), 1 p. blank, 1–336. — 7 plates.
This is a made-up volume consisting of the *Tale*, 1756 (see No. 242), to which the *Life of Swift*, 1762 (pp. [191]–336) has been added.

The / Works / Of / Dr. Jonathan Swift, / Dean of St. Patrick's, Dublin, / Volume XII. / Collected And Revised / By Deane Swift, Esq. / of Goodrich, in Herefordshire. / *Hæ tibi erunt artes.* Virgil. / — / Dublin: / Printed by George Faulkner. / — / MDCCLXV.

π^4, B–Ee^6, Ff^4 — 2 pp. (t. + bl.), III (misprinted V)–V (Contents), 1 p. blank, VII (misprinted VIII)–VIII (The Editors To The Reader), [1]–332.

The / Works / Of / Dr. Jonathan Swift, / Dean of St. Patrick's, Dublin, / Volume XIII. / Collected And Revised / By Deane Swift, Esq. / of Goodrich, in Herefordshire. / *Hæ tibi erunt artes.* Virgil. / — / Dublin: / Printed by George Faulkner. / — / MDCCLXV.

π^1, A^4, B–Bb^6, Cc^4 — 2 pp. (t. + bl.), 8 pp. (Contents), [1]–293, 3 pp. blank.

Volume XIV. / Containing / Letters / To And From / Dr. Jonathan Swift, / Dean of St. Patrick's, Dublin, / From / The Year 1703, to 1743. / With / Notes Explanatory and Historical, / By / The Rev. Thomas Birch, D.D.F.R.S. / John Hawkesworth, L.L.D. / And / The Editor, Mr. Thomas Wilkes. / = / Dublin: / Printed by George Faulkner, 1767.

Frontisp., a–d^6, B–Ii^6, Kk^2 — frontisp. (bust of Swift), 2 pp. (t. + bl.), 2 pp. (Dedication to Temple + bl.), [V]–VI (The Publisher To The Reader), [VII]–XI (Preface), 1 p. blank, I–XXXIII (Contents), 3 pp. blank, 1–375 + bl.

Volume XV. / Containing / Letters / To And From / Dr. Jonathan Swift, / Dean of St. Patrick's, Dublin, / From / The Year 1703, to 1743. / With / Notes Explanatory and Historical, / By / The Rev. Thomas Birch, D.D.F.R.S. / John Hawkesworth, L.L.D. / And / The Editor, Mr. Thomas Wilkes. / = / Dublin: / Printed by George Faulkner, 1767.

π^1, a^5, b–c^6, B^4, C–Cc^6 — 2 pp. (t. + bl.), [I]–XXXIV (Contents), [1]–294 + 2 pp. blank.

Volume XVI. / Containing / Letters / To And From / Dr. Jonathan Swift, / Dean of St. Patrick's, Dublin, / From / The Year 1703, to 1743. / With / Notes Explanatory and Historical, / By / The Rev. Thomas Birch, D.D.F.R.S. / John Hawkesworth, L.L.D. / And / The Editor, Mr. Thomas Wilkes. / — / With An / Appendix, / Containing many original Pieces. / = / Dublin: / Printed by George Faulkner, 1767.

d^6, c^8, B–X^6; A^6, b^6, C 1; D^{12}, E^6 — 2 pp. (t. + bl.), [I]–XXVI (Contents), [1]–239 + bl.; [1]–25 + bl. (Appendix); [27]–61 + bl. (Index).

Volume XVII. / Of The / Author's Works. / Containing / Letters, / Written By The Late / Dr. Jonathan Swift, / Dean of St. Patrick's, Dublin, / And / Several Of His Friends. / From The Year 1700 To 1742. / Published From The Originals; / Collected And Revised / By Deane Swift, Esq; / Of Goodrich In Hereford-shire. / — / To which is added, / Some Originals, never before published; / And / Illustrated with Historical and Explanatory Notes, / by the Publisher. / = / Dublin: / Printed by and for George Faulkner. / M.DCC.LXVIII.

Frontisp., A^4, b^6, B–Cc^6, Dd^4 — frontisp. (Stella), 2 pp. (t. + bl.), [III]–VI (Momus Mistaken), one leaf blank, [I]–X (Contents), one leaf blank, 2 pp. (title: Letters + bl.), [3]–286, blank leaf, [287]–305 + bl.

Volume XVIII. / Of The / Author's Works. / Containing / Letters, / Written By The Late / Dr. Jonathan Swift, / Dean of St. Patrick's, Dublin, / And / Several Of His Friends. / From The Year 1700 To 1742. / Published From The Originals; / Collected And Revised / By Deane Swift, Esq; / Of Goodrich In Hereford-shire. / — / To which is added, / Some Originals, never before published; / And / Illustrated with Historical and Explanatory Notes, / by the Publisher. / = / Dublin: / Printed by and for George Faulkner. / M.DCC.LXVIII.

π^1, A^6, b^2, B–Ff^6, Gg^4 — 2 pp. (t. + bl.), [I]–XV + bl. (Contents), [1]–341, 3 pp. blank.

Volume XIX. / Of The / Author's Works. / Containing / Letters, / Written By The Late / Dr. Jonathan Swift, / Dean Of St. Patrick's, Dublin, / And / Several Of His Friends. / From The Year 1700 To 1742. / Published From The Originals; / Collected And Revised / By Deane Swift, Esq; / Of Goodrich In Herefordshire. / — / To which is added, / Some Originals, never before published; / And / Illustrated with Historical and Explana-

(1)

TO THE
Athenian Society.
Moor-park, Feb. 14. 1691.

GENTLEMEN,

SINCE every Body *pretends to trouble you with their* Follies, *I thought I might claim the Priviledge of an* English-man, *and put in my share among the rest. Being last year in* Ireland, *(from whence I returned about half a year ago)* I *heard only a* loose talk of your Society, *and believed the design to be only some new* Folly *just suitable to the Age, which God knows, I little expected ever to produce any thing* extraordinary. *Since my being in* England, *having still continued in the Countrey, and much out of Company ; I had but little advantage of knowing any more, till about two Months ago* passing through Oxford, *a* very learned Gentleman *there, first shew'd me two or three of your* Volumes, *and gave me his Account and Opinion of you ; a while after, I came to this place, upon a Visit to* ———— *where I have been ever since, and have seen all the* four Volumes with their Supplements, *which answering my* Expectation. *The perusal has produced, what you find inclosed.*

As I have been somewhat inclined to this Folly, *so I have seldom wanted some-body to flatter me in it. And for the* Ode *inclosed, I have sent it to a Person of very great* Learning and Honour, *and since to some others, the best of my* Acquaintance, *(to which I thought* very proper to inure it for a greater light) *and they have all been pleased to tell me, that they are sure it will not be* unwelcome, *and that I should* beg the Honour of You *to let it be* Printed before Your next Volume *(which I think, is soon to be published,) it being so usual before most Books of any great value among* Poets, *and before it's seeing the* World, *I submit it wholly to the* Correction of your Pens.

I intreat therefore one of You would descend *so far, as to write two or three lines to me of your Pleasure upon it. Which as I cannot but expect from Gentlemen, who have so well shewn upon so many occasions, that greatest* Character *of Scholars, in being favourable to the* Ignorant, *So I am sure nothing at present, can more highly oblige me, or make me happier.*

    I am,

(Gentlemen)

Your ever most Humble,
and most
admiring Servant.

Jonathan Swift.

a   ODE

The Supplement to the Fifth Volume of the Athenian Gazette (no. 467). Swift's first appearance in print, *An Ode to The Athenian Society*, was advertised on the title-page and preceded by this letter. Swift's work occupied the first six pages of this issue which completed "the Entire Set for the Year 1691." (University of Pennsylvania)

1ᵃ

Merlinus Verax.

21. febr. 170⅞.

A Famous Prediction of *MERLIN*, the *British* Wizard; written above a Thousand Years ago, and relating to this present Year.

With Explanatory Notes. By *T. N.* Philomath.

LAST Year was publish'd a Paper of Predictions pretended to be written by one *Isaac Bickerstaff*, Esq; but the true Design of it was to Ridicule the Art of Astrology, and Expose its Professors as ignorant, or Impostors. Against this Imputation, Dr. *Partridge* hath vindicated himself in his Almanack for the present Year.

For a further Vindication of this famous Art, I have thought fit to present the World with the following Prophecy. The Original is said to be of the famous *Merlin*, who lived about a Thousand Years ago: And the following Translation is Two Hundred Years old; for it seems to be written near the End of *Henry* the Seventh's Reign. I found it in an Old Edition of *Merlin's* Prophecies; imprinted at *London* by *Johan Haukyns*, in the Year 1530, *Pag.* 39. I set it down Word for Word in the Old Orthography, and shall take Leave to subjoin a few Explanatory Notes.

> Seven and Ten addyd to nyne,
> Of Fraunce hir woe thys is the sygne,
> Tamys ribere twys y-frozen,
> Walke sans wetynge Shoes ne hozen.
> Then comyth foorthe, Ich understonde,
> From Toune of Stoffe to fattyn Londe
> An herdie Chiftan, woe the mozne
> To Fraunce, that ebere he was bozne.
> Than shall the Fyshe beweyle his Bosse;
> Noz shall grin Berris make up the Losse.
> Yonge Symnele shall agayne miscarrye:
> And Norways Pryd agayne shall marreye:
> And from the Tree where Blosums sele,
> Ripe fruit shall come, and all is wele.
> Reaums shall daunce honde in honde,
> And it shall be merye in olde Inglonde.
> Then olde Inglonde shall be noe moze,
> And no Man shall be sozie therefoze.
> Geryon shall have thzee Hedes agayne
> Till Hapsburge makyth them but twayne.

Expla-

A Famous Prediction of Merlin (no. 499). Narcissus Luttrell's copy, with his characteristic pricing and dating. From the Marquess of Bute broadside collection now at Harvard. (Courtesy of the Harvard College Library)

tory Notes, / by the Publisher. / = / Dublin: / Printed by and for George Faulkner. / M.DCC.LXVIII.

π^1, a^6, b^2, B–Gg^6, A–B^6, C^2, Hh^6 — 2 pp. (t. + bl.), I–XIV (Contents), 1–2 (Contents of the Appendix), [1]–360; [I]–II, 3–27 + bl.
Copies: Nat. Libr. of Ireland, and Penn.

⁎

Miscellanies (sm.8vo), 1742, &c.

The 1742 Edition:
After Motte's death (1738) the principal owners of the copyright of Swift's works in England were his partner and successor Charles Bathurst (with Gilliver) and Charles Davis (with Woodward), who had already experienced, and continued to feel, the result of Faulkner's competition, who sent his volumes into England. No doubt induced by their rival's success they resolved to co-operate to some degree for the reprint of Swift's works, and the outcome was the *Miscellanies*, sm. 8vo, 1742, consisting of:

(1) Vols. I–IV (Bathurst and Gilliver) corresponding with the four volumes of *Miscellanies* first published in 8vo, 1727 (Motte), 1727 (Motte), 1727 (Motte) and 1732 (Motte and Gilliver), but the distribution of the pieces over the four volumes modified, hence Vols. I and IV by Bathurst, Vols. II and III by Bathurst and Gilliver. Published July 3, 1742.

(2) Vols. V–VI (Woodward and Davis) corresponding with Vol. V, 8vo, 1735 (Davis).

(3) Vols. VII–IX (Davis and Bathurst) corresponding with *Political Tracts*, 2 vols., 8vo, 1738 (Davis), but also containing *An Essay On Polite Conversation*, published in 1738 by Motte and Bathurst, hence also Bathurst's name in the imprint.

(4) Vol. X (Dodsley) added in 1745.

(5) Vol. XI (Hitch, Davis, Dodsley, Cooper) added in 1746.

(6) *A Tale Of A Tub* (Bathurst) 1743.

(7) *Gulliver's Travels* (Bathurst) 1742.

It is strange to note that Vol. VIII, 1742, 1745, 1748, 1751 (first), 1751 (second), all have pp. 247–56 repeated in numbering; yet not two of them are the same printing.

66. This Sm. 8vo collection of 13 volumes, though the property of different booksellers, and in spite of the fact that the last two did not bear any sign to indicate that they belong to the group, forms a complete set of Swift's works. Their title-pages (all in red and black) are as follows:

Miscellanies / — / In / Four Volumes. / — / By Dr. *Swift*, Dr. *Arbuthnot*, / Mr. *Pope*, and Mr. *Gay*. / — / The Fourth Edition Corrected: / With Several Additional Pieces in / Verse and Prose. / — / Vol. I. / By Dr. *Swift*. / = / *London:* / Printed for Charles Bathurst, at the / *Cross Keys* opposite St. *Dunstan*'s Church, / *Fleetstreet*, MDCCXLII.

a^2, b^4, B–S^8 — 2 pp. (t. + bl.), 8 pp. (Preface), 2 pp. (Contents), [1]–269, 3 pp. advs.

Miscellanies. / — / The / Second Volume. / — / By Dr. *Swift*, Dr. *Arbuthnot*, / And Mr. *Pope*. / — / [ornament] / = / *London:* / Printed for Caarles [*sic*] Bathurst, at the / *Cross Keys*, and Lawton Gilliver, at / *Homer*'s Head, against St. *Dunstan*'s Church, / *Fleet-street*, MDCCXLII.

π^2, B–E^8, F–G^4, H^2, I–S^8, T^2, U^8 — 2 pp. (t. + bl.), 2 pp. (Contents), 5–88, 2 pp. (title: Martinus Scriblerus + bl.), [133]–308 (no break in the text).

Miscellanies. / — / The / Third Volume. / — / By / Dr. *Arbuthnot*, Mr. *Pope*, / And Mr. *Gay*. / — / [ornament] / = / *London:* / Printed for Charles Bathurst at the / *Cross Keys*, and L. Gilliver at *Homer*'s / Head opposite to St. *Dunstan*'s Church, / *Fleetstreet*, MDCCXLII.

π^2, B–R^8 — 2 pp. (t. + bl.), 2 pp. (Contents), [I]–VII + bl., 9–253, [1]–3 advs.

Miscellanies. / — / The / Fourth Volume. / — / Consisting of / Verses / By / Dr. *Swift*, Dr. *Arbuthnot*, / Mr. *Pope*, and Mr. *Gay*. / — / [ornament] / = / *London:* / Printed for Charles Bathurst at the / *Cross Keys* opposite to St. *Dunstan*'s Church, / *Fleetstreet*, MDCCXLII.

b^4, B–T^8, U^2 — 2 pp. (t. + bl.), 6 pp. (Contents), [1]–291 + bl.

Miscellanies, / — / The / The [*sic*] Fifth and Sixth Volumes. / — / By Dr. Swift and others. / — / The Third Edition Corrected: / With Several Additional Pieces in / Verse and Prose. / — / Vol. V. / = / *London,* / Printed for T. Woodward, / at the *Half-Moon* between the *Temple Gates;* / and C. Davis / against *Grays-Inn Gate, Holborn*. / — / MDCCXLII.

π^3, B–S^8, T^2 — 2 pp. (t. + bl.), 4 pp. (Contents), [1]–275 (advs. on verso). — The Nat. Libr. of Scotl. has a copy with two pages advs. preceding the t.p.

Miscellanies. / — / The / Sixth Volume. / — / By Dr. *Swift* and others. / — / [ornament] / = / *London,* / Printed for T. Woodward, / at the *Half-Moon* between the *Temple Gates;* / and C. Davis / against *Grays-Inn Gate, Holborn*. / — / MDCCXLII.

π^2, B–U^8, X^6 — 2 pp. (t. + bl.), 2 pp. (Contents), 1–316.

Miscellanies. / — / The / Seventh Volume. / — / By Dr. Swift. / — / The Second Edition. / — / [ornament] / = / *London:* / Printed for C. Davis, / against *Grays-Inn Gate, Holborn;* / and C. Bathurst, / opposite St. *Dunstan's Church, Fleetstreet*. / — / MDCCXLII.

π^2, B–X^8, Y^4 — 2 pp. (t. + bl.), 2 pp. (bl. + Contents), 1–326, 2 pp. blank.

Miscellanies. / — / The / Eighth Volume. / — / *By Dr*. Swift. / — / The Second Edition. / — / [ornament] / = / *London:* / Printed for C. Davis / against *Grays-Inn-Gate, Holborn*. / and C. Bathurst, / opposite St. *Dunstan's Church, Fleetstreet* / — / MDCCXLII.

A^2, B–X^8 — 2 pp. (t. + bl.), 2 pp. (Contents), 1–310 (247–56 repeated in numbering).

Miscellanies. / — / The / Ninth Volume. / — / *By Dr*. Swift. / — / The Second Edition. / — / [ornament] / = / *London:* / Printed for C. Davis; / against *Grays-Inn Gate, Holborn;* / and C. Bathurst, / opposite St. *Dunstan's Church, Fleetstreet*. / — / MDCCXLII.

π^2, B–S^8, T^4 — 2 pp. (t. + bl.), 2 pp. (Contents + bl.), [1]–278, 2 pp. blank.

Miscellanies. / — / The / Tenth Volume. / — / By Dr. Swift. / — / [ornament] / = / London: / Printed for R. Dodsley in Pall-mall. / — / M.DCC.XLV.

A^4, B–S^8, T^4 — 2 pp. (t. + bl.), III (Advertisement), 1 p. blank, V–VIII (Contents), 1–277, 3 pp. advs.

Miscellanies. / — / *By Dr*. Swift. / — / The / Eleventh Volume. / — / [ornament] / = / *London:* / Printed for C. Hitch, C. Davis, R. Dods- / ley, and M. Cooper. / — / MDCCXLVI.

A^4, B–U^8, X^2, two leaves (music) — 2 pp. (t. + bl.), [III]–VIII (Contents), [1]–304, 301–4, 4 pp. music.

A / Tale / Of A / Tub. / Written for the Universal Improvement / of Mankind. / — / *Diu multumque desideratum*. / — / To which is added, / An Account of a / Battle / Between The / Antient and Modern Books / in St. *James's* Library. / — / Basima eacabasa eanaa irraurista, diarba da caeotaba / fobor camelanthi. *Iren. Lib*. 1. *C*. 18. / — / — *Juvatque novos decerpere flores,* / *Insignemque meo capiti petere inde coronam,* / *Unde prius nulli velarunt tempora Musae*. Lucret. / — / The Tenth Edition. / With the Author's Apology; / And Explanatory Notes, by *W. W—tt—n*, B.D. / and others. / = / *London:* Printed for Charles Bathurst, / at the *Cross-Keys* in *Fleet-Street*. / MDCCXLIII.

Frontisp., π^1, B–Q^8, R 1 — frontisp., 2 pp. (t. + 'Treatises wrote' on verso), [I]–XVI (Apology), 5 pp. (Dedication to Sommers), 1 p. (The Book-seller to the Reader), [1]–8 (Epistle Dedicatory), 9–20 (Preface), 21–220. — 7 plates (offprints of the 1710 plates).

Travels / Into Several / Remote Nations / Of The / World. / — / In Four Parts. / — / By *Lemuel Gulliver*, / First a Surgeon, and then a Captain / of several Ships. / — / The Fourth Edition, Corrected. / = / *London:* / Printed for Charles Bathurst, at the / *Cross-Keys* in *Fleet-Street.* / MDCCXLII.

π^4, $2\pi^4$, a^2, B–Z^8 — 2 pp. (t. + bl.), 10 pp. (Contents), [1]–351 (advs. on verso) — 4 maps and 2 plans (offprints of the 1727, 12mo plates).
Copies: Penn.

67. *The 1747 Edition:*
The 1747 edition presents an irregular appearance as to dates, owing to the fact that about half of the volumes were not yet exhausted, and were therefore not reprinted till some years later (Vols. V–VI and VII–VIII–IX had already been reprinted in 1745; Vols. X and XI had only appeared for the first time in 1745 and 1746). The result is that various combinations may be found. See diagram after No. 69, *post*. The title-pages (again in red and black) are practically the same as those in the 1742 edition, save for modifications principally in the designation of the editions and in the imprints. Here is a list of them:
Sm. 8vo.

[Vol. I:] – – – – – / The Fifth Edition Corrected: / – – – – – – – / *London:* / Printed for Charle [*sic*] Bathurst, at the / *Cross Keys* opposite St. *Dunstan*'s Church, / *Fleetstret* [*sic*], MDCCXLVII.

a^2, 2b^4, B–S^8 — 2 pp. (t. + bl.), 8 pp. (Preface), 2 pp. (Contents), [1]–269, 3 pp. advs.

[Vol. II:] – – – – – / *London:* / Printed for Charles Bathurst, at the / *Cross Keys* opposite St. *Dunstan*'s Church, / *Fleetstreet*, and Charles Hitch in *Pa-* / *ter-noster-Row*, MDCCXLVII.

π^2, B–R^8, S^4 — 2 pp. (t. + bl.), 2 pp. (Contents), 5–268.

[Vol. III:] – – – – / *London:* / Printed for Charles Bathurst, at the / *Cross Keys* opposite St. *Dunstan*'s Church, / *Fleetstreet*, and Charles Hitch in *Pa-* / *ter-noster-Row*, MDCCXLVII.

π^2, B–R^8 — 2 pp. (t. + bl.), 2 pp. (Contents + bl.), [I]–VII + bl., 9–253, [1]–3 (advs.).

[Vol. IV:] – – – – / *London:* / Printed for Charles Bathurst, at the / *Cross Keys* opposite St. *Dunstan*'s Church, / *Fleetstreet*, MDCCXLVII.

b^4, B–T^8, U^2 — 2 pp. (t. + bl.), 6 pp. (Contents), [1]–291 + bl.

[Vol. V:] – – – – – / The Third Edition Corrected: / – – – – – – – / The / Fifth Volume. / = / *London,* / Printed for C. Davis, / against *Grays-Inn Gate, Holborn;* / and C. Bathurst, / opposite St. *Dunstan's Church, Fleetstreet.* / — / MDCCXLV.

π^3, B–S^8, T 1 — 2 pp. (t. + bl.), 4 pp. (Contents), [1]–274.

[Vol. VI:] – – – – / *London* / Printed for C. Davis, / against *Grays-Inn Gate, Holborn;* / and C. Bathurst, / opposite St. *Dunstan's Church, Fleetstreet.* / — / MDCCXLV.

π^2, B–U^8, X^4, Y^2 — 2 pp. (t. + bl.), 2 pp. (Contents), 1–316.

[Vol. VII:] – – – – – / The Third Edition. / – – – – – / *London,* / Printed for C. Davis, / against *Gray's-Inn Gate, Holborn;* / and C. Bathurst, / opposite St. *Dunstan's Church, Fleetstreet.* / — / MDCCXLV.

π^2, B–X^8, Y^4 — 2 pp. (t. + bl.), 2 pp. (Contents + bl.), 1–326, 2 pp. blank.

[Vol. VIII:] – – – – – / The Third Edition. / – – – – – / *London,* / Printed for C. Davis, / against *Grays-Inn-Gate, Holborn.* / and C. Bathurst, / opposite St. *Dunstan's Church, Fleetstreet.* / — / MDCCXLV.

A^2, B–X^8 — 2 pp. (t. + bl.), 2 pp. (Contents), 1–310 (247–56 repeated in numbering).

[Vol. IX:] – – – – – / The Third Edition. / – – – – / *London,* / Printed for C. Davis, / against *Grays-Inn Gate, Holborn;* / and C. Bathurst, / opposite St. *Dunstan's Church, Fleetstreet.* / — / MDCCXLV.

π^2, B–S^8, T^4 — 2 pp. (t. + bl.), 2 pp. (Contents + bl.), [1]–278, 2 pp. blank.

[Vol. X belonging to this set is Vol. X, 1745 — see No. 66, *ante.*]

[Vol. XI belonging to this set is Vol. XI, 1746 — see No. 66, *ante.*]

[Vol. XII:] – – – – / The Eleventh Edition. / – – – – – / *London:* Printed for Charles Bathurst, / at the *Cross-Keys* in *Fleet-Street.* / MDCCXLVII.

Frontisp., π^1, B–Q^8, R 1 — frontisp., 2 pp. (t. + 'Treatises wrote' on verso), [I]–XVI (Apology), 5 pp. (Dedication to Sommers), 1 p. (The Bookseller to the Reader), [1]–8 (Epistle Dedicatory), 9–20 (Preface), 21–220. — 7 plates (offprints of the 1710 plates).

[Vol. XIII:] – – – – – / The Fifth Edition, Corrected. / = / *London:* / Printed for Charles Bathurst, at the / *Cross-Keys* in *Fleet-Street.* / MDCCXLVII.

π^1, A^4, B–T^8, U^4 — 2 pp. (t. + bl.), 8 pp. (Contents), [1]–296. — 4 maps and 2 plans (offprints of the 1727, 12mo plates).
Copies: Penn.

67A. *Re-issued and reprinted volumes:*
Sm. 8vo.

Another issue of Vol. VI:

(1) [Vol. VI:] – – – – / *London,* / Printed for C. Davis, / against *Grays-Inn Gate, Holborn;* / and C. Bathurst, / opposite St. *Dunstan's Church, Fleetstreet.* / — / MDCCXLVI.

> Except for the title-page, this is the same printing as Vol. VI, 1745.
> Copies: Dobell, cat. 105, item 47, and Bibl. Arsenal, Paris.

Another edition of Vols. VII, VIII and IX (1748):

(2a) [Vol. VII:] – – – – / The Fourth Edition. / – – – – – / *London,* / Printed for C. Davis, / against *Gray's-Inn Gate, Holborn;* / and C. Bathurst, / opposite *St. Dunstan's Church, Fleetstreet.* / — / MDCCXLVIII.

π^2, B–X^8, Y^4 — 2 pp. (t. + bl.), 2 pp. (Contents + bl.), 1–326, 2 pp. blank.

(2b) [Vol. VIII:] – – – – / The Fourth Edition. / – – – – – / *London,* / Printed for C. Davis, / against *Gray's-Inn Gate, Holborn;* / and C. Bathurst, / opposite *St. Dunstan's Church, Fleetstreet.* / — / MDCCXLVIII.

A^2, B–X^8 — 2 pp. (t. + bl.), 2 pp. (Contents), 1–310 (247–56 repeated in numbering).

(2c) [Vol. IX:] – – – – / The Fourth Edition. / – – – – – / *London,* / Printed for C. Davis, / against *Gray's-Inn Gate, Holborn;* / and C. Bathurst, / opposite St. *Dunstan's Church, Fleetstreet.* / — / MDCCXLVIII.

π^2, B–S^8, T^4 — 2 pp. (t. + bl.), 2 pp. (Contents + bl.), [1]–278, 2 pp. blank.

Sm. 8vo:

Another edition of Vols. V and VI (1749):

(3a) [Vol. V:] – – – – / The Fourth Edition Corrected: / – – – – – – – / The / Fifth Volume. / = / *London,* / Printed for C. Davis, / against *Grays-Inn Gate, Holborn;* / and C. Bathurst, / opposite St. *Dunstan's Church, Fleetstreet.* / — / MDCCXLIX.

π^1, A^2, B–S^8, T 1 — 2 pp. (t. + bl.), 4 pp. (Contents), [1]–274.

(3b) [Vol. VI:] – – – – – / *London,* / Printed for C. Davis, / against *Grays-Inn Gate, Holborn;* / and C. Bathurst, / opposite St. *Dunstan's Church, Fleetstreet.* / — / MDCCXLIX.

π^2, B–U^8, X^6 — 2 pp. (t. + bl.), 2 pp. (Contents), 1–316 (X 5 signed y).

Another edition of Vol. XI (1749):
(4) [Vol. XI:] – – – – / *London,* / Printed for C. Hitch, C. Davis, / and R. Dodsley. / MDCCXLIX.

Sm. 8vo; A⁴, B–U⁸, X² — 2 pp. (t. + bl.), [III]–VIII (Contents), [1]–304, 301–4.
I have had two copies, one with, the other without, two unnumbered pages at the end, bearing a short *Life* of Swift.

Another edition of Vol. X (1750):
(5) [Vol. X:] – – – – / London: / Printed for R. Dodsley in Pall-mall. / — / MDCCL.

Sm. 8vo; A⁴, B–S⁸, T⁴, π² — 2 pp. (t. + bl.), III (Advertisement), 1 p. blank, V–VIII (Contents), 1–277, 3 pp. advs., 4 pp. music.

68. *The (first) 1751 Edition:*
The title-pages (again in red and black, with the exception of that of the *Tale,* Vol. [XII], which is in black only) are practically the same as those of the preceding editions. This list shows the modifications:

Sm. 8vo:
[Vol. I:] Miscellanies / By / Dr. Swift, Dr. Arbuthnot, / Mr. Pope, and Mr. Gay. / In / Four Volumes. / — / The Sixth Edition, Corrected: / With Several Additional Pieces in / Verse and Prose. / — / Vol. I. / By Dr. Swift. / = / *London,* / Printed for Charles Bathurst, / And sold by T. Woodward, C. Davis, / C. Hitch, R. Dodsley, and W. Bowyer. / MDCCLI.

a², b⁴, B–R⁸, S⁶ — 2 pp. (t. + bl.), [III]–X (Preface), [XI]–XII (Contents), [1]–268.

[Vol. II:] – – – – / *London,* / Printed for C. Bathurst, and C. Hitch. / And sold by T. Woodward, C. Davis, / R. Dodsley, and W. Bowyer. / MDCCLI.

π², B–R⁸, S⁴ — 2 pp. (t. + bl.), 2 pp. (Contents), 5–268.

[Vol. III:] – – – – – / *London,* / Printed for Charles Bathurst, / And sold by T. Woodward, C. Davis, / C. Hitch, R. Dodsley, and W. Bowyer. / MDCCLI.

π², B–Q⁸, R⁶ — 2 pp. (t. + bl.), 2 pp. (Contents), [I]–VII + bl., 9–252.

[Vol. IV:] – – – – / *London,* / Printed for Charles Bathurst, / And sold by T. Woodward, C. Davis, / C. Hitch, R. Dodsley, and W. Bowyer. / MDCCLI.

π², b², B–S⁸, T⁶ — 2 pp. (t. + bl.), [III]–VIII (Contents), 1–283 + bl.

Miscellanies. / — / The / Fifth Volume. / By Dr. Swift. / — / [ornament] / = / London. / Printed for T. Woodward, C. Davis, / C. Bathurst, and W. Bowyer. / MDCCLI.

[A]³, B–S⁸, T 1 — 2 pp. (t. + bl.), [III]–VI (Contents), [1]–274. — Copy: Texas.

Miscellanies. / — / The / Sixth Volume. / — / *By Dr*. Swift. / — / [ornament] / = / *London*, / Printed for T. Woodward, C. Davis, / C. Bathurst, and W. Bowyer. / MDCCLI.

π^2, B–U⁸, X⁶ — 2 pp. (t. + bl.), 2 pp. (Contents), 1–316. With the exception of the two leaves in front, sheet M (pp. 161–76), and sheet X (pp. 305–16), which are new, this is the same printing as Vol. VI, 1749 (No. 67A (3b)). —

[Vol. VII:] – – – – / The Fourth Edition. / – – – – / *London*, / Printed for C. Davis, / against *Gray's-Inn Gate, Holbourn;* / and C. Bathurst, / opposite St. *Dunstan's Church, Fleetstreet*. / — / MDCCLI.

π^2, B–X⁸, Y⁴ — 2 pp. (t. + bl.), 2 pp. (Contents + bl.), 1–326, 2 pp. blank.

[Vol. VIII:] – – – – / The Fourth Edition. / – – – – – / *London*, / Printed for C. Davis, / against *Gray's-Inn Gate, Holbourn;* / and C. Bathurst, / opposite *St. Dunstan's Church, Fleetstreet*. / — / MDCCLI.

π^2, B–X⁸ — 2 pp. (t. + bl.), 2 pp. (Contents), 1–310 (247–56 repeated in numbering).

[Vol. IX:] – – – – / The Fourth Edition. / – – – – – / *London*, / Printed for C. Davis, / against *Gray's-Inn Gate, Holborn*; / and C. Bathurst, / opposite St. *Dunstan's Church, Fleetstreet*. / — / MDCCLI.

π^2, B–S⁸, T⁴ — 2 pp. (t. + bl.), 2 pp. (Contents + bl.), [1]–278, 2 pp. blank.

[Vol. X belonging to this set is Vol. X, 1750 — see No. 67A (5), *ante*.]

[Vol. XI belonging to this set is Vol. XI, 1749 — see No. 67A (4), *ante*.]

[Vol. XII:] – – – – – / The Twelfth Edition. / – – – – / *London*: Printed for Charles Bathurst, at / the *Cross-Keys* in *Fleet-Street*. / MDCCLI.

Frontisp., π^1, B–Q^8, R 1 — frontisp., 2 pp. (title in black only + 'Treatises wrote' on verso), [I]–XVI (Apology), 5 pp. (Dedication to Sommers), 1 p. (The Bookseller to the Reader), [1]–8 (Epistle Dedicatory), 9–20 (Preface), 21–220 — 7 plates (offprints of the 1710 plates).

[Vol. XIII:] – – – – – / The Sixth Edition, Corrected. / = / London, / Printed for Charles Bathurst, / And sold by T. Woodward, C. Davis, / R. Dodsley, and W. Bowyer. / MDCCLI.

A^4, B–T^8, U^4 — 2 pp. (t. + bl.), [III]–VIII (Contents), [1]–296 — 4 maps and 2 plans (offprints of the 1727, 12mo plates).
Copies: Penn.

69. *The (second) 1751 Edition:*
Though many of the title-pages (again in red and black) of this (second) 1751 edition show similarity as regards 'edition', publishers, and year, with the preceding editions, this is an altogether different edition. This difference is at once perceptible, not only from the printer's errors and the paper used, but especially from the printer's ornaments.

[Vol. I:] Miscellanies. / — / In / Four Volumes. / — / By Dr. *Swift*, Dr. *Arbuthnot*, / Mr. *Pope*, and Mr. *Gay*. / — / The Fourth Edition Corrected: / With Several Additional Pieces in / Verse and Prose. / — / Vol. I. / By Dr. *Swift*. / = / *London:* / Printed for Charles Bathurst; / And sold by T. Woodward, C. Davis, / C. Hitch, R. Dodsley, and W. Bowyer. / — / MDCCLI.

Sm. 8vo:
a^2, b^4, B–S^8 — 2 pp. (t. + bl.), 8 pp. (Preface), 2 pp. (Contents), [1]–269, 3 pp. advs.

[Vol. II:] – – – – – / *London,* / Printed for Charles Bathurst, / And sold by T. Woodward, C. Davis, / C. Hitch, R. Dodsley, and W. Bowyer. / MDCCLI.

π^2, B–R^8, S^4 — 2 pp. (t. + bl.), 2 pp. (Contents), 1–264.

[Vol. III:] – – – – – / *London,* / Printed for Charles Bathurst, / And sold by T. Woodward, C. Davis, / C. Hitch, R. Dodsley, and W. Bowyer. / MDCCLI.

π^2, B–Q^8, R^6 — 2 pp. (t. + bl.), 2 pp. (Contents + bl.), [I]–VII + bl., 9–252.

[Vol. IV:] – – – – / *London,* / Printed for Charles Bathurst, / And sold by T. Woodward, C. Davis, / C. Hitch, R. Dodsley, and W. Bowyer. / MDCCLI.

π^2, b^2, B–S^8, T^6 — 2 pp. (t. + bl.), [III]–VIII (Contents), 1–283 + bl.

[Vol. V:] – – – – – / The Fifth Edition Corrected: / – – – – – – – / *London,* / Printed for C. Davis, / against *Grays Inn Gate, Holborn;* /

and C. Bathurst, / opposite St. *Dunstan*'s *Church*, *Fleetstreet*. / — / MDCCLI.

π^3, B–S^8, T 1 — 2 pp. (t. + bl.), 4 pp. (Contents), [1]–274.

[Vol. VI:] – – – – / *London:* / Printed for C. Davis, / against *Grays-Inn Gate*, *Holborn;* / and C. Bathurst, / opposite St. *Dunstan*'s *Church*, *Fleetstreet*. / — / MDCCLI.

π^2, B–U^8, X^6 — 2 pp. (t. + bl.), 2 pp. (Contents), 1–316.

[Vol. VII:] – – – – / The Fourth Edition. / – – – – / *London,* / Printed for C. Davis, / against *Gray's-Inn Gate*, *Holborn;* / and C. Bathurst, / opposite St. *Dunstan*'s *Church*, *Fleetstreet*. / — / MDCCLI.

π^2, B–X^8, Y^3 — 2 pp. (t. + bl.), 2 pp. (Contents + bl.), 326 (the leaf bearing 'Contents' was printed as Y 4).

[Vol. VIII:] – – – – / The Fourth Edition. / – – – – / *London:* / Printed for C. Davis, / against *Grays-Inn Gate*, *Holborn;* / and C. Bathurst, / opposite St. *Dunstan*'s *Church*, *Fleetstreet*. / — / MDCCLI.

A^2, B–X^8 — 2 pp. (t. + bl.), 2 pp. (Contents), 1–310 (247–56 repeated in numbering).

[Vol. IX:] – – – – / The Fourth Edition. / – – – – – / *London:* / Printed for C. Davis, / against *Gray's-Inn Gate*, *Holborn;* / and C. Bathurst, / opposite St. *Dunstan*'s *Church*, *Feetstreet* [*sic*]. / — / MDCCLI.

π^2, B–S^8, T^3 — 2 pp. (t. + bl.), 2 pp. (Contents + bl.), [1]–278 (the leaf bearing 'Contents' was printed as T 4).

[Vol. X:] – – – – / London: / Printed for R. Dodsley in Pall-mall. / — / MDCCL.

A^4, B–S^8, T^4 — 2 pp. (t. + bl.), III (Advertisement), 1 p. blank, V–VIII (Contents), 1–277, 3 pp. advs.

[Vol. XI:] Miscellanies. / — / The / Eleventh Volume. / — / By Dr. Swift. / — / [ornament] / = / London, / Printed for C. Hitch, C. Davis, / R. Dodsley, and W. Bowyer. / MDCCLI.

(1751): [A]^4, π^1, B–U^8, X^2 — 2 pp. (t. + bl.), [III]–VIII (Contents), 2 pp. (Life of Swift), 1–288. — Copy: Texas.

[Vol. XI:] – – – – / *London:* / Printed for C. Hitch, C. Davis, C. Bathurst, / R. Dodsley, and W. Bowyer. / MDCCLIII.

(1753): A⁴, B–U⁸, X³ — 2 pp. (t. + bl.), [III]–VIII (Contents), [1]–309 + bl. — 4 pp. music. (The Life of Swift is pp. 303–4.)

[Vol. XII:] – – -- – / The Tenth Edition. / *London:* Printed for Charles Bathurst, / and sold by T. Woodward, C. Davis, C. Hitch, / R. Dodsley, and W. Bowyer. / MDCCLI.

Frontisp., π¹, B–Q⁸, R 1 — frontisp., 2 pp. (t. + 'Treatises wrote' on verso), [I]–XVI (Apology), 5 pp. (Dedication to Sommers), 1 p. (The Bookseller to the Reader), [1]–8 (Epistle Dedicatory), 9–20 (Preface), 21–220. — 7 plates (offprints of the 1710 plates).

[Vol. XIII:] – – – – / The Fifth Edition, Corrected. / = / *London:* / Printed for Charles Bathurst, and Sold by / T. Woodward, C. Davis, C. Hitch, / R. Dodsley, and W. Bowyer. / MDCCLI.

π¹, A⁴, B–T⁸, U⁴ — 2 pp. (t. + bl.), 8 pp. (Contents), [1]–296. — 4 maps and 2 plans (offprints of the 1727, 12mo plates).

Notes to the preceding four editions:
I. The editions described in Nos. 66–9 represent the normal state; but there are also in existence copies in which the full titles are preceded by (extra) half-titles, after the following patterns:
[In Vol. XII:] — / The / Works / Of / Dr. *Swift.* / — / Tome I. / — / Containing A / *Tale* of a *Tub.* / And / An Account of a Battle between / The *Antient* and *Modern* Books in / St. *James*'s Library. / —
[In Vol. XIII:] — / The / Works / Of / Dr. *Swift.* / — / Tome II. / — / Containing The / Travels / Of / Capt. Lemuel Gulliver, / Into several remote Nations of the World. / —
[In Vol. I:] — / The / Works / Of / Dr. *Swift.* / — / Tome III. / — / Consisting of / Miscellanies / In / Verse. / — / 1.
[In Vol. II:] — / The / Works / Of / Dr. *Swift.* / — / Tome IV / — / Consisting of / Miscellanies / In / Prose. / — / 2.
And so on for Vols. III–IX = Tomes V–XI.
Penn possesses two such sets, 1742 and 1747, both eleven volumes, viz. *Tale, Gulliver,* vols. I–IX. From them we see that this is an early attempt to place the *Tale* and *Gulliver's Travels* in front, for the first time fully accomplished in the 12mo edition of 1751 (see No. 82, *post*).
Penn has a copy of Vol. XI, 1746, with an extra half-title leaf reading:
[headpiece] / The / Works / Of / Dr. *Swift.* / — / Volume the Thirteenth. / — / Consisting of / His Sermons; with some Letters / and Poems never before printed. / [tailpiece].
Curiously enough this is wrong, for this Vol. XI, 1746 does not contain the 'Sermons, Letters, and Poems' (which are in Vol. X), but 'Rules for Servants, Story Injured Lady, Letters, some prose pieces, and Poetry'.
There is also such a copy in Bibl. Arsenal, Paris. And I heard of a similar copy Vol. XI, 1749. Query: Are there copies of Vol. X in a similar state?
II. A close examination of the printer's ornaments in the 1742 and 1747 sets evinces the fact that there were two different printing-houses from which the volumes emanated: one (Bathurst's, where Vols. I–IV and XII–XIII were printed) characterized by a singular scarcity, the other (Davis's, where Vols. V–VI, VII–IX and XI were printed) by a great profusion of printer's

ornaments. This distinction, from which Vol. X must constantly be excluded (it belonged to another publisher), is also noticeable in the 1751 12mo edition (see No. 82, *post*). And in reliance upon this criterion, it would seem — in both cases again with the exception of Vol. X — that the first 1751 edition was entirely printed in Davis's, the second 1751 edition entirely in Bathurst's usual printing-house. This supposition finds some ground in an apparently closer union of all the publishers in 1751 than before, evinced by the occurrence of all their names in the title-pages of those volumes which originally bore the name of Bathurst only.

III. It is not always easy to account for the indication of 'edition' on the title-pages (see diagram after No. 69, *ante*). *The Fourth Edition Corrected* on the title-page of Vol. I, 1742, of course refers to the three 12mo editions 1731, 1733 and 1736. After this the 1747 and first 1751 editions have quite regularly: *The Fifth Edition Corrected* and *The Sixth Edition Corrected*. It is, however, strange to note that the second 1751 edition goes back to the 1742 edition, in being called *The Fourth Edition Corrected*.

The Third Edition Corrected on the title-page of Vol. V, 1742, has reference to Woodward and Davis's 12mo editions 1736 and 1738. The reprint of 1745 has, strangely enough, also *The Third Edition Corrected*, but after this those of 1749 and 1751 have regularly: *The Fourth Edition Corrected* and *The Fifth Edition Corrected*.

The Second Edition on the title-pages of Vols. VII–IX, 1742, evidently refers to Cooper's Vols. VII–IX, 1742 (No. 31, *ante*). After this the 1745 edition has *The Third Edition*, and the 1748 edition has *The Fourth Edition*; but why the two 1751 editions should both have *The Fourth Edition* again, is difficult to explain.

Nine editions of the *Tale* had preceded (see No. 236, *post*); therefore it is quite natural that the 1743 edition should be called *The Tenth Edition*, the 1747 one *The Eleventh Edition*, and the first 1751 one *The Twelfth Edition*. But the second 1751 edition has *The Tenth Edition*, which shows recurrence to 1743.

Gulliver's Travels 1742 is called *The Fourth Edition, Corrected* (for the preceding editions see note before No. 289, *post*), the 1747 edition *The Fifth Edition, Corrected*, the first 1751 one *The Sixth Edition, Corrected*. It is rather peculiar to find that after this the second 1751 edition is called *The Fifth Edition, Corrected*.

***

Works And Miscellanies (12mo), 1751

This edition is noteworthy as a link between the former *Miscellanies* (Nos. 66–69, *ante*) and the following *Works* (Hawkesworth, Nos. 87 &c., *post*), in being the first to place the *Tale* and *Gulliver's Travels*, hitherto forming the tail-end of the collection, in front, and also designating them on the title-pages as Volumes I, II–III in the set; and in being, for the first time, called (at least Vols. I–VII):

The / Works / Of / Dr. Jonathan Swift, / Dean of St. *Patrick*'s, *Dublin*.
But Vols. VIII–XIV are still entitled:
Miscellanies. / — / By Dr. *Swift*.
Owing to the fact that *Gulliver's Travels* is here printed in two volumes, there are 14 volumes, instead of the former 13. Their distribution is as follows:

(1) *Works:* Vol. I (*Tale*), Vols. II–III (*Gulliver's Travels*), Vols. IV–VII (the old Vols. I–IV, but the order of the volumes is altered). No mention of 'edition' on any of the title-pages.

Miscellanies (Sm. 8vo), 1742, &c.

Vol.							
I	1742 4th ed. corr.		1747 5th ed. corr.			1751 6th ed. corr.	1751 4th ed. corr.
I	1742		1747			1751	1751
III	1742		1747			1751	1751
IV	1742		1747			1751	1751
V	1742 3rd ed. corr.	1745 3rd ed. corr.			1749 4th ed. corr.		1751 5th ed. corr.
VI	1742	1745 1746			1749		1751
VII	1742 2nd ed.	1745 3rd ed.		1748 4th ed.		1751 4th ed.	1751 4th ed.
VIII	1742 2nd ed.	1745 3rd ed.		1748 4th ed.		1751 4th ed.	1751 4th ed.
IX	1742 2nd ed.	1745 3rd ed.		1748 4th ed.		1751 4th ed.	1751 4th ed.
X		1745			1750		
XI		1746		1749	1750		1751 1753
[XII]	1743 10th ed.		1747 11th ed.			1751 12th ed.	1751 10th ed.
[XIII]	1742 4th ed. corr.		1747 5th ed. corr.			1751 6th ed. corr.	1751 5th ed. corr.

(2) *Miscellanies:* Vols. VIII–XII are the old Vols. V–VI and VII–IX, but combined, after change of order, into one group, and designated on all the five title-pages as: *The Fifth Edition*. Then comes Vol. XIII (which is the old Vol. X), indicated on the title-page as: *The Fourth Edition*; and lastly Vol. XIV (which is the old Vol. XI) indicated as: *The Second Edition*.

All the volumes have half-titles (in Vols. I and II–III appropriate ones to the *Tale* and *Gulliver's Travels*, in the other volumes: 'Miscellanies. By Dr. Swift.'), except only Vols. V and VII, perhaps because in these two volumes the pieces by Pope, Arbuthnot and Gay were hidden away. Those in Vols. I–III follow the full title; those in the other volumes precede it. The title-pages are in black only.

82. The / Works / Of / Dr. Jonathan Swift, / Dean of St. *Patrick*'s, *Dublin*. / — / Vol. I. / — / Containing / A / Tale / Of A / Tub. / Written for the / Universal Improvement of Mankind. / = / *London:* / Printed for C. Bathurst, in *Fleet-street*. / — / MDCCLI.

12mo (in sixes):
Frontisp., π^2, a^6, π^4, B–Z^6, Aa^4 — frontisp., 2 pp. (t. + bl.), 2 pp. (title: Tale + 'Treatises wrote' on verso), I–XX (Apology), 6 pp. (Dedication to Somers), 2 pp. (The Bookseller to the Reader), 1–9 (Epistle Dedicatory), 10–24 (Preface), 25–261, 3 pp. blank. — 7 plates.

– – – – – Vol. II. / — / Containing / Capt. Lemuel Gulliver's / Travels into several remote / Nations of the World. / Parts I. and II. / = / – – – – –

Frontisp., A^{12}, B–U^6 — frontisp. (L. Gulliver), 2 pp. (t. + bl.), 2 pp. (title: Part I, Part II + bl.), [V]–VIII. (The Publisher To The Reader), [IX]–XIII (Contents), 1 p. blank, XV–XXIV (Verses), 1–224, 4 pp. advs. — 2 maps.

– – – – – Vol. III. / — / Containing / Capt. Lemuel Gulliver's / Travels into several remote / Nations of the World. / Parts III. and IV. / = / – – – – –

A^5, B–X^6, Y 1 — 2 pp. (t. + bl.), 2 pp. (title: Part III, Part IV + bl.), [V]–X (Contents), 3–244. — 2 maps and 2 plans.

– – – – – Vol. IV. / — / Consisting Of / Miscellanies / In Prose. / = / – – – – – –

Frontisp., π^2, B–Dd^6 — frontisp. (Swift), 2 pp. (title: Miscellanies Vol. IV + bl.), 2 pp. (t. + bl.), 8 pp. (Preface), 2 pp. (Contents), [1]–300, 2 pp. blank.

– – – – – Vol. V. / — / Consisting Of / Miscellanies / In Prose. / By Dr. Swift, Dr. Arbuthnot, / and Mr. Pope. / = / *London:* / Printed for C. Bathurst, in *Fleet-street*, / and C. Hitch, in *Pater-Noster-Row*. / — / MDCCLI.

Frontisp., A^2, B–Z^6, Aa 1 — frontisp. (Arbuthnot), 2 pp. (t. + bl.), 2 pp. (Contents), 3–263 + bl.

- - - - - Vol. VI. / — / Consisting Of / Miscellanies / In Prose. / By Dr. Swift, Dr. Arbuthnot, / Mr. Pope, and Mr. Gay. / = / - - - - - -

Frontisp., π^2, A^5, B–Z^6 (A 5 signed A 3) — frontisp. (Gay), 2 pp. (title: Miscellanies Vol. VI + bl.), 2 pp. (t. + bl.), 1 (Contents), 1 p. blank, 3 (title: Law is a Bottomless Pit.), 1 p. blank, V–X (Preface), 11–274.

- - - - - Vol. VII. / — / Consisting Of / Miscellanies / In Verse. / By Dr. Swift, Dr. Arbuthnot, / Mr. Pope, and Mr. Gay. / = / - - - - -

Frontisp., A^4, B–Y^6, Z 1 — frontisp. (Pope), 2 pp. (t. + bl.), 6 pp. (Contents), 3–255 + bl.

Miscellanies. / — / By Dr. *Swift*. / — / The / Eighth Volume. / — / The Fifth Edition. / — / [ornament] / = / *London:* / Printed for T. Woodward, C. Davis, / C. Bathurst, and W. Bowyer. / — / MDCCLI.

π^3, B–Ii^6, Kk^2 — 2 pp. (title: Miscellanies Vol. VIII + bl.), 2 pp. (t. + bl.), 2 pp. (Contents), 1–376.

- - - - - The / Ninth Volume. / — / The Fifth Edition. / — / [ornament] / = / *London:* / Printed for T. Woodward, C. Davis, / and W. Bowyer. / — / MDCCLI.

π^4, B–Dd^6, Ee^2 — 2 pp. (title: Miscellanies, Vol. IX + bl.), 2 pp. (t. + bl.), 3 pp. (Contents + bl.), [1]–315 + bl.

- - - - The / Tenth Volume. / — / The Fifth Edition. / — / [ornament] / = / *London:* / Printed for T. Woodward, C. Davis, / C. Bathurst, and W. Bowyer. / — / MDCCLI.

π^4, B–Z^6, Aa 1 — 2 pp. (title: Miscellanies, Vol. X + bl.), 2 pp. (t. + bl.), 4 pp. (Contents), 1–265 + bl.

- - - - The / Eleventh Volume. / — / The Fifth Edition. / — / [ornament] / = / *London:* / Printed for C. Davis and C. Bathurst. / — / MDCCLI.

π^3, B–Ff^6, Gg^2 — 2 pp. (title: Miscellanies, Vol. XI + bl.), 2 pp. (t. + bl.), 2 pp. (Contents + bl.), 1–340.

- - - - The / Twelfth Volume. / — / The Fifth Edition. / — / [ornament] / = / *London:* / Printed for T. Woodward, C. Davis, / C. Hitch, C. Bathurst, R. Dodsley, / and W. Bowyer. / — / MDCCLI.

π^3, B–Aa^6, Bb^2 — 2 pp. (title: Miscellanies, Vol. XII + bl.), 2 pp. (t. + bl.), 2 pp. (Contents + bl.), [1]–280.

– – – – – The / Thirteenth Volume. / — / The Fourth Edition. /—
/ [ornament] / = / *London:* / Printed for R. Dodsley in *Pall-mall.*
/ — / MDCCLI.

π^4, B–X^6, [Y]^2 — 2 pp. (title: Miscellanies, Vol. XIII + bl.), 2 pp. (t. +
bl.), 3 pp. (Contents + bl.), 1–240, 4 pp. advs.

– – – – The / Fourteenth Volume. / — / The Second Edition.
/ — / [ornament] / = / *London:* / Printed for C. Hitch, C. Davis,
/ R. Dodsley, and W. Bowyer. / — / MDCCLI.

π^4, B–Aa^6, Bb^4 — 2 pp. (title: Miscellanies, Vol. XIV + bl.), 2 pp. (t. +
bl.), 4 pp. (Contents), [1]–276 (misnumbered 221), 4 pp. advs. (Contains the
music, pp. 253–60, and the 'Life of Swift', pp. 275–6).
Copies: Penn.

There are two issues of this edition, one *without*, the other *with*, plates.
The plates occur in:
Vol. I: frontispiece and 7 plates.
Vols. II–III: frontispiece in Vol. II (portrait of Gulliver), 4 maps and
2 plans.
Vol. IV: frontispiece (portrait of Swift).
Vol. V: „   („   „ Arbuthnot).
Vol. VI: „   („   „ Gay).
Vol. VII: „   („   „ Pope).

But the plates do not form the only difference; at least in Vol. III sheets
K, L and M of the issue *with* plates show signs of considerable retouching
when compared with the same sheets of the issue *without* plates, resulting in a
widening-out of very full lines by the removal of part of them to the next
line, wherever necessary and possible.
Vol. I (the *Tale*) was also issued separately (see No. 239A).
Vols. II–III (*Gulliver*) may also have been treated in this way, but I have not
seen a copy.

**

Hawkesworth's Editions

The so-called Hawkesworth editions, later on and at various times completed by Deane Swift and John Nichols, appeared in four sizes, viz.:

(1) the 4to edition, begun in 1755.
(2) the large 8vo edition, begun in 1754–5; reprinted in 1768.
(3) the small 8vo edition, begun in 1760 (large crown paper); reprinted in
    1766 (ordinary crown paper).
(4) the 18mo edition, begun in 1765.

These editions all have a *Life* of Swift prefixed. The *Tale* and *Gulliver's
Travels* form the first volumes in each set. All the editions have copper-plates.
Those in the 4to, large 8vo and small 8vo editions (by I. S. Müller) are the
same, though not in number. In the 4to and the two large 8vo editions there
are 26, viz.: the usual 8 in the *Tale*; 10 in *Gulliver's Travels*, i.e. the usual 4 maps
and 2 plans (no portrait of Gulliver), but also 4 illustrations, one to each
'Part'; then 4 illustrations to *The History Of John Bull*; and lastly 4 illustrations

to the poetical part of the *Miscellanies*. Moreover there are 4 pages of *Cantata*. — In the small 8vo editions, however, there are only 14, the 4 illustrations in *Gulliver's Travels*, the 4 in *The History Of John Bull* and the 4 in the *Miscellanies* having been left out; but the 4 pages of *Cantata* are present.

In order to make the plates suitable for these various editions, it was of course from time to time necessary to effect erasures in the numbers and the volume- and page-indications at the top.

Furthermore, the plates in the 4to edition are distinguished by a large ornamental frame to fill up the 4to page.

The copperplates in the 18mo edition are the same as those in the 12mo edition (second issue) in 14 volumes, 1751 (see No. 82, *ante*), of course with the necessary erasures.

There are seven stages of publication to be distinguished in the production of the Hawkesworth editions (cf. diagram after No. 93, *post*).

First Stage:

In 1754–5 were published 6 volumes 4to (each volume containing two 'Parts'), and 12 volumes large 8vo. It seems that the latter edition was first begun, at least the title-pages of most of the 12 volumes have the year 1754 (Vol. I 1755, but half-title 1754; Vol. II 1754, but half-title 1755; Vols. III–IX all 1754; Vols. X–XII 1755), whereas those of the 4to edition have all 1755.

Apart from changes owing to extension or alteration of partnership, the printers and publishers were much the same as before.

In 1760 the 12 volumes were also published in a small 8vo size.

Second Stage:

The year 1762 saw an addition of two volumes (XIII and XIV) to the small 8vo edition, repeated for the 4to edition (Vol. VII) in 1763–4, and for the large 8vo edition (Vols. XIII and XIV) in 1764. The introductory *Advertisement* tells us that many of the pieces were reprinted from a Dublin edition (i.e. Faulkner's Vols. IX and X, 1758–62). The printer was W. Bowyer, Faulkner's friend; the imprint of Vol. VII, 4to edition, even has the names of both.

At the end of these volumes there was for the first time an *Index* for all the volumes printed up to that time, composed by J. Nichols, whose name we shall meet again further on.

Vol. VII, 4to, was reprinted in 1775. It does not contain the *Index*, which was placed, in its enlarged form, in Vol. IX, 1775 (see *Sixth Stage*).

Third Stage:

The year 1765 saw not only additions all along the line (Vol. VIII in 4to; Vols. XV–XVI in large 8vo; Vols. XV–XVII in small 8vo), all "collected and revised by Deane Swift, Esq., of Goodrich, in Herefordshire", and printed by a new man, W. Johnston; but in the same year also appeared a reprint of the 12mo edition of 1751 (see No. 82, *ante*), not in 14, as formerly, but in 12 volumes 18mo, to which 5 volumes (the 2 of Bowyer, and the 3 of Johnston) were now added, making 17 in all. The *Index* mentioned above (see *Second Stage*) was here placed at the end of Vol. XVII, and of course worked up so as to suit all the 17 volumes.

Fourth Stage:

In the next year, 1766, the small 8vo edition was reprinted, in 18 instead of the preceding 17 volumes. The extension of the last three volumes to four was owing to the insertion, in Vol. XV, of *The History Of The Four Last Years Of The Queen*. It was the first time that this piece was brought into the collection, and it occasioned a shifting of the materials and a different distribution over the volumes. The *Index*, lifted out of Vol. XIV, and enlarged so as to cover all the 18 volumes, was placed at the end of Vol. XVIII. — It is of some importance to note that, whereas the former 17 volumes had been printed on a 'large crown paper' (which gives them, especially if not too close cut, a broad look, almost like small quartos), these 18 volumes were printed on an 'ordinary crown paper', which made them slightly smaller than the former.

This is also the year of the first series of *Letters* ("with notes explanatory and historical, by John Hawkesworth, L.L.D."), 2 volumes in 4to, 3 volumes in large 8vo (the latter reprinted in the same year, with *A New Edition* on the title-page, and the contents differently distributed over the volumes), and probably a fourth edition: 3 volumes in small 8vo, belonging to the 'ordinary crown paper' edition in 18 volumes small 8vo, 1766. At least, Vol. XVIII, small 8vo, 1766, has this advertisement on verso of p. 283: "*Lately published,* Printed uniformly with this Edition, The Epistolary Correspondence of Dr. Swift. In Three Volumes". The next year, 1767, saw also 3 volumes in small 8vo (called *The Fifth Edition*) for the 'large crown paper' edition in 17 volumes small 8vo, 1760-2-5; and further 3 volumes in 18mo (called *The Sixth Edition*). In 1768 *The Seventh Edition* in small 8vo appeared, printed on 'ordinary crown paper', and therefore to be considered as a reprint of the supposed 'fourth'. And in 1769 *A New Edition* in large 8vo, a reprint of *A New Edition*, 1766. At the end of all these sets there is an *Index* covering the *Letters* in them.

Above I have assumed, on the ground of the advertisement "*Lately published,* &c.", that the 'fourth' edition is a small 8vo 'ordinary crown paper', 1766. But it may also have been a 4to edition. For Nichols's *Supplement*, 4to ed., 1779 (see *Seventh Stage*) says on verso of page XI, when speaking of Vols. X and XI, 4to, that "of these two volumes there have been two editions". One is, of course, the 1766, 4to ed., but when was the other? As long as I have not seen either another small 8vo, or another 4to edition, the question of the 'fourth' edition remains unsolved.

Fifth Stage:

In 1768 a new edition of the large 8vo edition appeared, not, however, of all the 16 volumes preceding the *Letters*, but of Vols. I–XIV only. It seems that Vols. XV–XVI, 1765, were not yet exhausted; but that a reprint of these two volumes in three (similar to that of Vols. XV–XVII in four volumes in the case of the small 8vo edition 1766) was even then in consideration, appears from the fact that the old *Index* in Vol. XIV was then lifted out of it. It was, however, not until 1775 (see *Sixth Stage*) that these three volumes at last came out.

In the year 1768 also appeared the second series of *Letters* ("collected and revised by Deane Swift, Esq. of Goodrich, in Herefordshire"), 2 volumes in 4to, and 3 volumes in large 8vo, followed in 1769 by 3 volumes in small 8vo (called *The Third Edition*), and in 1775 by 3 volumes in 18mo (called *A New Edition, Corrected*). Only the last set has an *Index*, covering all the 6 volumes of *Letters*.

Sixth Stage:

In 1775 John Nichols (and others) added another volume to Swift's works: Vol. IX in 4to, Vol. XVII in large 8vo (Vols. XV–XVI were reprinted at the same time — see *Fifth Stage*), and Vol. XVIII in 18mo. The principal piece in them, *The History Of The Four Last Years Of The Queen*, had already been inserted in Vol. XV, small 8vo, 1766 (see *Fourth Stage*); hence no corresponding volume in the small 8vo edition at this time. As to the enlarged *Index*, it was already present in the 18mo edition (Vol. XVII, 1765) and in the 'ordinary crown paper' small 8vo edition (Vol. XVIII, 1766), and therefore it was now only added at the end of Vol. IX, 4to and Vol. XVII, large 8vo. There is a second *Index* covering the four (4to) and six (large 8vo) volumes of *Letters*, which, for the 18mo edition, was inserted at the end of Vol. VI of the *Letters* printed the same year (see *Fifth Stage*).

The designation of the above volumes on the title-pages as Volume IX, Volume XVII and Volume XVIII respectively, shows that the volumes of *Letters* that had preceded them still stood outside the collection. They had simply been indicated as: *Letters* – – – – – – Volume I, II, III, IV, V, VI. But about this time Nichols included them as volumes into the collection, and binders then designated them as shown in the diagram after No. 92, *post*, on the backs of the volumes. However, there had been an earlier attempt in this direction. I possess a set of the first series of *Letters* in 18mo, 1767, which, in Vols. II and III, has half-titles: "Swift's Works. / Vol. XIX. / MDCCLXVII.", and: "Swift's Works. / Vol. XX. / MDCCLXVII." And another set, apparently bound after 1775, from which these half-titles have been removed.

In this year, 1775, Vol. VII, 4to, was reprinted. It does not contain the original *Index*, which, in its enlarged form, was now placed in Vol. IX.

Seventh Stage:

To complete the series Nichols added *A Supplement To Dr. Swift's Works* to the collection: 2 volumes large 8vo (1776 and 1779), 1 volume 4to (1779), 3 volumes small 8vo (1779), and 3 volumes 18mo (1779). On the title-pages these volumes are indicated as *Volume the First*, *Volume the Second* and *Volume the Third*, but in other places, i.a. at the foot of the first pages of new sheets, they are designated as volumes belonging to the collection and succeeding the *Letters* (see diagram after No. 92, *post*). At the end of the last volume of each set there is an *Index* covering this *Supplement*. (For a possible 26th volume, large 8vo, see No. 121, *post*).

One point remains to be discussed. When in 1766 the small 8vo edition was reprinted, new materials were added (principally *The History Of The Four Last Years Of The Queen*), and there were then 18 vols. instead of the preceding 17 vols. However, these new materials were not placed at the end (in Vol. XVIII), but in Vol. XV; hence a considerable re-arrangement (cf. *Fourth Stage*). The result is that ultimately the 1760 small 8vo set is complete in 26 vols. (without the *History*), the 1766 small 8vo set in 27 vols. (with the *History*). — In the case of the large 8vo reprint 1768, a different procedure was followed: in that year only Vols. I–XIV were reprinted, while Vols. XV–XVI were not reprinted until 1775, in which year Vol. XVII, containing the *History*, was added to the large 8vo edition for the first time (cf. *Fifth* and *Sixth Stages*). Vol. XVII must therefore belong to both large 8vo editions. The only peculiarity is that the 1754–5 large 8vo edition has then two *General Indexes*, one in Vol. XIV, and a more extensive one in Vol. XVII. But this can be no objection; the same peculiarity exists in the 4to edition, Vols. VII and IX. So that both large 8vo editions must be considered complete in 25 volumes.

87. *The 4to Edition:*

This edition has 14 volumes; nine of them are called *Works*, four are called *Letters*, and one is called *Supplement*.

The nine volumes of *Works* each consist of two (separately paged) 'Parts'.

The titles of the first 'Parts' are in red and black; those of the second 'Parts', as well as those of the volumes of *Letters* and *Supplement* are in black only.

The / Works / Of / Jonathan Swift, D.D. / Dean of St. Patrick's, Dublin, / Accurately revised / In Six Volumes, / Adorned with Copper-Plates; / With / Some Account of the Author's Life, / And / Notes Historical and Explanatory, / By John Hawkesworth. / = / London, / Printed for C. Bathurst, C. Davis, C. Hitch and L. Hawes, J. Hodges, / R. and J. Dodsley, and W. Bowyer. / — / MDCCLV.

The / Works / Of / Jonathan Swift, D.D. / Dean of St. Patrick's, Dublin. / Volume I. Part II. / = / London, / Printed for C. Bathurst, in Fleetstreet. / — / MDCCLV.

> 4to:
> Frontisp., π^1, A^4, A–E^4, F^2, A^4, a^4, b 1, B–Aa^4 — frontisp. (Tale), 2 pp. (t. + bl.), [1]–8 (Preface), [1]–40 (Life of Swift), 41–2 (Verses), 43 (Address), 1 p. blank, 2 pp. (title: Tale + bl.), [III]–XVI (Apology), XVII (Postscript), 1 p. (Treatises written), [1]–4 (Dedication to Sommers), 5 (The Bookseller To The Reader), 1 p. blank, [7]–12 (Epistle Dedicatory), [13]–22 (Preface), [23]–184. — 7 plates. π^1, a^4, A^2, A–Nn^4 — 2 pp. (t. + bl.), 2 pp. (title: Travels + bl.), [III]–XIII (Contents), [1] (The Publisher To The Reader), [2]–4 (Letter Gulliver to Sympson), [1]–286, 2 pp. blank. — 10 plates.

The / Works / Of / Jonathan Swift, D.D. / Dean of St. Patrick's, Dublin. / Volume II. Part I. / = / London, / Printed for C. Bathurst, in Fleetstreet. / — / MDCCLV.

> π^2, B–Gg^4 — 2 pp. (t. + bl.), 2 pp. (Contents + bl.), 5 pp. (Preface), 1 p. blank, [7]–231 + bl.

The / Works / Of / Jonathan Swift, D.D. / Dean of St. Patrick's, Dublin. / Volume II. Part II. / = / London, / Printed for C. Bathurst, in Fleetstreet. / — / MDCCLV.

> π^1, A 1, B–Aa^4 — 2 pp. (t. + bl.), 2 pp. (Contents + bl.), [1]–182, 2 pp. blank.

The / Works / Of / Jonathan Swift, D.D. / Dean of St. Patrick's, Dublin. / Volume III. Part I. / = / London, / Printed for C. Bathurst, in Fleetstreet. / — / MDCCLV.

> π^1, a^2, a^4, B–Bb^4 — 2 pp. (t. + bl.), [I]–III (Contents), 1 p. blank, 2 pp. (title: Law is a Bottomless Pit + bl.), [III]–VI (The Preface), 2 pp. (Contents + bl.), [1]–191 + bl. — 4 plates.

The / Works / Of / Jonathan Swift, D.D. / Dean of St. Patrick's, Dublin, / Volume III. Part II. / = / London, / Printed for C. Bathurst, in Fleetstreet. / — / MDCCLV.

π^1, b^3, B–Gg^4, Hh^3, Ii–Kk^4 — 2 pp. (t. + bl.), 6 pp. (Contents), 2 pp. (title: Miscellanies In Verse + bl.), 3–253 + bl. — 4 plates.

The / Works / Of / Jonathan Swift, D.D. / Dean of St. Patrick's, Dublin. / Volume IV. Part I. / = / London, / Printed for C. Davis, J. Hodges, and W. Bowyer. / — / MDCCLV.

π^1, A 1, a^2, B–Rr^4, Ss^3, 2 pp. (t. + bl.), 5 pp. (Contents + bl.), [1]–318. — 4 pp. music.

The / Works / Of / Jonathan Swift, D.D. / Dean of St. Patrick's, Dublin. / Volume IV. Part II. / = / London, / Printed for C. Davis, J. Hodges, and W. Bowyer. / — / MDCCLV.

π^1, a 1, B–Bb^4, π^2, Gg^4, Hh^2, Ii 1 — 2 pp. (t. + bl.), [I]–II (Contents), [1]–192, one page numbered 193–222, 1 p. blank, 2 pp. (title: Some Advice + bl.), [225]–237 + bl.

The / Works / Of / Jonathan Swift, D.D. / Dean of St. Patrick's, Dublin. / Volume V. Part I. / = / London, / Printed for C. Davis, J. Hodges, and W. Bowyer. / — / MDCCLV.

π^1, A 1, B–Kk^4, L 1 — 2 pp. (t. + bl.), 2 pp. (Contents), [1]–258.

The / Works / Of / Jonathan Swift, D.D. / Dean of St. Patrick's, Dublin. / Volume V. Part II. / = / London, / Printed for C. Davis, J. Hodges, and W. Bowyer. / — / MDCCLV.

A^2, B–Gg^4 — 2 pp. (t. + bl.), 2 pp. (Contents + bl.), [1]–232.

The / Works / Of / Jonathan Swift, D.D. / Dean of St. Patrick's, Dublin. / Volume VI. Part I. / = / London, / Printed for C. Davis, C. Hitch and L. Hawes, C. Bathurst, / R. and J. Dodsley, and W. Bowyer. / — / MDCCLV.

π^2, B–Dd^4, Ee 1 — 2 pp. (t. + bl.), 2 pp. (Contents + bl.), [1]–210.

The / Works / Of / Jonathan Swift, D.D. / Dean of St. Patrick's, Dublin. / Volume VI. Part II. / = / London, / Printed for C. Davis, C. Hitch and L. Hawes, J. Hodges, C. Bathurst, / R. and J. Dodsley, and W. Bowyer. / — / MDCCLV.

π^1, a^2, B–Ee^4, Ff 1 — 2 pp. (t. + bl.), [I]–III (Contents), 1 p. blank, [1]–218.

The / Works / Of / Jonathan Swift, D.D. / Dean of St. Patrick's, Dublin. / Volume VII. Part I. / = / London, / Printed for W. Bowyer, R. and J. Dodsley, and L Davis / and C. Reymers. / MDCCLXIV.

A⁴, B–Ff⁴, Gg³ — 2 pp. (h.t.: And Additional Volume + bl.), 2 pp. (t. + bl.), [V]–VI (Contents), 2 pp. (Advertisement + bl.), [1]–230.

The / Works / Of / Jonathan Swift, D.D. / Dean of St. Patrick's, Dublin. / Volume VII. Part II. / = / London, / Printed for W. Bowyer, R. and J. Dodsley, and L. Davis / and C. Reymers. / — / MDCCLXIII.

π¹, a 1, B–Ff⁴ — 2 pp. (t. + bl.), [III]–IV (Contents), [1]–221, 3 pp. blank.

The / Works / Of / Dr. Jonathan Swift, / Dean of St. Patrick's, Dublin. / Volume VIII. Part I. / Collected And Revised / By Deane Swift, Esq; / of Goodrich, in Herefordshire. / *Hæ tibi erunt artes*. Virgil. / = / *London:* / Printed for W. Johnston, in Ludgate-Street. / MDCCLXV.

A⁴, a–b⁴, B–Nn⁴ — 2 pp. (t. + 'Errata' on verso), III–XX (Subscribers Names), XXI–XXII (Contents), XXIII (The Editor To The Reader), 1 p. blank, [1]–278, 2 pp. blank.

The / Works / Of / Dr. Jonathan Swift, / Dean of St. Patrick's, Dublin. / Volume VIII. Part II. / Collected And Revised / By Deane Swift, Esq; / of Goodrich, in Herefordshire. / *Hæ tibi erunt artes*. Virgil. / = / London: / Printed for W. Johnston, in Ludgate-Street. / MDCCLXV.

A⁴, B–Nn⁴ — 2 pp. (t. + 'Errata' on verso), III–VIII (Contents), 1 p. blank, [1]–279 (adv. on verso).

The / Works / Of / Jonathan Swift, D.D. / Dean of St. Patrick's, Dublin. / Volume IX. Part I. / = / London, / Printed for W. Bowyer and J. Nichols, C. Bathurst, W. Strahan, / J. and F. Rivington, L. Davis, W. Owen, T. Longman, / J. Dodsley, T. Cadell, and E. Johnston. / MDCCLXXV.

[a]⁴, b³, B–Ee⁴ — 2 pp. (t. + bl.), III–IV (Contents), V–VIII (Advertisement), 2 pp. (title: The History + bl.), XI–XVI (Advertisement), 5 pp. (Preface + bl.), 9–213, 3 pp. blank.

The / Works / Of / Jonathan Swift, D.D. / Dean of St. Patrick's, Dublin. / Volume IX. Part II. / = / London, / Printed for W. Bowyer and J. Nichols, C. Bathurst, W. Strahan, / J. and F. Rivington, L. Davis, W. Johnston, W. Owen, / T. Longman, J. Dodsley, and T. Cadell. / MDCCLXXV.

π¹, Gg–L 11⁴, Mmm⁶, Nnn–Zzz⁴ — 2 pp. (t. + bl.), 5–236 (187–8 repeated in numbering), 4 pp. (*237, blank, title: A General Index, blank), 237–314.

Letters, / Written By The Late / Jonathan Swift, D.D. / Dean Of St. Patrick's, Dublin; / And / Several Of His Friends. / From The Year 1703 To 1740. / Published From The Originals; / With / Notes Explanatory And Historical, / By John Hawkesworth, L.L.D. / Volume I. / London: / Printed for R. Davis, in Piccadilly; T. Davies, in Russel-Street, Covent-Garden; / L. Davis and C. Reymers, in Holborn; and J. Dodsley, in Pall-mall. / MDCCLXVI.

 X: π^1, A^3, a^4, B–Zz^4 — 2 pp. (t. + bl.), 2 pp. (Dedication to Temple + bl.), [V]–VIII (Preface), IX–XVI (Contents), [1]–360.

Letters, / Written By The Late / Jonathan Swift, D.D. / Dean Of St. Patrick's, Dublin; / And / Several Of His Friends. / From The Year 1703 To 1740. / Published From The Originals; / With / Notes Explanatory And Historical, / By John Hawkesworth, L.L.D. / Volume II. / London: / Printed for R. Davis, in Piccadilly; T. Davies, in Russel-Street, Covent-Garden; / L. Davis and C. Reymers, in Holborn; and J. Dodsley, in Pall-mall. / MDCCLXVI.

 XI: A^4, B–Kk^4 — 2 pp. (t. + bl.), III–VIII (Contents), [1]–254, 2 pp. blank.

Letters, / Written By The Late / Jonathan Swift, D.D. / Dean Of St. Patrick's, Dublin; / And / Several Of His Friends. / From The Year 1710 To 1742. / Published From The Originals; / Collected And Revised / By Deane Swift, Esq. / Of Goodrich, In Herefordshire. / Volume III. / London, / Printed for C. Bathurst, H. Woodfall, W. Strahan, J. Rivington, / L. Davis and C. Reymers, W. Owen, R. Baldwin, T. Davies, / W. Johnston, T. Longman, and J. Hardy. / MDCCLXVIII.

 XII: a^4, B–Pp^4 — 2 pp. (t. + bl.), [III]–V (To Mr. William Johnston), 1 p. blank, VII–VIII (Contents), [1]–295 + bl.

Letters, / Written By The Late / Jonathan Swift, D.D. / Dean Of St. Patrick's, / Dublin; / And / Several Of His Friends. / From The Year 1710 To 1742. / Published From The Originals; / Collected And Revised / By Deane Swift, Esq. / Of Goodrich, In Herefordshire. / Volume IV. / London, / Printed for C. Bathurst, H. Woodfall, W. Strahan, J. Rivington, / L. Davis and C. Reymers, W. Owen, R. Baldwin, T. Davies, / W. Johnston, T. Longman, and J. Hardy. / MDCCLXVIII.

 XIII: A^4, B–Ss^4 — 2 pp. (t. + bl.), III–VIII (Contents), [1]–320. (*Erratum* slip pasted at foot of p. VIII of the Contents.)

A / Supplement / To / Dr. *Swift's* / Works, / Being / The Fourteenth In The Collection: / Containing / Miscellanies In Prose
And Verse, / By The Dean; / Dr. Delany, Dr. Sheridan, Mrs.
Johnson, / And Others, His Intimate Friends. / With / Explanatory Notes On All The Former Volumes, / And An Index, By
The Editor. / — / "Whoever in the three kingdoms has any books
at all, has Swift." / Chesterfield. / "I verily think, there are few
things he ever wrote, that he did not wish to be / "published
at one time or other." Delany. / = / London, / Printed For
J. Nichols: / And sold by H. Payne, in Pall Mall; and N. Conant,
in Fleet-street. / — / MDCCLXXIX.

XIV: a⁴, b², B–5 K⁴ — 2 pp. (t. + bl.), III–VIII (Advertisement), IX–XI
(Contents), 1 p. (adv.), [1]–800.

Reprint of Vol. VII, 1775:
The titles of the two 'Parts' are the same as before, except for the imprint
(twice):

– – – – – / London, / Printed for W. Bowyer and J. Nichols, /
L. Davis, and J. Dodsley. / MDCCLXXV.

4to; I–VI, 1–232.
  2 pp., 1–204.

88. *The Large 8vo Edition, 1754–5:*
The general title-page (in red and black) to the whole set is at the beginning
of the first volume and runs as follows:

The / Works / Of / Jonathan Swift, D.D. / Dean of St. Patrick's,
Dublin, / Accurately revised / In Twelve Volumes, / Adorned
with Copper-Plates; / With / Some Account of the Author's Life, /
And / Notes Historical and Explanatory, / By John Hawkesworth.
/ = / London, / Printed for C. Bathurst, C. Davis, C. Hitch / and
L. Hawkes, J. Hodges, R. and J. Dodsley, / and W. Bowyer.
/ — / MDCCLV.

Large 8vo;
π¹, A⁸, A–D⁸, E⁶, F², A⁸, a⁸, B–Y⁸, Z² — 2 pp. (t. + bl.), [1]–16 (Preface),
[1]–76 (Life of Swift), [77]–80 (Verses), 2 pp. (title: Tale + bl.), [III]–XXIX
(Apology), 1 p. (Treatises written), [1]–7 (Dedication to Sommers), 8–9 (The
Bookseller To The Reader), 1 p. blank, [11]–21 (Epistle Dedicatory), 1 p.
blank, [23]–41 (Preface), 1 p. blank, [43]–340. — 8 plates.
The title-pages of Vols. II–XII (in red and black) are after this pattern:

The / Works / Of / Dr. Jonathan Swift, / Dean of St. Patrick's,
Dublin. / Volume II. / = / London, / Printed for C. Bathurst, in
Fleetstreet. / — / MDCCLIV.

The variations are only in the imprints:
π¹, A⁴, a⁶, A–Ll⁸ — 2 pp. (t. + bl.), [1]–2 (The Publisher To The Reader),
[3]–8 (Letter Gulliver to Sympson), 2 pp. (bastard t. + bl.), [III]–XII
(Contents), [1]–542, 2 pp. blank. — 10 plates.

– – – – Volume III. / = / [imprint as in Vol. II].

π^2, b^8, C–Dd^8, Ee^4 — 2 pp. (t. + bl.), 2 pp. (Contents), 9 pp. (Preface), 1 p. (note), [1]–411 + bl. (G 8 (pp. 85–6) cancelled, but reprinted, provided with a footnote on p. [86], as H 1). π^1, A 1, B–U^8, X^2 — 2 pp. (t. + bl.), 2 pp. (Contents), [1]–307 + bl.

– – – – Volume IV. / = / [imprint as in Vol. II].

π^1, A 1, B–U^8, H^2 — 2 pp. (t. + bl.), 2 pp. (Contents), [1]–307 and bl.

– – – – Volume V. / = / London, / Printed for C. Bathurst, C. Hitch and C. Hawes. / — / MDCCLIV.

π^1, a^4, b^2, a^3, B–Y^8, Z^4 — 2 pp. (t. + bl.), 2 pp. (title: Law is a Bottomless Pit + bl.), [III]–IX (Preface), 1 p. blank, [XI]–XII (Contents), [I]–V (Contents 'John Bull'), 1 p. blank, [1]–344. — 4 plates.

– – – – Volume VI. / = / [imprint as in Vol. II].

π^1, b^2, c 1, B–U^8, X^2 — 2 pp. (t. + bl.), 6 pp. (Contents), [1]–307 + bl. — 4 plates.

– – – – Volume VII. / = / London, / Printed for C. Davis, C. Hitch and L. Hawes, / J. Hodges, C. Bathurst, R. and J. / Dodsley, and W. Bowyer. / — / MDCCLIV.

π^1, A^4, B–Ee^8 — 2 pp. (t. + bl.), 7 pp. (Contents + bl.), [1]–430, 2 pp. blank — 4 pp. music (numbered 432–5!).

– – – – Volume VIII. / = / London, / Printed for C. Davis, J. Hodges and W. Bowyer. / — / MDCCLIV.

π^1, a 1, B–Ee^8, Ff^4 — 2 pp. (t. + bl.), 2 pp. (Contents), [1]–440.

– – – – Volume IX. / = / [imprint as in Vol. VIII].

π^1, A 1, B–Gg^8, Hh^4, Ii 1 — 2 pp. (t. + bl.), 2 pp. (Contents), [1]–473 + bl.

– – – – Volume X. / = / [imprint as in Vol. VIII, but the year is MDCCLV].

A^2, B–Ee^8, Ff^4 — 2 pp. (t. + bl.), [III]–IV (Contents), [1]–438, 2 pp. blank.

– – – – Volume XI. / = / London, / Printed for C. Davis, C. Hitch and L. Hawes, / C. Bathurst, R. and J. Dodsley, / and W. Bowyer. / — / MDCCLV.

π^2, B–Aa^8, Bb^4 — 2 pp. (t. + bl.), 2 pp. (Contents), [1]–374, 2 pp. blank.

– – – – Volume XII. / = / [imprint as in Vol. VII, but the year is MDCCLV.]

π^1, a^2, B–Bb^8 — 2 pp. (t. + bl.), [I]–IV (Contents), [1]–383 + bl.
The title-page in Vol. XIII (in red and black) is:

The / Works / Of / Dr. Jonathan Swift, / Dean of St. Patrick's, Dublin. / Volume XIII. / = / London, / Printed for W. Bowyer, R. and J. Dodsley, / and L. Davis and C. Reymers. / MDCCLXIV.

π^1, π^1 (signed 'a'), π^1 (signed 'a 4'), π^1 (signed 'b'), B–Dd^8, Ee^6 — 2 pp. (t. + bl.), 2 pp. (title: Two Additional Volumes + bl.), [VII]–VIII (Contents), IX–X (Advertisement), [1]–428.
The title-page in Vol. XIV (in red and black) is:

The / Works / Of / Dr. Jonathan Swift, / Dean of St. Patrick's, Dublin. / Volume XIV. / With / An Index to the Whole. / = / [imprint as in Vol. XIII].

π^2, B–Aa^8, Bb^4, Cc^2 — 2 pp. (t. + bl.), [III]–IV (Contents), [1]–379 ('Errata' on verso).
The title-pages in Vols. XV–XVI (in red and black) are after this pattern:

The / Works / Of / Dr. Jonathan Swift, / Dean of St. Patrick's, Dublin. / Volume XV. / Collected And Revised / By Deane Swift, Esq; / of Goodrich, in Herefordshire. / *Hæ tibi erunt artes*. Virgil. / = / London: / Printed for W. Johnston, in Ludgate-Street. / MDCCLXV.

XV: A^8, a^8, B–Hh^8, Ii^4 — 2 pp. (t. + 'Errata' on verso), III–XXIV (Subscribers' Names), XXV–XXVII (Contents), 1 p. blank, XXIX–XXXI (The Editors To The Reader), 1 p. blank, [1]–486, 2 pp. blank.
XVI: A^4, B–Ee^8 — 2 pp. (t. + 'Errata' on verso), III–VIII (Contents), [1]–431 (adv. on verso).
The title-page in Vol. XVII (in red and black) is:

The / Works / Of / Dr. Jonathan Swift, / Dean of St. Patrick's, Dublin. / Volume XVII. / = / London, / Printed for W. Bowyer and J. Nichols, C. Bathurst, / W. Strahan, J. and F. Rivington, L. Davis, / W. Owen, T. Longman, J. Dodsley, / T. Cadell, and E. Johnston. / MDCCLXXV.

XVII: a^3; b^8; B 2–8, C–Mm^8, Nn^3, one folding leaf, Oo–Yy^8 — 2 pp. (title: An Additional Volume + adv. on verso), 2 pp. (t. + bl.), III–IV (Contents); V–X (Advertisement), 2 pp. (bastard t.: The History + bl.), XIII–XX (Advertisement); 3–680. — Leaf Tt 7 (645–6) slit as for cancellation; perhaps B 1 used for it.
The title-pages in the first set of *Letters*, Vols. XVIII–XX (in black only) are after this pattern:

Letters, / Written By The Late / Jonathan Swift, D.D. / Dean Of St. Patrick's, Dublin; / And / Several Of His Friends. / From The Year 1703 To 1740. / Published From The Originals; / With / Notes Explanatory And Historical, / By John Hawkesworth,

L.L.D. / Volume I. / London, / Printed for R. Davis, in Piccadilly; T. Davies, in Russel-Street, / Covent-Garden; L. Davis and C. Reymers, in Holborn; and / J. Dodsley, in Pall-mall. / MDCCLXVI.

> XVIII: A–Kk⁸, Ll⁴ — 2 pp. (t. + bl.), 2 pp. (Dedication to Temple + bl.), [V]–X (Preface), XI–XVI (Contents), [1]–520.
> XIX: A⁴, B–Bb⁸, Cc² — 2 pp. (t. + bl.), III–VIII (Contents), [1]–388.
> XX: A⁴, B–Aa⁸, Bb² — 2 pp. (t. + bl.), III–VII (Contents), 1 p. blank, [1]–371 + bl.
> The title-pages in the second set of *Letters*, Vols. XXI–XXIII (in black only) are after this pattern:

Letters, / Written By The Late / Jonathan Swift, D.D. / Dean Of St. Patrick's, Dublin, / And / Several Of His Friends. / From The Year 1710 To 1742. / Published From The Originals; / Collected And Revised / By Deane Swift, Esq. / Of Goodrich, In Herefordshire. / Volume IV. / London, / Printed for C. Bathurst, H. Woodfall, W. Strahan, / J. Rivington, L. Davis and C. Reymers, W. Owen, / R. Baldwin, T. Davies, W. Johnston, T. Longman, / and J. Hardy. MDCCLXVIII.

> XXI: a⁴, B–Cc⁸ — 2 pp. (t. + bl.), [III]–VI (To Mr. William Johnston), VII–VIII (Contents), [1]–400.
> XXII: π³, B–Dd⁸ — 2 pp. (t. + bl.), V–VIII (Contents), [1]–416.
> XXIII: a⁴, B–Ff⁸ — 2 pp. (t. + bl.), III–VIII (Contents), [1]–448.
> The title-page of the first volume of the *Supplement*, Vol. XXIV (in black only) is:

A / Supplement / To / Dr. *Swift's* / Works: / Being / A Collection Of / Miscellanies / In Prose and Verse, / By The Dean; / Dr. Delany, Dr. Sheridan, / And Others, his Intimate Friends. / With / Explanatory Notes, and an Index, by the Editor. / — / "I verily think, there are few things he ever wrote, that he did not / "wish to be published at one time or other." Delany. / = / *London*, / Printed for W. Bowyer and J. Nichols; and sold by / N. Conant, Successor to Mr. Whiston, in Fleet-street. / — / MDCCLXXVI.

> A–Xx⁸, Yy⁴ — 2 pp. (h.t. + adv. on verso), 2 pp. (t. + bl.), V–[X] (Advertisement), XI–XV (Contents), 1 p. blank, [1]–695 (advs. on verso).
> The title-page of the second volume of the *Supplement*, Vol. XXV (in black only) is:

A / Supplement / To / Dr. *Swift's* / Works: / Being / A Collection Of / Miscellanies / In Prose And Verse, / By The Dean; / Dr. Delany, Dr. Sheridan, Mrs. Johnson, / And Others, His Intimate Friends. / — / Volume The Second. / With Notes, And An Index, By The Editor. / — / "Whoever in the three kingdoms has any books at all, has / "Swift." Chesterfield. / "I verily think, there are few things he ever wrote, that he / "did not wish to be published at one time or other." Delany. / = / London, / Printed For J. Nichols: / Sold By H. Payne, Pall Mall; / And N. Conant, Fleet Street. / MDCCLXXIX.

> a⁴, b 1, B–S⁸, T⁴, U–Hh⁸, Ii⁶, Kk 1 — 2 pp. (h.t. + adv. on verso), 2 pp. (t. + bl.), V–VIII (Advertisement), IX–X (Contents), [1]–483, 3 pp. advs.
> For a possible 26th volume, see No. 121, *post*.
> Copies: Penn.

88A. (1). The first set of *Letters*, Vols. XVIII–XX, was reprinted in the same year, 1766. The title-page in the first volume (in black only) is as follows:

Letters, / Written By The Late / Jonathan Swift, D.D. / Dean Of St. Patrick's, Dublin, / And / Several Of His Friends. / From The Year 1703 To 1740. / Published From The Originals; / With / Notes Explanatory And Historical, / By John Hawkesworth, L.L.D. / In Three Volumes. / A New Edition. / Volume I. / London, / Printed for T. Davies, in Russel-Street, Covent-Garden; / R. Davis, in Piccadilly; L. Davis and C. Reymers, in / Holborn; and J. Dodsley, in Pall-mall. / MDCCLXVI.

> The title-pages (in black only) of the other two volumes are exactly the same, but they omit: "In Three Volumes. / A New Edition.", and are, of course, called: Volume II. and Volume III.
> Large 8vo:
> XVIII: A⁸, b⁸, B–Bb⁸, Cc⁴, Dd² — 2 pp. (t. + bl.), 2 pp. (Dedication to Temple + bl.), V–XI (Preface), XII–XXVIII (A General Table), XXIX–XXXII (Contents), [1]–396.
> XIX: A⁴, B–L⁸, N–O⁴, P–Ee⁸ — 2 pp. (t. + bl.), III–VIII (Contents); [1]–415 + bl.
> XX: A⁴, B–Dd⁸, Ee² — 2 pp. (t. + bl.), III–VIII (Contents), [1]–419 + bl.
> The first set of *Letters*, Vols. XVIII–XX, was again reprinted in the year 1769. The title-page in the first volume (in black only) is as follows:

(2) Letters, / Written By The Late / Jonathan Swift, D.D. / Dean Of St. Patrick's, Dublin, / And / Several Of His Friends. / From The Year 1703 To 1740. / Published From The Originals; / With / Notes Explanatory And Historical / By John Hawkesworth, L.L.D. / In Three Volumes. / A New Edition. / Volume I. / London, / Printed for T. Davies, in Russel-Street, Covent-Garden; / R. Davis, in Piccadilly; L. Davis and C. Reymers, in / Holborn; and J. Dodsley, in Pall-Mall. / MDCCLXIX.

> The title-pages (in black only) of the other two volumes are exactly the same, but they omit: "In Three Volumes.", and are, of course, called: Volume II. and Volume III.
> The same collations as those of 88A (1), but not the same printing. (Only the second volume collates: A⁴, B–Dd⁸.)
> Copies: Penn.

89. *The Large 8vo Edition*, 1768:

The general title-page (in red and black) to the whole set is at the beginning of the first volume and runs as follows:

The / Works / Of / Dr. Jonathan Swift, / Dean of St. Patrick's, Dublin, / Accurately revised / In Twelve Volumes, / Adorned with Copper-Plates; / With / Some Account of the Author's Life, / And / Notes Historical and Explanatory, / By John Hawkesworth, LL.D. /= / London, / Printed for W. Bowyer, C. Bathurst, W. Owen, / W. Strahan, J. Rivington, J. Hinton, L. Davis, / and C. Reymers, R. Baldwin, J. Dodsley, / S. Crowder and Co. and B. Collins. / MDCCLXVIII.

The title-pages of Vols. II–XIV (in red and black) are after this pattern:

The / Works / Of / Dr. Jonathan Swift, / Dean of St. Patrick's, Dublin. / Volume II. / = / London, / Printed for C. Bathurst, in Fleet-Street. / — / MDCCLXVIII.

The variations are only in the imprints:

– – – – Volume   III. / = / [imprint as in Vol. II]
– – – – Volume   IV. / = / [„   „ „   „   „]
– – – – Volume   V. / = / [„   „ „   „   „]
– – – – Volume   VI. / = / [„   „ „   „   „]
– – – – Volume   VII. / = / [imprint as in Vol. I]
– – – – Volume VIII. / = / [„   „ „   „   „]
– – – – Volume   IX. / = / [„   „ „   „   „]
– – – – Volume   X. / = / [„   „ „   „   „]
– – – – Volume   XI. / = / [„   „ „   „   „]
– – – – Volume   XII. / = / [imprint as in Vol. II]
– – – – Volume XIII. / = / London, / Printed for W. Bowyer, L. Davis and / C. Reymers, and J. Dodsley. / MDCCLXVIII.
– – – – Volume XIV. / = / [imprint as in Vol. XIII]

Large 8vo:
    I: A–Ff⁸, Gg² — 2 pp. (t. + bl.), [1]–16 (Preface), [1]–76 (Life of Swift), [77]–78 (Verses), 79–80 (address), 2 pp. (title: 'Tale' + bl.), [III]–XXIX (Apology), 1 p. (Treatises written), [1]–7 (Dedication tc Sommers), 8–9 (The Bookseller To The Reader), 1 p. blank, [11]–21 (Epistle Dedicatory), 1 p. blank, [23]–41 (Preface), 1 p. blank, [43]–340. — 8 plates.
    II: A⁸, b³, B–Cc⁸, Dd⁶ — 2 pp. (t. + bl.), 2 pp. (title: 'Travels' + bl.), [5]–6 (The Publisher To The Reader), [7]–12 (Letter Gulliver to Sympson), [XIII]–XXII (Contents), [1]–410, 2 pp. blank. — 10 plates.
    III: π², b⁸, C–Dd⁸, Ee⁴ — 2 pp. (t. + bl.), 2 pp. (Contents), 9 pp. (Preface), 1 p. (note), [1]–411 + bl. (G 8 (pp. 85–6) cancelled, but reprinted, provided with a footnote on p. [86], as H 1).

IV: A², B–Y⁸ — 2 pp. (t. + bl.), 2 pp. (Contents), [1]–335 + bl.

V: A², a⁸, B–Y⁸, Z⁴ — 2 pp. (t. + bl.), 2 pp. (title: Law is a Bottomless Pit + bl.), [I]–II (Contents of the whole volume), 2 pp. (title: Law is a Bottomless Pit + bl.), [III]–IX (Preface to John Bull), X (blank), [I]–IV (Contents of John Bull), [1]–344 — 4 plates.

VI: A⁴, B–U⁸, X² — 2 pp. (t. + bl.), 6 pp. (Contents), [1]–307 + bl. — 4 plates.

VII: π¹, A⁴, B–Ee⁸ — 2 pp. (t. + bl.), [III]–IX (Contents), 1 p. blank, [1]–431 + bl. — 4 pp. music.

VIII: a², B–Bb⁸, Cc 1 — 2 pp. (t. + bl.), [III]–IV (Contents), [1]–386.

IX: a², B–Gg⁸, Hh⁶ — 2 pp. (t. + bl.), [III]–IV (Contents), [1]–473, 3 pp. blank.

X: A², B–Ee⁸, Ff⁴ — 2 pp. (t. + bl.), [III]–IV (Contents), [1]–438, 2 pp. blank.

XI: π¹, a 1, B–Aa⁸, Bb⁴ — 2 pp. (t. + bl.), [III]–IV (Contents), [1]–375 + bl.

XII: π¹, a², B–Bb⁸ — 2 pp. (t. + bl.), [I]–IV (Contents), [1]–383 + bl.

XIII: π¹, a 3, B–Gg⁸ — 2 pp. (t. + bl.), V–VI (Contents), [1]–464.

XIV: a², b⁴, c², B–Gg⁸ — 2 pp. (t. + bl.), [III]–XV (Contents), 1 p. blank, [1]–461, 3 pp. blank.

The title-page in Vol. XV (in red and black) is:

The / Works / Of / Dr. Jonathan Swift, / Dean of St. Patrick's, Dublin. / Volume XV. / First Collected And Revised / By Deane Swift, Esq; / And Now Reprinted / With Additional Notes. / *Hæ tibi erunt Artes*. Virgil. / = / London, / Printed for C. Bathurst, W. Strahan, J. and F. / Rivington, L. Davis, W. and E. Johnston, / W. Owen, T. Longman, J. Dodsley, and T. Cadell. / MDCCLXXV.

A⁴, B–Hh⁸, Ii⁴ — 2 pp. (h.t. + bl.), 2 pp. (f.t. + bl.), V–VI (The Editors To The Reader), VII–VIII (Contents), 1–487 + bl.

The title-page in Vol. XVI is exactly the same, except for the omission of L. Davis in the imprint, and, of course, Volume XVI.

π², A⁴, B–Dd⁸, Ee⁶ — 2 pp. (h.t. + bl.), 2 pp. (f.t. + bl.), V–XI (Contents), 1 p. blank, 1–428.

For Vols. XVII–XXV, see No. 88, *ante*.

For a possible 26th volume, see No. 121.

Copies: Penn.

90. *The Small 8vo Edition*, 1760 ('large crown paper'):

The general title-page (in red and black) to the whole set is at the beginning of the first volume and runs as follows:

The / Works / Of / Dr. Jonathan Swift, / Dean of St. Patrick's, Dublin. / Accurately revised / In Twelve Volumes. / Adorned with Copper-Plates; / With / Some Account of the Author's Life, / And / Notes Historical and Explanatory. / By John Hawkesworth. / = / London, / Printed for C. Bathurst, C. Hitch and L. Hawes, / R. and J. Dodsley, L. Davis and C. Reymers, / J. Ward, R. Baldwin, S. Crowder / and Co. and W. Bowyer. / MDCCLX.

The title-pages of Vols. II–XII (in red and black) are after this pattern:

The / Works / Of / Dr. Jonathan Swift, / Dean of St. Patrick's, Dublin. / Volume II. / = / London, / Printed for C. Bathurst, in Fleetstreet. / MDCCLX.

The variations are only in the imprints:

– – – – Volume III. / = / [imprint as in Vol. II]

– – – – Volume IV. / = / [imprint as in Vol. II]

– – – – Volume V. / = / London, / Printed for C. Bathurst, C. Hitch and L. Hawes. / MDCCLX.

– – – – Volume VI. / = / [imprint as in Vol. II]

– – – – Volume VII. / = / [imprint as in Vol. I, but the name of C. Bathurst removed from the first place to the third]

– – – – Volume VIII. / = / London, / Printed for L. Davis and C. Reymers, J. Ward, R. / Baldwin, S. Crowder and Co. and W. Bowyer. / MDCCLX.

– – – – Volume IX. / = / London, / Printed for L. Davis and C. Reymers, and W. Bowyer. / MDCCLX.

– – – – Volume X. / = / [imprint as in Vol. VIII]

– – – – Volume XI. / = / [imprint as in Vol. VII]

– – – – Volume XII. / = / [imprint as in Vol. VII]

I: π^1, A–G^8, I–T^8, U^4, X^2 — 2 pp. (t. + bl.), I–XV (Preface), 1 p. (N.B.), [1]–71 (Life of Swift), [72]–73 (Verses), 74–5 (Address), 1 p. blank, 2 pp. (title: 'Tale' + bl.), [III]–XVII (Apology), 1 p. (Treatises written), [1]–4 (Dedication to Sommers), 5 (The Bookseller To The Reader), 1 p. blank, [7]–12 (Epistle Dedicatory), [13]–22 (Preface), [23]–190. — 8 plates.

    For a separate issue of the *Tale*, forming the greater part of this volume, see No. 243.

II: π^1, A–T^8, U^2 — 2 pp. (t. + bl.), 2 pp. (title: 'Travels' + bl.), III–IV (The Publisher To The Reader), V–X (Letter Gulliver to Sympson), XI–XVI (Contents), 1–292. — 6 plates.

    Also separately issued; see No. 311a.

III: π^2, B–S^8, T^4 — 2 pp. (t. + bl.), 2 pp. (Contents), 6 pp. (preface), 1 p. blank, 1 p. (note), [9]–277 (advs. on verso), 2 pp. blank.

IV: A^2, B–P^8 — 2 pp. (t. + bl.), 2 pp. (Contents + bl.), [1]–222, 2 pp. blank.

V: π^1, A–Q^8 — 2 pp. (t. + bl.), 2 pp. (Contents + bl.), 2 pp. (title: 'Law is a Bottomless Pit' + bl.), V–XI (Preface), 1 p. blank, XIII–XVI (Contents), 1–239 (adv. on verso).

VI: π^1, a^4, B–S^8 — 2 pp. (t. + bl.), 4 pp. (Contents), one leaf blank, [1]–271 + bl.

VII: π^1, A^2, B–U^8 — 2 pp. (t. + bl.), [I]–IV (Contents), [1]–304, 4 pp. music (numbered 432–5!).

VIII: π^1, A 1, B–P^8, Q^6 — 2 pp. (t. + bl.), 2 pp. (Contents + bl.), [1]–236.

IX: π^1, A 1, B–S^8, T^4 — 2 pp. (t. + bl.), 2 pp. (Contents), [1]–260 ([39]–48 and 45–54 repeated in numbering).

X: π^1, A 1, B–Q^8, R^4 — 2 pp. (t. + bl.), 2 pp. (Contents), [1]–246, 2 pp. blank.

XI: π^2, B–P^8 — 2 pp. (t. + bl.), 2 pp. (Contents + bl.), [1]–222, 2 pp. blank.

XII: π^1, A^2, B–P^8, Q^4 — 2 pp. (t. + bl.), [I]–III (Contents), 1 p. blank, [1]–232.

The title-page in Vol. XIII (in red and black) is:

The / Works / Of / Dr. Jonathan Swift, / Dean of St. Patrick's, Dublin. / Volume XIII. / = / London, / Printed for W. Bowyer, R. and J. Dodsley, / and L. Davis and C. Reymers. / MDCCLXII.

π^1, A^2, b 1, B–R^8 — 2 pp. (h.t. + bl.), 2 pp. (f.t. + bl.), [III]–IV (Contents), V–VI (Advertisement), [1]–256.

The title-page in Vol. XIV (in red and black) is:

The / Works / Of / Dr. Jonathan Swift, / Dean of St. Patrick's, Dublin. / Volume XIV. / With / An Index to the Whole. / = / [imprint as in Vol. XIII]

A^2, B–S^8, T^2 — 2 pp. (t. + bl.), [III]–IV (Contents), [1]–276.

The title-pages of Vols. XV–XVII (in red and black) are after this pattern:

The / Works / Of / Dr. Jonathan Swift, / Dean of St. Patrick's, Dublin. / Volume XV. / Collected And Revised / By Deane Swift, Esq; / of Goodrich, in Herefordshire. / *Hæ tibi erunt artes.* Virgil. / = / London: / Printed for W. Johnston, in Ludgate-Street. / MDCCLXV.

XV: π^1, A^8, a^6, B–P^8 — 2 pp. (h.t. + bl.), 2 pp. (f.t. + 'Erratum' on verso), III–XXIV (Subscribers' Names), XXV–XXVI (Contents), XXVII–XXVIII (The Editors To The Reader), [1]–224.

XVI: π^4, B–P^8 — 2 pp. (h.t. + bl.), 2 pp. (f.t. + 'Errata' on verso), 3 pp. (Contents), 1 p. blank, [1]–221, 3 pp. blank.

XVII: π^4, B–S^8 — 2 pp. (h.t. + bl.), 2 pp. (f.t. + 'Errata' on verso), 4 pp. (Contents), [1]–271 (adv. on verso).

The title-pages (in black only) of the first set of *Letters*, Vols. XVIII–XX, are after this pattern:

Letters, / Written By / Jonathan Swift, D.D. / Dean of St. Patrick's, Dublin, / And / Several Of His Friends. / From The Year 1703 To 1740. / Published From The Originals; / With / Notes Explanatory And Historical, / By John Hawkesworth, LL.D. / The Fifth Edition. / Volume I. / London, / Printed for T. Davies, in Russel-Street, Covent-Garden; / R. Davis, in Piccadilly; L. Davis and C. Reymers, / in Holborn; and J. Dodsley, in Pall-mall. / MDCCLXVII.

XVIII: A⁸, b⁸, B–U⁸ — 2 pp. (h.t. + bl.), 2 pp. (f.t. + bl.), 2 pp. (Dedication to Temple + bl.), [VII]–XI (Preface), 1 p. blank, XIII–XXXI (Contents), 1 p. (Errata), [1]–302, 2 pp. (adv. + bl.).

XIX: A⁴, B–U⁸, X⁴ — 2 pp. (t. + bl.), III–VIII (Contents), [1]–312.

XX: A⁴, B–T⁸, U⁶, Y⁸, Z⁴ — 2 pp. (t. + bl.), III–VIII (Contents), [1]–324.

The title-pages (in black only) of the second set of *Letters*, Vols. XXI–XXIII, are after this pattern:

Letters, / Written By The Late / Jonathan Swift, D.D. / Dean Of St. Patrick's, Dublin, / And / Several Of His Friends. / From The Year 1710 To 1742. / Published From The Originals; / Collected And Revised / By Deane Swift, Esq. / Of Goodrich, In Herefordshire. / The Third Edition / Volume IV. / London: / Printed for C. Bathurst, H. Woodfall, W. Strahan, / J. and F. Rivington, L. Davis and C. Reymers, W. / Owen, R. Baldwin, T. Davies, W. Johnston, T. Long- / man, and J. Hardy. MDCCLXIX.

XXI: a⁴, B–T⁸ — 2 pp. (t. + bl.), [III]–V (To Mr. William Johnston), 1 p. blank, VII–VIII (Contents), [1]–286, 2 pp. blank.

XXII: A⁴, B–T⁸ — 2 pp. (t. + bl.), III–VII (Contents), 1 p. blank, [1]–286, 2 pp. blank.

XXIII: a⁴, B–U⁸, X⁴ — 2 pp. (t. + bl.), III–VII (Contents), 1 p. blank, [1]–310, 2 pp. blank.

The title-pages (in black only) of the three volumes *Supplement*, Vols. XXIV–XXVI, are after this pattern:

A / Supplement / To / Dr. *Swift's* / Works: / Containing / Miscellanies In Prose And Verse, / By The Dean; / Dr. Delany, Dr. Sheridan, Mrs. Johnson, / And Others, His Intimate Friends. / With Explanatory Notes / On All The Former Volumes, / And An Index, By The Editor. / In Three Volumes. / — / Volume The First. / — / "Whoever in the three kingdoms has any books at all, / "has Swift." Chesterfield. / "I verily think, there are few things he ever wrote, that / "he did not wish to be published at one time or other." / Delany. / = / London, / Printed For J. Nichols: / Sold By H. Payne, Pall-Mall; / And N. Conant, Fleet-Street. / MDCCLXXIX.

XXIV: π², b⁶, C⁸, d–f⁸, g⁴, B–X⁸ — 2 pp. (h.t. + adv. on verso), 2 pp. (f.t. + bl.), V–XII (Advertisement), XIII–XIV (List of Desiderata), XV–XVI (Contents), XVII–LXXVI (Biographical Anecdotes), LXXVII–LXXX (A List of Spurious Productions), LXXI–LXXXVIII ('Dr. Swift's Remarks on'), [1]–320.

XXV: a², B–Gg⁸ — 2 pp. (t. + bl.), III–IV (Contents), [1]–464.

XXVI: a⁴, B–Cc⁸, Dd⁶ — 2 pp. (t. + bl.), III–VI (Contents), [1]–411 (advs. on verso). (I have seen a copy with two more pages of advs. at the end.)

91. *The Small 8vo Edition*, 1766 ('ordinary crown paper'):

The general title-page (in red and black) to the whole set is at the beginning of the first volume and runs as follows:

The / Works / Of / Dr. Jonathan Swift, / Dean of St. Patrick's, Dublin. / Accurately revised, / In Twelve Volumes. / Adorned with Copper-Plates; / With / Some Account of the Author's Life, / And / Notes Historical and Explanatory. / By John Hawkesworth. / = / London: / Printed for C. Bathurst, J. Rivington, W. Strahan, / B. Collins, J. Hinton, J. Dodsley, L. Davis / and C. Reymers, R. Baldwin, / and W. Bowyer. / M.DCC.LXVI.

> I: π^2, A–S^8, T^6 — 2 pp. (advs.), 2 pp. (t. + bl.), [II]–XV (Preface), 1 p.
> (notes), [1]–71 (Life of Swift), [72]–73 (Verses), 74–5 (Address), 1 p.
> blank, 2 pp. (title: 'Tale' + bl.), [III]–XVII (Apology), 1 p. (Treatises
> written), [1]–4 (Dedication to Sommers), 5 (The Bookseller To The
> Reader), 1 p. blank, [8]–12 (Epistle Dedicatory), [13]–22 (Preface),
> [23]–190. — 8 plates.

The title-pages in Vols. II–XVIII (in red and black) are after this pattern:

The / Works / Of / Dr. Jonathan Swift, / Dean of St. Patrick's, Dublin. / Volume II. / = / London, / Printed for C. Bathurst, in Fleet-Street. / MDCCLXVI.

> In Vol. XVIII with the addition of:
> "With an Accurate and Copious Index / to the whole Eighteen Volumes.",
> just over the double rule.
> The variations are only in the imprints:

– – – – Volume   III. / = / [imprint as in Vol. II]

– – – – Volume   IV. / = / [„   „ „   „   „]

– – – – Volume   V. / = / [„   „ „   „   „]

– – – – Volume   VI. / = / [„   „ „   „   „]

– – – – Volume   VII. / = / London, / Printed for T. Osborne, W. Bowyer, C. Bathurst, / W. Strahan, J. Rivington, J. Hinton, L. Davis / and C. Reymers, R. Baldwin, J. Dodsley, / S. Crowder and Co. and B. Collins. / MDCCLXVI.

– – – – Volume   VIII. / = / [imprint as in Vol. VII]

– – – – Volume   IX. / = / [„   „ „   „   „]

– – – – Volume   X. / = / [„   „ „   „   „]

– – – – Volume   XI. / = / [„   „ „   „   „]

– – – – Volume   XII. / = / [„   „ „   „   „]

– – – – Volume   XIII. / = / London, / Printed for W. Bowyer, L. Davis and / C. Reymers, and J. Dodsley. / MDCCLXVI.

– – – – Volume   XIV. / = / [imprint as in Vol. XIII]

– – – – Volume XV. / = / London, / Printed for W. Johnston, in *Ludgate-Street.* / MDCCLXVI.

– – – – Volume XVI. / = / [imprint as in Vol. XV]

– – – – Volume XVII. / = / [„ „ „ „ „]

– – – – Volume XVIII. / = / [„ „ „ „ „]

II: π^2, A–T^8, U^2 — 2 pp. (advs.), 2 pp. (t. + bl.), 2 pp. (title: 'Travels' + bl.), III–IV (The Publisher To The Reader), V–X (Letter Gulliver to Sympson), XI–XVI (Contents), 1–292. — 6 plates.

III: π^2, B–S^8, T^6 — 2 pp. (t. + bl.), 2 pp. (Contents), 7 pp. (Preface), 1 p. (note), [9]–284.

IV: π^2, B–P^8, Q^6 — 2 pp. (t. + bl.), 2 pp. (Contents), [1]–236.

V: A–Q^8 — 2 pp. (t. + bl.), 2 pp. (Contents + bl.), 2 pp. (title: Law is a Bottomless Pit + bl.), VII–XII (Preface), XIII–XVI (Contents), 1–240.

VI: a^4, B–R^8 — 2 pp. (t. + bl.), 5 pp. (Contents), 1 p. blank, [1]–256.

VII: A^3, B–Z^8 — 2 pp. (t. + bl.), [III]–VI (Contents), [1]–352. — 4 pp. music.

VIII: A^2, B–U^8 — 2 pp. (t. + bl.), [I]–II (Contents), [1]–301, 3 pp. blank.

IX: π^1, A 1, B–Z^8 — 2 pp. (t. + bl.), [I]–II (Contents), [1]–350, 2 pp. blank.

X: A^2, B–U^8, X^6 — 2 pp. (t. + bl.), [III]–IV (Contents), [1]–313, 3 pp. blank.

XI: a^2, B–T^8 — 2 pp. (t. + bl.), 2 pp. (Contents + bl.), [1]–285, 3 pp. blank.

XII: A^3, B–T^8 — 2 pp. (t. + bl.), [III]–VI (Contents), [1]–287 + bl.

XIII: π^2, A^2, B 2–8, C–T^8 — 2 pp. (h.t. + bl.), 2 pp. (f.t. + bl.), 2 pp. (Contents + bl.), [3]–286, 2 pp. blank.

XIV: π^1, A^4, B–U^8 — 2 pp. (t. + bl.), [III]–IX (Contents), 1 p. blank, [1]–304.

XV: π^1, b 1, B–T^8, U 1 — 2 pp. (t. + bl.), 2 pp. (Contents + bl.), [1]–290.

XVI: π^1, A^2, B–T^8, U^4 — 2 pp. (t. + bl.), [III]–V (Contents), 1 p. blank, [1]–296.

XVII: π^1, A^4, B–S^8, T 1 — 2 pp. (t. + bl.), [III]–X (Contents), [1]–274.

XVIII: A^3, B–S^8, T^4, U^2 — 2 pp. (t. + bl.), [III]–V (Contents), 1 p. blank, [1]–283 (adv. on verso).

The title-pages (in black only) of the first set of *Letters*, Vols. XIX–XXI are after this pattern:

Letters; / Written By / Jonathan Swift, D.D. / Dean Of St. Patrick's, Dublin, / And / Several Of His Friends. / From The Year 1703 To 1740. / Published From The Originals; / With / Notes Explanatory And Historical. / By John Hawkesworth, LL.D. / The Seventh Edition. / Volume I. / London: / Printed for T. Davies, in Russel-Street, Covent-Garden; / R. Davis, in Piccadilly; / L. Davis and C. Reymers, / in Holborn; / and J. Dodsley, in Pall-mall. / MDCCLXVIII.

XIX: A^8, a^8, B–U^8 — 2 pp. (h.t. + bl.), 2 pp. (f.t. + bl.), 2 pp. (Dedication to Temple + bl.), VII–XI (Preface), 1 p. blank, XIII–XVI (Contents), [XVII]–XXXI (A General Table Of The Letters), 1 p. blank, [1]–302, 2 pp. blank.

XX: A⁴, B–U⁸, X⁴ — 2 pp. (t. + bl.), III–VIII (Contents), [1]–312.
XXI: A⁴, B–X⁸ — 2 pp. (t. + bl.), III–VIII (Contents), [1]–320.
For Vols. XXII–XXVII, see Vols. XXI–XXVI, No. 90, *ante*.

92. *The 18mo Edition:*
The general title-page (in black only) to the whole set is at the beginning of the first volume and runs as follows:

The / Works / Of / Dr. Jonathan Swift, / Dean of St. *Patrick*'s, *Dublin*. / Accurately revised / In Twelve Volumes. / Adorned with Copper-Plates; / With / Some Account of the Author's Life, / And / Notes Historical and Explanatory. / By John Hawkesworth, LL.D. / = / *London:* / Printed for C. Bathurst, T. Osborne, / W. Bowyer, J. Hinton, W. Strahan, / B. Collins, J. Rivington, R. Bald- / win, L. Davis and C. Reymers, and / J. Dodsley. 1765.

18mo (in twelves and sixes alternately).

The second title in Vol. I and the titles in Vols. II–VI (all in black only) have all:

The / Works / Of / Dr. Jonathan Swift, / Dean of St. *Patrick*'s, *Dublin*. / —

followed in the successive volumes by:

Vol. I. / — / Containing / A / Tale / Of A / Tub. / Written for the / Universal Improvement of Mankind. / = / *London:* / Printed for C. Bathurst, in *Fleet-street*. / — / MDCCLXV.

π¹, A⁶–D⁶, [B]¹²–R⁶ — 2 pp. (series-title + bl.), 2 pp. (volume-title + bl.), [III]–XVII (Preface), 1 p. (note), [1]–48 (Life of Swift), [49]–51 (Verses), [52]–53 (Address), 1 p. blank, 2 pp. (title: 'Tale' + bl.), III–XXIII (Apology), 1 p. (Treatises written), [I]–VI (Dedication to Sommers), VII–VIII (The Bookseller to the Reader), 1–9 (Epistle Dedicatory), 10–24 (Preface), 25–256. — 8 plates.

Vol. II. / — / Containing / Capt. Lemuel Gulliver's / Travels into several remote / Nations of the World. / Parts I. and II. / = / *London:* / Printed for C. Bathurst, in *Fleet-street*. / — / MDCCLXV.

Vol. II. *Part II.* / — / Containing / Capt. Lemuel Gulliver's / Travels into several remote / Nations of the World. / Parts III. and IV. / = / *London:* / Printed for C. Bathurst, in *Fleet-street*. / — / MDCCLXV.

π¹, A¹²–Aa⁶ (two leaves between M 10 and 11) — 2 pp. (t. + bl.), [V]–VII (The Publisher To The Reader), 1 p. blank, IX–XVI (Letter Gulliver to Sympson), XVII–XXV (Contents), 1 p. blank, 2 pp. (h.t. + bl.), 1–200, 2 pp. (title: 'Vol. II. Part II.' + bl.), 2 pp. (h.t. + bl.), 201–408. — frontisp. (L. Gulliver) and 6 plates. [This volume is also found bound in two.]

Vol. III. / — / Consisting Of / Miscellanies / In Prose. / = / *London:* / Printed for C. Bathurst in *Fleet-street.* / — / MDCCLXV.

π^3, B^{12}–S^{12}, T^4 — 2 pp. (h.t. + bl.), 2 pp. (f.t. + bl.), 2 pp. (Contents), 7 pp. (Preface), 1 p. (note), [9]–316, 2 pp. advs., 2 pp. blank.

Vol. IV. / — / Consisting Of / Miscellanies / In Prose. / By Dr. Swift, Dr. Arbuthnot, / and Mr. Pope. / = / *London:* / Printed for C. Bathurst, in *Fleet-street*; / and J. Hinton, in *Newgate-street.* / — / MDCCLXV.

Frontisp., π^2, B^{12}–P^6, Q^4 — frontisp. (Swift), 2 pp. (t. + bl.), 2 pp. (Contents), [1]–257, 3 pp. blank.

Vol. V / — / Consisting Of / Miscellanies / In Prose. / By Dr. Swift, Dr. Arbuthnot, / Mr. Pope, and Mr. Gay. / = / *London:* / Printed for C. Bathurst, in *Fleet-street*; / and J. Hinton, in *Newgate-street.* / — / MDCCLXV.

Frontisp., A^8, B^{12}–P^6, Q^{10} — frontisp. (Arbuthnot), 2 pp. (t. + bl.), 2 pp. (Contents + bl.), 2 pp. (title: 'Law is a Bottomless Pit' + bl.), [VII]–XII (Preface), [XIII]–XVI (Contents), [1]–272.

Vol. VI. / — / Consisting Of / Miscellanies / In Verse. / By Dr. Swift, Dr. Arbuthnot, / Mr. Pope, and Mr. Gay. / = / *London:* / Printed for C. Bathurst, in *Fleet-street.* / — / MDCCLXV.

Frontisp., A^4, B^{12}–P^6, Q^4 — frontisp. (Gay), 2 pp. (t. + bl.), 5 pp. (Contents), 1 p. blank, [1]–260.

The title-pages (all in black only) of Vols. VII–XVII are after this pattern:

The / Works / Of / Dr. Jonathan Swift, / Dean of St. Patrick's, Dublin. / Volume VII. / = / London, / Printed for T. Osborne, W. Bowyer, / C. Bathurst, W. Strahan, J. Ri- / vington, J. Hinton, L. Davis and C. / Reymers, R. Baldwin, J. Dodsley, / S. Crowder and Co. and B. Collins. / MDCCLXV.

The variations are:

– – – – Volume XIII. / = / London, / Printed for W. Bowyer, L. Davis and / C. Reymers, and J. Dodsley. / MDCCLXV.

– – – – Volume XIV. / = / [imprint as in Vol. XIII)

– – – – Volume XV. / Collected and Revised by Deane Swift, Esq. / of Goodrich, in Herefordshire. / *Hæ tibi erunt Artes.* Virgil. / = / London, / Printed for W. Johnston, in *Ludgate-street.* / MDCCLXV.

– – – – Volume XVI. / [the rest as in Vol. XV].

– – – – Volume XVII. / Collected and Revised by Deane Swift,

Esq; / of Goodrich, in Herefordshire. / With an Accurate and Copious Index / to the whole Seventeen Volumes. / *Hæ tibi erunt Artes*. Virgil. / = / [imprint as in Vol. XV].

> VII: frontisp., π^1, A^3, B^{12}–U^{12}, X 1, Y^4 — frontisp. (Pope), 2 pp. (t. + bl.), [I]–VI (Contents), [1]–350, 8 pp. music.
> VIII: A^2, B^{12}–R^6, S^{10} — 2 pp. (t. + bl.), [I]–II (Contents), [1]–308.
> IX: π^1, A 1, B^{12}–X^6, Y 1 — 2 pp. (t. + bl.), [I]–II (Contents), [1]–361 + bl.
> X: A^2, B^{12}–T^6 — 2 pp. (t. + bl.), [I]–II (Contents), [1]–324.
> XI: π^1, a 1, B^{12}–R^6 — 2 pp. (t. + bl.), 2 pp. (Contents + bl.), [1]–286, 2 pp. blank.
> XII: A^3, B^{12}–R^6, S^4 — 2 pp. (t. + bl.), [I]–IV (misprinted VI) (Contents), [1]–296.
> XIII: π^1, A^2, B^{12}–R^6, S^2 — 2 pp. (h.t. + bl.), 2 pp. (t. + bl.), 2 pp. (Contents + bl.), 1–2 (Advertisement), [3]–291 + bl.
> XIV: π^1, A^4, B^{12}–R^6, S^8 — 2 pp. (t. + bl.), [I]–VII (Contents), 1 p. blank, [1]–304.
> XV: A^2, A 2, B^{12}–Q^{12}, R^4 — 2 pp. (t. + bl.), [III]–IV (The Editors To The Reader), [I]–II (Contents), [1]–281, 3 pp. blank.
> XVI: π^1, A^4, B^{12}–S^{12}, T^2 — 2 pp. (t. + bl.), [I]–VII (Contents), 1 p. blank, [1]–315 + bl.
> XVII: A^3, B^{12}–S^{12} — 2 pp. (t. + bl.), [III]–VI (Contents), [1]–309, 3 pp. blank.

The title-page in Vol. XVIII (in black only) is as follows:

The / Works / Of / Dr. Jonathan Swift, / Dean of St. Patrick's, Dublin. / Volume XVIII. / — / Let Ireland tell, how Wit upheld her cause, / Her trade supported, and supplied her laws; / And leave on Swift this grateful verse engrav'd, / "The rights a Court attack'd, a Poet sav'd!" / Behold the hand that wrought a Nation's cure, / Stretch'd to relieve the Idiot and the Poor; / Proud Vice to brand, or injur'd Worth adorn, / And stretch the ray to ages yet unborn. / Pope. / = / London, / Printed for W. Bowyer and J. Nichols, / C. Bathurst, W. Strahan, J. and F. / Rivington, L. Davis, W. Johnston, / W. Owen, T. Longman, J. Dodsley, / and T. Cadell. MDCCLXXV.

> a^2, B^{12}–Aa^{12}, Bb^4 — 2 pp. (t. + bl.), [III]–IV (Contents), [1]–428.
> The title-pages (in black only) in the first set of *Letters*, Vols. XIX–XXI, are after this pattern:

Letters, / Written By / Jonathan Swift, D.D. / Dean Of St. Patrick's, Dublin. / And / Several Of His Friends. / From The Year 1703 To 1740. / Published From The Originals; / With / Notes Explanatory And Historical, / By John Hawkesworth, LL.D. / The Sixth Edition. / Volume I. / London: / Printed for T. Davies, in Russel-street, Covent garden; / R. Davis, in Piccadilly; L. Davis and C. Reymers, / in Holborn; and J. Dodsley, in Pall-mall. / MDCCLXVII.

XIX: π^6, a^6, v^6, B^6–Ee^6, Ff^2 — 2 pp. (bl. + advs.), 2 pp. (h.t. Vol. XVIII + bl. — afterwards cancelled), 2 pp. (f.t. + bl.), 2 pp. (Dedication to Temple + bl.), VII–XI (Preface), 1 p. blank, XIII–XVI (Contents), [XVII]–XXXIII (A General Table), 1 p. blank, [1]–327 + bl.

XX: A^6, B^6–Ff^6, Gg^4 — 2 pp. (h.t. Vol. XIX + bl. — afterwards cancelled), 2 pp. (f.t. + bl.), V–XI (Contents), 1 p. blank, [1]–344.

XXI: A^6, B^6–Hh^6 — 2 pp. (h.t. Vol. XX + bl. — afterwards cancelled), 2 pp. (f.t. + bl.), V–XI (Contents), 1 p. blank, [1]–360.

The title-pages (in black only) in the second set of *Letters*, Vols. XXII–XXIV, are after this pattern:

Letters, / Written By / Jonathan Swift, D.D. / Dean Of St. Patrick's Dublin, / And / Several Of His Friends, / From The Year 1696 To 1742. / Published From The Originals; / Collected And Revised / By Deane Swift, Esq. / Of Goodrich In Herefordshire. / A New Edition, Corrected. / Volume IV. / London, / Printed for C. Bathurst, W. Strahan, / J. and F. Rivington, L. Davis, / W. and E. Johnston, W. Owen, R. / Baldwin, T. Longman, J. Dodsley, / and T. Cadell. MDCCLXXV.

XXII: a^2, B^{12}–Y^{12}, Z^4 — 2 pp. (t. + bl.), III–IV (Contents), 1–391 + bl.

XXIII: a^4, B^{12}–Y^{12}, Z^2 — 2 pp. (t. + bl.), III–VIII (Contents), 1–388.

XXIV: a^{12}, b^6, b^3, B^{12}–Y^6 (E has 5 leaves only) — 2 pp. (t. + bl.), III–XXXVI (General Contents Of The Twenty-four Volumes), XXXVII–XLI (Contents), 1 p. blank, 1–370.

The title-pages (in black only) in the three volumes *Supplement*, Vols. XXV–XXVII, are after this pattern:

A / Supplement / To / Dr. *Swift's* / Works: / Containing / Miscellanies In Prose And Verse, / By The Dean; / Dr. Delany, Dr. Sheridan, Mrs. Johnson, / And Others, His Intimate Friends. / With Explanatory Notes / On All The Former Volumes, / By The Editor. / In Three Volumes. / — / Volume The First. / — / London, / Printed For J. Nichols: / Sold By H. Payne, Pall-Mall; / And N. Conant, Fleet-Street. / MDCCLXXIX.

XXV: a^9, c^{12}, d^6, e^{12}, B^{12}–X^6 — 2 pp. (t. + bl.), I–XI (Advertisement), 2 pp. (List of Desiderata), 1 p. (advs.), [XI]–XII (Contents), XIII–LXXII (Biographical Anecdotes), [1]–359 + bl.

XXVI: d^2, B^{12}–Dd^6 — 2 pp. (t. + bl.), III–IV (Contents), [1]–468.

XXVII: a^4, B^{12}–Bb^{12} — 2 pp. (t. + bl.), III–VII (Contents), 1 p. (advs.), [1]–428, 4 pp. advs.

Copies: Penn.

***

Scotch and Irish Editions

(*See diagram after No. 100, post*)

93. *Scotch Edition*, 1752:

The title-page of the first collected Scotch edition of Swift's Works says "The Seventh Edition", and "Reprinted from the Dublin Copy", which

The Hawkesworth Editions

			Small 8vo		
Stage	4to	Large 8vo	Large Crown Paper	Ordinary Crown Paper	18mo
First Stage	1755 Works I–VI	1754–5 Works I–XII	1760 Works I–XII		1765 Works I–XVII
Second Stage	1763–4 Works VII	1764 Works XIII–XIV	1762 Works XIII–XIV		
Third Stage	1765 Works VIII	1765 Works XV–XVI	1765 Works XV–XVII		
Fourth Stage	1766 Letters (X–XI) Reprinted (when?)	1766 Letters (XVIII–XX) / 1766 (A New Edition) / 1769 (A New Edition)	1767 Letters (5th ed.) (XVIII–XX)	1766 Works I–XVIII / 1766 Letters 3 vols. (?) / 1768 Letters (7th ed.) (XIX–XXI)	1767 Letters (6th ed.) (XIX–XXI)
Fifth Stage	1768 Letters (XII–XIII)	1768 Works I–XIV ⟶ / 1768 Letters (XXI–XXIII)	1769 Letters (3rd ed.) (XXI–XXIII) / (XXII–XXIV)	(XXII–XXIV)	1775 Letters (A New Ed. corr.) (XXII–XXIV)
Sixth Stage	1775 Works IX / 1775 Works VII (reprint)	1775 Works XV–XVI ⟶ / 1775 Works XVII		1775 Works XVIII	1775 Works XVIII
Seventh Stage	1779 Supplement (XIV)	1776 Supplement (XXIV) / 1779 Supplement (XXV)	1779 Supplement (XXIV–XXVI)	1779 Supplement (XXV–XXVII)	1779 Supplement (XXV–XXVII)
	(14 vols.)	(25 vols.) For a possible 26th vol, see No. 121, *post*.	(26 vols.)	(27 vols.)	(27 vols.)

clearly refers to Faulkner's "The Sixth Edition, revised and corrected", 8 vols., 12mo, 1747, &c. (see No. 51, *ante*). Indeed, comparison shows that these two editions resemble each other in the smallest details.

Series-title:

The / Works / Of / Jonathan Swift, / D.D.D.S.P.D. / In Eight Volumes. / Containing / [*First column:*] I. His Miscellanies / in Prose. / II. His Poetical Wri- / tings. / III. The Travels of / Captain Lemuel Gul- / liver. / IV. Papers relating to / Ireland, and the / Drapier's Letters. / V. The Conduct of / [*Second column:*] the Allies, and the / Examiners. / VI. The Publick Spi- / rit of the Whigs, *&c.* / with Polite Conver- / sation. / VII. Letters to and / from Dr. Swift. / VIII. Directions to / Servants, Sermons, / Poems, *&c.* / The Seventh Edition. / Reprinted from the Dublin Copy. / Edinburgh: / Printed by Hamilton, Balfour, and Neill. / M,DCC,LII.

12mo (in sixes):

The / Works / Of / Jonathan Swift, / D.D.D.S.P.D. / Volume I. / Containing / Miscellanies / In / Prose.

(*first state*, 8 vols.): frontisp., π^6, B–Bb^6 — frontisp. (Swift), 2 pp. (series-title 8 vols. + bl.), 2 pp. (volume-title + bl.), [V]–X (Preface), [XI]–XII (Contents), [1]–287 + bl.
(*second state*, 9 vols.): frontisp., π^7, a–b^6, B–Bb^6 — frontisp. (Swift), 2 pp. (series-title 9 vols. + bl.), 2 pp. (List of the 9 vols.), 2 pp. (volume-title + bl.), [V]–X (Preface), [XI]–XII (Contents), [V]–XXVIII (Life of Swift), [1]–287 + bl.

The / Works / Of / D. *Jonathan Swift.* / Volume II. / Containing / His Poetical Writings. / *Dublin* printed; and *Edinburgh* reprinted, / For G. Hamilton & J. Balfour, & L. Hunter / at *Edinburgh;* and A. Stalker, at *Glasgow;* and / sold by them and other Booksellers. / M,DCC,LII.

*$*^4$, A–Ii^6 — 2 pp. (t. + bl.), 2 pp. (Advertisement), 4 pp. (Contents), [1]–384.

The / Works / Of / D. *Jonathan Swift.* / Vol. III. / Containing / Travels / Into Several / Remote Nations of the World. / In Four Parts, *viz.* / [*First column:*] I. A Voyage to Lil- / liput. / II. A Voyage to Brob- / dingnag. / III. A Voyage to La- / puta, Balni-bar- / [*Second column:*] bi, Luggnagg, / Glubbdubdrib, / and Japan. / IV. A Voyage to the / Country of the / Houyhnhnms. / By Lemuel Gulliver, first a Surgeon, and / then a Captain, of several Ships. / — — *Retroque* / *Vulgus abhorret ab his.* / *Dublin* printed; and *Edinburgh* reprinted, / For G. Hamilton & J. Balfour, and L.

Hunter, at / *Edinburgh;* and A. Stalker, at *Glasgow;* and sold by / them and other Booksellers.

π^2, *_{*}*^{4}, A^4, B–Cc^6, Dd 1 — 2 pp. (t. + bl.), 2 pp. (Advertisement + bl.), [I]–V (Letter Gulliver to Sympson), 1 p. blank, [VII]–VIII (The Publisher to the Reader), 8 pp. (Contents), [1]–302.

The / Works / Of / D. *Jonathan Swift,* / Vol. IV. / Containing / A Collection of Tracts, / Relating To / *Ireland*; / Among which are, / The Drapier's Letters / To The / People of Ireland, / Against / Receiving Wood's Half-pence; / Also, / Two Original Drapier's Letters. / [imprint as in Vol. III, but with the year: M,DCC,LII. added at foot]

π^4, B–Ff^6, Gg^2 — 2 pp. (t. + bl.), 2 pp. (Advertisement), 4 pp. (Contents), 2 pp. (title: 'A Letter' + bl.), [I]–II (The Publisher's Advertisement To The Reader), 1–316 (21–4 omitted in numbering).

The / Works / Of / D. *Jonathan Swift.* / Vol. V. / Containing / I. The Conduct of the Allies. / II. The Examiner, from N° 13. / *Dublin* printed; and *Glasgow* reprinted, / For A. Stalker, at *Glasgow;* and G. Hamilton and / J. Balfour, and L. Hunter, at *Edinburgh;* and sold / by them and other Booksellers.

π^1, A–Cc^6, Dd^5 — 2 pp. (t. + bl.), 2 pp. (The Publisher's Preface), 2 pp. (title: Conduct + bl.), 2 pp. (Preface), [7]–306, 2 pp. (Contents + bl.), 10 pp. Index, 4 pp. advs. [Dd^6 probably used as full title.]

The / Works / Of / D. *Jonathan Swift.* / Vol. VI. / Containing / The Public Spirit of the Whigs; / and other Pieces of Political Writ- / ings; with Polite Conversa- / tion, *etc.* / [imprint as in Vol. V]

π^2, A–Ee^6, Ff^4 — 2 pp. (t. + bl.), 2 pp. (Contents + bl.), 2 pp. (The Publisher's Preface), [3]–342, 2 pp. blank.

The / Works / Of / D. *Jonathan Swift.* / Vol. VII. / Containing / I. Letters to and from Dr. J. / Swift, D.S.P.D. from the Year / 1714, to 1738. / II. Some Free Thoughts upon the / present State of Affairs. / [imprint as in Vol. V]

a^6, A–X^6 — 2 pp. (t. + bl.), 8 pp. (Contents), one leaf blank, [1]–224, 2 pp. (title: 'Some Free Thoughts' + bl.), 2 pp. (Advertisement To The Reader + bl.), 1–23 + bl.

The / Works / Of / D. *Jonathan Swift.* / Vol. VIII. / Containing / Directions to Servants; / And / Other Pieces in Prose and / Verse, published in his life- / time, with several poems and let- / ters never before printed. / [imprint as in Vol. V, but the word "sold" misprinted "also"] a⁴, A–Hh⁶ — 2 pp. (t. + bl.), 2 pp. (Advertisement + bl.), 4 pp. (Contents), [1]–386, 2 pp. advs.

In the same year, presumably even during the process of printing, it was resolved to add a ninth volume:

The / Works / Of / D. *Jonathan Swift*. / Volume IX. / Containing / [*First column:*] I. A Tale of a Tub: / Written for the uni- / versal Improvement of / Mankind. / II. A Battle between / the antient and mo- / [*Second column:*] dern Books in / St. James's Library. / III. A Discourse con- / cerning the Mecha- / nical Operation / of the Spirit. / *Diu multumque desideratum.* / With the Author's Apology; / And explanatory Notes, by *W. W-tt-n*, B. D. / and Others. / Basima eacabasa eanaa irraurista, diarba da caeotaba / fobor camelanthi *Iren. lib.* I. *c.* 18. / — *Juvatque novos decerpere flores,* / *Insignemque meo capiti petere inde coronam,* / *Unde prius nulli velârunt tempora Musae.* Lucret. / *Edinburgh:* / Printed for G. Hamilton & J. Balfour, and L. Hun- / ter, at *Edinburgh;* and A. Stalker, at *Glasgow;* and / sold by them and other Booksellers. / M,DCC,LII.

a–b⁶, A–R⁶ — 2 pp. (t. + bl.), [III]–XVIII (Apology), [XIX]–XXIII (Dedication to Sommers), [XXIV] (The Bookseller to the Reader), [1]–7 + bl. (The Epistle Dedicatory), [9]–19 + bl. (The Preface), [21]–136 (Tale); 2 pp. (title of the 'Battle' + bl.), [139]–140 (The Bookseller to the Reader), [141]–142 (The Preface Of The Author), [143]–172 (Battle); 2 pp. (title of the 'Discourse' + bl.), 2 pp. (The Bookseller's Advertisement + bl.), [177]–199 + bl. (Discourse), 2 pp. (Errata + bl.), 2 pp. (Treatises wrote + bl.).

This volume was also issued separately with a different title; see No. 240.

The addition of this ninth volume caused some alteration in the prefatory matter of Vol. I, namely: The series-title mentioning 8 vols. was cut away (the volume-title was preserved), and a double leaf was inserted, bearing new series-title mentioning 9 vols., and a list of short contents of the 9 vols. Moreover, a *Life* of Swift (pp. V–XXVIII) was inserted before the text. The new series-title is:

The / Works / Of / D. *Jonathan Swift*. / In Nine Volumes. / The Seventh Edition. / To which is prefixed, / The Doctor's Life, with Remarks on his Wri- / tings, from the Earl of *Orrery* and others, not / to be found in any former Edition of his Works. / *Dublin* printed; and *Edinburgh* reprinted, / For G. Hamilton & J. Balfour, and L. Hunter, / at *Edinburgh;* and A. Stalker, at *Glasgow;* and / sold by them and other Booksellers. / M,DCC,LII.

In 1753 a tenth volume was added, which in the 'Advertisement', p. [3], boasts this advantage over "any of the *London* editions of Dr. *Swift*'s works", that in this volume the works of his friends are kept apart:

A / Supplement / To / Dr. *Swift*'s / Works. / Containing, / I. Miscellanies, by Dr. Arbuthnot. / II. Several Pieces, by Dr. Swift and Mr. Pope. / III. Poems on several Occasions. / *Edinburgh:* / Printed for G. Hamilton and J. Balfour. / M,DCC,LIII.

A–Ff⁶ — 2 pp. (t. + bl.), 2 pp. (Advertisement + bl.), [5]–6 (Contents), 2 pp. (title: 'Law is a Bottomless Pit' + bl.), [9]–12 (Preface), [13]–347 + bl. [This volume was also issued with a different title, with the names of Midwinter and Tonson in the imprint. Query: Did the other nine volumes also appear with new titles Midwinter and Tonson?]

Copies: The Bodl. (2699 f 182. 1–8) has a 9 vol. set, with Vol. I in the second state, but Vol. IX is missing. Penn has a 10 vol. set, with Vol. I in the second state, but the series-title 8 vols. has been preserved(!). The Stadtbibl., Leipsic, has a 9 vol. set, the same as Penn's, but Vol. X is wanting.

94. *Another edition,* 1757:

The / Works / Of / Dr. Jonathan Swift, / Dean of St Patrick's, Dublin. / Accurately corrected by the best editions. / With / The author's Life and Character, / Notes historical, critical, and explanatory; / Tables of Contents, and Indexes. / More complete than any preceding edition. / In Eight Volumes. / *Edinburgh:* / Printed for G. Hamilton, J. Balfour, & L. Hunter. / — / M,DCC,LVII.

The volume-titles are after this pattern:

The / Works / Of / Dr. Jonathan Swift, / Dean of St Patrick's, Dublin. / Vol. I. / *Edinburgh:* / Printed for G. Hamilton, J. Balfour, & L. Hunter. / — / M,DCC,LVII.

12mo (in sixes):

I: a–k⁶, π¹, A–Dd⁶, Ee² — 2 pp. (series-title + bl.), 2 pp. (volume-title + bl.), [V]–CXV (Life of Swift, Characters and Accounts from Orrery, Deane Swift, and Mrs. Pilkington), 1 p. (Contents), CXVII–CXIX (Criticism), 1 p. blank, CXXI–CXXII (Account of a Monument), 2 pp. (title: 'Tale' + bl.), [III]–[XVI] (Apology), 2 pp. ('Treatises written' + bl.), [XIX]–XXII (Dedication to Sommers), 2 pp. (The Bookseller to the Reader + bl.), [1]–7 (Epistle Dedicatory), 1 p. blank, [9]–18 (Preface), [19]–304.

II: a⁴, A–Ii⁶, Kk⁴ — 2 pp. (t. + bl.), [III]–VIII (Contents), [3]–392, 2 pp. blank.

III: π², A–Hh⁶ — 2 pp. (t. + bl.), [III]–IV (Contents), [1]–372.

IV: a⁴, A–Ii⁶ — 2 pp. (t. + bl.), [III]–VIII (Contents), [1]–388.

V: π², A–Kk⁶, Ll² — 2 pp. (t. + bl.), 2 pp. (Contents), 3–402.

VI: π¹, a³, A–Ii⁶ — 2 pp. (t. + bl.), [III]–VIII (Contents), [1]–384.

VII: π², A–Kk⁶, Ll⁴ — 2 pp. (t. + bl.), [III]–IV (Contents), [1]–404.

VIII: π¹, a³, A–Hh⁶ — 2 pp. (t. + bl.), [III]–VIII (Contents), 3–338, 34 pp. Indexes (unnumbered), 2 pp. blank.

Judging from the names in the imprint, this is the successor of the Edinburgh–Glasgow edition of 1752 in 10 vols. (No. 93, *ante*). The number of the volumes is reduced from 10 to 8.

However, the arrangement of the materials is altogether different; in this respect this edition shows the same classing of the pieces in volumes as the 1756 Scotch edition (No. 95, *post*), though not the same order of the volumes themselves.

In 1766 John Balfour added 3 vols. of *Posthumous Works*, containing the same pieces as Hawkesworth's Vols. XIII–XVII, sm. 8vo. Each volume has two titles, after these patterns:

The / Posthumous / Works / Of / Dr *Jonathan Swift*, / Dean of St Patrick's, Dublin. / Volume I. / Edinburgh: / Printed for John Balfour. / — / M,DCC,LXVI.

The / Works / Of / Dr *Jonathan Swift*, / Dean of St Patrick's, Dublin. / Volume IX. / Edinburgh: / Printed for John Balfour. / — / M,DCC,LXVI.

12mo (in sixes):
    I (IX): π^7, B–Dd^6, Ee^2 — 2 pp. (series-title + bl.), 2 pp. (volume-title + bl.), III–IV (Advertisement), V–VI (Contents), [1]–322.
    II (X): π^4, A–Ff^6 — 2 pp. (series-title + bl.), 2 pp. (volume-title + bl.), III–V (Contents), 1 p. blank, [1]–345, 3 pp. blank.
    III (XI): π^5, A–Aa^6, Bb^2 — 2 pp. (series-title + bl.), 2 pp. (volume-title + bl.), III–VII (Contents), 1 p. blank, [1]–290, 2 pp. blank.
Copies: Edinb. Univ. Libr., and Penn.

Scotch Edition, 1756:
95. The / Works / Of / Dr Jonathan Swift, / Dean of St Patrick's, Dublin. / Accurately corrected by the best editions. / With / The author's Life and Character; / Notes historical, critical, and explanatory; / Tables of Contents, and Indexes. / More complete than any preceding edition. / In Eight Volumes. / Edinburgh and Glasgow: / Printed for A. Kincaid & A. Donaldson, Yair / & Fleming, and W. Gordon, *Edinburgh;* and / R. Urie, J. Gilmour, and D. Baxter, *Glasgow.* / MDCCLVI.

The volume-titles are after this pattern:

The / Works / Of / Dr Jonathan Swift, / Dean of St Patrick's, Dublin. / Volume I. / [imprint as above]

12mo (in sixes):
    I: a–l^6, m^5, A–Cc^6, Dd 1 — 2 pp. (series-title + bl.), 2 pp. (volume-title + bl.), [V]–XX (The Editor's Preface), [XXI]–XXX (The Family Of Swift), [XXXI]–CXXXIX (Life of Swift, Characters and Accounts from Orrery, Deane Swift, and Mrs. Pilkington), 1 p. (Contents, Addenda, Erratum), [CXLI]–CXLII (Criticism by Orrery), [1]–314.
    II: π^2, A–Kk^6, Ll^2 — 2 pp. (t. + bl.), 2 pp. (Contents, Addenda), 3–402.
    III: π^2, A–Hh^6, Ii^2 — 2 pp. (t. + bl.), 2 pp. (Contents), 3–377 + bl.
    IV: π^4, A–Ii^6, Kk–Ll^2 — 2 pp. (t. + bl.), 6 pp. (Contents), 3–392, 2 pp. Notes.
    V: a^4, A–Hh^6 — 2 pp. (t. + bl.), 6 pp. (Contents), 3–373 + bl.
    VI: a^4, A–Hh^6 — 2 pp. (t. + bl.), [III]–VIII (Contents), [1]–372.
    VII: π^2, A–Kk^6, Ll^4 — 2 pp. (t. + bl.), [III]–IV (Contents), [1]–404.
    VIII: π^2, b^2, C 1, A–Ii^6, Kk^4 — 2 pp. (t. + bl.), [III]–IX (Contents), 1 p. (Addenda, Errata), [1]–355, 37 pp. Indexes (unnumbered).
For three additional volumes, see No. 97A.
Copies: Penn.

96. *Another edition*, 1761:

The / Works / Of / Dr Jonathan Swift, / Dean of St Patrick's, Dublin. / Accurately corrected by the best editions. / With / The author's Life and Character; / Notes historical, critical, and explanatory; / Tables of Contents, and Indexes. / More complete than any preceding edition. / In Eight Volumes. / Edinburgh: / Printed for A. Donaldson, at Pope's Head. / MDCCLXI.

The volume-titles are after this pattern:

The / Works / Of / Dr Jonathan Swift, / Dean of St Patrick's, Dublin. / Volume I. / Edinburgh: / Printed for A. Donaldson, at Pope's Head. / MDCCLXI.

Vol. VI has the date misprinted: MDCCLIX.
12mo (in sixes):
I: a–m⁶, A–Cc⁶— 2 pp. (series-title + bl.), 2 pp. (volume-title + bl.), [V]–XX (The Editor's Preface), [XXI]–XXX (The Family Of Swift), [XXXI]–CXXXIX (Life of Swift, Characters and Accounts from Orrery, Deane Swift, and Mrs. Pilkington), 1 p. (Contents, Erratum), [CXLI]–CXLII (Criticism by Orrery), [1]–314.
II: a², A–Kk⁶, Ll⁴ — 2 pp. (t. + bl.), 2 pp. (Contents), [5]–406, 2 pp. blank.
III: π², A–Hh⁶, Ii² — 2 pp. (t. + bl.), [III]–IV (Contents), [5]–379 + bl.
IV: a⁴, A–Ii⁶, Kk⁴ — 2 pp. (t. + bl.), [III]–VII (Contents), 1 p. blank, 3–392, 2 pp. blank.
V: a⁴, A–Hh⁶ — 2 pp. (t. + bl.), [III]–VII (Contents), 1 p. blank, 3–373 + bl.
VI: a³, A–Hh⁶ — 2 pp. (t. + bl.), [III]–VI (Contents), [1]–371 + bl.
VII: π², A–Ll⁶, Mm 1 — 2 pp. (t. + bl.), [III]–IV (Contents), [1]–410.
VIII: a⁴, A–Kk⁶, Ll⁴ — 2 pp. (t. + bl.), [III]–VIII (Contents), [1]–365, 37 pp. Indexes (unnumbered).
For three additional volumes, see No. 97A.
Copies: Penn.

Another issue, 1766:
In 1766 this edition was provided with new title-pages, as follows:

The / Works / Of / Dr Jonathan Swift, / Dean of St. Patrick's, Dublin. / With / The Author's Life and Character; / Notes Historical, Critical, and Explanatory; / and Tables of Contents, and Indexes. / More complete than any preceding Edition. / — / In Eight Volumes. / — / Accurately corrected by the best Editions. / = / Edinburgh: / Printed for A. Donaldson, and sold at his / Shops in London and Edinburgh. / — / MDCCLXVI.

The volume-titles are after this pattern:

The / Works / Of / Dr. Jonathan Swift, / Dean of St. Patrick's, Dublin, / Volume I. / = / Edinburgh: / Printed for A. Donaldson, and sold at his / Shops in London and Edinburgh. / — / MDCCLXVI.

The collation is exactly the same, except Vol. I:

π^2, a^3, b–f^6 (some of the leaves wrongly signed), A–Cc^6 — 2 pp. (series-title + bl.), 2 pp. (volume-title + bl.), [V]–X (The Editor's Preface), [XXI]–LXI (Life of Swift, Accounts by Mrs. Pilkington), 1 p. blank, 1 p. (title: 'Tale'), 1 p. (Contents), [LXV]–LXVII (Criticism), 1 p. blank, [1]–314.

As a result of considerable alterations, the prefatory matter (i.e. everything before page 3, which is the first leaf of sheet A) was reprinted; the rest of the book is the same printing in the two issues.

Copies: Penn.

97. *Another edition, 1768:*

The former 8 volumes were reprinted in 10, while at the same time 3 new volumes were added (derived from 'Falconer', who had derived from Hawkesworth, Vols. XIII–XVII, sm. 8vo). There are four (or rather five) issues, differing principally in the imprints:

(1a) *First issue*, 1768 (thin and small paper):

The / Works / Of / Dr Jonathan Swift, / Dean of St. Patrick's, Dublin. / With / The Author's Life and Character; Notes / Historical, Critical, and Explanatory; Tables of / Contents, and Indexes. / More complete than any preceding Edition. / — / In Thirteen Volumes. / — / Accurately corrected by the best Editions. / = / Edinburgh: / Printed for A. Donaldson, and sold at his Shop / (N° 195.) in the Strand, London; / and at Edinburgh. / = / M.DCC.LXVIII.

The volume-titles I–X are after this pattern:

The / Works / Of / Dr. Jonathan Swift, / Dean of St. Patrick's, Dublin. / — / Volume I. / — / = / Edinburgh: / Printed for A. Donaldson, and sold at his Shops / in London and Edinburgh. / = / M.DCC.LXVIII.

[In Vols. I (volume-title), II and VI, the imprint has: Printed for A. Donaldson, &c.; in the other volumes: Printed by A. Donaldson, &c.]

12mo (in sixes):

I: a–e^6, f^3, A–Bb^6 — 2 pp. (series-title + bl.), 2 pp. (volume-title + bl.), V–IX (The Editor's Preface), 1 p. blank, XI–LXI (Life of Swift, Accounts by Mrs. Pilkington), LXII–LXIV (Criticism), 1 p. (title: 'Tale'), LXVI (Contents), [1]–297, 3 pp. blank.

II: π^2, A–Ff^6, Gg^2 — 2 pp. (t. + bl.), 2 pp. (Contents + bl.), [1]–351 + bl.

III: a^2, A–Ee^6, Ff^4 — 2 pp. (t. + bl.), III–IV (Contents), 1–343 + bl.

IV: a^3, A–Ii^6, Kk^4 — 2 pp. (t. + bl.), III–V (Contents), 1 p. blank, 1–390, 2 pp. blank.

V: a^4, A–Gg^6, Hh^4 — 2 pp. (t. + bl.), I–VI (Contents), 1–366, 2 pp. blank.

VI: a^4, A–Dd^6 — 2 pp. (t. + bl.), III–VIII (Contents), 1–324.

VII: a^2, b^2, A–Ee^6, Ff^4 — 2 pp. (t. + bl.), III–VII (Contents), 1 p. blank, [1]–344.

VIII: a^2, b^2, A–Ii^6, Kk^4 — 2 pp. (t. + bl.), III–VIII (Contents), 1–391 + bl.

IX: a^3, A–Gg^6, Hh^4 — 2 pp. (t. + bl.), III–VI (Contents), 1–367 + bl.

X: a⁶, A–Hh⁶, Ii² — 2 pp. (t. + bl.), III–XI (Contents), 1 p. blank, [1]–342, 34 pp. Indexes (unnumbered).

The titles in Vols. XI–XIII are after this pattern:

The / Works / Of / Dr. Jonathan Swift, / Dean of St. Patrick's, Dublin. / = / Volume XI. / = / = / Edinburgh: / Printed by A. Donaldson, and sold at his / Shops in London and Edinburgh. / = / MDCCLXVIII.

XI: a³, A–Ii⁶ — 2 pp. (t. + bl.), III–IV (Advertisement), V–VI (Contents), 1–383 + bl.

XII: a³, A–Ii⁶, Kk⁴ — 2 pp. (t. + bl.), [III]–VI (Contents), [1]–390, 2 pp. blank.

XIII: a⁴, A–Cc⁶, Dd² — 2 pp. (t. + bl.), III–VII (Contents), 1 p. blank, 1–314, 2 pp. blank.

(1b) *First issue*, 1768 (thick and large paper):
Penn has a set, the same printing as above, but on thick and large paper, measuring 7 × 4½ inches, the thin and small set being 6⅝ × 4 inches. But this is not the only difference. The sheets of the Sm. P. issue are in sixes, those of the L.P. one in fours. Moreover, the collation of Vol. I of the latter shows two pages more, owing to the fact that the leaf before the text (pp. [LXV]–LXVI) in the former, bearing title 'A Tale Of A Tub', and 'Contents of Vol. I', has been replaced by a double leaf (Contents + blank, title + blank) in the latter. At the end of Vol. XIII, on p. [315], there is a 'Note for the Binder' concerning a faulty signature, which is not in the Sm. P. issue. And lastly, slight corrections have been effected in the L.P. issue, proving it to be later than the Sm. P. one.

(2) *Second issue*, 1768:
Exactly the same printing as the first issue (thin and small paper), with the exception only of this series-title in Vol. I:

The / Works / Of / Dr. Jonathan Swift, / Dean of St. Patrick's, Dublin. / With / The Author's Life and Character; Notes / Historical, Critical, and Explanatory; Tables / of Contents, and Indexes. / More complete than any preceding Edition. / — / In Thirteen Volumes. / — / Accurately corrected by the best Editions. / = / Edinburgh: / Printed by Alexander Donaldson. / Sold at his Shop, No. 48, East corner of St. Paul's / Church-yard, London; and at Edinburgh. / = / M.DCC.LXVIII.

Copy: B.M. 12272 aaa 16.

(3) *Third issue*, 1768:
Exactly the same printing as the first issue (thin and small paper). The title-pages are the same as those in the first issue, except for the imprints. Those in Vols. I (series-title), II and X are:

Edinburgh: / Printed for Eben. Wilson, Bookseller in / Dumfries. / = / M.DCC.LXVIII.

Those in Vols. I (volume-title), III–IX are:

Edinburgh: / Printed for Eben. Wilson, Bookseller in Dumfries. / = / M.DCC.LXVIII.

> Those in Vols. XI–XIII are the same as those in the first issue.
> Copy: Penn.

(4) *Fourth issue*, 1774:
In 1774 the set (thin and small paper) was again provided with new title-pages after this pattern in all the 13 volumes:

The / Works / Of / Dr Jonathan Swift, / Dean of St Patrick's, Dublin. / In Thirteen Volumes. / Volume I. / Edinburgh: / Printed for John Donadlson [*sic*], Corner of Arundel / Street, Strand, London. / = / MDCCLXXIV.

> [The misprint Donad*l*son occurs in the imprints of all the 13 vols.]
> The two original titles have been replaced by one only, as above.
> Copy: Penn.

97A. *Another issue of Vols. XI–XIII, 1768 (see 97 (1)):*
In this issue all the signs to mark them as Vols. XI–XIII have been removed, so as to make them suitable for addition to the preceding 8 vol. editions of 1756, 1761 and 1766 (see Nos. 95 and 96 (1) and (2), *ante*). The titles in these three volumes are:

The / Works / Of / Dr. Jonathan Swift, / Dean of St. Patrick's, Dublin. / = / A New Edition, Corrected. / = / = / Edinburgh: / Printed by A. Donaldson, and sold at his / Shops in London and Edinburgh. / = / MDCCLXVIII.

> The modifications are:
> (1) The volume-indications at the top of the *Contents* and at the foot of the first page of each new sheet were removed (by mistake preserved at the foot of p. 1 in the first volume).
> (2) On the last page of each volume the words: "*The End of the Eleventh (Twelfth, Thirteenth) Volume.*" were altered into simply: "*The End.*"
> (3) The heading of the *Index* at the end of Vol. III was altered from: "Index. To Volumes XI. XII. XIII." into: "Index. To Volumes IX. X. XI."
> (4) The blank leaf at the end of the third volume after p. 314 was used for printing 'Note For The Binder' on.
> Copy: Penn.

98. *Irish Edition*, 1758:
(1) The / Works / Of / Dr. Jonathan Swift, / Dean of St. Patrick's Dublin. / Accurately corrected by the best Editions. / With / The Author's Life and Character; / Notes historical, critical, and explanatory; / Tables of Contents, and Indexes. / More complete than any preceding Edition. / — / In Nine Volumes. / — / Vol. I. / = / Dublin: / Printed for G. and A. Ewing, in *Dame-street*. / — / MDCCLVIII.

> The volume-titles are after this pattern:

The / Works / Of / Dr. Jonathan Swift, / Dean of St. Patrick's Dublin. / Volume I. / Containing: / A Tale of a Tub. / The Battle of the Books. / Sermons. I. On the Trinity. / II. On Mutual Subjection. / III. On the Testimony of the Conscience. / IV. On Brotherly Love. / V. The Difficulty of Knowing One's Self, &c. / = / Dublin: / Printed for G. and A. Ewing, in *Dame-street.* / — / MDCCLVIII.

> 12mo:
> Frontisp., π^2, a^2, A 2–12, B–T^{12} — frontisp. (Swift), 2 pp. (series-title + bl.), 2 pp. (volume-title + bl.), 4 pp. (Subscriber's Names), 1 p. (The Dublin Editor's Preface), [IV]–XIII (Preface to Mr. Hawkesworth's Edition), XIII–XVIII (The Scotch Editor's Plan), [XIX]–XXVIII (The Family of Swift), [XXIX]–CXXXVII (Life of Swift, etc.), 1 p. (Contents), [CXXXIX]–CXL (Criticism), [1]–314, 2 pp. blank.

The contents mentioned on the title-pages are as follows:

[Vol. II:] The Preface to Pope and Swift's Miscellanies. / Contests, &c. in Athens and Rome. / The Public Spirit of the Whigs. / The Conduct of the Allies. / Some Remarks on the Barrier-Treaty. / The Examiner. / Advice to the October Club.

> π^2, A–Q^{12}, R^8 — 2 pp. (t. + bl.), 2 pp. (Contents), 3–402.

[Vol. III:] A Proposal for the Use of Irish Manufactures. / The Drapier's Letters. / The Intelligencer. / Papers relating to Irish Affairs, &c.

> π^2, A–Q^{12}, R^4 — 2 pp. (t. + bl.), 2 pp. (Contents), 1–392.

[Vol. IV:] Travels of Capt. Gulliver. / Bickerstaff's Predictions. / 'Squire Bickerstaff detected. / The Wonderful Wonder of Wonders. / A Proposal for Improving the English Tongue. / Thoughts on Various Subjects.

> a^4, A–Q^{12}, R^8 — 2 pp. (t. + bl.), [III]–VIII (Contents), 3–400, 2 pp. blank.

[Vol. V:] Memoirs of Martinus Scriblerus. / A Key to the Lock. / Thoughts on Various Subjects. / The History of John Bull. / The Art of Political Lying. / An Account of the Poisoning of Edmund Curll. / A Rumour of the Day of Judgment.

> a^4, A–P^{12}, Q^6 — 2 pp. (t. + bl.), 6 pp. (Contents), 3–373 + bl.

[Vol. VI:] Miscellanies / In / Verse.

> π^3, B–Q^{12}, R^8 — 2 pp. (t. + bl.), [III]–VI (Contents), [1]–375 + bl.

[Vol. VII:] Miscellanies in Verse. / A Letter to a young Clergyman. / An Essay on Modern Education. / A Letter to a young Lady on her Marriage. / A Preface to Bp. Burnet's Introduction, &c. / Polite Conversation. In three Dialogues. / Directions to Servants.

π^2, A–R^{12} — 2 pp. (t. + bl.), [III]–IV (Contents), [1]–405, 3 pp. blank.

[Vol. VIII:] Letters to and from Dr Swift. / Thoughts on Various Subjects. / Defence of the Lady's Dressing-Room. / The Last Will of Dr Swift.

a^4, A–O^{12}, P^8 — 2 pp. (t. + bl.), [III]–VIII (Contents), [1]–355, 2 pp. blank (207–211 omitted in numbering).

[Vol. IX:] The History of the four last Years of the Queen. / Letters to Governor Hunter. / The Craftsman and Answer. / On Good-Manners and Good-Breeding.

π^2, A^8, B–M^{12}, N^6, O 1, P–R^{12}, S^8 — 2 pp. (t. + bl.), 2 pp. (Contents + bl.), 2 pp. (title: 'The History' + bl.), III–XIV (Advertisement), [3]–330, 37 pp. Indexes (unnumbered), 3 pp. advs.

The *Preface* says: "The Edition of the Works of Dr. Swift now preparing for the Public is, for the greater Part, taken from a second Edition printed in *Scotland* in 1756"; and, indeed, it shows exactly the same arrangement, both as to materials and volumes, with the addition of a ninth volume.

Vol. IX had to serve two purposes: the full volume was destined to form Vol. IX of the above edition; and the greater part of it, namely *The History Of The Four Last Years Of The Queen* (pp. [I]–XIV, [3]–282), was to be sold separately (see No. 813, *post*). This is clear not only from the absence of volume indications at the foot of the first page of each new sheet (present in all the other 8 vols.), but also from the fact that after p. 282 (where the *History* ends) a new sheet begins, so that everything before p. I (two leaves: title Vol. IX and *Contents*) and after p. 282 could easily be kept or dropped as necessity required.

Copies: Penn.

(2) *Another issue*, 1767:

In 1767 the 9 volumes were provided with new title-pages, Vols. X–XI (a selection from Hawkesworth's Vols. XIII–XVII) and Vols. XII–XIV (the first set of *Letters*) were added, while the next year Vols. XV–XVII (the second set of *Letters*) completed the set.

The engraved titles (within a decorated frame, and showing a portrait of Swift) in all the 17 volumes are after this pattern:

The / *Works* / Of / *Jonathan Swift*. / D.D: D.S.P.D. / *With* / Notes Historical And Critical — / By *J. Hawkesworth*. L.L.D. / And Others. / Vol. I. / *Printed for* J. Williams *Dublin 1767*.

Besides the above engraved title Vols. X–XVII have other titles, viz.: In Vols. X–XI:

The / Works / Of / Dr. Jonathan Swift, / Dean of St. Patrick's, Dublin. / Volume X. [XI.] / Collected And Revised / By Deane

Swift, Esq; / of Goodrich, in Herefordshire. / *Hæ tibi erunt artes.*
Virgil. / = / Dublin: / Printed For J. Williams, In Skinner-Row.
/ — / MDCCLXVII.

> X: π^6 (the 3rd and 4th signed A), B–N^{12}, O^8 — 2 pp. (engraved title +
> bl.), 2 pp. (second title + bl.), 6 pp. (Contents), 2 pp. (The Editors
> To The Reader), [1]–304.
> XI: π^2, B–L^{12}, M^6 — 2 pp. (engraved title + bl.), 2 pp. (second title +
> bl.), 1–252.
> In Vols. XII–XIV:

Letters, / Written By The Late / Jonathan Swift, D.D. / Dean
Of St. Patrick's, Dublin; / And Several Of His Friends. / From The
Year 1703 To 1740. / Published From The Originals; / With /
Notes Explanatory And Historical, / By John Hawkesworth,
L.L.D. / Volume I. [II. III.] / Dublin: / Printed For James Williams
In Skinner-Row. / M,DCC,LXVII.

> XII: π^3, A^8, B–O^{12}, P^6 — 2 pp. (engraved title + bl.), 2 pp. (second title
> + bl.), 2 pp. (Dedication to Temple + bl.), [III]–VII (Preface), 1 p.
> blank, IX–XIII (Contents), [1]–324.
> XIII: π^1, A^4, B–L^{12}, M^8 — 2 pp. (engraved title + bl.), 2 pp. (second title
> + bl.), III–VIII (Contents), [1]–255 + bl.
> XIV: π^1, A^3, B–K^{12}, L^6, M 1 — 2 pp. (engraved title + bl.), 2 pp. (second
> title + bl.), III–VI (Contents), [1]–230.
> In Vols. XV–XVII:

Letters, / Written By The Late / Jonathan Swift, D.D. / Dean
Of St. Patrick's, Dublin, / And Several Of His Friends. / From The
Year 1710 To 1742. / Published From The Originals; / Collected
And Revised / By Deane Swift, Esq. / Of Goodrich In Hereford-
shire. / Volume I. [II. III.] / = / Dublin: / Printed For J. Williams
In Skinner-Row. / — / MDCCLXVIII.

> 12mo:
> I–IX: The same as the first issue. — [In Vol. I, by the removal of the
> two titles and 4 pp. of *Subscribers Names*, and the insertion of the new
> title, the order becomes regularly: [I]–CXL, 1–314. There is no
> frontispiece as in the first issue. — At the end of Vol. IX one leaf
> bearing advertisements has been removed, but that could not be
> done with the first of the 3 pp. advertisements, as it forms the verso
> of the last page of the *Index*, so that this verso still bears advertise-
> ments of books published by George and Alexander Ewing, the
> former owners of this edition.]
> XV: π^5, B–K^{12}, L^2 — 2 pp. (engraved title + bl.), 2 pp. (advs.), 2 pp.
> (second title + bl.), [III]–V (To Mr. William Johnston), VI (mis-
> printed VIII) (Contents), [1]–218 (217–18 misprinted 283–4), 2 pp.
> advs.
> XVI: π^1, A^4, B–K^{12}, L^8 — 2 pp. (engraved title and bl.), 2 pp. (second
> title and bl.), III–VII (Contents), 1 p. blank, [1]–231 and bl.
> XVII: π^1, A^4, B–M^{12}, N^2 — 2 pp. (engraved title + bl.), 2 pp. (second
> title + bl.), III–VII (Contents), 1 p. blank, [1]–266, 2 pp. blank.
> The two sets of *Letters*, Vols. XII–XIV and XV–XVII, both have Vol. I,

II, III at the foot of the first page of each new sheet, which shows that they were also sold separately. As a matter of fact, Penn has these two sets (in contemporary binding, and both labelled: Swift's Letters, Vol. I, Vol. II, Vol. III), without the engraved titles that belong to the full set.

Copies: Penn.

99. *Another edition, 1774:*

In 1774 the number of 17 vols. was reduced to 15, by the distribution of the original Vols. X and XI, 1767, partly over the works (Vols. I–IX), partly over the correspondence (Vols. X–XV). There are no *Contents* or *Indexes*. In all the 15 volumes the first page of each new sheet has the volume-number at foot.

The engraved titles (again within a decorated frame, also showing a portrait of Swift, but different and presenting a much better likeness than the 1767 one) in all the 15 volumes are after this pattern:

The / Works / Of / Jonath.^{n} Swift, D.D.: D.S.P.D. / With / Notes Historical and Critical / By / J. Hawkesworth, L.L.D. / and others. / Vol. I. / Printed for J. Williams, / Dublin: 1774.

There are no second titles in Vols. X–XV, as in 1767–68 (No. 98, *ante*).

12mo:

I: π^1, a–e^{12}, f^6, B–O^{12}, P^2 — 2 pp. (t. + bl.), 1 p. (The Dublin Editor's Preface), [II]–XII (The Family of Swift), [XIII]–CXXIX (Life of Swift, etc.), [CXXX]–CXXXI (Criticism), 1 p. blank, [1]–314, 2 pp. blank.

II: π^1, A–Q^{12}, R^9, S^2 — 2 pp. (t. + bl.), 3–7 (Preface Miscellanies 1727), 8–402.

III: π^1, A–Q^{12}, R^4 — 2 pp. (t. + bl.), 1–392.

IV: π^1, a^4, A–R^{12}, S^2 — 2 pp. (t. + bl.), [III]–X (Contents), 3–414.

V: π^1, A–P^{12}, Q^6, R^4 — 2 pp. (t. + bl.), 3–382.

VI: π^1, B–Q^{12}, R^6, S^2 — 2 pp. (t. + bl.), [1]–375 + bl.

VII: π^1, A–R^{12}, S^2 — 2 pp. (t. + bl.), [1]–412.

VIII: π^1, B–T^{12}, U^6, X^4 — 2 pp. (t. + bl.), [1]–450, 2 pp. blank.

IX: π^1, B–P^{12} — 2 pp. (t. + bl.), III–X (Advertisement), [1]–326, 2 pp. blank.

X: π^1, B–O^{12} — 2 pp. (t. + bl.), [1]–310, 2 pp. blank.

XI: π^1, B–O^{12} — 2 pp. (t. + bl.), [1]–312.

XII: π^1, B–O^{12} — 2 pp. (t. + bl.), [1]–312.

XIII: π^1, B–O^{12} — 2 pp. (t. + bl.), [1]–312.

XIV: π^1, B–N^{12} — 2 pp. (t. + bl.), [1]–288.

XV: π^1, B–L^{12} — 2 pp. (t. + bl.), [1]–239 + bl.

Copies: Penn.

100. *Scotch Edition* (four issues: 1778, 1780, 1781, 1784):

(1) *First issue*, 1778:

The title-pages in the 18 vols. are after this pattern:

The / Works / Of / Jonathan Swift, D.D: D.S.P.D. / With / Notes Historical and Critical, / By / J. Hawkesworth, L.L.D. / And Others. / — / Vol. I. / — / Edinburgh: / Printed by Mrs Mundell, Old Excise-Office; / by David Willison, Craig's Close;

and by / Churnside and Wilson, Royal Bank Close; / the Publishers.
1778.

12mo (in sixes):
I: π^2, A–Nn^6, π^1 — 2 pp. (t. + bl.), III–IV (Contents), [1]–2 ('The
    Editor's Preface), [3]–17 (The Family Of Swift), 18–180 (Life of
    Swift, etc.), [181]–182 (Criticism), 2 pp. (title: 'Tale' + bl.), 185–204
    (Apology), 205 (Treatises written), 206–11 (Dedication to Sommers),
    211–12 (The Bookseller to the Reader), 213–21 (Epistle Dedica-
    tory), 222–35 (Preface), 236–433 + bl.
II: π^2, A–Qq^6, Rr^4 — 2 pp. (t. + bl.), III–IV (Contents), [1]–474, 2 pp.
    blank.
III: π^2, A–Oo^6 — 2 pp. (t. + bl.), III (Contents), 1 p. blank, [1]–444.
IV: π^2, A–Nn^6, Oo^4 — 2 pp. (t. + bl.), III–IV (Contents), [1]–439 + bl.
V: a^6, A–Oo^6, Pp^4 — 2 pp. (t. + bl.), 2 pp. (title: 'Travels' + bl.),
    V–XII (Contents), [1]–450, 2 pp. blank.
VI: a^3, A–Hh^6, Ii^2 — 2 pp. (t. + bl.), [III]–VI (Contents), [1]–375 + bl.
    (373–5 misnumbered 403–5).
VII: a^4, A–Bb^6 — 2 pp. (t. + bl.), [III]–VIII (Contents), [1]–297, 3 pp.
    blank.
VIII: a^6, A–Hh^6, Ii^4 — 2 pp. (t. + bl.), III–IX (Contents), 1 p. blank,
    2 pp. (title: 'Miscellanies In Verse' + bl.), [1]–378, 2 pp. blank.
IX: a^6, A–Hh^6, Ii^4 — 2 pp. (t. + bl.), III–IX (Contents), 1 p. blank,
    2 pp. (title: 'Miscellanies In Verse, Continued' + bl.), [1]–377,
    3 pp. blank.
X: a^2, A–Mm^6, Nn^4 — 2 pp. (t. + bl.), [III]–IV (Contents), [1]–427
    + bl.
XI: a^3, A–Mm^6 — 2 pp. (t. + bl.), III–VI (Contents), [1]–419 + bl.
XII: a^2, A–Pp^6, Qq 1 — 2 pp. (t. + bl.), [III]–IV (Contents), 2 pp.
    (title: 'The History' + bl.), VII–XVI (Advertisement), [1]–446.
XIII: Three leaves (the 2nd signed a 3), A–Nn^6, Oo^4 — 2 pp. (t. + bl.),
    [V]–VIII (Contents), [1]–439 + bl.
XIV: Three leaves (the 2nd signed a 3), A–Nn^6, Oo^4 — 2 pp. (t. + bl.),
    [V]–VIII (Contents), [1]–440.
XV: a^6, A–Nn^6, Oo^4 — 2 pp. (t. + bl.), [III]–XII (Contents), [1]–440.
XVI: a^6, A–Nn^6 — 2 pp. (t. + bl.), [III]–IX (Contents), 1 p. blank,
    2 pp. (title: 'Dean Swift's Correspondence' + bl.), [1]–431 + bl.
XVII: a^4, A–Ii^6, Kk^2 — 2 pp. (t. + bl.), [III]–VIII (Contents), [1]–387
    + bl.
XVIII: a^4, A–Gg^6, Hh^4 — 2 pp. (t. + bl.), [III]–VIII (Contents),
    [1]–308, 56 pp. Index.

(2) *Second issue*, 1780:
    Unfortunately I possess only three odd volumes (X, XI and XV) of this
issue. The title-pages are after this pattern:

The / Works / Of / Jonathan Swift, D.D: D.S.P.D. / With /
Notes Historical And Critical, / By / J. Hawkesworth, L.L.D. /
And Others. / — / Vol. X / = / *London:* / Printed for J. Dodsley,
and / W. Payne. / — / M.DCC.LXXX.

(3) *Third issue*, 1781:
    The title-pages are after this pattern:

The / Works / Of / Jonathan Swift, D.D: D.S.P.D. / With / Notes Historical And Critical, / By / J. Hawkesworth, L.L.D. / And Others. / — / In Eighteen Volumes. / — / Vol. I. / = / London: / Printed for A. Millar, J. and R. Tonson, / E. Dilly, J. Hinton, J. Hodges, / J. Wren, R. Cadell, and / P. Dodsley. / MDCCLXXXI.

(4) *Fourth issue*, 1784:
   The title-pages (misleadingly saying 'A New Edition') are after this pattern:

The / Works / Of / Jonathan Swift, D.D. / Dean Of St. Patrick's, Dublin: / Including The Whole Of His / Posthumous Pieces, Letters, &c. / A New Edition, / Accurately Revised, And Arranged In The Most / Natural And Proper Order; / With / An Account of the Author's Life, / And / Notes Historical, Critical, And Explanatory, / *By J. Hawkesworth, LL.D. and others.* / — / Adorned With Copperplates. / — / Vol. I. / — / London: / Printed for Charles Elliot, Edinburgh. / — / MDCCLXXXIV.

   The 1784 issue has a half-title, preceding full-title, in each volume; moreover it has copper-plates. Neither have been included in the above collations. The plates are: frontisp. (portrait of Swift) and 8 plates in Vol. I (*Tale*); 4 maps, 2 plans and 4 illustrations in Vol. V (*Gull. Travels*); 4 plates in Vol. VII (*John Bull*); 4 plates in Vol. VIII (*Poetry*).
   Preface and arrangement of this edition (4 issues) are the same as those of the 1774 Dublin edition (No. 99, *ante*).
   Copies: Penn.

Scotch and Irish Editions

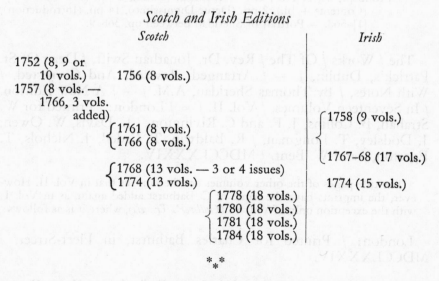

Scotch		Irish
1752 (8, 9 or 10 vols.) 1756 (8 vols.)		
1757 (8 vols. — 1766, 3 vols. added)		
	1761 (8 vols.) 1766 (8 vols.)	1758 (9 vols.)
		1767–68 (17 vols.)
	1768 (13 vols. — 3 or 4 issues) 1774 (13 vols.)	
	1778 (18 vols.) 1780 (18 vols.) 1781 (18 vols.) 1784 (18 vols.)	1774 (15 vols.)

***

Sheridan's Edition, 1784

   The desultory way of publication of the Hawkesworth editions of Swift's Works — the *Works* (in which the pieces by Pope, Arbuthnot and Gay were still present) followed by the *Letters*, and these by the *Supplement* (also containing pieces by others) — had been owing to the fact that the property of Swift's Works had hitherto been vested in no fewer than five different sets of proprietors. These copyright obstacles were now removed by Sheridan (J. Nichols, *Illustrations*, Vol. V, 394). "The first thing to be done in this edition", he says in his *Preface* before Vol. II, "was, to disembroil these Works from the chaos in which they have hitherto appeared, and reduce them into some regular order under proper heads"; after which he briefly gives the contents of the several volumes. And he concludes this enumeration thus: "The 17th and last volume, consists of Martinus Scriblerus; John Bull, and various other Pieces in prose and verse, published in Pope's Miscellanies. As these Pieces are admirable in themselves, and as it is well known that Swift had a great share in some of the most capital, tho', according to his usual practice, he never claimed any, but let his friends Arbuthnot and Pope enjoy the whole reputation as well as profit arising from them; and as these have always made a part of Swift's Works, where only they are now to be found collected, it was thought proper to add this volume to the rest."

119. The / Life / Of The / Rev. Dr. Jonathan Swift, / Dean Of St. Patrick's, Dublin. / — / By Thomas Sheridan, A.M. / — / Vol. I. / = / London: / Printed for C. Bathurst, W. Strahan, B. Collins, / J. F. and C. Rivington, L. Davis, W. Owen, J. Dodsley, / T. Longman, R. Baldwin, T. Cadell, J. Nichols, / T. Egerton, and W. Bent. / MDCCLXXXIV.

8vo:
    Frontisp., π^2, A–Nn^8, Oo^4 — frontisp. (Swift), 2 pp. (t. + bl.), 2 pp.
        (Contents + bl.), 2 pp. (Detur Dignissimo), 14 pp. (Introduction),
        [1]-568. — Portrait of Sheridan between pp. 368–9.

The / Works / Of The / Rev. Dr. Jonathan Swift, / Dean Of St. Patrick's, Dublin. / — / Arranged, Revised, And Corrected, / With Notes, / By Thomas Sheridan, A.M. / — / A New Edition, / In Seventeen Volumes. / Vol. II. / = / London: / Printed for W. Strahan, B. Collins, J. F. and C. Rivington, / L. Davis, W. Owen, J. Dodsley, T. Longman, / R. Baldwin, T. Cadell, J. Nichols, T. Egerton, / and W. Bent. / MDCCLXXXIV.

The title-pages of the other volumes are the same as that in Vol. II. However, the imprints have the name of C. Bathurst added again, as in Vol. I; with the exception only of Vol. VI (*Gulliver's Travels*), where it is as follows:

London: / Printed for Charles Bathurst, in Fleet-Street. / MDCCLXXXIV.

II: π^2, A–Ee^8 — 2 pp. (t. + bl.), 2 pp. (Dedication to Henry Grattan
    + bl.), 15 pp. (Preface), 1 p. (Contents), 2 pp. (title: 'Tale' + bl.),
    [III]–XXI (Apology), 1 p. (Treatises written), [1]–5 (Dedication to
    Sommers), 6–7 (The Bookseller To The Reader), 1 p. blank, [9]–16

(Epistle Dedicatory), [17]–29 (Preface), 1 p. blank, [31]–509 + bl. (282–509 numbered 100 too high).

III: a², B–Hh⁸, Ii⁴, π¹ — 2 pp. (t. + bl.), 2 pp. (Contents + bl.), [1]–489 + bl.

IV: π², B–Gg⁸ — 2 pp. (t. + bl.), 2 pp. (Contents + bl.), [1]–463 + bl.

V: A², B–Ii⁸ — 2 pp. (t. + bl.), 2 pp. (Contents), [1]–495 + bl.

VI: a⁷, B–Aa⁸, Bb⁴ — 2 pp. (t. + bl.), 2 pp. (title: 'Travels' + bl.), [V]–XIV (Contents), [1]–375 + bl.

VII: A⁴, B–Ff⁸ — 2 pp. (t. + bl.), 6 pp. (Contents), [1]–448.

VIII: π², B–A⁸, Bb⁶ — 2 pp. (t. + bl.), 2 pp. (Contents), [1]–378, 2 pp. blank.

IX: π², B–Ff⁸, Gg⁴ — 2 pp. (t. + bl.), 2 pp. (Contents + bl.), [1]–454, 2 pp. blank.

X: π², B–Ee⁸, Ff 1 — 2 pp. (t. + bl.), 2 pp. (Contents + bl.), [1]–433 + bl.

XI: A⁴, B–Ii⁸ — 2 pp. (t. + bl.), 6 pp. (Contents), [1]–495 + bl.

XII: A⁴, B–Ii⁸ — 2 pp. (t. + bl.), 6 pp. (Contents), [1]–496.

XIII: A⁴, B–Hh⁸ — 2 pp. (t. + bl.), 6 pp. (Contents), [1]–479 + bl.

XIV: π², B–Cc⁸, Dd² — 2 pp. (t. + bl.), 2 pp. (Contents + bl.), [1]–404.

XV: π², B–Ee⁸, Ff⁴ — 2 pp. (t. + bl.), 2 pp. (Contents + bl.), [1]–440.

XVI: a², B–Cc⁸, Dd–Ee⁴ — 2 pp. (t. + bl.), 2 pp. (Contents), 1–415 + bl., 4 pp. music.

XVII: π², B–Ii⁸, Kk² — 2 pp. (t. + bl.), 2 pp. (Contents), [1]–499 + bl.

Copies: Penn.

Vol. I was also issued separately; second edition 1787 (see No. 1368, *post*). *A Catalogue of a Select Collection of Ancient and Modern Books,* – – – *sold during the Year 1789, At Edwards's, No. 102, Pall-mall, London* has the following items:

3986 Swift's Works, by Sheridan 17 vol. 1787.

3987 The same, 17 vol. elegantly bound 1787.

Whether the year 1787 refers to the whole set, or to Vol. I only, which was reprinted in 1787 (see No. 1368), I cannot say, as I have never seen or heard of a whole set dated 1787.

For a possible 18th volume, see No. 121, *post*.

Nichols's Editions

129. The / Works / Of The / Rev. Jonathan Swift, D.D., / Dean Of St. Patrick's, Dublin. / *Arranged By Thomas Sheridan, A.M.* / With / Notes, Historical And Critical. / = / A New Edition, In Nineteen Volumes; / Corrected And Revised / *By John Nichols, F.S.A. Edinburgh And Perth.* / = / Volume I. / = / London: / Printed For J. Johnson, J. Nichols, R. Baldwin, Otridge And / Son, J. Sewell, F. and C. Rivington, T. Payne, R. Faulder, / G. And J. Robinson, R. Lea, J. Nunn, W. Cuthell, T. Egerton, / Clarke And Son, Vernor And Hood, J. Scatcherd, T. Kay, / Lackington Allen And Co., Carpenter And Co., Murray / And Highley, Longman And Rees, Cadell Jun. And Davies, / T. Bagster, J. Harding, and J. Mawman. / — / 1801.

The title-pages in the other volumes are the same, except for the volume-number. Moreover, the imprints in some cases show a widening-out, causing a different line-division.

8vo:

I: a⁵, B–Nn⁸ — 2 pp. (h.t. + printer's name on verso), 2 pp. (f.t. + bl.), 2 pp. (Dedication to Francis Rawdon Hastings + 2 quotations on verso), V–VIII (Advertisement), IX (Contents), 1 p. blank, 2 pp. (title: Life of Swift by Sheridan + bl.), III–IV (Detur Dignissimo), V–XVIII (Introduction), 1–540, 1 p. (Pedigree), 1 p. (Printer's name). — Portrait of Swift between h.t. and f.t.

II: a–b⁸, c⁷, B–Dd⁸, Ee⁶ — 2 pp. (t. + printer's name on verso), [III]–IV (Contents), V–XLVI (General Preface), 2 pp. (title: 'Tale' + bl.), III–IX (Advertisement), 1 p. blank, XI–XXII (Analytical Table), 23–40 (Apology), 41 (Treatises written), 42–6 (Dedication to Sommers), 47–8 (The Bookseller To The Reader), 49–56 (Epistle Dedicatory), 57–69 (Preface), 1 p. blank, 71–428.

III: π², B–Ff⁸, Gg² — 2 pp. (t. + printer's name on verso), 2 pp. (Contents + bl.), 2 pp. (title: 'The Examiner' + bl.), 3–456.

IV: π², B–Ee⁸, Ff⁴ — 2 pp. (t. + printer's name on verso), 2 pp. (Contents + bl.), 1 p. (title: 'The History'), [II]–IV (Advertisement 1775), [V]–XIV (Advertisement 1758), [XV]–XX (The Author's Preface), [21]–440.

V: π², B–Gg⁸, Hh⁴ — 2 pp. (t. + printer's name on verso), [III]–IV (Contents), [1]–471 + bl.

VI: a⁸, B–Z⁸, Aa⁴ — 2 pp. (t. + printer's name on verso), [III]–VIII (Contents), IX–X (The Publisher To The Reader), XI–XVI (Letter Gulliver to Sympson), [1]–357, 3 pp. blank. — Two plates.

VII: a⁴, B–Ee⁸, Ff² — 2 pp. (t. + printer's name on verso), [III]–VII (Contents), 1 p. blank, [1]–436.

VIII: a³, B–Ee⁸, Ff⁴ — 2 pp. (t. + printer's name on verso), [III]–V (Contents), 1 p. blank, [1]–438, 2 pp. blank.

IX: π², B–Dd⁸, Ee⁶ — 2 pp. (t. + printer's name on verso), [III]–IV (Contents), [1]–426, 2 pp. blank.

X: π², B–Cc⁸ — 2 pp. (t. + printer's name on verso), 2 pp. (Contents + bl.), [1]–397, 3 pp. blank.

XI: a⁴, B–Hh⁸, I⁴ — 2 pp. (t. + printer's name on verso), [III]–VIII (Contents), [1]–486, 2 pp. blank.

XII: a⁴, B–Ii⁸ — 2 pp. (t. + printer's name on verso), [III]–VIII (Contents), [1]–495 + bl.

XIII: a⁴, B–Gg⁸, Hh⁴ — 2 pp. (t. + printer's name on verso), III–VIII (Contents), [1]–472.

XIV: π², B–Bb⁸, Cc 1 — 2 pp. (t. + printer's name on verso), 2 pp. (Contents + bl.), [1]–385 + bl.

XV: π², B–Ee⁸ — 2 pp. (t. + printer's name on verso), [III]–IV (Contents), 1–431 + bl.

XVI: π², B–Aa⁸, Bb⁴ — 2 pp. (t. + printer's name on verso), III–IV (Contents), [1]–375 + bl.

XVII: π², B–Hh⁸ — 2 pp. (t. + printer's name on verso), [III]–IV (Contents), [1]–480.

XVIII: a⁴, B–Gg⁸ — 2 pp. (t. + printer's name on verso), [III]–VII (Contents), 1 p. blank, [1]–464.

XIX: a³, B–Bb⁸, Cc⁶ — 2 pp. (t. + printer's name on verso), [III]–V (Contents), VI (Addendum), [1]–396.

It seems that only Vol. I has a half-title (referring to the whole set); at least, so it is in the B.M. copy, the Bibl. Nat. Paris copy, and the Penn copy. The Forster copy has not any half-title, not even in Vol. I.

There is also a Large Paper issue.

130. *Another Edition* (12mo, 1803):

The / Works / Of The / Rev. Jonathan Swift, D.D. / Dean Of St. Patrick's, Dublin. / *Arranged By Thomas Sheridan, A.M.* / With / Notes, Historical And Critical. / = / A New Edition, In Twenty-Four Volumes; / Corrected And Revised By / *John Nichols, F.A.S. Edinburgh & Perth.* / = / Volume I. / = / *London:* / Printed For J. Johnson, John Nichols And Son, / R. Baldwin, Otridge And Son, F. And C. Rivington, / T. Payne, R. Faulder, G. And J. Robinson, R. Lea, / J. Nunn, W. Cuthell, J. Walker, T. Egerton, / Clarke And Son, Vernor And Hood, J. Scatcherd, / T. Kay, Lackington Allan And Co. Carpenter / And Co. Longman And Rees, Cadell And / Davies, S. Bagster, J. Harding, R. H. Evans, *and* / J. Mawman. / — / 1803.

The title-pages of the other volumes are the same as that in Vol. I, except for the volume-number. The imprints are also the same; however, sometimes we find the names of Murray and Highley added, while T. Bagster takes the place of S. Bagster; and the line-division is sometimes different.

12mo (in sixes):

I: π^4, b–f^6, G–DD^6, EE^2 — 2 pp. (h.t. + printer's name on verso), 2 pp. (t. + bl.), 2 pp. (Dedication to Hastings + bl.), 2 pp. (Contents + bl.), IX–XIV (Advertisement), XV–LIX (General Preface), 1 p. blank, 2 pp. (title: 'Life of Swift' + bl.), 63–4 (Detur Dignissimo), 65–77 (introduction), 1 p. blank, 79–323 (printer's name on verso). Frontisp. (Swift) between the two titles.

II: π^4, B–EE^6, FF^4 — 2 pp. (h.t. + printer's name on verso), 2 pp. (t. + bl.), 2 pp. (Contents + bl.), 1 leaf blank, 1–330, 2 pp. blank.

III: A^4, B–EE^6, FF^4 — 2 pp. (h.t. + printer's name on verso), 2 pp. (t. + bl.), [V]–[VII] (Contents), 1 p. blank, [1]–331 + bl.

IV: A^4, B–FF^6 — 2 pp. (h.t. + printer's name on verso), 2 pp. (t. + bl.), [V]–VII (Contents), 1 p. blank, [1]–334, 2 pp. blank.

V: π^2, B–EE^6, FF^4 — 2 pp. (h.t. + printer's name on verso), 2 pp. (t. + bl.), [1]–329 + bl., 2 pp. (Contents + bl.).

VI: A^4, B–HH^6 — 2 pp. (h.t. + printer's name on verso), 2 pp. (t. + bl.), 1 leaf blank, [VII]–VIII (Contents), [1]–359 + bl.

VII: A^4, B–EE^6 — 2 pp. (h.t. + printer's name on verso), 2 pp. (t. + bl.), 1 leaf blank, 2 pp. (Contents + bl.), [1]–324.

VIII: π^3, B–EE^6 — 2 pp. (h.t. + printer's name on verso), 2 pp. (t. + bl.), [III]–IV (Contents), [1]–322, 2 pp. blank.

IX: A^4, B–FF^6 — 2 pp. (h.t. + printer's name on verso), 2 pp. (t. + bl.), [V]–XII (Contents), [1]–334, 2 pp. blank. — Two plates, the same as those in Vol. VI, 1801 — see No. 129.

X: π^1, A^4, B–FF^6 — 2 pp. (h.t. + printer's name on verso), 2 pp. (t. + bl.), [III]–VII (Contents), 1 p. blank, [1]–335 + bl.

XI: π^5, B–HH^6, II^4 — 2 pp. (h.t. + printer's name on verso), 2 pp. (t. + bl.), [VII]–XII (Contents), [1]–366, 2 pp. blank.

XII: π^4, B–CC^6, DD^2 — 2 pp. (h.t. + printer's name on verso), 2 pp. (t. + bl.), [V]–VII (Contents), 1 p. blank, [1]–315 + bl.

XIII: π^4, B–CC^6 — 2 pp. (h.t. + printer's name on verso), 2 pp. (t. + bl.), [V]–VII (Contents), 1 p. blank, [1]–298, 2 pp. blank.

XIV: A^4, B–HH^6 — 2 pp. (h.t. + printer's name on verso), 2 pp. (t. + bl.), 1 leaf blank, [V]–VI (Contents), [1]–360.

XV: π^4, b 1, B–BB^6, CC^2 — 2 pp. (h.t. + printer's name on verso), 2 pp. (t. + bl.), [V]–IX (Contents), 1 p. blank, [1]–291 + bl.

XVI: π^4, b 1, B–CC^6 — 2 pp. (h.t. + printer's name on verso), 2 pp. (t. + bl.), [V]–X (Contents), [1]–299 + bl.

XVII: π^5, B–U^6, X^4 — 2 pp. (h.t. + printer's name on verso), 2 pp. (t. + printer's name on verso), [III]–VIII (Contents), 1 leaf blank, [1]–233, 3 pp. blank.

XVIII: π^4, B–GG^6, HH^4 — 2 pp. (h.t. + printer's name on verso), 2 pp. (t. + printer's name on verso), [III]–VI (Contents), [1]–354, 2 pp. blank.

XIX: A^5, B–BB^6, CC 1 — 2 pp. (h.t. + printer's name on verso), 2 pp. (t. + bl.), [V]–IX (Contents), 1 p. blank, [1]–289 + bl.

XX: π^4, b 1, B–CC^6, DD 1 — 2 pp. (h.t. + printer's name on verso), 2 pp. (t. + bl.), [V]–X (Contents), [1]–302.

XXI: π^4, B–Ff^6, Gg^2 — 2 pp. (h.t. + printer's name on verso), 2 pp. (t. + bl.), 2 pp. (Contents), 1 leaf blank, [1]–340.

XXII: π^3, B–GG^6, HH^4 — 2 pp. (h.t. + printer's name on verso), 2 pp. (t. + bl.), [III]–IV (Contents), [1]–354, 2 pp. blank.

XXIII: π^3, B–KK^6 — 2 pp. (h.t. + printer's name on verso), 2 pp. (t. + bl.), [V]–VI (Contents), [1]–359 + bl.

XXIV: π^3, B–NN^6 — 2 pp. (h.t. + printer's name on verso), 2 pp. (t. + bl.), [V]–VII (Contents), 1 p. blank, [1]–420.

Vols. III (*Tale*) and IX (*Gulliver's Travels*) were also issued separately (see Nos. 249 and 333, *post*).

Copies: Penn.

131. *Another Edition* (8vo, 1808):

The / Works / Of The / Rev. Jonathan Swift, D.D. / Dean Of St. Patrick's, Dublin. / *Arranged By Thomas Sheridan, A.M.* / With / Notes, Historical and Critical. / = / A New Edition, In Nineteen Volumes; / Corrected And Revised By / *John Nichols, F.S.A. Edinburgh And Perth.* / = / Vol. I. / — / *London:* / Printed For J. Johnson; J. Nichols and Son; R. Baldwin; Otridge And Son; / F. C. And J. Rivington; T. Payne; R. Faulder; G. Robinson; Wilkie And / Robinson; R. Lea; J. Nunn; Cuthell And Martin; J. Walker; T. Egerton; / Clarke And Son; Vernor, Hood And Sharpe; Scatcherd And Letterman; / Lackington, Allen, And Co.; J. Carpenter; Longman, Hurst, Rees, And Orme; / Cadell And Davies; W. Miller; J. And A. Arch; S. Bagster; J. Murray; / J. Harding; R. H. Evans; And J. Mawman.

The title-page has no year, but at the foot of the *Dedication* and of the *General Preface* there is: June 1808.

The title-pages of all the other volumes are the same as that in Vol. I, except for the volume-number. Like the title in Vol. I those in Vols. VII, VIII and IX have no year; all the others have 1808. The imprints show slight differences.

8vo:

I: π^7, b–c^8, d 1–7, e–n^8, B–Ee^8, Ff 1 — 2 pp. (t. + bl.), 2 pp. (Dedication to Hastings + bl.), 2 pp. (Contents + bl.), [IX]–XIII (Advertisement), 1 p. blank, [XV]–LXII (General Preface), [LXIII]–CCVI (Barrett's Essay), [1]–433 (Life of Swift), [434] (printer's name only). — Frontisp. (Swift); deathbed portrait of Swift before page [LXIII].

For a separate issue of Barrett's Essay, see No. 136.

II: π^2, B–Hh^8, Ii^2 — 2 pp. (t. + printer's name on verso), [III]–IV (Contents), [1]–484.

III: π^3, B–Ii^8 — 2 pp. (t. + printer's name on verso), [V]–VII (Contents), 1 p. blank, [1]–495 + printer's name on verso.

IV: π^2, B–Ll^8 — 2 pp. (t. + printer's name on verso), 2 pp. (Contents + bl.), [1]–528.

V: π^2, B–Ii^8 — 2 pp. (t. + printer's name on verso), [III]–IV (Contents), [1]–495 + bl.

VI: π^2, B–Ii^8, Kk^6 — 2 pp. (t. + printer's name on verso), [III]–IV (Contents), [1]–507 + bl.

VII: π^5, A–2H^8 — 2 pp. (t. + bl.), [V]–XI (Contents), 1 p. blank, [1]–496. — Two plates, the same as those in Vol. VI, 1801 — see No. 129.

VIII: π^3, B–2H^8, 2I^4 — 2 pp. (t. + bl.), [V]–VII (Contents), 1 p. blank, [1]–486, 2 pp. blank.

IX: π^3, B–2G^8, 2H^6 — 2 pp. (t. + bl.), [V]–VII (Contents), 1 p. blank, [1]–474, 2 pp. blank.

X: π^4, B–GG^8, HH^6 — 2 pp. (t. + printer's name on verso), 6 pp. (Contents), [1]–473 (Errata on verso), 2 pp. blank.

XI: π^4, B–FF^8, GG^6 — 2 pp. (t. + printer's name on verso), [III]–VIII (Contents), 1–459 + bl.

XII: A^4, B–GG^8 — 2 pp. (t. + printer's name on verso), [III]–VII (Contents), 1 p. blank, 1–463 (printer's name on verso).

XIII: A^4, B–EE^8, FF^6 — 2 pp. (t. + printer's name on verso), [III]–VIII (Contents), [1]–443 + bl.

XIV: a^3, B–DD^8, EE^6 — 2 pp. (t. + printer's name on verso), [III]–VI (Contents), 1–426, 2 pp. blank.

XV: π^2, B–EE^8 — 2 pp. (t. + printer's name on verso), [III]–IV (Contents), [1]–431 + bl.

XVI: π^4, B–FF^8, GG^2 — 2 pp. (t. + bl.), [III]–VIII (Contents), [1]–452.

XVII: π^3, B–FF^8, GG^6, HH–MM^8 — 2 pp. (t. + bl.), [V]–VIII (Contents), [1]–540.

XVIII: π^1, b^2, B–GG^8, HH^6 — 2 pp. (t. + bl.), [III]–V (Contents), 1 p. blank, [1]–474, 2 pp. blank.

XIX: π^3, B–FF^8, GG^4 — 2 pp. (t. + bl.), [V]–VII (Contents), 1 p. blank, [1]–453, 3 pp. blank.

This is Penn's copy, which has no half-title in any of the volumes. The Forster copy has half-titles in Vols. I, VII, VIII and IX. Query: Are half-titles essential to all the volumes?

132. *Another Edition* (12mo, 1812–13):

The / Works / Of The / Rev. Jonathan Swift, D.D. / Dean Of St. Patrick's, Dublin. / Arranged By / *Thomas Sheridan, A.M.* / With / Notes, Historical And Critical. / = / A New Edition, In Twenty-Four Volumes. / Corrected and Revised / *By John Nichols,*

F.A.S. / Edinburgh and Perth. / = / Volume I. / [ornament] / *New York:* / Published By William Durell And Co. / — / 1812.

The titles of all the 24 volumes are the same, except for the volume-numbers. The year is 1812 for Vols. I–XIV, 1813 for Vols. XV–XXIV.
12mo:

I: A^6, $B-N^{12}$, O^6, P^2 — 2 pp. (h.t. + bl.), 2 pp. (f.t. + bl.), 2 pp. (Dedication + bl.), 2 pp. (Contents + bl.), [9]–12 (Advertisement), [13]–55 (General Preface), 1 p. blank, 2 pp. (h.t. + bl.), 59–317 + bl. — Pages 313–14 omitted in numbering.

II: π^1, $A-N^{12}$, O^8 — 2 pp. (h.t. + bl.), 2 pp. (f.t. + bl.), 2 pp. (Contents + bl.), [5]–328.

III: π^3, $A-N^{12}$, O^{10} — 2 pp. (h.t. + bl.), 2 pp. (f.t. + bl.), 2 pp. (Contents), 2 pp. (h.t. Tale + bl.), 3–331 + bl. — Also issued separately; see No. 251.

IV: π^3, $A-H^{12}$, I^8, $K-O^{12}$, P^4 — 2 pp. blank, 2 pp. (t. + bl.), [V]–VI (Contents), 2 pp. (h.t. + bl.), [3]–334, 2 pp. blank.

V: π^3, $A-O^{12}$ — 2 pp. (h.t. + bl.), 2 pp. (f.t. + bl.), 2 pp. (Contents + bl.), 2 pp. (h.t. + bl.), 3–334, 2 pp. blank.

VI: π^4, A^8, $B-P^{12}$, Q^6 — 2 pp. blank, 2 pp. (h.t. + bl.), 2 pp. (f.t. + bl.), [VII]–VIII (Contents), 2 pp. (h.t. + bl.), [3]–361, 3 pp. blank.

VII: π^3, $A-B^{12}$, C^8, $D-O^{12}$ — 2 pp. (h.t. + bl.), 2 pp. (f.t. + bl.), 2 pp. (Contents + bl.), 2 pp. (h.t. + bl.), 3–324, 4 pp. blank.

VIII: π^3, $A-N^{12}$, O^6 — 2 pp. (h.t. + bl.), 2 pp. (f.t. + bl.), 2 pp. (Contents + bl.), 2 pp. (h.t. + bl.), [3]–322, 2 pp. blank.

IX: π^6, A^8, $B-O^{12}$, P^6 — 2 pp. blank, 2 pp. (h.t. + bl.), 2 pp. (f.t. + bl.), [VII]–XI (Contents), 1 p. blank, 2 pp. (h.t. + bl.), [3]–4 (Publisher to Reader), 5–9 (Letter), 1 p. (Note), [11]–338, 2 pp. blank. — Also issued separately; see No. 343.

X: A^4, $B-P^{12}$, Q^8 — 2 pp. (h.t. + bl.), 2 pp. (f.t. + bl.), [V]–VIII (Contents), [1]–352.

XI: π^4, $A-Q^{12}$, R^6 — 2 pp. (h.t. + bl.), 2 pp. (f.t. + bl.), [V]–VIII (Contents), [1]–396.

XII: π^3, $[A]-C^{12}$, D^8, $E-O^{12}$ — 2 pp. (h.t. + bl.), 2 pp. (f.t. + bl.), [V]–VI (Contents), 2 pp. (h.t. + bl.), 3–325, 3 pp. blank.

XIII: π^3, A^8, $B-N^{12}$, O^6 — 2 pp. (h.t. + bl.), 2 pp. (f.t. + bl.), [V]–VI (Contents), 2 pp. (h.t. + bl.), 3–314, 2 pp. (colophon imprint + bl.).

XIV: π^3, A^8, $B-P^{12}$, Q^6 — 2 pp. (h.t. + bl.), 2 pp. (f.t. + bl.), [V]–VI (Contents), 2 pp. (h.t. + bl.), [3]–361, 1 p. (colophon imprint), 2 pp. blank.

XV: π^4, A^8, $[B]-N^{12}$, O^2 — 2 pp. (h.t. + bl.), 2 pp. (f.t. + bl.), [V]–VIII (Contents), [1]–308.

XVI: π^4, $A-N^{12}$, O^2 — 2 pp. (h.t. + bl.), 2 pp. (f.t. + bl.), [V]–VIII (Contents), [1]–315, 1 p. (colophon imprint).

XVII: π^4, $A-L^{12}$, M^{10} — 2 pp. (h.t. + bl.), 2 pp. (f.t. + bl.), [V]–VIII (Contents), [1]–284.

XVIII: π^4, $A-C^{12}$, D^{10}, $E-N^{12}$, O^2 — 2 pp. (h.t. + bl.), 2 pp. (f.t. + bl.), [V]–VI (Contents), 2 pp. blank, [1]–311 + bl.

XIX: π^4, $A-L^{12}$, M^8 — 2 pp. (h.t. + bl.), 2 pp. (f.t. + bl.), [V]–VIII (Contents), [1]–279 + bl.

XX: π^4, $A-M^{12}$, N^8 — 2 pp. (h.t. + bl.), 2 pp. (f.t. + bl.), [V]–VIII (Contents), [1]–304.

XXI: π^3, $A-O^{12}$, P^4 — 2 pp. (h.t. + bl.), 2 pp. (f.t. + bl.), [V]–VI (Contents); [1]–342, 2 pp. blank.

XXII: π^3, A–B^8, C–P^{12}, Q^{10} — 2 pp. (h.t. + bl.), 2 pp. (f.t. + bl.),
   [V]–VI (Contents), [1]–363 + bl.
XXIII: π^3, A–B^{12}, C^{10}, D–P^{12}, Q^{10} — 2 pp. (h.t. + bl.), 2 pp. (f.t. +
   bl.), [V]–VI (Contents), 2 pp. (h.t. + bl.), [3]–374, 2 pp. blank.
XXIV: π^3, A^{10}, B–H^{12}, I–R^6, S^4, T^2 — 2 pp. (h.t. + bl.), 2 pp. (f.t. +
   bl.), [V]–VI (Contents), 2 pp. (h.t. + bl.), [3]–305, 3 pp. blank.
Copy: Am. Antiq. Soc., Worcester (Mass.).

138. The / Works / Of / Jonathan Swift, D.D. / Dean Of St.
Patrick's, Dublin; / Containing / Additional Letters, Tracts, And
Poems, / Not Hitherto Published; / With / Notes, / And / A Life Of
The Author, / By / Walter Scott, Esq. / = / Volume I. / = /
Edinburgh: / Printed For Archibald Constable And Co. Edin-
burgh; / White, Cochrane, And Co. And Gale, Curtis, And Fenner,
/ London; And John Cumming, Dublin. / — / 1814.

The titles of all the other volumes are the same, except for the volume-
numbers.
There are also L. P. copies.
8vo:
   I: π^8, A–Hh^8, Ii^3, a–i^8 — 2 pp. (h.t. + printer's name on verso), 2 pp.
      (f.t. + bl.), [V]–X (Advertisement), [XI]–XV (Contents), 1 p.
      blank, [1]–502, [I]–CXLIV. — Frontisp. (Swift), and one plate.
   II: π^3, A–2E^8 — 2 pp. (h.t. + bl.), 2 pp. (f.t. + bl.), [VII]–VIII (Con-
      tents), [1]–446, 2 pp. blank.
   III: π^3, A–2D^8, 2E^6 — 2 pp. (h.t. + bl.), 2 pp. (f.t. + bl.), [V]–VI
      (Contents), [1]–444.
   IV: π^3, A–2G^8 — 2 pp. (h.t. + bl.), 2 pp. (f.t. + bl.), [VII]–VIII
      (Contents), [1]–478, 2 pp. blank.
   V: π^3, A–2C^8, 2D^2 — 2 pp. (h.t. + bl.), 2 pp. (f.t. + bl.), 2 pp. (Con-
      tents + bl.), [1]–420 (last page misnumbered 418).
   VI: π^3, A–2E^8, 2F^6 — 2 pp. (h.t. + bl.), 2 pp. (f.t. + bl.), [V]–VI
      (Contents), [1]–458, 2 pp. blank.
   VII: π^4, A–Oo^8 — 2 pp. (h.t. + bl.), 2 pp. (f.t. + bl.), [V]–VII (Con-
      tents), 1 p. blank, [1]–592.
   VIII: π^3, A–2E^8 — 2 pp. (h.t. + bl.), 2 pp. (f.t. + bl.), [V]–VI (Con-
      tents), [1]–446, 2 pp. blank.
   IX: π^4, A–2I^8, 2K^3, 2L^8, 2M^4, 2N 1 — 2 pp. (h.t. + bl.), 2 pp. (f.t. +
      bl.), [V]–VII (Contents), 1 p. blank, [1]–544.
   X: π^4, A–Oo^8, Pp^2 — 2 pp. (h.t. + bl.), 2 pp. (f.t. + bl.), [V]–VIII
      (Contents), [1]–595 + bl.
   XI: π^3, A–2D^8 — 2 pp. (h.t. + printer's name on verso), 2 pp. (f.t. +
      bl.), 2 pp. (Contents + bl.), 1–429, 3 pp. blank.
   XII: π^3, A–2F^8, 2G^2 — 2 pp. (h.t. + bl.), 2 pp. (f.t. + bl.), 2 pp.
      (Contents + bl.), [1]–467 + bl.
   XIII: π^4, A–Hh^8 — 2 pp. (h.t. + bl.), 2 pp. (f.t. + bl.), [V]–VII (Con-
      tents), 1 p. blank, [1]–493, 3 pp. blank.
   XIV: π^5, A–Hh^8, Ii^6 — 2 pp. (h.t. + bl.), 2 pp. (f.t. + bl.), [V]–IX
      (Contents), 1 p. blank, [1]–507 + bl.
   XV: π^5, A–Ff^8, Gg^4, *1 — 2 pp. (h.t. + bl.), 2 pp. (f.t. + bl.), [V]–IX
      (Contents), 1 p. blank, [1]–473 + bl.
   XVI: π^5, A–Gg^8, Hh^2 — 2 pp. (h.t. + bl.), 2 pp. (f.t. + bl.), [V]–X
      (Contents), [1]–483 + bl.

XVII: π^5, A–Ee^8, Ff^6 — 2 pp. (h.t. + bl.), 2 pp. (f.t. + bl.), [V]–X
  (Contents), [1]–460.
XVIII: π^5, A–Ff^8, Gg^4, Hh 1 — 2 pp. (h.t. + bl.), 2 pp. (f.t. + bl.),
  [V]–IX (Contents), 1 p. blank, [1]–473 + bl.
XIX: π^2, b^4, A–Mm^8, Nn^2 — 2 pp. (h.t. + bl.), 2 pp. (f.t. + bl.),
  [V]–XI (Contents), 1 p. blank, [1]–457 + bl., [I]–CVI.
Copies: B.M. 134 O 11, and Penn.

MEMOIRS.

From the
PEACE concluded 1679.

TO THE

Time of the Author's Retirement from Publick Busineſs.

By Sir WILLIAM TEMPLE *Baronet.*

Et Ille quidem plenus annis abiit, plenus honoribus, illis etiam quos recuſavit. Plin. Epiſt. Lib. 2. Epiſt. 1.

Publiſh'd by *Jonathan Swift*, D.D.

LONDON:
Printed for BENJAMIN TOOKE,
at the *Middle-Temple Gate* in *Fleet-ſtreet.* MDCCIX.

A

T A L E

OF A

T U B.

Written for the Univerfal Improvement of Mankind.

Diu multumque defideratum.

Samuel To which is added, *Eyre*

An ACCOUNT of a

B A T T E L

BETWEEN THE

Antient and Modern BOOKS in St. *James's* Library.

Bafima eacabafa eanaa irrauᵣifta, diarba da caeotaba fobor camelanthi. *Iren. Lib.* 1. *C.* 18.

——— *Juvatque novos decerpere flores,*
Infignemque meo capiti petere inde coronam,
Unde prius nulls velarunt tempora Mufæ. Lucret.

The Fifth EDITION: With the Author's Apology and Explanatory Notes. By *W. W--tt--n*, B. D. and others.

LONDON : Printed for *John Nutt,* near *Stationers-Hall.* M DCC X.

A Tale of a Tub (no. 222). The fifth edition, the first to include the "Author's Apology" and Wotton notes. The copy of Samuel Eyre. (University of Pennsylvania)

SECTION II

SMALLER COLLECTIONS

✠✠

1A. A / Meditation / Upon A / Broom = Stick, / And / *Somewhat Beside;* / Of / The Same Author's. / — / — — *Utile dulci.* / — / *London:* / Printed for *E. Curll,* at the *Dial* and *Bible* against / St. *Dunstan*'s Church in *Fleetstreet;* and sold by / *J. Harding,* at the *Post-Office* in St. *Martins-Lane.* / 1710. / (Price 6 *d.*)

> 8vo (in fours); π^4, B–D^4 — 2 pp. (h.t. + advs. on verso), 2 pp. (f.t. + bl.), 5–7 + bl. (A Meditation Upon A Broom-Stick), 9–18 (Baucis and Philemon), 19–25 (The Humble Petition of Frances Harris), 26 (To Mrs. Biddy Floyd), 27–9 (The History of Vanbrugh's House), 30 (Advertisement + book advs.), 2 pp. blank.
> Copies: Forster, Rothschild 2008, and B.M. C 28 b 11 (5) lacking h.t.
> The B.M. copy has this MS. note on title: "Given me by John Cliffe, Esq.; who had them of the Bp. of Kilalla, in Ireland, whose Daughter he married & was my Lodger. — E. Curll." — It is an unauthorized edition.
> Appeared about April 6, 1710 (adv. in *The Post Boy*).
> Though no copy has been discovered, Elr. Ball thinks it probable that the *Broomstick* was in print before Nov. 1708 (*Corresp.* I, 315, n. 3).

Another issue of 1A:

3. Miscellanies / By / Dr. *Jonathan Swift.* / *Viz.* / I. A Meditation upon a Broom-Stick / according to the Style and Manner of / the Honourable Robert Boyle's / Meditations. / II. Baucis and Philemon, Imitated / from the VIII. Book of *Ovid.* / III. To their Excellencies the Lords Justices / of *Ireland,* / — — The Humble Petition of *Frances Harris,* / Who must Starve, and Die a Maid if it miscarries. / IV. To Mrs. Biddy Floyd. / V. The History of Vanbrugh's House. / To all which is prefix'd, / A Complete Key to the Tale of a Tub. / — / *London,* / Printed for E. Curll, at the *Dial and Bible* / against St. *Dunstan*'s *Church* in *Fleetstreet,* 1711. / (Price 1 *s.*)

> [Title within double-lined frame]
> 8vo (in fours); π^2, B–E^4, F^2; the rest as above — 2 pp. (title: Miscellanies + bl.), 2 pp. (To The Reader), 1–28 (Some Annotations And Explanatory Notes Upon The Tale of a Tub), 29–34 (An Examination), 35–6 (Mr. Wotton's Remarks); the rest as above.
> Copy: B.M. 12350 b 16.
> This is a made-up volume, consisting of *A Meditation,* &c., preceded by *A Complete Key,* &c. (No. 1004), of which the title has been cut away and replaced by the title: *Miscellanies,* &c.
> Appeared before May 14, 1711, possibly in April (see *Journal to Stella*).

Another edition of 1A:

1. A / Meditation / Upon A / Broom – – Stick, / And / *Somewhat Beside;* / Of / The Same Author's. / — / – – – – – *Utile dulci.* / — / *London,* / Printed for E. Curll at the *Dial* and *Bible* / against St. *Dunstan*'s Church in *Fleet-* / *street,* 1710. / (Price 2 *d.*)

8vo; A⁸ — 2 pp. (t. + *Advertisement* on verso), [3]–4 (Meditation), 5–10 (Baucis and Philemon), 11–14 (To Their Excellancies, &c. The Humble Petition of Frances Harris), 14 (To Mrs Biddy Floyd), 15–16 (The History Of Vanbrugh's House).

The Humble Petition, &c. is in smaller type than the other pieces, which may be an indication that this 2 *d.* edition came after the 6 *d.* one.

Copy: Penn. — There are also copies in Forster (8937–19 D 18) and in the B.M. (239 i 7), but both are incomplete; the former lacking pp. 15–16, the latter pp. [1]–4. The B.M. copy is included in a collection of separately paged pamphlets, bound together and provided with a new general title-page, as follows:

A / Collection / Of Original / Poems, / Translations, and Imitations, / By / Mr. Prior, Mr. Rowe, Dr. Swift, / And other Eminent Hands. / — / [ornament] / — / *London:* / Printed for E. Curll, at the *Dial and Bible* / against St. *Dunstan*'s Church in *Fleet-street,* 1714. / (Price Five Shillings.)

Another edition or issue of 1A:

1B. A / Complete Key / To The / *Tale* of a *Tub:* / With some Account of the / Authors, / The Occasion and Design of Writing it, / and Mr. *Wotton*'s Remarks Examined. / — / The Second Edition, Corrected. / — / To which are added the Following / Miscellanies, / *Viz.* / I. A Meditation upon a *Broomstick* accord- / ing to the Stile and Manner of the Ho- / nourable *Robert Boyle*'s Meditations. / II. *Baucis* and *Philemon,* Imitated from the / VIIIth Book of *Ovid.* / III. The Humble Petition of *Frances Harris,* / Who must Starve, and Die a Maid, if it miscarries. / IV. To Mrs. *Biddy Floyd.* / V. The History of *Vanbrugh*'s House. / — / *London,* Printed for *E. Curll,* at the *Dial* and / *Bible* against St. *Dunstan*'s Church in *Fleetstreet.* 1713. / (Price Sixpence.)

8vo (in fours); [B]–D⁴ — 2 pp. [t. + To The Reader, on verso), [1]–21, [22].
Copy: Forster 8937–19 D 18. Incomplete; contains only *A Complete Key,* &c.; unfortunately the *Miscellanies* are lacking.
'The Second Edition, Corrected.' apparently refers to 'A Complete Key' only, and the 'Miscellanies' may be a re-issue of the edition recorded under (2).

***

16. A / Second Collection / Of / Miscellanies. / — / Written by Jonathan Swift, D.D. / — / [ornament] / — / *London:* / Printed for J. Roberts, near the *Oxford-Arms* / in *Warwick-Lane.* mdccxx.

8vo (in fours); π²; A–G⁴; π⁴, B–D⁴; A², B–D⁴, E²; π², a⁴, B–C⁴, D²; π², B–M⁴, N², B–C⁴, D², A⁴, A⁴ — 2 pp. (h.t. + bl.), 2 pp. (f.t. + bl.); 2 pp.

(title: 'Art of Punning, 2nd ed.' + bl.), 3 pp. (Dedication to Sir John Scrub), 4 pp. (verse), 1 p. (addendum to preface), I–XIII (Preface), 1 p. blank, 1–27, 4 pp. (another Preface), 1 p. blank; 2 pp. (h.t. 'The Right of Precedence, 2nd ed.' + letter concerning authorship on verso), 2 pp. (f.t. + bl.), 5–32; 2 pp. (title: 'A Defence of English Commodities' + bl.), 2 pp. (Preface), 1–28; 2 pp. (h.t. 'The Swearer's Bank' + bl.), 2 pp. (f.t. + bl.), [I]–VIII (Dedication, entitled: 'Essay on Bubbles', 1–15 (advs. on verso), 17–19 + bl.; 2 pp. (title: 'Letters, Poems, Tales' + bl.), 2 pp. (Contents), [1]–92, [1]–19 (advs. on verso), 8 pp. advs., 8 pp. advs.

This is a made-up volume (only h.t. and f.t. in front being new), consisting of the pieces mentioned. It is an unauthorized edition. The fifth pamphlet is itself a made-up volume (see sep. works, 1718). Only 'A Decree &c.' (No. 610) is genuine; the rest is doubtful (see Nos. 895, 899, 614, 615–17, 610). Cf. Case, No. 316.

Copy: Yale.

Fourth edition:
19. Miscellanies, / Written / By Jonathan Swift, D.D. / Dean of St. *Patrick*'s, *Dublin*. / *Viz*. / I. The Art of Punning. / II. The Right of Precedence. / III. Advice to a Young Poet. / IV. The Swearer's Bank. / V. A Defence of *English-Commodities*. / VI. An Imitation of Horace. / VII. Letters, Poems, Tales, &c. / — / The Fourth Edition. / — / *London:* / Printed in the Year M.DCC.XXII. / Price 2 *s*. 6 *d*.

[Title within double-lined frame.]
12mo; π^4, [A]–I^{12}, K^8 — 2 pp. (frontisp. portrait of Swift), 2 pp. (t. + bl.), 3 pp. (Contents), 1 p. (advs.), [I]–XXVII + bl., 1–204.
'A Decree &c.' (No. 610), 'Epilogue to a Play for the Weavers' (No. 625), 'An Elegy on Demar' (No. 611), and 'An Imitation of Horace' (No. 757), all included in the 'Letters, Poems, Tales, &c.', are genuine; the rest is doubtful.

Some copies contain, at the beginning (after the 6 pp. of prefatory matter) or at the end (after p. 204), two pieces that do not belong to this volume, namely: *The Benefit Of Farting* and *The Wonderful Wonder Of Wonders*, both separately paged. See No. 906.

19A. *Fifth edition:*
Miscellanies, / Written / By *Jonathan Swift*, D.D. / Dean of St. Patrick's, *Dublin*. / *Viz*. / I. The Art of Punning. / II. The Right of Precedence. / III. Advice to a Young Poet. / IV. The Swearer's Bank. / V. The Benefit of Farting. / VI. The Wonder of Wonders. / VII. An Imitation of Horace. / — / The Fifth Edition. / = / *London:* / Printed in the Year 1736.

12mo; π^1, A–F^{12}, G^{10} — 2 pp. (t. + bl.), [I]–XXI, one page unnumbered, [23]–164. — Frontisp. (Swift). This book was also used to form the second part of:

Mr. *Pope*'s / *Literary Correspondence*. / — / Volume the Third. / / — / With Letters *To*, and *From*, / [*First column:*] *The Duke of*

Shrewsberry, / *Lord* Lansdowne, / *Bishop of* St. Asaph, / *Sir* Berkeley Lucy, / [*Second column:*] *Dean* Swift, / *Lady* Chudleigh, / *Mrs.* Manley, / *Mrs.* Thomas, *&c.* / — / The Second Edition. / — / [monogram] / = / *London:* / Printed for E. Curll, at *Pope*'s *Head*, in / *Rose-Street, Covent-Garden.* M.DCC.XXXV.

12mo; A⁶, B–E¹², F⁶ — 2 pp. (frontisp. Pope), 2 pp. (t. + bl.), [V]–XII (To the Subscribers, etc.), [I]–86, 2 pp. (plate: 'Landsdowne' + bl.), [89]–107, one page unnumbered [the rest as above].

Contrary to the mention in the title, there are no letters to or from Swift in it.

Copy: Penn; cf. Griffith, No. 404.

57. In 1737–38–39 Johann Andreas Rüdigern published at 'Berlin und Leipzig' three volumes entitled:

Eine / Sammlung / allerhand auserlesener / Moralischer und Satyrischer / Meister-Stücke, / Aus dem Englischen übersetzt. / Erste Probe. / — — — — —

— — — — — / Andere Probe. / — — — —

— — — — — / Die Dritte Probe, / — — — —

The title of the first volume is in red and black, those of the other two in black only.

The first volume has a frontisp. portrait of Swift, properly belonging to the second; the third volume has one of Addison. Some of the nine pieces contained in the second volume are translations of pieces by Swift taken from the *Miscellanies*, 5th ed., 1736 (see No. 19, *ante*).

Title of the second volume:

Eine / Sammlung / allerhand auserlesener / Moralischer und Satyrischer / Meister-Stücke, / Aus dem Englischen übersetzt, / Andere Probe. / 1. Ars Pun-ica: sive Flos Linguarum. Die Kunst der Wort- / Spiele &c. in 79. Regeln gezeiget, von dem berühmten Swift. / 2. Das Recht des Vor-Rangs zwischen den Medicis u. Rechts- / Gelehrten unparteyisch entschieden von eben demselben. / 3. Wohlgemeinter Rath an einen jungen Poeten &c. von eben / demselben / 4. Die Schwörers-Banco &c. von eben demselben. / 5. Die Wohlthat des Fa - ns erkläret, oder die funda- / ment-all Ursache der Kranckheiten, denen das schöne Ge- / schlecht so sehr unterworffen &c. a Posteriori bewiesen &c. von / eben demselben. / 6. Das wundervolle Wunder der Wunder, als eine genaue / Beschreibung der Geburt, Auferziehung, Lebens, Art, Reli- / gion, Staats-Kunst, Gelehrsamkeit &c. meines A - - es von / eben demselben. / 7. Ein Paar Dutzend wohlgetroffene Characters, oder sinn- / reiche Schildereyen &c. eines Anonymi. / 8. Convivium Sybariticum, oder, des Trimalchio Fest, eine / Nachahmung Titi Petronii Arbiters, von Addison. / 9. Mahomet

Alis erdichteter Traum, wodurch er den schwel- / gerischen
Scham Abbas bekehret, von Littleton. / Aufgeweckten Gemûthern
beyderley Ge- / schlechts statt eines Nach-Confects bey Tisch /
aufgesetzt. / — / Berlin und Leipzig, / Bey Johann Andres Rûdigern,
1738.

Sm. 8vo; A⁷, B–U⁸, X⁴ — 2 pp. (t. + bl.), 2 pp. (title: Ars Punica + quotation on verso), 2 pp. (title: Dedication + bl.), 6 pp. (Dedication), [15]–328.
Copy: Penn.

*
* *

24. *Miscellanea.* / In / Two Volumes. / — / *Never before
Published.* / — / *Viz.* / I. *Familiar Letters* written to Henry / Cromwell *Esq*; by Mr. Pope. / II. Occasional Poems by Mr. Pope, /
Mr. Cromwell, Dean Swift, *&c.* / III. Letters from Mr. Dryden, to /
a Lady, in the Year 1699. / — / Volume I. / — / *London:* / Printed
in the Year, 1727. / Price 5 *s.*

12mo; A–P⁶ — 2 pp. (frontisp. portrait of Pope), 2 pp. (t. + bl.), 2 pp.
(To *Henry Cromwell*, Esq;), 3 pp. (To The Editor), 3 pp. (The Preface),
[1]–155, 3 pp. (*Explanation* + *Errata*), 6 pp. (The Table), 4 pp. (advs.).
Contains (pp. 88–119): *Cadenus* and *Vanessa*, A Law Case. *By* Dean Swift.

Miscellanea. / The Second Volume. / I. An Essay upon Gibing. /
With a Project for its Improvement. / II. The Praise of Women. /
Done out of *French.* / III. An Essay on the *Mischief* / of giving
Fortunes with *Women* in / Marriage. / IV. *Swifteana:* Or / Poems
by Dean Swift, and seve- / ral of his Friends. / V. *Laus Ululæ.* The
Praise of / Owls. Translated from the *Latin,* / By a *Canary* Bird.
/ — / [ornament] / — / *London:* / Printed in the Year, 1727.

12mo: π⁴, B–I⁶, K²; π¹, A², 2B–I⁶, 2K³ — 2 pp. (frontisp. portrait of
Swift), 2 pp. (t. + bl.), 2 pp. (To Mr. *Alexander Pope*), 2 pp. (title Essay on
Gibing + bl.), [1]–99 + bl.; 2 pp. (title Laus Ululae + vignette on verso),
[I]–IV (To The Jocund Reader), I–II (Preface), [3]–101 + bl.
The two volumes were published early in June 1726.
For 'Cadenus and Vanessa' see No. 657.
The *Swifteana* cover page, 67–99, contains five pieces ascribed to Swift:
(1) The Broken Mug. A Tale. (2) The Dean's Answer (to: A Rebus on Dean
Swift. By Vanessa). (3) Swift's answer to a Riddle by Dr. Delany. (4) The
Journal. (5) His Grace's Answer to Smedley's Petition to the Duke of
Grafton. — Only No. 1 is doubtful.
The collation of Vol. II, as recorded above, corresponds with the pieces
mentioned on the title-page; but in other copies the place of *Laus Ululae* is
taken by remainder copies of the following pamphlets:

(A) *Court* / Poems. / In / Two Parts. / — / *By Mr.* Pope, *&c.* / — /
[ornament] / — / *London:* / Printed for E. Curll in the *Strand.* 1726.
/ (Price 1 *s.*)

(a) 12mo; π^1, B^{12} (B 2 signed A 2) — 2 pp. (t. + bl.), 2 pp. (Advertisement By the Bookseller. — dated at end: *London*, 1717), 1, 4–24 (no catchword at foot).

(b) 12mo; D^5 — [25]–34.

Note: A (a) is a remainder copy of the first half of:

Court Poems / In Two Parts Compleat. / To which are added, / [2 titles] / — / By Mr. Pope. / — / [ornament] / *London:* / Printed for R. Burleigh, 1719. / Price One Shilling.

12mo; π^1, B^{12} (B 2 signed A 2); B–C^6, π^3 — 2 pp. (t. + bl.), 2 pp. ('Advertisement By the Bookseller,' dated at end: *London*, 1717), 1, 4–24 (no catchword at foot); 1–26, 4 pp. (advs.).

Griffith mentions two variants (Nos. 174, 175) of this book, differing in the placing of the headpieces only:

Variant a (No. 174): B 1 recto (an urn), p. 13 (a bird), p. 17 (scrolls and leaves).

Variant b (No. 175): B 1 recto (a bird), p. 13 (scrolls and leaves), p. 17 (an urn).

Copies:

Variant a: Harvard — Case 295b.

Variant b: Harvard (2 copies) — Case 295c, and Penn (2 copies). It also forms part of *Mr. Pope's Literary Correspondence* (Curll), Vol. IV, 12mo, 1736 (cf. my 56).

This 'Court Poems, R. Burleigh, 1719' must not be confounded with Griffith 180, which has exactly the same title, but is quite different, as appears from the following collation:

12mo (in half-sheets); π^2; A^2, B–C^6; π^1, D 1, B–C^6 — 2 pp., 25–6; 4 pp., 1–22, 2 pp. (advs.); 4 pp., 1–24.

(The first two leaves misbound above, were intended to be folded coverwise about all the others).

It appears to be a re-issue of *Pope's Miscellany*, Second Edition, London, R. Burleigh, 1717 (Griffith No. 90), followed by *Pope's Miscellany*, The Second Part, London, R. Burleigh, 1717 (Griffith No. 89).

(B) Poems On Several Occasions. / By N. Rowe, Esq; / The Third Edition. / London: Printed for E. Curll, at the Dial and / Bible against St. Dunstan's Church in Fleet-street. / MDCCXIV.

(a) 12mo; [A]^{12}, B^6 — 2 pp. (frontisp.), 2 pp. (t. + bl.), 1–32 (*Finis.* at foot).

(b) 12mo; C^5 — 33–42.

I have seen neither the above, nor the first and second editions. The first edition of Rowe's *Poems*, 1714, seems to be: 4to; π^2, [A]–D^4, E^3 — 2 pp. (h.t. + advs.), 2 pp. (The Exceptionable Passages + adv.), 2 pp. (t. + bl.), [3]–37 (advs. on verso). Copy: B.M. 11643 bbb 20 (1).

Possibly the second edition is a 12mo, 1–32, of which the above may be a re-issue, to which pp. 33–42 were added.

Cf. Case's article in *Modern Philology*, XXIV, Feb. 1927, p. 298, and Griffith Add. 35c. Yale has a copy lacking the first two leaves.

(C) Original / Poems / And / *Translations*. / By / *Mr.* Hill, *Mr.* Eusden, *Mr.* / Broome, *Dr.* King, &c. / — / *Never before Printed*.

/ — / [ornament] / *London*, / Printed for E. Curll, at the *Dial* and *Bible* against / St. *Dunstan's* Church in *Fleet-street*. 1714.

12mo; π^1, B–C⁶, D⁵ — 2 pp. (t. + bl.), 1–33 (advs. on verso). Cf. Case's article in *Modern Philology*, XXIV, Feb. 1927, p. 299; Case, *Poet. Misc.*, No. 275; Griffith No. 33.

(B) and (C) were re-issued in 1715, when the frontispiece of (b) was preserved, but the two titles were cancelled, and replaced by the following new one:

The / *Elzivir* Miscellany: / Consisting of Original / Poems, / Translations, and Imitations. / By the most Eminent Hands, / *Viz.* / [*First column:*] *Mr*. Rowe, / *Mr*. Shippen, / *Dr*. King, / *Mr*. Sewell, / [*Second column:*] *Mr*. Hill, / *Mr*. Eusden, / *Mr*. Broome, / *Mr*. Jones. / — / The Second Edition. / — / [ornament] / — / *London*, / Printed for E. Curll, at the *Dial and Bible* against / St. *Dunstan's* Church in *Fleet-street*. 1715. / Price 2 *s*. 6 *d*.

Cf. Griffith, Add. 45c; Case 283b.

Some copies have 'Elzivir' on the title-page, others 'Elzevir'.

Frontispieces, titles, and sections may have been preserved or cancelled; shiftings of them may occur. The result is that all kinds of combinations are met with, some of which follow here:

Copies (in all of them the first part is the same):

Penn: + Laus.
     + A (a + b) + C.
     + A (a) + B (a + b) + C.
Griffith 178: + Laus.
     179: + A (a + b) + B (a) + C.
     180: + A (a) + B (a + b) + C — This is the Grolier Club copy, cat. No. 7. It lacks frontisp. + title *Elzivir*.
B.M.: + Laus.
Bodl.: + Laus.
Yale: + Laus.
     + A (a) + B (a + b) + C. [2 copies. One of them has frontisp. + title *Elzivir* preserved.]
     + A (a) + b) + C.
Harvard: + Laus (2 copies).
     + (all after the first part lacking, but a note says that it once contained *Court Poems*, which was removed and bound separately).
     + A (a + b) + C.
Prof. Boys: + C + B (b).

Ralph Straus, *The Unspeakable Curll*, London, 1927, p. 278, says that *Swifteana* (Vol. II) was also published separately. I have not seen or heard of such a copy, unless it is the one owned by Prof. R. C. Boys, University of Michigan, which appears to be a copy of *Miscellanea*, Vol. II, but with the frontispiece portrait of Swift, followed by the 'Swifteana' title, which is G 4 (pp. [67–68]) and has been removed from its proper place to be placed in front.

The two volumes *Miscellanea* were followed by two volumes *Whartoniana*, and one volume *Atterburyana*, all five dated 1727, and marked as Vol. I (II, III, IV, V) at the foot of the first page of each new sheet. The first of the two volumes *Whartoniana* contains some pieces ascribed to Swift, viz.: one genuine: *An Excellent New Song Archbishop of Dublin* (No. 1153, *post*), and two doubtful: *Ireland's Warning*, and *A Poem Upon R — — r* (No. 652, *post*). Here follows its title:

Whartoniana: / Or, / Miscellanies, / In / *Verse* and *Prose*. / By The / *Wharton* Family, / And / Several other Persons of *Distinction*. / — / *Never before Published*. / — / Volume I. / — / *London:* / Printed in the Year, 1727. / (Price 5 *s*.)

12mo; frontisp. portrait of Wharton, 2 pp., I–VII (advs. on verso), 1–185, 3 pp. *Contents*.

The two volumes *Whartoniana* were re-issued, with a *Life* of Wharton, and a new title: *The Poetical Works of Philip Late Duke of Wharton*; &c. *London: Printed for William Warner* (n.d.).

The B.M. Catalogue says: 1731?

They were again re-issued: *The Works of Philip Late Duke of Wharton*; &c. *The Third Edition, London, F. Noble and J. Duncan*, 1740.

Cf. Case, Nos. 347(1)a and (2)a, 347(1)b and (2)b, 347(1)c and (2)c.

A bookseller's catalogue says: *The Life And Writings Of Philip Late Duke of Wharton. Booksellers of London and Westminster. 1732.* — 2 vols. 8vo. — frontisp. portrait of Wharton by C. Jervis, engr. by G. Vertue.

* *

38A. The / Drapier's *Miscellany*, / In / Verse and Prose. / Consisting / Of several scarce Pieces of that cele- / brated *Author*; none of which / were ever in any Collection before. / [*First column:*] I. A modest Proposal for / preventing the Children / of poor People from be- / ing a Burthen to their / Parents, &c. / II. The Journal of a *Dub-* / *lin* Lady. A Poem. / III. A Poem to his present / Majesty King George, / in *Lilliputian* Verse. / IV. Namby Pamby. A / Poem. / [*Second column:*] V. A faithful Inventory of / the Houshold [*sic*] Goods of / D—S—T, lent / to the Bishop of M— / VI. An Elegy on the much / lamented Death of Mr. / Demar. / VII. A Letter written in / Behalf of the Parishion- / ers to a Minister, who / used several hard Words / in his Sermon. / — / [ornament]; / — / *Dublin:* / Printed by and for James Hoey, at the *Pamphlet-* / *Shop* in *Skinner-Row*, opposite to the *Tholsel*.

Sm. 8vo (in fours); [A]–E⁴ — 2 pp. (t. + bl.), 3–40.

Contains (on pp. 36–40) an eighth item, not mentioned on the t.p.: *An Elegy on the much lamented Death of Matthew Buckinger*.

Copies: Texas; R.I.A. (Hal. Tracts, Box 187, Tract 8).

Pieces I, II, VI are by Swift.

Scott, *Works* I, 401 n., 414 n. refers to this *Miscellany*. From the fact that Scott's quotation of Piece VII differs much from the text of that piece in the above *Miscellany*, Harold Williams concludes that there may have been another edition, which cannot have been the following (see the title).

Another edition:

38. The / Drapier's *Miscellany*. / Consisting / Of several scarce Pieces of that cele- / brated *Author;* some of which / were never in any Collection before. / [*First column:*] I. A Prologue spoke by / Mr. *Elrington* at the *The-* / *atre-Royal* in behalf of the / *Weavers*. / II. An Epilogue to a / Play for the Benefit of / the *Weavers* in *Ireland*. / III. The Journal of a *Dub-* / *lin* Lady. A. Poem. / IV. A Poem to his present / Majesty King George, / in *Lilliputian* Verse. / V. Namby Pamby. A / Poem. / VI. A faithful Inventory of / [*Second column:*] the Houshold Goods of / D—S—T, lent / to the Bishop of *M* — — — — — / VII. An Elegy on the much / lamented Death of Mr. / Demer. / VIII. An Elegy on the / much lamented Death of / Matthew Buck- / inger, the famous Lit- / tle Man, (without Arms / or Legs. / IX. A Libel on D – – – D – – – – / and a certain great Lord. / — / [ornament] / — / *Dublin:* / Printed by and for James Hoey, at the *Pamphlet-* / *Shop* in *Skinner-Row*, opposite to the *Tholsel*, 1733.

12mo (in fours and twos alternately); [A]–G⁴ — 2 pp. (t. + bl.), [3]–5 (Prologue), 6–8 (Epilogue), 8–19 (Journal Dublin Lady), 20 (Poem), 21–4 (Namby Pamby), 25–6 (Inventory), 26–8 (Elegy Demer + Epitaph), 29–33 (Elegy Buckinger + Epitaph), 34–8 (Libel), 2 pp. advs. (the advs. start in the middle of p. 38).
    Copy: B.M. C 71 bb 15.4 (lacks the last leaf).
    Pieces II, III, VII, IX are by Swift.

⁎⁎⁎

55A. Poems / On / Several Occasions. / — / By J.S, D.D, D.S.P.D. / — / [monogram] / = / *Dublin:* / Printed by and for George Faulkner, / Printer and Bookseller, in *Essex-street*, / opposite to the Bridge, M.DCC.XXXV.

This is a separate issue of the *Works*, Vol. II, 12mo in sixes, 1735 (see No. 49), from which the volume-title title has been cut away and replaced by the above title. The volume-indication at the foot of the first page of each sheet is still present.
    Copy: own.

55. The Poetical / Works, / Of / *J.S.D.D.D.S.P.D.* / Consisting Of / Curious Miscellaneous Pieces, both / Humourous and Sa- tyrical. / = / Reprinted from the Second *Dublin* Edition, with / Notes and Additions. / = / *Quivis Speret idem.* Hor. / = / [orna- ment] / = / Printed in the Year. / — / MDCCXXXVI.

12mo; frontisp., [A]⁴, B–N¹², O⁸ — frontisp. (Swift in medallion), 2 pp. (t. + bl.), 3 pp. (Advertisement), 3 pp. (Contents), 1–304.
    Copy: Penn.
    This volume seems to be a pirated reprint of Faulkner's Vol. II, 12mo (No. 49). As the title says, there are more notes than in Faulkner's edition,

and two pieces added: 'Verses by Dr. Delany', and its answer: 'Verses by Dr. S—.'

55B. Poems / On / Several Occasions. / — / By J.S., D.D., D.S.P.D. / — / [monogram] / = / *Dublin:* / Printed by and for George Faulkner, / Printer and Bookseller, in *Essex-street*, opposite to the Bridge, M.DCC.XXXVII.

This is a separate issue of the *Works*, Vol. II, 8vo, 1737 (see No. 42), from which the volume-title has been cut away and replaced by the above title.

Copy: Mr. P. S. O'Hegarty, Dublin.

Letters, 1736–37

56. New / Letters / Of / Mr *Alexander Pope,* / And Several of his Friends. / — / Vellem Nescire Litteras! / *Cum desiderio Veteres, Revocamus Amores; / atque olim missas, flemus Amicitias.* / — / [ornament] / — / *London:* / Printed, *Anno Reformationis,* 1737.

8vo; π^2, B–E^8, F^2 — 2 pp. (t. + bl.), [I]–II (*To My Subscribers encore.*), [1]–66, 2 pp. (Curll's advs.). — Portrait of Bolingbroke between pp. 16–17.

Contains (pp. 1–7, 8–15) two letters: Pope to Swift, Aug. 1723, and Bolingbroke to Swift, undated, postscript to the former and here printed as a separate letter. Though the year in the imprint is 1737, the book appeared Nov. 1736 (cf. Griffith, No. 429).

Probably secretly handed to the press by Pope to suggest that the letters in Swift's hands were not safe, and thus create for himself a pretext for a genuine edition of his own.

Cf. *Corresp.* VI, 202.

This book was incorporated (same printing) into:

Mr Pope's / *Literary Correspondence.* / — / Volume the Fifth. / — / With Letters of / [*First column:*] Lord Bolingbroke. / Lord Lansdowne. / Sir Samuel Garth. / [*Second column:*] Mrs Eliza Justice. / William Bromley, Esq; / Pieces of Mr. Walsh. / [monogram] / *London:* / Printed for E. Curll, at *Pope's* Head, in *Rose-Street* / *Covent-Garden.* M.DCC.XXXVII.

8vo; π^1 (this is R 1); π^2, π^1 (this is the first F 2), B–E^8, F 1; F–Q^8, R 2–8, π^8 — 2 pp. (title: Mr. Pope's Literary Correspondence + bl.); 2 pp. (title: New Letters + bl.), [I]–II (*To My Subscribers encore.*), 2 pp. (Curll's advs.), [1]–66; [65]–250, [251], 252 (misprinted 242), 2 pp. (*Advertisement*), 1–16 (Curll's advs.), — Portrait of Bolingbroke between pp. 16–17. Published June 1737.

This is the B.M. copy (12274 i 12); it contains, besides the two letters mentioned before, three more: Swift to Pope, Sept. 20, 1723, Pope to Swift, Dec. 10, 1725, and Swift to Peterborow, undated (Elr. Ball, *Corresp.* IV, 466 dates it [1733]).

Griffith No. 462 is the same book, *without* the title 'New Letters, &c.', the 2 pp. Curll's advs., the 2 pp. *Advertisement* and the 16 pp. Curll's advs.; but *with* a frontisp. portrait of Swift. Moreover it has Walsh's *Works* added at the end: π^4, A–B^8, C^7, D–E^8, F^6, G^4 — 8 pp., [I]–XII, [1]–86.

56A. *Another edition,* a reprint of part of the preceding book:

Letters / From / Alexander Pope, Esq; / And the Right Hon. the / Lord Bolingbroke, / To the Reverend / Dr. Swift, D.S.P.D. / To which is added / Almahide, / A / Poem / By The / Lord Bolingbroke. / = / London: Printed. / Dublin: Reprinted by and for George / Faulkner, Bookseller in Essex-street, / M.DCC.XXXVII.

Sm. 8vo; A⁸, B⁴ — [1]–22, Blank leaf.
[Title and collation taken from Griffith, No. 453.]

56B. *Another edition:*

Letters / Of / Mr. Alexander Pope, / And Several of his Friends. / [Vignette: portrait, head of Pope] / London: / Printed by J. Wright for J. Knapton in Ludgate-street, / L. Gilliver in Fleet-street, J. Brindley in New Bond- / street, and R. Dodsley in Pall-mall, MDCCXXXVII.

[Title in red and black.]
4to; π⁴, b–d⁴, e², B–Dd⁴, *Dd⁴ inserted between Dd³ and Dd⁴, Ee–Ss⁴, Tt² — 36 pp., [9]–222, 215–332.
[Title and collation taken from Griffith, No. 454. For a variant of this 4to, for the L. P. folio, and the Sm. folio, see Griffith, Nos. 455, 456, 457 — all May 19, 1737.]
Contains (pp. 322–32) four letters: Pope to Swift, Aug. 1723; its postscript Bolingbroke to Swift, undated; Swift to Pope, Sept. 20, 1723; and Pope to Swift, Dec. 10, 1725. The letter Swift to Peterborow, undated, is not in it.
There is a note at the top of p. 322, reading:
"P.S. Since the foregoing Sheets were printed off, the following Letters having been published without the Consent of their Writers, we have added them, tho' not in the order of time."
Griffith 457 remarks: "Thus the four letters purported to be reprinted from Curll's *Literary Correspondence* series" (see No. 56, above).

56C. *Another edition:*

The / Works / Of / Alexander Pope, Esq; / — / Vol. VI. / Containing the Remainder of / His Letters. / — / [ornament] / — / London: / Printed for J. Roberts in Warwick lane. / MDCCXXXVII.

[Title in black and red.]
Sm. 8vo; π¹, B–H⁸, I 1–2, *I 3–5 (this half-sheet inserted between I 2 and I 3), I 3–8, K–T⁸, U⁴, X⁶ — 2 pp. (t. + bl.), [1]–116, 117–24 (misprinted 217–24 = *I 3–6), [117]–308. — Contains the above five letters. Published, together with Vol. V, June 17, 1737.
This is Griffith 461.

Letters, 1741

In 1736–7 only a few letters to and from Swift had been published (see Nos. 56, 56a, 56b). In 1741 appeared several more. The mystery surrounding their publication was discovered by Dilke (*The Papers Of A Critic*, 1875, Vol. I, *passim.*), and retold at great length by Elwin (*The Works of Alexander Pope*, Vols. I, VII, VIII). See also *Corresp.*, VI, 156–76, 197–202, and

Appendix I; Griffith, Nos. 519, 529, 530, 531, 532, 533, 534. The facts are briefly as follows:

After some vain attempts Pope, through Orrery, had at last (July 1737 — see *Corresp*. VI, 39) succeeded in recovering from Swift the letters he had for many years written to Swift. Three years later, about May–July 1740, Swift received "a printed volume, without title-page, preface, or other introduction, containing the version of the correspondence between Pope, Gay, Boling-broke, and himself"; together with an unsigned letter stating that this volume was submitted to him for inspection, and was not to be published without his approbation. Soon after (July 1740), Swift, no doubt recognizing Pope's hand in this secret business, gave Faulkner leave to reprint these letters for publication in Dublin, from the mysterious copy received. On July 29, 1740, Faulkner informed Pope of this permission (Elwin, *op. cit.*, VIII, 416–17), and while Pope, for his own purposes, was delaying his answer to this news, Faulkner began to set up his type (this must have been his 8vo edition — see note under No. 64); but after he had only finished the first two sheets and after a correspondence with Pope and Orrery extending over several months and revealing Pope's opposition to the plan, he stopped and withheld his edition until Pope's own quarto and folio editions, which were then in course of preparation, should have been published in London. They appeared in the middle of April 1741 (*The Works Of Mr. Alexander Pope, In Prose, Vol. II.*); but before that date, early in 1741, Pope had caused the clandestine volume to be published (see third state, below), in order to suggest that its appearance had compelled him to publish his own authorized editions. Soon after, Curll entered the lists. His *Dean Swift's Correspondence, &c.*, must have appeared about May–June 1741, for on June 4 Pope filed a bill against Curll for piratically publishing the letters. And a few weeks later two Dublin editions were announced in the *Dublin News Letter*: the so-called Exshaw volume was advertised in the issue of June 16, 1741, and Faulkner's *Letters*, 8vo, in that of June 20, 1741. [Dilke, *op. cit.*, I, 328, quotes the two advertisements, and Griffith, Nos. 532, 533, quotes from Dilke; but Griffith applies the second advertisement to Faulkner's 12mo, whereas it clearly refers to Faulkner's 8vo, not recorded by Griffith.] Faulkner's *Letters*, 12mo, must have appeared still later. And finally, probably late in 1741, though no advertisement concerning the book has been found earlier than the end of June 1742 (see Griffith, No. 560), the clandestine volume was re-issued as Vol. VII of the sm. 8vo edition of *The Works of Alexander Pope, 1741*.

After this, these 'Swift' Letters, to which later on more were added, were regularly reprinted in the collected works of Swift, and in those of Pope.

Here follow the several editions in the order of their publication:

1580. *First state.*
[*Caption-title* on page [1]]:
= / Letters / To and From / Dr. *Jonathan Swift*, &c. / From the Year 1714 to 1737. / —.

Sm. 8vo; B–O⁸ — [1]–208. — No prefatory matter.
This must have been the original printing, of which, however, no copy has been found. Probably none has survived.

1581. *Second state.*
[*Caption-title* on page [1]]:
= / Letters / To and From / Dr. *Jonathan Swift*, &c. / From the Year 1714 to 1737. / —

Sm. 8vo; B 1–3, *B⁸ (replacing B 4–5), B 6–8, C–O⁸ — [1]–6, 7–22, 11–16, 17–208. — No prefatory matter.

Copy: Harvard (last leaf lacking).

The 'clandestine' volume must have been one of this description. Pope, pretending ignorance, had asked for a sight of it, and when it had been sent him for inspection, he wrote to Orrery on Dec. 27, 1740 (see Elwin and Courthope VIII, 466) about its "interpolated halfsheets and quartersheets", and "asterisks". These words must refer to sheet *B (see Note 1, below). When Pope had returned it to Orrery, the latter told him on Jan. 12, 1741 (see Elwin and Courthope VIII, 496) that "of the printed [i.e. the clandestine] volume there came only from page 23", which cannot refer to page 23 (C 4), but must refer to B 6–8, whose pagination had apparently been altered by Pope from 11–16 into something like 23, 24, 25, 26, 27, 16, probably in ink. Leaves B 1–3 and sheet *B had evidently been kept by Pope.

60. *Third state.*

Letters / Between / Dr. *Swift*, Mr. *Pope*, &c. / — / From the Year 1714 to 1736. / — / Publish'd from a Copy Transmit- / ted from *Dublin*. / = / *London:* / Printed for T. Cooper, in the Year / Mdccxli.

Sm. 8vo; π², B 1–3, *B⁸ (replacing B 4–5) [B 6–8 lacking], C–O⁸ — 2 pp. (t. + bl.), 2 pp. (To the Reader + bl.), [1]–6, 7–22 (replacing 7–10), [11]–16 lacking], 17–208. — With prefatory matter.

Published early in 1741.

Copies: Yale, and Penn.

It is hard to account for the absence of B 6–8, unless owing to carelessness of someone in the printing-house.

Fourth state.

Re-issued (see No. 64A).

Copy: Harvard.

Notes:

(1) Sheet *B⁸ (replacing B 4–5) reprints the last two lines of Letter III, and Letter IV entire; it takes up as *a new element* the long letter (numbered V) of Jan. 10, 1721, from Swift to Pope, of which Pope wrote to Orrery on Oct. 17, 1740 (Elwin, VIII, 432) that he could swear he had never received it from Swift (which may be literally true, though it need not mean that he had not acquired it in time for insertion into the 'clandestine' volume); and it *reprints* the first part (26 lines) of the original Letter V. After this the three leaves B 6–8 regularly continue the second part of the original Letter V, Letter VI entire, and the first part (23 lines) of Letter VII.

(2) In the first state there must have been 81 letters, in the second and following there are 82 letters, two of them numbered V.

(3) For a fuller discussion see two articles in *The Library*, March 1939, 465–85, and June–Sept. 1943, 74–86, by Prof. Maynard Mack (The First Printing Of The Letters Of Pope And Swift), and Mr. Vinton A. Dearing (New Light On The First Printing Of The Letters Of Pope And Swift). Also see *The Correspondence of Alexander Pope*, edited by George Sherburn, I, xi–xxv.

60A. The / Works / Of / Mr. *Alexander Pope*, / In Prose. / — / Vol. II. / — / [vignette portrait of Pope] / *London:* / Printed for J. and P. Knapton, C. Bathurst, and / R. Dodsley, M.DCC.XLI.

Large folio; A–B², c–d²; A–X², *Y–*Z², *Aa–*Dd², Y–Z², Aa–Ss², Tt 1, Uu–Xx²; Ffff–Iiii²; π², B–T²; Ggg–Ttt², Uuu 1 (first leaf of this sheet), *Uuu–*Xxx²; *Bb–*Cc²; π¹, Aaaa–*Ffff²; Uuu 2 (second leaf of this sheet), Xxx–Zzz², Aaa²—2 pp. (h.t. + bl.), 2 pp. (f.t. + bl.), [V]–VI (The Booksellers to the Reader); 10 pp. (title: Letters + Contents), [1]–108, 85–173 + bl. (Letters); 2 pp. (title), [299]–312 (Thoughts On Various Subjects); 2 pp. (title: Tracts Of Martinus Scriblerus And Other Miscellaneous Pieces + Directions to Binder, on verso), 2 pp. (The Booksellers To The Reader + bl.), [1]–70, 2 pp. (Contents of Martinus Scriblerus); [187]–248 (Art Of Sinking); [259]–266 (Memoirs of P. P. Clerk of this Parish); [255]–280 (Guardians); [241]–257 + bl. (Key to the Lock). Published Apr. 16, 1741.

This is the B.M. copy (834 bb 4). Sm. folio and quarto copies were issued about the same time, largely from the same type (see Griffith, Nos. 529–31).

At the beginning of the *Contents* there is this note: "N.B. Those letters which have an Asterisk * prefixed, are added in this, and not in the Dublin Edition". The starred letters, all from Swift to Pope, are Nos. 61, 63, 66, 77, 87, and 88. The last two had been written since the bulk had been sent in July 1737; the other four are of earlier date, and had no doubt been found by Pope since.

Contains Letters 1–89; letter 89 (Orrery to Pope, Oct. 4, 1738) not listed in the Contents.

Passages marked with commas occur in Letters 75, 77, 81, 84, 86, 87, 88.

61. Dean *Swift's* / *Literary Correspondence*, / For Twenty-four Years; from 1714 to 1738. / Consisting of Original Letters *To* and *From* / [*First column:*] Mr. Pope, / Dr. Swift, / Mr. Gay, / Lord Bolingbroke, / [*Second column:*] Dr. Arbuthnot, / Dr. Wotton, / Bishop Atterbury, / D. & Dss. of Queensbury. / [monogram] / *London:* / Printed for E. Curll, at *Pope's-Head*, in *Rose-* / *Street*, *Covent-Garden*. M.DCC.XLI. / Price 4 *s.* Sewed, 5 *s.* Bound.

8vo; π², A–T⁸, U–X⁴ — 2 pp. (t. + bl.), 2 pp. (Preface By The Editor), [1]–228 'Letters'), [229]–284 (History of the Deluge [by Arbuthnot, 1697]), 285–307 (Classical Remarks Atterbury to Dr. Freind), [308]–310 (Letter Crichton to Curll), [1]–6 (book advs.), 4 pp. (book advs.). — Frontisp. portrait of Swift.

    Copy: B.M. 12274 i 1.

    Published ca. June 1, 1741.

    Contains letters, including the six "starred" ones.

Griffith No. 532 says they "are a reprint of the Dublin edition, with some omissions of parts previously published". With Dilke I think it more probable that Curll reprinted from Pope's quarto, though the 'Preface By The Editor' would suggest that he had the disposal of a Faulkner copy in its original state, before publication, as well. There are 'Notes and Translations' in Faulkner, not in Cooper. Curll has even more than Faulkner.

62. Letters To and From the Rev. Dr. Swift, D.S.P.D., From The Year 1714 To 1738. To which are added several Notes and Translations not in the London Edition. Dublin: For Ed. Exshaw.

The above title partly derived from Dilke I, 328, and Griffith, No. 532, partly from a copy of the 1746 re-issue (see below). — "There can be no doubt", says Dilke, "that this Exshaw edition was printed by Faulkner."
Contains letters 1–81 (2x Letter V), 82–8 (inferred from the 1746 re-issue).
Published June 15, 1741 (see Dilke I, 328).
Cf. No. 51, and see note under No. 64.

62A. *Re-issued, with a new title-page:*
Letters / To and From / Dr. J. Swift, D.S.P.D. / From The / Year 1714, to 1738. / To which are added, / Several Notes and Transla- / tions not in the *London* Edition. / = / *Dublin:* / Printed by and for George Faulkner, / M,DCC,XLVI.

12mo; [A]⁴, B–T⁶, U² — 2 pp. (t. + bl.), 6 pp. (Contents), [1]–182 (Letters), 183–97 (Supplement), 198–220 (Some Free Thoughts). — Chain-lines of t.p. vertical, of the rest of the book horizontal.
Copy: Nat. Libr. of Ireland, Dublin (see No. 51, *ante*).
Copies of both issues were owned (or seen) by Charles Wentworth Dilke (*The Papers Of A Critic*, London, 1875, I, 328), but since Dilke's time no copy of the Exshaw edition can be traced. Contains letters 1–81 (2x letter 5), 82–8 (letter 88: Orrery to Pope, Oct. 4, 1738, not mentioned in the Contents).

62B. Letters / To and From / Dr. J. Swift, D.S.P.D. / From The / Year 1714, to 1738. / To which are added, / Several Notes and Translations / not in the *London* Edition. / = / *Dublin:* / Printed by and for George Faulkner, / MDCCXLI.

8vo; π⁸, B–S⁸, T⁴; U⁸, X²; 2U–X⁸, 2C² — 2 pp. (advs.), 2 pp. (t. + bl.), 11 pp. + bl. (*Contents*), [1]–280 (*Finis.* at foot); 281–300 (*Supplement — Finis.* at foot); 2 pp. (title *Some Free Thoughts* + bl.), 2 pp. (*Advertisement to the Reader* + bl.), 1–32 (*Finis.* at foot).
Contains letters 1–81 (2x Letter V), 82–8.
Published June 20, 1741 (but printed earlier).
Re-issued in 1746 (see No. 44), with one letter added (leaf *T = pp. 301–2): Swift to Pope, April 28, 1739.
Cf. No. 44, and see note under No. 64.

64. Letters / To and From / Dr. J. Swift, D.S.P.D. / From The / Year 1714, to 1738. / = / [monogram] / = / *Dublin*; / Printed by and for George Faulkner, / — / MDCCXLI.

12mo; π⁶, B–L¹²; M¹², N 1–2; N 3–6, O⁶, P⁴ — 2 pp. (advs.), 2 pp. (t. + bl.), 8 pp. (Contents), [1]–240 (*Finis.* at foot); 241–56 (*Supplement — Finis.* at foot); 2 pp. (title *Some Free Thoughts* + bl.), 2 pp. (*Advertisement to the Reader* + bl.), 1–22 (*Finis.* at foot), 2 pp. blank.
Contains letters 1–81 (2x Letter VII), 83–9 (no letter 82).
Published later than June 20, 1741.
Copy: Penn.
Cf. No. 51, and see note below.

Note: As regards the last three editions, Faulkner's 8vo must have been printed first. This is proved by its composition. It consists of four units. First, pp. 1–280 (B–S⁸, T⁴), containing Letters I–LXXXI, were printed. [A copy of these sheets was once in the possession of Orrery (given to him by Faulkner), who wrote some MS. notes on the inside of the front cover and on the first page of the text (see Dilke, *Papers Of A Critic*, I, 326–7 note). Afterwards, in 1860, a Mr. James Pink, of Bristol, owned it, but it cannot now be found. — Curll may have had another copy of the original sheets (see No. 61).] Next, 4 pp., 1–32 (U–X⁸, C²), bearing 'Some Free Thoughts', were added, as an afterthought. Then pp. 281–300 (U⁸, X²), entitled 'Supplement' and containing seven more letters, namely the six 'starred' ones, and one more (Orrery to Pope, Oct. 4, 1738, the latest in the series), all derived from Pope's folio edition (see No. 60A, *ante*), were inserted as a second afterthought. And lastly the prefatory matter (one sheet of 16 pp., unsigned) was prefixed to the whole. The first three units have all *Finis.* at the end.

The conclusion to be drawn from the signatures is that the first and second units must have been printed off before the appearance of Pope's folio edition, that is before April 16, 1741. The seventh letter in the 'Supplement' (Letter LXXXVIII) was apparently a very late addition, proved by the fact that it is not listed in the 'Contents' (neither is it called for in the Contents of Pope's folio edition), and by its cramped position at the end. It would even seem that X 1–2 (pp. 297–300) were reprinted to make its addition possible.

As the type of both the Exshaw volume (or rather its 1746 re-issue) and Faulkner's 12mo has not been set thus separately, they must have been printed after Faulkner's 8vo, and from it.

The Exshaw volume, apart from its different size, shows resemblance, not as Griffith says (No. 532) with Faulkner's 12mo, but with his 8vo edition (both, in the title-page, refer to "the *London* Edition"; both have two Letters numbered V). This shows their relationship. — But Faulkner's 12mo is a different thing. The title-page intimation of "Several Notes and Translations not in the *London* Edition" has been discarded. The mistake of two Letters numbered V, has been corrected into two Letters numbered VII (the second is the postscript of the first). Another improvement is, that *Some Free Thoughts*, &c., which in the Exshaw volume awkwardly started on a verso, here correctly begins on a recto.

Pope's folio and quarto editions have a note at the beginning of the 'Contents', saying: 'N.B. Those letters which have an Asterisk * prefixed, are added in this, and not in the Dublin Edition.' The asterisk accompanies letters 61, 63, 66, 77, 87, and 88, which in the Dublin edition are the first six of the 'Supplement'. The note is either based on the *supposition* only that the Dublin edition would and could not contain the starred letters, or it refers to a Dublin edition that had really appeared before April 16, 1741, which must then have been an earlier issue (without 'Supplement' and 'Some Free Thoughts') of either Faulkner's 8vo or the Exshaw volume, probably the latter, as a reply to and in competition with the Cooper volume (No. 60, *ante*).

64A. The / Works / Of / Alexander Pope, Esq; / — / Vol. VII. / — / Containing the Third and Last Part of / Letters, / Between / Him and Dr. Swift. / — / [ornament] / = / London: / Printed for T. Cooper, M.DCC.XLI.

[Title in black and red.]

Sm. 8vo; a⁴, [A]–B⁸; C–K⁸, L⁴; M–P⁸, Q⁴ — 2 pp. (t. + *The Booksellers to the Reader* on verso), 10 pp. (Contents), [1]–27, 16; 17–152; 153–224.

This is a re-issue of No. 60. Everything before sheet C, and after sheet L, is new; sheets C–K⁸, L⁴ (pp. 17–152) are the same printing as the corresponding ones in No. 60, *ante*, but H 6 and I 3–6 are cancels. — [A] 1 and [A] 2 wrongly signed b and b 2. — Text begins on A 3; sig. C begins on the second p. 17.

Copy: Harvard.

Griffith, No. 560, quotes the advertisement in the *Evening Post* of June 29, 1742 ("This Day is publish'd . . ."); but Mack, *The Library*, 483, n. 2, says that this edition "may well belong to 1741, as the title-page suggests".

This volume contains letters 1–5, 5–88, against the 81 in No. 60, *ante*.

The following notes are from Griffith No. 560: 'Starred' letters are: the second letter 5, 60, 62, 65, 76, 86, 87, 88. Passages in quotation marks are in letters 74, 76, 80, 83, 85, 86, 87, 88.

On p. 3 there is note quoted from the 'Dublin Edition'. A note on the second p. 19 ends with: "now first correctly published." In the folio 1741, p. 27, another sentence follows, viz.: "This note is taken from the Dublin Edition."

Leaf H 6 (pp. 107–8), an insert, has a brief note not in the folio 1741.

P. 158 has a note quoted from the 'Dublin Edition', the same as the note on p. 118 of the folio 1741.

P. 223 is misnumbered 229.

Letter 88 (pp. 223–4) from Orrery to Pope is letter 89 in the folio 1741 not listed in the Contents.

84. Letters / Of / Lord Bolingbroke / To / Dr. Jonathan Swift, D.S.P.D. / *Glasgow:* / Printed by R. Urie, MDCCLII.

12mo (in sixes); [A] 1–2, a², A 3–6, B–G⁶, H⁴ — 2 pp. (t. + bl.), 2 pp. (Adv. + bl.), 4 pp. (Contents), 5–89 + bl., 2 pp. advs.

Copy: B.M. 10921 aa 30.

Contains 14 letters, mostly from Bolingbroke to Swift, but also some from Swift to Bolingbroke, and some from Pope to Bolingbroke.

103. *The Universal Museum and Complete Magazine*, for the year 1766, contains some letters to and from Swift (pp. 299, 472–3).

118. The / Epistolary Correspondence, / Visitation Charges, / Speeches, And Miscellanies, / Of The Right Reverend / Francis Atterbury, D.D. / Lord Bishop Of Rochester. / With Historical Notes. / How pleasing Atterbury's softer hour! / How shin'd the soul, unconquer'd in the Tower!" / Pope. / — / Volume The Second. / — / London, / Printed By And For J. Nichols: / And Sold By C. Dilly, In The Poultry. / MDCCLXXXIII.

8vo; I–V + bl., blank leaf, 1–456.

This volume contains five letters from Swift to Atterbury (pp. 34, 39, 45, 49 and 53).

There are five volumes in all: Vols. I–IV, *Correspondence*; Vol. V, *Miscellaneous Works*. They appeared in 1783, 1783, 1784, 1787, and 1790 respectively.

120. Literary Relics: / Containing / Original Letters / From / King Charles II. King James II. / The Queen Of Bohemia, / Swift,

Berkeley, Addison, Steele, / Congreve, The Duke Of Ormond, / And Bishop Rundle. / To which is prefixed, / An Inquiry / Into / The Life Of Dean Swift. / — / By George-Monck Berkeley, Esq; / L.L.B. In The University Of Dublin, F.S.S.A. / A Member Of St Mary Magdalen Hall Oxford, / And Of The Inner Temple London. / — / London: / Printed For C. Elliot and T. Kay, N° 332. Strand; / And C. Elliot Parliament Square, Edinburgh. / M,DCC,LXXXIX.

8vo; π^4, b–d^8, A–Cc^8 — 2 pp. (h.t. + bl.), 2 pp. (f.t. + bl.), 1 p. (Dedication to John Monck Mason), 1 p. blank, [VII]–XII (Preface), [XIII]–LVI (Life of Swift), [1]–415 + bl.
Copy: Penn.
Contains, besides the *Inquiry* (see title), some letters from and to Swift.

Second edition:
Literary Relics: / Containing / Original Letters / From / King Charles II. King James II. / The Queen Of Bohemia, / Swift, Berkeley, Addison, Steele, / Congreve, The Duke Of Ormond, / And Bishop Rundle. / To which is prefixed, / An Inquiry / Into / The Life Of Dean Swift. / — / By George-Monck Berkeley, Esq. / L.L.B. In The University Of Dublin, F.S.S.A. / A Member Of St. Mary Magdalen Hall, Oxford, / And Of The Inner Temple, London. / — / Second Edition, / Revised and Corrected. / — / London: / Printed for T. Kay (late Elliot and Kay), No. 332, / opposite Somerset House, Strand; / And W. Creech, Edinburgh. / — / MDCCXCII.

8vo; π^3, b–d^8, A–Cc^8 — 2 pp. (t. + bl.), 2 pp. (Dedication + bl.), [VII]–XII (Preface), [XIII]–LVI (Life), [1]–415 + bl.
Copy: U.L.C. (no h.t.).

58. A / Supplement / To / Dr. *Swift*'s / And / Mr. *Pope*'s Works. / Containing / I. Miscellanies, by Dr. Arbuthnot. / II. Several Pieces, by Dr. Swift and Mr. / Pope. / III. Poems on Several Occasions. / Now first Collected into One Vol. / — / This Volume contains all the Pieces in Verse and / Prose published by Dr. Swift and Mr. Pope in / their Miscellanies, which are not printed in Mr. / Faulkner's Edition of the Dean's Works in / Six Volumes, or Mr. Pope's in Four Volumes. / = / *Dublin:* / Printed by S. Powell, / For Edward Exshaw at the *Bible* on *Cork-hill*, / over-against the *Old-Exchange*. MDCCXXXIX.

12mo; π^3, a 2–4, A–O^{12}, P^8 — 2 pp. (t. + bl.), 4 pp. ('Contents' covering 2 pp. and 2 lines of the third page, followed by 'Books printed for Edward Exshaw'), 6 pp. ('Preface'), [3]–354.
Originally there were eight pages of prefatory matter (a^4), bearing title (2 pp.) and 'Preface' (6 pp.). Then the title [a 1] was cut away (stub visible), and before the remaining 'Preface' (a 2–4) were placed one double-leaf [bearing new title (2 pp.) and 2 pp. of the 'Contents'], followed by one single

leaf [bearing the rest of the 'Contents', and 'Books printed for Edward Exshaw']. I have possessed two copies: in one the six new pages have been placed before the six old ones, in the other the six old pages have been inserted inside the double-leaf of the new matter. The former arrangement is the correct one, because the catchword 'Law' on the last page of the *Preface* corresponds with the first word on p. [3]. The *Preface* is the same text as that in *Miscellanies* Vol. I, 1727 (No. 25, *ante*), mentioning more volumes, and signed and dated 'Jonath. Swift. Alex. Pope. Twickenham, May 27, 1727.'

Copies: Penn and own.

65. A New / Miscellany / In Prose and Verse. / Containing, / Several Pieces never before made public. / — / *By the Reverend Dr. Swift*, Dean *of St.* / Patrick's, / *The Hon. Mr. Holles St. John*, / And other Eminent Hands. / — / [ornament] / — / London: / Printed for T. Read, in *Dogwell-Court, White-* / *Fryers, Fleet-Street.* MDCCXLII. / (Price One Shilling).

8vo (in fours); π^1, B–H^4, I^3 (I 4 probably used as title-page) — 2 pp. (t. + bl.), [1]–62.

Contains: A Letter to Mrs. Prat (by Swift), The Hard Duty of Dean Swift's Curate, On Phillis, To Strephon, Horace Book I Ode XI Imitated, Horace Book II Ode XVI Imitated, On the Dinners of Dr. Swift, Dean of St. Patrick's.

Copy: Forster 8562 (34 A 30).

**

59. The / Poetical / Works / Of / Dr. Jonathan Swift, / Dean of St. Patrick's, Dublin. / — / In Two Volumes. / — / Vol. I. / = / London: / Sold by A. Manson, R. Dilton, J. Thom- / son, H. Gray, T. Nelson, and / P. Bland.

12mo; π^3, A–K^{12} — 2 pp. (t. + bl.), [III]–V (Contents), 1 p. blank, [1]–239 + bl. — Frontisp. (Swift). π^3, A–K^{12} — 2 pp. (t. + bl.), [III]–V (Contents), 1 p. blank, [1]–240.

Copy: Penn.

The inclusion of "Toland's Invitation" (not reprinted in collections until 1755) and the absence of catchwords, a mid-century innovation by the Foulis Press at Glasgow, suggests a date in the 1760's.

Sermons

70. Three / Sermons: / I. On Mutual Subjection. / II. On Conscience. / III. On the Trinity. / — / *By the Reverend Dr. Swift*, / *Dean of St.* Patrick's. / — / [ornament] / = / *London:* / Printed for R. Dodsley in *Pall-Mall:* / And Sold by M. Cooper in *Pater-* / *noster-* / *Row.* 1744. / [*Price* 1 *s.* 6 *d.*]

4to; A–H^4 — 2 pp. (t. + bl.), [3]–64 (text). — Misprint 'Subordination' in last line of p. 34.

Published Oct.–Nov. 1744.

Another [second] *edition:*

The title-page is exactly the same as that of the first edition, but the collation is different:

4to; π^1, A–G^4, H^3 (see *Note* below). — 2 pp. (t. + bl.), [1]–62 (text). — Misprint ('Subordination' in last line of p. 32).

Later copies of this edition have the misprint corrected into 'Subornation', apparently effected during the press-work while the type was still standing.

Note: The [second] edition is printed in a narrower measure than the first, and shows some differences in punctuation, especially in the last page. Its title was probably printed on leaf H 4, and then cut away and placed in front, in order to start the text on the first page of a signature. This improvement, the correction of the misprint, and the occasional addition of a fourth sermon to the two states of the [second] edition but not to copies of the first edition, afford the only clues to the probable sequence of these two editions.

Title of the fourth sermon:

— / The / Difficulty / Of / Knowing One's Self. / A / Sermon. / —.

4to; [I]–M^4 — 2 pp. (t. + bl.), [67]–94, 2 pp. advs.

On the authenticity of this fourth sermon see *Prose Works*, Vol. IX, 103–6. Published July 9, 1745, but I do not agree with the supposition that it should also have been published separately, i.e. with pagination 2 pp., [1]–28, 2 pp.

Copies:

First ed.: B.M. 4473 f 24 (1), and Penn (2 copies).

[Second] ed. ('Subordination'): No separate copy seen.

    With 4th Sermon added: U.L.C. (Hib. 5.744.4).

[Second] ed. ('Subornation'): Bodl. I.I. 53Th9, B.M. 1025 f 3 (1), and Penn.

    With 4th Sermon added: Bodl. Godw. Pamph. 74(8), U.L.C. 8.31.15(1), B.M. 226 f 2 (9) [title 'Three Sermons' lacking], Chapin Libr., and Penn.

71. Three / Sermons: / I. On Mutual Subjection. / II. On Conscience. / III. On the Trinity. / — / *By the Reverend Dr. Swift,* / *Dean of St.* Patrick*'s* / — / [ornament] / = / *Dublin:* / Printed by and for George Faulkner, / — / M,DCC,XLIV.

8vo; A–C^8, D^4 — 2 pp. (t. + bl.), 3–54, 2 pp. advs.

Copy: Penn.

Another edition:

Three / Sermons: / I. On Mutual Subjection. / II. On Conscience. / III. On the Trinity. / — / By the Reverend Dr. *Swift*, Dean of / St. *Patrick*'s, *Dublin.* / — / [monogram] / = / Dublin: / Printed by George Faulkner, 1751.

8vo; [A]–B^8, C^7 — 2 pp. (t. + bl.), 3–46.

Copy: T.C.D. (47 h. 137).

Another edition:

Four / Sermons: / I. On Mutual Subjection. / II. On Conscience. / III. On the Trinity. / IV. The Difficulty of Knowing / One's Self. / — / By the Reverend Dr. *Swift*, Dean of / St. *Patrick*'s, *Dublin.* / — / [ornament] / = / *Dublin,* / Printed by George Faulkner. / — / MDCCLX.

8vo; π^1 (probably F 2 used as such), B–E⁸, F¹ — 2 pp. (t. + bl.), 1–66.
Copies: U.L.C. and Bodl.

72. *German translation:*
Dr. / Jonathan Swifts / einige / Predigten. / Aus dem Englischen
übersetzt. / [ornament] / — / Hamburg und Leipzig. 1758.

8vo; 2 pp., 8 pp. (*Vorrede*), 3–72. — This is a separate issue of the last
part of Vol. III of *Satyrische und ernsthafte Schriften*, 1758 (see No. 101, *post*);
only the leaves before the text are new.
Copy: Preuszische Staatsbibl., Berlin.

73. The / Sermons / Of the Reverend / Dr. Jonathan Swift, /
Dean of St. Patrick's, Dublin. / Carefully Corrected. / Glasgow: /
Printed for Robert Urie. / MDCCLXIII.

12mo; 8 pp., 3–336.
Copy: own.

74. The / Sermons / Of the Reverend / Dr. Jonathan Swift, /
Dean of St. Patrick's Dublin. / A New Edition, Corrected. /
Glasgow: / Printed by William Smith. / Sold at his Shop in
Saltmercat; by W. Gray, / J. Dickson, and C. Elliot, Edinburgh. /
MDCCLXXVI.

12mo (in sixes); π^2, B–Y⁶, Z⁴ — 2 pp. (t. + bl.), 1 p. (Foreword), 1 p.
(Contents), [13]–260. — Pp. 185 and 188 misnumbered 285 and 288. — Con-
tains nine sermons.
Copy: Glasgow Univ. Libr.

75. *German translation:*
Des berühmten / Dechant Swifts / sämmtliche / Predigten /
aus / dem Englischen übersezt / und / mit Vorrede und einigen
Anmerkungen / begleitet / von / Friedrich Wilhelm Streit, /
Pastor Primar. und Superintendent zu Ronneburg / der Teutschen
und Lateinischen Gesellschafft / zu Jena Mitglied. / — / Ronneburg
und Leipzig, / bey Heinrich Gottlieb Rothen, / 1776.

Sm. 8vo; *⁶, A–P⁸, Q² — 2 pp. (t. + bl.), 8 pp. (Vorrede), 2 pp. (Inhalt),
[1]–244. — Contains twelve sermons.
Copy: Penn.

76. The / Sermons / Of / Dr. J. Swift, / Dean Of St. Patrick's,
Dublin. / To Which Is Prefixed / The Author's Life: / Together
With His / Prayer For Stella, / His / Thoughts / On, And / Project
/ For The / Advancement Of Religion. / Vol. I. / London: /
Sold by R. Dampier, J. Thompson, W. / Manson, T. Davidson,
and P. / Watson.

The second volume has the same title, except: Vol. II.

12mo; a–b¹², c⁶, B–H¹² — 2 pp. (t. + bl.), [III]–IV (Contents), 2 pp. (title: 'Account Life of Swift' + bl.), VII–XXXVI (Life), [XXXVII]–XLII (A Prayer For Stella), [XLIII]–LIV (Thoughts On Religion), [LV]–LIX (Further Thoughts On Religion), 1 p. blank, [1]–192.

π², A–I¹², K⁶, L² — 2 pp. (t. + bl.), [III]–IV (Contents), [1]–165 + bl., [167]–231 + bl. (Project Advancement of Religion).

No year. *Prose Works*, XII, 189 says: 1790?

Thorp, cat. 498 (1938), item 996, mentions a Third Edition.

Copy: Penn.

79. The / Story / Of The / Injured Lady. / Being a true Picture of / Scotch Perfidy, Irish Poverty, / and English Partiality. / With / Letters and Poems / Never before Printed. / — / By the Rev. Dr. Swift, D.S.P.D. / — / *London*, / Printed for M. Cooper, at the *Globe* in / *Pater-Noster-Row*. MDCCXLVI. / [Price One Shilling.]

8vo; π², A–D⁸, E² — 2 pp. (t. + bl.), [III]–IV (Contents), 1–68.

Copies: Forster, and B.M. 1203 i 10.

Contains: Story Injured Lady, with The Answer, Letters to and from Dr. Swift, The Beasts Confession, Verses made for Women who cry Apples, To Love, Lines written on a very old Glass, Verses cut by two of the Dean's Friends, On another Window, The Author's manner of Living, An Epigram on Woods's Brass-Money, Part of the 9th Ode of the 4th Book of Horace, A Love Poem from a Physician, Verses upon the late Countess of Donegal, An Epigram on Scolding.

***

79A. Poems / On Several / Occasions. / By / J. Swift, D.D, D.S.P.D. / = / [monogram] / = / *Dublin:* / Printed by George Faulkner, in *Essex-Street*. / — / M,DCC,XLVII.

This is a separate issue of the *Works*, Vol. II, 12mo, 1747 (see Nos. 51 and 51A), from which the volume-title has been cut away and replaced by the above title.

Copies: Univ. of Michigan (Hubbard Coll.), and Birrell and Garnett's cat. No. 12, item 601.

81. A / Supplement / To The / Works / Of The / Most celebrated Minor Poets. / Namely, / [*First column:*] E. of Roscommon, / —— Dorset, / —— Hallifax, / —— Godolphin, / Lord Somers, / Dr. Sprat, Bishop of / Rochester, / [*Second column:*] Sir Samuel Garth, / George Stepney, Esq; / William Walsh, Esq; / Thomas Tickell, Esq; / and / Ambrose Phillips, Esq; / To which are added, / Pieces omitted in the Works of / [*First column:*] Sir John Suckling, / Mr. Otway, / Matthew Prior, Esq; / [*Second column:*] Dr. King, / and / Dean Swift. / = / *London:* / Printed for F. Cogan, at the *Middle Temple Gate*, / *Fleet Street*. MDCCL.

8vo; π^2; a^4; B–S^8, F^6; A–F^8; 2A–F^8 — 2 pp. (bl. + 'To the Publick' on verso), 2 pp. (f.t. + bl.); 8 pp. 'Contents' of all the three volumes (sometimes inserted here, sometimes in front of Vol. I); [1]–284 (beginning with title: 'Supplement Part I); [1]–95 + bl. (Beginning with title: 'Supplement Part II'); 2 pp. (title Supplement Part III + bl.), 3–96.

In the first section A–F^8, A 7–8 are cancelled, and replaced by a new double-leaf, while 93, and in some copies 79, are unnumbered. The second section A–F^8 contains the pieces by Swift, with the following title:

A / Supplement / To The / Works / Of / Dr. *Swift.* / Part III.

Copies: B.M. 992 d 7, Harvard, Yale, own.

This volume is the third volume belonging to: The Works Of The most celebrated Minor Poets. Namely, Wentworth, Earl of Roscommon; Charles, Earl of Dorset; Charles, Earl of Halifax; Sir Samuel Garth; George Stepney, Esq; William Walsh, Esq; Thomas Tickell, Esq. Never before collected and publish'd together. In Two Volumes. London: Printed for F. Cogan, at the Middle Temple Gate. MDCCXLIX.

The 'To the Publick' (on verso of leaf before the f.t.) attacks the publishers of a rival edition (*The Works Of Celebrated Authors*, 2 vols., 1750), who in their preface had first attacked those of *The Works Of The most celebrated Minor Poets*, 2 vols., 1749.

Case, No. 467 (3)(a) says that "a two-volume edition of this miscellany was published in Dublin in 1751". I have not seen it.

83. A / Supplement / To The / Works / Of / Dr. *Swift.* / — / [ornament] / = / *London:* / Printed for F. Cogan, at the *Middle Temple* / *Gate, Fleet-street.* 1752.

8vo; π^3, B–K^8, L^7 — 2 pp. (t. + bl.), V–VI (To The Publick), VII–VIII (Contents), [1]–158.

Copy: B.M. 12269 bb 15 (probably lacks h.t. and leaf at the end).

Contains pieces by Swift, some genuine, some doubtful.

85. Das Buch / Der Weisheit und der Tugend, / Oder die / Verfassung / Des / Menschlichen Lebens, / Aus einer Indianischen Handschrift eines / alten Braminen übersezt, und aus China nach / Londen an den Herrn Grafen von Chesterfield / gesandt. / Nebst einem Anhang / Sinnreicher Gedanken / Des berühmten Herrn / Pope und Swift. / [   ]ntlich aus dem Englischen übersezt. Straszburg, 1752. / = / [   ]ts, Amand König, Buchhåndler.

Sm. 8vo; [ )( ]^7,)( )(^{8}, A–Q^8 — 2 pp. (t. + bl.), 1 p. (Auf die Verfassung, &c.), 23 pp. (Vorrede des Ubersetzers), 4 pp. (Register), 1 p. (bastard title), [2] (Vorbericht des Englischen Herausgebers), 3–256. — Left hand foot corner of title mutilated.

Copy: Univ. Libr. Amsterdam (231 G 20). Though the special title on p. [233] mentions Pope only: "Sinnreiche Gedanken des berühmten Mr. Pope Uber allerhand Materien, aus dem Englischen übersezt.", these *Thoughts* are partly Pope's (pp. 235–46), partly Swift's (pp. 246–52).

101. Satyrische / und / ernsthafte / Schriften, / von / Dr. Jonathan Swift. / Erster Band. / [vignette] / Hamburg und Leipzig, 1756.

Except for the volume-numbers, the vignettes, and the years, the titles of the other volumes are the same. Vol. III has "Mit Kupfern." under the vignette, and Vols. IV–VIII have a rule just over the imprint. The years are:

– – – – / Zweyter Band. / – – – – – – – – – 1756.

– – – – / Dritter Band. / – – – – – – – – – 1758.

– – – – / Vierter Band. / – – – – – – – – – 1760.

– – – – / Fůnfter Band. / – – – – – – – – – 1761.

– – – – / Sechster Band. / – – – – – – – – 1761.

– – – – / Siebender Band. / – – – – – – – – 1763.

– – – – / Achter und lezter Band. / – – – – 1766.

8vo:

I: [ )( ]⁸,)( )(⁸,)( )( )(⁸, a–c⁸, d², A–Ee⁸, Ff⁴ — 2 pp. (t. + bl.), 46 pp. (Vorrede), [1]–52, [1]–455 + bl.

II: [ )( ]⁸,)( )(⁸,)( )( )(⁴, A–Cc⁸ — 2 pp. (t. + bl.), 38 pp. (Vorrede), [1]–416.

III: [ )( ]⁸, [A]–Y⁸, Z², [a]–d⁸, e⁴ — 2 pp. (t. + bl.), 12 pp. (An den Leser), 2 pp. (title: 'Swifts Mahrgen von der Tonne' + bl.), [1]–355 + bl., [1]–72. — 9 plates.

IV: [ )( ]⁷, [A]–Cc⁸, Dd⁶ — 2 pp. (t. + bl.), [III]–VI (An den Leser), 8 pp. (Innhalt), [1]–428.

V: [ )( ]⁸, A–Ee⁸, Ff¹⁰ — 2 pp. (t. + Latin quotation on verso), 14 pp. (Schreiben), [1]–462, 6 pp. (Inhalt). — 4 plates.

VI: π², A–Bb⁸, Cc⁴ — 2 pp. (t. + bl.), 2 pp. (Innhalt + bl.), [1]–406, 2 pp. blank.

VII: π¹, A–T⁸, U⁷, X–Cc⁸ — 2 pp. (t. + bl.), 1–412, 2 pp. blank (177–8 omitted, 209–10 (misprinted 101) repeated in numbering).

VIII: π¹, A–Cc⁸, Dd⁷, Ee–Hh⁸, Ii² — 2 pp. (t. + bl.), [1]–496, 1 p. (Innhalt), 1 p. (Drukfehler).

The above set is Penn's.

I possess a copy of Vol. II, exactly the same printing as the one mentioned above, only with different imprint, namely: Zůrich, bey Orell und Compagnie, 1756.

Vol. IV seems to occur with the year 1759 on the title-page (information supplied by Henning Oppermann, Basel).

The translation is by Diakon Waser.

Reprinted and reissued volumes:

– – – – / Erster Band. / [vignette] / — / Zweyte Auflage. / — / Hamburg und Leipzig, 1760.

8vo; I–XLVIII, 1–52, 1–455 + bl.
Copy: Freiburg.

– – – – – / Erster Band. / [vignette] / — / Dritte Auflage. / — / Zůrich, bey Orell, Geszner und Comp. 1766.

8vo; [ )( ]–)( )( )(^{8}, a–c^8, d^2; A–Ee^8, Ff^4 — 2 pp. (t. + bl.), III–XLVIII, [1]–52, [1]–455 + bl. — Not the same printing as the 2nd ed.
Copies: B.M. 12271 df 2, Freiburg, and Bibl. Nat. Paris.

– – – – – / Zweyter Band. / [vignette] / — / Hamburg und Leipzig, 1760.

8vo; 40 pp., 1–416.
Copies: Freiburg, and Bibl. Nat. Paris.

– – – – – / Zweyter Band. / [vignette] / — / Zürich, bey Orell, Geszner, Füeszlin und Comp. 1772.

8vo; [ )( ]^8,)( )(^{8},)( )( )(^{4}, A–Dd^8 — 2 pp. (t. + bl.), 38 pages, [1]–432.
Copy: B.M.

– – – – / Dritter Band. / — / Zweyte Auflage. / — / [vignette] / Mit Kupfern. / Hamburg und Leipzig, 1759.

8vo; [ )( ]^5; a–d^8, c^4; π^1, [A]–X^8 — 2 pp. (t. + bl.), 8 pp. (An den Leser); [1]–72 (Sermons); 2 pp. (title *Tale* + bl.), [1]–332, 2 pp. (Nachschrift + bl.), 2 pp. blank. — Nine plates.
Copy: B.M. — Other copies (Freiburg and Bibl. Nat. Paris) have the *Tale* before the *Sermons*.

– – – – / Fünfter Band. / [vignette] / — / Zürich, bey Orell, Geszner, Füeszlin und Comp. 1772.

8vo; [ )( ]^8, π^3, A–Hh^8, Ii^4 — 2 pp. (t. + quotation on verso), 14 pp. (Letter), 6 pp. (Inhalt), 1–500, 4 pp. advs. — Four plates.
Copies: B.M., and Freiburg.
For separate editions of Vol. III (*Tale*), Vol. III, last part (*Sermons*), and Vol. V (*Gulliver's Travels*), see Nos. 275, *post*; 72, *ante*; 429–31, *post*.

101A. Miscellanies: / Or / Essays / Literary, Political, and Moral. / By the Reverend / Dr. Jonathan Swift, / D.S.P.D. / Glasgow: / Printed for Robert Urie.

12mo; I–IV (t. + bl., 2 pp. Contents), [3]–259 + bl., 2 pp. advs.
Contains *Discourse Athens and Rome, Proposal English Tongue, Letter Young Clergyman, Letter Young Lady, Argument Abolishing Christianity, Project Advancement Religion, On Good Manners, Hints Essay Conversation.*
The year must be later than 1755, as notes from Orrery, Deane Swift, and Hawkesworth have been inserted.
Copy: own.

104. An / Appendix / To / Dr. Swift's Works / And Literary Correspondence. / Improved / From an Edition printed by / Mr. Faulkner: / And now first published, April 1767. / = / London, / Printed for W. B. and sold by S. Bladon, in / *Pater-noster-Row.* MDCCLXVII.

8vo; [A]², B–C⁸ — 2 pp. (t. + bl.), [III]–IV (Contents), [1]–32.
Copy: B.M. 12270 b 2.

105. The / Historical Works / Of the Reverend / Dr. Jonathan Swift, / D.S.P.D. / In Three Volumes. / Volume I. / Containing / The History of the four last / Years of the Queen. / Glasgow: / Printed for Robert Urie. / MDCCLXIX.

– – – – – / Volume II. / Containing / The History of England, from / the Death of William the Con- / queror, to the Accession of Hen- / ry the Second. / – – – –

– – – – – / Volume III. / Containing / The Memoirs of Cap. Creighton. / – – – –

12 mo; 2 pp., I–X, 11–302.
12 pp., 3–272.
I–XII, 13–227 + bl.

Presumably all these three volumes are old ones re-issued. As to Vol. III, I am sure of it (see No. 708, *post*); while the arrangement of the first leaves in the other two volumes is such (the titles are separate leaves, and the stubs of leaves cancelled are clearly visible) that it becomes highly probable.

***

106. Travels / Into / Remote Nations / Of The / World. / — / By Lemuel Gulliver, / First a Surgeon and then a Captain of seve- / ral Ships. / — / [ornament] / = / Printed in the Year 1771.

8vo (in fours); π¹, A–Ii⁴, K⁴ (should be Kk⁴), L⁴ (should be Ll⁴), M⁴ (should be Mm⁴), N⁴ (should be Nn⁴), M⁴ (should be Oo⁴) — The signatures are Numb. 1. A to Numb. 37. M (should be Oo) — 2 pp. (t. + bl.), [1]–40 (Verses), 41–293 (Travels), 3 pp. blank.
Copies: B.M. 12613 dd 12, and Penn.
Contains: 1. *Baucis and Philemon.* 2. *A Letter to a very Young Lady on her Marriage.* 3. *Verses on the Death of Dr. Swift.* 4. *On Censure.* 5. *Mary the Cook-Maid's Letter to Dr. Sheridan.* 6. *Voyage to Lilliput.* 7. *Voyage to Brobdingnag.*

107. Poems / Of / Dr. Jonathan Swift, / Dean Of Saint Patrick's, / Dublin. / Volume I. / Edinburgh: / Printed for J. Balfour and W. Creech. / — / M,DCC,LXXIII.

The second volume has the same title, except: Volume II.
In both volumes the above title is preceded by another:

The / British Poets. / Vol. XXXI. [XXXII.] / Edinburgh: / Printed for J. Balfour and W. Creech. / — / M,DCC,LXXIII.

16mo (in eights):
π⁴, A–N⁸ — 2 pp. (t. + bl.), 2 pp. (t. + bl.), [V]–VII (Contents), 1 p. blank, [1]–208.

π^4, A–N^8 — 2 pp. (t. + bl.), 2 pp. (t. + bl.), [V]–VI (Contents), 2 pp. (title: 'Miscellanies' + bl.), [1]–207, one page unnumbered.

Copy: Penn. There are 42 volumes in all (editor, Dr. Blair).

108. Poems / Of / Dr. Jonathan Swift, / Dean Of Saint Patrick's, / Dublin. / In / Two Volumes. / Vol. I. / Glasgow: / Printed By Robert & Andrew Foulis, / Printers To The University, / M.DCC.LXXIV.

The second volume has the same title, except: Vol. II.
12mo (in sixes):
π^2, A–P^6, Q^4 — 2 pp. (t. + bl.), 2 pp. (Contents), 2 pp. (title: 'Miscellanies' + bl.), [3]–188.
π^1, A–O^6, P^2 — 2 pp. (t. + bl.), 2 pp. (title: 'Miscellanies' + bl.), [3]–172.
Copy: Penn.

109. A / Collection / Of The / English Poets, / Containing The Poetical Works Of / [*First column:*] Pope. / Dryden. / Swift. / Prior. / Gay. / [*Second column:*] Shenston. / Pomfret. / Gray & Littleton. / Thomson. / Young. / In Twenty Volumes. / Volume VII. / Aberdeen: / Printed For, And Sold By J. Boyle. / M.DCC.LXXVI.

The other volume has the same title, except: Volume VIII.
In both volumes the above title is followed by another:

Poems / Of / Dr. Jonathan Swift, / Dean Of Saint Patrick's, / Dublin. / In / Two Volumes. / Vol. I. [Vol. II.] / Aberdeen: / Printed For, And Sold By J. Boyle. / M.DCC.LXXVI.

Sm. 12mo (in sixes):
π^3, A–P^6, Q^4 — 2 pp. (1st t. + bl.), 2 pp. (2nd t. + bl.), 2 pp. (Contents), [1]–188.
π^3, A–O^6, P^2 — 2 pp. (1st t. + bl.), 2 pp. (2nd t. + bl.), 2 pp. (Contents), [1]–172.
Copy: Bodl. 12 θ 646.

110. The / Poetical Works / Of / Dr. Jonath. Swift, / Dean Of St. Patrick's, Dublin. / In Four Volumes. / With The Life Of The Author. / = / . . . . . Two Chiefs, the guardians of thy name, / Conspire to raise thee to the point of fame. / Ye future Times! I heard the silver sound, / I saw the Graces form a circle round: / Each where she fix'd attentive seem'd to root, / And all but Eloquence herself was mute. / From out her breast ('t was there the treasure lay) / She drew thy Labours to the blaze of day; / Then gaz'd, and read the charms she could inspire, / And taught the list'ning audience to admire . . . . . / Then here, she cries, let future ages dwell, / And learn to copy where they can't excel . . . . . / O Swift! if fame be life (as well we know / That bards and heroes have esteem'd it so) / Thou can'st not wholly die; thy

Works will shine / To future times, and life in fame be thine.
Parnell. / = / Vol. I. / Edinburg [*sic*]: / At The Apollo Press, By
The Martins. / *Anno* 1778.

> The other three titles are the same, except: Vol. II., Vol. III., Vol. IV.
>
> In each volume the title as above is followed by another, appropriate to that volume.
>
> Sm. 12mo (in sixes):
>
> π^2 of thicker paper, [A]–S^6 — 2 pp. (portrait of Swift), 2 pp. (frontisp.), 2 pp. (t. + bl.), 2 pp. (t. + bl.), [V]–CLVI (Life), 157–215 (Contents on verso).
>
> π^1, [A]–U^6, X^4 — 2 pp. (frontisp.), 2 pp. (t. + bl.), 2 pp. (t. + bl.), [5]–247 + bl.
>
> π^1, [A]–T^6, U^3 — 2 pp. (frontisp.), 2 pp. (t. + bl.), 2 pp. (t. + bl.), [5]–233 + bl.
>
> π^1, π^2, A–R^6, S^3 — 2 pp. (frontisp.), 2 pp. (t. + bl.), 2 pp. (t. + bl.), [1]–209 + bl.
>
> Copy: B.M. 1066 b 23–24.

111. *Another edition:*

> The same titles as in the 1778 edition, but with the following imprint:

London: / Printed Under The Direction Of J. Bell, / British
Library, Strand, / Bookseller To His Royal Highness / The Prince
Of Wales. / 1787.

> Sm. 12mo (in sixes):
>
> A–R^6, S^3 — 2 pp. (t. + bl.), 2 pp. (t. + bl.), [V]–CLII, [153]–209 ('Contents' on verso). — Two frontispieces.
>
> A–U^6 — 2 pp. (t. + bl.), 2 pp. (t. + bl.), [5]–238, 2 pp. blank. — Frontisp.
>
> A–T^6 — 2 pp. (t. + bl.), 2 pp. (t. + bl.), [5]–221 + bl., 5 pp. 'Contents' + bl. — Frontisp.
>
> A–R^6 — 2 pp. (t. + bl.), 2 pp. (t. + bl.), [5]–203 + bl. — Frontisp.
>
> Begun in 1776, the whole collection, in both these editions, seems to consist of 109 volumes, to which 18 vols. of *Translations* were added, making 127 vols. in all.
>
> Copy: Penn.

112. *Another edition:*

The Poets Of Great Britain from Chaucer to Churchill. London,
Samuel Bagster, 1807. 12mo. 124 vols. in 61. (Reprint of John
Bell's edition, 1777).

> Swift's poems are in two double volumes (4 titles, numbered 56, 57, 58, 59), entitled: "Poetical Works of Jonathan Swift, with Life of the Author by Samuel Johnson". Portrait and engraved title to each volume. [Information kindly supplied by Messrs. Blackwell, Oxford].

113. The / Works / Of The / English Poets. / With / Prefaces, /
Biographical And Critical, / By Samuel Johnson. / — / Volume
The Thirty-Ninth. / — / London: / Printed By J. Nichols; / For
C. Bathurst, J. Buckland, W. Strahan, J. Riving- / ton And Sons,

T. Davies, T. Payne, L. Davis, W. Owen, / B. White, S. Crowder,
T. Caslon, T. Longman, / B. Law, E. And C. Dilly, J. Dodsley,
H. Baldwin, / J. Wilkie, J. Robson, J. Johnson, T. Lowndes, / T.
Becket, G. Robinson, T. Cadell, W. Davis, / J. Nichols, F. New-
bery, T. Evans, J. Rid- / ley, R. Baldwin, G. Nicol, Leigh And /
Sotheby, J. Bew, N. Conant, / J. Murray, W. Fox, J. Bowen. /
MDCCLXXIX.

The second volume has the same title, except: Volume The Fortieth.
Sm. 8vo; π^1, a^2, B–Aa^8 — 2 pp. (frontisp. Swift), 2 pp. (f.t. + bl.), 2 pp.
(h.t. + bl.), 1–368.
a^2, B–Bb^8 — 2 pp. (f.t. + bl.), 2 pp. (h.t. + bl.), 1–384.
Copy: B.M. 11601 cc 4.
The whole collection comprises 68 volumes, namely 56 vols. Works
(1779), 2 vols. Index (1780), 10 vols. Prefaces (1779–81), to which in 1790,
9 vols. were added, making 77 vols. in all.
Heads engraved by Bartolozzi, etc.
In a dealer's catalogue I found a copy of 68 vols. (56 + 2 + 10) with
another imprint: London, H. Hughes, 1779–81.

114. *Another edition:*
The / Works / Of The / English Poets. / With / Prefaces, /
Biographical And Critical, / By Samuel Johnson. / — / Volume
The Forty-Second. / — / London: / Printed By T. Spilsbury And
Son; / For J. Buckland, J. Rivington And Sons, T. Payne And /
Sons, L. Davis, B. White And Son, T. Longman, B. Law, / J.
Dodsley, H. Baldwin, J. Robson, C. Dilly, T. Cadell, / J. Nichols,
J. Johnson, G. G. J. And J. Robinson, / R. Baldwin, H. L. Gard-
ner, P. Elmsly, T. Evans, / G. Nicol, Leigh And Sotheby, J. Bew,
N. Conant, / J. Murray, J. Sewell, W. Goldsmith, W. Richardson,
/ T. Vernor, W. Lowndes, W. Bent, W. Otridge, T. And / J.
Egerton, S. Hayes, R. Faulder, J. Edwards, G. And / T. Wilkie,
W. Nicoll, Ogilvy And Speare, Scatcherd / And Whitaker, W. Fox,
C. Stalker, E. Newbery. 1790.

The second and third volumes have the same titles, except: Volume The
Forty-Third., and: Volume The Forty-Fourth.
Sm. 8vo:
π^1, a^1, B–X^8 — 2 pp. (h.t. + bl.), 2 pp. (f.t. + bl.), 2 pp. (t. + bl.),
3–319 + bl.
π^1, a^1, B–X^8 — 2 pp. (h.t. + bl.), 2 pp. (f.t. + bl.), 2 pp. (t. + bl.),
3–319 + bl.
π^1, a^1, B–U^8, X^3 — 2 pp. (h.t. + bl.), 2 pp. (f.t. + bl.), 2 pp. (t. + bl.),
3–309 + bl. [Swift ends on p. 129; Broome follows].
Copy: B.M. 238 d 3–5.
There are in this edition 75 vols. in all.

116. *The* / *Beauties of Swift:* / *or, the* / *Favorite Offspring* / *of* /
Wit & Genius. / *No writer can easily be found that has borrowed so* /
little, or that in all his excellencies & all his defects has / *so well*

maintained his claim to be considered as original. | D.ʳ Johnson. |
[vignette portrait of Swift] | London. | *Printed for G: Kearsley
Fleet Street —— 1782. | Harmar script.* | Price Half a Crown Sewed.

12mo; π¹, A⁶, Aa⁶ b⁶ (c² between b 5 and b 6), B–Z⁶ — 2 pp. (t. + bl.),
1 p. (To Samuel Johnson), 1 p. (Preface, Advertisement), [III]–XXXVIII
(Life of Swift), 2 pp. (Contents), [1]–264.
Copy: Penn.
Second issue:
Exactly the same printing, except that the title-page, over the vignette, has:
Second Edition.

117. *Dublin edition:*
The | Beauties Of Swift: | Or, The | Favourite Offspring | Of |
Wit And Genius. | — | No Writer can easily be found that has
borrowed so little, or that | in all his excellencies and all his defects
has so well maintained | his claim to be considered as original. |
Dr. Johnson. | — | Dublin: | Printed by J. and R. Byrn, (18),
Sycamore-Alley, | For Messrs. Walker, Wilson, Burton, Cash, |
And J. Byrn. M.DCC.LXXXIII.

12mo; A–L¹² (two leaves between [A] 1 and A 2) — 2 pp. (t. + bl.),
[I]–IV (Contents). 1 p. (To Samuel Johnson), 1 p. (Preface), [V]–XXXVI
(Life of Swift), [1]–228.
Copy: Penn.

121. Miscellaneous | Pieces, | In Prose And Verse. | By | The
Rev. Dr. Jonathan Swift, | Dean Of St. Patrick's, Dublin. | Not
Inserted In Mr. Sheridan's Edition | Of The Dean's Works. |
London: | Printed For C. Dilly, In The Poultry. | MDCCLXXXIX.

8vo; [a]⁴, B–P⁸, Q⁷, R⁸, S⁴ — 2 pp. (t. + bl.), 2 pp. (Advertisement),
[V]–VI (List), 2 pp. (Contents), [1]–262.
Copy: B.M. 633 g 18.
Of this volume the editor, John Nichols, says that it may be used as the
18th vol. of Sheridan's, or the 26th vol. of Hawkesworth and Nichols's
edition.

122. Elegant Extracts: | *or useful and entertaining | Passages in
Prose | Selected for the |* Improvement of Scholars | *at Classical &
other Schools |* in the | Art of Speaking, | *in |* Reading, Thinking,
Composing; | *and in the |* Conduct of Life. | [ornament] | Μύϑων τε
ῥητῆρ' ἔμεναι, πρηκτῆρα τε ἔργων. | Hom: | *A New Edition.* |
London. Printed for Charles Dilly.

[Engraved title on thicker paper.]
Large 8vo; π¹, A⁸, b⁴, B–3H⁸, 3I⁴ — 2 pp. (t. + bl.), I (Advertisement To
The Last Edition), 1 p. blank, [III]–IV (Preface To The First Edition),
V (Advertisement To The Second Edition), VI–XVI (Introduction), 8 pp.
(Contents), [1]–856.
Contains: *Some Letters from and to Swift* (519–25), *A Dialogue between Mr.
Addison and Dr. Swift. From the Dialogues of the Dead* (542–3), *Extracts from*

Scriblerus and Bathos (575–85), *Humorous Scene between Dennis the Critic and the Doctor* (670–2), *Voyages to Lilliput and Brobdingnag* (700–60). Compiled by the Rev. Dr. Vicesimus Knox, headmaster of Tunbridge school.

Copy: Penn.

122A. *Another edition:*

Elegant Extracts: / Or, / *useful and entertaining* / Passages in Prose, / Selected for the Improvement / of Young Persons: / *being similar in Design to* / Elegant Extracts in Poetry. / — / [ornament] / Studio Fallente Laborem. *Hor.* / London: / *Printed for B. Law, J. Johnson, C. Dilly, C. G. & J. Robinson, T. Cadell, W. Richardson,* / *J. Sewell, F. & C. Rivington, R. Baldwin, J. Edwards, R. Faulder, Ogilvy & Son, J. Cuthell,* / *Clarke & Son, W. Lowndes, B. & J. White, G. & T. Wilkie, J. Walker, F. Wingrave, P. Wynne,* / *T. N. Longman, T. Cadell, Junr. & W. Davies, J. Scatcherd, W. Bent, T. Kay, Vernor &* / *Hood, D. Walker, J. Anderson, Lackington & Allen, G. Kearsley, T. Boosey, W. Miller,* / *Lee & Hurst, Murray & Highley, S. Bagster, J. Hamilton & G. Cawthorne.* — 1797.—

[Engraved title on thicker paper.]
Large 8vo; π^1, A^8, b^4, B–4B^8 — 2 pp. (t. + bl.), [I]–III ('Advertisement To The Seventh And Last Edition', dated at the end: March 1, 1797.), IV ('Preface To The First Edition.'), V ('Advertisement To The Second Edition.' and 'Advertisement To The Third And Fourth Editions.'), [VI]–XVI (Introduction), 8 pp. (Contents), [1]–1120.
Copy: Penn.

123. Extracts, / *Elegant, Instructive, and Entertaining,* / in Poetry; / *from the most approved Authors:* / Disposed Under Proper Heads, / With a View / to the / *Improvement and Amusement* / of / Young Persons: / *being similar in design to* / Extracts in Prose. / — / [vignette] / [Latin quotation from Cicero] / London: *Printed for Messrs. Rivingtons, Longman, Law, Dodsley, Whites, Johnson,* / *Robinsons, Cadell, Murray, Richardson, Baldwin, Bew, Goldsmith, Faulder, Hayes,* / *Ogilvy & Cº. Bent, Scatcherd & Cº. Vernor, Wynne, Wilkie, Lowndes, Evans & Kearsley.* / 1791.

[Title decorated with flourishes.]
Large 8vo; 8 pp., 1–472, 1–472.
The second set of 472 pages contains 18 poetical pieces by Swift (pp. 275–90).

The difficulty is that the specific editions are not mentioned on the title-pages, but something may be learned from the Prefaces and Advertisements. As to the *Prose*, the 'New Edition' recorded above was apparently the fourth, the 1797 edition the seventh. The first edition was in 12mo, the second in 8vo (possibly 1770 and 1784; nothing by Swift in them yet). When the third edition of the *Prose* appeared, an edition (probably the first) of the *Verse* had just been published; and an enlarged edition (probably the second) of the *Verse* came out with the fourth edition of the *Prose.* In 1794 there were: 2 vols. *Prose*, 2 vols. *Poetry*, 1 vol. *Epistles.* (1st ed. 1790). In 1797 there were: 1 vol. *Prose* (7th ed. — see above). 1 vol. *Poetry*, 1 vol. *Epistles.*

There were further editions in 1801, 1803, 1809. Afterwards rival editions appeared: In 1810–16 (?) there was one of 18 vols. in 16mo (36 parts, with 36 engraved vignette titles), consisting of 6 vols. *Prose*, 6 vols. *Verse*, 6 vols. *Epistles* (John Sharpe, n.d.). And in 1823–7 there was one of 12 vols. in 12mo (Chiswick Press, by C. Whittingham), partly called *Elegant Extracts*, and partly *New Elegant Extracts* (edited by R. A. Davenport, meant not for schoolboys but for grown-up readers).

124. Dean Swift's / Tracts / On The / Repeal Of The Test Act, / Written, And First Published, In / Ireland, In The Years 1731–2, / *viz.* / I. The Presbyterians Plea of Merit in order to take off / the Test, impartially examined. / II. The Advantages proposed by Repealing the Sacra- / mental Test, impartially considered. / III. Queries relating to the Sacramental Test. / — / London: / Reprinted At The Logographic Press; / And Sold By / J. Walter, No. 169, Opposite Bond Street, Piccadilly. / — / M.DCC.XC.

8vo; π^2, B–D^8, E^2 — 2 pp. (h.t. + bl.), 2 pp. (f.t. + bl.), [1]–50, 2 pp. advs. Copy: B.M. 8132 dd 1 (8).

126. Roach's / Beauties of the Poets / Of / Great Britain. / *Carefully Selected & Arranged* / From the Works of / *The most Admired Authors,* / Particularly. / [*First column:*] Milton, / Pope, / Dryden, / Thomson, / Addison, / Goldsmith, / Johnson, / Young, / [*Second column:*] Blair, / Gray, / Prior, / Shenstone, / Mallet, / Cowper, / Collins, Parnell, / [*Third column:*] Beattie, / Moore, / Chatterton, / Buckingham, / Duncombe, / Armstrong, / Percy, / Cotton, / &c. &c. / In Six Volumes / Vol. I. / [illustration] / London. / Printed *by* J. Roach, *at the* Britannia Printing Office. / *Woburn Street, New Drury Theatre Royal. 1794.*

[Decorated title.]
The other titles are the same, except for the volume-numbers.
Size: 12mo (in sixes).
Vol. IV contains *Dean Swift's Curate* (p. 24), Vol. V (third section, with special title: N.° XX) *On the Death of Dr. Swift* (pp. 28–47), *Mrs. Harris's Petition* (pp. 51–6), and *Mary the Cook-Maid's Letter to Dr. Sheridan* (pp. 57–9).

125. The / Works / Of The / *British Poets.* / With / Prefaces, / Biographical And Critical, / *By Robert Anderson, M.D.* / = / *Volume Ninth;* / Containing / [*First column:*] Swift, / Thomson, / Watts, / Hamilton, / [*Second column:*] Philips, (A.) / West, (G.) / Collins, / Dyer, / [*Third column:*] Shenstone, / Mallet, / Akenside, And / Harte. / = / London: / Printed For John & Arthur Arch; / And For Bell & Bradfute, / And J. Mundell & Co. Edinburgh. / — / 1795.

Large 8vo; π^1, π^1, a^8, b^1, A–3L^8, 3M^2 — 2 pp. (decorated title on thicker paper bearing illustration from Swift's 'Baucis and Philemon', + bl.), 2 pp. (above title + bl.), 2 pp. (title as below + bl.), [III]–XVIII, [1]–915 + bl.

The 'Swift' part in this volume has the following title:

The / Poetical Works / Of / Jonathan Swift, D.D. / Containing / [*First column:*] Cadenus And Vanessa, / Odes, / Epistles, / Epigrams, / Songs, / [*Second column:*] Satires, / Epitaphs, / Characters, / Aenigmas, / Rebuses, / *&c. &c. &c.* / To which is prefixed / *The Life Of The Author.* / = / O Swift! if fame be life (as well we know / That bards and heroes have esteem'd it so) / Thou canst not wholly die: thy works will shine / To future times, and life in fame be thine! / Parnell's Verses To Swift On His Birth-Day. / = / Edinburgh: / Printed by *Mundell And Son*, Royal Bank Close. / *Anno* 1794.

Large 8vo; 2 pp. (t. + bl.), III–XVIII, 1–170.
There are 13 vols, all 1795, and a 14th vol. of 'Fugitive Poetry' (1807), but I have not seen the latter.

127. Swift's und Arbuthnot's / vorzüglichste / prosaische Schriften, / satyrischen, humoristischen / und andern Inhalts. / — / Erster Band. / [vignette] / — / Leipzig, / in der Weygandschen Buchhandlung, / — / 1798.

Sm. 8vo:
I: π^1,)(^{2}, a–b^8, c^4, A–K^8, L^7, M–O^8, P^6 — 2 pp. (t. + bl.), 3 pp. (Vorrede), 1 p. (Inhalt), [I]–XL (Swift's Leben), [1]–234.
II: π^1, A–P^8, Q^2 — 2 pp. (t. + bl.), 2 pp. (Inhalt), [3]–244.
III: A–Q^8 — 2 pp. (t. + bl.), [3]–254, 2 pp. (Inhalt).
IV:)(^{6}, A–P^8, Q^4 — 2 pp. (t. + bl.), 4 pp. (Vorrede), 6 pp. (Inhalt), [1]–234, 2 pp. blank.
V: π^2,)(^{2}, A–E^8, F^6, G–Q^8, R^6 — 2 pp. (bl. + title: 'Gulliver'), 2 pp. (t. + bl.), 4 pp. (Inhalt), [1]–263 + bl.
VI: π^1,)(^{4}, A–R^8, S^4 — 2 pp. (bl. + title: 'Gulliver'), 2 pp. (t. + bl.), 6 pp. (Inhalt), [1]–276, 2 pp. advs., 2 pp. blank.
The same title in all the six volumes, but the second, fourth and sixth have no vignette, while the year of the last four is 1799. The title of the sixth volume has 'Mit Kupfern.' just over the imprint, but there are no plates, unless the three vignettes are meant.
The only illustration in the Penn copy is in the text of Vol. VI on p. 32.

128. The Works Of The Poets Of Great Britain And Ireland, with Prefaces Biographical and Critical. 1800. Large 8vo; 8 or 9 vols.

Contains 26 pp. of the Biography of Swift, and 184 pp. of his Poems. It is Johnson's Works of the Poets, and the publisher is Andrew Miller, Strand, London [Information kindly supplied by Thomas C. Godfrey, York].

133. Gleanings / From The / *Writings Of The Celebrated* / Dean Swift. / Consisting / Chiefly Of His Humorous Pieces. / To Which Is Added, / Some Account Of The Author. / — / [ornament, containing monogram TH] / = / London: / *Printed by J. Cundee, Ivy*

Lane, / For T. Hurst, Paternoster Row; / J. Dingle, Bury; T. Richards, Plymouth; H. Holmes, and T. Both- / amley, Leeds; and T. Coombe, Leicester. / — / 1802.

Small 12mo (in sixes); π^5, B–Aa^6, π^1 — 2 pp. (t. + bl.), [III]–IX (Life of Swift), 1 p. (Contents), [1]–277 ('Character of Swift' on verso). — Frontisp. (Swift).
Copy: Penn.

134. The / Works / Of The / British Poets, / Collated With The Best Editions: / By / *Thomas Park*, F.S.A. / — / Vol. XVI. / — / Containing / The First And Second Volumes / Of / *Swift.* / = / *London:* / Printed For J. Sharpe, Opposite Albany, / Piccadilly; And Sold By / W. Suttaby, Stationers' Court, Ludgate Street / — / 1808.

The same title in Vol. XVII, except:
– – – – / Vol. XVII. / — / Containing / The Third And Fourth Volumes / Of / *Swift.* / = / – – – –

Each of these two volumes contains two separately paged parts, again called 'volumes', with appropriate titles, after the following pattern:

The / Poetical Works / Of / *Jonathan Swift,* / Dean Of St. Patrick's, Dublin. / Collated With The Best Editions: / By / *Thomas Park, Esq. F.S.A.* / In Four Volumes. / — / Vol. I. / = / *London:* / Printed at the Stanhope Press, / By Charles Whittingham, / *Union Buildings, Leather Lane*; / For J. Sharpe; And Sold By W. Suttaby, / Stationers' Court, Ludgate Street. / — / 1806.

The same titles in Vols. II, III, IV, except for the volume-numbers; while the address under the name of Charles Whittingham in these three volumes is: 103, *Goswell Street*;
The year of my own copy Vol. IV. is 1806; that of the B.M. copy is 1807.
16mo (in eights):
π^4, B^4, C–L^8, M^6 — 2 pp. (h.t. + printer's name on verso), 2 pp. (series-title + bl.), 2 pp. (volume-title + bl.), 2 pp. (Contents), [5]–166, 2 pp. blank. — Frontisp.
π^3, B–L^8, M^2 — 2 pp. (volume-title + bl.), [III]–VI (Contents), [5]–167 + bl. — Frontisp.
π^6, B^2, C–M^8, N^4 — 2 pp. (h.t. + printer's name on verso), 2 pp. (series-title + bl.), 2 pp. (volume-title + bl.), [III]–VII (Contents), 1 p. blank, [5]–173, 3 pp. blank. — Frontisp.
π^4, B–K^8, L^2 — 2 pp. (volume-title + bl.), [III]–VII (Contents), 1 p. blank, [5]–150, 2 pp. blank. — Frontisp.
The whole collection (1805–12) seems to consist of: *Poets*, 84 vols. in 42; *Supplement*, 12 vols. in 6; *Johnson's Lives*, 7 vols. in 4; *Translations*, 16 vols. in 8. Together 119 vols. in 60.
In an antiquarian book catalogue I found: 70 vols., 1808–15; in another: 108 vols in 54, 1808–18, general titles all dated 1818.

135. *Another edition* (100 vols. in 50):

The / British Poets: / With The Most / *Approved Translations* / Of The / Greek And Roman Poets, / With / Dissertations, Notes, &c. / = / *The Text collated with the best Editions,* / By Thomas Park, Esq. F.S.A. / — / Illustrated By A Series Of Engravings, By The / Most Eminent Artists. / — / *In One Hundred Volumes.* / Vols. XXXV. XXXVI. / Containing The Poetical Works Of / Swift. In 4 Volumes. / Vols. 1. 2. / = / *London:* / Printed For J. Sharpe. / — / 1810–1824.

The same title for the other volume, except:
– – – – / Vols. XXXVII. XXXVIII. / – – – – – – – / Vols. 3. 4. / – – – – –

Each of these two volumes contains two separately paged parts, again called 'volumes', with appropriate titles, after the following pattern:

The / Poetical Works / Of / *Jonathan Swift,* / Dean Of St. Patrick's, Dublin. / Collated With The Best Editions: / By / *Thomas Park, Esq. F.S.A.* / — / In Four Volumes. / Vol. I. / = / *London:* / Printed at the Stanhope Press, / By C. Whittingham; / For John Sharpe, Piccadilly; Suttaby, Evance, / And Fox, Stationers' Court; And Taylor And / Hessey, Fleet Street. / — / 1814.

The same titles in Vols. II, III, IV, except for the volume-numbers.
18mo:
frontisp., 2 pp., I–IV, 5–166, bl. leaf; frontisp., I–IV, 5–167 + bl. frontisp., 2 pp., I–VI, 7–175 + bl.; frontisp., I–VI, 7–152.
Copy: Bibl. Nat. Paris.

137. The / Works / Of The / English Poets, / *From Chaucer To Cowper;* / Including The / Series Edited, / With / Prefaces, Biographical And Critical, / *By Dr. Samuel Johnson:* / And / The Most Approved Translations. / = / The / Additional Lives / By *Alexander Chalmers,* F.S.A. / = / In Twenty-One Volumes. / Vol. XI. / [*First column:*] Lansdowne, / Yalden, / Tickell, / Hammond, / [*Second column:*] Somervile, / Savage, / Swift. / = / *London:* / Printed For J. Johnson; J. Nichols And Son; R. Baldwin; F. And C. Rivington; W. Otridge And Son; / Leigh And Sotheby; R. Faulder And Son; G. Nicol And Son; T. Payne; G. Robinson; Wilkie And / Robinson; C. Davies; T. Egerton; Scatcherd And Letterman; J. Walker; Vernor; Hood, And Sharpe; / R. Lea; J. Nunn; Lackington, Allen, And Co.; J. Stockdale; Cuthell And Martin; Clarke And Sons; / J. White And Co.; Longman, Hurst, Rees, And Orme; Cadell And Davies; J. Barker; John Richardson; / J. M. Richardson; J. Carpenter; B. Crosby; E. Jeffery; J. Murray; W. Miller; J. And A. Arch; Black, / Parry, And Kingsbury; J. Booker; S. Bagster; J. Harding; J. Mackinlay; J. Hatchard; R. H. Evans; / Matthews And Leigh; J. Mawman; J.

Booth; J. Asperne; P. And W. Wynne; and W. Grace, Deighton /
and Son at Cambridge, And Wilson And Son At York. / — / 1810.

Large 8vo; I–XIII (including h.t., before f.t.) + bl., 1–535 + bl.
Swift's pieces comprise pp. 343–535, including *Life of Swift* by Dr. Johnson,
pp. 345–66.

SECTION III

A TALE OF A TUB, &C.

++

Though this work always goes by the title of *A Tale Of A Tub*, it contains two more pieces, one mentioned in the title (*An Account of a Battel, &c.*), the third not (*A Discourse Concerning the Mechanical Operation Of The Spirit*).

217. A / Tale / Of A / Tub. / Written for the Universal Improve- / ment of Mankind. / — / *Diu multumque desideratum.* / — / To which is added, / An Account of a / Battel / Between The / Antient and Modern Books / in St. *James's* Library. / — / Basima eacabasa eanaa irraurista, diarba da caeo- / taba fobor camelanthi. *Iren. Lib. I. C. 18.* / — / —— *Juvatque novos decerpere flores,* / *Insignemque meo capiti petere inde coronam,* / *Unde prius nulli velarunt tempora Musae.* Lucret. / — / *London:* / Printed for *John Nutt,* near *Stationers-Hall.* / MDCCIV.

[Title within double-lined frame.]

8vo; A⁶, B–X⁸, Y² — 2 pp. (bl. + Treatises writ), 2 pp. (t. + bl.), 6 pp. (To The Right Honourable, John *Lord Sommers.*), 2 pp. (The Bookseller To The Reader.), 1–11 (The Epistle Dedicatory), 1 p. blank, 13–31 (The Preface), 1 p. blank, 33–221 + bl. (Tale); 2 pp. (title of the 'Battel' + bl.), 2 pp. (The Bookseller To The Reader.), 2 pp. (title of the 'Discourse' + bl.), 2 pp. (The Bookseller's Advertisement + bl.), 283–322 (Discourse), 2 pp. blank.

Published May 10, 1704 (see *Term Catalogues*).

Copies may occur with the leaf *Treatises writ by the same Author, &c.* [A1] facing *The Epistle Dedicatory* [p. 1], owing to a wrong folding of the double leaf A1 and A6. (See for a similar case No. 297, *post*.)

Copy: Penn.

Harvard has two copies of the first edition: one has on p. 320, 11.9–10 "for the *furor Uterinus.* Persons", the other "for the furor   Persons", the space for "*Uterinus*" having been left blank.

218. *Second edition:*

Same title and collation as those of the first edition, except:

— — — — — / The Second Edition Corrected. / — / *London:* Printed for *John Nutt,* near *Stationers-* / *Hall.* MDCCIV.

Copy: Penn.

219. *Third edition:*

Same title and collation as those of the first edition, except:

— — — — — / The Third Edition Corrected. / — / *London:* Printed for *John Nutt,* near *Stationers-* / *Hall.* MDCCIV.

Some sheets (H and N) are the same printing as the corresponding ones in the second edition.

Copy: Penn.

165

220. *Fourth edition:*
Same title and collation as those of the first edition, except:

– – – – / The Fourth Edition Corrected. / — / *London:* Printed for *John Nutt*, near *Stationers-* / *Hall*. MDCCV.

Copy: Penn.

221. *Dublin edition* (fourth):
Same title as that of the first London edition (only, the word 'Tub' is followed, not by a full stop, but by a colon; 'Battel' is spelt 'Battle'; *velarunt* is misspelt *velarnnt*) except:

– – – – – – / The Fourth Edition Corrected. / — / *Dublin*, Re-Printed; and are to be Sold / only at *Dick*'s and *Lloyd*'s Coffee-Houses, and / at the Printing-Press in *Fishamble-street*. 1705.

Sm. 8vo; A–H⁸, I⁴, K–M⁸, N⁴ — 2 pp. (bl. + Treatises writ), 2 pp. (t. + bl.), 4 pp. (To The Right Honourable, John *Lord Sommers*.), 2 pp. (The Bookseller To The Reader.), 1–6 (The Epistle Dedicatory), 7–17 (The Preface), 1 p. blank, 19–124 (Tale); 2 pp. (title of the 'Battel' + bl.), CXXVII (The Bookseller to the Reader.), CXXVIII (The Preface Of The Author.), 129–56 (Battel); 2 pp. (title of the 'Discourse' + bl.), 159 (The Bookseller's Advertisement.), 160–82 (Discourse). — B 4 signed A 4.
Copy: Penn.

222. *Fifth edition:*
Same title as that of the first edition, except:

– – – – – / The Fifth Edition: With the Au- / thor's Apology and Explanatory Notes. / By *W. W--tt--n*, B.D. and others. / — / *London:* Printed for *John Nutt*, near / *Stationers-Hall*. MDCCX.

8vo; A⁸, a⁸, B–Y⁸, L⁴ — a pp. (t. + Treatises wrote, on verso), 22 pp. (An Apology *For the*, &c.), 6 pp. (To The Right Honourable, John *Lord Sommers*.), 2 pp. (The Bookseller To The Reader.), 1–12 (The Epistle Dedicatory), 13–31 (The Preface.), 1 p. blank, 33–241 + bl. (Tale); 2 pp. (title of the 'Battel' + bl.), 2 pp. (The Bookseller To The Reader.), 2 pp. (The Preface Of The Author.), 249–99 + bl. (Battel); 2 pp. (title of the 'Discourse' + bl.), 2 pp. (The Bookseller's Advertisement. + bl.), 305–44 (Discourse). — A 2 and A 4 signed A 3 and a 2. — Frontisp. and 7 plates. There are also Large Paper copies.
Copy: Penn.

This edition contains *marginal notes* (which had already appeared in the first four editions), and (for the first time) the *Apology*, the *Explanatory Notes* (footnotes, partly by Swift himself, partly derived from Wotton), and the *plates*. The latter are: frontispieces to the *Tale* (signed B. Lens delin: J. Sturt sculp.) and to the *Battle*, and six others facing pp. 35, 56, 121, 138, 192, and 233.

The original plan was a page-for-page reprint, with the *Explanatory Notes* not as footnotes as they now appear in this fifth edition, but placed at the end of the book, by themselves. This is proved by the plates in a copy in the Forster library, subscribed to face pp. 35, 55, 111, 127, 178 and 214, i.e. the corresponding pages in the first four editions. A further proof is supplied by the following separate edition of the *Apology* and the *Explanatory Notes:*

223. An | Apology | For The | Tale of a' Tub. | — | With | Explanatory | Notes | By | *W. W-tt-n*, B.D. | And others. | — | *London*; | Printed for John Morphew near | *Stationers-Hall*. MDCCXI.

[Title within double-lined frame.]
8vo (in fours); A⁴, b–c⁴, D–F⁴, G² — 2 pp. (t. + bl.), 24 (Apology), 25–51 (Explanatory Notes), 1 page blank. A 2 and b 2 signed A 3 and b 3.
"The 'Apology' (pp. 3–24) is an offprint from ed. 5 with page numbers added. The 'Explanatory Notes' are the footnotes in ed. 5, but are printed in a body in the same type as the text of edd. 1–5. . . . The explanation of the date 1711 may be that the type had been kept standing in order to form along with an offprint of the 'Apology' a supplement to the earlier editions of the *Tale*." (*A Tale Of A Tub*, ed. Guthkelch and Nichol Smith, 1958, pp. LXVIII–LXX.)
The *Explanatory Notes By W. W—tt—n, B.D.* were derived from the last pages ('Observations') of the last section ('A Defense') in:
Reflections Upon Ancient and Modern Learning. To which is now added A Defense Thereof, In Answer to the Objections of Sir W. Temple, and Others. With Observations upon the Tale of a Tub. By William Wotton, B.D. &c. Third Edition Corrected. London: Printed for Tim. Goodwin, at the Queen's Head, against St. Dunstan's Church in Fleetstreet. MDCCV.
8vo; 6 pp., I–XXXII, 2 pp., 1–541, 3 pp. advs. ["A Defense, &c." is pp. 471–541; "Observations upon The Tale of a Tub" is pp. 517–41]. — Cf. No. 999.
The 'Defense' and the 'Observations' were also published separately:
A Defense Of The Reflections Upon Ancient and Modern Learning, In Answer to the Objections Of Sir W. Temple, and Others. With Observations upon The Tale of a Tub.
8vo (in fours); A–H⁴, I⁶ — 2 pp. (h.t. + Advertisement on verso), 2 pp. (f.t. + bl.), 1–69, 3 app. advs. — Pages 37–40 repeated in numbering.
Copies: Forster, and B.M. 833 e 14 (2) and Rothschild, where the description is given as A–I⁴, [—] 2.
For Curll's *Complete Key To The Tale Of A Tub*, see No. 1004, *post*.

***

Small 12mo Editions of 1711

224. (1) A | Tale | Of A | Tub. | Written for the Universal Im- | provement of Mankind. | — | *Diu multumque desideratum.* | — | To which is Added, | An Account of a Battel | between the Antient and Modern | Books in St. *James*'s Library. | — | Basima eacabasa eanaa irraurista, diarba da | caeotaba fobor camelanthi. *Iren. lib.* 1. *c.* 18. | — | —— *Juvatque novos decerpere flores,* | *Insignemque meo capiti petere inde coronam,* | *Unde prius nulli velarunt tempora Musae.* Lucret. | — | *Anno* M.DCC.XI.

Sm. 12mo; A–N¹² — 2 pp. (bl. + Treatises writ), 2 pp. (t. + bl.), 5–11 + bl. (To The Right Honourable John Lord Sommers.), 13–14 (The Bookseller To The Reader.), 15–24 (The Epistle Dedicatory), 25–41 (The

Preface.), 1 p. blank, 43–213 + bl. (Tale); 2 pp. (title of the 'Battel' + bl.), 217–18 (The Bookseller To The Reader.), 219–20. (The Preface Of The Author.), 221–66 (Battel), 2 pp. blank, 2 pp. (title of the 'Discourse' + bl.), 271 (The Bookseller's Advertisement.), 1 p. blank, 273–310 (Discourse), 2 pp. blank. — No plates.

Copy: Penn.

225. (2) *Another edition:*

Same title, and same collation. — Penn has two copies, one without plates, the other with 8 plates, the same as those in the fifth edition 1710, but on a smaller scale.

226. (3) *Another edition:*

Same title, but the word 'camelanthi' misprinted 'camelaanthi'. Same collation. No plates.

Copy: Penn.

227. (4) *Another edition:*

Same title and collation, but *Juvatque* printed *Juvat que*. Plates as in No. 2 above.

Notes: 1. The above four editions resemble each other so much — page for page, and line for line — that at first sight they seem to be the same. However, they are all different printings. Besides variations in the lettertypes (for instance the capital U, which appears as U[and U; and the italic capital W, which appears as *W* and *VV*) the difference is i.a. distinguishable by the following points:

No. 1 has:

p. 69, l. 3 from foot: 'Vein'.

p. 207, l. 5 from foot: 'uicely'.

No. 2 has:

p. 16, l. 3 from top: '*Highnoss*'.

p. 50, l. 1 from top: 'your'.

No. 3 has:

p. 69, l. 7 from foot: 'Pans'.

p. 164, l. 21 from top: '*videre*'.

No. 4 has:

p. 176, l. 1 from foot: 'Studant'.

p. 177, ll. 1–2 from top: 'sqee-zing'.

I have purposely selected variations that do not occur in the corresponding places in the other volumes.

2. Plates occur in editions No. 2 (apparently not in all copies) and No. 4; not in the others. Exactly the same plates, i.e. the same off-prints, appear again in the 6th edition of the *Tale*, 1724, printed for S. Tooke and B. Motte (see No. 230, *post*), only with different page-inscriptions at foot to suit the different pagination.

3. None of the four editions has the new matter of the fifth 8vo edition, 1710 (*Apology*, and *Explanatory Notes* at foot). But Penn has copies of editions No. 2, No. 3 and No. 4 with *A Complete Key*, 3rd ed., 1714, bound in at the end. This 3rd edition of the *Key*, 1714, occurs in two different shapes (see No. 1004, *post*); the Penn copies of editions No. 2 and No. 3 have it in the first, that of edition No. 4 in the second shape. It clearly served the double purpose of addition to a 1714 Curll edition of the *Tale* (see No. 228, *post*), and to the previous 1711 editions. — The Guildhall Library even possesses a 1711 copy of the *Tale*, with *A Complete Key*, 4th ed., 1724, bound in (see No. 1004, *post*). The 6th ed. of the *Tale*, 1724, (Tooke and Motte) cannot have had any need for this *Key*, as it has the *Apology* in front, and the *Explanatory*

Notes at foot. This makes me think there may have been a 'Curll' edition of the *Tale* in 1724 (see No. 231, *post*).

4. The above details are too slight to base on them any conclusion as to the sequence of these four editions. Yet I venture to suppose that No. 1 was published by Curll, and that on its appearance the real owner of the copyright, Tooke, had No. 2 printed, resembling its rival in the smallest details, and adding soon after the plates to outdo his competitor. No. 3 I take to be a reprint of No. 1 (or the reverse); likewise No. 4 of No. 2. And the two third editions of the *Key* may constitute a further case of rivalry, in which Curll's example was again at once followed by Tooke.

228. *Another edition* in 12mo, 1714 (Curll?):

Blackwell's cat. 197, item 1410, says: "Swift, A Tale of a Tub, 1714, with a complete Key to the Tale of a Tub, 1714, 2 vols. in 1, 12mo, etc." — I have not seen such a copy (see No. 227, *ante*, note 3).

***

229. *An edition printed in Holland*, 1720, which is the first to contain the *History Of Martin* (see No. 17, *ante*).

230. *Sixth edition:*

A / Tale / Of A / Tub. / Written for the Universal Im- / prove-ment of Mankind. / — / *Diu multumque desideratum.* / — / To which is added, / An Account of a / Battel / Between The / Ancient and Modern Books / in St. *James*'s Library. / — / Basima eacabasa eanaa irraurista, diarba da / caeotaba fobor camelanthi. *Iren. Lib*. 1. *C*. 18. / — / —— *Juvatque novos decerpere flores,* / *Insignemque meo capiti petere inde coronam,* / *Unde prius nulli velarunt tempora Musae.* Lucr. / — / The Sixth Edition: With the / Author's Apology and Explanatory Notes. / By *W. W - - tt - - n*, B.D. and others. / — / *London:* Printed for *S. Tooke* and *B. Motte,* / at the *Middle Temple Gate, Fleet-street.* 1724.

Sm. 12mo; A⁶, B–O¹², P⁴ — 2 pp. (t. + bl.), III–XXII (Apology), XXIII–XXVIII (To The Right Honourable John *Lord Sommers*.), XXIX–XXX (The Bookseller To The Reader.), XXXI–XL (The Epistle Dedi-catory), XLI–LVI (The Preface.), 1–184 (Tale); 2 pp. (title of the 'Battle' + bl.), 187–8 (The Bookseller To The Reader.), 189–90 (The Preface Of The Author.), 191–234 (Battle); 2 pp. (title of the 'Discourse' + bl.), 237 (The Bookseller's Advertisement.), 1 p. blank, 239–73 (Discourse), 3 pp. blank. — Eight plates, the same off-prints as those in two of the 1711 editions (see Nos. 224–7, *ante*), but six of them differently inscribed to suit the different pagination.

Copy: Penn.

231. *Another 'Curll' edition* in 12mo, 1724(?):

See No. 227, *ante*, note 3.

232. *Dublin edition* (seventh):

A / Tale / Of A / Tub. / Written for the Universal Improvement / Of / Mankind. / — / *Diu multumque desideratum.* / — / To which is added, / An Account of a Battle between the Anti- / ent and

Modern Books in St. *James*'s Library. / Also / A Discourse concerning the Mechanical O- / peration of the Spirit, in a Letter to a
/ Friend. A Fragment. / — / Basima eacabasa èanaa irraurista,
diarba da caeo- / taba fobor camelanthi. *Iren. Lib.* 1. *C.* 18. / — /
— — *Juvatque novos decerpere floros,* / *Insignemque meo capiti petere*
inde coronam, / *Unde prius nulli velarunt tempora Musae.* Lucr. / — /
The Seventh Edition: With the Author's / Apology and Explana-
tory Notes. / By *W. W - - - - tt - - - - - n*, B.D. and Others. / — /
Dublin: Printed by A. Rhames for W. Smith / at the *Hercules* in
Dame-street, 1726.

Sm. 12mo (in sixes); A–L⁶ — 2 pp. (t. + bl.), III–XX (Apology), XXI–
XXV (To The Right Honourable John *Lord* Sommers.), XXVI–XXVII
(The Bookseller To The Reader.), XXVIII–XXXV (The Epistle Dedicatory),
XXVI–XLIX (The Preface.), 1 p. blank, 1–154 (Tale); 2 pp. (title of the
'Battle' + bl.), 157–8 (The Bookseller To The Reader.) 159–60 (The
Preface Of The Author.), 161–96 (Battle); 197 (title of the 'Discourse'),
198 (The Bookseller's Advertisement.), 199–226 (Discourse). — The title
of the 'Battle', wrongly dated MDCCXXIV. — Frontisp. (ship and dolphin),
unsigned.
Copy: Penn.

233. *Seventh edition:*
A / Tale / Of A / Tub. / Written for the Universal Improve- /
ment of Mankind. / — / *Diu multumque desideratum.* / — / To
which is added, / An Account of a / Battel / Between The / Antient
and Modern Books / in St. *James*'s Library. / — / Basima eacabasa
eanaa irraurista, diarba da caeotaba / fobor camelanthi. *Iren. Lib.*
1. *C.* 18. / — / —— *Juvatque novos decerpere flores,* / *Insignemque*
meo capiti petere inde coronam, / *Unde prius nulli velarunt tempora*
Musae. Lucret. / — / The Seventh Edition. / With the Author's
Apology; / And Explanatory Notes, by *W. W - - tt - - n*, B.D. /
and Others. / — / *London:* Printed for Benj. Motte, at / the *Middle-*
Temple Gate, in *Fleet-street.* / M.DCC.XXVII.

12mo; A–K¹², L² — 2 pp. (t. + *Treatises wrote* on verso), 16 pp. (Apology),
5 pp. (To The Right Honourable John *Lord Sommers.*), 1 p. (The *Bookseller*
to the *Reader.*), 1–8 (Epistle Dedicatory), 9–20 (The Preface.), 21 (misprinted
24) — 152 (Tale); 2 pp. (title of the 'Battel' + bl.), 155–6 (The Bookseller
To The Reader.), 157–8 (The Preface Of The Author.), 159–89 + bl.
(Battel); 2 pp. (title of the 'Discourse' + bl.), 193–4 (The Bookseller's
Advertisement.), 195–220 (Discourse). — Frontisp. and 7 plates (the same
off-prints as those in the 6th ed., but retouched and with different page-
inscriptions).
Copy: Penn.

234. *Eighth edition:*
The same title-page as that of the seventh edition, except:

- - - - - / The Eighth Edition. / With the Author's Apology. /
And Explanatory Notes, by *W. W - - tt - - n*, B.D. / and Others.

| — | London: Printed for Benj. Motte, at | the *Middle-Temple Gate,* in *Fleetstreet,* | MDCCXXXIII.

The same collation as that of the seventh edition, No. 233, but a different printing. — The running-title on p. 218 misprinted *A Fragetnt*; page-number 219 misprinted 249. — Frontisp. and 7 plates (the same offprints as those in the 7th edition, and again retouched).
Copy: Penn.

235. *Another edition* (printed in Holland ?):
A Tale | Of A Tub: | Written for the universal Improvement | of Mankind. | *Diu multumque desideratum.* | To which is added, | An Account of a Battel between | the *Antient* and *Modern* Books in | *St. James*'s Library. | — | Basima eacabasa eanaa irraurista, diarba da | caetoba fobor camelanthi. *Iren. lib.* 1. *c.* 18. | — — *Juvatque novos decerpere flores,* | *Insignemque meo capiti petere inde coronam,* | *Unde prius nulli velarunt tempora Musae.* Lucret. | — | A new Edition, with the Author's Apo- | logy, and Explanatory Notes, | by *W. Wotton* B.D. & others. | [ornament] | London. | M.DCC.XXXIV.

Sm. 8vo; π^2, A–S^8, I^2 — 2 pp. (t. + *Treatises wrote* on verso), 2 pp. (The Bookseller's Advertisement on this new Edition.), 1–6 (To The Right Honourable John Lord Somers.), 7–8 (The Bookseller To The Reader.), 9–16 (The Epistle Dedicatory), 17–30 (The Preface.), 31–180 (Tale); 1 p. (title of the 'Discourse'), 1 p. (The Bookseller's Advertisement.), 183–213 + bl. (Discourse); 2 pp. (title of the 'Battel' + bl.), 217–18 (The Bookseller *to the* Reader., and The Preface Of The Author.), 219–55 (Battel); 256–74 (An Apology *For the Tale of a Tub,* &c.), 275–92 (A Table), 292 (Errors & Omissions). — C 1 not signed. The *Table* contains *The History of Martin.*
Penn has a French translation in MS. (large 4to; 115 leaves) of this 1734 edition, of the *Tale* only, which shows a different text from the French editions of 1721, &c. (Nos 263, &c., *post*), and has as far as I know, never been published. Its title reads:
Conte du Tonneau | Ecrit pour L'instruction universelle du genre humain | Diu multumq; &c. | .... Juvatque &c. | Nouvelle édition | avec L'Apologie de l'auteur, et des nottes par | Mr. Wotton B.D. et autres. | A Londres 1754.

235A. *Another issue:*
Exactly the same printing, only the title-page has been renewed. It is the same as in the 1734 copy, except for a double rule under 'Of A Tub:', while the imprint is as follows:

– – – – | London. | *Printed for* R. Wilson, | MDCCL.
Copy: Penn.

236. *Ninth edition:*
The same title-page and collation as those of the seventh and eighth editions (only 'Battel' spelt 'Battle'), except:

– – – – | The Ninth Edition. | With the Author's Apology. And Explanatory Notes, by *W. W - - tt - - n,* B.D. | and Others. | = | *London:* Printed for Charles Bathurst, at | the *Middle-Temple-Gate,* in *Fleet-Street.* | M.DCC.XXXIX.

Eight new plates, representing the same subjects as before, but copied in reverse; all inscribed: J Mynde sculp.
Copy: Penn.

237. *Dublin edition* (eighth):

A / Tale / Of A / Tub. / Written for the / Universal Improvement / Of / *Mankind.* / — / *Diu multumque desideratum.* / — / To which is added, / An Account of a Battle between the / Antient and Modern Books in St. *James*'s Li- / brary. / Also / A Discourse concerning the Mechanical / Operation of the Spirit, in a Letter to a / Friend. A Fragment. / — / Basima eacabasa eanaa irraurista, diarba da caeotaba fobor came- / lanthi. *Iren. Lib.* 1. *C.* 18. / — / —— *Juvatque novos decerpere flores,* / *Insignemque meo capiti petere inde coronam,* / *Unde prius nulli velarunt tempora Musae.* Lucr. / The Eighth Edition: With the Author's Apology / and Explanatory Notes. / By *W. W* - - - - *tt* - - - - *n*, B.D. and Others. / — / *Dublin:* / Printed by S. Powell, / For W. Smith at the *Hercules* in *Dame-street*, and G. / Faulkner in *Essex-street*, MDCCXLI.

12mo; A–L¹² — 2 pp. (t. + bl.), III–XIX (Apology), XX–XXIV (To The Right Honourable John *Lord* Sommers.), XXV–XXVI (The Bookseller To The Reader.), XXVII–XXXIV (The Epistle Dedicatory), XXXV–XLVII + bl. (The Preface.), 49–195 + bl. (Tale); 2 pp. (title of the 'Battle' + bl.), 199–200 (The Bookseller To The Reader.), 201–2 (The Preface Of The Author.), 203–36 (Battle); 237 (title of the 'Discourse'), 238 (The Bookseller's Advertisement.), 239–64 (Discourse). — Eight plates.
Copy: Penn.

238. For editions of the *Tale* in 1743 (10th ed.), 1747 (11th ed.), 1751 (12th ed.), 1751 (10th ed.), and further in Swift's *Works*, see Nos. 66, &c., *ante*.

239. *Edinburgh edition* (twelfth):

A / Tale / Of A / Tub. / Written for the universal Improve- / ment of Mankind. / *Diu multumque desideratum.* / To which are added, / An Account of a Battle between / The Ancient and the Modern / Books in St. *James*'s Library; and, / A Discourse concerning the Mechani- / cal Operation of the Spirit. / With the Author's Apology; and, / Explanatory Notes, by *W. Wotton*, B.D. and others. / Basima eacabasa eanaa irraurista, diarba da caeotaba fobor ca- / melanthi. *Iren. l.* 1. *c.* 18. / —— *Juvatque novos decerpere flores,* / *Insignemque meo capiti petere inde coronam,* / *Unde priùs velârunt tempora musae.* Lucret. / The Twelfth Edition. / *Edinburgh:* / Printed by W. Sands, A. Murray, and J. Cochran. / For William Gay *junior.* / Sold by G. Crawfurd, W. Gordon, and J. Brown, / *Edinburgh*; J. Barry, *Glasgow*; and T. Glas, *Dundee.* / MDCCL.

12mo; π², a⁶, b⁶, A–R⁶, S⁴ — 2 pp. (t. + bl.), 2 pp. (Treatises wrote + bl.), [III]–XVIII (Apology), [XIX]–XXIV (To The Right Honourable John Lord Sommers.), [XXV]–XXVI (The Bookseller To The Reader.), [1]–8

(The Epistle Dedicatory), 9–20 (The Preface.), [21]–142 (Tale); 2 pp. (title of the 'Battle' + bl.), [145]–146 (The Bookseller To The Reader.), [147]–148 (The Preface Of The Author.), [149]–180 (Battle); 2 pp. (title of the 'Discourse' + bl.), 2 pp. (The Bookseller's Advertisement. + bl.), 185–209 (Discourse), 3 pp. blank. — Frontisp. and 7 plates (all inscribed 'T. Smith Sculp').
Copy: Penn.

239A. A / Tale / Of A / Tub. / Written for the Universal Improvement / of Mankind. / — / *Diu multumque desideratum.* / — / To which is added, / An Account of a / Battle / Between the Antient and Modern Books / in St. James's Library. / — / Basima eacabasa eanaa irraurista, diarba da caeotaba / fobor camelanthi. *Iren. Lib.* 1. *C.* 18. / — / — — *Juvatque novos decerpere flores,* / *Insignemque meo capiti petere inde coronam,* / *Unde prius nulli velarunt tempora Musae.* Lucret. / — / With the Author's Apology. / And Explanatory Notes, by *W. W-tt-n,* B. D. / and Others. / — / *London:* / Printed for C. Bathurst in *Fleet-street.* / — / MDCCLI.

This is a separate issue of *Works*, Vol. I, 12mo in sixes, 1751 (see No. 82), after cancellation of the volume-title. It has the frontisp. and 7 plates.
Copy: B.M. 102314 ggg 21.

240. *Edinburgh and Glasgow edition* (thirteenth):
A / Tale of a Tub. / Written for the universal Improve- / ment of Mankind. / *Diu multumque desideratum.* / To which are added, / An Account of a Battle between / the Ancient and the Modern / Books in St. *James*'s Library; and, / A Discourse concerning the Mechani- / cal Operation of the Spirit. / With the Author's Apology; and, / Explanatory Notes, by *W. Wotton,* B.D. and others. / Basima eacabasa eanaa irraurista, diarba da caeotaba fobor / camelanthi. *Iren. l.* 1. *c.* 18. / —— *Juvatque novos decerpere flores,* / *Insignemque meo capiti petere inde coronam,* / *Unde priùs nulli velarunt tempora Musae.* Lucret. / The Thirteenth Edition. / *Edinburgh:* / Printed for G. Hamilton & J. Balfour, and L. Hun- / ter, at *Edinburgh*; / and A. Stalker, at *Glasgow*; and / sold by them and other Booksellers. / M,DCC,LII.

This is a separate issue of *Works*, Vol. IX, 12mo in sixes, 1752 (see No. 93), with title-page cancelled and renewed.
Copy: Penn.

241. *Glasgow edition* (thirteenth):
A / Tale / Of A / Tub. / Written for the universal Improvement / of Mankind. / *Diu multumque desideratum.* / To which are added, / An Account of a Battle between the / Ancient and the Modern Books in / St. *James*'s Library; and, / A Discourse concerning the Mechanical / Operation of the Spirit. / With the Author's Apology; and, / Explanatory Notes, by *W. Wotton,* B.D. and others. / Basima eacabasa, eanaa irraurista, diarba da caeotaba fobor ca- /

melanthi. *Iren. l.* 1. c. 18. | —— *Juvatque novos decerpere flores,* | *Insignemque meo capiti petere inde coronam,* | *Unde prius nulli velarunt tempora musae.* Lucret. | The Thirteenth Edition. | *Glasgow:* | Printed by R. Urie. MDCCLIII.

Sm. 8vo; A–Ff⁴ — 2 pp. (t. + bl.), 2 pp. (Treatises wrote + bl.), [V]–XIX + bl. (Apology), [XXI]–XXV + bl. (To The Right Honourable John Lord Sommers.), [XXVII]–XXVIII (The Bookseller To The Reader.), [29]–35 + bl. (The Epistle Dedicatory), 37–47 + bl. (The Preface.), [49]–166 (Tale); 2 pp. (title of the 'Battle' + bl.), [169]–170 (The Bookseller To The Reader.), 2 pp. (The Preface Of The Author. + bl.), [173]–202 (Battle); 2 pp. (title of the 'Discourse' + bl.), 2 pp. (The Bookseller's Advertisement. + bl.), 207–30 (Discourse), 2 pp. advs. — Frontisp. and 7 plates.

This seems to be the successor of the Edinburgh edition (twelfth), 1750 (No. 239, *ante*), as the frontisp. and plates are the same offprints as in that edition (in my copy the page-inscriptions of the 5th, 6th and 7th plates have been erased and renewed, while those of the 2nd, 3rd and 4th have been altered with a pen, to suit the new pagination).

Copy: Penn.

241A. A | Tale Of A Tub. | Written for the | Universal Improvement | Of | Mankind. | *Diu multumque desideratum.* | To which is added, | An Account of a Battle between the Antient and | Modern Books in St. *James's* Library. | Basyma cacabasa eanaa, irraumista diadarba caeota bafober ca- | melanthi. | — *Juvatque novos decerpere flores,* | *Insignemque meo capiti petere inde coronam,* | *Unde prius nulli velarunt tempora Musae.* Lucret. | With the Author's Apology; | And Explanatory Notes, by *W. Wotton,* B. D. | and others. | London: | Printed for Charles Bathurst, at the *Cross- | Keys* in Fleetstreet. | MDCCLIVl

This is a separate issue of *Works,* Vol. I, Part I, 4to, 1755 (see No. 87), from which the volume-title and the prefatory matter, pp. [1]–[44], have been removed.

242. *Dublin edition* (ninth):

A | Tale | Of A | Tub. | Written for the | Universal Improvement | Of | Mankind. | — | *Diu multumque desideratum.* | — | To which is added, | An Account of a Battle between | the Antient and Modern Books in | St. *James's* Library. | Also | A Discourse concerning the Mechanical | Operation of the Spirit, in a Letter to | a Friend. A Fragment. | — | Basima eacabasa eanaa irraurista, diarba da caeotaba fobor ca- | melanthi. *Iren. Lib.* 1. *C.* 18. | — | — *Juvatque novos decerpere flores,* | *Insignemque meo capiti petere inde coronam,* | *Unde prius nulli velarunt tempora Musae.* Lucr. | — | The Ninth Edition: With the Author's Apology | and Explanatory Notes. | By *W. Wotton,* B.D. and Others. | — | Dublin: | Printed for G. Faulkner in *Essex-street.* MDCCLVI.

18mo (in sixes); π^2 [inserts, as explained below] A^6, b–d^6, B–Q^6, R^4 [R 5 & 6 cancelled], S–Z^6, Aa–Ff^6, Gg^2 — 2 pp. (t. + bl.), III–XVIII (Apology), XIX–XXIII + bl. (To The Right Honourable John *Lord* Sommers), XXV–XXVI (The Bookseller To The Reader), XXVII–XXIII + bl. (The Epistle Dedicatory), XXXV–XLVII + bl. (The Preface), 1–125 + bl. (Tale); 2 pp. (title of the 'Battle' + bl.), 129–30 (The Bookseller To The Reader), 131–2 (The Preface Of The Author), 133–62 (Battle); [163] (title of the 'Discourse' + bl.), [164] (The Bookseller's Advertisement), 165–89 (Discourse), 3 pp. blank or advs. (?) — Frontisp. and 7 plates.

The titles of the *Tale*, the *Battle*, and the *Discourse* are all dated 1756. The presence of 'Vol. XI.' at the foot of the first leaves of sheets B, E, H, L, O, R (not of the intervening sheets) proves not only that it is an 18mo in sixes, but also that this volume was intended as Vol. XI of a set. As, however, this set was only printed in 1762 (see No. 53, *ante*), this book could provisionally only be sold separately. The composition of Vol. XI, 1762 (No. 53, *ante*) betrays what happened in that year, namely: A double leaf, bearing title Vol. XI, 1762, and *Contents* Vol. XI, was placed before above title. The last two leaves of the book (p. 189 + 3 pp. blank or advs. ?) were cut away (the two stubs are clearly visible), after which pp. 189–336 were added (p. 189 bears the last few lines of the text, p. [190] is blank, pp. [191]–336, S 2 through Gg 2, are the *Life of Swift*, dated 1762).

Copy: Penn.

243. A / Tale Of A Tub. / Written for the / Universal Improvement / Of / Mankind. / *Diu multumque desideratum.* / To which is added, / An Account of a Battle between the Antient and / Modern Books in *St. James*'s Library. / Basyma cacabasa eanaa, irraumista diarbada caëota bafobor came- / lanthi. *Iren. Lib.* I. *C.* 18. / —— *Juvatque novos decerpere flores,* / *Insignemque meo capiti petere inde coronam,* / *Unde prius nulli velarunt tempora Musae.* Lucret. / With the Author's Apology; / And Explanatory Notes, by *W. Wotton,* B.D. and / others. / London: / Printed for Charles Bathurst, at the *Cross-Keys* / in *Fleet-Street.* / MDCCLX.

Sm. 8vo; π^2, B–N^8, O^6 — 2 pp. (t. + bl.), [III]–XVI (Apology), XVII (Postscript), 1 p. (Treatises written), [1]–190. — Frontisp. and 7 plates.

Copies: B.M. 12330 ccc 30, and Penn.

This is a separate issue of the *Works*, Vol. I, sm. 8vo, 1760 (see No. 90), with the omission of the volume-title and the prefatory matter I–[XVI], [1]–[76], while the volume-indications at the foot of the first page of each new sheet have been removed, and the signatures indicated by new capitals.

244. A / Tale Of A Tub. / Written for the / Universal Improvement / Of / Mankind. / — / *Diu multumque desideratum.* / — / To which is added, / An Account of a Battle between the / Ancient and Modern Books in St. *James's* / Library. / Also / A Discourse concerning the Mechanical / Operation of the Spirit, in a Letter / to a Friend. A Fragment. / — / Basyma cacabasa eanaa irraumista, diarbada caeota bafobor / camelanthi. *Iren. Lib.* I. *C.* 18. / — / —— *Juvatque novos decerpere flores,* / *Insignemque meo capiti petere inde* *coronam,* | *Unde prius nulli velarunt tempora Musae.* Lucret. | — | With the Author's Apology; | And | Explanatory Notes, | By *W. Wotton,* B.D. and Others. | — | Dublin: | Printed by G. Faulkner, in Parliament-Street. | MDCCLXIX.

> This is a separate issue of the *Works,* Vol. XX, 8vo, 1769 (see No. 47), from which the first leaf (t. + bl.) has been cut away. At the foot of the first page of each new sheet there is: 'Vol. XX.'
> Copy: Penn.

245. A | Tale Of A Tub. | Written for the | Universal Improvement | Of | Mankind. | — | Diu multumque desideratum. | — | To which is added, | An Account of a Battle between the Ancient | and Modern Books in St. James's Library. | Also | A Discourse concerning the Mechanical Operation | of the Spirit, in a Letter to a Friend. | A Fragment. | — | Basyma cacabasa eanaa irraumista, diarbada caeota bafobor | camelanthi. Iren. Lib. 1. C. 18. | — | —— Juvatque novos decerpere flores, | Insignemque meo capiti petere inde coronam, | Unde prius nulli velarunt tempora Musae. Lucret. | — | With the Author's Apology; | And | Explanatory Notes, | By *W. Wotton,* B.D. and Others. | — | Dublin: | Printed by G. Faulkner, in Parliament-Street. | MDCCLXXI.

> This is a separate issue of the *Works,* Vol. XX, 12mo, 1771 (see No. 52), from which the first leaf (t. + bl.) has been cut away. At the foot of the first page of each new sheet there is: 'Vol. XX.'

246. A | Tale Of A Tub. | Written for the | Universal Improvement | Of | Mankind. | *Diù multumque desideratum.* | To which is added, | An Account of a Battle between the Ancient and | Modern Books in *St. James*'s Library. | Basyma cacabasa eanaa, irraumista diarbada caëota bafobor | camelanthi. *Iren. Lib.* 1. *C.* 18. | —— *Juvatque novos decerpere flores,* | *Insignemque meo capiti petere inde coronam,* | *Unde priùs nulli velarunt tempora Musae.* Lucret. | With the Author's Apology; | And Explanatory Notes, by *W. Wotton,* B.D. | and others. | Paris: | Printed by Didot senior. | Sold by {Pissot, | Barrois junior,} Booksellers. | Quai des Augustins. | MDCCLXXXI.

> Sm. 12mo; π^3, A–N^{12}, O^2 — 2 pp. (h.t. + bl.), 2 pp. (bl. + advs.), 2 pp. (f.t. + bl.), [1]–315 (*Errata* on verso).
> Copies: Bibl. Nat. Paris, and Heidelberg.

247. A | Tale of a Tub. | Written for the Universal Improvement | of Mankind. | — | *Diu multumque desideratum.* | — | To Which Is Added An | Account of a Battle | Between the Antient and Modern | Books in St. James's Library. | By Dr. Swift. | Basima eacabasa eanaa irraurista, diarba da caeotaba | fobor camelanthi. Iren. lib. 1 c. 18. | — | —— *Juvatque novos decerpere* *flores,* | *Insegnemque meo capiti petere inde coronam,* | *Unde prius nulli velarunt tempora Musae.* Lucret. | — | In Two Volumes. | — | Vol. I. | = | London: | Printed for Joseph Wenman, | No. 144, Fleet-Street. | M.DCC.LXXXI.

Same title in the second volume, except for the volume-number.
18mo; frontisp., 3–95 + bl.
frontisp., 3–94.
Copy: Forster (8550–34 D. 12).

248. Tale Of A Tub, | Written For The Universal | Improvement Of Mankind. | *Diu multumque desideratum.* | To which are added, | An Account Of A Battle | Between The | Ancient And Modern Books. | In St. James's Library. | And a Discourse, concerning the Mechanical | Operations Of The Spirit. | With the Author's Apology, and Explanatory Notes, | By W. Wotton, B.D. And Others. | = | Basima eacabasa eanaa irraurista, diarba da caeotaba fobor camelanthi. | Iren. l. 1. c. 18. | — Iuvatque novos decerpere flores, | Insignemque meo capiti petere inde coronam, | Unde prius nulli velarunt tempora musae. Lucret. | = | Cooke's Edition. | = | [ornament] | = | Embellished With Superb Engravings. | = | London: | Printed for C. Cooke, No. 17, Paternoster-Row, | And sold by all the Booksellers in | Great-Britain.

Sm. 12mo (in sixes); π^2, A–C^6, D^4, 2A 3–6, 2B–2S^6, 2T^2 — 2 pp. (h.t. + bl.), 2 pp. (f.t. + bl.), [1]–44 (Life of Swift), [I]–[LII], [53]–216. — Two frontispieces (illustrated title, and a portrait of Swift), dated 1798 and 1797; moreover three plates, dated 1798, 1798 and 1797 (pp. 71, 95, 110.)
Copy: Penn.

249. A Tale Of A Tub. | Written For The | Universal Improvement | Of | Mankind. | *Diu multumque desideratum.* | To Which Is Added, | An Account Of A Battle | Between The | Ancient And Modern Books | In | *St. James's Library.* | With The Author's Apology; | And | Explanatory Notes, | By | *W. Wotton, B.D. And Others.* | = | *London:* | Printed For J. Johnson, John Nichols And Son, | R. Baldwin, Otridge And Son, F. And C. Rivington, | T. Payne, R. Faulder, G. And J. Robinson, R. Lea, | J. Nunn, W. Cuthell, T. Egerton, Clarke And Son, | Vernor And Hood, J. Scatcherd, T. Kay, Lacking- | ton Allan And Co. Carpenter And Co. Murray | And Highley, Longman And Rees, Cadell Jun. And | Davies, T. Bagster, J. Harding, And J. Mawman. | — | 1803.

This is a separate issue of the *Works*, Vol. III, 12mo in sixes, 1803 (see Nos. 130), with the following alterations: The volume-number has been removed from the foot of each new sheet; the 8 pages in front are new; the text of pp. 277–8 has been distributed over 3 pages (277–9), and the rest of the book (pp. 279–331) has been rejected,
Copy: Penn,

250. A / Tale Of A Tub, / Written / For The Universal Improvement / Of / *Mankind.* / = / Diu Multumque Desideratum. / = / To which is added, / An Account Of A Battle / Between The / *Ancient and Modern Books* / In St. James's Library. / — / With / The Author's Apology, / And / *Explanatory Notes, By W. Wotton,* B.D. / And Others. / = / Basyma cacabasa eanaa irraumista, diarbada caëota bafobor / camelanthi. *Iren. Lib.* 1. *C.* 18. / —— Juvatque novos decerpere flores, / Insignemque meo capiti petere inde coronam, / Unde prius nulli velarunt tempora Musae. *Lucret.* / = / *London:* / Printed For Thomas Tegg, / 111, Cheapside. / = / 1811.

12mo; π^2, B–O^{12}, P^6 — 2 pp. (t. + bl.), 2 pp. ('Treatises wrote' + bl.), [1]–322, 2 pp. ('Directions for placing the Plates' + bl.). — Frontisp. and six plates.
There is also a Large Paper issue, with the 7 plates coloured.

251. A / Tale Of A Tub. / Written For / The Universal Improvement / Of / Mankind. / *Diu multumque desideratum.* / To Which Is Added, / An Account Of A Battle / Between / The Ancient And Modern Books / In St. James's Library. / With The Author's Apology; / And / Explanatory Notes, / By W. Wotton, B.D. And Others. / [ornament] / New-York: / Published By William Durell And Co. / C. S. Van Winkle, *Printer.* / — / 1812.

This is a separate issue of the *Works*, Vol. III, 12mo, 1812 (see No. 132), from which the first four leaves have been removed and replaced by the above title-leaf (with Latin quotations on verso), while everything after p. 235 + bl. has been dropped.
Copy: Am. Antiq. Society, Worcester (Mass.).

***

262. *French adaptation:*
Les Trois / Justaucorps, / *Conte Bleu,* / Tiré de l'Anglois du Révérend / Mr. Jonathan Swif [*sic*], / *Ministre de l'Eglise Anglicane, Docteur / en Théologie & Doïen de la Cathédrale / de St. Patrice de Dublin.* / Avec Les / Trois Anneaux, / Nouvelle tirée de Bocace. / [ornament] / A Dublin. / M.DCC.XXI.

[Title in red and black.]
Sm. 8vo; [∗]², A–E⁸, F⁴ — 2 pp. (t. + bl.), 2 pp. (Avertissement), 1–88.
Copy: B.M. 12316 bbb 31.
A pencil note on the title of the B.M. copy says: par René Macé. *Les Trois Justaucorps* is pp. 1–79; it is only an adaptation. Both paper and type look so much like those of the "T. Johnson" books printed at The Hague (see No. 17,

ante), and so absolutely different from any Dublin type of that time, that I should not be surprised if "A Dublin" were only a blind.

***

[Though the several editions of the French, German, and Dutch translations of the *Tale* are properly Collections — several of Swift's smaller pieces having been printed with them —, we have inserted them here for the sake of order.]

***

French Translations Published In Holland

263. Le Conte / Du / Tonneau / Contenant tout ce que les / Arts, & les Sciences / Ont de plus Sublime, / Et de plus Mysterieux. / Avec plusieurs autres Piéces très- / curieuses. / Par le fameux Dr. Swift / Traduit de l'Anglois. / Tome Premier. / [ornament] / A La Haye, / Chez Henri Scheurleer, / M.DCC.XXI.

The title to the second volume is the same, except: Tome Second. The ornament is different.

[Titles in red and black.]

12mo; $*^4$, $*^9$, A–M^{12}, N^7, O^6 — 2 pp. (t. + bl.), 6 pp. (Dedicace), 16 pp. (Preface Du Traducteur), [1]–300, 12 pp. (Table Des Matieres). — Pages 287–88 repeated in numbering. — $*1$ cancelled.

π^1, $*^6$, A^4, B–M^{12}, N^7, O^5 — 2 pp. (t. + bl.), 12 pp. (Preface Du Traducteur), 1–286, 10 pp. (Table Des Matieres).

There are also Large Paper copies (Bibl. Nat. Paris Y^2 70827–28). This is the first French translation of the *Tale*. It was done by Justus van Effen, and is based on the 1720 English edition printed in Holland (see No. 17, *ante*). It contains *The History Of Martin*, &c., but Van Effen doubts its authenticity. — Vol. I contains the *Tale*, the *Battle*, and the *Discourse*; in Vol. II there are the same prose pieces as in the second part of the 1720 English ed., printed in Holland (see No. 17), together with the *Project For The Advancement Of Religion*; but no poetical pieces. — Copies, as a rule, have no plates; however, I have seen a copy with 8 plates, the same as those in the next edition (1732), but probably they do not really belong to it.

Copy: Penn.

264. *Another edition of Vols. I and II:*

Le Conte / Du / Tonneau, / Contenant tout ce que les / Arts, & les Sciences / Ont de plus Sublime, / Et de plus Mysterieux; / Avec plusieurs autres Pieces très- / curieuses. / Par Jonathan Swift, / *Doïen de St. Patrick en Irlande.* / Traduit de l'Anglois. / *Tome Premier.* / [ornament] / *A La Haye,* / Chez Henri Scheurleer, / M.DCC.XXXII.

The second volume has the same title, except: *Tome Second.* [Titles in red and black].

12mo; π^9, $**^2$, A–M^{12}, N^8, O^5 — 2 pp. (t. + bl.), 4 pp. (Dedicace), 16 pp. (Preface Du Traducteur), [1]–300, 12 pp. (Table Des Matieres). — Pp. 287–8 repeated in numbering.

π^1, *^{6}, A^4, B–M^{12}, N^8, O^4 — 2 pp. (t. + bl.), 12 pp. (Preface Du Traducteur), [1]–286, 10 pp. (Table Des Matieres). Frontisp. and seven plates. —
*3 and 4 bound between A 2 and A 3 in Penn copy.

265. In 1733 a third volume was added:
Traité / Des Dissensions / Entre Les Nobles Et Le Peuple, /
Dans les Républiques d'Athenes & / de Rome, &c. / L'Art De
Ramper En Poesie; / Et / L'Art Du Mensonge / Politique; /
Traduits de l'Anglois de Mr. Swift. / Pour servir de Suite au / Conte
Du Tonneau. / [ornament] / A Amsterdam, / Aux Dépens de la
Compagnie. / M.DCC.XXXIII.

> [Title in red and black.]
> 12mo; π^2 *^{8}, A–L^{12}, M^8, N^4 — 2 pp. (h.t. + bl.), 2 pp. (t. + bl.), I–XI
> (Avertissement), 5 pp. (Table), [1]–280, 8 pp. (advs.).
> Copy: Penn.

266. *Another edition of Vol. III:*
Traité / Des Dissensions / Entre Les Nobles Et Le Peuple /
Dans les Republiques d'Athenes & de / Rome, &c. / L'Art De
Ramper En Poesie, / Et / L'Art Du Mensonge / Politique; /
Traduits de l'Anglois de M. Swift. / [ornament] / A Alethoba-
thopseudopolis. / Chez Bold Truth, ruë du Mock, vis-à-vis / le
Bathos, à la Societé. / — / M.DCC.XXXIII.

> [Title in red and black.]
> 12mo (in eights and fours alternately); π^1, a^8, A–H — 2 pp. (t. + bl.),
> [I]–XV (Avertissement), 1 p. Errata, [1]–364, 4 pp. (Table).
> Copy: Penn.
> Sybil Goulding, *Swift En France*, 1924, p. 190, mentions an edition with
> the same imprint, but with the addition: ". . . . Bathos, et se trouve à Paris
> chez J.-F. Joffe, rue Saint-Jacques." — I have not seen a copy.

267. *Another edition of Vols. I and II:*
Le Conte / Du / Tonneau, / Contenant tout ce que les / Arts &
les Sciences / Ont de plus Sublime / Et de plus Misterieux; / Avec
plusieurs autres Piéces très- / curieuses. / Par Jonathan Swift, /
Doyen de St. Patrick en Irlande. / Traduit de l'Anglois. / Nouvelle
Edition revûë & corrigée. / Tome Premier. / [ornament] / A La Haye, /
Chez Henri Scheurleer, / M.DCC.XLI.

> The title of the second volume is the same, except: *Tome Second.*
> [Titles in red and black.]
> 12mo; *^{9}, **^{2}, A–M^{12}, N^8, O^6 — 2 pp. (t. + bl.), 4 pp. (Dedicace), 16 pp.
> (Preface Du Traducteur), [1]–300, 10 pp. (Table Des Matieres), 2 pp. advs. —
> Pp. 287–88 repeated in numbering.
> π^1, *^{6}, A^4, B–N^{12} — 2 pp. (t. + bl.), 12 pp. (Preface Du Traducteur),
> [1]–286, 10 pp. (Table Des Matieres).
> Frontisp. and 7 plates (same offprints as those in the 1732 ed. — see
> No. 264, *ante*).

Penn has such a copy, with leaves P 1–3 (Table des Matieres) added from the Swiss edition of 1756.

After some time Scheurleer's stock of plates was apparently exhausted, and to supply the want, he provided his remaining copies with the plates of the 'Lausanne & Geneve' edition, 1742 (see No. 281, *post*).

From this time dates a certain co-operation between Scheurleer and Bousquet & Co. (cf. Nos. 268 and 282, as well as No. 270, Vol. III, and 283, *post*).

268. *Another edition of Vol. III:*

Traité / Des Dissensions / Entre Les Nobles Et Le Peuple, Dans les Républiques d'Athenes & / de Rome, &c. / L'Art De Ramper En Poesie, / Et / L'Art Du Mensonge / Politique; / *Traduits de l'Anglois de Mr.* / Jonathan Swift, / *Pour servir de* Suite *au* / Conte Du Tonneau. / [ornament] / A La Haye, / Chez Fred Henri Scheurleer. / — / MDCCXLIX.

[Title in red and black.]
12mo; π^2, $*^8$, A–L^{12}, M^8 — 2 pp. (h.t. + bl.), 2 pp. (f.t. + bl.), I–XI (Avertissement), [XII]–XVI (Table), [1]–280.
Copy: Kon. Bibl. (187 M. 9).
For another issue see No. 282.

269. *Another edition of Vols. I and II:*
The titles, in black only, are the same as those in the 1721 edition (No. 263, *ante*), except for the imprint:

– – – – / A La Haye, / Chez Henri Scheurleer. / — / M.DCC.LV.

12mo; $[*]^{12}$, [A]–N^{12} — 2 pp. (t. + bl.), 4 pp. (Dedicace), [I]–XVI (Preface Du Traducteur), 2 pp. (Catalogue Traites), [1]–312. — A 2 signed A.
π^2, $*^6$, A^4, B–N^{12} — 2 pp. (h.t. + bl.), 2 pp. (f.t. + bl.), [I]–XII (Preface Du Traducteur), [1]–296.
Frontisp. and 7 plates, new ones, representing the same subjects as before, but reversed.
Copy: Penn.

270. *Another issue of Vols. I, II and III:*
Le Conte / Du / Tonneau, / Contenant tout ce que / Les Arts Et Les Sciences / Ont de plus Sublime / Et de plus Mystérieux; / *Avec plusieurs autres Pièces très-curieuses.* / Par le fameux Dr Swift. / *Traduit de l'Anglois.* / Tome Premier. / [ornament] / A La Haye, / Chez Henri Scheurleer. / = / *M.DCC.LVII.*

The title in the second volume is the same, except: Tome Second.
That in the third volume is:

Traité / Des Dissentions / Entre Les Nobles / Et Le Peuple, / Dans les Républiques d'Athenes & de / Rome, &c. / L'Art De Ramper En Poësie; / Et L'Art / Du Mensonge Politique. / *Traduits de l'Anglois* / De M. Jonathan Swift, / Pour servir de Suite / Au Conte Du Tonneau. / [ornament] / A La Haye, / Chez Henri Scheurleer. / = / *M.DCC.LVII.*

[All three title in red and black.] Vols. I and II are the same printing as Vols. I and II recorded in No. 269; the 8 plates are also identical. In Vol. I the original full-title leaf has been replaced by a double leaf (h.t. and f.t.). Penn has two copies of Vol. I, 1757; in one leaf [A] 1 bearing bastard-title, dated M.DCC.LV., has been preserved, in the other it has been cancelled. In Vol. II the h.t. and f.t. have been replaced by new ones.

Vol. III is the same printing as Vol. III, No. 283; only the h.t. and f.t. have been renewed.

Copy: Penn.

*
* *

German Translations

271. Des berühmten / Herrn D. Schwifts / Måhrgen / Von der / Tonne, / Zum allgemeinen Nutzen des / menschlichen Geschlechts / abgefasset, / Nebst einem vollståndigen Begriffe / einer allgemeinen Gelehrsamkeit, / Aus dem Englischen ins Teutsche übersetzet. / I. Theil. / — / Basima racabasa ranaa irraurista, diarba da / carotaba fobor camelanthi. Iren libr. I. c. 18. / — / — — *Juvatque novos decerpere flores,* / *Insignemque meo capiti petere inde coronam,* / *Unde prius nulli velarunt tempora Musae.* / Lucret. / — / Altona. 1729. / Auf Kosten guter Freunde.

Anderer Theil / des Måhrgens / von der / Tonne, / So / Zum allgemeinen Nutzen / des menschlichen Geschlechts / abgefasset worden, / Von / Einem gewissen elenden Scribenten, / Insgemein genant / Der Autor des Ersten. / — / Aus dem Englischen ins Teutsche übersetzet. / — / Altona 1729. / Auf Kosten guter Freunde.

Sm. 8vo; a⁷, B⁴, A–P⁸, Q² — 2 pp. (t. + bl.), 9 pp. (Dedication), 11 pp. (Vorrede des Ubersetzers), [1]–244. — Frontisp. and six plates.

[ )( ]⁷, A–P⁸ — 2 pp. (t. + bl.), 12 pp. (Vorrede des Ubersetzers), [1]–240. — Frontisp. (save in Vol. I, Sig. B is signed b).

Vol. I contains the *Tale*, Vol. II the *Battle*, the *Discourse*, the *Meditation on a Broomstick*, *Thoughts on Various Subjects*, the *Tritical Essay*, the *Argument against the Abolishing of Christianity*, the *Project for the Advancement of Religion*, and the *Bickerstaff Pamphlets*. — The translation is by G. Chr. Wolf.

Copy: Penn.

272. *Another edition,* 1737:

The titles and collations are the same as in 1729, except for the year, which in both volumes is 1737. — The plates, though the same in number and representing the same subjects, are all new, with the exception of the frontisp. to Vol. II, which is the same offprint as that of 1729.

Copy: Penn.

273. *Another issue:*

Des berühmten / Herrn D. Schwifts / Måhrgen / von der / Tonne, / Zum allgemeinen Nutzen des menschlichen / Geschlechts abgefasset, / Nebst einem / Vollståndigen Begriffe einer allgemeinen Gelehrsamkeit, / Aus dem Englischen ins Teutsche übersetzet.

/ Erster Theil. / — / Basima racabasa ranaa irraurista, diarba da carotaba / fobor camelanthi. Iren lib. 1. c. 18. / — / Lvcret. / – – – – Juvatque novos decerpere flores, / Insignemque meo capiti petere inde coronam, / Unde prius nulli velarunt tempora Musae. / = / Altona, 1748. / Auf Kosten guter Freunde.

Anderer Theil / Des / Måhrgens / von der / Tonne, / So zum allgemeinen Nutzen / des menschlichen Geschlechts / abgefasset worden, / Von / Einem gewissen elenden Scribenten, / Insgemein genannt / Der Autor des Ersten. / — / Aus dem Englischen ins Teutsche übersetzet. / — / [ornament] / = / Altona, auf Kosten guter Freunde, 1748.

Exactly the same printing and plates as the 1737 ed.; only the two titles are new.
Copy: Penn.

274. Wahrhaffte / und merckwürdige Lebens- / Beschreibung Joris Pines / von Dublin aus Irrland bürtig, / Worinnen. / Dessen Ankunft und 70. jähriger / Auffenthalt auf einer wüsten Insul Sůd-Lan- / des, mit seinen vier Weibern, als einer schwar- / tzen und drey weiszen; Auch seine daselbst gehab- / ten Erstaunenswürdigen Avanturen, Ver- / mehrung seines Geschlechts, angefangene, und von seinen Nachkommen den Pinesern fortge- / setzte Viel-Weiberey, dessen Testament und / Gesetze, Zwiespalt seiner Kinder, / derselben nothwendige / Blut-Schande. / Ingleichen deren Bekanntschafft und / Handel mit den Sůd-Låndern beyder Sitten / und wunderliche Lebens-Art ausführlich / beschrieben wird. / Aus dem Englischen übersetzet. / Dritte Aufflage. / — / Anno MDCCXXXIV.

[Title in red and black.]
8vo;)o(⁷, B–Cc⁸ — 2 pp. (t. + bl.), 5 pp. (Vorrede), 8–14, 17–384 (no break in text).
Copy: Penn.
Contains (pp. 320 — end): *Fortsetzung des Pines Geschichte*, which is an almost literal translation of the allegory of the three brothers Peter, Martin and Jack in Swift's *Tale* (Sections II, IV, VI and XI).
Dr. Hermann Ullrich *Robinson und Robinsonaden*, Teil I (Litterarhistorische Forschungen, VII. Heft, Weimar, 1898), mentions on p. 118 four editions: 1726, 1729, 1734 (Schneeberg, bey C. W. Fulden. — Apparently different from the 3rd ed. mentioned above), and 1744. I have not seen any of them, and can therefore not say whether they also contain the translation of the allegory.
Pp. 8–320 is a greatly enlarged version of a much earlier work, which appeared in 1668, in English, French, German and Dutch. Its English title is: *The Isle of Pines, Or A late Discovery of a fourth Island in Terra Australis, Incognita. Being a true Relation of – – – – Incognita etc. London, 1668.* — Sm. 4to; 2 pp., 1–9 + bl. (B.M. B 671 (15)).

275. Dr. Jonathan Swifts / Måhrgen / von der / Tonne. / Nebst übrigen / dazu gehörigen Schriften. / Von neuem aus dem Englischen übersezt. [*sic*] / [vignette] / Mit Kupfern. / Hamburg und Leipzig, 1758.

> This book, which contains the *Tale*, the *Battle*, and the *Discourse*, occurs in two different shapes:
>
> (1) One is a separate issue of Vol. III of *Satyrische und ernsthafte Schriften*, 1758 (see No. 101, *ante*), and collates:
> 8vo; [∗]⁴, A 2–8, B–Y⁸, Z 1 — 2 pp. (t. + bl.), 6 pp. (Vorrede), [3]–354. — Frontisp. and 8 plates.
> Copy: B.M. 12613 dd 10 and Penn.
> (2) The other is a separate issue of Vol. III of *Satyrische und ernsthafte Schriften*, 1759 (see No. 101, *ante*), and collates:
> 8vo; [∗]⁴, A–X⁸ — 2 pp. (t. + bl.), 6 pp. (Vorrede), [1]–332, 4 pp. blank. — Frontisp. and 8 plates.
> Copy: Penn.
> Only the 8 pp. of prefatory matter are new; they are the same printing in (1) and (2).

277. Dr. Jonathan Swifts / Måhrchen / von der / Tonne. / Eine neue Uebersetzung mit Erläuterungen / von / dem Verfasser der Briefe eines reisenden / Franzosen. / [vignette] / — / Zürich, bey Orell, Geszner, Füszli und Comp. / 1787.

> Sm. 8vo; π⁸, B–P⁸, Q² — 2 pp. (t. + editor's note on verso), 1 p. (title: 'Måhrchen'), 1 p. ('Abhandlungen'), [5]–242, 2 pp. blank.
> Copy: Penn.
> Contains only the *Tale* and the *Battle*. The note on verso of title says that this new translation is by K. Risbeck, i.e. Joh. Kasp. Riesbeck. Cf. No. 433.

∗
∗ ∗

Dutch Translation

279. Vertelsel / Van De / Ton, / Behelzende Het Merg / Van Alle / Kunsten En Weetenschappen. / Geschreeven Tot Algemeen Nut / Des Menschelyken Geslachts. / *Mitsgaders een Verhaal.* / Van Den Strydt Der / Boeken. / In De Boekzaal Van St. James. / *Door den beroemden* / Dr. Swift. / *Uit het Engelsch vertaalt door* / P. le Clercq. / [vignette] / t'Amsterdam, / *Voor Rekening van de Compagnie.* / M.D.CC.XXXV.

> [Title in red and black.]
> Sm. 8vo; (∗)⁸, ∗–∗∗∗⁸, A–V⁸, X⁴ — 2 pp. (h.t. + 'Verklaaring Der Tytel-plaat' on verso), 2 pp. (f.t. + bl.), 10 pp. (Voorreden Van Den Vertaaler), 2 pp. (Lyst), 9 pp. (Oxdragt aan Sommers), 14 pp. (Opdragt aan Prins Nazaat), 25 pp. (Voorreden Van Den Schryver), 1–325, 1 p. Errata, 2 pp. blank. — Frontisp. and six plates.
> Copy: Penn.
> *Another edition:*
> The same title-page (except that there are no full stops behind '*Verhaal*' and 'Boeken'), the same collation, and the same plates as the edition just

mentioned. But it is not the same printing, as is easily visible from the list of *Errata* on verso of p. 325, here called: 'Drukfeilen'.

Second volume:

Vertelsel / Van De / Ton, / Behelsende Het Merg / Van Alle / Kunsten En Weetenschappen. / *Mitsgaders eenige* / Keurige Stukken, / *Van den beroemden* / Dr. Swift. / Vertaald door / P. le Clercq. / [ornament] / Te Utrecht, / By Arnoldus Lobedanius / Boekverkoper 1743.

[Title in black only.]
Sm. 8vo; *⁸, A–Dd⁸ — 2 pp. (t. + bl.), 12 pp. (Voorreden Van Den Overzetter), 2 pp. (Errata), [1]–426. (Pp. 283–8 repeated in numbering).
Copy: Penn.
Another issue of the second volume:
The title-page has been cancelled and replaced by one exactly the same, with this difference:

– – – – Clercq. / II. Deel. / [ornament] / – – – –.

Moreover, the 2 pp. *Errata* have been cancelled, and replaced by 4 pp. *Errata*, enlarged, and inserted at the end of the volume.
Copy: Penn.
Vol. I contains the *Tale* and the *Battle*; Vol. II the *Bathos*, the *Art of Political Lying*, the *Argument against the Abolishing of Christianity*, the *Discourse Athens and Rome*, the *Meditation on a Broomstick*, the *Project for the Advancement of Religion*, the *Tritical Essay*, and the *Discourse Mechanical Operation of the Spirit*.

***

280. *French adaptation:*
Productions / D'Esprit; / *Contenant* / Tout Ce Que Les Arts / Et Les Sciences Ont De Rare / Et De Merveilleux. / *Ouvrage Critique & sublime, composé par le* / *Docteur* Swift, & *autres personnes rem-* / *plies d'une érudition profonde. Avec des* / Notes *en plusieurs endroits.* / Traduit par Monsieur***. / Inde priùs nulli velarunt tempora Musae. / *Lucret.* / *Premiere Partie.* / [ornament] / A Paris, / Chez Gregoire-Antoine-Dupuis, / Grand' Salle du Palais, au Saint-Esprit. / — / M.DCC.XXXVI. / *Avec Privilege Du Roy.*

12mo; a¹², b⁶, A–I¹², K⁸, π¹, L⁴, M–X¹², Y⁸, Z² — 2 pp. (t. + bl.), [III]–XI (Preface Du Traducteur), 1 p. (ornament), XIII–XXXV (Preface De L'Auteur), 1 p. (Approbation), [1]–232, 2 pp. (title the same as above, only: *Seconde Partie.*), 233–498, 2 pp. unnumbered.
Copy: Penn.
This is an adaptation of Van Effen's translation, by l'abbé Saunier de Beaumont, in the shape of letters.

***

French Translations Published In Switzerland

281. Le Conte / Du / Tonneau, / Contenant tout ce que les / Arts Et Les Sciences / *Ont de plus* Sublime & *de plus* / Mysterieux;

/ Avec plusieurs autres Pieces très curieuses. / *Par* / Jonathan Swift, / *Doïen de St. Patrick en Irlande*. / *Nouvelle Edition*, / Ornée de Figures en taille douce, & aug- / mentée d'un Troisieme Volume. / *Traduit de l'Anglois*. / Tome Premier. / [ornament] / A Lausanne & à Geneve, / Chez Marc-Mich. Bousquet & Comp. / — / MDCCXLII.

The title of the second volume is the same, except: Tome Second. There is a different ornament.

Traité / Des Dissensions / Entre Les Nobles Et Le Peuple, / Dans les Républiques d'Athènes & / de Rome, &c. / L'Art De Ramper En Poesie; / *Et* / L'Art Du Mensonge / Politique; / *Traduits de l'Anglois de* / Mr. Jonathan Swift. / Pour servir de Suite au / Conte Du Tonneau. / [ornament] / A Lausanne & à Geneve, / Chez Marc-Mich. Bousquet & Comp. / — / MDCCXLII.

[Titles all three in red and black.]
12mo; π^1, *[3]–9, **^{2}, A–M^{12}, N^8, O^2, P^3 — 2 pp. (t. + bl.), 16 pp. (Preface Du Traducteur), [1]–312. (287–8 repeated in numbering).
π^1, *^{6}, A^4, B–N^{12} — 2 pp. (t. + bl.), 12 pp. (Preface Du Traducteur), [1]–296.
π^2, *^{8}, A–L^{12}, M^8 — 2 pp. (h.t. + bl.), 2 pp. (f.t. + bl.), I–XI (Avertissement), [XII]–XVI (Table), [1]–280.
Frontisp. and seven plates.
See note under No. 267.

282. *Another issue* of Vol. III:
Traité / Des Dissensions / Entre Les Nobles Et Le Peuple, / Dans les Républiques d'Athenes & / de Rome, &c. / L'Art De Ramper En Poesie, / Et / L'Art Du Mensonge / Politique; / *Traduits de l'Anglois de Mr.* / Jonathan Swift, / *Pour servir de* Suite *au* / Conte Du Tonneau. / [ornament] / A Lausanne, / Chez Marc-Mich. Bousquet & Comp. / — / MDCCL.

[Title in red and black.]
12mo; π^2, *^{8}, A–L^{12}, M^8 — 2 pp. (h.t. + bl.), 2 pp. (f.t. + bl.), I–XI (Avertissement), [XII]–XVI (Table), [1]–280.
This is exactly the same printing as No. 268; only the year of the h.t. and the imprint of the f.t. have been altered in the type.

283. *Another edition of Vol. III:*
Traite / Des Dissensions / Entre Les Nobles Et Le Peuple, / Dans les Republiques d'Athenes & / de Rome, &c. / L'Art De Ramper En Poesie; / *Et* / L'Art Du Mensonge / Politique; / *Traduits de l'Anglais de* / Mr. Jonathan Swift. / Pour servir de Suite au / Conte Du Tonneau. / [ornament] / A Lausanne & à Geneve. / Chez Marc-Mich. Bousquet & Comp. / — / M.DCC.LV.

[Title in black only.]
12mo; π^2, *[2]–11, A–L^{12}, M^8 — 2 pp. (h.t. + bl.), 2 pp. (f.t. + bl.),
I–XI (Avertissement), [XII]–XVI (Table), [1]–280.
See also No. 270.

284. *Another edition of Vols. I and II:*

Le Conte / Du / Tonneau, / Contenant tout ce que les / Arts Et
Les Sciences / *Ont de plus* Sublime & *de plus* / Mysterieux; / Avec
plusieurs autres Pieces très curieuses. / *Par* / Jonathan Swift, /
Doïen de St. Patrick en Irlande. / *Nouvelle Edition,* / Ornée de Figures
en taille douce, & aug- / mentée d'un Troisieme Volume / Traduit
de l'Anglais. / Tome Premier. / [ornament] / A Lausanne & à
Geneve, / Chez Marc-Mich. Bousquet & Comp. / — / MDCCLVI.

The title of the second volume is the same, except: Tome Second. The
ornament is a different one.
[Titles in red and black.]
12mo; π, *^{6}, **^{2}, A–M^{12}, N^8, O^2, P^3 — 2 pp. (t. + bl.), 16 pp. (Preface
Du Traducteur), [1]–312. (Pp. 287–8 repeated in numbering).
    π, *^{6}, A^4, B–N^{12} — 2 pp. (t. + bl.), 12 pp. (Preface Du Traducteur),
[1]–296.
Frontisp. and seven plates (the same as those in No. 281).
Copy: Penn.

285. *Another edition of Vol. III:*

Traité / Des Dissentions / Entre Les Nobles Et Le Peuple, /
dans le Républiques d'Athènes & / de Rome, &c. / L'Art De
Ramper En Poesie; / *Et* / L'Art Du Mensonge / Politique, / *Traduits de l'Anglois de* / Mr Jonathan Swift, / Pour servir de Suite
au / Conte Du Tonneau. / [ornament] / A Lausanne Et à Geneve, /
Chez Marc Chapuis & Compag. / — / MDCCLXIV.

[Title in black only.]
12mo; π^2, *^{6}, **^{4}, A–M^{12}, L^8 — 2 pp. (h.t. + bl.), 2 pp. (f.t. + bl.),
V–XV (Avertissement), XVI–XX (Table), [1]–280.
Copy: Penn.

Criticism, Imitations, &c.

997. Some Remarks On The Tale of a Tub. &c. London: A. Baldwin, 1704.
(see No. 834, *ante*).
    Also in Vol. I of: The Original Works Of William King, LL.D. &c. London,
N. Conant, MDCCLXXVI. — 3 vols., sm. 8vo.

998. The Tale of a Tub, Revers'd, &c. With a Character of the Author.
London, A. Baldwin, MDCCV. — 12mo, 16 pp., 1–110.

1000. Satyrical Reflections On The Vices and Follies of the Age. Containing,
I. &c. London, Benj. Bragge. 1707. — 4to; 1–24. — Contains (pp. 13–14)
No. III: A Tale of two Tubs [in verse].

1003. A New Tale Of A Tub, concerning One Goody Law, Old Father Discipline, and Young Master Nicodemus. Printed for Witwould Wiseacre (ca. 1710). — Sm. 4to.

1004. A Complete Key To The Tale of a Tub; With some Account of the Authors, The Ocasion and Design of Writing it, and Mr. Wotton's Remarks examin'd. London: Edmund Curll, 1710. &c. — 8vo; 4 pp., 1–36. [By Dr. Thomas Swift?] — Penn has two copies: one has 'Ocasion', the other 'Occasion'. For another issue, and the Second Edition, see No. 3, *ante*.

Third ed.: A Complete Key To The Tale of a Tub. The Third Edition. London: Printed in the Year M.DCC.XIV. — Sm. 12mo; 1–36.
Copy: Penn.

Another third ed.: The title is the same, but the ornament is different (a basket of flowers) with only a single rule instead of a double one under it. The collation is also the same, but the printing is clearly different.
Copy: Penn.

Fourth ed.: A Complete Key To The Tale of a Tub. The Fourth Edition. London: Printed in the Year M.DCC.XXIV. — Sm. 12mo; 1–36. — Copy: Guildhall.

1005. A Morning's Discourse Of A Bottomless Tubb, Introducing the Historical Fable Of The Oak And Her Three Provinces; &c. London: John Morphew. 1712. — 8vo; 8 pp., 1–160.
Copy: Penn.
[Anonymous attack on the 'Tale' and its author.]

1039. A Vindication Of The Present M——y, &c. London, Printed in the Year M.DCC.XI. — 8vo; 1–52. — Contains favourable references to Swift's *New Journey to Paris*, *A Tale Of A Tub*, and *The Examiner*.
Copy: Penn.

1007. A Tale, And No Tale: That is to say, A Tale, and No Tale of a Tub. &c. London: J. Roberts. 1715. — 8vo; 1–24.

1008. A Tale Of A Bottomless Tub. &c. London: J. Roberts. 1723. — Folio; 1–12.

Also forms part of a made-up miscellany: A Collection Of Original Poems. Viz. [7 titles] The Second Edition. London, J. Roberts, 1724. (See Case, No. 329.)

920. The Longitude Discover'd; A Tale. By the Author of the Deluge, and Bottomless Tub; Tales. [quotation from Dryden] [ornament] London: J. Roberts, &c. 1726. Price 6d.
Folio; [A]–C² — 2 pp. (t. + bl.), 3–12.
Copy: Clark.
Dublin edition: — Dublin: Thos. Hume, &c. N. D.
Sm. 8vo; 2 pp. (t. + bl.), 3–15 + bl.

1009. Tale Of A Tub Bottled off and Moraliz'd. Or, An Heroicomick Oration. With A Touch upon the Times. &c. London; J. Roberts. M.DCC. XXXVI. — Folio; 1–10. — Copy: Penn.

1011. A Tale of Two Tubs: Or, The B – – – – – rs in Querpo. &c. London: Printed in the Year, 1749.
8vo; frontisp., 1–47 + bl.
Copy: Bodl.
There seems to be another edition: — Printed for A. Price, jun. near Ludgate, 1749.
8vo; h.t., frontisp., 1–55 + bl.

1012. A New Tale Of An Old Tub: Or, The Way to Fame. &c. London: M. Cooper. MDCCLII. — 8vo; 2 pp., 1–94. — Copy: Forster.

1013. The Battle Of The Players. In Imitation of Dean Swift's Battle of the Books. &c. London: W. Flexney. MDCCLXII.

8vo; π^2, B–F^8 — 2 pp. (t. + bl.), 3–4 (Names), [5]–52.

Copy: B.M. 641 d 31 (14).

Third ed.: – – – – – The Third Edition. &c. London: R. Richards. MDCCLXII. — 8vo; 2 pp., 2 pp. *Dedication*, 3–52.

1014. A New Tale Of A Tub, Written For The Delight And Instruction Of Every British Subject In Particular, And All The World In General. &c. London: J. Ridgway. 1790. — 12mo; 4 pp., I–IV, 1–128. [MS. note on title: "by John Pinkerton, Esq."]

1014A. Dobell Cat. 104, 1948, lists: "Emancipation, or Peter, Martin and the Squire, a tale in rhyme, to which is added a short account of the Irish Catholics, *folding coloured plate*, 8vo, 1808."

'By The Author Of A Tale Of A Tub', &c.

833. Mully of Mountown. A Poem. By the Author of the Tale of a Tub. London, 1704. — Folio; 4 pages. — There are copies with the year misprinted 1702. — The author is William King.

Also in: A New Collection Of Poems Relating to State Affairs, &c. London, MDCCV. — 8vo; 16 pp., 1–591 + bl.

See further No. 834, *post*.

834. The Fairy Feast, Written by the Author of A Tale of a Tub, And The Mully of Mountown. London: 1704. — Folio; 1–12. — Contains only 'The Fairy Feast', the word 'Author' referring to the 'Tale' and the 'Mully' together. — The author is William King.

Both 'Mully' and 'The Fairy Feast' (with a different title, namely: 'Orpheus and Euridice') also in:

Some Remarks On The Tale of a Tub. To which are Annexed Mully of Mountown, And Orpheus and Euridice. By the Author Of The Journey to London. London: A. Baldwin, 1704. — 8vo; 10 pp., 1–63, 2 pp. (advs.) + bl.

Also both in: Miscellanies In Prose And Verse. By William King. London: B. Lintott and H. Clements. — 8vo; 32 pp., 1–536, 2 pp. [The year is 1705]. — Later ed.: 2 vols., 8vo, N.D.

Also both in: A Miscellany Of Poems. Viz Mully of Mountown. By Dr. King. Phoenix-Park. By Mr Ward I. Orpheus and Euridice. Dublin: Edwin Sandys for George Grierson. MDCCXVIII. — 12mo; 4 pp., 3–34.

Also both in Vol. III of: The Original Works Of William King, LL. D. &c. London, N. Conant, MDCCLXXVI. — 3 vols., sm. 8vo. — Later ed.: 2 vols., 16mo, 1781.

836. The Swan Tripe-Club In Dublin. A Satyr. &c. Printed at Dublin, Sold by the Booksellers in London and Westminster, MDCCVI. — 4to; 1–20. — Elr. Ball, *Swift's Verse*, 58–9, says that it is not by Swift.

Copy: Penn.

Another ed.: The Tripe Club. A Satyr. &c. By the Author of the Tale of a Tub. London: Jacob Tonson, Sold by the Booksellers of London, and Westminster. MDCCVI. — 4to; 1–20.

Another ed.: The Swan Tripe-Club: A Satyr, On The High-Flyers; In The Year 1705. London: Booksellers of London and Westminster, 1710. — 8vo; 1–16. [This ed. was also included in Warner's Vol. II, 1717. See No. 522, *post.*]

839. The Art of Cookery: A Poem. In Imitation of Horace's Art of Poetry. By the Author of a Tale of a Tub. &c. London: Booksellers of London and Westminster. 1708. — Folio; 2 pp., 1–22. — Copy: Gilbert Coll., Dublin.

The author is William King.

Another ed.: The Art of Cookery &c. with some Letters to Dr. Lister and others &c. Lintott, N.D. [1715] — 8vo. — 2nd ed., London, 1719. 8vo, engraved frontisp.

Also in further editions of King's Works (cf. No. 834, *ante*).

1001. The Second Part of the Tale of a Tub, In Imitation of Horace's Art of Poetry. &c. Bp [*sic*] the Author of the Tale of a Tub. London: Printed for B. Lintott: And, Re-printed for M. G. at Essex-street Gate, Dublin, 1708. Price 12d. — 8vo; 2 pp., 1–70.

1002. The History Of Addresses. By One very near a Kin to the Author of the Tale of a Tub. &c. London, Printed in the Year 1709. — 8vo; 16 pp., 1–244, 8 pp. *Index.* — The author was John Oldmixon. Copy: Penn.

1002A. The History of Addresses. With Remarks serious and comical. In which a particular Regard is had to all such as have been presented since the Impeachment of Dr. Sacheverell. Part II. 1711 (Baker).

1002B. The / Instructive Library: / Or, An / Entertainment for the Curious, The / Improvement of the Learned, the / Information of the Ignorant, The / Satisfaction of all Good Men, and / the Confusion of the Bad. / — / [Quotation: 1 line in Latin] / — / By a Friend of the Author of the / Tale of a Tub / Dedicated to *Isaac Bickerstaffe* esq; / — / Printed for the Man in the Moon. 1710.

16 pp. of a fictitious library, the titles satirizing all manner of celebrities. 8vo; A⁸ — 1–16. — Copy: Clark.

1002C. *TORY ANNALS* / Faithfully extracted out of / Abel Roper's / Famous WRITINGS. / Vulgarly call'd / Poſt-Boy and Supplement. / FROM / *March* 1710. to *December* 1711. / ... / [single rule] / *Revis'd and Emprov'd by the Author of the* Tale of a Tub: / [single rule] / To be continu'd Annually. / [single rule] /*Et haec olim meminiſſe juvabit.* Virg. / [single rule] / *LONDON:* / Printed, and ſold by the Bookſellers in *Great* / *Britain.* 1712. Price 1 *s.*

8vo; 8 pp., 100 pp. — Copy: Chapin Library.

1035. A Town Eclogue Or, A Poetical Contest Between Toby And A Minor-Poet Of B—tt—n's Coffee-House; &c. Inscrib'd to the Author of the Tale of a Tub. &c. London: Ferdinando Burleigh and A. Dodd. — 8vo; 2 pp., 1–18.

Pickering & Chatto, cat. 304, item 210, has this note: "A contemporary owner has noted that Toby is *Swift*, a Minor Poet is John Dunton, and dates it 1714. He has also annotated the text referring to Steele. The bookseller was Lintott; he refers to the minor poet as D—ton. Dunton's whig leanings are also referred to."

1082. Essays Divine, Moral, and Political: Viz. I. Of Religion [*sic*] in General. II. Of Christianity. III. Of Priests. IV. Of Virtue. V. Of Friendship. VI. Of Government: VII. Of Parties. VIII. Of Plots. By the Author of the Tale of a Tub, sometime the Writer of the Examiner, and the Original Inventor of the

Band-Box-Plot. &c. London: Printed in the Year, 1714. — 8vo; 2 pp., I–XIV, 1–82. Frontisp. [Contains an attack on Swift. Ascribed to Thomas Burnet; also to Steele.]

Another copy with the misprint rectified, and a full stop after 'Government', instead of the colon. — Both copies are Penn's.

Second edition: — Collected from the Works of J. S – – t, D – – of St. P – – k, and Author of the Tale of a Tubb. Second edition. London: J. Baker, 1715. — 8vo.

(From Maggs' cat. 653, item 1367.)

887. The Dignity, Use and Abuse of Glass-Bottles. Set forth in A Sermon Preach'd to an Illustrious Assembly, And now Publish'd for the Use of the Inferiour Clergy. By the Author of the Tale of a Tub. London: Booksellers of London and Westminster, 1715. — 8vo; 1–24. — Copy: U.L.C. — There seem to be at least two more editions (3rd ed., 1752), but I have not seen them.

893. The Agreeable Variety. In Two Parts. &c. London: G. Strahan &c., MDCCXVII. — 8vo; 12 pp., 1–338, 1 p. + bl. [Part II, dropped title, on p. 199]. — Contains on p. 150 and pp. 179–80, two very short pieces 'From the Author of A Tale of a Tub', beginning: "Let your Discretion moderate your Cost", &c. (12 lines)

"Let your Discretion moderate your Cost", &c. (12 lines)
"A real Grief with silent Steps proceeds", &c. (6 lines)

Re-issued, and called second and third edition, in 1724 and 1742 (cf. Griffith, Nos. 87, 145, 557).

SECTION IV

GULLIVER'S TRAVELS

✠✠✠

'Motte' Editions

The first five editions of *Gulliver's Travels* were all published by Benjamin Motte. They form a group together, and give rise to the following observations:
Sequence and denomination:

(1) A edition (1st 8vo ed.), publ. 28 Oct. 1726.
(2) AA edition (2nd 8vo ed.), publ. medio Nov. 1726.
(3) B edition (3rd 8vo ed.), publ. Dec. 1726.
(4) Second Edition (4th 8vo ed.), publ. May 4, 1727.
(5) [Third Edition] (1st 12mo ed.), with the year 1727, but published early in 1728. — Re-issued 1731.

The first three editions, long considered different *issues* only, have been proved to be separate *editions* (see Lucius L. Hubbard, *Contributions*, 1922; and Harold Williams, *The Library* for Dec. 1925, and *Gulliver's Travels* for the First Edition Club, 1926). Both Hubbard and Williams say that these three 8vo editions were followed in 1727, first by a 12mo, then by another 8vo edition. I cannot quite agree with them. It is correct to say, as both do, that the 12mo edition was *printed* before the 8vo edition, because a comparison of the texts shows that the former has *not* the literal corrections mentioned in the *Errata* of Ford's letter to Motte of Jan. 3, 1727, whereas The Second Edition *has* them, which shows the time of *printing* before and after that date. However, it is not the *printing*, but the *publication*, which concerns us here. Publication of The Second Edition took place on May 4, 1727 (adv. in *The Post Boy* of that date). And publication of the 12mo edition cannot have taken place until after Dec. 28, 1727, the date for the four illustrations exactly suiting them as they occur for the first time in the 12mo edition. As long, therefore, as no copies have turned up without them — and although several copies have gone through my hands, I have never seen one — I prefer to stick to the following order:

(*a*) three 8vo editions in 1726, hitherto distinguished as A, AA and B, of which only Vol. II of the second edition is described as *The Second Edition*.

(*b*) one 8vo edition in 1727, with *The Second Edition* on the title-page of Vol. I, and *The Second Edition, Corrected* on that of Vol. II.

(*c*) one 12mo edition in 1727 (or rather in the beginning of 1728); and the same edition, consisting of exactly the same sheets, but with new title-pages, bearing the year 1731. Neither of them has any indication of edition on the title-pages.

This sequence has the advantage of being the conventional one. Pope, Swift and Ford all meant the 1727 8vo edition, when they spoke of the 'second' edition (cf. *Corresp.*, III, 381; V, 26, 37; and 'A Letter from Gulliver to Sympson', dated April 2, 1727, for the first time printed in Faulkner's *Works*, Vol. III, 1735, where Gulliver says: "I have sent you some Corrections, which you may insert, if ever there should be a second Edition.") The fact that Bathurst, Motte's partner and successor and therefore not to be considered as an outsider, placed *The Fourth Edition, Corrected* on the title-page in 1742, shows his opinion, however wrong it may be for the rest, that three

A

Complete Key

TO THE

TALE of a *TUB*;

With some Account of the

AUTHORS,

The Ocasion and Design of Writing it,
and Mr. WOTTON's *Remarks* examin'd.

*Is This pamphlet is severely censur'd
in the Postscript to the Apology of
the Tale of y*^e *Tub 1710? But This
seems to be wrote in
defence of the
Author.*

LONDON:
Printed for EDMUND CURLL at the *Dial and*
Bible against St. *Dunstan's* Church in
Fleetstreet. **1710.** Price *6d.*

Where may be had *A Meditation upon a Broomstick*,
and somewhat beside, *utile dulci*; by one of the
Authors of the *Tale of a Tub.* Price *6d.*

I

1194

A

MEDITATION

UPON A

Broom--Stick,

AND

Somewhat Beside ;

OF

The Same A U T H O R's.

----*Utile dulci.*

L O N D O N,

Printed for E. CURLL at the *Dial* and *Bible*
against St. *Dunstan's* Church in *Fleet-
street,* 1710.

(Price 2 d.)

editions had then preceded. And as to Motte himself, he may of course have been responsible, as Mr. Williams asserts (*The Library*, Dec. 1925, p. 261), for the placing of *The Second Edition* on the title-page of Vol. II of the AA edition, though, considering the circumstance that this edition was produced in haste, it may very well have been the printer who did it. At any rate it is noteworthy that this procedure was not continued in the case of the B edition, and that after it the 'Second' edition was very definitely described as *The Second Edition* and *The Second Edition, Corrected*. Nor can the latter description be explained as meaning: 'the corrected second (AA) edition'. Apart from the consideration that there should have been no comma in that case, this interpretation would be contrary to fact, for it is not the 'corrected second (= AA) edition', but rather the 'corrected first (= A) edition'. The only alternative is that the words in question mean: this is (absolutely) the second edition, the three preceding editions of 1726 counting as one, and compared with them corrections (from Ford's *Errata*) have been made in this one.' This is not only the usual explanation in similar cases, but in this special case, I think, the only correct one.

On the above considerations I think it advisable to stick to the well-established practice of calling the three 1726 editions *first* (A, AA and B), the 1727 8vo edition *second*, and the 1727 (= 1731) 12mo edition *third*; after which Bathurst's 1742, 1747 and 1751 editions as *fourth*, *fifth* and *sixth* follow in regular sequence.

Contents:

The work consists of four 'Voyages', distinguished as Parts I, II, III and IV respectively. Each of the *Motte* editions has two 'Volumes', each volume containing two 'Parts'.

Titles:

There are five titles: a general title in Vol. I, serving both as general title to the whole work and as general title to Vol. I; moreover two special titles, one to each of the two 'Parts' of Vol. I; further a general title to Vol. II, and a special title to Part IV, but no special title to Part III. All the five titles are within double-lined frames.

Portrait:

There is a frontispiece portrait of Gulliver in all the copies of the A, AA, and B editions, and in some copies of the Second Edition and of the two 12mo issues, all from the same plate, but in different states:

(1) the first has the inscription "*Captain Lemuel Gulliver*, of Redriff Aetat, suae 58." on a tablet under the oval (in all L. P., and in the earlier Sm. P. copies of the A edition);

(2) the second has the same inscription round the oval, the tablet bearing a Latin inscription (in the later Sm. P. copies of the A edition, in all the copies of the AA and B edition, and in the earlier copies of the second), but it has been retouched;

    (a) printed on paper with *vertical* chainlines (in the later copies of the Second Edition);

    (b) printed on paper with *horizontal* chainlines in the later copies of the 1727, 12mo edition, and in the earlier copies of its 1731 re-issue; also in a few L. P. copies of the A edition, in which they form a late insertion, and two of which are now known: the Ham House copy, and the Pierpont Morgan copy (with MS. corrections in the hand of Charles Ford).

So there is no portrait in the middle copies of the Second Edition, the earlier ones of the 1727, 12mo edition, and the later ones of its 1731 re-issue.

The Ham House *Gulliver*, a very exceptional copy sold at Sotheby's on June 21, 1938, to the American Rosenbach Co., who resold it to its present owner, Lord Rothschild, is a L. P. copy in the original boards, totally uncut, measuring 251 × 150 mm., apparently the only copy existing in this state. The original purchaser, the fourth Earl of Dysart, has written inside the front cover: "Read through 2 vol. at Tunbridge in July 1731 — Dysart." I have not seen it, but the description in Sotheby's sale-catalogue, supplemented by information kindly supplied by them and Lord Rothschild would suggest that the portrait was specially made for this copy. It is in the third state (*b*), printed on a very large sheet of paper, cut to size: 251 × 150 mm. It has led me to an examination of my own copies of the 1727 and 1731, 12mo issues, of each of which I have possessed one with and one without the portrait. It appears that these two portraits are also the third state (*b*). Hence I conclude that, after the portraits in the second state still present in the earlier copies of the Second Edition had been exhausted, and after an interval during which no portrait was available, the portraits in the third state (*a*) and (*b*) came into being, and were applied as mentioned above. They must therefore belong to a time between the second half of 1728, and 1731.

Four maps and two plans:
There are four maps (one to each of the four Parts) and two plans (in Part III), in all the Motte editions. Those in the four 8vo editions are from larger-size plates; they do not occur again. Those in the two 12mo editions are from smaller-size plates; they were used again by Bathurst in the *Gullivers* belonging to the *Miscellanies*, 1742, &c. (Nos. 66–9, *ante*), but those in the separate Bathurst editions, 1748, &c. (Nos. 304–6, *post*) are from different plates.

Illustrations:
The two 12mo editions have four illustrations, one to each Part, which were used again by Bathurst in 1748, &c. (Nos. 304–5, *post*).

Verses:
In his letter to Swift of Feb. 18, 1727, Pope mentions three verses (Nos. 3, 1, 4 below), which supplemented by a fourth (No. 2 below) first appeared as a separate publication (about March 1727 — cf. *Corresp.*, III, 380–1):

Several / Copies / Of / Verses / On Occasion of / Mr. *Gulliver's* / Travels. / — / Never before Printed. / — / [ornament] / — / London: / Printed for Benj. Motte, at the *Middle Temple* / Gate in Fleet-street. MDCCXXVII.

8vo; [A]–D⁴, 2 pp. (h.t. + bl.), 2 pp. (f.t. + bl.), 5–30, 2 pp. blank.
The 26 pages text (pp. 5–20), containing four *Verses* (1. To Quinbus Flestrim. 2. The Lamentation. 3. To Mr. Lemuel Gulliver. 4. Mary Gulliver To Capt. Lemuel Gulliver.), after removal of the page numbers and the signatures, were then compressed, from the type that had been kept standing, to 20 pages. Next new page indications and signatures ( )(and a, b respectively) were introduced, while the last page was provided with the catchword 'Part,' after which these 20 pages were placed before the text of the *Second Edition* of the Travels.
Later on, one more verse was added (5. The Words of the King of Brobdingnag.), in the separate publication by the insertion of a double-leaf, signed * (numbered 17, 14, 15, 16) between pages 16 and 17, and in the other

case by the addition of a double-leaf, signed ✳ (again marked)(, and provided with the catchword 'Part' on the 4th page) placed after the 20 pages.

Variants occur, the result of wrong mating. My own copy of the *Second Edition* has the 4 Verses of the second issue, the 5th of the first issue. Griffith No. 190 (a) mentions a copy of the *Second Edition* in the Lefferts Collection (Harvard), which has Verses 1, 2, 3 of the second issue, followed by Verses 3, 4 of the first issue, so that Verse 3 occurs twice, while Verse 5 is absent.

In the 12mo edition there were at first no *Verses* at all, but later on they were also inserted into it, reprinted and all five at once together, in the order 1, 2, 5, 3, 4. They are mentioned on the title-page of the Second Edition, not on that of the 12mo edition.

In Faulkner's edition of the *Travels* (Vol. III of the *Works*), 1735, verses 1, 2 and 4 are ascribed to Arbuthnot, Pope, and Gay; but the latest criticism (Normal Ault, *New Light On Pope*, London, 1949, p. 231 etc.) gives all five to Pope. Cf. Nos. 293, 294, 1224.

Pagination:
The A, AA and 'Second' editions have separate pagination to each 'Part', the B edition and the two 12mo issues have continuous pagination to each 'Volume'.

Further details:
Each of the five editions shows various irregularities. Some of the more important and characteristic ones have been hereafter appended to the editions separately. As a rule these so-called 'points', together with the title-pages and collations, will suffice to determine copies; but for a fuller discussion of mistakes, misprints, signatures, founts, etc., and the conclusions to be drawn from them, see Hubbard, and Williams, in their works mentioned above.

289. *The A edition:*
1. General title to the whole work as well as to Vol. I:

Travels / Into Several / Remote Nations / Of The / World. / — / In Four Parts. / — / By *Lemuel Gulliver*, / First a Surgeon, and then a Cap- / tain of several Ships. / — / Vol. I. / — / *London*: / *Printed for* Benj. Motte, *at the* / *Middle* Temple-Gate *in* Fleet-street. / MDCCXXVI.

2. Special title to Part I:
Travels / Into Several / Remote Nations / Of The / World. / — / Part I. / A Voyage to *Lilliput*. / — / [ornament] / — / *London*: / Printed in the Year MDCCXXVI.

3. Special title to Part II:
Travels / Into Several / Remote Nations / Of The / World. / — / By *Captain* Lemuel Gulliver. / — / Part II. / A Voyage to Brob-dingnag. / — / *London*: / Printed in the Year, MDCCXXVI.

4. General title to Vol. II:
Travels / Into Several / Remote Nations / Of The / World. / — / By *Captain* Lemuel Gulliver. / — / Part III. / A Voyage to Laputa,

Balnibarbi, / Glubbdubdrib, Luggnagg and / Japan. / Part IV. / A Voyage to the Houyhnhnms. / — / *London:* / Printed for Benjamin Motte, at the / *Middle-Temple-Gate.* MDCCXXVI.

5. Special title to Part IV:

Travels / Into Several / Remote Nations / Of The / World. / — / *By Captain* Lemuel Gulliver. / — / Part IV. / A Voyage to the Houyhnhnms. / — / *London:* / Printed in the Year, MDCCXXVI.

[Titles all five in double-lined frame]

8vo; A–K⁸, L²; [π]³, 2B–L⁸, M² — 2 pp. (1st title + bl.), 2 pp. (titles of the 4 parts + bl.), [V]–IX + bl. (The Publisher To The Reader), 2 pp. (2nd title + bl.), [XIII]–XVI (Contents of Part I), [1]–148 (Lilliput); 2 pp. (3rd title + bl.), 4 pp. (Contents of Part II), [1]–164 (Brobdingnag).

A³, B–K⁸, L⁴, M²; 2A⁴, 2B–N⁸, O⁴ — 2 pp. (4th title + bl.), 4 pp. (Contents of Part III), [1]–155 + bl. (Laputa); 2 pp. (5th title + bl.), 6 pp. (Contents of Part IV), [1]–199 + bl. (Houyhnhnms).

Frontisp. portrait of Gulliver (first or second state), 4 maps and 2 plans.

Note: Besides the ordinary small-paper copies there are also some copies printed on "a Royal Paper," which, Hubbard, *Contributions*, p. 28, says, "represent an intermediate if not the final printing of the first edition". This is a question perhaps impossible to decide. The only available evidence points in the other direction. Judging from the ornaments, type, and page numbers, the four Parts were printed in four different printing-houses; and the order of printing of the L. P. and Sm. P. sheets, not only as groups, but even as separate units, may have differed in these four printing-houses. Only as to leaf E in Part IV can we say with certainty that its L. P. printing preceded its Sm. P. printing — see point (5) below. On this point my article, "The Publication of Gulliver's Travels", in *The Dublin Magazine*, Jan. 1948, p. 26 wants correction.

L. P. copies should have the portrait in the first state; Sm. P. copies have it either in the first or second state.

Some L. P. copies (Ham House, and Pierpont Morgan) have it in the third state (*b*).

Distinguishing marks between L. P. and Sm. P. copies are:

(1) Part I, p. 17, l. 22: 'Potio' in L. P., 'Potion' in Sm. P. copies.

(2) Part II, p. 39: Certain letters at the beginning of ll. 1–4 have failed to print in L. P. copies; not so in Sm. P. ones.

(3) Part IV, p. 50: In L. P. copies (B. M., Forster, Bodl., U.L.C., Armagh) the first letters of the words 'sold' and 'til' in ll. 10 and 11 have entirely dropped out, these words therefore reading 'old' and 'ill'; but by mistake the compositor has reinserted the 's' three lines higher up, so that the word 'trea-ted' reads 'trea-sted'. In Sm. P. copies the 's' and 't' show dislocation only, but they have not dropped out.

(4) Part IV, p. 62: In L. P. copies the page number is misprinted 26, in Sm. P. copies correct 62.

(5) Part IV, leaf 2E 8 (pp. 63–4) is a cancel in Sm. P. copies, not in L. P. ones. Page 64, l. 1 in L. P. copies has 'ours and give', while the catchword on that page is 'frequent'; in Sm. P. copies the three words are 'ours or give', and the catchword has been altered into 'sufficient' to avoid tautology with 'frequent' some lines higher up, the result being that it no longer corresponds with the first word on p. 65, which was and remained 'frequent'. — This proves this sheet L. P. to have preceded Sm. P.

(6) Part IV, p. 90, l. 18: In L. P. copies 'carryon', in Sm. P. ones 'car ryon', or 'carry on'.

A more doubtful point is:

Part III, p. 90, ll. 12–14: Some Sm. P. copies have two misspelt words ('Conspir*i*cies' and 'turbul*a*ncy'); others, together with all L. P. copies, have correctly 'Conspir*a*cies' and 'turbul*e*ncy'.

The following details, common to Sm. P. and L. P. copies alike, can only serve as distinguishing marks between the A and AA editions:

(1) Part I, p. 35, l. 5: All the A ed. copies have correctly 'Subsidies', where the AA ed. ones have 'Subsid*u*es'.

(2) Part III, p. 74: All the A ed. copies have this page misnumbered '44', where the AA ed. ones have correctly '74'.

(3) Part III, leaf G 6 (pp. 91–2): In all the A ed. copies this leaf is a cancel ("Part III" at foot); in the AA ed. ones not.

(4) Part IV, p. 52, l. 1: In all the A ed. copies 'buth is'; in AA ed. copies 'but his'.

The following, which have often been mentioned as 'points', occur in both A and AA ed. copies, and can therefore be no 'points' at all:

(1) Part I, pp. 62 and 64: Three times the number 1724 is wrong for 1728. The number is correct in the B and following editions.

(2) Part I, p. 145, ll. 8–9: *Lilliput* is wrong for *Blefuscu*. Only correct in the 'Second' edition.

(3) Part III, p. 94: The seventh chapter is misnumbered 'Chap. V.'. Wrong in all the *Motte* editions.

(4) Part III, p. 114, ll. 6–7: The word 'singular' appears as 'ngu-lar'. However, in some of the AA edition copies this misprint has been corrected, apparently during the press-work, for it occurs in sheet I, which is identical in the A and AA editions (see note under the AA ed.).

Sm. P. copy: Penn.

290. *The AA edition:*

Titles 1, 2 and 3 are the same printing as those in the A edition; 4 and 5 are different:

4. General title to Vol. II:

Travels / Into Several / Remote Nations / Of The / World. / — / *By Captain* Lemuel Gulliver. / — / Part III. / A Voyage to Laputa, Balnibarbi, / Glubbdubdrib, Luggnagg, and / Japan. / Part IV. / A Voyage to the Houyhnhnms. / — / The Second Edition. / — / *London:* / Printed for Benjamin Motte, at the / *Middle-Temple-Gate.* M.DCC.XXVI.

5. The special title to Part IV is at first sight the same as that in the A edition, but a closer view shows that the word 'Voyage' is printed with capitals in the A edition, and with ordinary letters in the AA edition. For the rest they have the same appearance.

[Titles all five in double-lined frame]

8vo; A–K⁸; [π]³, B–L⁸, M² — 2 pp. (1st title + bl.), 1 p. (titles of the 4 parts), [IV]–VIII (The Publisher To The Reader), 1 p. (2nd title), [X]–XII (Contents of Part I), [1]–148 (Lilliput); 2 pp. (3rd title + bl.), 4 pp. (Contents of Part II), [1]–164 (Brobdingnag).

A³, B–K⁸, L⁵; A⁴, B–N⁸, O⁴ — 2 pp. (4th title + bl.), 4 pp. (Contents of Part III), [1]–154 (Laputa); 2 pp. (5th title + bl.), 6 pp. (Contents of Part IV), [1]–199 + bl. (Houyhnhmms).

Frontisp. portrait of Gulliver (second state), 4 maps and 2 plans. Set from the A edition.

Here are some misprints:

Part I, p.   3, l. 19: 'two' (for 'too')
       p. 16, l.   5: 'understook' (for 'understood')
       p. 27, l.   9: 'momentuous' (for 'momentous')
       p. 35, l.   5: 'Subsidues' (for 'Subsidies')
       p. 44, l.   7: 'two and fro' (for 'to and fro')
       p. 63, ll. 1–2: 'Ar-ties' (for 'Ar-ticles')
Part II, p. 163, l. 16: 'Gooss' (for 'Goose')
Part III, p. 79, l.   5: 'Abstience' (for 'Abstinence')
       p. 80, ll. 3–4: 're-received' (for 're-ceived')
       p. 89, l.   7: 'strick' (for 'strict')
       p. 89, l. 19: 'tinture' (for 'Tincture')
Part IV, p. 10, l. 16: 'Wondet' (for 'Wonder')
       p. 37, l.   2: 'Languxge' (for 'Language')

Note: Sheets I and K of Part III, and sheet N of Part IV, appear to be the same printing as the corresponding sheets in the A edition; with, however, some minor corrections effected during the press-work.

Sheet I of Part IV occurs in two different settings, distinguishable i.a. by widening out of text (pp. 119, 120, 122) and the absence of 'Part IV' at the foot of page 113 in one of them. Neither of these settings is the same as the corresponding sheet in the A edition (cf. Hubbard, *Contributions*, pp. 32, 34).

Hubbard also says that copies of the AA edition occur with title 4 of the B edition (*op. cit.*, 17, 24, 29).

Copy: Penn.

291. *The B edition:*
1. General title to the whole work as well as to Vol. I:

Travels / Into Several / Remote Nations / Of The / World. / — / In Four Parts. / — / By *Lemuel Gulliver*, / first a Surgeon, and then a Captain / of several Ships. / — / Vol. I. / — / *London:* / *Printed for* Benj. Motte, *at the Middle* / Temple-Gate *in* Fleet-street. / M,DCC,XXVI.

2. Special title to Part I:

Travels / Into Several / Remote Nations / Of The / World. / — / By *Captain* Lemuel Gulliver. / — / Part I. / A Voyage to Lilliput. / — / *London:* / Printed in the Year, MDCCXXVI.

3. Special title to Part II:

The same as the corresponding one in the A edition, but not the same printing.

4. General title to Vol. II:

Travels / Into Several / Remote Nations / Of The / World. / — / By *Captain* Lemuel Gulliver. / — / Vol. II. / — / Part III. / A Voyage to Laputa, Balnibarbi, / Glubbdubdrib, Luggnagg, and / Japan. / Part IV. / A Voyage to the Houyhnhnms. / = / *London:*

/ Printed for Benjamin Motte, at the / *Middle-Temple-Gate.*
Mdccxxvi.

5. Special title to Part IV:
The same as the corresponding one in the AA edition, but no comma
behind the word 'Year'.
[Titles all five in double-lined frame]
8vo; A–K^8; L^3, M–X^8, Y^1 — 2 pp. (1st title + bl.), 1 p. (titles of the 4
parts), [IV]–VIII (The Publisher To The Reader), 2 pp. (2nd title + bl.),
2 pp. (Contents of Part I), [1]–148 (Lilliput), 2 pp. (3rd title + bl.), 4 pp.
(Contents of Part II), [149]–310 (Brobdingnag).
A^3, B–K^8, L^5; M–Aa^8 — 2 pp. (4th title + bl.), 4 pp. (Contents of Part III),
[1]–154 (Laputa), 2 pp. (5th title + bl.), 6 pp. (Contents of Part IV), [155]–
353 + bl. (Houyhnhnms).
Frontisp. portrait of Gulliver (second state), 4 maps and 2 plans. Set from
the AA edition.
Note: In this edition Vol. I has nineteen misnumbered pages: one in sheet
E (66 for 68), ten in sheet N, and eight in sheet Q. — Copies occur in which
the four *Keys* mentioned in No. 1215, *post*, have been bound in, usually one at
the end of each 'Part'.
Needless to say that they form no integral part of the *Travels* proper.
Copy: Penn.

292. In 1727 a spurious third volume was published:
Travels / Into Several / Remote Nations / Of The / World. / — /
By Capt. Lemuel Gulliver. / — / Vol. III. / — / *Accidit in Puncto,
quod non speratur in Anno.* / *Gaudent securi narrare pericula nautae.* /
— / *London:* / Printed in the Year M.DCC.XXVII.

Travels / Into Several / Remote Nations / Of The / World. / — /
By Captain Lemuel Gulliver. / — / Vol. III. Part II. / A Voyage
to Sevarambia, &c. / — / *London:* / Printed in the Year
MDCCXXVII.

[Titles within double-lined frame]
8vo; [A]^4, B–H^8, I^4, 2A^4, 2B–L^8 — 2 pp. (h. t. + bl.), 2 pp. (1st title + bl.),
4 pp. (Contents of Part I), [1]–20 (Introduction), 21–118 (Second Voyage to
Brobdingnag, and Voyage to Sporunda); 2 pp. (2nd title + bl.), 5 pp. + bl.
(Contents of Part II), [1]–159 + bl. (Voyages to Sevarambia, Monatamia,
Batavia, The Cape, and England). — Frontisp. P. 113–20 misnumbered
111–18.

Part I (*A Second Voyage To Brobdingnag,* and *A Voyage To Sporunda*) is an
imitation; Part II (*A Voyage to Sevarambia*) has been stolen from: *The History
Of The Sevarites or Sevarambi,* By one Captain Siden (i.e. Denis de Veiras, or
Denys Vairasse d'Alais), London, / Printed for Henry Brome, 12mo, 2 vols.,
1675–9 (French translation 1677–9, Dutch 1682, German 1689).
The reason why I have included this volume here is, not only that in
antiquarian catalogues it is frequently offered with the two volumes of the
genuine *Travels,* but principally because the translations generally, at least
during the 18th century, add it to the genuine work.
Copy: Penn.

293. *The Second Edition:*
1. General title to the whole work as well as to Vol. I:

Travels / Into Several / Remote Nations / Of The / World. / — / In Four Parts. / — / By *Lemuel Gulliver,* / First a Surgeon, and then a Captain / of several Ships. / — / To which are prefix'd, / Several Copies of Verses Expla- / planatory [*sic*] and Commendatory; never be- / fore printed. / — / Vol. I. / — / The Second Edition. / — / *London:* / *Printed for* Benj. Motte, *at the* Middle / Temple Gate *in* Fleet-street. MDCCXXVII.

2. Special title to Part I:
The same as the corresponding one in the A edition, but the ornament is different, and the year is MDCCXXVII.

3. Special title to Part II:

Travels / Into Several / Remote Nations / Of The / World. / — / Part II. / A Voyage to *Brobdingnag.* / — / [ornament] / — / *London:* / Printed in the Year MDCCXXVII.

4. General title to Vol. II:

Travels / Into Several / Remote Nations / Of The / World. / — / *By Captain* Lemuel Gulliver. / — / Part III. / A Voyage to Laputa, Balnibarbi, / Glubbdubdrib, Luggnagg and / Japan. / Part IV. / A Voyage to the Houyhnhnms. / — / Vol. II. / — / The Second Edition, Corrected. / — / *London:* / Printed for Benjamin Motte, at the *Middle-* / *Temple-Gate.* MDCCXXVII.

5. Special title to Part IV:

Travels / Into Several / Remote Nations / Of The / World. / — / *By Captain* Lemuel Gulliver. / — / Part IV. / A Voyage to the Houyhnhnms. / = / *London:* / Printed in the Year, MDCCXXVII.

[Titles all five in double-lined frame]

8vo; [A1], 2^{2-7}, b⁴, *², A^{2-8}, B–K⁸; [L]–U⁸, X⁴, Y 1 — 2 pp. (1st title + bl.), 20 pp. (4 verses), (4 pp. (1 verse)), 1 p. (titles of the 4 parts), [IV]–VIII (The Publisher To The Reader), 1 p. (2nd title), [X]–XII (Contents of Part I), [1]–148 (Lilliput); 2 pp. (3rd title + bl.), 4 pp. (Contents of Part II), [1]–164 (Brobdingnag).

A⁴, B–K⁸, L⁴, M²; A⁴, B–N⁸, O⁴ — 2 pp. (bl. + advs.), 2 pp. (4th title + bl.), 4 pp. (Contents of Part III), [1]–155 + bl. (Laputa); 2 pp. (5th title + bl.), 6 pp. (Contents of Part IV), [1]–199 + bl. (Houyhnhnms).

Frontisp. portrait of Gulliver (second state in the earlier, third state (*a*) in the later copies; in between, during a time of temporary exhaustion, copies were sold without the portrait), 4 maps and 2 plans.

Set from the A edition.

The *Verses* occur in two shapes:
(1) 20 pp. (a^{2-7}, b⁴), marked)(at the top; catchword on the last page is 'Part'. — Contains 4 *Verses.* (2) 24 pp. (a^{2-7}, b⁴, *²), the same 20 pp. with

4 added, also marked)(at the top; catchword on the last of the 4 pages again 'Part'. — Contains 5 *Verses*.

For separate editions of the *Verses*, see No. 1224, *post.*, and note before 289.

Copies: (1) with 20 pp. *Verses*: Forster 9599 (the tail-piece on the 12th page shows a flaming fire pointing downwards). (2) with 24 pp. *Verses*: Forster 7087, Bodl., and Penn (tail-piece on the 12th page shows a flaming fire pointing upwards).

Here are some misprints:

Part   I, p. 138, ll. 21–22: 'im-possile' (for 'im-possible')
Part II, p.   3, l.   19: 'hurlling' (for 'hulling')
Part III, p.   5, l.   10: 'tryed' (for 'tyed')
          p. 36, l.   13: 'course' (for 'Cause')
          p. 105, l.   8: 'think' (for 'thin')
          p. 155, l.   11: 'found' omitted
Part IV, p.   5, ll. 1–2: 'ex-postuled' (for 'ex-postulated')
          p. 36, l.   17: 'greet' (for 'great')
          p. 45, l.   18: 'himself' (for 'myself')
          p. 120, ll. 23–24: 'Act-vity' (for 'Act-ivity')
          p. 139, l.   18: 'Smilies' (for 'Similes')

Notes:

1. This is the first Motte edition (after the A, AA, B editions, and 12mo printing) to contain emendations in the spirit of Ford's *Errata*; hence 'The Second Edition', and 'The Second Edition, Corrected' on the title-pages. As to the authority of its text, see No. 302, *post.*

2. Hubbard, *Contributions*, 133, mentions a rebound copy of the "Second" edition with 8 pp. book-advertisements (for Stephen Austen, 1728) at the end of Vol. II. Likewise Penn has a copy in contemporary binding of the B edition with 4 pp. book-advertisements (by J. Walthoe, 1726) at the end of Vol. II. It is of course plain that suchlike insertions have nothing to do with the book itself.

294. [*Third edition*], 1727, in 12mo:

Travels / Into Several / Remote Nations / Of The / World. / — / In Four Parts. / — / By *Lemuel Gulliver*, / first a Surgeon, and then a Captain / of several Ships. / — / Vol. I. / — / *London:* / *Printed for* Benj. Motte, *at the Middle* / Temple-Gate *in* Fleet-street. / M,DCC,XXVII.

Travels / Into Several / Remote Nations / Of The / World / — / *By Captain* Lemuel Gulliver. / — / Part I. / A Voyage to Lilliput. / — / *London:* / Printed in the Year, MDCXXVII. [*sic*]

Travels / Into Several / Remote Nations / Of The / World / — / *By Captain* Lemuel Gulliver. / — / Part II. / A Voyage to Brob-dingnag. / — / *London:* / Printed in the Year, MDCXXVII. [*sic*]

Travels / Into Several / Remote Nations / Of The / World. / — / *By Captain* Lemuel Gulliver. / — / Vol. II. / — / Part III. / A Voyage to Laputa, Balnibarbi, / Glubbdubdribb, Luggnagg, and / Japan. / Part IV. / A Voyage to the Houyhnhnms. / = / *London:*

/ Printed for Benjamin Motte, at the / *Middle-Temple-Gate*.
M.DCC.XXVII.

Travels / Into Several / Remote Nations / Of The / World. / — /
By Captain Lemuel Gulliver. / — / Part IV. / A Voyage to the
Houyhnhnms. / — / [ornament] / = / *London:* / Printed in the
Year M.DCC.XXVII.

> [Titles all five in double-lined frame]
> 12mo; A⁶, a⁶, B–M¹² — 2 pp. (1st title + bl.), 2 pp. (titles of the 4 parts +
> bl.), [III]–VI (The Publisher To The Reader), 2 pp. (2nd title + bl.), 2 pp.
> (Contents of Part I), ([I]–XII (Verses)), [1]–121 + bl. (Lilliput), 2 pp. (3rd
> title + bl.), 4 pp. (Contents of Part II), [129]–264 (Brobdingnag).
> A³, B–M¹², N³ — 2 pp. (4th title + bl.), 4 pp. (Contents of Part III),
> [1]–117 + bl. (Laputa), 2 pp. (5th title + bl.), 4 pp. (Contents of Part IV),
> [125]–269 + bl. (Houyhnhnms).
> Four maps and two plans; also four illustrations (each representing three
> scenes, except the third), one to each 'Part'.
> Earlier copies have no *Verses*, but later ones have them. Earlier copies
> have no portrait of Gulliver, but later ones have it in the third state (*b*).
> I possess a copy without either *Verses* or portrait. Penn has one (an entirely
> uncut one, in contemporary half-calf boards covered with paper of chintz
> design, probably the only copy in existence in this state) with both *Verses*
> and portrait.
> Cf. No. 1224, and note before No. 289.
> Set from the B edition.
> This edition, though *printed* before the 'Second' edition (No. 293, *ante*),
> was *published* after it, early in 1728. See note before No. 289, *ante*.

295. *Second issue*, 1731:
Travels / Into Several / Remote Nations / Of The / World. / — /
In Four Parts. / — / By *Lemuel Gulliver*, / First a Surgeon, and
then a Captain of / several Ships. / — / Vol. I. / = / *London:* /
Printed for Benjamin Motte, at the *Middle* / *Temple-Gate in Fleet-*
Street. / M.DCC.XXI.

Travels / Into Several / Remote Nations / Of The / World / — /
By Captain Lemuel Gulliver. / — / Part I. / A Voyage to Lilliput.
/ — / *London:* / Printed in the Year, MDCXXVII. [*sic*]

Travels / Into Several / Remote Nations / Of The / World. / — /
By Captain Lemuel Gulliver. / — / Part II. / A Voyage to Brobdingnag. / = / *London:* / Printed in the Year M.DCC.XXXI.

Travels / Into Several / Remote Nations / Of The / World. / — /
By Captain Lemuel Gulliver. / — / Vol. II. / — / Part III. / A
Voyage to Laputa, Balnibarbi, / Glubbdubdribb, Luggnagg, and /
Japan. / Part IV. / A Voyage to the Houyhnhnms. / = / *London:*
/ Printed for Benjamin Motte, at the *Middle-* / *Temple-Gate.*
M.DCC.XXXI.

Travels / Into Several / Remote Nations / Of The / World. / — / *By Captain* Lemuel Gulliver. / — / Part IV. / A Voyage to the Houyhnhnms. / = / *London*: / Printed in the Year M.DCC.XXXI.

[Titles all five in double-lined frame]
This is exactly the same printing as the 1727 edition in 12mo (No. 294); only the original titles 1, 3, 4 and 5 have been cut away and replaced by new ones. The second title, with the misprinted year, has by mistake been preserved in some copies; in others it has been cancelled. The four maps, two plans, and four illustrations are also the same.

Earlier copies have the *Verses*; later ones lack them.

Earlier copies have the portrait of Gulliver in the third state (*b*): in later ones it is absent.

Penn has a copy with the *Verses* and the portrait.

Cf. No. 1224, and note before No. 289.

***

Serial Editions

296. Numb. 251. / The Penny / London Post. / — / Friday, November 25, 1726. / — /

[The text, in two columns, is headed:]

We shall omit for some time the Life of / Don Quixote to give Place for the Travels / of Captain Lemuel Gulliver into several re- / mote Parts of the World, which have been / lately published, and bore so considerable a / Share in almost every Conversation both in / Town and Country, not only from the Repu- / tation of their suppos'd Author, but the vast / Variety of Wit and Pleasantry with which the / several Relations are interpos'd; that those / who have not the Convenience of reading / them at the Price they are now sold, may / not be debarr'd so delightful an Entertain- / ment, we shall begin them in this Paper in / the Manner following, and continue them till / the whole is finished. / Travels into several remote Nations of the / World. In four Parts. By Lemuel Gulliver, / first a Surgeon, and then a Captain of seve- / ral Ships.

[At end of this Numb. 251, at foot of p. 4:]

London: Printed by T. Read behind the *Sun-Tavern* in *Fleet-Street*. Where *Adve* [*sic*] / *tisements* are taken in. And compleat Setts had.

This periodical appeared on Mondays, Wednesdays and Fridays. Each number has two quarto-size leaves. The only copy known, an incomplete set, is in the possession of Lord Rothschild, Merton Hall, Cambridge, with whose kind permission these particulars are here given. The numbers containing 'Gulliver's Travels' are Nos. 252–67 (No. 252 misprinted "Numb. 251." as above; No. 259 missing), dated Nov. 25, 28, 30, Dec. 2, 5, 7, 9, 14, 16, 19,

21, 23, 26, 28, 30; so that the story only reaches the middle of Chap. VI of Lilliput.

296A. Parker's Penny Post. Numb. 246 / — / *Monday* November 28 1726. / — /

[The text, in two columns, follows immediately under this, and is headed:]

The Travels of Capt. *Gulliver*, who was first a Sur- / geon, then a Captain of divers Ships, whereby / he sail'd into several remote Parts of the World; / which have been lately publish'd, having for their / Variety of Wit and pleasant Diversion, become / the general Entertainment of Town and Coun- / try, we will insert here in small Parcels, to / oblige our Customers, who are otherwise, not cap- / able of reading them at the Price they are sold.

[At end of this Numb. 246, at foot of p. 4:]

London, Printed by *George Parker*, at the *Star* and *Ball*, in Salisbury-Court, where / Advertisements are taken in.

This periodical appeared on Mondays, Wednesdays and Fridays. Each number consists of two quarto-size leaves, numbered 1–4. The last number containing *Gull. Travels* was: Numb. 390 Friday November 3, 1727.
Copy: B.M. Burney Coll. 27*b*, 29*b*.

***

Dublin Editions

297. Travels / Into Several / Remote Nations / Of The / World. / — / In Four Parts. / — / By *Lemuel Gulliver*, / First a Surgeon, and then a Captain / of several Ships. / — / Vol. I. / — / *In this Impression, several* Errors *in the* / London *Edition are Corrected.* / — / *Dublin:* / Printed by and for J. Hyde, Book- / seller in *Dames's Street*, 1726.

The title of the second volume is exactly the same, except: Vol. II.
[Both titles in double-lined frame]
12mo; [A]⁶, B–F¹², G⁶; π³, H–N¹² — 2 pp. (t. + bl.), 4 pp. (3 pp. The Publisher to the Reader + bl.), 4 pp. (Contents of Parts I and II), 2 pp. blank, [1]–62 (Lilliput), 63–131 + bl. (Brobdingnag); 2 pp. (t. + bl.), 4 pp. (Contents of Parts III and IV), [133]–195 + bl. (Laputa), 197–274 (Houyhnhnms), 2 pp. blank.
Frontisp. portrait of Gulliver (inscription round the oval), 4 maps and 2 plans.
The above copy is in the Univ. of Michigan (Hubbard Collection), but it lacks the portrait. Mr. Harold Williams owns another copy (formerly in the possession of the late Mr. M. J. Ryan, Dun Laoghaire, Co. Dublin), which has the blank leaf A 6 turned outside so that it appears before the title.

The *Dublin Weekly Journal*, Numb. LXXXVII, Sat. Nov. 26, 1726, p. 342, has an adv. reading: *In the Press, and will be published next week*, Travels, etc.

Sold by G. Risk, G. Ewing and W. Smith in Dame's Street. And the next number, Sat. Dec. 3, 1726, p. 348 has: *Just Publish'd*, etc. (as before). — From these, as well as from the imprints of Nos. 298, 299, it appears that Risk, Ewing and Smith were booksellers only, and not printers. But the Hyde copy (297) has 'Printed by and for' in the imprint, from which it may be concluded that the two advertisements above can only refer to the Hyde copy, which was therefore published about Dec. 2, 1726.

As to the authority of its text it is noteworthy that, even some months before Motte's Second Edition (No. 293), it is the first edition to contain some alterations in the spirit of Ford's *Errata*. For Swift's opinion of Hyde, see *Corresp.* III 438, IV 56. See also note, No. 302.

298. Travels / Into Several / Remote Nations / Of The / World. / — / In Four Parts, *viz.* / Part I. A Voyage to Lilliput. / Part II. A Voyage to Brobdingnag. / Part III. A Voyage to Laputa, Bal- / nibarbi, Luggnagg, Glubdub- / drib and Japan. / Part. IV. A Voyage to the Country of the / Houyhnhnms. / — / By *Lemuel Gulliver*, / First a Surgeon, and then a Captain of several Ships. / — / With Cuts and Maps of the Author's Travels. / — / *Dublin:* / Printed for G. Risk, G. Ewing, and / W. Smith in *Dame-street*, MDCCXXVII.

Travels / Into Several / Remote Nations / Of The / World. / — / Part I. / A Voyage to *Lilliput.* / — / [ornament] / — / *Dublin:* / Printed for G. Risk, G. Ewing, and W. Smith in / *Dame-street*, MDCCXXVII.

Travels / Into Several / Remote Nations / Of The / World /. — / By *Captain* Lemuel Gulliver. / — / Part II. / A Voyage to Brob- dingnag. / — / [ornament] / — / *Dublin:* / Printed for G. Risk, G. Ewing, and W. Smith in / *Dame-street*, MDCCXXVII.

Travels / Into Several / Remote Nations / Of The / World. / By *Captain* Lemuel Gulliver. / — / Part III. / A Voyage to Laputa, Balnibar- / bi, Glubbdubdrib, Luggnagg / and Japan. / Part IV. / A Voyage to the Houyhnhnms. / — / *Dublin:* / Printed for G. Risk, G. Ewing, and W. Smith / in *Dame-street*, MDCCXXVII.

Travels / Into Several / Remote Nations / Of The / World. / — / By *Captain* Lemuel Gulliver. / — / Part IV. / A Voyage to the Houyhnhnms. / — / [ornament] / — / *Dublin:* / Printed for G. Risk, G. Ewing, and W. Smith in / *Dame-street*, MDCCXXVII.

8vo (in fours); A–I⁴, K²; π², B², C–L⁴; π², B–L⁴; π³, B–M⁴ — 2 pp. (1st title + bl.), 2 pp. (The Publisher To The Reader), 2 pp. (2nd title + bl.), 2 pp. (Contents of Part I), [1]–68 (Lilliput); 2 pp. (3rd title + bl.), 2 pp. (Contents of Part II), [1]–75 + bl. (Brobdingnag); 2 pp. (4th title + bl.), 2 pp. (Contents of Part III), [1]–79 + bl. (Laputa); 2 pp. (5th title + bl.), 4 pp. (Contents of Part IV), [1]–88 (Houyhnhnms). — Frontisp. portrait of Gulliver, 4 maps and 2 plans.

I possess two copies, a complete L. P. one (2 vols. — pages 63 and 64 of Part I misnumbered 65 and 66) and an incomplete Sm. P. one (Vol. I only — page numbers correct 63 and 64), differing in size and paper.

The former, a cut copy, is 18 × 12¼ cm.; it has been printed on a larger, thinner and smoother paper.

The latter, also a cut copy, is 16 × 10⅓ cm.; it has been printed on a smaller, thicker and rougher paper.

The B.M. copy (12611 h 5), a cut one, is like my 2 vol. copy, but it has another misnumbered page in Part I (51 misnumbered 52), where my copy has correct 51.

Mr. Harold Williams owns a copy, a cut one, 17 × 10½ cm., which is like my Vol. I copy (page numbers 51, 63, 64 all correct).

Penn has a copy with the two volumes bound as one.

299. Travels / Into Several / Remote Nations / Of The / World. / — / In Four Parts, *viz.* / Part I. A Voyage to Lilliput. / Part II. A Voyage to Brobdingnag. / Part III. A Voyage to Laputa, Balni- / barbi, Luggnagg, Glubdubdrib and / Japan. / Part IV. A Voyage to the Country of the / Houyhnhnms. / — / By *Lemuel Gulliver*, / First a Surgeon, and then a Captain of several Ships. / — / The Second Edition. / — / With Cuts and Maps of the Author's Travels. / — / *Dublin:* / Printed by S. P. for G. Risk, G. Ewing, / and W. Smith in *Dame's-street*, / MDCCXXVII.

Travels / Into Several / Remote Nations / Of The / World. / — / Vol. I. / — / Containing / Part I. A Voyage to Lilliput. / Part II. A Voyage to Brobdingnag. / — / By *Lemuel Gulliver*, / First a Surgeon, and then a Captain of several Ships. / — / With Cuts and Maps of the Author's Travels. / — / *Dublin:* / *Printed by* S. P. *for* G. Risk, G. Ewing, / *and* W. Smith, *in* Dame's-street, / MDCCXXVII.

Travels / Into Several / Remote Nations / Of The / World. / — / Vol. II. / — / Containing / Part III. A Voyage to Laputa, Balni- / barbi, Luggnagg, Glubdubdrib and / Japan. / Part IV. A Voyage to the Country of the / Houyhnhnms. / — / By *Lemuel Gulliver*, / First a Surgeon, and then a Captain of several Ships. / — / With Cuts and Maps of the Author's Travels. / — / *Dublin:* / Printed by S. P. for G. Risk, G. Ewing, / and W. Smith in *Dame's-street*, / MDCCXXVII.

12mo; [A]⁶, b², B–Aa⁶, Bb⁴ — 2 pp. (1st title + bl.), 2 pp. (2nd title + bl.), 2 pp. (The Publisher to the Reader), 10 pp. (Contents), [1]–133 + bl., [135–136] (3rd title + bl.), [137]–283 (advs. on verso). — Page 91, logically 14, has sign. 13, but should not be signed at all. — Frontisp. portrait of Gulliver, 4 maps and 2 plans (the same offprints as those in the preceding edition).

Copies: Harold Williams, and Yale (lacking 1st title, portrait, maps and plans — this copy has a portrait and 2 maps, none of these three belonging to it).

Cf. Prof. H. C. Hutchins, *The Review Of English Studies*, III, 1927, pp. 466–73; Harold Williams, *The Library*, IX, 1929, pp. 187–96.

Abridged Edition

300. Travels / Into Several / Remote Nations / Of The / World. / — / *By Capt*. Lemuel Guliver. [*sic*] / — / *Faithfully Abridged*. / — / [ornament] / — / *London:* / Printed for J. Stone, against *Bedford Row*, and / R. King, at the *Prince's-Arms* in St. *Paul*'s / Church-Yard. MDCCXXVII.

There is one more title, belonging to 'Brobdingnag':

Travels / Into Several / Remote Nations / Of The / World. / — / *By Capt*. Lemuel Gulliver. / — / Part II. / *A Voyage to* Brob-dingnag. / — / [ornament] / — / *London:* / Printed in the Year MDCCXXVII.

12mo; A⁴, B–G¹², H⁸; 2B–H¹², I⁶ — 2 pp. (1st title + bl.), 4 pp. (The Publisher of the Abridgment, To The Reader.), 2 pp. (Contents of Part I), [1]–67 + bl. (Lilliput), 2 pp. (2nd title + bl.), 71–4 (Contents of Part II), [75]–159 + bl. (Brobdingnag); [1]–100 (Laputa), 101–75 + bl. (Houhyn-hnms), 3 pp. advs. + bl. — Frontisp. portrait of Gulliver. — Parts III and IV have only dropped titles, and no Contents.

Copies: Nat. Libr. of Wales; Univ. of Mich. (Hubbard Coll.); and Penn.

301. *Another issue:*

Penn has a copy in which the two leaves I 5–6 (3 pp. advs. + bl.) have been cut away (stubs visible), and replaced by two double-leaves ([1]–8 = A Key And Compleat Index To Captain *Gulliver*'s Travels). —.

The Univ. of Michigan (Hubbard Coll.) has a copy in which not the 3 pp. advs. + bl., but the 2 pp. Contents of Part I have been cut away, and replaced by the 8 pp. Key and Compleat Index.

The B.M. copy (12604 bb 1) has the 8 pp. Key and Compleat Index, but both the 3 pp. advs. + bl., and the 2 pp. Contents of Part I have been cancelled. Moreover it lacks the portrait.

302. Travels / Into Several / Remote Nations of the *World*. / In Four Parts, *viz*. / [*First column:*] I. A Voyage to Lil- / liput. / II. A Voyage to Brob- / dingnag. / III. A Voyage to La- / [*Second column:*] puta, Balnibarbi, / Luggnagg, Glubb- / dubdrib and Japan. / IV. A Voyage to the / Country of the / Houyhnhnms. / — / By *Lemuel Gulliver*, first a Sur- / geon, and then a Captain of several Ships. / — / – – – – – *Retro*; / *Vulgus abhorret ab his.* / — / In this Impression several Errors in the *London* and / *Dublin* Editions are corrected. / — / *Dublin:* / Printed by and for George Faulkner, / Printer and Bookseller, in *Essex-Street*, / opposite to the Bridge. MDCCXXXV.

This is a separate issue of *Works*, Vol. III, 1735, 12mo in sixes (see No. 49); the 'Vol. III' title has been replaced by the above 'Travels' title. The pagination of the text has been altered: [1]–312, 313–16, 336 + bl.

Copy: Danielson.

Query: Was there also a similar separate issue of the 8vo ed.?

303. For the editions of *Gulliver's Travels* in 1742 (4th ed.), 1747 (5th ed.), 1751 (6th ed.), 1751 (5th ed.), and further in Swift's *Works*, see Nos. 66, &c., *ante*.

⁎

'Bathurst' Editions

Apart from the several Bathurst editions of *Gulliver's Travels* included in sets, and extending from 1742 to 1784 (see Nos. 66–119, *ante*), Bathurst also printed some separate editions:

304. Travels / Into Several / Remote Nations / Of The / World. / — / In Four Parts. / — / By *Lemuel Gulliver*, / first a Surgeon, and then a Captain / of several Ships. / — / Vol. I. / — / *London*: / Printed for Charles Bathurst, at / the *Cross Keys* in *Fleet-street*. / M,DCC,XLVIII.

Travels / Into Several / Remote Nations / Of The / World. / — / By *Lemuel Gulliver*, / First a Surgeon, and then a Captain of / several Ships. / — / Vol. II. / = / *London*: / Printed for Charles Bathurst, at the / *Cross-Keys*, in *Fleet-Street*. / MDCCXLVIII.

12mo; A⁶, B–M¹² — 2 pp. (t. + bl.), [III]–VI (The Publisher To The Reader), 2 pp. (titles of the 4 parts + bl.), 3 pp. (Contents of Part I) + bl., [1]–128 (Lilliput), 129–264 (Brobdingnag).
A⁶, B–N¹² — 2 pp. (t. + bl.), [III]–XI (Contents of Parts III and IV) + bl., [1]–124 (Laputa), [125]–283 (Houyhnhnms), 5 pp. advs.
Four illustrations (off-prints of the 1727 12mo ed.), no maps or plans.
The *Contents* of Part II are absent, apparently by error of the compositor.
The running-title of Laputa has, by mistake, been carried on into Part IV as far as p. 144.
Copy: Penn. — Cf. for further details *The Library*, Vol. IX, 1929 (No. 1550, *post*).

305. Travels / Into Several / Remote Nations / Of The / World. / — / In Four Parts. / — / By *Lemuel Gulliver*, / First a Surgeon, and then a Captain of / several Ships. / — / Vol. I. / — / [ornament] / = / *London*: / Printed for Charles Bathurst, at the / *Cross-Keys*, in *Fleet-Street*. / — / M.DCC.LVII.

The title of the second volume is the same, except: Vol. II.
12mo; A⁶, B–M¹² — 2 pp. (t. + bl.), [III]–VI (The Publisher To The Reader), [VII]–XII (Contents of Parts I and II), [1]–128 (Lilliput), 129–64 (Brobdingnag).
A⁶, B–N¹² — 2 pp. (t. + bl.), [III]–XI (Contents of Parts III and IV), 1 p. blank, [1]–124 (Laputa), [125]–283 (Houyhnhnms), 5 pp. advs.
Four illustrations (off-prints of the 1727 12mo ed.), no maps or plans.
Copy: Penn.

306. Travels / Into Several / Remote Nations / Of The / World. / — / In Four Parts. / — / By *Lemuel Gulliver*, / First a Surgeon, and then a Captain of / several Ships. / — / Vol. I. / — / [ornament] / = / *London:* / Printed for Charles Bathurst, at the / *Cross-Keys*, in *Fleet-Street.* / — / M.DCC.LXVII.

> The title of the second volume is the same, except: Vol. II.
> 12mo; I–XII, 1–268.
>   I–X, 1–290.
> Four illustrations (off-prints of the 1727 12mo ed.), no maps or plans.

306A. *Another issue:*
> The same collations and titles, except for the year, which in the first volume
> is M.DCC.LXXVII., in the second M.DCC.LXXVI.
> No illustrations, maps, or plans.

**

Other Editions

307. Travels / Into Several / Remote Nations / Of The / World. / In Four Parts. / [*First column:*] Part I. A Voyage to *Lilliput*, where- / in are described the Customs and / Manners of those diminutive Peo- / ple the *Lilliputians*, five of whom / the Captain put at one Time, in / his Coat-Pocket. / Part II. A Voyage to *Brobdingnag*, / describing the Customs and Man- / ners of those Gigantick People, the / [*Second column:*] jointed Babies of whose Children / were as big as the Giants at *Guild*- / *Hall.* / Part III. A Voyage to *Laputa*, or / a strange Country of *Mathematici*- / *ans*, to *Balnibarbi, Glubbdubdribb,* / *Luggnagg* and *Japan.* / Part IV. A Voyage to the *Houy*- / *hnhnms*, or a Nation of *Horses.* / — / *By* Captain Lemuel Gulliver, *First a Surgeon,* / *and then a Captain of several Ships.* / — / *London:* / Printed and Sold by the Booksellers of *London* and *Westminster.*

> 4to (in twos); π^1, [A]–Uuu² [signed: No 2. B to No 66. Uuu — These
> signatures start on p. 5, and end on p. 261] — 2 pp. (t. + bl.), [1]–264. —
> Text in double columns.
> Copy: B.M. 12613 h 7. The catalogue says: 1750(?).

307A. Travels / Into Several / Remote Nations / Of The / World. / In Four Parts. / *By* Lemuel Gulliver, *first a* Surgeon, / *and then a* Captain *of several* Ships. / *Edinburgh:* / Printed by Hamilton, Balfour, and Neill, / for W. Gray *junior.* M,DCC,LII.

> Sm. 12mo (in sixes); *⁶, A–Gg⁶ — 2 pp. (t. + bl.), [III]–IV (The Publisher
> To The Reader), 8 pp. (Contents), [1]–359 + bl.
> Copy: Penn.

308. Travels / Into / Several remote Nations of the World; / By Lemuel Gulliver. / First a Surgeon, and then a Captain of several Ships. / In Four Parts. / Part I. A Voyage to Lilliput. / Part II. A Voyage to Brobdingnag. / Part III. A Voyage to Laputa,

Balnibarbi, Lugg- / nagg, Glubbdubdrib, and Japan. / Part IV.
A Voyage to the Country of the Houyhnhnms. / = / London, /
Printed for C. Bathurst. / — / MDCCLV.

> This is a separate issue of *Works*, Vol. I. Part II., 4to, 1755 (see No. 87),
> from which the volume-title has been removed.
> Copy: Penn.

308A. Travels / Into / Several remote Nations of the World; /
By Lemuel Gulliver, / First a Surgeon, and then a Captain of
several Ships. / In Four Parts. / Part I. A Voyage to Lilliput. /
Part II. A Voyage to Brobdingnag. / Part III. A Voyage to Laputa,
Balnibarbi, / Luggnagg, Glubbdubdrib, and Japan. / Part IV. A
Voyage to the Country of the / Houyhnhnms. / = / London, /
Printed for C. Bathurst. / — / MDCCLV.

> This is a separate issue of *Works*, Vol. II, large 8vo, 1755 (see No. 88),
> from which the volume-title has been removed.

309. Travels / Into Several / Remote Nations of the World. / In
Four Parts. / [*First column:*] I. A Voyage to Lil- / liput. / II. A
Voyage to Brob- / dingnag. / III. A Voyage to / Laputa, Balni- /
[*Second column:*] barbi, Luggnagg, / Glubbdubdrib, / and Japan. /
— / By Lemuel Gulliver, first a Surgeon, / and then a Captain, of
several Ships. / — / —— *Retroq*; / *Vulgus abhorret ab his.* / — /
[ornament] / = / Dublin: / Printed by George Faulkner, in Essex-
Street. / — / MDCCLVI.

> This is a separate issue of *Works*, Vol. III, 18mo in sixes, 1756 (see No. 53),
> with slight alteration in the title. — 'Vol. III.' at foot of several pages.
> Copy: own.

310. The / Travels and Adventures / Of / Capt. Lemuel Gulliver. / Shewing / How he was cast upon unknown Land, / where
the Inhabitants were but six In- / ches high; the Customs of the
Coun- / try, Court, King, &c. and the Author's / Exploits, and
surprising Return. / [Illustration of Gulliver lying on the ground
with the pigmies round him] / Printed in Aldermary Church Yard,
London.

> Sm. 12mo size; no signatures —: 1–24. — Page 2 misnumbered 20. —
> Besides the illustration in the title there are some more in the text. — Con-
> tains *Lilliput* only. — Not dated, a very cheap production (chapbook).
> Copy: B.M. T 1854 (2).

311. Travels / Into Several / Remote Nations / Of The / World.
/ In Four Parts. / By *Lemuel Gulliver*, first a Sur- / geon, and then
a Captain of several Ships. / *Glasgow*, / Printed by James Knox,
and sold at his Shop near the / Head of the Salt-mercat. / — /
MDCCLIX.

12mo (in sixes); A–Bb⁶, Cc 1—2 pp. (t. + bl.), 4 pp. (Contents), [3]–298.
Copy: Penn.
Hubbard, *Contributions*, 139, mentions an edition with exactly the same
title and collation, except for the year, which is: M.DCC.LXV.

311A. Travels / Into Several / Remote Nations / Of The /
World; / By Lemuel Gulliver, / First a Surgeon, and then a Captain
of several Ships. / In Four Parts. / Part I. A Voyage to Lilliput. /
Part II. A Voyage to Brobdingnag. / Part III. A Voyage to Laputa,
Balnibarbi, / Luggnagg, Glubbdubdrib, and Japan. / Part IV. A
Voyage to the Country of the / Houyhnhnms. / = / London: /
Printed for C. Bathurst. / — / MDCCLX.

This is a separate issue of *Works*, Vol. II, sm. 8vo, 1760 (see No. 90), from
which the volume-title has been cut away.
Copy: Mich. P.R. 3724 G 8.

312. Travels / Into Several / Remote Nations / Of The / World.
/ In Four Parts. / By Lemuel Gulliver, / First a Surgeon, and then
a Captain of several Ships. / *Glasgow:* / Printed for Robert Urie,
MDCCLXIV.

12mo; I–VIII, 3–289, 1 p. advs.
Copy: own.

313. Same title as 311A, except a full stop after 'World.', and the year
MDCCLXVI.
This is a separate issue of *Works*, Vol. II, sm. 8vo, 1766 (see No. 91), from
which the leaf of advs. and the volume-title, as well as the volume-indications
at the foot of the first page of each new sheet have been removed.

314. Travels / Into Several / Remote Nations / Of The / World.
/ In Four Parts. / By Captain Lemuel Gulliver. / Volume First. /
London, / Printed for P. Turnbull in St *Paul*'s Church-yard. /
MDCCLXVI.

The title of the second volume is the same, except: Volume Second.
8vo; π², A–M⁸, N⁴ — 2 pp. (t. + bl.), III–XV (Verses), 1 p. (title of the
four parts), [XVII]–XVIII (The Publisher to the Reader), [1]–86 (Lilliput),
2 pp. (Contents of Part I), [1]–95 (Brobdingnag), 2 pp. (Contents of Part II),
1 p. blank.
π¹, O–Bb⁸, Cc⁴, Dd² — 2 pp. (t. + bl.), [1]–87 (Laputa), 3 pp. (Contents
of Part III), [1]–109 (Houyhnhnms), 4 pp. (Contents of Part IV), 1 p. blank.
Copy: Penn.

314A. Travels / Into / Several Remote Nations of the / World; /
/ By Lemuel Gulliver, / First a Surgeon, and then a Captain of
several Ships. / In Four Parts. / Part I. / A Voyage to Lilliput. /
Part II. / A Voyage to Brobdingnag. / — / Vol. I. / — / Edinburgh:

/ Printed by David Willison, and sold by / the Booksellers in Town. / M,DCC,LXX.

The title of the second volume is the same, except:

– – – – – / Part III. / A Voyage to Laputa, Balnibarbi, Lugg- / nagg, Glubbdubdrib, and Japan. / Part IV. / A Voyage to the Country of the Houyhnhnms. / — / Vol. II. / — / – – – – –

Sm. 12mo (in sixes); π^1, a^6, b 1, A–S⁶, T⁵ — 2 pp. (t. + bl.), 5–6 (The Publisher to the Reader), 7–13 (Letter Gulliver to Sympson), 14 (note), XV–XVIII (Contents Parts I and II), [1]–108 (Gulliver), [109]–226 (Brobdingnag).
[a]⁵, A–U⁶ — 2 pp. (t. + bl.), III–VII (Contents Parts III and IV), 3 pp. blank, [1]–109 (Laputa), [110]–240 (Houyhnhnms).
Copy: own.

316. For an edition 1771, see No. 106, *ante*.

317. The / Adventures / Of / Capt. Gulliver, / In A / Voyage / To the Islands of / Lilliput & Brobdingnag. / — / Abridged from the Works of / The Celebrated Dean Swift. / = / Darlington: / Printed by John Sadler. 1773.

Very Sm. 8vo (in fours); [A]–C⁴, D² — 2 pp. (t. + bl.), 3–28. — A chapbook. In spite of what the title says, it contains *Lilliput* only.
Copy: Bodl. (Godw. Pamph. 2863 (3)).

318. Travels / Into Several / Remote Nations / Of The / World. / In Four Parts. / By / Lemuel Gulliver. / First A / Surgeon, / And Then A / Captain / Of / Several Ships. / Volume First. / London: / Printed for John Bell, N° 132. Strand. / M.DCC.LXXIV.

The second volume has the same title, except: Volume Second.
12mo; A–U⁶, X⁴ — 2 pp. (h.t. + bl.), 2 pp. (f.t. + bl.), [V]–VIII (The Publisher To The Reader), [IX]–XVI (Letter Gulliver to Sympson), XVII (note), 1 p. blank, [XIX]–XXII (Contents Parts I and II), [23]–130 (Lilliput), [131]–248 (Brobdingnag).
A–U⁶, X⁴ — 2 pp. (h.t. + bl.), 2 pp. (f.t. + bl.), [V]–X (Contents Parts III and IV), [11]–118 (Laputa), [119]–248 (Houyhnhnms).
Copy: Penn.

318A. *Another issue:*
Only the full title cancelled and replaced by another with the following modification:

— / Volume First. / = / Edinburgh: / Printed in the Year M.DCC.LXXV.

The f.t. of the second volume modified in the same way.
Copy: own.

319. The / Travels / Of / Lemuel Gulliver; / *First A Surgeon* / And Then / Captain Of Several Ships. / Containing His / *Voyages* /

To / Lilliput and Brobdingnag. / — / —— *Retroq;* / *Vulgus abhorret ab his.* / — / *Dublin:* / Printed by P. Wogan, Old-Bridge.

18mo (in twelves and sixes alternately); [A]¹² — K⁶ — 2 pp. (frontisp.), 2 pp. (t. + bl.), 2 pp. (The Publisher to the Reader), [7]–86 (Lilliput), 87–173 (Brobdingnag), [174]–[180] (three poems). — One more illustration (woodcut) on p. 11.

Copy: Nat. Libr., Dublin. The copy is close shaved, and it may be that the year at foot of title-page has been cut off. The catalogue says: 177–?.

320. Travels / Into Several / Remote Nations / Of The / World. / By *Lemuel Gulliver.* / Vol. I. / *Paris,* / M.DCC.LXXIX.

The title of the second volume is the same, except: Vol. II.
16mo; I–VI, 1–100, 101–215 + bl.
      2 pp., 1–106, 107–244.
Copies: Heidelberg, Bibl. Nat. Paris, and Bibl. St. Geneviève, Paris.

321. Travels / Into Several / Remote Nations / Of The / World. / — / In Four Parts. / — / By Lemuel Gulliver, / First a Surgeon, and then a Captain of / several Ships. / — / Vol. I. / = / London: / Printed for Joseph Wenman, / No. 144, Fleet-Street. / M.DCC.LXXX.

The titles in the second and third volumes are the same, except: Vol. II., and Vol. III.
Sm. 12mo; [A]–D¹², E⁴ — 2 pp. (bl. + frontisp.), 2 pp. (t. + bl.), [V]–VIII (Publisher to Reader), 9–104.
[A]⁸, B–E¹² — 2 pp. (bl. + frontisp.), 2 pp. (t. + bl.), 5–112.
[A]–D¹², E⁸ — 2 pp. (bl. + frontisp.), 2 pp. (t. + bl.), 5–112.
Copy: B.M. 12614 a 2.

322. Travels / Into Several / Remote Nations / Of The / World. / By / Lemuel Gulliver, / First A Surgeon, And Then A Captain Of Several Ships. / In Two Volumes. / By Dean Swift. / [ornament] / London: / Printed for Harrison and Co. No. 18, Paternoster-Row. / MDCCLXXXII.

8vo (in fours); π³, B–R⁴, S³ — 2 pp. (t. + bl.), 2 pp. (Publ. to Reader + bl.), [5]–140. — Text in double columns. — Four full-page illustrations, one to each 'Part'. Moreover the two plans of *Laputa* in the text (pp. 79 and 85).
Copy: B.M. 1207 c 3 (2).
This is Vol. IX of Harrison's "Novelist's Magazine" (23 vols., 1781–88).
Hubbard, *Contributions,* 143, mentions a reprint 1792, by the same publishers.

323. The / Lilliputian Library, / Or / Gullivers Museum / In Ten Volumes. / Containing / [*First column:*] Lectures On Morality / Historical Pieces / Interesting Fables / Diverting Tales / Miraculous Voyages / [*Second column:*] Surprising Adventures / Remarkable Lives / Poetical Pieces / Comical Jokes / Useful Letters. /

The whole forming / A / Complete System / of Juvenile Knowledge / for / the Amusement and Improvement / of all / Little Masters and Misses, / Whether in Summer or Winter, Morning, / Noon or Evening / by / Lilliputius Gulliver / Citizen of Utopia and Knight of the most noble ordre [*sic*] of / human prudence / — / Vol. I–V. / — / Berlin / Sold by Chr. Fridr. Himburg. 1782.

> The second volume has the same title, except: Vol. VI–X.
> 12mo; frontisp., 2 pp., 1–96, 1–98, 1–98, 1–98, 1–100.
>   4 pp., 7–96, 1–92, 1–100, 1–102, 1–96.
> Contains in Vol. II, pp. 5–56, a much abridged version of *Lilliput* and *Brobdingnag.*
> Copies: B.M., and Sächsische Landesbibl., Dresden.

325. The / Travels / Of / Lemuel Gulliver, / Into Several / Remote Nations / Of The / World. / Who Was First A / Surgeon, / And Then A / Captain / Of / Several Ships. / — / In Four Parts. / — / — / *Falkirk:* / Printed By Thomas Cheap. / — / M.DCC.LXXXVII.

> 12mo (in sixes); A–Ff⁶, Gg² — 2 pp. (t. + bl.), [III]–VIII (Contents), [9] (Note, signed Orrery), [10] (blank), [11]–12 (The Publisher to the Reader), [13]–18 (Letter Gulliver to Sympson), [19]–93 (Lilliput), [94]–175 (Brobdingnag), [176]–252 (Laputa), [253]–344 (Houyhnhnms), 345–52 (3 poems).
> Copy: Penn.

Another issue:

324. The / Travels / Of / Lemuel Gulliver, / Into Several / Remote Nations / Of The / World. / Who Was First A / Surgeon, / And Then A / Captain / Of / Several Ships. / — / In Four Parts. / — / *Illustrated With Copperplates.* / Edinburgh: / Printed for C. Elliot. / — / M.DCC.LXXXVII.

> The same printing; only the title-leaf is new. Moreover four illustrations, four maps, and two plans. All ten the same as those in Vol. V of Swift's *Works,* Elliot, 1784 (see No. 100).
> Copy: Nat. Libr. of Ireland.

326. Travels / Into Several / Remote Nations / Of The / World. / In Four Parts, *viz.* / I. *A Voyage to* Lilliput. / II. *A Voyage to* Brobdingnagg. / III. *A Voyage to* Laputa, Balnibarbi, Lugg- / nagg, Glubbdubdrib, *and* Japan. / IV. *A Voyage to the Country of the* Houyhnhnms. / = / By Lemuel Gulliver, / First a Surgeon, and then Captain of several Ships. / = / —— *Retroq;* / *Vulgus abhorret ab his.* / — / Dublin: / Printed by P. Wogan, No. 23, Old-Bridge. / — / M,DCC,XCII.

> 12mo; [a]⁴, A–M¹², N⁸ — 2 pp. (t. + bl.), [III]–VIII (Contents), [3]–306.
> Copy: Nat. Libr., Dublin.

327. The / Travels / Of / Lemuel Gulliver; / First A Surgeon, And Then Captain / Of Several Ships. / Containing His / Voyages To Lilliput / And / Brobdingnag. / Dublin: / Printed By C. M. Warren, / 21, Upper Ormond Quay.

Sm. 12mo (in sixes); [A]–M⁶ — 1 p. (title), [2] –144. — In yellowish cover, the front-cover bearing illustration of Gulliver lying on the ground surrounded by pigmies (verso blank); the back-cover has recto blank, the verso has "Books printed and published by C. M. Warren." The cover is not counted in the pagination.
Copy: Nat. Libr. of Ireland.

328. The / Travels / Of / *Lemuel Gulliver*, / Into / Several Remote Nations Of / The World. / Who Was / First A Surgeon, And Then A Captain / Of Several Ships. / = / *In Two Volumes.* / = / Vol. I. / [ornament] / Edinburgh: / Printed For And Sold By The Booksellers. / — / MDCCXCIII.

The other title is the same, except: Vol. II.
18mo; 12 pp. (h.t. + bl., quotation + bl., f.t. + bl., 6 pp. *Contents*), 13–204.
12 pp. (h.t. + bl., f.t. + bl., 8 pp. *Contents*), 1–228.
Copy: University Library, Leipsic.

329. Thoughts / On / War, / Political, Commercial, Religious, / And / Satyrical; / = / By Josiah Tucker, / Dean Of Gloucester, / William Law M.A. / And / Jonathan Swift, / Dean Of St. Patricks. / = / London. / Printed In The Year MDCCXCIII, / By Darton And Harvey, Gracechurch-Street.

12mo (in sixes); π², B–E⁶, F⁴ — 2 pp. (h.t. + bl.), 2 pp. (f.t. + bl.), [1]–54, 2 pp. blank. — Pp. 51–4 contain a quotation from *Gulliver's Travels*, Voyage IV.
Copy: Bodl. Godw. Pamph. 232.

329A. The / Adventures / Of / Captain Gulliver, / In A / Voyage / To the Islands of / Lilliput, / And / Brobdingnag. / Abridged from the Works of / The celebrated Dean Swift. / Adorned With Cuts. / = / New-York: / Printed and Sold by W. Durell, / No. 19, Queen-Street.

16mo (in eights); [A]⁸ — ? — 4 pp. (cover, frontisp., title-page, alphabet), 5–16 (the rest of the book is lacking). — Frontisp. and two illustrations in the text.
Copy: Am. Antiq. Soc., Worcester (Mass.).
The date is supposed to be 1793.

329B. The / Adventures / Of / Captain *Gulliver*, / In A / *Voyage* / To the Islands of / *Lilliput* & *Brobdingnag*. / Abridged from the Works of / The celebrated Dean Swift. / Adorned With Cuts. /

/ = / Boston: / Printed and sold by S. Hall, No. 53, Cornhill. / 1794.

> Sm. 8vo; π⁸, B–H⁸ — 2 pp. (cover), 2 pp. (frontisp.), 2 pp. (t. + bl.), 7–119 + bl., 6 pp. advs., 2 pp. (cover). — Several illustrations in the text.
> Copies: Libr. of Congress; Am. Antiq. Soc., Worcester (Mass.), lacking frontisp. and pp. 97–100.

329C. The / Adventures / Of / Captain Gulliver, / In A / Voyage / To The Islands Of / Lilliput And Brobdingnag. / Abridged from the Works of / The Celebrated Dean Swift. / Adorned With Cuts. / = / London, Printed for E. Newbery [179–?].

> 123 pages; illustrations — 11½ cm.
> Copy: Michigan.

Another issue:
Same title, except:

—— / London: / Ptinted [*sic*] for J. Harris, (Successor to E. New- / bery,) the Corner of St. Paul's Church-Yard: / By E. Hensted, Great New-Street, Fetter- / Lane. / = / (Price Six-pence.)

> Very sm. 8vo (11½ cm.); [A]–H⁸ — 2 pp. (t. + bl.), 3–123 + bl., [I]–IV (advs.), — Several illustrations in the text.
> Copies: Michigan, and Univ. Bibl., Nymegen.

330. Travels / Into Several / Remote Nations / Of The / *World.* / By Lemuel Gulliver. / First a Surgeon, and then a Captain, of several Ships. / Two Volumes In One. / By Dean Swift. / = / Cooke's Edition. / = / [ornament] / = / Embellished With Superb Engravings. / = / London: / Printed for C. Cooke, No. 17, Pater-noster-Row / And sold by all the Booksellers in / Great-Britain and / Ireland.

> Sm. 12mo (in sixes); [A]–Aa⁶ — 2 pp. (t. + bl.), [III]–IV (Publ. to Reader), [5]–287 + bl. — Frontisp. and three plates; two plans (Laputa) in the text.
> Copies: Mich. P.R. 3724 G 8; Forster D 14 A 46 misses frontisp.

Another issue (?):
Same title and collation, except: London, Printed for C. Cooke, by J. Adlard [1800 ?].
Plates dated 1795–1800.
Copy: Michigan.

Another issue (?):
Same title and collation [1801 ?] — Plates dated 1797–1801.
Copy: Michigan.
Hubbard, *Contributions*, 175, says: "There were two editions, each with four plates after R. Corbould, by Hawkins, and Warren. In the earlier ed. these plates are dated 1795–97; in the later, 1797, 1798, 1800 and 1801, and partly re-engraved. In the later ed. the last p. has a list of books."

331. The / Travels / Of / Lemuel Gulliver, / Into Several / Remote Nations / Of The / World; / Who Was First A / Surgeon, / And Then A / Captain / Of / Several Ships. / By The Dean / *D. Jonathan Swift.* / — / Dresden, 1800. / Printed For C. and F. Walther.

> Sm. 8vo; [1]⁶, A–Dd⁸, Ee 1 — 2 pp. (t. + bl.), 10 pp. (Contents), [1]–3 (The Publisher To The Reader), [4]–10 (Letter Gulliver to Sympson), [11]–434.
> Copy: Penn.

332. From an antiquarian book catalogue:
Miniature Books — Lilliputian Folio Editions of Gulliver's Travels, Robinson Crusoe, etc., 8 vols. R. Snagg, 1801–2. — Size 1¾ × 1¼ inches.

332A. The / Adventures / Of / Captain Gulliver, / In A / *Voyage To The Island Of* / Lilliput. / Abridged *from the* Works *of the* / Celebrated Dean Swift. / [ornament] / First Worcester Edition. / [ornament] / = / Worcester, (*Massachusetts*) / *Printed by J. Thomas, Jun.* / Sold Wholesale and Retail by him. — *November,* / 1802.

> 16mo (in eights); [A]–D⁸ — 2 pp. (cover + verso blank), 2 pp. (t. + bl.), [5]–59, 2 pp. (poems), 2 pp. (illustrations), 1 p. (verso of back-cover).
> Copy: Am. Antiq. Soc., Worcester (Mass.).

333. Travels / Into Several / Remote Nations / Of The / World, / By / Lemuel Gulliver, / First a Surgeon, and then a Captain, of several Ships. / *By Jonathan Swift, D.D.* / Dean Of St. Patrick's, Dublin. / A New Edition. / = / *London:* / Printed for J. Johnson, John Nichols and Son, / R. Baldwin, Otridge and Son, F. and C. Rivington, / T. Payne, R. Faulder, G. and J. Robinson, R. Lea, J. Nunn, / W. Cuthell, J. Walker, T. Egerton, Clarke and Son, / Vernor and Hood, J. Scatcherd, T. Kay, Lackington / Allan and Co. Carpenter and Co. Murray and Highley, / Longman and Rees, Cadell and Davies, T. Bagster, / J. Harding, *and* J. Mawman. / — / 1803.

> This is a separate issue of *Works,* Vol. IX, 12mo in sixes, 1803 (see No. 130), but the volume indications have been removed from the foot of the first page of each new sheet, while the two titles "Works" have been replaced by two titles "Travels", and the heading "Contents Of The Ninth Volume" on page [V] altered into "Contents."
> Copy: Penn.

334. The / Travels / Of / Lemuel Gulliver, / Into / Several Remote Nations Of The / World. / Who Was / First A Surgeon, And Then A Captain, / Of Several Ships. / = / *In Two Volumes.* / = / Vol. I. / — / Edinburgh: / *Printed by* Alex. Jardine, / *Back of Gavin Loch's Land, Forrester's Wynd.* / = / 1803.

12mo (in sixes); [a]⁶, A–K⁶, L⁴ — 2 pp. (t. + bl.), 3 pp. (Contents), 1 p. (quotation from Orrery), [VII]–XII, [1]–128.
The title in the second volume is the same, except: Vol. II.
π³, A², B–M⁶, N³ — 2 pp. (t. + bl.), 4 pp. (Contents), [1]–142.
Copy: B.M. 12611 dd 4.

335. Travels / Into Several / Remote Nations / Of The / World. / By Lemuel Gulliver. / First a Surgeon, and then a Captain of several Ships. / By Dean Swift. / A new Edition in two volumes. / — / Vol. I. / — / Paris: / Printed for Theophilus Barrois junior, / Bookseller, Quay Voltaire, n°. 3. / 1804.

12mo; A–H¹² — 2 pp. (t. + bl.), [III]–IV ('The Publisher To The Reader), [5]–190, 2 pp. blank.
The second volume has the same title, except: Vol. II.
[A]–H¹², I⁶ — 2 pp. (t. + bl.), [3]–202, [1]–2 (advs.).
Copy: Penn.

1582. Voyages and Travels of Capt. L. Gulliver, 4 parts, Tabart's Improved Edition, coloured plates, orig. wrappers, 1805 (from Sotheby's catal. July 21, 1947, item 40).

336. *Gulliver's* / Travels / into several / Remote Nations Of The World. / — / By Jonathan Swift, D.D. / Dean of St. Patrick's, Dublin. / — / *With A Sketch Of His Life.* / = / London: / Printed For J. Walker; / J. Johnson; J. & J. Richardson; R. Faulder & Son; F. C. / & J. Rivington; Vernor, Hood, and Sharpe; R. Lea; J. / Nunn; Cuthell & Martin; E. Jeffery; Lackington, / Allen, & Co.; Lane, Newman, & Co.; Longman, Hurst, / Rees, & Crme; Cadell and Davies; Wilkie & Robinson; / J. Booker; Black, Parry, & Kingsbury; H. D. Symonds; / J. Asperne; R. Scholey; and J. Harris. / — / 1808.

Sm. 12mo; π², π¹, a⁶, B–O¹², P⁵ — 4 pp. of thicker paper (bl. + frontisp. + ornamented t. + bl.), 2 pp. (f.t. + printer on verso), 6 pp. (Contents), 6 pp. (Life), [I]–[XIV], [15]–322.
Copy: B.M. 12206 aaa 11.
The 1st and 5th leaves of each sheet are signed, e.g. D and D 2, etc.
Belongs to the series: 'Walker's British Classics'.

336A. *Another issue* (?):
Same title and collation, except: London, Printed for J. Walker and co. - - - - - by S. Hamilton, Weybridge, Surrey, 1815.
Copy: Michigan.

Another issue (?):
337. Gulliver's / Travels / Into Several / Remote Nations Of The World. / — / By Jonathan Swift, D.D. / *Dean of St. Patrick's, Dublin.* / — / With A Sketch Of His Life. / — / London: / Printed for J. Walker; / F. C. and J. Rivington; J. Nunn; Longman, Hurst, / Rees, Orme, and Brown; Cadell and Davies; / G. and W.

B. Whittaker; J. Richardson; Newman / and Co.; Lackington and Co.; Black, Kingsbury, / Parbury, and Allen; J. Black and Son; Sher- / wood, Neely, and Jones; / Baldwin, Cradock, and / Joy; J. Robinson; E. Edwards; and B. Rey- / nolds: / By S. Hamilton, Whitefriars. / — / 1819.

> Tall 12mo; two leaves of thicker paper, a⁶, B–O¹², P⁶ — 2 pp. (bl. + frontisp.), 2 pp. (illustrated title + bl.), 2 pp. (above title + bl.), 6 pp. (Contents), 4 pp. (Life of Swift), 2 pp. (title: 'Travels' + bl.), [III]–VI (Preface), [VII]–VIII (The Publisher To The Reader), [IX]–XIV (Letter Gulliver to Sympson), [15]–322, 2 pp. blank.
> Copies: B.M. 12604 aa 5, Michigan, and Penn.

338. The / Surprizing Adventures / Of / Captain Gulliver / in a / Voyage / *To the Kingdom of* / Lilliput. / [ornament] / Glasgow. / *Published by* / Lumsden & Son *at their* / Toy Book Manufactory. / *Price Six Pence.*

> [Decorated title (flourishes).]
> 18mo; 1–52 (including frontisp., before f.t.). — Six illustrations in the text.
> Hubbard, *Contributions*, 167, mentions an edition of the same size, the same collation, and the same title, except for the imprint: Philadelphia, published by B. C. Buzby, No. 2 Nh. 3 St., 1808.

339. Travels / Into Several / Remote Nations / Of The / World. / = / In Four Parts. / = / By Lemuel Gulliver: / First A Surgeon, And Then A Captain Of / Several Ships. / = / Vol. I. / = / Phila- delphia: / Printed For Mathew Carey, / No. 122, Market Street.

> 12mo (in sixes); [A]–F⁶, H–K⁶, L² — 2 pp. (t. + bl.), [III]–V (Publisher to Reader), 1 p. blank, [7]–112. — Frontisp. — Sheet G lacking, but no text missing. — Contains 'Gulliver' only.

Travels / Into Several / Remote Nations / Of The / World. / = / Voyage To Brobdingnag, Complete. / = / By Lemuel Gulliver: / First A Surgeon, And Then A Captain Of / Several Ships. / = / Philadelphia: / Printed For Mathew Carey, / No. 122, Market Street. / — / 1809.

> 12mo (in sixes); [A]⁴, B–I⁶, K⁸ — 2 pp. (t. + bl.), [3]–119 + bl. — Frontisp.
> Copies: Michigan; and Am. Antiq. Soc., Worcester, Mass. (vol. 2 only).

339A. *Another issue:*
Voyages / To / Lilliput / And / Brobdingnag. / — / By Lemuel Gulliver: / First a Surgeon, and then a Captain of a Vessel. / — / In Two Volumes. / Vol. I. / Voyage To Brobdingnag Complete. / — / Philadelphia: / Printed For Mathew Carey, / No. 126, Market Street. / — / 1809.

Voyages / To / Lilliput / And / Brobdingnag. / — / By Lemuel Gulliver: / First a Surgeon, and then a Captain of a Vessel. / — / In Two Volumes. / — / Vol. II. / Voyage To Lilliput Complete. / — / Philadelphia: / Printed For Mathew Carey, / No. 126, Market Street. / — / 1809.

> These two volumes are the same printing as the preceding two; only the titles are new. But these titles are wrong, the first volume containing 'Gulliver', the second 'Brobdingnag'.
> Copy: Am. Antiq. Soc., Worcester, Mass.
> From the above it appears that about 1808–9 Carey moved from Market Street 122 to Market Street 126, and that therefore the volumes with title 'Travels' must be earlier than those with titles 'Voyages'. Judging from the titles 'Travels' it would seem that the original plan was four parts, but that this plan was abandoned, after which the titles 'Travels' were cancelled and replaced by the new (though faulty) titles 'Voyages'.

340. The / Adventures / Of / Captain Gulliver, / In A Voyage To / The Lilliputian Country: / *Where the Inhabitants are* / Only About / Six Inches High. / [woodcut] / *Falkirk:* / Printed By T. Johnston. / 1808.

> [Title within decorated frame.] [Chapbook.] Sm. 8vo size, no sigs. — 1 p. (title), [2]–24.
> Copy: U.L.C. (Hib. 8.808.1).

341. Travels / Into Several / Remote Nations / Of The / World, / By / *Lemuel Gulliver.* / First a Surgeon, and then a Captain of several Ships. / By Jonathan Swift, D.D. / Dean Of St. Patrick's, Dublin. / = / *A New Edition.* / = / Gainsborough: / Printed By and For H. Mozley. / 1809.

> Sm. 12mo (in sixes); π^1, [A]^4, B–Bb^6 — 2 pp. (bl. + frontisp.), 2 pp. (t. + bl.), [III]–VIII (Contents), [1]–287 + bl. — Two plans to 'Laputa' in the text.
> Copies: B.M. 012612 de 9, and own.

342. The / Adventures / Of / *Captain Gulliver,* / In a Voyage to / The Lilliputian Country: / Where the Inhabitants are / Only about / *Six Inches High.* / [ornament] / *Lancaster:* / Printed by C. Clark, Market-Place. / 1809.

> 16mo; 1–16. [Chapbook]
> Contains *Lilliput* only. Printed on very light green paper.

343. Hubbard, *Contributions*, 168, mentions an edition 1812 (12mo; I–XII incl. front., 1–338), which is a separate issue of Vol. IX of "The Works – – – – Sheridan — Nichols – – – – 24 vols. – – – New York, Durell and Co. 1812" (see No. 132, *ante*). The half-title reads: "The British Classics: Volume the fifty-third, containing the ninth volume of Swift's works. 1812."

344. Popular Romances: / Consisting Of / Imaginary Voyages And Travels. / — / Containing / Gulliver's Travels, / Journey To

The World Under Ground, / The Life And Adventures Of Peter
Wilkins, / The Adventures Of Robinson Crusoe, / And / The
History Of Automathes. / = / To Which Is Prefixed / An Intro-
ductory Dissertation, / By / Henry Weber, Esq. / = / Edinburgh:
/ *Printed by James Ballantyne and Company*, / For John Ballantyne
And Company, Silvester Doig And / Andrew Stirling, Edinburgh;
/ Longman, Hurst, Rees, Orme, And Brown, / And John Murray,
London. / — / 1812.

> Large 8vo; 4 pp. (h.t. and f.t.), I–XV + bl. (*Contents*), XVII–XLIII + bl.
> (*Introduction*), 1–638.
> Contains *Gulliver's Travels* (pp. 1–114).
> Copy: Bibl. Nat. Paris (Inv. Y² 74081).

345. The / Adventures / Of / *Captain Gulliver*, / In A Voyage
To / Lilliput. / = / Edinburgh: / Printed and Published by G.
Ross. / — / 1814.

> 16mo (in eights); π^8, B–C⁸ — 2 pp. (cover), 2 pp. (t. + bl.), [5]–47, 48
> (verso of cover). — Text of 47 printed on 46 and the reverse. — Illustrations
> (black) in the text, and on inside front cover by way of frontispiece.
> Copy: B.M. 012806 de 31.

Another issue:
The / Adventures / Of / *Captain Gulliver*, / In A Voyage To /
Lilliput. / = / Glasgow: / Published by / J. Lumsden & Son, /
1814.

> Same printing as before.
> Copy: B.M. 12804 deb 5 (1).

346. *Another edition:*
Adventures / Of / Captain Gulliver, / In A Voyage To / *Lilliput*.
/ [ornament] / *Edinburgh*. / Printed and published by / G. Ross.

> Collation and illustrations the same as in No. 345. Pp. 46–7 are correct.
> On the recto of the front cover there is: "Ross's Juvenile Library". — This
> is B.M. 012808 e 20. There is another copy B.M. 12804 de 59 (6), exactly the
> same printing, except for the cover, which is different both in colour and in
> print.

Another issue:
The / Adventures / Of / Captain Gulliver, / In A Voyage To /
Lilliput. / [ornament] / *Glasgow;* / Published by J. Lumsden &
Son. / 1815.

> Same printing as preceding edition.
> Copy: B.M. 12804 de 59 (3).

347. The / Adventures / Of / *Cap. Gulliver*. / In A Voyage To /
Lilliput. / — / Stirling: / Printed and Sold by C. Randall.

12mo size; no signatures — [1]–24.
A very cheap production.
Copy: B.M. 1078 k 17 (2). The catalogue says 1815 (?).

Dutch Translations

Like the English original the first Dutch translation consists of four parts in two volumes. There are four titles, one to each 'Part', all in red and black. These four titles are the same but for the appropriate alteration of the 'Voyage' and the 'Part', while the vignettes are all different:

366. (1) Reisbeschryving / Na Verscheyde Afgelegene / Natien In De Wereld. / Reys Na / Lilliput, / Door / Lemuel Gulliver / *Eerste Deel.* / [vignette] / *In's Gravenhage* / by Alberts & Van Der Kloot. / — / MDCCXXVII.

(2) – – – – – – / Reys Na / Brobdingnag, / – – – – – – – – / *Tweede Deel.* / – – – – –

12mo; π^2, $*^2$, A–E^{12}, F 1–7, F 8 cancelled and replaced by a double leaf with a single leaf (title) inserted, F 9–12, G–L^{12}, M^{10} — 2 pp. (both blank), 2 pp. (t. + bl.), 4 pp. (De Uitgeever aan den Lezer), 1–135 + bl., 2 pp. (t. + bl.), 1 p. blank, 136–284.

(3) – – – – – – / Reys Na / Laputa, Balnibarbi, / Luggnagg, Glubbdub- / drib En Japan; / – – – – – – / *Derde Deel.* / – – – –

(4) – – – – – – / Reys Na 'T Land Der / Houyhnhnms, / – – – – – – / *Vierde Deel.* / – – – –

π^2, A–E^{12}, F^{10}, π^2, A–G^{12}, H^2 — 2 pp. (both blank), 2 pp. (t. + bl.), 1–139 + bl., 2 pp. (both blank), 2 pp. (t. + bl.), [1]–172.
Frontisp. portrait of Gulliver, 4 maps and 2 plans; moreover 4 illustrations, one to each 'Part'.
The catalogue of the Bibl. Maatsch. Ned. Letterk.; Leiden, says that the translator was C. van Blankesteyn.
In the library of the Univ. of Michigan (Hubbard Coll.) there is a copy which, after the first title-page, has a printed leaf of dedication, reading:

Aan / Onse Broeder / Thomas Van Dalen, / Vendumeester Van's Gravenhage, / Leesgierige Liefhebber / Der / Historien, Reyzen, &c. / Werd / Deeze Koddige En Vermakelyke / Reyze / Naar Verscheyde / Onbekende Landen, / Door / Lemuel Gulliver / Ontdekt, / Met Veel Genegentheyd / Opgedragen, / Door / Zyn Ed: / Dienstbereyde / Broeders / Alberts En Van Der Kloot.

Though several copies have gone through my hands, I have never seen one with this extra leaf. In the Penn copies the blank leaf and the title-leaf form a double-leaf (chainlines horizontal), into which the portrait (chainlines horizontal) has been inserted. In the 'Hubbard' copy the portrait and leaf of dedication apparently form a double-leaf (chainlines vertical), into which the title-leaf (chainlines horizontal) has been inserted after removal of its blank companion-leaf.

This translation and the French one published at The Hague (No. 371, *post*), which are the first *Gullivers* containing illustrations, must have appeared at about the same time (Jan. 1727), as appears from some of the plates in these two editions. For a discussion see note under No. 371, *post*.

There are signs of haste during the production. The word "Reisbeschryving" (in the singular) in the four titles should have been in the plural; while the word "Deel" (meaning both 'volume' and 'part') gives rise to confusion, for in the titles it means 'Part', and at the top of the maps it means 'Volume'. But there is another error of a more serious character. Part I ended on p. 135; the compositor continued the text for Part II on its verso, thus leaving no room for the title of Part II to be inserted. Unfortunately F 8 (pp. 135–6) was in the middle of a sheet, and to remedy the mistake, F 8 had to be cancelled (stub visible). It was replaced by a double leaf (135; blank; blank; 136), and the title of Part II (turn-over visible) was placed between the two blanks. The result — the beginning of Part II on the verso of a leaf of which the recto is blank — remains a strange sight. To avoid a renewal of this trouble the pagination of Vol. II was made separate for the two Parts.

367. *Another issue:*
There are copies in which pp. 1–120 of Vol. I have been reset. The difference is easily distinguishable by the printer's ornaments and the capital at the beginning of chapter I, the type-size of the headlines, and variations in spelling. The first issue has 'gepresen' in the first line of page 3 (in some copies of this issue this page is numbered, in others not), and 'yf' in the last line of page 7; the second issue has 'gepreezen' (this page is numbered), and 'lyf'. My presumption is that, while the volume was in course of printing, it was resolved — perhaps as a result of the enormous sale of the work in England — to print more copies than originally intended. However, the type of pp. 1–120 having already been distributed, it had to be reset.
Copy: Penn.

368. In 1728 a third volume appeared, consisting of a translation of the spurious Vol. III, 1727 (see No. 292, *ante*), followed by a translation of the four *Keys*, 1726 (see No. 1215, *post*).
There is one general title (in red and black) to the whole volume, another (in black only) to the second part, and four special titles (all in black), i.e. one to each of the four *Keys*.

Reys / Na Verscheide Ver Afgelegene / Volkeren / Der / Wereld, / Door / Kap: Lemuel Gulliver. / Met De / Sleutel, / Op deszelfs vier Eerste Reyzen. / *Derde en laatste Deel.* / [vignette] / In 's Gravenhage, / By Alberts & Van Der Kloot. / — / MDCCXXVIII.

12mo; ∗[10], A–Q[12], R[4] — 2 pp. (t. + bl.), 18 pp. ('Inleyding'), 1–391 + bl. — Frontisp. portrait of Gulliver (same offprint as in No. 366), and 2 illustrations.
Copy: Penn.

369. [h.t. whole work] Gulliver's / *Reizen.* / Vier Deelen. [f.t. whole work] *L. Gulliver's* / Reize / Naar / Lilliput, Brobdingnag,

La- / puta, Balnibarbi, Lugg- / nagg, Glubbdubdrib, / Japan En
Het Land Der / Houyhnhnms. / *Vier Deelen* / Met Plaaten. /
[ornament] / Te Amsterdam, / By W. Houtgraff, / Boekverkoper
in de Hartestraat, in de / Dubbelde Kelder. 1791.

[f.t. Part I] *L. Gullivers* / Reize / Naar / *Lilliput.* / [ornament] / *Te
Amsterdam*, / By W. Houtgraaff, / Boekverkoper in de Hartestraat,
in de / dubbelde Kelder, 1790.

Very sm. 8vo; π^1, $*^2$, A–G^8, H 1 — 2 pp. (t. + bl.), [III]–VI (Contents),
[1]–114.

[f.t. Part II] *L. Gulliver's* / Reize / Naar / Brobdingnag. / [orna-
ment] / *Te Amsterdam*, / By W. Houtgraaff, / Boekverkoper in de
Hartestraat, in de / Dubbelde Kelder. 1791.

[*]^3, A–H^8, I^4 — 2 pp. (t. + bl.), [III]–VI (Contents), [1]–136.

[h.t. Part III] Gulliver's / *Reizen.* / Derde Deel. [f.t. Part III]
L. Gulliver's / Reize / Naar / *Laputa*, / Enz. / [ornament] / *Te
Amsterdam*, / By W. Houtgraaff, / Boekverkoper in de Hartestraat,
in de / Dubbelde Kelder. 1791.

[*]^4, A–H^8 — 2 pp. (h.t. + bl.), 2 pp. (f.t. + bl.), [V]–VIII (Contents),
[1]–128 (on p. 32 map of Balnibarbi in the text).

[h.t. Part IV] Gulliver's / *Reizen.* / Vierde Deel. [f.t. Part IV]
L. Gulliver's / Reize / In Het Land Der / Houyhnhnms. / [ornament]
Te Amsterdam, / By W. Houtgraaff, / Boekverkoper in de Hartestraat,
in de / Dubbelde Kelder. 1791.

[*]^6, A–K^8, π^2 — 2 pp. (h.t. + bl.), 2 pp. (f.t. + bl.), [V]–XII (Contents),
[1]–158, 2 pp. (*Bericht Aan Den Binder*), 2 pp. (h.t. to the whole work + bl.),
2 pp. (general t. to the whole work + bl.). Six plates, one given with Part I,
one with Part II, two with Part III (one of them destined for Part II), two
with Part IV (one of them destined for Part I).

Note: This is the shape in which the four Parts were originally issued.
But the *Bericht Aan Den Binder* — besides giving instructions as to the placing
of the plates (two in Part I opposite pp. 6 and 46, two in Part II, opposite
pp. 9 and 52, one in Part III, opposite p. 9, and one in Part IV, opposite p. 33)
— says that in binding the four parts into one volume, all the titles before
each 'Part' (that is 6 titles in all) have to be cancelled, the *Contents* of the four
'Parts' have to be placed consecutively before the text, and the general title
with its half-title (given to buyers with Part IV, at the end of that 'Part') have
to be put in front. After these instructions have been carried out, the *Bericht*
itself becomes superfluous, and copy in its new state should therefore collate:
4 pp. (h.t. and general t.), [III]–VI, [III]–VI, [V]–VIII, [V]–XII, [1]–114,
[1]–136, [1]–128, [1]–158. — 6 plates.
Copy: Penn.

370. *Another issue:*
Exactly the same printing as the first issue, but *all* the titles cut away and replaced by six new ones:

[Title for Parts I and II:] *L. Gulliver's* / Reize. / I. en II. Deel.

[Title for Part I:] *L. Gulliver's* / Reize / Naar / Lilliput. / Eerste Deel. / [ornament] / *Te Amsterdam, by* / J. B. Elwe, / MDCCXCII.

[Title for Part II:] Gulliver's / *Reizen.* / Tweede Deel.

[Title for Parts III and IV:] *L. Gulliver's* / Reize. / III. en IV. Deel.

[Title for Part III:] *L. Gulliver's* / Reize / Naar / Laputa, / Enz. / Derde Deel. / [ornament] / *Te Amsterdam, by* / J. B. Elwe, / MDCCXCII.

[Title for Part IV:] Gulliver's / *Reizen.* / Vierde Deel.

Very sm. 8vo; 2 pp. (1st title + bl.), 2 pp. (2nd title + bl.), [III]–VI, [1]–114; 2 pp. (3rd title + bl.), [III]–VI, [1]–136; 2 pp. (4th title + bl.), 2 pp. (5th title + bl.), [V]–VIII, [1]–128; 2 pp. (6th title + bl.), [V]–XII, [1]–158. — Six plates.

This is B.M. 012639 de 13. It has, as well as another I saw, by mistake preserved the leaf *Bericht Aan Den Binder.* Lotgevallen van kapitein Gulliver. Verkorte uitgave – – – – 's Gravenhage, Nederlands che maats chappy van schoone kunsten, bestuurder J. J. van Ryckevorsel, 1841.

2 vols. in 1 — frontispieces, illustrations, plates — 17½ × 13 cm. — Biblistheek von de jeugd. — Title vignette. — Copy: Michigan.

French Translations (The Hague)

371. (1) Voyages / Du Capitaine / Lemuel Gulliver, / En / Divers Pays / Éloignez. / Tome Premier. / *Premiere Partie.* / Contenant le Voyage de Lilliput. / [ornament] / *A La Haye,* / Chez P. Gosse & J. Neaulme. / *MDCCXXVII.*

(2) – – – – – / Tome Premier. / *Seconde Partie.* / Contenant le Voyage de Brobdingnag. / [other ornament] / – – – – –

(3) – – – – / Tome Second. / *Premiere Partie.* / Contenant le Voyage de Laputa, Balnibarbi, / Glubbdubdribb, Luggnagg, & Japon. / [other ornament] / – – – – –

(4) – – – – / Tome Second. / *Seconde Partie.* / Contenant le Voyage au Pays des / Houyhnhnms. / [ornament, the same as that on title-page of second voyage] / – – – – –

[Titles all four in red and black.]
12mo; [*]⁴, A–D¹², E 1–5, π¹, E 6–12, F–H¹², I¹⁰ — 2 pp. (t. + bl.), 4 pp. (Table), 2 pp. (advs. and 'Avertissement Au Relieur'), [1]–105 + bl., 2 pp.

(t. + bl.), [107]–212. (+)⁴, A–D¹², E 1–2, π¹, E 3–12, F–I¹², K² — 2 pp. (t. + bl.), 6 pp. (Table), [1]–99 + bl., 2 pp. (t. + bl.), [101]–220. — Frontisp. portrait of Gulliver, 4 maps, 2 plans, 4 illustrations.

This translation appeared in Jan. 1727 (cf. S. Goulding, *Swift En France*, 1924, pp. 57–8). As regards the plates in this French translation and the Dutch one (No. 366, *ante*), the 4 maps and 2 plans are different, which — at least for the 4 maps — is but natural, as they bear French and Dutch names respectively. Still, the occurrence of some Dutch names in the French maps (where the original English maps have English names) points to priority of the Dutch ones. The other 5 plates, however, are all the same printing. Two of them, the portrait and the illustration to Lilliput, are worth a closer examination. Both have a space at the foot, the former bearing the name "L. Gulliver.", the latter left blank. But both show traces of erasure of an earlier inscription. In the latter the words "Voyages De Gulliver" are still faintly visible. This justifies the conclusion that, after these two plates were finished in their original state, the two publishing firms came to an agreement to let them and the other 3 plates serve for both editions. Consequently the engraver effected the erasures, placed "L. Gulliver." in the space under the portrait, left the space under the 'Lilliput' plate blank, made the three remaining plates, and provided the four illustrations with the indications Fig. I, Fig. II, Fig. III, Fig. IV; all this suited the two editions equally well.

About the middle of 1727 the French translation went into a second edition (see No. 372, *post*), but it is curious to observe that the publishers had not then the disposal of the old plates, for the plates in this second edition are all new. Yet the old plates had not been destroyed, for the old portrait appeared again in 1728 (Nos. 368, *ante*, and 373, *post*), while *all* the original plates were used again in 1730 (No. 374, *post*), and again, retouched, in 1741 (No. 375, *post*).

Copy: Penn.

372. *Another [second] edition of Vols. I and II (1727):*
The titles (red and black) and the collations are the same as those of the [first] edition (No. 371, *ante*), with this addition just above the ornament:

Nouvelle Traduction / plus ample, plus exacte, & plus fidéle, que / celle de Paris, avec Figures, & Cartes / Geographiques.

Moreover, the line-division of the third title is slightly different:

– – – – – / Contenant le Voyage de Laputa, / Balnibarbi, Glubb-dubdribb, / Luggnagg, & Japon. / – – – –

My own copy lacks the second and fourth titles; the Bibl. Nat. Paris copy (Y² 17908) has Volume II only (with third and fourth titles). So that I cannot guarantee the second title, not having seen a copy with it.

The type of this edition is smaller than that of the [first]. As the first Paris translation (see Nos. 383–5, *post*) appeared about the middle of April 1727, this one must belong to May or later.

Copy: Penn.

373. In 1728 a third volume was added, consisting of a translation of the spurious Vol. III, 1727 (see No. 292, *ante*), followed by a translation of the four *Keys*, 1726 (see No. 1215, *post*). There is one general title (in red and black) to the whole volume, another (in black only) to the second part, and four special titles (all in black), i.e. one to each of the four *Keys*.

Voyages / Du Capitaine / Lem. Gulliver / En / Divers Pays /
Eloignes. / *Tome Troisieme*. / Contenant les Voiages de Brobdin- /
gnag & des Sevarambes, & la / Clef des deux Tomes précédens. /
[ornament] / *A La Haye* / — / Chez P. Gosse & J. Neaulme. /
M.DCC.XXVIII.

12mo; π^1, $*^4$, $*^{12}$, A–O^{12} — 2 pp. (t. + bl.), 8 pp. (Table), 22 pp. (Introduction), 2 pp. (both blank), 1–336. In some copies the blank leaf is to be
found before the title. — Frontisp. portrait of Gulliver, 2 illustrations (all
three the same offprints as those in No. 368, *ante*).
Copy: Penn.

374. *Another [third] edition of Vols. I, II and III* (1730):
Voyages / Du Capitaine / Lemuel Gulliver, / En / Divers Pays /
Eloignez. / Tome Premier. / Contenant le Voyage de Lilliput. /
[ornament] / *A La Haye*, / Chez Gerard Van Der Poel. /
MDCCXXX.

— — — — — — / Tome Second. / Contenant le Voyage de Laputa,
Balnibarbi, / Glubbdubdribb, Luggnagg, & Japon. / [ornament] /
— — — — — —

— — — — — / Tome Troisieme. / Contenant les Voyages de Brobdingnag & / des Sevarambes, & la Clef des deux / Tomes précédens. /
[ornament] / — — — — —

[Titles in red and black.]
12mo; $*^4$, A–H^{12}, I^{10} — 2 pp. (t. + bl.), 6 pp. ('Table' and 'Avertissement
Au Relieur'), 1–105 + bl., [107]–212. [t]^4, A–I^{12}, K^2 — 2 pp. (t. + bl.),
6 pp. ('Table'), [1]–99 + bl., [101]–220.
Frontisp. portrait of Gulliver, 4 maps, 2 plans, 4 illustrations (all eleven
the same offprints as those in No. 371, *ante*).
There are no titles to Parts II and IV. — Volume III is exactly the same
printing and has the same plates as Vol. III, 1728 (No. 373, *ante*); only the
title-page is new.
Copy: Penn.

375. *Another [fourth] edition of Vols. I, II and III* (1741):
The titles (red and black), the collations, and the plates (retouched) are
the same as those in the third edition (No. 374, *ante*), with the following
deviations in all three titles:
(1) No comma after the name: 'Lemuel Gulliver'
(2) The word 'Pays' spelled 'Païs'
(3) The imprint is:
A La Haye, / Chez Jean Swart, / Libraire dans le Toornstraat. / *MDCCXLI.*
There is no frontispiece portrait of Gulliver before Vol. III.
Penn has two copies of Vol. III, 1741. One is entirely new; in the other the
Introduction (22 pages) and the last sheet (sheet O, pp. 313–36) are the same
printing as the corresponding units in the 1728 and 1730 issues (Nos. 373 and
374, *ante*).

376. *Another [fifth] edition of Vols. I, II and III* (1762):
There are three title-pages, one to each volume, all in red and black:

Voyages / Du Capitaine / Gulliver / En / Divers Pays / Éloignés. / Tome Premier. / [ornament] / A La Haye, / Chez Jean Swart, Libraire, / dans le Toornstraat. / = / M.DCC.LXII.

12mo; π^2, a^8, b^2, A–F^{12}, G^5 — 2 pp. (t. + bl.), 2 pp. (Dedication to Madame La Marquise D**), I–XVI (Preface Du Traducteur), 3 pp. (Table, 1 p. blank), [1]–77, [78]–154.

π^1, *^{2}, A–G^{12}, H^8 — 2 pp. (t. + bl.), 4 pp. (Table), [1]–75 + bl., [77]–183 + bl.: π^1, a^8, b^2, A–K^{12} — 2 pp. (t. + bl.), 16 pp. (Introduction), 4 pp. (Table), [1]–238, 2 pp. blank.

The second title has: Tome Second.

The third title has: Tome Troisieme. / *Avec la Clef des deux Tomes précédens.* The ornaments are all three different.

Besides the general title there are in Vol. III four special ones (in black only), one to each *Key*.

Six illustrations, two to each volume.

This edition shows a great difference with its predecessors: the text in Vol. III has remained the same, but that of Vols. I and II is not the full one of the four preceding 'Hague' editions, but the abridged adaptation of the 'Paris' editions (see note under Nos. 383–5, *post*), even to the *Epitre à Madame la Marquise D** and the *Préface du Traducteur* before Vol. I. — Also the four illustrations in Vols. I and II are imitations of the corresponding ones in the 'Paris' editions; while the two illustrations in Vol. III are the same as those in the preceding 'Hague' editions of Vol. III, but new ones, and much poorer.

Copy: Penn.

377. *Another [sixth] edition of Vols. I, II and III* (1765):
The titles (in red and black) are the same as those in the [fifth] edition, only the word "Éloignés" is three times in italics, and the word "précédens" is spelt "précédents", while the year is M.DCC.LXV.

12mo; π^2, A–H^{12} — 2 pp. (t. + bl.), 2 pp. (Dedication to Madame La Marquise D**), I–XIII (Preface Du Traducteur), 1 p. blank, 1–87, 88–174, 3 pp. (Table), 1 p. blank.

π^1, A–H^{12}, I^8 — 2 pp. (t. + bl.), [1]–83 + bl., 85–204, 4 pp. (Table).

π^1, A–M^{12} — 2 pp. (t. + bl.), 15 pp. (Introduction), 1 p. blank, [1]–257 + bl., 4 pp. (Table), 1 p. blank, [1]–264 + bl., 4 pp. (Table).

Six illustrations, two to each volume.

Text the same as in the [fifth] edition. — The plates are also the same, but they are new ones, slightly better than those in the [fifth] edition.

Copy: Penn.

378. *Another [seventh] edition of Vols. I, II and III* (1767):
The titles (all in black only), the collations, the plates, and the text are the same as those of the [fifth] edition, but the year is: M.DCC.LXVII.

Copy: Penn.

379. *Another [eighth] edition of Vols. I, II and III* (1773):
The titles (all in black only), the collations, the plates, and the text are the same as those of the [fifth] edition, but the year is: M.DCC.LXXIII.

Copies: Bibl. St. Geneviève, Paris, and Penn.

380. *Another [ninth] edition of Vols. I, II and III* (1777):
The titles (all in black only), the collations, the plates, and the text are the same as those of the [fifth] edition, but the year is: M.DCC.LXXVII.
Copy: Dr. S. West-Goulding.

381. *Another [tenth] edition of Vols. I, II and III* (1778):
Voyages / Du Capitaine / Gulliver, / *En* / Divers Pays / *Eloignés* / = / Tome Premier. / = / *Nouvelle Edition.* / [ornament] / A La Haye, / Chez Jean Swart, Libraire, dans / le Toornstraat. / ≡ / M.DCC.LXXVIII.

The second title has: Tome Second.
The third title has: Tome Troisiéme. / = / *Avec la Clef des deux Tomes précédens.*
[Titles all in black only.]
8vo; [A]–M⁸, π² — 2 pp. (t. + bl.), 2 pp. (A Madame), I–XIV (Preface), 1–174, 4 pp. (Table).
π¹, A⁷, B–N⁸, π¹ — 2 pp. (t. + bl.), [1]–204, 4 pp. (Table).
π¹, A–S⁸ — 2 pp. (t. + bl.), 15 pp. + bl. (Introduction), [1]–267 + bl., 4 pp. (Table).
Six illustrations, two to each volume, very crude. — Text as in the [fifth] edition.
Copy: B.M. 12808 p 2.

**

382. Voyages / *Imaginaires,* / Romanesques, Merveilleux, / Allégoriques, Amusans, / Comiques et Critiques. / *Suivis des* / Songes et Visions, / *Et des* / Romans Cabalistiques.

Voyages / *Imaginaires,* / Songes, Visions, / et / Romans Cabalistiques. / *Ornés de Figures.* / = / Tome Quatorzième. / = / Seconde division de la première classe, contenant / les Voyages Imaginaires *merveilleux.* / [ornament] / A Amsterdam, / *Et se trouve à Paris,* / Rue et Hotel Serpente. / = / M.DCC.LXXXVII.

Voyages / Du Capitaine / Lemuel Gulliver, / *Par le docteur Swift,* / Traduits par l'abbé Desfontaine.

8vo; [a]–b⁸, A–Bb⁸ — 2 pp. (1st title + Contents on verso), 2 pp. (2nd title + bl.), 2 pp. (3rd title + bl.), [VII]–XIV (Avertissement), [XV]–XXXII (Preface), [1]–90, 91–182, 183–269, 270–395, [396]–400 (Table). — Two plates (one to Part I, and one to Part IV).
Copy: B.M. 303 g 3.
The whole collection, 1787–89, consists of 36 vols. and 3 vols. *Supplement*; together 39 vols. Each volume has two plates, except vol. III, which has none, and vols. VII, VIII, IX, which have 3, 2, and 1 plates respectively; together 76 plates. The plates were also issued separately, on large and thicker paper.

**

French Translations (Paris)

383. Voyages / De / Gulliver. / *Tome Premier.* / [ornament] / A Paris, / Chés Hypolite-Louis Guerin, / ruë Saint Jacques, à S.

Thomas / d'Aquin, vis-à-vis S. Yves. / — / M.DCC.XXVII. / *Avec Privilege Du Roy.*

The title of the second volume is the same, except: *Tome Second.*

12mo (in eights and fours alternately); [*]⁸, **⁴, ***⁸, ****⁴, A–V⁴ (in eights and fours alternately), X⁴ — 2 pp. (t. + bl.), 3 pp. (Dedication to Madame La Marquise D***), 1 p. blank, VII–XLI (Preface Du Traducteur), 5 pp. (Table), 2 pp. (both blank), [1]–123 + bl., [125]–248.

*⁴, A–Aa⁴ (in eights and fours alternately), Bb² — 2 pp. (t. + bl.), 5 pp. (Table), 1 p. blank, [1]–119 + bl., [121]–289, 3 pp. ('Approbation', 'Privilege Du Roy', and 'Errata').

Four illustrations, one to each 'Part'.

Copies: Bibl. Nat. Paris, and Penn.

In the *Neue Zeitungen Von Gelehrten Sachen* of Dec. 4, 1727, N. XCVII, p. 963, there is an announcement under Paris, saying that the first edition of Desfontaines is sold off, and that a new edition in smaller print has appeared. In the same number on p. 976 it is said that within a month 1500 copies of the first edition have been sold. And in N. XXVI, March 29, 1728, p. 246, there is a review of this edition.

The *Privilège Du Roy* mentioned on the title-pages and printed at the end of 'Tome Second' had been given (20 Mars 1727) to Hypolite-Louis Guerin, who, the next day, "faisait part du present Privilege aux Sieurs Gabriël Martin & Jacques Guerin". In accordance with this participation the first edition (same printing) appeared with two other imprints on the titles of both volumes:

384. – – – – – / A Paris, / Chés Gabriel Martin, / ruë S. Jacques, vis-à-vis la ruë / du Plâtre, à l'Etoile. / — / M.DCC.XXVII. / *Avec Privilege Du Roy.*

Copy: Bibl. Nat., Paris.

385. – – – – – / A Paris, / Dans la boutique de la V. Coustelier, / chés Jacques Guerin, / Quay des Augustins. / — / M.DCC.XXVII. / *Avec Privilege Du Roy.*

Copy: Penn.

When compared with the first 'Hague' edition (see No. 371, *ante*) it appears: (1) that this edition came out three months later, April 1727 (cf. S. Goulding, *Swift En France*, 1924, p. 60); (2) that, whereas the 'Hague' translation was a complete one, this was only an abridgement and adaptation, made by the abbot Pierre-François Guyot Desfontaines; (3) that this 'Paris' edition did not add Vol. III; (4) that plates 1 and 3 point to complete, plates 2 and 4 to partial imitation of the corresponding ones in the 'Hague' edition, while the portrait, the 4 maps, and the 2 plans were not included.

386. *Seconde Edition, revûe & corrigée:*

Voyages / De / Gulliver. / *Tome Premier.* / *Seconde Edition, revûe & corrigée.* / [ornament] / A Paris, / Chez Hippolyte-Louis Guerin, / ruë S. Jacques, à S. Thomas / d'Aquin, vis-à-vis S. Yves. / — / M.DCC.XXVII. / *Avec Approbation & Privilege du Roi.*

The title of the second volume is the same, except: *Tome Second.*

12mo (in eights and fours):

[*]⁸, **⁴, ***⁸, ****², A–Y⁴, Z⁴, Aa², Bb 1 — 2 pp. (t. + bl.), 3 pp. (A Madame, + bl.), VII–XXXIX (Preface), 5 pp. (Table), [1]–138, 139–277 + bl.

[a]⁴, A–Dd⁸ — 2 pp. (t. + bl.), 5 pp. (Table + bl.), [1]–134, [135]–325, 3 pp. (Approbation, &c.).

Four illustrations.

Copies: B.M. 012612 e 9, and Bibl. Arsenal, Paris (8° B 29, 853).

Like the first edition (Nos. 383–5, *ante*) the second appears in two other shapes, the difference being again in the imprints only:

387. – – – – – / A Paris, / Chez Gabriel Martin, ruë / S. Jacques, vis-à-vis la ruë / du Plâtre, à l'Etoile. / — / M.DCC.XXVII. / *Avec Approbation & Privilege du Roi.*

Copy: Forster 8558 (34 D 14).

388. – – – – / A Paris, / Dans la boutique de la V. Coustelier, / chés Jacques Guerin, / Quay des Augustins. / — / M.DCC.XXVII. / *Avec Approbation & Privilege du Roi.*

Copy: Bibl. Arsenal, Paris (8° B 29, 852).

389. *Seconde Edition:*

Voyages / De / Gulliver. / *Tome Premier.* / *Seconde Edition.* / [ornament] / A Paris, ruë S. Jacques. / Chez { Gabriel Martin, vis-à-vis / la ruë du Plâtre, à l'Etoile. / Hyppolite-Louis Guerin, / à S. Thomas d'Aquin, vis-à-vis S. Yves. / Et Quay des Augustins, / Dans la boutique de la V. Coustelier, / chez Jacques Guerin. / — / M.DCC.XXVII. / *Avec Privilege Du Roy.*

The second title is the same, except: *Tome Second.*

Sm. 12mo (in eights and fours alternately); *⁸, **⁴, ***⁴, ****¹, A–O⁴ (in eights and fours alternately), P⁴; π¹, Q⁸, R–Hh⁸ (in eights and fours alternately), Ii⁴ — 2 pp. (t. + bl.), [III]–IV (Dedication to Madame La Marquise D**), V–XXVIII (Preface Du Traducteur), 6 pp. (Table of the four Parts), [1]–87, 88–176; 2 pp. (title, numbered 177 + bl.), 177–259, 260–379, 3 pp. ('Approbation' and 'Privilege Du Roy'). — Four illustrations (the same offprints as those of the first edition, but very slightly shortened at top, and differently inscribed).

The type of this edition is smaller than that of the first; the pagination is consecutive for the two vols.

Copy: Penn.

390. Another *Seconde Edition, revûë & corrigée:*

Voyages / De / Gulliver. / *Tome Premier.* / *Seconde Edition, revûë & corrigée.* / [ornament] / *A Mildendo,* / Chez les Freres Pigmeos. / — / *Avec Privilége de l'Empereur de Lilliput.* / 1727.

The second volume has the same title, except: *Tome Second.*

Tall 12mo (in eights and fours alternately); [*]⁸, **⁴, ***⁸, ****², A–Z⁴ (in eights and fours alternately), Aa², Bb 1 — 2 pp. (t. + bl.), 3 pp. (Dedication to Madame La Marquise D***), 1 p. blank, VII–XXXIX (Preface Du Traducteur), 5 pp. (Table), 1–138, 139–277 + bl.

[a]⁴, A–Dd⁸ (in eights and fours alternately) — 2 pp. (t. + bl.), 5 pp. (Table), 1 p. blank, 1–134, 135–325, 3 pp. blank.

Four illustrations (new ones, representing the same scenes, but in reversed order).

Penn has a copy that once belonged to Hypolite-Louis Guerin (the publisher of the other editions), apparent from his autograph signature HL.G. at the end of the *Préface*, p. XXXIX. Query: Does this mean that he was the publisher of this edition as well? And was the facetious imprint, derived from the text itself, simply a blind? And if so, for what purpose?

391. *Voyages de Gulliver* – – – Paris, J. Guérin, 1737. — 2 vols. in 1; 12mo; plates. [Mentioned by Sybil Goulding, *Swift En France*, 1924, p. 192]

392. Voyages / De / Gulliver, / *Traduits par M. l'Abbé Desfontaines.* / Nouvelle Edition. / *Tome Premier.* / [ornament] / *A Paris,* / Chez la Veuve Damonneville & Musier fils, / quai des Augustins, au coin de la rue / Pavée, à Saint Etienne. / = / M.DCC.LXII. / *Avec Privilege Du Roi.*

The title of the second volume is the same, except: Tome Second.
16mo; I–XXXVI, 1–156, 157–322.
2 pp., 1–150, 151–380.
Four illustrations.
Copy: Bibl. Nat. Paris (Y² 70842–43).

393. *Voyages de Gulliver* – – – – Paris, chez Guérin et Delatour, 1762. — 2 vols. 12mo; plates. [Mentioned by Sybil Goulding, *Swift En France*, 1924, p. 192]

394. Voyages / De / Gulliver, / *Traduits par M. l'Abbé des Fontaines.* / Nouvelle Edition. / Tome Premier. / [vignette] / *A Paris,* / Chez Jean-Baptiste-Guillaume Musier, / fils, Libraire, Quai des Augustins, au coin / de la rue Gist-le-Coeur. / = / M.DCC.LXXII. / *Avec privilege du Roi.*

The title of the second volume is the same, except: Tome Second., and an ornament instead of the vignette.
12mo; π², A¹², b², A–L¹², M⁶ — 2 pp. (h.t. + bl.), 2 pp. (f.t. + bl.), [i]–II (Dedication to Madame La Marquise D**), [III]–XXVIII (Preface Du Traducteur), [1]–135, [136]–271, [272]–275 (Table), 1 p. blank.
π², A–N¹², O² — 2 pp. (h.t. + bl.), 2 pp. (f.t. + bl.), [1]–129, [130]–314, 2 pp. ('Approbation' and 'Privilege Du Roi').
Copy: Penn.

395. *Voyages de Gulliver*. A Paris, chez Musier, 1776. — 2 vols. 12mo; plates. [Mentioned by Sybil Goulding, *Swift En France*, 1924, p. 192]

396. Voyages / *Du Capitaine* / Gulliver, / *En* / Divers Pays /
Eloignés. / — / Tome Premier. / — / [ornament] / *A Rouen,* / De
L'Imprimerie Privilégiée. / = / M.DCC.LXXIX.

The title of the second volume is the same, except: Tome Second.
That of the third volume is again the same, but it has: Avec la clef des
deux Tomes précédents. / — / Tome Troisieme.
12mo; a¹², A–F¹², G⁵ — 2 pp. (h.t. + bl.), 2 pp. (f.t. + bl.), [V]–VI
(Dedication to Madame La Marquise D**), [VII]–XXI (Preface Du Traducteur), XXII–XXIV (Table), [1]–77, [78]–154.
π⁴, A–G¹², H⁸ — 2 pp. (h.t. + bl.), 2 pp. (f.t. + bl.), V–VIII (Table),
[1]–75 + bl., [77]–183 + bl.
a¹², A–K¹² — 2 pp. (h.t. + bl.), 2 pp. (f.t. + bl.), V–XX (Introduction),
XXI–XXIV (Table), [1]–238, 2 pp. blank.
Copy: Penn.
Six illustrations, two to each volume.

396A. Voyages / *Du Capitaine* / Lemuel Gulliver. / Par Le Doc-
teur Swift. / Traduits par l'Abbee Desfontaine. / = / Tome
Premier. / = / Avec figures. / [ornament] / A Avignon, / Chez
Jean-Albert Joly, Imprimeur- / Libraire. / — / 1793.

The title of the second volume is the same, except: Tome Second.
Sm. 12mo (in sixes); [a]⁴, b², A–N⁶, O⁴ — 2 pp. (t. + bl.), [III]–IV
(Dedication to Madame La Marquise D**), [V]–XVI (Preface Du Traducteur), [1]–80, [81]–160, 161–3 (Table), 1 p. blank.
π² (the second signed A), B–R⁶ — 2 pp. (t. + bl.), [3]–80, [81]–190,
191–4 (Table), 2 pp. blank.
Six illustrations, two belonging to Vol. I, two to Vol. II, and two properly
belonging to Vol. III, but here placed as frontispieces to Vols. I and II, which
makes me believe there should be a Vol. III.
Copy: Penn.

396B. Voyages / De / Gulliver, / Traduits De Swift, / *Par
l'Abbé Desfontaines.* / Tome Premier. / [ornament] / A Paris, / Chez
J. B. G. Musier, Libraire, rue / Pavée André-des-Arcs, No. 8. /
— / L'An IVᵉ. de la République francaise.

The title of the other three parts are the same, except: Tome Second.,
Tome Troisieme., Tome Quatrieme.
Sm. 12mo (in sixes); π², A–N⁶; π², A–L⁶, π² — 2 pp. (h.t. + bl.), 2 pp.
(f.t. + bl.), [5]–30 (Preface), [1]–130; 2 pp. (h.t. + bl.), 2 pp. (f.t. + bl.),
[3]–134, 4 pp. Table.
π², A–K⁶, L²; π², A–P⁶ — 2 pp. (h.t. + bl.), 2 pp. (f.t. + bl.), [1]–124;
2 pp. (h.t. + bl.), 2 pp. (f.t. + bl.), [1]–175, [176]–180 (Table).
Four illustrations as frontispieces, one to each 'Part', between h.t. and f.t.
Copy: Penn.

397. Voyages / De Gulliver. / — / Tome Premier. / [monogram]
/ A Paris, / De L'Imprimerie / De Pierre Didot L'Aîné. / An V.
1797.

The second volume has the same title, except: Tome Second.

12mo (in sixes); π^2, a–c^6, 1–12^6, 13^2, 14^4, 15–26^6, 27^2 — 2 pp. (h.t. + bl.) 2 pp. (f.t. + bl.), 2 pp. (h.t. for Part I + communication that only 100 copies have been printed on L. P.), 2 pp. (f.t. for Part I + bl.), [V]–VI (A Madame), [VII]–XXXVI (Preface), [1]–148, 2 pp. (h.t. for Part II + bl.), 2 pp. (f.t. for Part II + bl.), [153]–303 + bl.

1–12^6, 13^2, 14^4, 15–31^6, 32^1 — 2 pp. (h.t. + bl.), 2 pp. (f.t. + bl.), 2 pp. (h.t. for Part III + bl.), 2 pp. (f.t. for Part III + bl.), [5]–148, 2 pp. (h.t. for Part IV + bl.), 2 pp. (f.t. for Part IV + bl.), [153]–358.

Frontisp. between the first two titles of the first volume, and 9 plates.

Copy: B.M. 837 c 2 (has no h.t. and f.t. for 'Tome Second Première Partie').

There seem to be copies on Large Vellum Paper, or Large Holland Paper, with the plates *before* and *with* "letters and dates".

Hubbard, *Contributions*, 157–8 and 159–60, says that this edition was reprinted in 1860: Voyages de Gulliver. A Paris, An MDCCCLX. — 2 v.; pp. XXXV, 152; 153–308, and 148; 149–360. 10 plates by le Febvre, engraved by Masquelier; cm. 16½ (uncut). Title-page in red and black; title-page has monogram. General half-title, with imprint. (Like Didot ed. of 1797, but has half-title for each Part.) Only 150 copies.

I have noted two copies sold at Sotheby's: one on "papier velin", the plates each in four states (with and before letters and the etchings), the other, an L. P. copy (only 100 so issued), the plates each in two states (preliminary etched and before letters).

397A. Voyages au capitaine Gulliver, en divers pays eloignes. Nouvelle edition — Rouen, Labbey, 1797.

> 4 vols, 16mo:
> 2 pp. (h.t. + bl.), 2 pp. (f.t. + bl.), [I]–XXIV, [25]–244.
> 2 pp. (h.t. + bl.), 2 pp. (f.t. + bl.), [V]–VIII, [1]–269 + bl.
> 2 pp. (h.t. + bl.), 2 pp. (f.t. + bl.), [V]–XXXII, [1]–180.
> 2 pp. (h.t. + bl.), 2 pp. (f.t. + bl.), [I]–II, [1]–153 + bl.
> Frontisp. in each volume.
> Copy: Michigan.
> Vol. III contains the spurious third volume, Vol. IV the four Keys.

398. Voyage / De / Gulliver, / A Lilliput. / [ornament] / A Paris, / Chez Tiger, Libraire, rue du Petit-Pont- / Saint-Jacques, au coin de celle de la / Huchette. *Au Pilier Littéraire*. / De L'Imprimerie De P. Didot L'Aîné.

– – – – – – – / A Brobdingnag. / – – – – –

– – – – – – – / A Laputa, / Aux Balnibarbes, A Luggnagg, A / Gloubbdoubrid, Et Au Japon. / – – – –

– – – – – – – / Au Pays / Des Houyhnhnms. / – – – –

> 18mo (in twelves and sixes alternately):
> A^{12}–F^6 — 2 pp. (t. + 'Avis' on verso), [3]–106, 2 pp. blank.
> A^{12}–F^6 — 2 pp. (t. + 'Avis' on verso), [3]–108.
> A^{12}–F^6 — 2 pp. (t. + 'Avis' on verso), [3]–106, 2 pp. blank.

A^{12}–F^6 — 2 pp. (t. + 'Avis' on verso), [3]–108.
Frontisp. in each volume.
Copies: Bibl. Nat. Paris, and Penn.

398A. *Another edition:*
The same collation and the same titles, except for the imprints, which in all four volumes are:

A Paris, / Chez Tiger, Imprimeur-Libraire, / rue du Petit-Pont, n°. 10. / [ornamental rule].

At first sight these two editions seem to be the same offprints; but a closer examination shows them to be from different settings. This edition has been set from the preceding one; several lines have been widened-out, upper case has often been replaced by lower case, types are sometimes different (*v* and v), misprints have been corrected. The paper is different, but the frontispieces are from the same plates. Probably No. 398 is earlier, as Tiger is there a 'Libraire' only, whereas in No. 398A he is an 'Imprimeur-Libraire'.
Copy: Penn.

399. Voyages / De / Gulliver, / Traduits De Swift, / Par *Desfontaines. | Nouvelle Edition | Revue, corrigée, et ornée de gravures. |* Tome Premier. / — / A Paris. / L'An VII De La République Française.

The second volume has the same title, except: Tome Second.
18mo (in twelves and sixes alternately); π^2, a^{12}, B^{12}–K^6 — 2 pp (h.t. + bl.), 2 pp. (f.t. + bl.), [1]–16 (Preface Du Traducteur), [17]–96, [97]–178, 2 pp. (Table).
π^1, A^{12}–L^6 — 2 pp. (f.t. + bl.), [1]–78, [79]–190, 2 pp. (Table).
Two illustrations (one to Part I, and one to Part III). — [An VII = 1798–9].
Copy: Penn.

400. Voyages / De / Gulliver, / Traduits De Swift, / Par L'Abbé Des Fontaines. / Troisième [altered with pen into: Première] Partie. / [monogram] / A Paris, / A La Librairie Économique, / rue de la Harpe, n° 94, ancien collége d'Harcourt. / 1807.

The other title is the same, except: Quatrième [altered with pen into: Seconde] Partie.
16mo; 8 pp. (h.t., illustration, f.t., illustration), 1–252.
8 pp. (h.t., illustration, f.t., illustration), 1–271 + bl.
The text is complete, but the titles have been tampered with. For the full-titles see above; as to the half-titles, they were originally marked (in print) 3 and 4, but these figures were altered into 1 and 2, both in ink and in print.
Copy: Bibl. Arsenal, Paris (8° B 29, 860).

401. Voyages / *De* / Gulliver, / *Traduits De L'Anglais, De* Swift, / Par l'Abbé Des Fontaines. / *Edition ornée de douze Gravures.* / Tome Premier. / [illustration] / A Paris, / *Chez* Billois, *Libraire, Quai des Augustins, N°. 31.* / 1813.

The second volume has the same title, except: Tome Second.

Sm. 12mo (in sixes); [1]–18⁶, 19³ — 2 pp. (h.t. + printer's name on verso), 2 pp. (f.t. + bl.), [3]–18 (Preface Du Traducteur), [19]–118, [119]–218, [219]–222 (Table).

1³, 2–20⁶, 21³ — 2 pp. (h.t. + printer's name on verso), 2 pp. (f.t. + bl.), [3]–98, [99]–234, [235]–238 (Table).

This edition is complete with a 'Tome Troisième' and a 'Tome Quatrième', containing "Le Nouveau Gulliver", for which see No. 1238, *post.* — The "douze Gravures" mentioned in the four titles comprise two to each volume, and the four title-illustrations.

Copy: Penn.

Another issue:
The same titles, collations, and plates, but with imprint:

– – – – | A Paris, | *Chez* Genets *jeune, Libraire, Rue Dauphine,* N.° *14.* | 1813.

German Translations

425. Des | Capitains | Lemuel Gulliver | Reisen | in unter- schiedliche entfernte und unbe- | kandte Länder. | Erster Theil. | In sich haltend die Reisen | nach | Lilliput | und | Brobdingnac. | Ihrer Seltsamkeit und Anmuth wegen | aus dem Englischen in das Teutsche mit | Fleisz übersetzet. | Mit Kupfern gezieret. | — | Hamburg, | Gedruckt und verlegt von sehl. Thomas von Wierings Er- | ben bey der Börse im güldnen A, B, C. 1727. | Ist auch in Leipzig bey Philip Herteln zu bekommen.

Des | Capitains | Lemuel Gulliver | Reisen | in unterschiedliche entfernte und unbe- | kandte Länder | Zweiter Theil. | In sich fassend | Die Reisen nach Laputa, Bal- | nibarbi, Glubbdubdribb, | Luggnagg, Japon und dem | Lande der Houyhnhnms. | Wegen der besondern darin befindlichen | Staats- und Sitten- Lehren | aus dem Englischen ins Teutsche mit Fleisz | übersetzet. | Mit Kupfern erläutert. | — | Hamburg, | Gedruckt und verlegt von sehl. Thomas von Wierings Er- | ben bey der Börse im güldnen A, B, C. 1727 | Ist auch in Leipzig bey Philip Herteln zu bekommen.

Des | Capitains | Lemuel Gulliver | Reisen | in | unterschied- liche entfernte und unbekandte | Länder. | Dritter und Letzter Theil. | In sich haltend | Dessen zweite Reise nach Brobding- | nagg, und von dar nach Spo- | runda, Severambia, | Monatamia &c. &c. | Nebst | des Hrn. *Carolini,* eines Venetianis. Edelmanns, | Schlüssel | oder Erklärung derer in beyden vorgehenden | Thei- len beschriebenen vier Reisen. | Wegen ihrer Seltsamkeit, An- muth und Zusammenhän- | gung mit denen vorigen aus dem Englis. ins Teutsche mit | Fleisz übersetzet, und mit Kupfern ge- zieret. | — | Hamburg, | Gedruckt und verlegt von seel. Thomas von Wierings Erben, / im güldnen A.B.C. bey der Börse. 1728. / Ist auch in Leipzig bey Philip Hertel zu bekommen.

[All three titles in red and black.]
Sm. 8vo;):(⁸, A–O⁸ — 2 pp. (t. + bl.), 8 pp. (Vorrede), 6 pp. (Register), 1–112, 113–223 + bl.
):(⁴, A–O⁸ — 2 pp. (t. + bl.), 4 pp. (Register), 1–105, 106–224.
2 pp., 1–304.
Two maps (Parts I and II), two plans (Part III), six illustrations (two to each volume).
One copy I have seen has in sheet A (pp. 1–16) of Vol. I, the page-number — (1) —; 'nützlichers' on p. 2, l. 29; and 'und welches einer' on p. 8, l. 11; whereas my own copy has no page-number, 'nützliches', and 'die einer'. It appears that the latter sheet properly belongs to the second edition, 1733. Whether this is only an irregularity, or whether there are more such copies, I cannot say.
Copy: Penn.

426. *Second edition:*
The three titles (again in red and black) are practically the same as before, except:

[Vol. I] – – – – – Teutsche mit Fleisz / übersetzet, und mit Kup-fern gezieret. / Die zweite Auflage. / — / Hamburg, / Gedruckt und verlegt von seel. Thomas von Wierings Er- / ben bey der Börse, im güldnen A, B, C. 1733. / Ist auch in Leipzig bey Philip Herteln zu bekommen.

[Vol. II] – – – – – / übersetzet. / Die andere Auflage. / Mit Kup-fern. / — / Hamburg, / Gedruckt und verlegt von sehl. Thomas von Wierings Er- / ben bey der Börse im güldnen A, B, C. 1735. / Ist auch in Leipzig bey Philip Hertel zu bekommen.

[Vol. III] Exactly the same as in 1728; only the year is 1731.

Sm. 8vo;):(⁸, A–O⁸ — 2 pp. (t. + bl.), 9 pp. (Vorrede), 5 pp. (Register), [1]–112, 113–223 + bl.
):(⁴, A–O⁸, P² — 2 pp. (t. + bl.), 6 pp. (Register), 1–105, 106–227 + bl.
π¹, A–T⁸, U² — 2 pp. (t. + bl.), 1–16 (Einleitung), 17–308.
Ten plates, the same as before.
Copy: Penn.

427. *Third edition:*
Des / Capitains / Lemuel Gulliver / Reisen / in unterschiedliche entfernte und unbe- / kandte Länder. / Erster Theil. / In sich hal-tend die Reisen / nach / Lilliput / und / Brobdingnac. / Ihrer Selt-samkeit und Anmuth wegen / aus dem Englischen in das Teutsche mit Fleisz / übersetzet, und mit Kupfern gezieret. / Die dritte Auflage. / — / Hamburg, / Gedruckt und verlegt von seel. Thomas von Wierings Er- / ben, bey der Börse, im güldnen A, B, C. 1739. / Ist auch in Leipzig in Hertels Handlung zu bekommen.

Des / Capitains / Lemuel Gulliver / Reisen / in unterschiedliche entfernte und unbe- / kannte Lånder / Zweiter Theil. / In sich fassend / Die Reisen nach Laputa, Bal- / nibarbi, Glubbdubdribb, / Luggnagg, Japon und dem / Lande der Houyhnhnms. / Wegen der besondern darin befindlichen / Staats- und Sitten-Lehren / aus dem Englischen ins Teutsche mit Fleisz / übersetzet. / Die dritte Auflage. / Mit Kupfern. / — / Hamburg, / Gedruckt und verlegt von sel. Thomas von Wierings Erben / bey der Börse im güldnen A, B, C. 1739. / auch in Leipzig in Hertels Handlung zu bekommen.

Des / Capitains / Lemuel Gulliver / Reisen, / in / unterschied- liche entfernte und unbekannte / Länder. / Dritter und Letzter Theil. / In sich haltend / Dessen zweite Reise nach Brobding- / nagg, und von dar nach Spo- / runda, Severambia, / Monatamia &c. &c. / Nebst / des Hrn. Carolini, eines Venetianis. Edelmanns, / Schlüssel / oder Erklårung derer in beyden vorgehenden / Theilen beschriebenen vier Reisen. / Wegen ihrer Seltsamkeit, Anmuth und Zusammenhån- / gung mit denen vorigen aus dem Englis. ins Teutsche mit / Fleisz übersetzet, und nun zum drittenmahl aufge- legt. / — / Hamburg, / Gedruckt und verlegt von seel. Thomas von Wierings Erben, / im güldnen A.B.C. bey der Börse. 1746.

[All three titles in red and black.] Collations and plates the same as in No. 426, but a different printing.
Copy: Penn.

428. *Another third edition* of Vols. I and II, also 1739:
This is a different printing. The collations and plates are the same, but the title-pages are slightly different. The modifications are:

[Vol. I] unbe- / kannte	(for: unbe- / kandte	)
sel.	(for: seel.	)
Erben, /	(for: Er- / ben,	)
[Vol. II] Lånder.	(no stop	)
besonders	(for: besondern	)
Erben,	(no comma	)
Börse,	(no comma	)
Ist	(printed before 'auch')	

Copy: Penn.

428A. Des Capitain / Lemuel Gullivers / Reisen / In / Neu entlegene Lånder, / Erster und Anderer Theil, / Oder / Erste, zweyte, dritte und vierdte Reise / nach Lilliput, Brobdingnag, Laputa, Balnibarbi, Glubbdubdribb, Luggnagg, Japan und / in des Land derer Houyhnhnms, / Wegen derer besondern darinne befindli- / chen Staats = und Sitten = Lehren, / Aus dem Frantzôs. ins Teutsche übersetzt, / Nebst vielen Kupffern, und einem An = / hange, in welchem die darinne enthaltene / Sachen in einem

Gedichte erörtert / werden. / = / Leipzig, / Bey Johann Christoph Coernern, / An. 1728.

Des Capitain / Lemuel Gullivers / Reisen / In / Neu = entlegene Länder, / Ersten Theils / Erste Abtheilung, / Die Reise nach Lilliput / enthaltend. / [ornament] / = / Leipzig, / Bey Johann Christoph Coernern, / An, 1728.

– – – – – / Ersten Theils / Andere Abtheilung, / – – – – – – Brobdingnag / – – – – – – – – / An. 1728.

– – – – / Andern Theils / Erste Abtheilung, / – – – – Laputa, Bal- / nibarbi, Glubbdubdribb, Luggnagg / und Japon enthaltend. / – – – – – – / An. 1728.

– – – – / Andern Theils / Andere Abtheilung, / – – – – in das Land derer / Houyhnhnms enthaltend. / – – – – – / An. 1728.

[The general title in red and black, the four 'Part' titles in black only.]
Sm. 8vo; π^{10} (see below), π^1, A–H^8, I^4; π^1, a–i^8; A–H^8, I^4; a–k^8, 1^4; m^4— 2 pp. (both blank), 2 pp. (bl. + portrait Gulliver), 2 pp. (general title + bl.), 8 pp. (Dedication to Hanns Carl von Kirchbach), 6 pp. (Vorrede, dated: Leipziger Michaeli = Messe 1727); 2 pp. (title Part I + bl.), 1–134 (127–8 repeated in numbering); 2 pp. (title Part II + bl.), 1–144; 2 pp. (title Part III + bl.), 3–136; 2 pp. (title Part IV + bl.), 3–168; 8 pp. (Anhang). — Frontisp. portrait of Gulliver, and ten plates, viz. 4 maps, 2 plans, and 4 illustrations.
The gathering of the ten leaves of prefatory matter is rather curious. There are two separate double-leaves, not gathered together: the first is bl. + bl. + first page 'Vorrede' (signed)(2) + second page 'Vorrede'; the second is the other four pages of the 'Vorrede' (the first of these four signed)(3). Within the first of these double-leaves have been gathered one double-leaf separately, bearing portrait of Gulliver and general title, both unsigned; followed by two double-leaves, gathered together, bearing the 'Dedication', and signed $*^{1-4}$.
As to text and plates this German translation is based on the 1727 The Hague French translation (see No. 371, *ante*).
The *Anhang* is a rather poor performance.
The 'Vorrede' says (1) that at the French court this work has been so well received that M. de Marinaux has been ordered to make a comedy based on Gulliver, and that M. Romansi is to perform it on the Italian stage (2) that Vol. III will be published soon. (I have not seen it. Did it ever appear?)
The *Neue Zeitungen Von Gelehrten Sachen* of Dec. 4, 1727, N. XCVII, p. 976 announces this edition as having just appeared, and dates it 1727.

429. Lemuel Güllivers / sämtliche / Reisen. / Aus dem Englischen des berühmten Dr. Swifts / von neuem übersezt. / Mit Kupfern. / [vignette, representing Gulliver] / — / Hamburg und Leipzig. 1761.

8vo;)((^{8}, A–Ff^8 — 2 pp. (t. + bl.), [III]–XV (Vorrede), 1 p. (Latin quotation), (1)–462, 2 pp. blank. — Four illustrations, one to each 'Part'.
Copy: Penn. — This is a separate issue of Vol. V of *Satyrische und ernsthafte Schriften*, 1761 (see No. 101, *ante*). The text ([1]–462) is the same printing

(only: 'V. Theil.' removed from foot of first page of each new sheet), but the prefatory matter is new. — In the *Vorrede* the translator condemns preceding translations as having been based on a French translation (the 'Hague' one), in its turn based on the English original which had been tampered with in the press, so that they contained double mistakes; whereas he praises his own, translated direct from the English text corrected by the author himself (Faulkner's?). This translator knows how to appreciate Swift: he defends Swift's intentions in *Gulliver's Travels* against stupid critics, i.a. Orrery and Young.

430. *Second edition:*
The same collation, plates, and title as those of No. 429, *ante*, except:

– – – – / [vignette, representing Gulliver] / Zweyte Auflage. / — / Hamburg und Leipzig, 1762.

This is exactly the same printing as No. 429, *ante* ('V. Theil.' has been preserved at foot of first page of each new sheet), except for the prefatory matter, which is new.
Copy: Bayerische Staatsbibl., München.

431. *Third edition:*
Lemuel Gûllivers / sâmtliche / Reisen. / Aus dem / Englischen des Dr. Swifts übersezt. / Mit Kupfern. / [ornament] / Dritte Auflage. / — / Zûrich, bey Orell, Geszner, Fûeszlin und Comp. 1772.

8vo; I–XVI, 1–500, 4 pp. (advs.). — Four plates.
This is no doubt a separate issue of Vol. V of *Satyrische und ernsthafte Schriften*, 1772 (see No. 101, *ante*).

432. Lemuel Gûllivers / Reise / nach Lilliput / — / aufs neue / frei verdeutscht / von / C. H. K . . . . n. / = / Kopenhagen 1786. / bey Ole Hegelund, / und in Kommiszion bey Korte in Flensburg.

12mo; 1–103 + bl.
Copy: University Library, München, and Michigan.

433. Lemuel Gullivers / Reisen / zu verschiedenen / entfernten Nationen. / Aus dem / Englischen des D. Jonathan Swift / neu übersetzt / von dem / Verfasser der Briefe eines reisenden Franzosen / durch Deutschland. / [vignette] / = / Zûrich, bey Orell, Geszner, Fûszli und Comp. 1788.

Sm. 8vo; π^{12}, B–Bb^8, Cc^3 — 2 pp. (t. + bl.), [III]–VIII (Inhalt), 2 pp. (title Part I + bl.), [3]–92, 2 pp. (title Part II + bl.), 95–194, 2 pp. (title Part III + bl.), 197–288, 2 pp. (title Part IV + bl.), 291–406 (misnumbered 306).
The translator is Joh. Kasp. Riesbeck (cf. No. 277).
Copies: Stadtbibl., Leipsic, and Penn.

434. Lemuel Gulliver's / Reisen / 1^r Band. / [portrait Gulliver] / Reise nach Lilliput. / — / Leipzig, / in der Tuniussischen Buchhandlung 1804.

– – – – / 2ᴿ Band. / [illustration] / Reise nach Brobdingnag. / – – –

– – – – / 3ᴿ Band. / [illustration] / Reise nach Laputa. / – – – –

– – – – / 4ᴿ Band. / [illustration] / Reise ins Land der Houyhnhnms. / – – – –

> Sm. 8vo; 2 pp., III–VIII, 1–176.
>   2 pp., 1–194.
>   2 pp., III–X, 1–179 + bl.
>   2 pp., 1–220.
> The first two pages of each 'Part' are the title-pages as above; they are
> entirely engraved (on thicker paper).
> Copy: Preuszische Staatsbibl., Berlin.

435. *Another issue* (only the titles renewed):
Lemuel Gulliver's / Reisen / zu verschiedenen bisher / unbekann-
ten Völkern / des Erdbodens. / [illustration] / Von neuem aus dem
Englischen übersetzt. / Erster Band. / Reise nach Liliput. / — /
Leipzig 1810 / bei J. L. Hinrichs.

– – – – / Zweiter Band. / Reise nach Brobdingnag. / — / Leipzig,
/ bei J. L. Hinrichs. / 1810.

– – – – / Dritter Band. / Reise nach Laputa. / — / Leipzig, / bei
J. L. Hinrichs / 1810.

– – – – / Vierter Band. / Reise ins Land der Houyhnhnms. / — /
Leipzig, / bei J. L. Hinrichs. / 1810.

436. Lemuel Gulliver's / Reisen / zu verschiedenen bisher / un-
bekannten Vôlkern / des Erdbodens. / — / Von neuem aus dem
Englishchen ûbersetzt. / Erster Band. / — / Reise nach Liliput.
/ — / Leipzig, 1811.

> The titles to the second, third and fourth volumes are the same, except:

– – – – – / Zweyter Band. / — / Reise nach Brobdingnag. / – – – –

– – – / Dritter Band. / — / Reise nach Laputa. / – – – – –

– – – / Vierter Band. / — / Reise ins Land der Houyhnhnms. / – –

> Sm. 8vo; 2 pp. (f.t.), 1–128 (beginning with h.t.), I–IV (*Inhalt*).
>   2 pp. (f.t.), 1–142 (beginning with h.t.), I–IV (*Inhalt*).
>   2 pp. (f.t.), 1–132 (beginning with h.t.), I–IV (*Inhalt*).
>   2 pp. (f.t.), 1–160 (beginning with h.t.), I–IV (*Inhalt*).
> Four frontispieces (one to each 'Part').

**

Italian Translation

436A. Viaggj / Del Capitano / Lemuel Gulliver / In diversi
Paesi lontani. / *Traduzione dal Franzese* / Di F. Zannino Marsecco. /

Tomo Primo. / Parte Prima, / *Contenente il Viaggio di* Lilliput. / [Ornament] / In Venezia, MDCCXXIX. / Per Giuseppe Corona, / A S. Gio: Grisostomo, all'Insegna del Premio. / Con Lic. De' Superiori, *e* Privileg.

The title of the second volume is the same, except:

– – – – – / Tomo Secondo. / Parte Terza, / *Contenente il Viaggio di Laputa, Balni- / barbi, Glubbdubdribb, Luggnagg, / e del Giapone.*

12mo; 2 pp. (t. + bl.), 2 pp. (Lo Stampatore, etc.), 2 pp. (Tavola – – – di Lilliput.), 2 pp. (Tavola – – – di Brobdingnag.), 1–244. — Frontisp. (portrait) and 2 plates.
2 pp. (t. + bl.), 2 pp. (Tavola – – – di Laputa, etc.), 4 pp. (Tavola – – – degli Houyhnhnms.), 1–247 + "Libri – – – vendono alla – – – Giuseppe Corona – – – ", on verso). — Two plates, one plan.
Copy: Michigan.

442. Viaggi / Del Capitano / Lemuel Gulliver / In diversi Paesi lontani. / Traduzione dal Franzese. / Di F. Zannino Marsecco. / Tomo Primo. / Parte Prima. / *Contenente il Viaggio di* Lilliput / [vignette] / In Venezia, MDCCXLIX. / Appresso Giovanni Tevernin. / All' Insegna della Providenza / *Con Liacenza de' Superiori, c Privilegio.* / Del Duca di Setmoneta.

Viaggi / Del Capitano / Lemuel Gulliver / Tomo Secondo. / Parte Terza, / *Contenente il Viaggio di Laputa, Balni- / barbi, Glubbdubdribb, Luggnagg, / e del Giapone.*

12mo; π^6, A–R^{12}, 2 pp. (bl. + frontisp.), 2 pp. (t. + bl.), V–XII (Adv. to Reader + Contents), 1–204, 2 pp. (second t. + bl.), 207–408.
Copy: B.M. C 59 fff 15.

***

Danish Translations

443. Kapitain / Lemuel Gullivers / Reise / til / Lilleput / eller / til de smaae Folk. / Skreven paa Engelsk / af / den berømte / Dr. Jonathan Swift, / og / deraf i det Danske oversat. / — / *Imprimatur, Mart. Hübner.* / = / Kiøbenhavn 1768, / trykt hos August Friderich Stein.

Sm. 8vo; [ )( ]^8, A–F^8, G^4 — 2 pp. (t. + Latin quotation on verso), 4 pp. (Richard Sympson's preface), 2 pp. (translator's preface), 4 pp. (Contents), 4 pp. (Quinbus Flestrin), [1]–104.
Copies: Bibl. Nat. Paris (Inv. Y^2 70953), and Penn.
In the preface the translator promises the *Voyage to Brobdingnag,* if *Lilliput* is well received. It appeared in 1775:

Capitain / Lemuel Gullivers / Reise / til / Brobdingnag / eller / de Store Folk. / = / Skreven paa Engelsk / af den berømte / Dr.

Jonathan Swift, / og / deraf i det Danske oversat / ved / C. Hamming. / = / Kiøbenhavn 1775. / Trykt hos August Friderich Stein, boende / i Skidenstrædet No. 171.

12mo; 4 pp., 1–140.
Copy: Bibl. Nat. Paris (Inv. Y² 70954).

443A. Lemuel Gullivers reise nach Lilliput, aufs neue frei verdeutscht von C.H.K. . . .n [i.e. Krôgen] Kopenhagen, O. Hegelund; Flensburg, In kommission bey Korte, 1786.
Copy: Michigan.

***

Swedish Translation

445. Capitain / Lemuel / Gullivers / Resor, / Til åtskillige långt bort belägne / Land; / Beprydde med Kopparstycken. / Förra Delen / Tålkad ifrån Fransyskan. / [ornament] / — / Andra Uplagan. / — / Wästerås, / Tryckt hos Joh. Laur. Horrn, på desz / bekostnad, år 1772.

Capitaine / Lemuel Gullivers / Resor / Til åtskillige långt bort belägne / Land; / Beprydde med Kopparstycken; / Senare Delen / Tålkad ifrån Fransyskan. / [ornament] / — / Wästerås, / Tryckt hos Joh. Laur. Horrn, på desz / bekostnad, år 1772.

Sm. 8vo;)(⁸, A–I⁸, K⁴ — 2 pp. (t. + bl.), 14 pp. (Fôretal), [1]–75, 76–150, 2 pp. advs.
[A]⁴, B–M⁸ — 2 pp. (t. + bl.), 8 pp. (Fôrklaring), [3]–68, 69–160, 161–73 (An examination of Mandeville's *Fable of the Bees*), 3 pp. advs.
Four plates, by way of frontisp. to each of the four Parts.
Copy: B.M. 12612 aa 7.

***

Russian Translation

[In Russian characters; the translation in English is as follows:]

450. Travels / of the Gullivers, / Book I. / containing / *the voyage* / to Lilliput, / translated / by Erofej Korzjawin. / — / *Second Edition.* / [ornament] / — / *Part I.* / — / In the University Printing-house / of the year 1780.

The titles of the other three parts are the same, except:

– – – – / Book II. / – – – – / to Brodinjag, / – – – – / *Part II.* / – – –

– – – – / Book III. / – – – – / to Laputa, to Balnibarbi, / to Glubdubdrib, to Lugnag / And to Japan, / – – – – – – / *Part III.* / – – –

– – – – / Book IV. / – – – – / to Houyhnhnm's Land. / – – – –
– – / Part IV. / – – – –

8vo; 1–120.
    2 pp., 1–125 + bl.
    2 pp., 1–107.
    2 pp., 1–150.
Copy: Bibl. Nat. Paris (Y^2 70955–8).

**
*

Portuguese Translation

459A. Viagens / De / Gulliver / A Varios / Paizes Remotos, /
Traduzidas / Por / J. B. G. / — / Tomo Primeiro. / — / [ornament] /
Coimbra: / Na Real Imprensa Da Universid. / — / Anno De
M.DCC.XCIII. / *Com licenca da Real Mesa da Commissao Ge-* / *ral*
sobre o Exame, e Censura dos Livros. / — / *Vende-se em Coimbra em*
Casa de Joao Te- / *dro Aillaud.*

The title of the second volume is the same, except: Tomo Segundo.
Sm. 8vo; π^2, *^{8}, A–H^{VIII}, A–H^8 — 2 pp. (h.t. + bl.), 2 pp. (f.t. + bl.),
16 pp. (Preface), 1–128, [1]–125 + 3 pp. blank.
π^2, A–G^8, H^4, A–K^8, L^4 — 2 pp. (h.t. + bl.), 2 pp. (f.t. + bl.), [1]–118,
2 pp. blank, [1]–167 + bl.
Copy: T.C.D. 25 ee 23.

**
*

Gulliveriana

1215. Lemuel Gulliver's Travels Into Several Remote Nations Of The
World. Compendiously methodized, for publick Benefit; with Observations
and Explanatory Notes throughout. &c. London: Printed in the Year
MDCCXXVI. — 8vo; frontisp., general t. + bl., 2 pp. *Verses,* 1–29, 3 pp. advs.;
1–32; 1–32; 1–28; 16 pp. advs. (Curll). [Each of the four sections, called 'Keys',
has a special title.]
Ralph Straus, *The Unspeakable Curll,* 1927, p. 283 says that *The Evening Post,*
Sept. 21, 1727 has this advertisement: *A Compleat Key to Gulliver's Travels.* A
New Impression. [This is probably the above, after the four 'Keys' had first
appeared separately.] — These *Keys* (without the frontisp., the general title, and
the 2 pp. of *Verses,* and the 16 pp. advs. at the end) are sometimes found bound
up with the genuine *Travels,* one at the end of each of the four *Parts.* It seems
that this practice first began with the B edition (No. 291, *ante*).
Dublin ed.: A Key, Being Observations And Explanatory Notes, Upon The
Travels Of Lemuel Gulliver. &c. London Printed, and Re-printed in Dublin,
for G. Risk &c., MDCCXXVII. — 12mo; 2 pp., 1–17 + bl. [This is the first
'Key'.]
The Brobdingnagians. &c. [same imprint] — 12mo; 1–22. [This is the second
'Key'.] — I have not seen the third and fourth; were they ever reprinted in
Dublin?
Copies: Penn.

1216. Gulliver Decypher'd: Or Remarks On a late Book, intitled, Travels
Into Several Remote Nations of the World. &c. London: J. Roberts. —

8vo (in fours); π^3, a^4, B–G^4, π^1 — 2 pp. (h.t. + bl.), 2 pp. (f.t. + bl.), V–XII (Prefatory Discourse concerning Decyphering), 2 pp. advs., 1–49 + bl. — Copies: U.L.C., and B.M. C 116 b 2 (1). — [An attack on Swift, Pope, and Arbuthnot.]

The Second Edition, with a complete Key: The same printing, only the leaves bearing h.t. and f.t. have been removed, and replaced by a double leaf bearing the new title and *The Key* (referring to "Gulliver Decypher'd" itself, not to "Gulliver's Travels").

Copy: B.M. 12613 bb 12.

1217. The Blunder of all Blunders, On the Wonder of all Wonders. Or, Gulliver devour'd by Butterflies: Or, the Fops Observation on Lilliput, &c. Dublin: Printed in the Year 1726. &c. — Folio; 1 page (2 columns) — Copy: B.M. 839 m 23 (154).

1218. A Letter From A Clergyman to his Friend, With an Account of the Travels Of Capt. Lemuel Gulliver: &c. London: A. Moore, M.DCC.XXVI. — 8vo (in fours); [A]–B^4, C^3 — 2 pp. (t. + bl.), 3–22 — Copy: B.M. C 116 b 2 (2), Penn.

1219. For '*Gulliver's Travels*, Vol. III, 1727', see No. 292, *ante.*

1220. The Devil to pay at St. James's, &c. London, A. Moore, MDCCXXVII. — Sm. 4to; 1–15 + bl. (pp. 14 and 15 misnumbered 12 and 9). — Contains a reference to Swift and Gulliver. Copy: Penn.

1221. Memoirs Of The Court of Lilliput. Written by Captain Gulliver. – – – – – Published by Lucas Bennet – – – – London: J. Roberts. M.DCC.XXVII. — 8vo (in fours); [A]–K^4 — 2 pp. (t. + bl.), III–VIII, 1–159 + bl. — Copy: B.M. — [Lucas Bennet = Mrs. Eliza Heywood?].

Second ed.: – – – – The Second Edition. – – – – [Same title and collation (same printing) as those of the first ed.] — Copy: Forster.

Dublin ed.: – – – – – – Dublin: S. P. for George Risk &c., MDCCXXVII. — 16mo; I–V + bl., 1–64, 1 p. advs. + bl. — Copy: Nat. Libr. Dublin.

1222. A Voyage To Cacklogallinia: With a Description of the Religion, Policy, Customs and Manners, of that Country. By Captain Samuel Brunt. London: J. Watson. 1727. — 8vo; frontisp., 2 pp., 1–167 + bl. — This is a satire on the *South Sea Bubble*, and an imitation of *Gulliver's Travels*.

Republished with an introduction by Marjorie Nicolson, for the Facsimile Text Society, New York, 1940. For German translations, see No. 54.

Another German translation: Reise des Capitain Samuel Brunt nach Kaklogallinien und in den Mond. Nach dem Englischen des Swift frei übersetzt. Berlin, 1799. bei Karl August Nicolai, Sohn, &c. — 12mo; 1–158. — Copy: Preuszische Staatsbibl., Berlin.

Russian translation: Moskwa, University Printinghouse, N. Nowikow, 1788. — 8vo; [1]–246. — Copy: Penn.

1224. Several Copies Of Verses On Occasion of Mr. Gulliver's Travels. Never before Printed. London: Benj. Motte. MDCCXXVII. — 8vo; 1–30. — Contains 4 poems. Copy: Penn.

Second issue: The same as the first, with 4 pp. added, to be inserted between pp. 16 and 17. These 4 pp. are numbered 17, 14, 15, 16. Catchword on the fourth page is 'To'. — Contains 5 poems. [For these Verses included in *Gulliver's Travels*, 2nd ed. 1727 (8vo) and 3rd ed. 1727–31 (12mo), see note before No. 289, and Nos. 293–4, *ante*.]

Dublin ed.: Poems Occasion'd by Reading the Travels Of Captain Lemuel Gulliver, Explanatory And Commendatory. Dublin: J. Hyde, 1727. — 12mo; 1–16. — Contains 4 poems.

Another ed.: Poems occasioned by Reading the Travels of Captain Lemuel Gulliver, Explanatory and Commendatory. — Very large folio; 1 page (3 columns). — Contains 4 poems.

1225. The Totness Address, Versified, With The Original Address, as presented to his Majesty. &c. Dublin: George Faulkner, 1727. — Folio; 2 pages. [The 'Original Address' is an avowal of loyalty to King George I by the people of Totnes, Devon.]

Another ed.: – – – – – – – London: H. Whitridge. M.DCC.XXVII. — Folio; 1–11 + bl. — The B.M. (163 m 62) has a 4th ed. of this, 1727; and one of Maggs's catalogues mentions a 6th ed. Whitridge, folio, 1727.

Also in: Poems On Several Occasions. London: Printed for the Author, And sold by L. Gulliver &c., 1729. — 2 vols., 8vo. — 'The Totness Address Versified' is in Vol. II, pp. 137–45. [Same printing only different titles: Poems On Several Occasions. In Two Volumes. By Mr. Joseph Mitchell. Vol. I. [Vol. II.] London: Harmen Noorthouck &c. M.DCC.XXXII.]

There is a 'Second Part' [1739]. — See No. 1250, *post*.

1226. The Totness Address Transversed by Capt. Gulliver, 1727. — Cf. R. Straus, *The Unspeakable Curll*, 284.

1227. Two Lilliputian Odes: The First, On the Famous Engine &c. The Second, Inviting a Bookseller, &c. London: S. Pigmy, for Tom. Thumb, 1727. — 8vo; 1–24.

1228. A Lilliputian Ode On King George the IId's and Queen Caroline's happy Accession to the Throne. Printed by J. Gowan &c., 1727. — Folio; 1 page.

1229. The Little Beaus Speech To His Ex——y the Lord Lieu—t, And Lady C—R—T, On Their Late Arrival. Paraphras'd. &c. John Little, 1727. — Folio; 1 page. [In so-called Lilliputian verse.]

Cf. Elr. Ball, *Swift's Verse*, 234.

1230. A Poem to his Majesty King George II on the present State of Affairs in England &c. By the Rev. Dr. J. Swift, Dean of St. Patrick's, Dublin. Dublin: Little George Faulkner 1727. [In so-called Lilliputian verse.]

Cf. Elr. Ball, *Swift's Verse*, 235; Wilde, *The Closing Years of Dean Swift's Life*, 1849, p. 174.

1231. Seasonable Reflections Address'd To the Citizens of Dublin, by Captain Gulliver. London: Printed, and Dublin Re-printed, George Faulkner, 1727. — Folio; 1 page. — Copy: T. C. D. — Cf. Herbert Davis, *The Drapier's Letters*, 1935, p. 333.

1232. A Cursory View Of The History of Lilliput For these last forty three Years, &c. London: A. Moore. MDCCXXVII. — 8vo; 1–24.

1233. The Anatomist Dissected: &c. By Lemuel Gulliver, Surgeon and Anatomist to the Kings of Lilliput and Blefuscu, and Fellow of the Academy of Sciences in Balnibarbi. &c. Westminster: A. Campbell, &c. 1727. — 8vo; 2 pp., 1–34.

Second ed.: – – – – The Second Edition. – – – – – – Same title and collation as those of the first ed.

1234. An Account of the State of Learning In The Empire of Lilliput. &c. Faithfully Transcribed out of Captain Lemuel Gulliver's General Description of the Empire of Lilliput, mention'd in the 69th Page of the First Volume of his Travels. London: J. Roberts. MDCCXXVIII. — 8vo (in fours); π^4, B–D^4, E^3 — 2 pp. (h.t. + bl.), 2 pp. (f.t. + bl.), 5–37 + bl. — Copy: B.M. 12331 bbb 42 (3).

1235. The Masquerade, A Poem. &c. By Lemuel Gulliver, Poet Laureat to the King of Lilliput. London, J. Roberts, and A. Dodd. MDCCXXVIII. — 8vo; 4 pp., 1–11 + bl.

1236. A Lullaby For the D – – n of St. P – – ks: Or, The D – – n fed with his own Spoon. &c. An Huze: Or, The D – – n's Answer To The Lullaby. &c. Brobdignagg Printed, by Lamuel Hnhmyontrams, Printer to his Majesty of Laputa. — Folio; 1 page. — Copy: U. L. C. [The Bradshaw Catalogue dates this 1728, Elr. Ball, *Swift's Verse*, 290, 385–8, says 1734.] — Written in derision of Swift and Delany.

Also in: The Trader's Garland, Composed Of Five Excellent New Songs. I. – – – – II. – – – – III. – – – – IV. The answer from the B— to the D – – – V. The D— Reply to the B—. Licensed and entered according tn [*sic*] order. — 16mo; 1–8. [IV and V are the pieces meant.]

1237. The Lilliputian Widow. A Poem Address'd to the Chester-Ladies. London, John Brown, 1729. — 12mo; 1–24.

1238. Le Nouveau Gulliver, Ou Voyage De Jean Gulliver, Fils Du Capitaine Gulliver. Traduit d'un Manuscrit Anglois, Par Mr. l'Abbé de L. D. F. Tome I. [II.] A Paris, Chez La veuve Clouzier Et François le Breton. M.DCC.XXX. — 12mo; 32 pp., 1–262, 6 pp.; and 8 pp., 1–259 + bl. — Copy: own. — This is an imitation of the original *Travels*, by Pierre-François Guyot Desfontaines. Copy: Penn.

Another ed.: Practically the same titles. — 12mo; 22 pp., 1–230; and 4 pp., 1–227 + bl. — Copy: Penn.

Another ed.: – – – – – – A Amsterdam, Aux dépens de la Compagnie. M.DCC.XXX. — 12mo; 4 pp., 24 pp., 1–204; and 4 pp., 4 pp., 1–190. — Copy: Penn.

English translation: The Travels Of Mr. John Gulliver, Son to Capt. Lemuel Gulliver. Translated from the French, By J. Lockman. Vol. I. [II.] London: Sam. Harding. MDCCXXXI. — 12mo; frontisp., 6 pp., I–IV, 1–10, I–VI, 1–212; and 2 pp., I–IV, 1–198. — Copy: Penn.

Dutch translation: De Nieuwe Gulliver, Of Reize Van Joan Gulliver, Zoon Van Den Kapitein Gulliver. Uit het Fransch vertaalt. Eerste Deel. [Twede Deel.] In s'Gravenhage, By Isaac Van Der Kloot, MDCCXXXI. — 12mo; frontisp., 34 pp., 1–232; and frontisp., 4 pp., 7–219 + bl. — Copy: own.

German translation: Der Neue Gulliver, oder Die Reise J. Gullivers, Sohnes des Capitain Lemuel Gullivers, Aus einem Engländischen MSSt. ehedem in die Frantzösische Sprache übersetzet durch den Herrn Abt de Fontenelle, und numehr bestmöglichst verteutschet von Selimantes. Erster und Andrer Theil. Hamburg, Gedruckt und verlegt von seel. Thomas von Wierings Erben bey der Börse, im güldnen A, B, C. 1731. Ist auch in Leipzig bey Philip Hertel zu bekommen. — 12mo; frontisp., 44 pp. (the last bearing a large number of "Errata Typographica"), 1–318. — I saw this copy in private hands.

Another ed. of this German translation, also 1731, distinguishable i.a. by the following differences in the title-page: (1) 'Französische' has no *t* (2) 'nunmehr' with an *n* (3) comma after 'Erben' (4) ABC. 1731. (5) Ist auch in Leipzig in Hertels

Handlung zu bekommen. The collation is the same, but the 44th page (before the text) is blank. — Copies: B.M., and Penn.

Another (earlier) German translation: In the *Vorrede des Teutschen Uebersetzers*, dated March 6, 1731 in both the editions just mentioned, the translator speaks of another translation which appeared "ausser Mesz-zeit, zu Berlin, Frankfurt, Leipzig und Altona." Besides being a different work from what the title indicates, it shows numerous errors and omissions, of which several examples are given. "Ob nun eine solche Traduction Wohlgerathen heissen kônne, wie dem Hrn. Verfasser des gelehrten Articuls in dem Hamburgischen Corres-pondenten sub. 26 Jan. zu schreiben gefallen hat, daran darf nicht erst ein eifriger Cartesianer zweifeln." Apparently this poor translation belongs to the end of 1730.

French translation: Voyages De Jean Gulliver, Fils Du Capitaine Gulliver, Traduits d'un Manuscrit Anglais, Par l'Abbé Des Fontaines. Édition ornée de douze Gravures. Tome Troisième. [Tome Quatrième.] A Paris, Chez Billois &c. 1813. — Sm. 12mo (in sixes); 4 pp., 1–4, V–XIV, 1–188; and 4 pp., 1–175 + bl. (four plates, two to each vol.). — These two volumes form part of the edition "Voyages De Gulliver", 1813 (No. 401, *ante*). Copy: Penn.

French translation: Le Nouveau Gulliver, Ou Voyage De Jean Gulliver, Fils Du Capitaine Gulliver. Tome Premier. [Tome Deuxième.] Paris. Lebigre Frères &c. 1833. — 16mo (in eights); h.t., frontisp., f.t., 1–145 + bl.; and h.t., frontisp., f.t., 1–124. Copy: Penn.

1239. An Excellent New Ballad On The Wedding of Pritty Miss S – – lly to Jolly Old J – – – o. By Captain Gulliver. Xʳ· 2021 [or 3031 (?) – copy in B.M. is close-cropped] AD 1730. — Folio; 1 page.

1240. A Letter From Martin Gulliver, To George Faulkner, Printer. &c. Printed in the Year MDCCXXX. — 16mo size; no signatures — 2 pp. (t. + bl.), [3]–8.
Copy: Forster 8562.

1241. Threnodia: Or, An Elegy On the unexpected and unlamented Death Of The Censor: &c. Written Originally by Martin Gulliver, &c. Printed in the Year 1730. — 12mo; 1–8.

1242. The Censoriad: A Poem. Written Originally by Martin Gulliver. (see No. 690, *ante*).

1243. The Heraldiad; A Satyr upon a certain Philosopher. &c. By Martin Gulliver. &c. Printed in the Year, 1730. — Folio; 1 page.

1244. The Asiniad: A Second Satire upon a certain Wooden-Man revived by Martin Gulliver. Printed in the Year 1730.
8 pp. in verse.
Copy: Barry Brown — see his List No. 31A.

1245. The Art of Beauing: In Imitation Of Horace's Art of Poetry. Addres'd To a Certain Lord. By Martinus Gulliverianus. &c. The Third Edition. London Printed, And Dublin: Reprinted by J. Watts &c. M,DCC,XXX. — 12mo; 6 pp., 1–17 + bl.

1246. The Proctor's Banquet: A Pindarick Ode. By Martin Gulliver. Dublin: Printed in the Year, MDCCXXXI. — 12mo; 1–8. — I saw this copy in private hands.

1247. The Gentleman's Magazine.

Vol. III, 1733, pp. 463–5, contains: The Maxims of the Laputan Projectors Applied to the British Parliament.

Vol. VIII, June 1738, to Vol. XVI, Oct. 1746, have from time to time: Political News from Lilliput. Continued for 8 years, 1738–45.

Samuel Johnson: Debates In Magna Lilliputia (see Gosse, Hist. E. L. 18th cent. 285).

Vol. IX, 1739, pp. 55–9, contains: A Defence of Mr. Gulliver's Voyages. Truth Asserted, or, A Demonstration that the Relations in Mr. Gulliver's Voyages are No Fiction. By Jonathan Wagstaff.

1248. A Poem Upon Musick. By Mr. John Waldron. Dublin: James Hoey, 1733. — 8vo; I–VI, 2 pp., 9–24. — Pages 19–20 are a dedication to Swift; pp. 21–4 are: The Hoop-Peticoat, In Lilliputian Verse. Written by Mr. John Waldron, in immitation of D—n S—t. &c.

1249. Critical Remarks On Capt. Gulliver's Travels. By Doctor Bantley. &c. Printed at Cambridge, and sold by L. G. in London, MDCCXXXV. — 8vo; 10 pp., 1–33 + bl.

1250. The second Part of Totness Address. — Folio; 1 page. — [This is a satirical ballad on the speech of King George II at the opening of Parliament, Feb. 1, 1739] — Cf. No. 1225, ante.

Another issue (different title): The Speech Englished, A New Ballad. — Folio; 1 page.

1251. Nicolai Klimii Iter Subterraneum Novam Telluris Theoriam Ac Historiam Quintae Monarchiae Adhuc Nobis Incognitae Exhibens E Bibliotheca B. Abelini. Hafniae & Lipsiae, Sumptibus Iacobi Preussii. MDCCXLI. — 12mo; bl. leaf, frontisp., t. + bl., map, 1–380. Two more plates. [Inspired by *Gulliver's Travels*. The author is Ludwig Holberg.]

Danish, German, French, and Dutch translations in 1741, English in 1742.

German copy: Penn; Dutch copies 1744 and 1761: Penn.

1252. Lezione su D'un Vitello a due teste Dell' Accademico Delle Scienze, Colle Note Di Lemuel Gulliver. — 4to; 4 pp., 1–44. — [This is a satire on: "Lezione Di Michelangiolo Ruberti Dell' Accademia delle Scienze Sulla Testa Monstruosa D'Un Vitello. Napoli MDCCXXXXV."]

1253. The Pleasures and Felicity Of Marriage, Display'd in Ten Books: Containing &c. By Lemuel Gulliver. The Second Edition. London, J. Robinson. 1745. — 12mo; frontisp., 2 pp., I–XII, 1–84. Ten plates.

1254. Le Micromégas de Mr. De Voltaire, &c. A Londres, J. Robinson et W. Meyer, M.DCC.LII. — 12mo; 2 pp., 1–257 + bl. — This was inspired by *Gulliver's Travels*.

German translation: Mikromegas. aus dem Französischen des Herrn von Voltaire übersetzt. &c. Dresden, Georg Conrad Walther, 1752. — 12mo; 12 pp., 1–52.

English translation: Micromegas: A Comic Romance. &c. London: D. Wilson and T. Durham. MDCCLIII. — 12mo; 2 pp., 1–252.

1255. Lilliput. A Dramatic Entertainment. &c. London: Paul Vaillant. MDCCLVII. — 8vo; I–VI, 2 pp., 1–39 (*Epilogue* on verso). — A play founded on *Gulliver's Travels*. By David Garrick.

Also in Vol. 6 of Coll. of Esteemed Farces, 1792.

1256. Baron Munchausen's Narrative Of His Marvellous Travels And Campaigns In Russia. &c. Oxford: Printed for the Editor, &c. MDCCLXXXVI. — 16mo; 4 pp., I–IV, 5–49 + bl. — The author of this imitation of *Gulliver's Travels* is Rudolf Erich Raspe (1737–94). Later editions have altered the title into: 'Gulliver Revived, &c.'
Copy: Penn.
There was also 'A Sequel to the Adventures Of Baron Munchausen, Containing his expedition into Africa. &c. London. H. D. Symonds, and J. Owen. MDCCXCII. — Sm. 8vo; 1–243 + bl. Frontisp. and 19 plates.' — Another ed. 1793; another (New Edition) 1796. English: 1st ed. 1785; 2nd Oxford 1786 (see above); 7th ed. 1793; 8th ed.; 2 vols. sm. 8vo, London, G. Kearsley, 1799–1801 (second part entitled 'A Sequel'); 1810 (chapbook); 1889 (illustrated by A. Crowquill); 1895 (T. Seccombe). German translation (by Gottfried August Bürger), 1786; French, 1787; Dutch, 1790, 1827.

1257. Modern Gulliver's Travels. Lilliput: Being A New Journey To That Celebrated Island. Containing a faithful Account — from 1702 to 1796 &c. By Lemuel Gulliver, Jun. &c. London: T. Chapman, 1796. — 12mo; I–VIII, 1–226. (By H. Whitmore.)

1258. The Flapper. A Periodical Work. Vol. I. From Tuesday, Feb. 2, 1796, to Saturday, Sep. 10, 1797. They forgot several Times what they were about, 'till their Memories were again roused by their Flappers. Gulliver's Voyage to Laputa. Dublin: R. E. Mercier and Co. — Folio; 2 pp., I–II, 1–216. — Vol. II starts with Saturday, Sep. 17, 1796, and ends with Saturday, Feb. 4, 1797 (pp. 1–84). The two volumes contain 75 numbers of 4 pp. each.

1259. Lilliput in Caricature, by Woodward, Pigmy Revels or All alive at Lilliput, London, 1800, 9 plates in Folio, oblong, with hundreds of caricatures of Lilliputians, in colours. [From an antiq. book cat.]

1260. The Liliputian History, Containing A particular Account of the Government, Laws, Customs and Manners of that celebrated Nation, &c. London: W. Tringham &c. [ca. 1800]. — 16mo; frontisp., 2 pp., 1–101 + bl. Ten more plates.

1261. The Voyages and Discoveries of Crusoe Richard Davis, &c. London, S. Fisher (1801). — 12mo; engr. frontisp. — A curious intermingling in the style of Rob. Crusoe, Gulliver's Travels (i.a. the floating island), and Peter Wilkins.

1262. Cabinet of Lilliput. Instructive Stories; &c. London, J. Harris &c. 1802. — 10 vols., 32mo. — [contains nothing by Swift].

1263. The Eo-Nauts, Or The Spirit Of Delusion, &c. Edited By Lemuel Gulliver, Esq. &c. London: C. Chapple. 1813. — 8vo; col. frontisp., I–VII + bl., 1–48.

1264. A Voyage To Locuta; &c. By Lemuel Gulliver, Jun. &c. London: J. Hatchard. 1818. — 12mo; I–VII + bl., 9–47 (*Errata* on verso). Frontisp. and five plates.

1265. Gulliver's Last Voyage, Describing Ballymugland, Or The Floating Island. Second Edition. London: William Cole. 1825. — 8vo; 1–79 + bl.

1266. Sequel To Gulliver's Travels. An Eulogy. By Lemuel Gulliver. &c. London: J. Jaques &c. 1830. — 8vo; 1–16.

1267. Reize Naar Het Land Der Boggdhufz. Onuitgegeven Fragment Van Lemuel Gulliver, In Het Licht Gegeven Door Henrik Van Brakel. Amsterdam, Wed. R. Stemvers, 1848. — 8vo; 8 pp., 1–39 + bl. — Copies: Bibl. Royale, Brussels, and Penn.

1268. Illustrated Memoir Of An Eventful Expedition Into Central America; &c. Described By John L. Stephens, Esq., And Other Travellers. &c. London: R. S. Francis. 1853. — 12mo; frontisp., 2 pp., I–VIII, 1–36. Five plates, and four illustrations in the text. [The title on the cover is: "The History Of The Aztec Lilliputians".] — Copy: Penn.

1269. The Auto-Biography Of Master Henry Bundy, Known As The King Of The Lilliputians, &c. G. & H. Gilmour, Winchester. [1856]. — 16mo; 1–8. — Copy: Penn.

1270. O Gulliver Dos Meninos, Augmentado Com Outras Viagens: Obra escrita para seu recreio Por José Da Fonseca. Pariz Vᵃ J.-P. Aillaud, Guillard E Cᵃ, 1864. — 12mo; 4 pp., 1–196. Two coloured plates. — Copy: Bibl. Nat. Paris.

1271. Tweede Reis naar Lilliput. Onuitgegeven vervolg op "Gulliver's Reizen." &c. Utrecht. Firma P. H. Reyers (H. de Vroede). 1899. — 8vo.

1272. Gulliver Joe By Jonathan Quick Dean of St. Rattrick's Isbister & Company Limited London 1903 — 8vo; 1–108, 4 pp. advs. — Illustrated. [A political satire.]

1273. The Monthly Review Vol. XII. July–September 1903 London: John Murray — Very large 8vo; 8 pp., 1–194, &c. — Contains: Gulliver's Last Voyage (pp. 1–17). [A satire on Chamberlain.]
Reprint: Gulliver's Last Voyage Reprinted from The Monthly Review, July 1903 — 8vo; 1–42.

1274. The Land Of Unreason. A Satire. By Dean Gulliver. &c. London: Simpkin, Marshall & Co., Limited. MCMV. — 8vo; 6 pp., 1–148.

1275. Laputa Revisited By Gulliver Redivivus In 1905 London Hirschfeld Brothers Ltd. MCMV — 8vo; 8 pp., 1–124.
Third ed.: – – – – MCMVI — 8vo; 6 pp., 1–120, 2 pp. advs.

**

1423. Swift's Description Of A Storm, In The Voyage To Brobdingnag. &c. – – – – copied from Sturmy. ("Compleat Mariner", pp. 17, 18, in his "Mariner's Magazine." Fol. 1669.) Both writers are quoted below. E. H. Knowles. — Single 4to leaf, printed on one side. Two columns, the first headed 'Swift', the second 'Sturmy'. At foot: Printed At The "Advertiser" Office, Castle End, Kenilworth. [The B.M. catalogue dates it 1868. *Notes & Queries* of March 7, 1868, 4th Series, Vol. I, 223, contains a short question by E. H. Knowles, Kenilworth, whether anyone has yet noted the above similarity.]

1450. Quellen Zu Dean Jonathan Swift's 'Gulliver's Travels' (1727), by E. Honncher, in *Anglia*, 1888, pp. 397–456.

1458. Quellen Zu Swift's Gulliver (diss. Rostock), von Theodor Borkowsky, Halle A. S., Ehrhardt Karras, 1893 — 8vo; 4 pp., 1–45 + bl. — Also in *Anglia*, 1893, pp. 345–89 (also as a separate offprint).

1459. A criticism of Borkowsky's Quellen Zu Swift's Gulliver, by O. Glöde, in *Englische Studien* 1893, pp. 461–3.

1471. Swift's Gulliver und seine franzosischen Vorganger, von Dr. Paul Thierkopf, in *Dreiszigster Jahresbericht* uber die Guericke = Schule, Magdeburg, E. Baenschjun., 1899 (pp. 2, 1–26).
See further Landa's List 1900, etc.

SECTION V

SEPARATE WORKS

✦✦✦

467. To The / Athenian Society. / *Moor-park*, Feb. 14, 1691.
Ode. / To The / Athenian Society.

Printed in:
The / Supplement / To The / Fifth Volume / Of The / Athenian
Gazette; / Resolving / All the most Nice and Curious Questions
propo- / sed by the Ingenious of either Sex. / To which is prefixt /
The New Project concerning the / Natural & Artificial Rarities /
Of / England. / As Also / An Ode / To The / Athenian Society.
/ — / London, / Printed for *John Dunton* at the Raven in the *Poultrey*,
where is to / be had the *First, Second, Third, Fourth*, and *Fifth
Volumes* of the / *Athenian Gazette*, (and the *Supplements* to 'em)
compleating the / Entire Set for the Year 1691. (or single ones to
this time.)

[Title in double-lined frame.]
Folio; π^2, a 1, B–G^2, H 1 — 2 pp. (t. + bl.), 2 pp. (The Preface to the
Fifth Supplement), 1 (To The Athenian Society — *Moor-park*, Feb. 14, 1691;
signed *Jonathan Swift.*), 2–6 (Ode. To the Athenian Society.), 7–26 (The
Supplement etc.), 27 (misnumbered 26)–28 (An Account &c.).
Copies: B.M. Burney 103A, and Penn.
It would seem that the 'Ode' was also published separately.
Dr. J. Starkey kindly drew my attention to his copy of John Dunton's
magazine *The Complete Library: or, News for the Ingenious*, May 1692–Dec.
1692, London, Printed for John Dunton at the Raven in the Poultrey, 1692,
sm. 4to, which on p. 350, the last page of the Sept. issue, has this advertise-
ment: "Books newly Printed for John Dunton at the Raven in the Poultrey:
An Ode to the Athenian Society." I have not seen or heard of a copy.
John Dunton edited *The Athenian Gazette* (started in 1689), afterwards
called *The Athenian Mercury* (from March 24, 1690–91 onwards). In 1703 *The
Athenian Oracle* appeared; it is a selection from the *Athenian Mercuries:* 1st ed.
1703, 2 vols.; 2nd ed. 1704, 3 vols.; Vol. I, 1706, 3rd ed.; *Supplement*, 1710
(see below); 3rd ed. 1728, 4 vols.
Letter and *Ode* reprinted (pp. 111–19) in:
A Supplement To The Athenian Oracle: Being A Collection Of the
Remaining Questions And Answers In The Old Athenian Mercuries. – – – –
To which is prefix'd The History of the Athenian Society, And an Essay
upon Learning. – – – London: Printed for Andrew Bell – – – – 1710.
8vo; 6 pp. (bl. + frontisp., explanation frontisp. + The Publisher to the
Reader, t. + bl.), 1–76 (History), 77–110 (Essay), 111–19 (Swift's Letter +
Ode), 119–487 (questions and answers), 1 p. blank, 14 pp. (Table + advs.),
2 pp. blank.
Copy: Penn.

468. *Reprinted* (different title), without the Letter:

Sphinx: | A | Poem, | Ascrib'd to Certain | *Anonymous Authors.* | — | By the Rev'd. Dean S—t. | — | *Cedite Romani Scriptores, cedite Graii.* | — | [ornament] | — | *Dublin:* | Printed in the Year 1724. 5.

> [Title within double-lined frame.]
> 12mo size; no signatures — 2 pp. (t. + bl.), 3–14. — Signed at foot of p. 14: Jonathan Swift.
> Copy: B.M. C 71 bb 15 (6).

Temple's Letters, Miscellanea, and Memoirs, edited by Swift

469. To His | Most Sacred Majesty | William III. | King of *England, Scot-* | *land, France,* and | *Ireland,* &c. | These Letters of Sir *W. Tem-* | *ple* having been left to my | Care, they are most hum- | bly presented to Your | Majesty by | *Your Majesty's most dutiful* | *and obedient Subject.* | *Jonathan Swift.* | The | Publisher's Epistle | To The | Reader.

> These two pieces occur in Vol. I of:
> Letters Written by Sir W. Temple, Bart. And Other Ministers of State, Both at Home and Abroad. – – – – In Two Volumes. – – – – Published by Jonathan Swift Domestick Chaplain to his Excellency the Earl of Berkeley, one of the Lords Justices of Ireland. London: J. Tonson, – – – – and A. and J. Churchil – – – – and R. Simpson – – – – MDCC. Two vols. 8vo; frontisp. portrait of Temple, 10 pp., 1–520; 2 pp., 1–360. — There are also copies printed on thick paper.
> Copy: Penn.

470. *Also in the French translation:*

> Lettres De Mr. Le Chevalier Guill. Temple, Et Autres Ministres D'Etat, Tant en Angleterre que dans les Pais Etrangers. – – – – publices par Jonathan Swift, Chapelain de son Exc. le Comte de Berkeley, un des Lords Regens du Royaume d'Irlande. – – – Tome I. [Tome II.]. A La Haye, Chez Henri Van Bulderen – – – – M.DCC. Two vols. 12mo; 12 pp., 1–470 (286–7 and 379–[382] repeated in numbering); 2 pp., 3–384.

471. *Also in another issue of the preceding two volumes:*

> Collations and titles the same as those of the preceding edition, except for the imprint:

– – – – | A La Haye, | Chez Jean van Duren, Marchand | Libraire dans le Poote, près du Plyn. | — | M.DCC.XI.

> Copy: B.M. 10920 b 8.

472. The | Preface.

> This occurs in:
> Letters To The King, The Prince of Orange, The Chief Ministers of State, And Other Persons. By Sir W. Temple, Bart. Being the Third and Last

Volume. Published by Jonathan Swift, D. D. London: Printed for Tim. Goodwin – – – – and Benj. Tooke – – – – 1703.

8vo; 8 pp., 1–550.
Copy: Penn.

473. The Publisher to the / Reader.

This occurs in:
Miscellanea. The Third Part. – – – – By the late Sir William Temple, Bar. Published by Jonathan Swift, A. M. Prebendary of St. Patrick's, Dublin. London, Printed for Benjamin Tooke – – – – 1701.

8vo; 8 pp., 1–368.
Copy: Penn.
There is a Dutch translation of the above volume: *Nagelaten Schriften Van Den Ridder W. Temple*, Utrecht, Anthony Schouten, 1704, 12mo, but though the *Bericht Aan Den Lezer* mentions Swift's name, it is not the translation of his *The Publisher to the Reader*.

474. The / Preface.

This occurs in:
Memoirs. Part III. – – – By Sir William Temple Baronet. – – – –. Publish'd by Jonathan Swift, D.D. London: Printed for Benjamin Tooke – – – MDCCIX.

8vo; 2 pp., I–XIV, 1–173 + bl., 1–43, 7 pp. advs.
Copy: Penn.

475. *Also in another edition:*
Memoirs. Part III. – – – – By Sir William Temple Baronet. – – – – Publish'd by Jonathan Swift, D.D. London: Printed and Sold by the Booksellers of London and Westminister, 1709.

8vo; 1–37, 10 pp. + bl.

476. *Also in the French translation:*
Nouveaux Memoires Du Chevalier Guillaume Temple, – – – – Publiez avec une Preface par le Docteur Jonathan Swift. On Y A Joint La Vie Et Le Caractere Du Chevalier G. Temple par un de ses Amis particuliers. – – – A La Haye, Chez Jean van Duren. Adrien Moetjens. M.C.CC.XXIX.

12mo; [I]–LXXX, 1–172.

477. Starting with 'The Works Of Sir William Temple, Bart.', 2 vols., folio, 1720, these Prefaces, &c. were also printed in succeeding editions of Temple's Works.

*_**

478. A / Discourse / Of The / *Contests* and *Dissensions* / Between The / Nobles and the Commons / In *Athens* and *Rome*, / With The / Consequences they had upon both those / States. / — / —— *Si tibi vera videtur* / *Dede manus*; *& si falsa est accingere contra*. Lucret. / — / London: / Printed for *John Nutt* near *Stationers-Hall*. 1701.

4to; A–H⁴ — 2 pp. (t. + bl.), 3–62, 2 pp. blank.
Copy: Penn.

Another issue or edition:

The same title and collation as the first issue, but partly a different printing. The difference is at once visible from the fact that the first issue has the rules on the title-page both in two parts, the second both in one. There are several more differences, only a few of the more characteristic of which are:

P. 9, l. 7, first issue: 'be worth nothing.'; second issue: 'be worth remarking.'

P. 38, first issue: no side-note to l. 4; second issue: side-note 'De bello civili, l. 1.'

Pp. 41 and 44, first issue: page numbers in square brackets; second issue: in round brackets.

For a fuller treatment, see Dr. H. Teerink, *Swift's Discourse Contests Athens and Rome*, 1701, in *The Library*, 5th Series, Vol. IV, No. 3, Dec. 1949, 201–5.

Reprinted (verso of Ee — recto of Gg 3 — pp. 210–29) *in:*

A / Collection / Of / State Tracts / Publish'd during the / Reign / Of / King William III. / Vol. III. and Last. / *In which is Inserted* (*being now first printed from the Manuscript*) / A Vindication of the late Revolution, in Answer to / two Memorials, and a Protestation against the Peace of *Res-* / *wick*, and to other Papers publish'd in K. *James's* Name. / With A / Table of the several Tracts in this Volume, / And an Alphabetical Index of Matters. / London, / Printed in the Year M.DCC.VII.

[Title in black and red.]
Copy: T.C.D. (RR. cc. 14).
The title halfway p. 210 reads:

A Discourse of the Contests *and* Dis- / sensions *between the Nobles and the Commons in* / Athens *and* Rome, *with the Consequences they* / *had upon both those States.*

Another edition:

A / Discourse / Of The / *Contests and Dissentions* / Between the / Nobles and the Commons / In / *Athens* and *Rome,* / With The / Consequences they had upon both those / States. / — / — *Si tibi vera videtur* / *Dedemanus*; *& si falsa est accingere contra.* Lucret. / — / [ornament] / — / Printed in the Year, 1728.

8vo (in fours); [A]–H⁴ — 2 pp. (h.t. + bl.), 2 pp. (f.t. + bl.), 1–59 + bl. — D 2 wrongly signed C 2.
Copies: New York Public Libr., and Am. Antiq. Soc. Worcester (Mass.).
This edition was printed at Boston (Mass.), and made by direction of Governor William Burnet (cf. Evans 3108: Thomas-Price).

Contemporary Criticism

1020. The Sourse Of Our Present Fears Discover'd, &c. The Second Edition. London, B. Bragg, 1706. — 12mo; 8 pp., 1–94. — Pp. 48–75 contain a criticism

The W--df-r Prophecy.

ABOUT three Months ago at *W--nd--r*, a poor Knight's Widow was buried in the Cloyfters. In digging the Grave, the Sexton ftruck againft a fmall Leaden Coffer, about half a Foot in length, and four Inches wide. The poor Man expecting he had difcovered a Treafure, opened it with fome difficulty ; but found only a fmall Parchment, rolled up very faft, put into a Leather Cafe; which Cafe was tied at the top, and fealed with a St. *George*, the Impreffion on black Wax, very rude and *Gothick*. The Parchment was carried to a Gentleman of Learning, who found in it the following Lines, written in a black Old *Englifh* Letter, and in the Orthography of the Age, which feems to be about Two hundred Years ago. I made a fhift to obtain a Copy of it; but the Tranfcriber, I find, hath in many Parts alter'd the Spelling to the Modern way. The Original, as I am informed, is now in the Hands of the Ingenious Dr. *W*——, F. R. S. where, I fuppofe, the Curious will not be refufed the Satisfaction of feeing it.

The Lines feem to be a fort of Prophefie, and written in Verfe, as old Prophefies ufually are, but in a very Hobling kind of Meafure. Their Meaning is very dark, if it be any at all; of which the Learned Reader can judge better than I : However it be, feveral Perfons were of Opinion, that they deferved to be Publifhed, both as they difcover fomewhat of the Genius of a former Age, and may be an Amufement to the prefent.

When a holy black Suede, the Son of Bob,
With a Saint at his Chin, and a Seal in his Fob ;
Shall not fee one New-Years-day in that Year,
Then let old Englond make good Chear :
Windfor and Briftow then shall be
Jóyned together in the Low-Countree.
Then shall the tall black Daventry Bird
Speak againft Peace right many a Word;
And fome shall admire his conyng Witt,
For many good Groats his Tongue shall flitt :
But fpight of the Harpy that crawls on all four,
There shall be Peace, pardie, and War no more.
But Englond muft cry aack and well a Day,
If the Stick be taken from the dead Sea.
And dear Englond, if ought I underftond,
Beware of Carrots from Northumberlond.
Carrots fown Thyn a deep root may get,
If fo be they are in Sommer fet :
Their Conyngs mark thou, for I have been told,
They Affaffine when young, and Poifon when old.
Root out thefe Carrots, O Thou, whofe Name
Is backwards and forwards always the fame ;
And keep clofe to Thee always that Name,
Which backwards and forwards is allmoft the fame.
And Englond wouldft thou be happy ftill,
Bury thofe Carrots under a Hill.

Printed in the Year, 1711.

The Windsor Prophecy (no. 555). Swift's attack on the Duchess of Somerset is known in three early editions, none having priority. This edition shares the black letter with roman for emphasis with another edition from which it differs in type. A third edition is set exclusively in roman. (University of Pennsylvania)

3.ᵈ A N

Hue and Cry

A F T E R

Dr. S⎯⎯T;

Occasion'd by a True and Exact
Copy of Part of his own *Diary,*
found in his Pocket - Book,
wherein he has set down a
faithful Account of himself,
and of all that happen'd to him
for the last Week of his Life.
Thought to be writt by himself, a comical acc.ᵗ

𝔗𝔥𝔢 𝔖𝔢𝔠𝔬𝔫𝔡 𝔈𝔡𝔦𝔱𝔦𝔬𝔫.

L O N D O N:

Printed for *J. Roberts,* near the *Oxford
Arms* in *Warwick-lane.* 1714.
7. August.

An Hue and Cry after Dr. S--t (no. 1081). A witty parody of Swift
emanating from the jubilant Whig pamphleteers upon the death of
Queen Anne on August 1, 1714. (University of Pennsylvania)

of Swift's *Discourse Athens and Rome* (No. 478, *ante*). — I have not seen a copy
of the first ed.

The Third Edition, much Enlarg'd. 1706. — 8vo; 6 pp., 1–92.

***

Bickerstaff Tracts

483. Predictions / For The / Year 1708. / Wherein the Month
and Day of the / Month are set down, the Persons / named, and
the great Actions and / Events of next Year particularly / related,
as they will come to pass. / — / *Written to prevent the People of*
England *from* / *being further impos'd on by vulgar Almanack-* / *makers.*
/ — / *By* Isaac Bickerstaff *Esq*; / = / Sold by *John Morphew* near
Stationers-Hall. / MDCCVIII.

> 8vo (four leaves); A⁴ — 1 p. (title), 2–8.
> Appeared at the end of Jan. 1708.
> Copies: Lambeth 110 B 3 (5), and Penn.

484. *Another edition:*
Predictions for the Year 1708. / Wherein the Month and Day of
the Month are set down, the / Persons named, and the great
Actions and Events of next / Year particulary [*sic*] related, as
they will come to pass. / *Written to prevent People from being further*
Impos'd on by vulgar / *Almanack Makers.* / — / *By* Isaac Bickerstaff,
Esq; / — /

> 4to; A⁴ — 1–8. — Text begins immediately under the title.
> Copy: B.M. 8610 c 16.

485. *Another edition:*
Predictions for the Year 1708. / Wherein the Month and Day of
the Month are set / down, the Persons named, and the great
Actions and / Events of next Year particularly related, as they /
will come to pass. / — / *Written to prevent the People of* England
from being further Im- / *pos'd on by vulgar Almanack-makers.* / — /
By Isaac Bickerstaff, *Esq*; / — /

> 8vo (four leaves); A⁴ — Text begins immediately under the title; pp. 4–5
> in smaller type than the rest.
> At foot of p. 8:

London: Printed and Sold by *Hen. Hills,* in *Black-fry-* / *ars,* near
the Water-side. 1708.

> Copy: Penn.

486. *Another edition:*
Esquire *Bickerstaff*'s / Most strange and wonderful / Predictions
/ For the Year 1708. / Wherein the Month and Day of the Month
are set / down, when several most surprizing Accidents / shall

certainly come to pass, as particularly that | the present *French* King shall Die on the 29th of | *July.* The Pope to Die the 11th of *September.* The | *Dauphin* the *French* King's Son to Die on the 7th of | *May.* That *Partridge* the famous Astrologer is to | Die on 29th of *March.* On the 23d of *May* a fa- | mous Actor of the Play-house will Die a ridiculous | Death suitable to his Vocation. Upon the 26th of | *August* will arrive from *Flanders* such a welcome | Express of Victory, that a Thousand Bonfires will | be made in *London* for Joy of the News, and in the | same Month a noble Admiral will gain immortal | Honour, by obtaining a signal Victory at Sea. On | the 6th of *June* the City of *Paris* will be Burnt down | to the Ground. Towards the end of *August* will be | great Mischief done in *Bartholomew-Fair*, by the | tumbling down of a Booth; with several other | strange Things too tedious here to be related. | — | *Licensed accordiug* [*sic*] *to Order.* | — | *London*, Printed for T. *Wise*, near *Fleet-street*.

8vo size (four leaves); no signatures — 1 p. (title), 2–8. — Pp. 2, 3, and 4 (first half) are in smaller type than the rest.
Copies: Guildhall (Tract 8. 2), and Penn.

487. *Another edition:*
Esquire *Bickerstaff's* | Most Strange and Wonderful | Predictions | For the Year 1708. | Wherein the Month and Day of the Month are set | down, when several most surprizing Accidents shall | certainly come to pass, as particularly that the | present *French* King shall die on the 29th of *July.* | The Pope to die the 11th of *September.* The *Dau-* | *phine* the *French* King's Son to die on the 7th of | *May.* That *P—idge*, the famous Astrologer, is | to die on the 29th of *March.* On the 23d. of *May* | a Famous Actor of the Play-house will die a ridi- | culous Death suitable to his Vo-cation. Upon the | 26th of *August* will arrive from *Flanders*, such a | welcome Express of Victory, that a Thousand | Bonfires will be made in *London* for Joy of the | News: And in the same month a noble Admiral | will gain immortal Honour, by obtaining signal | Victory at Sea. On the 6th of *June* the City of | *Paris* will be burnt down to the Ground. Towards | the End of *August* will be great mischief done in | *Bartholomew-Fair*, by the tumbling down of a *Booth.* | With several other strange things too tedious here | to be Related. | — | *Licensed according to Order.* | — | Printed by *W. B.* 1708.

8vo size; no signatures — 1 p. (title), 2–8.
Copy: Forster 8937 — 19 D 12.

488. *Another edition:*
Esquire *Bickerstaff's* | Most strange and wonderful | Predictions | For the Year, 1708. | Wherein the Month and Day of the Month

are set / down, when several most surprizing Accidents / shall certainly come to pass, as particularly that / the present *French* King shall Die on the 29th of / *July*. The Pope to Die the 11th of *September*. The / *Dauphin* the *French* King's Son to dye on the 7th of / *May*. That *Partridge* the famous Astrologer is to / dye on the 29th of *March*. On the 23d of *May* a fa- / mous Actor of the Play-house will die a ridiculous / death, suitable to his Vocation. Upon the 26th of / *August*, will arrive from *Flanders* such a wel- / come / Express of Victory, that a Thousand Bonfires will / be made in London for Joy of the News, and in the / same Month a Noble Admiral will gain immortal / Honour, by obtaining a signal Victory at Sea. On / the 6th of *June* the City of *Paris* will be burnt down / to the Ground. Towards the end of *August* will be / great Mischief done in Bartholomew-Fair, by the / tumbling down of a Booth; with several other / strange Things too tedious here to be related. / — / Licensed according to Order. / — / Sold by *John Stiles*: 1708.

Sm. 4to; [A]⁴ — 1 p. (title), 2–8.
Copy: Bodl. Ashm. 1819 (26).

489. *Another edition:*
Predictions for the Year 1708. / Giving an Account of all the Remarkable Events that shall happen in *Europe* this / Year; as Battles, Sieges, *&c*. The Month, Day and Hour of the Death of *John* / *Partridge*, Astrologer, Cardinal *Noailles*, Archbishop of *Paris*, the *Dauphine*, / young Prince of *Asturias*, the *Pope*, *French* King and other Princes, Also the un- / timely and Natural Ends of Persons in *London*, Accidents to some Generals, and the / Death of others in Battle, with the Confutation of common Almanack-Makers in / General. By *Isaac Bickerstaff*, Esq;

4to size; π², no signature, no pagination. — Text begins immediately under the title.
At foot of the fourth page:

London Printed: and Reprinted and Sold at the *Union* Coffee-House on Cork-Hill.

Copy: T.C.D. (P.hh 3.9).

490. *Dutch translation:*
Wonderlijke / Prognosticatie / Ofte / Voorsegginge, / Wat in dit Jaar 1708. zal voorvallen. / Waar in de Maand, en den / dag van de Maand uytgedrukt, de Personen / genoemt, en de groote Actien en uitkom- / sten van 't selve Jaar bysonderlyk ver- / haalt wor- den, zoo als deselve sullen / komen te gebeuren. / *Zynde geschreven om het Volk van* Engelant *te waarschouwen, dat / zy door de gemeene*

Almanachmakers niet worden bedrogen. | Door | Isaak Bickerstaff,
Schiltknaap. | [ornament] | In 's Gravenhage, gedrukt by Gillis
van Limburg, | Boekdrukker in de Papestraat, 1708, | *Na de
Engelse Copye*.

> Small 4to; [A]⁴ — 8 pages (no pagination).
> Copy: Kon. Bibl. (pamphlet 15653).

491. *Another Dutch translation:*

Wonderlijke Prognosticatie ofte Voorzegginge, | Wat in dit
Jaar 1708. zal voorvallen: Waar in de Maand, en den dagh van de
| Maand uytgedrukt, de Persoonen genoemt, en de groote Actien
en uytkomsten van | 't zelve Jaar bysonderlyk verhaalt worden,
zoo als de selve sullen komen te gebeuren | Zynde geschreven om
het Volk van Engelant te waarschouwen, dat sy door de ge- |
meene Almanach-makers niet worden bedrogen. Door Isaak Bik-
kerstaf, Schiltknaap.

> Sm. 4to size; no signatures, no pagination, 4 pages. — Text begins
> immediately under the title.
> At foot of the fourth page:

Door Isaak Bickerstaf, Schiltknaap. | Gedrukt, na de Copy van
's Gravenhage, by Gillis van Limburg.

> Copy: Kon. Bibl. (pamphlet 15654).

492. *Another Dutch translation:*

Wonderlyke Prognosticatie ofte Voorzegginge, | Wat in dit
Jaar 1708. zal voorvallen: Waar in de Maand, en den dag van de
Maand uytgedrukt, de Persoonen | genoemt, en de groote Actien
en uytkomsten van 't selve Jaer bysonderlijk verhaald worden,
soo als de selve | sullen komen te gebeuren. Zijnde geschreven om
het Volk van Engelandt te waarschouwen, dat sy door de ge- |
meene Almanach-makers niet worden bedrogen.

> 4to size; A² — 4 unnumbered pages (double columns). — Text begins
> immediately under the title.
> At foot of the fourth page:

[*Under 2ⁿᵈ column only:*] Door Isaak Bickerstaf, Schiltknaap.

[*Under both columns:*] Gedrukt na de Copy van 's Gravenhage,
by Gillis van Limburg.

> Copy: B.M. 3911 aaa 64 (26).

493. *German translation:*

Wundersahmes | Prognosticon | Oder | Prophezeyung | Was in
diesem 1708 ten Jahr geschehen soll. | Wobey nebst dem Monath
auch der eigentli- | che Tag, und bey einigen gar der Ort und die

Stunden / ausgedruckt, die Personen genennet, auch alle sonst vorfallende / grosse Sachen desselben Jahrs specialiter erzehlet sind, / so wie dieselbe kůnfftighin sich zutragen werden / Beschrieben / durch / Isaac Bickerstaff, Edelmann. / — / Nach der zu London gedruckten Copia.

4to; [ )( ]⁴ — 2 pp. (t. + bl.), six unnumbered pages.
Copy: B.M. 594 b 33.
Cf. No. 1021, *post*.

494. An / Answer / To / Bickerstaff. / *Some Reflections upon Mr. Bickerstaff's Predictions for the / Year* MDCCVIII. / By A Person Of Quality.

I have not seen a copy of the original pamphlet, but it was printed in Swift's *Works*, Vol. VIII Part I, 4to ed., 1765, pp. 232–7. Contents and style almost certainly prove it to be by Swift himself. Prof. Davis, *Prose Works*, Vol. II, p. xii, points to an unmistakable allusion to *A Tale of a Tub*, a possible reason for its not having been printed at the time. Internal evidence shows that it was written seven weeks before Partridge's predicted death, i.e. about Feb. 7, 1708; and that the *Predictions* had appeared nine days before that, i.e. at the end of Jan. 1708. It contains an invitation to Partridge to publish an answer, which duly appeared during the next three weeks (see No. 1022, *post*).

495. The / Accomplishment / Of the First of / Mr. *Bickerstaff's* Predictions: / Being an / Account / Of the Death of Mr. / Partrige, / The Almanack-Maker, upon the 29th Inst. / — / *In a Letter to a Person of Honour.* / — / London: Printed in the Year, 1708.

Small 4to; 1–4. — Appeared March 30, 1708. — Copy: Armagh.

1648. A / Continuation / Of The / Prdictions [*sic*] / For the Remaining Part of the / YEAR 1708. / From the Month of *September*, till the / Month of *March*, which compleats the whole / Year; wherein the Month, and day of the Month / are set down, the Persons nam'd, and the great / Actions and Events of the next year, / particular- / ly related as they will come to pass. / — / Written to prevent the People of *England*, from be- / ing farther impos'd on by Vulgar *Almanack-Makers*. / — / By ISAAC BICKERSTAFF, *Esq*; / — / *LONDON:* / Printed and Sold by *H. Hills* in *Black Fryars*, near / the Waterside. 1708.

8vo; 2 pp. (t. + bl.), 2–8. — Copy: Texas.

1649. RENVERSEMENT / DES / PREDICTIONS / FRIVOLLES / D' ISAAC BICKERSTAF, / GENTILE-HOMME / *Ou la deffense de la Vie des Personnes sacrées, / que ce faux devin a vainement / attaquées,* /Par Monsieur du Belastre Astrologue. / [device: armillary sphere] / A LUNEVILLE, / Chez LUCIDOR DE SOLEILMONT, / à l'enseigne de l'observatoire. / [rule] / M. D. CCVIII.

8vo; A⁸, B⁵ (B 1, 2, 3 are single leaves; B 4, 5 are a double-leaf). — Copy: Harvard. [By Jean Brusle' de Montplainchamp — W. A. Eddy, S.P., XXIX (1932), 29–40.]

496. An Elegy on Mr. *Patrige*, the Almanack-maker, who Died on the 29th of / this Instant *March*, 1708.

Very large folio; 1 page (2 columns). — Text within thick black border. At foot of second column:

London: Printed in the Year 1708.

Appeared March 30, 1708.
Copy: B.M. C. 40 m 11 (74).

497. *Another edition:*
An Elegy / On Mr. *Patrige*, the Almanack- / Maker, who Died on the 29th of *March* last, 1708.

Folio; 1 page (2 columns).
At foot of page:

Edinburgh Re-printed in the Year 1708.

Copies: B.M. 12350 m 18 (4), and Nat. Libr. of Scotl. (22).

1647. *Adaptation:*
An Elegy, on Dr. *John Whalley*, who departed this Life / on the 17th, of *January*, 1724, in the 71st Year of his age.

[Title and text in heavy black frame.]
Folio; 1 page (2 columns).
Copy: Lord Rothschild.
This is an adapted version of the 'Elegy' (with the exception of ll. 95–102), reprinted and distributed at Dublin on the death (Jan. 17, 1724) of the Dublin astrologer Dr. John Whalley, who was the publisher of the *Dublin News Letter*.

498. A / Vindication / Of / *Isaac Bickerstaff* Esq; / Against / What is Objected to Him by / Mr. *Partridge*, in his Almanack / for the present Year 1709. / — / *By the said* Isaac Bickerstaff *Esq*; / — / [ornament] / — / *London:* / Printed in the Year MDCCIX.

8vo (four leaves); A⁴ — 2 pp. (t. + bl.), 3–8.
Copies: B.M., and Penn.
This piece was referred to in the *Tatler* of April 12, 1709; it had been elicited by Partridge's *Almanack for 1709*, which had appeared in Nov. 1708.

15. The pieces recorded in Nos. 483, 495, 498 and 496 were reprinted in Vol. V, pp. 289–324, of:

The / Lucubrations / Of / *Isaac Bickerstaff* Esq; / — / In Five Volumes. / — / To which are added, (in order to render the / Work Compleat) / I. Mr. Bickerstaff's Predictions for / the Year 1708. / II. The Accomplishment of his Pre- / diction as to the Death of Dr. *Partridge*. / III. His Vindication, against Dr. *Par- / tridge*'s Objections in his Almanack of / 1709. / IV. An Elegy on

the Death of Dr. / *Partridge.* / — / *London,* / Printed for E. Nutt,
A. Bell, J. Darby, / A. Bettesworth, J. Pemberton, / J. Hooke,
C. Rivington, R. Crut- / tenden, T. Cox, J. Battley, F. Clay, / and
E. Symon. M.DCC.XX.

Copy: B.M. 12274 f 12. (5 vols., all 1720).

There is a 12mo edition, 5 vols., 1712, but I have not seen it. Apparently
the last volume is: "The Lucubrations of Isaac Bickerstaff, Esq.; By W.
H—n, Esq.; Dr. S—t, A. H—y, Esq., deceased: and several other hands.
Vol. V." (Aitken, *The Life Of Richard Steele,* II, 425). It contains Harrison's
Tatlers, and may contain the four pieces mentioned above.

The Bodleian has a five vol. set, 12mo, 1720–23–23–23–27; the fifth volume,
called 'The Third Edition' on the title-page, has the four pieces (pp. 289–
324). — There seems to be a set of 5 vols. 12mo, London, 1728. I have not
seen it.

There is a French translation of the *Tatler,* entitled: *Le Babillard, Ou Le
Nouvelliste Philosophe.* &c., Amsterdam, 1724–35; 2 vols., 12mo. Vol. I has
the first three of the four pieces mentioned above (pp. 15–52).

There is a Dutch translation of the *Tatler,* entitled: *De Snapper, Of De
Britsche Tuchtmeester,* &c., 4 vols. 12mo, 1733–33–34–52. Vol. IV has the
first three of the four pieces mentioned above (pp. 317–54). — Copy: Univ.
Libr. Amsterdam (XX565).

Reprinted, all the four pieces (the *Accomplishment* is here called: *A Revenue
Officer's Letter to a Lord*), and one more: *Squire Bickerstaff Detected* (No. 1025).

511. A / Letter / From A / Member of the / House of Commons
/ In / Ireland / To A / Member of the / House of Commons / In /
England, / Concerning the / *Sacramental Test.* / — / *London:* /
Printed for *John Morphew,* near *Stationers-Hall,* 1709.

4to; [A]–C⁴, D² — 2 pp. (t. + bl.), 3–28.
Copy: B.M. T 1754 (7).
Published ca. Jan. 1, 1709 (see *Corresp.,* I, 130–1 n.).
Cf. *Prose Works,* Vol. II, pp. XXIII, XXXIX, 281.

512. *Another edition:*
= / *A Letter from a Member of the* House *of* / Commons *in* Ireland, *to a Member of the* House *of* / Commons *in* England, *concerning
the* Sacramental / Test.

4to (in twos); A–B² — [1]–8. Text begins at once under the title.
At foot of the first page:

Price One Penny.

At foot of the eighth page:

Re-printed in *Dublin,* and Sold by the Booksellers. Price One
Penny.

Copy: Nat. Libr. Dublin. This copy is badly cropped, so that the page
numbers 1 (if there was one), 2, and 3 are absent.

512A. *Another edition:*

A / Letter / From A / Member / Of The / House of Commons / In / *Ireland,* / To A / Member / Of The / House of Commons / In / *England,* / Concerning the *Sacramental Test.* / — / Written in the Year 1708. / — / Printed in the Year MDCCXXXIII.

8vo; [B]⁸, C⁴ — 2 pp. (t. + bl.), [I]–II (The Publisher's Advertisement To The Reader), [1]–20 (text).

This is a separate issue of the first tract of Faulkner's Vol. IV of the *Works,* 1735 (see No. 41). It is the same printing, only the signatures on the title (Vol. IV. B) have been removed, but the signatures B 2 on p. [I], Vol. IV. C on p. 13, Vol. IV. C 2 on p. 15, and the catchword 'A' on p. 20 have been preserved.

Copy: Penn.

499. A Famous Prediction of *Merlin,* the *British* Wizard; / written above a Thousand Years ago, and relating to this / present Year. / With Explanatory Notes. By *T. N.* Philomath.

Folio; 2 pages. — Woodcut portrait at top of page, inscribed: Merlinus Verax.

At foot of second page:

London: *Printed and Sold by* A. Baldwin, *near the Oxford-Arms in Warwick-* / *Lane.* MDCCIX.

Copy: Rothschild. 2002.

500. *Another edition:*

A Famous Prediction of *Merlin,* the *British* Wizard; / written above a Thousand Years ago, and relating to this present Year. / With Explanatory Notes. By *T. N.* Philomath.

Folio; 2 pages. — Woodcut at top, inscribed: Merlinus Verax.
At foot of second page:

London: / Printed and Sold by *H. Hills,* in *Black-fryars* near the Water-side, 1708.

Copy: Harold Williams. Harvard has another edition which differs only by saying: London: Printed in the year, MDCCIX.

501. *Another edition:*

A Famous Prediction of *Merlin,* the *British* / Wizard; written above a Thousand Years ago, / and relating to the present Year. / With Explanatory Notes, By *T. N.* Philomath.

Folio; 2 pages.
At foot of second page:

London, Printed by *A. Baldwin: Edinburgh* Re-printed by *James Watson* 1709.

Copy: Nat. Libr. of Scot. (22).

502. *Also in:*

Dean *Swift's* | True, Genuine, and Authentic Copy | Of that most Strange, Wonderful, and Surprizing | Prophecy | Written by | Saint *Patrick*, | The Patron of Ireland, | Above a Thousand Years ago: | Faithfully Translated | From the *Irish* Original above two hundred | Years since, in the Reign of K. *Henry* VII. | Now publish'd with Explanatory Notes. | — | The Second Edition. | To which is subjoin'd, | Æsculapius: An Imitation of Lucian. | — | Pope, Nixon, Swift, *the Public now explore;* | *Who tell such Things as ne'er were told before:* | Three Kingdoms-*Fate,* | *Prophetic Truths decree;* | Thrice *happy* Britain *in Her Sages* Three. | — | Dublin printed, by W. Faulkener. | Reprinted at London, by E. Curll, at *Pope's-Head,* | in *Rose-Street, Covent-Garden,* 1740. Price 6*d.* | *Where may be had,* | I. Nixon's Cheshire Prophecy at Large. Price 6*d.* | II. Seventeen Hundred Thirty Nine: A Rhapsody. By | way of Sequel to Seventeen Hundred Thirty Seven and | Eight: Written by Mr. Pope. Price 6*d.*

> 8vo (in fours); [A]–C⁴, D³ — 2 pp. (t. + advs. on verso), [3]–8, [1]–22.
> Copy: B.M. 8631 bb 34.

> *Reprinted,* as an example of ancient typography, *in:*
> Ames, *Typographical Antiquities,* 1749.

> *Reprinted,* as an example of ancient typography, *in:*
> Philip Luckombe, *Concise History of Printing,* 1770, p. 60.
> Monck Mason, *The History and Antiquities of St. Patrick's,* 1820, p. 252, 1st col., says that Ames was duped into the belief that the *Prophecy,* which Swift pretended to have quoted from Johan Haukyns's *Merlin's Prophecies,* London, 1530, p. 39 (a work that never existed), was a genuine one; that this mistake was copied by Luckombe; but that his successor Herbert was not to be imposed upon so easily, and rectified the error. Dr. Johnson was likewise duped, supposing the Explanatory Notes alone to have been the work of Swift. — Cf. *Poems,* 102.

508. A | Project | For The | Advancement of Religion, | And The | *Reformation of Manners.* | — | By a Person of Quality. | — | *O quisquis volet impias* | *Caedes, & rabiem tollere civicam:* | *Si quaeret* *pater urbium* | *Subscribi statuis, indomitam audeat* | *Refraenare licentiam.* Hor. | = | London: | Printed for *Benj. Tooke,* at the *Middle-Temple-* | *Gate* in *Fleet-street.* M.DCC.IX.

> [Title in double-lined frame.]
> 8vo (in fours); A–H⁴ — 2 pp. (t. + bl.), 3–62, 2 pp. blank.
> Copies: Guildhall (Tracts 7 (5)), B.M. 527 i 1 (1), and Penn.
> Published beg. of April (referred to in the *Tatler,* April 20, 1709).

509. *Another edition:*

A | Project | For The | Advancement of Religion, | And The | *Reformation of Manners.* | — | By a Person of Quality. | — | O *quisquis volet impias | Caedes, & rabiem tollere civicam: | Si quæret pater urbium | Subscribi statuis, indomitam audeat | Refrænare licentiam. | Hor. | — | London: | Printed and Sold by H. Hills*, in *Black-fryars*, near the | Water-side. For the Benefit of the Poor. 1709.

> 8vo; [A]⁸, B⁴ — 1 p. (title), 2–24.
> Copies: Nat. Libr. of Scotl. LC 568.9, and Guildhall Pam. 936.

510. *Another edition:*
A | Project | For The | Advancement of Religion | And The | *Reformation of Manners.* | — | By a Person of Quality. | — | *O quisquis volet impias | Caedes, & rabiem tollere civicam: | Si quaeret pater urbium | Subscribi statuis, indomitam audeat | Refraenare licentiam.* | Hor. | = | *Edinburgh* | Reprinted by the Heirs and Successors of | *Andrew Anderson*, Printer to the Queens | most Excellent Majesty *Anno Dom.* 1709.

> [Title in double-lined frame.]
> 8vo; [A]–B⁸, C⁴ — 2 pp. (t. + bl.), 3 pp. + bl. (Dedication), 7–39 + bl.
> Copy: U.L.C. (9.56.18⁷).

78. A Modest | Address | To the Wicked | Authors | Of The | Present Age. | Particularly the Authors of | *Christianity not founded on Argument;* | And Of | *The Resurrection of Jesus considered; in* an- | swer to the Trial of the Witnesses. | — | By H.F. Esq; | — | *Dublin* Printed; | *London* Reprinted; and sold also by the | Booksellers of *Oxford* and *Cambridge.* | MDCCLXV. | (*Price One Shilling and Six-pence.*)

> 8vo; 2 pp. V–XII, 9–107 + bl.
> Contains retouched versions of *Arguments Against Abolishing Christianity*, and *A Project For The Advancement Of Religion.* The third piece is not by Swift. — The date seems to be a misprint for MDCCXLV.
> Copy: B.M. 115 e 64.

Another issue:
Dean *Swift*'s | Legacy | To The | Wicked Authors | Of The | Present Age. | In Three Parts. | The two First containing Arguments against abo | lishing Christianity; and a Project for the Ad- | vancement of Religion, and the Reformation of | Manners: both new Modell'd, and adapted to | the present Times. | The Third consisting of some New and Tritical Re- | flections on *Freethinking*, and *Freethinkers:* Also | Animadversions and Remarks *variorum.* | — | *Publish'd, according to the* Dean's *Appointment*, | By H.F. Esq; | — | Dublin printed; | London reprinted, and sold by the Booksellers there, | and in *Oxford* and *Cambridge*. | [Price 1 *s.* 6 *d.*]

> 8vo (in fours); π¹, B–D⁴, E², F–N⁴, O² — 2 pp. (t. + Advertisement on verso), 9–34, 39–107 + bl.

Copy: B.M. 1076 g 45.

Comparison of the two issues reveals that in the second the title-page, B 1 (pp. 9–10), E 1–3 (pp. 33–8), and K 2 (pp. 75–6) have been cancelled, and replaced by a new title-page (unsigned), and three new leaves: pp. 9–10 (signed B), pp. 33–4 (signed E), pp. 75–6 (unsigned). The rest has remained unchanged, except for the *Dedication* (pp. V–XII), which has been entirely left out.

Also reprinted as part of No. 76.

513. Numb. 1 | The Tatler. | — | By *Isaac Bickerstaff* Esq; | — | *Quicquid agunt Homines nostri Farrago Libelli.* | — | *Tuesday, April* 12. 1709.

Folio; 2 pages (double columns).
At foot of second page:

London: Printed for the Author, 1709.

From Numb. 5, this was altered into:

Sold by *John Morphew* near *Stationers-Hall;* where *Advertisements* are taken in.

Published three times a week, on Tuesday, Thursday and Saturday, in 271 numbers, from April 12, 1709 to Jan. 2, 1711 inclusive. Afterwards were sold two extra titles (*The Lucubrations of Isaac Bickerstaff Esq.*, Vol. I, 1710, and ditto Vol. II, 1711), Dedications, Preface, and Indexes, intended for those who wished to bind the original papers in volumes. — Cf. George A. Aitken, *The Life Of Richard Steele*, 2 vols., London, 1889.

Continued, twice a week, on Tuesday and Saturday, in 52 numbers, from Jan. 13, 1711 to May 19, 1711 inclusive, by William Harrison, Swift's protégé (numbering 1–6, 285–330). —

For Harrison's 'Tatler' see R. C. Elliott, "Swift's Little Harrison, Poet and Continuator of the Tatler", in *Studies in Philology*, XLVI, Oct. 4, 1949, pp. 544–59.

Opinions on Swift's share in the 'Tatler' differ. Cf. T.Sc. IX, pp. [XV], 3–66; *Poems*, pp. LII, 124, 136, 1087; *Prose Works*, II, pp. [V]–VI, XXV, etc.

According to the latest critics, Williams and Davis, the following pieces are by Swift: *Verse:* Nos. 9, 238, 301 (Swift and Harrison); *Prose:* Nos. 230, 5 and 20 (both in Harrison's 'Tatler'); 21, 31, 67, 68, 249, 258, 1, 2, 8, 28 (the last four in Harrison's 'Tatler'). Prof. Davis is sure of Nos. 230, 5, 20 only; of the rest he expresses himself with some reserve.

For some more continuations, and several reprints, see Aitken's *Life Of Steele*, II, 404, &c., and Powell Stewart's *British Newspapers And Periodicals 1632–1800* (in Texas University), Austin, 1950, Nos. 262–3.

514. *Edinburgh edition:*

Numb. 3. | The Tatler. | — | By *Isaac Bickerstaff* Esq; | — | [Two lines of Latin quotation. Tull. de Sen.] | — | Advertisement. | At *the Desire of some Knowing Gentlemen, this Paper is in time-coming to be Re-* | *printed at* Edinburgh, *beginning with That dated at* London *the 6th instant,* | *and shall be Publish'd Thrice a Week, in a few Hours after the Arrival of each* London | *Post, when he comes in* Monday *and*

Wednesday *Night*. Advertisements, *relating | to Affairs in* Scotland, *are to be insert in it, at easier Rates, by far, than hitherto | and will be taken in at the Shop of* James Watson *the Printer, next Door to the |* Red-Lyon, *opposite to the* Lucken-booths; *where the several Copies of this Paper, | from the above date, may be had. | — |* From *Wednesday, February* 15, to *Friday February* 17, 1710.

> Folio; 2 pages. No pagination, unless cut away.
> At foot of second page:

London *Printed, and Re-printed at* Edinburgh, *by* James Watson, *and Sold at | his Shop next Door to the* Red-Lyon *opposite to the* Luckenbooths. 1710.

> Copy: Texas. — This copy consists of Nos. 3–22 (Friday, Feb. 17, 1710 — Monday, April 3, 1710), Nos. 33–4 (Thursday, April 27, 1710 — Monday, May 1, 1710), Nos. 36–46 (Thursday, May 4, 1710 — Monday, May 29, 1710), Nos. 48–165 (Thursday, June 1, 1710 — Sat., March 3, 1711).
> This reprint appears to have been begun when No. 130 of the London edition appeared, the Edinburgh edition being called "No. 1", and so to the end. (G. A. Aitken, *The Life Of Richard Steele*, II, 404.) The B.M. seems to possess one number only: No. 31, Thursday, April 20 to Monday, April 24, 1710 (corresponding with No. 160 of the London ed., Saturday, April 15 to Tuesday, April 18), but for the present this copy is nowhere to be found.

515. *Dublin edition:*
Vol. I. (37) Numb. 10 | The Tatler. | — | By *Isaac Bickerstaff*, Esq; | — | — *Sapientia prima est | Stultitia caruisse* —— Hor. | — | *Wednesday, May* 24th, 1710.

> 4to; k² — 37–40.
> At foot of p. 40:

Dublin: Re-Printed by *Edwin Sandys* in *Essex-street*, 1710.

> I have only seen this one number (copy: T.C.D. P.hh.3.7). Its contents show it to be No. 173 of the London ed. (Thursday, May 18, 1710), so that No. 1 of the Dublin ed. must have started with No. 164 of the original issue.

Some Bickerstaffiana

1022. Mr. Partridge's Answer To Esquire Bickerstaff's Strange and Wonderful Predictions For The Year 1708. &c. London: E. Beer. 1708.
8vo (four leaves); [A]⁴ — 1 p. (title), 2–8.
Copy: Penn. — On p. 2 Partridge says that Bickerstaff will be proved a liar, "if he lives but till the 30th of the next Month", which dates this pamphlet Feb. 1708. — See also No. 494, *ante*.

1021. Unverfängliche Gedancken Uber Die unlängst im Druck heraus gekommene aus der Englischen Sprache übersetzte Wundersame Prophezeyung. Gedruckt, Den 24. Martii Anno 1708. — 4to size; no signatures — 1 p. (title), 3 pp. (text). — Copy: B.M. 594 b 34 — These 'Thoughts' were elicited by the German translation recorded in No. 493, *ante*.

1023. L – – – – – – – – N Bewitch'd: Or, The Town Turn'd upside down. Lonon [*sic*]: Printed in the Year, 1708. — 16mo; 1–8. — Contains prophecies for all the twelve months of the year, from January to December. — Copy: Tregaskis.

1024. Bickerstaffe's Prediction Confirm'd In The Death Of Partridge, The Almanack-Maker, the 29th day of this instant, March, at 13 minutes past 11 at night. With farther Predictions for the Months of October, November, and December 1708 – – – – – London Printed: And Sold by J. Morphew – – – – – 1708.

4to; 1–4. (Imprint at foot of page 4.)

Must have appeared, according to the title, on 30 or 31 March 1708. Copy mentioned in Birrell & Garnett's catalogue No. 12, item 556. I have not seen it, but the title suggests either Swift or one of his friends.

1025. Squire *Bickerstaff* Detected; / Or, The / *Astrological Impostor* Convicted, / By / *John Partridge*, / Student in Physick and Astrology. / — / Part I. / — /

8vo; A⁴ — 1–7, 8 (Advertisement). — Text begins at once under the title. On p. 3: A True and Impartial Account Of The Proceedings Of Isaac Bickerstaff, Esq; Against Me —.

Copy: B.M. 718 g 14 (8), Penn.

Internal evidence shows that this cannot have appeared before July 1708. It is supposed to have been written by Yalden, Rowe, and Congreve.

The Lucubrations of Isaac Bickerstaff, Esq. Astrologer (i.e. *The Tatler*, 1709–11). By Steele and others.

The Whisperer – – – By Mrs. Jenny Distaff, half-sister to Isaac Bickerstaff, Esq. London, 1709.

1026. Mr. Partridge's Judgment and Opinion of this Frost. Foretelling &c. Printed for J. Bagnall. 1709. — 8vo; 1–8. — On p. 5 the author says that he would not have written this, if he had not feared that the public might be again imposed upon by one of his enemies. — As the name Partridge is here spelt "with the want of a letter", this is probably one of the "impudent forgeries, by a breed of villains, and wholly without my knowledge or consent", as Partridge calls them in a later Almanack (1714).

1585. The Tory Tatler – – – London, 1709.

1586. The Tattling Harlot — London, 1709.

1587. The Famous Prophesie of the White King and the Dead Man Explain'd – – – By Isaac Bickerstaff. London, 1710 (?).

1027. Bickerstaff's Almanack: Or, A Vindication of the Stars, &c. London: Printed for the Company of Stationers, Anno Aerae Christianae 1710. — 12mo; 47 unnumbered pages + bl.

840. A / Letter / To / *Isaac Bickerstaff*, Esq; / Occasion'd by the / Letter / To The / Examiner. / — / [ornament] / — / *London*, / Printed in the Year M.DCC.X.

8vo; [A]⁸ — 2 pp. (t. + bl.), 3–16. — Copy: B.M. T 1761 (24).

1589. Titt for Tatt – – – By Jo. Partridge, Esq. London, 1710.

1590. Partrige and Bickerstaf — London, 1710 (?).

1591. A Bickerstaff's Burying — By Mrs. Susanna Centlivre. London, 1710.

1593. A Testimonial of the Death of Mr. Partridge — By Jeremy Wagstaff. London, 1710.

1594. Bickerstaff's Aesop — London, 1710.

1595. A Good Husband for Five Shillings, or, Esquire Bickerstaff's Lottery for the London Ladies — By Isaac Bickerstaff. London, 1710.

1028. The British Visions: Or, Isaac Bickerstaff's Twelve Prophecies For The Year 1711. — 16mo; 1–23 + bl. — This has been attributed to Defoe.
    Another edition: The British Visions: Or, Isaac Bickerstaff Senr; Being Twelve Prophecies For The Year 1711. &c. Printed first in the North, And now Reprinted at London; &c. John Baker. 1711. —
    8vo; A^8 — 1 p. (title), 1 p. (Preface), 3–16. — Copies: T.C.D., and Penn.

1029. Predictions For the Year 1712. By Isaac Bickerstaff, Esq; &c. Printed in the Year, 1712. —
    8vo; [A]^8 — 2 pp. (t. + bl.), 3–16. — Copy: Penn.

1596. Merlin Reviv'd; Or, Strange & Wonderful Predictions – – – – Also an Account of a Blazing Star – – – – Together with The Author, J. P.'s Advice To Isaac Bickerstaff. Esq. Printed for John Morphew, 1711. 8vo. — Continues the Swift-Partridge feud. — Signed at end: J. P.
    Copy: P. M. Hill's cat. 38, item 341.

1597. August the Second, One Thousand Seven Hundred and Thirty Eight. A Prediction; In the Manner of Many. By Bickerstaff the Younger.
    Pr. for T. Cooper, 1738. Folio.

1030. That Part Of The Last Will And Testament Of Isaac Bickerstaff, Esq; Deceased; Which Relates To The Publick: Together with his Strange and Wonderful Prophecies; All to be fulfill'd in the Year, 1725. To which is Added An Important Meditation On A Staff. A Fragment. Published in Pursuance of the said Will by Gabriel Bickerstaffe, Esq; His nephew and Executor. – – – – – London; Printed and Sold by A. Moor, near St Paul's. MDCCXXV. — 8vo; 1–36. — Catalogue Birrell & Garnett, No. 12, item 556.

1031. That Part of the Last Will and Testament Of Isaac Bickerstaff, Esq; Which relates to the Publick: With His Strange and Wonderful Prophecies, To be fulfilled in the Years 1738, & 9. To which is Added, An Important Meditation on a Staff. A Fragment. Published in Pursuance of the said Will, By Gabriel Bickerstaff, Esq; His Nephew, and Executor. &c. London, Printed, and Sold by T. Cooper, &c., and the Booksellers of London and Westminster. MDCCXXKVII. [*sic*] — 8vo; 1–99 + bl.

Imitation:
    Benjamin Franklin's 'Poor Richard' (see J. F. Ross, "The Character Of Poor Richard: Its Source And Alteration", in PMLA, LV (Sept. 1940), No. 3, pp. 785–94).

***

Baucis and Philemon; *To Mrs. Biddy Floyd*; *The Humble Petition of Frances Harris*

516. = / *Baucis* and *Philemon*, / *Imitated from* Ovid.

Sm. 4to; no signatures [1]–8. — Text begins at once under the title. At foot of p. 8:

Printed *An. Dom.* MDCCIX. / Price Two-Pence.

Copies: B.M. 11633 e 56, and Bodl. (Rawl. 203.5).

517. *Another issue:*
Penn has another issue, which has "He'll talk" in l. 19 on p. 7, where the above copy has "He'd talk". Moreover, this copy has only 'Printed *An. Dom.* MDCCIX.' at foot of p. 8, without the addition 'Price Two-Pence'.

520. *Also in:*
Poetical Miscellanies: / The / Sixth Part. / Containing a / Collection / Of / *Original Poems,* / With Several / New Translations. / — / *By the most Eminent Hands.* / — / *London,* / Printed for *Jacob Tonson,* within *Grays-Inn* / Gate, next *Grays-Inn* Lane. 1709. / — / *Where you may have the Five former Parts.*

[Title within double-lined frame.]
8vo; π^1, A^4, B–T^8, U^7; X–Rr^8, Ss^6; Aaa–Bbb^8 — one leaf (frontisp.), 1–172, 177–224, 221–98; 301–632; [721]–751 + bl.
Contains: Baucis and Philemon (pp. 237–48), On Mrs. Biddy Floyd [English and Latin] (pp. 249–51).
This is Vol. VI, 1st edition, of a 6 vol. set, called Dryden's or Tonson's *Miscellanies*. The other volumes first appeared in 1684, 1685, 1693, 1694, 1704. A fourth edition, differing considerably from the earlier editions, was published in 1716, a fifth in 1727.
Griffith No. 1 says: "Pages 299–300 may have been a blank leaf (= U 8) thrown away by the binder." There are two states: One has Hh 8 (= pp. 475–6) 'A Translation'; Mm 3 verso, ll. 3, 5, 6 incompletely printed; Ss = 8 leaves. Another (B.M. 1076 k 28) has 'An Imitation'; ll. 3, 5, 6 complete; Ss = 6 leaves (pp. 621–32).
There is another copy (B.M. 1077 1.39), the same as the other B.M. copy, but pp. 475–6 both blank.
Pp. 221–4 repeated in numbering; no break in the text.

518. *Also in:*
Miscellaneous / Works / By / The Right Honourable / The / *Earl of* Roscommon. / — / [ornament] / = / *London:* / Printed in the Year MDCCIX.

[Title within double-lined frame.]
8vo; [A]–K^8, L^7, M^9, N 1, π^1 — 2 pp. (t. + bl.), [3]–190, 4 pp. (Contents) 2 pp. advs. (Curll).
Copy: B.M. 1081 m 3 (2).
This is the second volume of *The Works of Rochester and Roscommon,* &c. The Third Edition. To which is added, A Collection of Miscellaneous

10—J.S.

Pieces. London. E. Curll. 1709. It contains *Baucis and Philemon* (pp. 129–39), *The Humble Petition of Frances Harris* (pp. 175–81), and *On Mrs. Biddy Floyd* (p. 187).

The *Works of Rochester and Roscommon* were reprinted in 1711 (London, J. Bradford). The B.M. copy (12314 aaa 1 (2)) has only Part I (12mo; 1–24, in very small type). Possibly the missing part or parts also contain the three pieces just mentioned.

519. *Also in* (pp. 145–52):

Poems / On / *Several Occasions.* / By the Earls of / Roscommon, / And / Dorset, &c. / — / [ornament] / = / *London:* / Printed for *E. Curll*, MDCCXIV.

> [Title in double-lined frame.]
> 12mo; π^2, [A]–G^{12}, H^{10} — 2 pp. (t. + bl.), 2 pp. (Table), 3–187 + bl. — Frontisp. portrait.
> Copy: B.M. 11633 aa 57.

521. *Another edition:*

Baucis and *Philemon;* / A / Poem. / On the ever lamented Loss / Of the two *Yew-Trees*, / In the Parish of *Chilthorne*, / Near the / County Town of *Somerset*. / Together with / Mrs. *Harris*'s Earnest Petition. / — / By the *Author of the* Tale of a Tub. / — / As also / An Ode upon *Solitude*. / — / By the *Earl of* Roscommon. / — / *London:* / Printed and Sold by *H. Hills*, in *Black-fryars*, near / the Water-side. 1709.

> 8vo; A^8 — 2 pp. (t. + bl.), 3–16.
> Copy: Penn.

522. *Another edition:*

Baucis and *Philemon:* / — / A / Poem / On the Ever-lamented Loss of the / Two Yew-Trees, / In the Parish of *Chilthorne*, near the / Count [*sic*]-Town of *Somerset*. / Together with / Mrs. *Harris*'s Earnest Petition: / And an Admirable Recipe. / — / By the *Author of* The Tale of a Tub. / — / As Also / An Ode upot [*sic*] *Solitude:* / By the *Earl of* Roscommon. / — / *London:* / Printed, and Sold by *H. Hills*, in *Black-Fryars*, near / the Water-side, 1710.

> 8vo; [A]^8 — 2 pp. (t. + bl.), 3–16.
> Copies: B.M. (11603 d. 15), and Bodl. (G. Pamph. 1278. 18).
> *Another state:*
> The title has correctly: 'County' and 'upon'.
> Copy: Forster, and Penn.
> *Another issue:*
> In 1717 the remaining copies of this edition, together with several other pamphlets, were combined so as to form two volumes, provided with the following titles:
> A Collection Of the Best English Poetry, By Several Hands. Viz. [seventeen names, among them Dr. Swift] In Two Vol's Octavo. London: – – – – T. Warner – – – 1717. Price 10 *s*.

A Collection Of the Best English Poetry, By Several Hands. Vol. II. London: – – – T. Warner – – – 1717.

The first volume has nothing by Swift, but the second contains: *Baucis and Philemon* (Hills, 1710). — Cf. Case, 294.

Also in:

605. The Bee. A Collection Of Choice Poems. Part I. – – – – London. – – – T. Ilive – – – S. Popping – – – – A. Boulter – – – – MDCCXV.

Contains: *Mrs. Harris's Petition.*

There are two more parts: 'Part II. London. W. Hunter, &c.', and 'Part III. London.', both 1715, but neither has anything by Swift. Cf. Case, No. 282.

Also in:

1584. The Virgin Muse. Being a Collection of Poems From our most Celebrated English Poets. Designed for the Use of Young Gentlemen and Ladies, At Schools – – – – By James Greenwood – – – London, – – – – T. Varnam and J. Osborne – – – R. Halsey – – – J. Brotherton – – – Jonas Brown – – – 1717.

Contains: Baucis and Philemon (pp. 161–6).

Second edition (same printing), 1722.

Third edition, 1731.

Cf. Case, No. 304.

523. *Also in:*

Four / Poems. / First / *Baucis* and *Philemon*, / — / *By* Jonatan [*sic*] Swift, *D.D.* / — / Second / On the Day of Judgment. / — / *By the Earl of* Roscommon. / — / Third / On *Rome's Pardons.* / — / *By the Earl of* Rochester. / — / Fourth / On the taking Port St. *Mary's* in / *Spain,* by the late Duke of Ormond. / To which is added, / Two Tales: The fair *Nun,* / and the *Widow's* Wile. / — / *London:* Printed in the Year, 1725–26.

Sm. 8vo (in fours); A–C⁴ — 2 pp. (t. + bl.), 3–24. — Pages 3–7 are *Baucis and Philemon.*

Copy: Penn.

Also in:

A Collection Of Merry Poems: Consisting of Facetious Tales, Epigrams, &c. From Oldham, Brown, Prior, Swift, And other Eminent Poets; With some from the Weekly Papers and Miscellanies. – – – – The Second Edition – – – – London: – – – T. Cooper – – – 1736. (Price One Shilling and Sixpence.)

Contains, pp. 76–80, Baucis and Philemon.

Copy: Harvard. — cf. Case 403(b).

I have not seen the first edition.

MLN, Vol. XLVII, 1932 contains:

C. M. Webster, "Hudibras and Swift [Baucis And Philemon]."

523A. *Apollo* Outwitted. *To the Honourable Mrs.* Finch, *under her Name of* Ardelia, Written, 1709.

The catalogue of the Gilbert Coll., Dublin, mentions a broadside, n.d., but it seems to have been mislaid.

525. Numb. 1. / The Examiner: / Or, / Remarks upon Papers and Occurrences. / — / To be continu'd Weekly. / — / Thursday, *August* 3. 1710.

Folio; 2 pages.
At foot of second page:

London: Printed for John Morphew, near *Stationers-Hall*, 1710.

Vol. I, Nos. 14–45 and the first half of 46 are by Swift. Also: Vol. II, No. 34, July 24, 1712 (*Remarks on the Bp. of S. Asaph's Preface*), Vol. III, No. 16, Jan. 16, 1712–13 (*An Appendix to the Conduct of the Allies; and Remarks on the Barrier Treaty*), and Vol. III, No. 21, Feb. 2, 1712–13 (*A Complete Refutation of the Falsehoods alleged against Erasmus Lewis, Esq.*).

Copies: B.M. 627 m 20, and Penn.
Temple Scott IX, 69, has this note:
"The first number of 'The Examiner' was issued on August 3rd, 1710, and the paper was continued until July 26th, 1711 (52 numbers). On December 6th, 1711, William Oldisworth revived it, and issued it weekly until December 18th, 1712, after which date it was published twice a week until July 26th, 1714, though it occasionally happened that only one was issued in a week. The last number was No. 19 of the sixth volume, so that Oldisworth edited vols. II., III., IV., V. and what was published of Vol. VI. (47, 50, 50, 50, and 19 numbers). The death of the Queen put an end to the publication."
Perhaps 'The Examiner. London: Printed for James Roberts, in Warwick-lane, 1714' (later numbers were printed for E. Griffis, or printed and sold by Edm. Powell) was a continuation. Texas has Nos. 1 (Nov. 3, 1714), and 4–12 (Nov. 13–Dec. 11, 1714).
See Powell Stewart, *British Newspapers And Periodicals 1632–1800* (Austin, 1950), 68.

Edinburgh reprint:
Numb. 8. / The Examiner: / — / From *Wednesday, September* 20, to / *Tuesday, September* 26, 1710. / — / [One line Latin quotation from Hor.] / —

Folio; 2 pages. No pagination, unless cut away.
At foot of page:

Edinburgh: *Reprinted by* James Watson, *and sold at his Shop opposite to the* Lucken-booths.

Copy: Texas. — This copy consists of Vol. I, Nos. 8–11 (Tuesday, Sept. 26 1710 — Saturday, Oct. 28, 1710), No. 13 (Saturday, Nov. 4, 1710), No. 17 (Monday, Dec. 4, 1710), Nos. 22–5 (Friday, Jan. 5, 1711–Tuesday, Jan. 30, 1711), No. 28 (Saturday, Feb. 17, 1711), No. 30 (Tuesday, March 6, 1711), No. 30 [*sic*] (Monday, March 12, 1711), Nos. 32–3 (Thursday, March 22, 1711 — Friday, March 23, 1711).
Imprint as given above, except in Nos. 9, 28, 30, 30 [*sic*], 32–3, where '*Reprinted*' is replaced by '*Printed*'.

Dublin edition:
(Reprint without the advertisements of the London edition):
Vol. I. (1) Numb. 1. / The Examiner. / Or, / Remarks upon Papers and Occurrences / — / *To be Continu'd Weekly.*

4to; 1–4. — The following numbers are paged consecutively, 5–8, 9–12, &c. No imprint at foot of p. 4.
At foot of p. 8:

— | *Dublin: Printed by C. Carter at the Old Post-Office in Fish-shamble-* | *street,* 1711.

Copy: Nat. Libr. of Ireland. — This copy consists of Vol. I, Nos. 1–52, pp. 1–204 (Monday, Aug. 14, 1710–Wednesday, Aug. 15, 1711), Vol. II, Nos. 1–47, pp. 1–184 (Thursday, Dec. 13, 1711–Tuesday, Nov. 4, 1712), and Vol. III, No. 29 only, pp. 113–16 (Thursday, April 9, 1713).

Texas has i.a. Vol. III complete, Nos. 1–29 (Saturday, Nov. 8, 1712–Thursday, April 9, 1713). — See Powell Stewart, 69.

526. *Another Dublin edition* (reprint without the advertisements of the London edition):

Vol. I. (1) *Numb*. I. | The Examiner: | Or, | Remarks upon Papers and Occurrences. | — | *To be Continu'd Weekly.* | — | *Monday,* August 14, 1710.

4to; 1–4. — The following numbers are paged consecutively, 5–8, 9–12, &c.
At foot of p. 4:

Dublin Printed at the Old Post-Office in Fish-shamble-Street.

At foot of p. 8:
The same 'C. Carter' imprint as above.
Copy: T.C.D. TTL. 73. — This copy has the same numbers as the above Nat. Libr. of Ireland copy, except Vol. III, No. 29. —
All the numbers (except No. 1) have 'C. Carter' in the imprint, but Nos. 10, 11, 13, 17, 23 have 'D. Tompson' (see next entry).

526A. *Another Dublin edition* (reprint without the advertisements of the London edition):

Numb. I. | The Examiner. | Or, | Remarks upon Papers and Occurrences. | — | *To be continued Weekly.* | — | *Monday, August the 14th,* 1710.

4to; [1]–4. — The following numbers are paged consecutively, 5–8, 9–12, &c.
At foot of p. 4:

This Paper being Numb. Ist, Printed in England, will be continued here as | it comes from thence, if it finds Encouragement. | *At* Daniel Tompson's, *next Door to the Tom of Lincoln, in West-Church* | *street in Smith-Field, where there's a Rowling-Press, ready to Print* | *all sorts of Copper-Pleats, as Tobacco Bills, and This Indenture, of different* | *Sizes of Text-Hand, and Lottery Pictures, at reasonable Rates.* | — |

Dublin: *Re-printed in Channel-Row.* for D. Tompson, 1710.
Copy: T.C.D. (unfortunately Vol. I Numbers 1–12 only). — All the numbers have the 'Tompson' imprint, but Nos. 3, 6 and 8 have no imprint. No. 8 has two long book-advertisements, not present in the other edition(s).

Note: At any rate Nos. 1–12 are different printings. Possibly Nos. 10, 11, 13, 17, 23 ('Tompson') in the preceding entry are intruders in the 'Carter' set; or some time after the beginning Carter and Tompson may have joined issue. The imprints always say: 'Printed *by* Carter', and 'Printed *for* Tompson'.

Collected edition:

4. The | Examiners | For The | Year 1711. | To which is prefix'd, | A Letter to the *Examiner*. | = | —— *Si quis* | *Opprobriis dignum latraverit, integer ipse,* | *Solventur risu tabulae: tu missus abilis.* | = | *London:* | Printed for *John Morphew,* near *Sta-* | *tioners-Hall*; and *A. Dodd,* at the | *Peacock* without *Temple-Bar.* 1712.

[Title within double-lined frame.]
16mo; I–XVI, 1–306, 12 pp. *Index*, 2 pp. advs.
The first number of the 'Examiner' (not by Swift) elicited: A Letter To The Examiner. Printed in the Year, 1710. — 8vo; [A]⁸ — 2 pp. (t. + bl.), 3–16.
In its turn it elicited:
A Letter To Isaac Bickerstaff, Esq; Occasion'd by the Letter To The Examiner. London, Printed in the Year M.DCC.X. — 8vo; [A]⁸ — 2 pp. (t. + bl.), 3–16.
Because the original No. 13 (by Atterbury) was omitted, Swift's numbers became 13–44 and the first half of 45.

Contemporary criticism

1033. The Case Of The Present Convocation Consider'd; In Answer to the Examiner's Unfair Representation of it, and Unjust Reflections upon it. &c. London: John Churchill. 1711. — 8vo; 1–24. — A reply to Swift's *Examiner*, No. 22, Dec. 28, 1710. — Ascribed to W. Wotton.

1034. A Letter To A Member Of The October-Club: Shewing, That to yield Spain to the Duke of Anjou by a Peace, wou'd be the Ruin of Great-Britain. &c. London; A. Baldwin. 1711. — 8vo; I–VI, 3–75 + bl. — Contains some passages against Swift's writings in *The Examiner*.
The Second Edition, with Additions. London; A. Baldwin. 1711. — 8vo; I–VI, 1–42.

1034A. Bouchain, In A Dialogue Between the Late Medley and Examiner. &c. London, A. Baldwin. M.DCC.XI. — 8vo (in fours); A–E⁴, F² — 2 pp. (t. + bl.), 3–43 + bl.
Second ed.: – – – – The Second Edition. – – – M.DCC.XI. — Same collation.
Answered by:

852. The D. of M—h's Vindication: In Answer to a Pamphlet Lately Publish'd, called [Bouchain, or a Dialogue between the Medley and the Examiner.] London: John Morphew, 1711. — 8vo; 1–16.
Second ed.: – – – – The Second Edition Corrected. – – – 1711. — Same printing, except for the title, and two advs. added at foot of p. 16.
Again answered by:

852A. The Duke of M – – – – – h's Vindication. In Answer to a Pamphlet falsely so called. &c. London, A. Baldwin, 1712.
Copies: Penn.

1036. The Present State Of Wit, &c. London, 1711. — 8vo; 3–23 + bl. (B.M. copy, probably h.t. missing).
   Also in: An English Garner, &c. Vol. VI, 1883.
   Contains a favourable criticism of the 'Examiner'.

1036A. A Few Words Upon the Examiner's Scandalous Peace. London: Printed in the Year, M.DCC.XI. — 8vo (in fours); [A]–C⁴ — 2 pp. (t. + bl.) 3–22, 2 pp. blank.

1036B. Reflections Upon The Examiner's Scandalous Peace. London: A. Baldwin, 1711. — 8vo (in fours); [A]–C⁴ — 2 pp. (t. + bl.), 3–22, 2 pp. blank.

1037. An Elegy On The Death of the Examiner, Who departed this Mortal Life, on Thursday, the 25th of July, 1711, at John Morphew's, near Stationer's-Hall. — 8vo; 4 pages. (from Dobell's cat. 105, item 202).

1075. Two Letters Concerning the Author Of The Examiner. London: A. Baldwin, MDCCXIII. — 8vo (in fours), A–C⁴ — 2 pp. (t. + bl.), 3–21, 3 pp. blank.
   Copy: Penn.

1575. The Examiner Examin'd. In A Letter To The Englishman: Occasion'd by the Examiner of Friday, Dec. 18, 1713. &c. London: J. Roberts, 1713. — 4to; [A]⁴, B² — 2 pp. (t. + bl.), [3]–12.

1576. An Answer to the Examiner's Cavils against the Barrier Treaty of 1709. To which are added, the Articles of the New Barrier Treaty that relate to the Hanover Succession, both in Latin and English. London, 1713. — 8vo.

1577. The Blessings of Peace. Being The Examiner, Upon Occasion of Her Majesty's most Gracious Speech To Her Parliament, April the 9th, 1713. Dublin, Edward Waters, 1713. Sm. 8vo (in fours); π⁴, B⁴ — 2 pp. (t. + bl.), 13 unnumbered pages (unless cut off by close cropping) + bl.

1578. A Letter To The Examiner, Suggesting Proper Heads, For Vindicating his Masters. London: J. Moore, 1714.
   Price 6 d. — 8vo (in fours); π¹, B–E⁴ — 2 pp. (t. + bl.), 1–31 + bl.
   Another ed.: Same title. London: J. Moore, 1714. Price 3 d.
   8vo (in fours); [A]–D⁴ — 2 pp. (t. + bl.), 3–31 + bl.

1579. A Letter To The Examiner; &c. London, S. Popping, 1715. — 8vo (in fours); [A]–D⁴ — 2 pp. (t. + bl.), 3–32.

***

524. The | Virtues | Of | *Sid Hamet* the Magician's | Rod.

Sm. folio; 2 pages.
At foot of second page:

London, Printed: for John Morphew, near | *Stationers-Hall*, MDCCX,

Published ca. Oct. 9, 1710 (see *Journal to Stella*, Oct. 4 and 14).
Copy: Penn. — The B.M. copy (1876 f 1 (50)) is close-cropped at top, so that 'The' has been cut off.

Another edition:
The | Virtues | Of | *Sid Hamet* the Magician's | Rod.

Sm. folio; 1 page (2 columns).
At foot of page:

London Printed, and Re-Printed in Dublin, 1710.

On verso:

The | *Devil a Barrel better Herring*; | Or, A | Merry Dialogue | Between | In and Out.

Copy: Texas Univ.

Character Earl Of Wharton

527. A Short | Character | Of | His Ex. *T. E.* of *W*. | L.L. of *I*——. | With | An Account of some smaller Facts, du- | ring His Government, which will not | be put into the Articles of Im- peach- | ment. | = | *London:* | Printed for *William Coryton*, Book- seller, at the | *Black-Swan* on *Ludgate-hill*. 1711.

Sm. 8vo; A–B⁸ — 2 pp. (t. + bl.), 3–29, 3 pp. blank. — B 4 signed B 3.
Copy: Penn.
The second part of this pamphlet: "An Account of some smaller Facts" was written by an understrapper.
This piece was first printed privately, but no copy seems to have survived (Cf. *Prose Works*, III, pp. XX, 277 — *Journal to Stella*, Dec. 8, Jan. 1).
Though dated 1711, it appeared in the first week of Dec. 1710 (see *Journal to Stella*, Dec. 8, 1710). The date at the beginning of the text, *August* 30, 1710, is a blind.
There seems to be a Dublin edition, and an answer to it (*Corresp.*, I, 233–4 n., 235 n.). I have seen neither.

529. *Another issue:*
A Short | Character | Of | His Ex. *T.E.* of *W*. | LL. of *I*——. | With | An Account of some smaller Facts, du- | ring His Government, which will not | be put into the Articles of Impeach- |

ment, | = | *London:* | Printed for *William Coryton*, Bookseller, at the | *Black Swan* on *Ludgate-hill*. 1711. | Price 4*d*.

Copy: Penn.

528. *Another issue:*

A short | Character | Of | His Ex. *T.E.* of *W*. | LL. of *I* — — — — —. | With | An Account of some smaller Facts, du- | ring His Government, which will not | be put into the Articles of Impeach- | ment. | = | *London:* | Printed for *William Coryton*, Bookseller, at the | *Black-Swan* on *Ludgate-hill*, 1711. | Price 4*d*.

A close examination of the above three issues has shown that they are the same printing, except for the first sheet (pp. 1–16, including the title), which shows all kinds of minor differences.

In some copies the 4 of 4*d* in the imprint has been altered with a pen into 6, probably by the publisher when he saw the quick sale of this pamphlet.

530. *Another edition:*

— | A Short | Character | Of | His Ex. *T.E.* of *W*. | L.L. of *I* — — — — — — | With an Account of some smaller Facts, | during his Government, which will not | be put into the Articles of Impeachment.

[Text begins at once under this.]
Sm. 8vo (in fours); π^4, B–C^4 — 1–24.
At foot of p. 24:

London. | Printed for *William Coryton*, Booksellor [*sic*] at the | *Black Swan* on *Ludgate-Hill*, 1711.

Copy: B.M. 10816 a 16.

531. *Another edition:*

A | Short Character | Of the Late | M — — — — — s of *W* — — — — — — — *n*. | Together with | An Account of some Smaller | Facts, during his G — — — — — — — — — t in | *I* — — — — — — — — *d*, which would scarce | have reach'd to an *Impeach-* | *ment*. | — | Extracted from an *Irish Manuscript*, | By | The Author of the *Tale of a Tub*. | — | *London:* | Printed for John More, near St. *Paul's* | *Church-yard;* and Sold by most Booksellers | in *London* and *Westminster*. pr. 4*d*.

8vo (in fours); π^1, A–C^4 — 2 pp. (h.t. + bl.), 2 pp. (f.t. + bl.), 1–20, 1 p. advs. + bl.
Copy: Penn.
As the title says: 'the Late M — — — — — s of W — — — — — — n' and Wharton died in 1715, this edition must be 1715 or later.

532. *Another issue:*

A | Short Character | Of the Late | M — — — — — s of *W* — — — — — — *n*. | Together with | An Account of some Smaller | Facts, during his G — — — — — — — t in | *I* — — — — — — — — *d*, which would scarce | have reach'd to an *Impeach-* | *ment.* | — | Extracted from an *Irish Manu-script,* | By | The Author of the *Tale of a Tub.* | — | *London:* | Printed, and Sold by *A. Dodd* without *Temple-* | *bar,* and *E. Smith* at the *Royal-Exchange,* | and most Booksellers of *London* and *West-* | *minster.* Price 4*d.*

> 8vo; [A]–C⁴. — The same printing as No. 531, except for the t.p.
> There is no h.t.; apparently the original h.t. and f.t. have been cut away, and replaced by above new title.
> Copy: New York Publ. Libr. (Berg Coll.)

534. Some | Remarks | Upon A | Pamphlet, | Entitl'd, | [*A Letter to the Seven Lords* | *of the Committee, appointed* | *to Examine* Gregg.] | — | By the Author of the Examiner. | — | [ornament] | — | *London,* | Printed for *John Morphew,* near *Statio-* | *ners-Hall.* 1711. (Price 3*d.*)

> [Title within double-lined frame.]
> 8vo (in fours); A–C⁴ — 2 pp. (t. + bl.), 3–24.
> Published Aug. 18 (adv. in *The Daily Courant*).
> Copy: Penn.
> The author of 'A Letter' was John Oldmixon.

535. *Dublin edition:*
Some | Remarks | Upon A | Pamphlet, | Entitl'd, | [*A Letter to the Seven Lords of* | *the Committee, appointed to* | *Examine* Gregg.] | — | By *the Author* of the Examiner. | — | [ornament] | — | *Dublin,* Re-Printed by *E. Waters,* in *Essex-street,* for | *J. Hyde,* Bookseller on *College-Green,* 1711.

> 8vo (in fours); [A]–D⁴ — 2 pp. (t. + bl.), 3–31 + bl. — Page-number 30 is printed upside down.
> Copy: Marsh Cas. XI, 1 (3).

536. A New | Journey to Paris: | Together with some | *Secret Transactions* | Between the | Fr – – – h K – – – g, | And An | Eng – – – Gentleman. | — | *By the Sieur du Baudrier..* | — | Translated from the French. | — | *London,* | Printed for *John Morphew,* near *Statio-* | *ners-Hall.* 1711. (Price 2*d.*)

> [Title within double-lined frame.]
> 8vo; A⁸ — 2 pp. (t. + bl.), 2 pp. (The Translator To The Reader), 5–16.
> Published Sept. 11, 1711 (adv. in *The Daily Courant,* and *The Post Boy*).
> Copy: Penn.
> *Second edition:*
> Same title, except:

– – – – French. | — | The Second Edition, Corrected. | — | *London,* | – – – – – –

Copy: Penn.

Except for the title-page this is exactly the same printing as the first edition, with only a few slight corrections in the type, the principal of which is the alteration of, 'Fifty Pistoles' in l. 2 on p. 16 into 'Twenty Pistoles'.

Published Sept. 18, 1711 (adv. in *The Post Boy*, again on Sept. 20).

Third edition:

Copy not seen; its existence may be assumed from newspaper advertisements in *The Post Boy*, Nov. 1–3, 1711, and in the *Examiner*, Jan. 17–24, 1711/12.

537. *French translation:*

Relation / Du / Voyage / Que Fit / Monsieur P—r, / Gentilhomme Ang—s, à la Cour Fr—e, / en Juillet 1711. / *Au sujet de la Négociation de Paix.* / [ornament] / *Traduit de l'Anglois.* / Imprimé à Londres pour Jean Morphew, Libraire. / l'an M.DCC.XI.

Sm. 4to; [A]⁴, B³ — 2 pp. (t. + bl.), 3–14.
Copy: Kon. Bibl., pamphlet 15962.
Criticism: See 1039.

The Conduct Of The Allies

539. The / *Conduct* / Of The / Allies, / And Of The / Late Ministry, / In / Beginning and Carrying on / The / Present War. / = / —— *Partem tibi Gallia nostri* / *Eripuit: partem duris Hispania bellis:* / *Pars jacet Hesperia: totoq; exercitus orbe* / *Te vincente perit* —— / *Odimus accipitrem quia semper vivit in armis.* / —— *Victrix Provincia plorat.* / = / London, / Printed for *John Morphew,* near *Statio-* / *ners-Hall.* 1712.

[Title in double-lined frame.]
8vo; A–F⁸ — 2 pp. (t. + bl.), 3 pp. + bl. (The Preface), 7–96.
Though the year in the imprint is 1712, this piece appeared Nov. 27, 1711.

Second edition:

The / *Conduct* / Of The / Allies, / And Of The / Late Ministry, / In / Beginning and Carrying on / The / Present War. / — / —— *Partem tibi Gallia nostri* / *Eripuit: partem duris Hispania bellis:* / *Pars jacet Hesperia: totoq; exercitus orbe* / *Te vincente perit. Terris fudisse cruorem* / *Quid juvat Arctois, Rhodano, Rhenoq; subactis?* / *Odimus accipitrem quia semper vivit in armis.* / —— *Victrix Provincia plorat.* / — / The Second Edition, Corrected. / — / London, / Printed for *John Morphew,* near *Statio-* / *ners-Hall.* 1711.

[Title within double-lined frame.]
Collation the same as that of the first edition.

Third edition:

Title and collation the same as those of the second edition, except:

— / The Third Edition, Corrected. / —

Fourth edition:
Title and collation the same as those of the second edition, except:

— / The Fourth Edition, Corrected. / —

Fifth edition:
Title the same as that of the second edition, except:

— / The Fifth Edition, Corrected. / —

8vo (in fours); A–F⁴ — 2 pp. (t. + bl.), 2 pp. (The Preface), 5–48.
Sixth edition:
Title the same as that of the second edition, except:

— / The Sixth Edition, Corrected. / – – – – – – 1712.

Collation the same as that of the fifth edition.

Seventh edition:
Title the same as that of the second edition, except:

— / The Seventh Edition, Corrected. / – – – – – – – 1712.

Collation the same as that of the fifth edition.

Eighth edition:
Title the same as that of the second edition, except:

— / The Eighth Edition, Corrected. / – – – – – – 1713.

Collation the same as that of the fifth edition.
Note: But for slight alterations while the type was still standing, the first four editions are from the same setting. The same is the case with the 5th, 6th and 7th editions. But the 8th is a different setting.

The fourth and all the following editions have a short Postscript at the end, recording the addition of a few new lines "in the 38th (21st) Page, which mentions the *Succession.*"
Cf. *Journal to Stella,* 478, n. 16.
Copies of all the eight editions are at Penn.

540. *Dublin edition:*
The / Conduct / Of The / Allies, / And Of The / Late Ministry, / In / Beginning and Carrying on / The / Present War. / = / ——
Partem tibi Gallia nostri / *Eripuit: Partem duris Hispania bellis:* / *Pars jacet Hesperia: totoq; exercitus orbe* / *Te vincente perit* —— / *Odimus accipitrem quia semper vivit in armis.* / —— *Victrix Provincia plorat.* / = / *Dublin,* / Re-Printed for *John Hyde* Bookseller / in *Dames-street.* 1712.

[Title in double-lined frame.]
8vo; A–D⁸, E⁴ — 2 pp. (t. + bl.), 2 pp. (The Preface), 5–72.
Reprinted from the 1st, 2nd or 3rd London edition; the additional lines are not in it.
Copies: T.C.D. (PPP 23.5), and Penn.

541. *Another Dublin edition:*
The Conduct / Of The / Allies, / And Of The / Late Ministry, / In Begining [*sic*] and Carrying on the / Present War. / — / ——

Partem tibi Gallia nostri | Eripuit: Partem duris Hispania bellis: | Pars jacet Hesperia: totoq; exercitus orbe | Te vincente perit. Terris fudisse cruorem | Quid juvat Arctois, Rhodano, Rhenoq; subactis? | Odimus accipitrem quia semper vivit in armis. | — Victrix Provincia plorat. | Sola, Novum, Dictuq; Nefas, Harpyia Celaeno | Prodigium canit, & tristes denuntiat Iras. Virg. | — | The Fourth Edition, Corrected. | — | *London:* Printed by John Morphew: | And Re-printed by Edward Waters in *Essex-street,* | at the Corner of *Sycamore-Alley,* Dublin, 1712.

[Title within double-lined frame.]
Sm. 8vo (in fours); π^4, B–G^4 — 2 pp. (t. + bl.), 2 pp. (Preface), 5–54 (39 and 40 repeated in numbering) — F begins on the second p. 39, G on p. 47.
Copy: Marsh Cas XI 16 (3).
Another Dublin edition (or issue?):
Title and collation are the same as those of the preceding edition, except:
(1) the misprint 'Begining' has been corrected
(2) the second quotation (2 lines from Virgil) has been omitted
(3) — | The Fifth Edition, Corrected. | — | *London:* Printed by John Morphew: | And Re printed by Edward Waters in *Essex-street* | at the Corner of *Sycamore-Alley.* Dublin, 1712.
(4) Page number 26 is printed upside down.
Copies: Nat. Libr. Dublin, and U.L.C. (Hib. 8.712.5^1).

542. *Edinburgh edition:*
The | *Conduct* | Of The | Allies, | And Of The | Late Ministry, | In | Beginning and Carrying on | The | Present War. | — | —— *Partem tibi Gallia nostri | Eripuit: partem duris Hispania bellis: | Pars jacet Hesperia: totoque exercitus orbe, | Te vincente perit* —— | *Odimus accipitrem quia semper vivit in armis.* | —— *Victrix provincia plorat.* | — | *Edinburgh:* | Re-printed by Mr. *Robert Freebairn,* and sold at his Shop in | the Parliament-Closs, 1711.

8vo (in fours); [A]–G^4 — 2 pp. (t. + bl.), 1 p. (Preface), 4–56.
Copy: Nat. Libr. of Scotl. L.C. 668.3.
Another Edinburgh edition (or issue?):
Title and collation are the same as those of the preceding edition, except:
(1) – – – – Ministry, | In The | Beginning – – – –
(2) No long dashes before '*Partem*', after '*perit*', and before '*Victrix*', but a series of very small dashes.
(3) The year is 1712.
Copy: Nat. Libr. of Scotl. (L.C. 618.1).

543. *Another edition* (different title):
Good Queen Anne *vindicated,* | And | The Ingratitude, Insolence, *&c.* | Of Her | Whig Ministry | And The | Allies | Detected and Exposed, in the Beginning and | Conducting of the War. | The | Englishman's Memorial: | Containing | A *short History* of the Land Wars we have | been engaged in, with unanswerable Arguments, |

proving 'tis not the Interest of *England* to be con- / cerned, as a Principal, in a Land War, upon any / Pretence whatsoever; —— Mind The Sea. / With / Remarks on the new Ways of raising Money, *&c*. (un- / known to our Ancestors, and which our Posterity will / curse us for;) / Also / Many important Matters relative to the *British* Affairs, worthy / of the Attention of the Publick at this Juncture. / *By the* Author *of* the Dissertation on Parties. / *London*, / Printed for and sold by W. Owen, at *Temple-Bar*. 1748. / (Price One Shilling.)

8vo (in fours); π^2, B–K^4 — 2 pp. (t. + adv. on verso), 2 pp. (f.t. + bl.), 1–72.
Copy: Penn.

544. *Another edition:*
Good Queen Anne *vindicated*, / And The / Ingratitutde, Insolence, *&c*. / Of Her / Whig Ministry / And The / Allies / Detected and Exposed, in the Beginning / and Conducting of the War. / The Groans of Old England: / Containing / A *short History* of Land Wars and those we have / been engaged in, with unanswerable Arguments, / proving 'tis not the Business of *England* to be con- / cerned, as a Principal, in a Land War, upon any / Pretence what-soever; —— Mind The Sea. / With Remarks on the new Ways of raising Money, *&c*. / (unknown to our Ancestors, and which our Posterity / will curse us for;) / Also many important Matters relative to the *British* Affairs, / worthy of the Attention of the Publick at this Juncture. / *By that worthy Patriot Dean* Swift, / Whose Name will be always rever'd by the Patrons of / Liberty and Publick Spirit. / *London*, / Printed and sold by W. Owen, at *Temple-Bar*, and at / *Oxford, Manchester, Edinburgh* and *Dublin*. 1748.

8vo (in fours); π^1, B–K^4 — 2 pp. (t. + bl.), 1–72.
Copies: U.L.C. (X 25.26), and Penn.

1660. *Another edition:*
Good Queen Anne *vindicated*, / And / The Ingratitude, Insolence, *&c*. / Of Her / Whig Ministry / And The / Allies / Detected and Exposed, in the Beginning and / Conducting of the War. / The / Englishman's Memorial: / Containing / A *short History* of the Land Wars we have / been engaged in, with unanswerable Arguments, / proving 'tis not the Interest of *England* to be con- / cerned, as a Principal, in a Land War, upon / any Pretence whatsoever Mind The Sea. / With / Remarks on the new Ways of raising Money, *&c*. (unknown / to our Ancestors, and which our Posterity will curse us / for;) / Also / Many important Matters relative to the *British* Affairs, worthy / of the Attention of the Publick at this Juncture.

/ *By the* Author *of* the Dissertation on Parties. / = / *London:* / Printed by M. Cooper, in *Pater-noster-Row.* / — / MDCCXLVIII.

8vo; [A]–C⁸ — [1] (title), [2]–48.
Copy: Nat. Libr. of Ireland, Dublin.

545. *French translation* of the above:

Apologie / *De La* / Reine Anne, / *Où l'on examine la conduite de ses* / *Ministres pendant la guerre,* & / *celle des Alliés de la Grande-Bre-* / *tagne.* / Par M. Swift, / Doyen de Saint Patrice de Dublin. / *Traduite De L'Anglois,* / *Par M.L.B.C.D.G.* / [ornament] / A Bruxelles, / *Et se trouve à Paris,* / Chez Le Jay, Libraire, Quai de Gêvres, / au Grand Corneille. / = / M.DCC.LXIX.

12mo; aˣᴵᴵ, bᴵᴵ, A–Kˣᴵᴵ — 2 pp. (t. + bl.), [III]–XXVIII (Preface), [1]–240. — aV signed aIV.
Copies: Bibl. Nat. Paris, and Penn.
The title-page as given above is not the original one, but an insert. In the Penn copy the original title page (forming a double-leaf with leaf aXII) was not cut away, but pasted to the inside of the front of the paper cover enveloping the book; after disengagement the reason was revealed, namely, because it mentioned the translator not in initials only, but in full: *Par M. le Beau, Commissaire des guerres.*
For the rest the two title-pages are the same (only *PARIS*, and *Paris,*).

547. *French translation:*

Lettres / Et / Memoires / Sur La Conduite / De La / Presente Guerre / Et Sur Les / Negociations De Paix. / *Tome I.* / *Seconde Edition, corrigée* & *augmentée.* / [ornament] / A La Haye, / Chez T. Johnson, Marchand Libraire. / — / M.DCC.XII.

The title of the second volume is the same, except:

– – – – Paix. / *Tome II.* / [ornament] / A La Haye, / – – – – –

[Titles in red and black.]
8vo; [*]–**⁸, ***⁷, A–Dd⁸ — 2 pp. (t. + bl.), [III]–XII (Avertissement Du Libraire), [XIII]–XLVI (Lettre Écrite A Mᴿ ***), 1–430, 2 pp. (Liste Des Pièces).
[*]⁸, **², A–G⁸, H⁶ — 2 pp. (t. + bl.), 2 pp. (Avertissement Du Libraire), [V]–XVIII (Lettre A L'Examinateur), 2 pp. (second title: 'La Conduite Des Alliez' + bl.), 1–4 (Préface De L'Auteur Anglois), 5–122, 1 p. advs. + bl.
In the second volume, the 2 pp., 1–4, 5–122 contain *The Conduct of the Allies,* with the following title:

La / Conduite / Des / Alliez / Et De / L'Ancien Ministere / D'Angleterre, / Par raport à la présente Guerre. / *Traduit de l'Anglois.* / — / —— *Partem tibi Gallia nostri* / *Eripuit: partem duris Hispania Bellis:* / *Pars jacet Hesperia: totoque exercitus orbe* / *Te vincente perit. Terris fudisse cruorem* / *Quid juvat Arctois Rhodano,*

Rhenoque subactis? | *Odimus accipitrem quia semper vivit in armis.* |
—— *Victrix Provincia plorat.*

> Copies: B.M. 808 b 32, and Kon. Bibl. (lacking last leaf in Vol. II).
> I have not seen the first edition of these two volumes.

548. *Another French translation:*
La | Conduite | Des Alliez, | Et | Du Dernier Ministere, | En
commençant & en continuant | la Guerre. | *Traduit d'un Imprimé
Anglois, intitulé,* | The Conduct of the Allies, and of the late |
Ministry, in Beginning and carrying on / the Present War. Second
Edition cor- | rected. | Chez Jean Morphew, à Londres 1711. |
[ornament] | A Liege, | Chez Guillaume-Henry Streel. | 1712.

> 8vo; [A] 1, π², A 2–8, B–D⁸, E⁵ — 2 pp. (t. + Latin quotation on verso),
> 4 pp. (Preface), 3–74.
> Copy: B.M. 1093 d 10.

549. *Another French translation:*
Traduction | D'Un | Ecrit Anglois | intitulé, | *La Conduite des
Alliez, & du dernier* | *Ministere, en commençant & en conti-* | *nuant la
Guerre.* | Imprimé chez Jean Morphew, à Londres 1711. | — |
A Liege, | Chez Guillaume-Henry Streel. | 1712.

> 8vo; 1–73 (verso blank), 74, 3 pp. blank [mistake in printing].
> Copy: Mazarine, Paris.

550. *Another French translation:*
Manifeste | Pour | Le Ministere | Present | D'Angleterre, |
Traduit d'un Ecrit Anglois, | intitulé, | *La Conduite des Alliez, &*
du dernier | *Ministere, en commençant & en conti-* | *nuant la Guerre.*
| Imprimé chez Jean Morphew, à Londres 1711. | — | A Liege, |
Chez Guillaume-Henry Streel. | 1712.

> 8vo; 1–74.
> This is the same printing as the preceding volume, with new title, and the
> mistake in the pagination corrected.
> Copy: Mazarine, Paris (2 copies).

551. *Another French translation:*
La | Conduite | Des Alliez, | Et Du | Ministere | Precedent, | En
commençant & en continuant | la presente Guerre. | *Traduit De
L'Anglois.* | Septiéme Edition, corrigée. | —— *Partem tibi Gallia
nostri* | *Eripuit: partem duris Hispania bellis,* | *Pars jacet Hesperia:*
totoque exercitus orbe | *Te vincente perit. Terris fudisse cruorem* | *Quid
juvat Arctois. Rhodano, Rheno'que subactis:* | *Odimus Accipitrem,*
quia semper vivit in armis. | —— *Victrix Provincia plorat.* | A Londres,
chez Jean Morphew. 1712. | [ornament] | A Luxembourg, | Chez
André Chevalier. | — | 1712.

Sm. 8vo; *⁶, A–E⁸, F² — 2 pp. (t. + bl.), I–VII (Lettre), VIII–X (Prèface), 1–84.

At first published by itself, this pamphlet was the same year bound together with seven others (all paged separately). The new general title is:

552. Recueil / De / Quelques / Pieces / Nouvelles. / Concernant les Affaires du / Tems present, qui ont pa- / rües en Angleterre & en / Hollande. / *La Pluspart Traduites De* / *L'Anglois.* / [ornament] / M.D.CC.XII.

Sm. 8vo; 2 pp. (t. Recueil + bl.), 2 pp. (t. Conduite + bl.), I–VII (Lettre), VIII–X (Prèface), 1–84; 1–48; 1–44; 1–75 + bl.; 1–40; 1–17 + bl.; 1–7 + bl., 1–8.

The [2 pp., I–X, 1–84] pages are *La Conduite Des Alliez*, &c.; the [1–48] pages are *Remarques Sur Le Traité De La Barriere*, &c. (see No. 563, *post*).
Copy: Bibl. Nat. Paris (Nc 2443 bis).

553. *Spanish translation:*
Conducta / De Los Aliados, / Y De El Ultimo Ministerio / Desde El Principio A La Continuacion / De La Guerra. / Impresso En Londres / en Casa de Juan Morphew, / Año de 1711. / Traducido En Francés, / Y Nuevamente Impresso En Lieja / En La De Enrique Streel, / Año de 1712. / Y Ultimamente En Madrid / En la Imprenta Real, por Joseph Rodriguez, / Año de 1712. / — / B.D.M.

[Title in decorated frame.]
4to; [A]–F⁴, G² — 2 pp. (t. + Latin quotation with translation into Spanish, on verso), 1–50.
Copy: B.M. T 1303 (19).

Contemporary Criticism Conduct Allies, and Barrier Treaty:

1040. Remarks On A False, Scandalous, and Seditious Libel, Intituled, The Conduct of the Allies, &c. London, A. Baldwin, 1711.
8vo (in fours); π⁴, A–E⁴ — 2 pp. (h.t. + bl.), 2 pp. (f.t. + bl.), 3 pp. (Preface), 1 p. (blank), 1–40.
Copy: Penn.

1045. Remarks upon Remarks: Or The Barrier-Treaty And The Protestant Succession Vindicated. In Answer to the False and Treasonable Reflections of the Author of The Conduct of the Allies. &c. London: A. Baldwin. 1711. — 8vo; 2 pp., 1–43 + bl.
Second ed.: London, A. Baldwin, 1712.

1041. The Allies And The Late Ministry Defended against France, And the Present Friends of France. In Answer to a Pamphlet, Intituled, The Conduct of the Allies. &c. London, A. Baldwin. 1711.
8vo (in fours); π¹, B–F⁴, G³ — 2 pp. (t. + bl.), 1–46 — G 4 probably used as title-leaf.
Copy: Penn.

The Allies And The Late Ministry Defended against France, And the Present Friends of France. Part II. Containing a Vindication of the Barrier-Treaty, &c. London: A. Baldwin. 1711. — 8vo; 4 pp. (h.t. and f.t.), 1–71 + bl.

There are two more Parts (III and IV); the author of the four parts was Dr. Francis Hare.

There were more editions, i.a. 3rd ed., 4 parts, 1711–12.

Dutch translation of Part II: De Geallieerden en de Laatstvoorgaande Engelsche Ministers Verdeedigd, Tegen Vrankrijk, en de tegenwoordige Vrinden van Vrankrijk. Behelzende Eene Verdeediging van het Tractaat der Barriere, &c. Amsterdam, Robert Blokland, 1712. — 12mo; 1–106.

French translation of Parts I and II: Défense Des Hauts Alliez Et Du Dernier Ministere De La Grande-Bretagne; Contre La France et ses Partisans. Pour servir de Réponse à un Livre qui a pour Titre La Conduite des Alliez & du dernier Ministére dans la présente Guerre. Premiere Partie, Ou Critique générale de cet Ouvrage, &c. [no imprint].

— — — — — — Second Partie, Contenant la défense du Traité de Barriére & de celui de Portugal. &c. [no imprint].

8vo; 1–88, 89–196. [The sigs. in both Parts are: 'Tom. III', which suggests two preceding 'Tomes'].

1042. A Defence Of The Allies And The Late Ministry: Or, Remarks On The Tories New Idol. Being A Detection of the Manifest Frauds and Falsities, in a late Pamphlet, Entituled, The Conduct of the Allies. &c. London: J. Baker. 1712. — 8vo (in fours); π^1, B–F^4, G^3 — 2 pp. (t. + bl.), 1–46. — G 4 probably used as title-leaf.

1046. A Further Search Into The Conduct Of The Allies, And The Late Ministry, As To Peace and War. &c. London: John Morphew. 1712. — 8vo (in fours); [A]–K^4 — 2 pp. (t. + bl.), 3–77, 3 pp. blank.

1043. Natural Reflections Upon The Present Debates About Peace And War. &c. London: John Morphew. MDCCXII. — 8vo; 2 pp. (h.t.), 1–76 (beginning with f.t.) [Pp. 65–76 are a later addition]. — Contains references to *The Conduct Of The Allies*, the *Defence Of The Allies*, and the *Vindication Of The Present Ministry*.

1044. A Full Answer To The Conduct of the Allies: To which is added, some Observations On The Remarks on the Barrier Treaty. By the same Author. London: Printed in the Year MDCCXII.

8vo; A–F^8 — 2 pp. (t. + bl.), 3–95 + bl.

Copy: Penn.

Dutch translation: Bondig Antwoord Op het Tractaat, genaemt Het Gedrag Der Geallieerden, &c. — Waer by geroegt syn eenige Observatien en Aanmerkingen op het Traktaat van de Barriere, &c. — [no imprint] — 8vo; [A]–H^8, I^4 — 2 pp. (t. + bl.), 3–135 + bl.

1048. The Dutch Barrier Our's: Or The Interest Of England and Holland Inseparable. With Reflections on the Insolent Treatment the Emperor and States-General have met with from the Author of the Conduct, and his Brethren. &c. London: Printed in the Year, 1712. — 8vo; 1–20. — By John Oldmixon.

Also an ed.: Baldwin, 1712.

French translation: Discours Sur La Barriere Des Hollandais, &c. Rotterdam, Jean Hofhout, 1712. — 12mo; 1–39 + bl.

Another French translation: Discours Sur La Barriere Des Hollandais, &c. Rotterdam, Jean Hofhout, 1712. Et se vend, A Bruxelles, chez T'Serstevens. — 12mo; 1–40.

1049. Some Remarks On The Letters Between the L—d T – – – – – nd, And Mr. Se – – – tary B – – le. In A Letter To The Author Of The Remarks on the Barrier-Treaty. London, John Morphew, 1712. — 8vo; 1–22, 1 p. advs. + bl. [Contains, besides much praise, the complaint that the author of *Remarks On The Barrier Treaty* has not been severe enough, the contents falling far short of what the title promises; after which at some length suggestions are made for a possible 'second Part'. — Cf. the title of the following Dublin ed.].

Dublin edition: The Second Part Of The Remarks On The Barrier Treaty, Being Some Remarks On The Letters Between &c. (as above). London John Morphew: And Re-printed by Edward Waters &c. Dublin, 1712. — 12mo; 1–23 + bl.

Edinburgh edition: Some Remarks On The Letters Between &c. (as above). Edinburgh, Robert Freebairn. 1712. — 8vo; 1–14, 1 p. advs. + bl.

Copy: Penn.

1047. The Barrier-Treaty Vindicated. London: A. Baldwin. MDCCXII. — 8vo; 12 pp., 1–200. [There is a 3rd ed., 1713].

Answered by: Remarks On The Barrier-Treaty Vindicated. In A Letter To The Author. London: John Morphew. MDCCXIII. — 8vo; 1–32. [Dilke, *Papers Of A Critic*, I, 361, who ascribes this to Bolingbroke, thinks that it is a Vindication of Swift's *Remarks On The Barrier Treaty*, whereas in reality it contains Remarks on the preceding pamphlet]. Also ascribed to Lord Townshend, also to Francis Hare.

Copy: Penn.

1047A. A Letter To The Examiner concerning the Barrier-Treaty vindicated; sm. 8vo, 32 pp. — From an antiq. book-catalogue.

1047B. The Examiner, Vol. III, No. 16, (Jan. 16, 1712–13) contains an 'Appendix to the Conduct Allies, and Barrier Treaty' (see No. 525, note; cf. *Journal to Stella*, Jan. 15, 1712–13).

554. An Excellent New Song, / Being The / *Intended Speech of a famous Orator / against Peace.*

Sm. folio; 2 pages.
Published Dec. 6, 1711 (cf. *Journal to Stella*, Dec. 5).
Another edition (?):
The Earl of Nottingham's *Speech to the Honourable House of Lords*; London, printed by J. Tomson, *near* Covent-Garden, 1711.

No copy found. Mentioned in *Poems*, 142, where the question is put whether this is a pirated reprint. The real printer was found to be Andrew Hind, living in Peterborough-Court, near Fleet-Street. He was taken into custody, but discharged after about four weeks, on Jan. 19, 1712.

555. The W – – ds-r Prophecy.

Sm. folio; 1 page.
At foot of page:

Printed in the Year, 1711.

Copies: B.M. (two copies) C20 f2 (235), and 1871 f3 (22); U.L.C. Syn 3.71.4(4), and Penn.
Published Dec. 24, 1711.

556. *Another edition:*

The same as above, but different printing (smaller type).
Copy: B.M. G. 1390 (10).

This piece consists of an introduction in prose, followed by the prophecy
in verse. The above two editions have the 'Prophecy' partly in black letter
and partly roman letter.

Poems, 145, mentions another edition with the text of the 'Prophecy'
entirely in roman. On my asking Mr. Williams for its location, he said he
could not find it in his notes. Where is it?

556A. *The Post Boy*, Dec. 27, 1711, contains an obituary notice concerning
Mrs. Anne Long, caused to be inserted into it by Swift (cf. *Journal to Stella*,
446, n. 21; and see Swift's *Account-Book*, No. 508, Vict. & Alb. Museum,
containing a memorandum to the same effect).

For Swift's contributions to *Post Boy* and *Evening Post* see Davis, Vol. VI,
p. 196, etc.

557. Some / Advice / Humbly Offer'd to the / Members / Of
The / *October Club*, / In A / Letter / From A / Person of Honour. /
= / *London*, / Printed for *John Morphew*, near *Stationers-* / *Hall*,
1712. Price 2 *d*.

[Title within double-lined frame].
8vo; A⁸ — 2 pp. (t. + bl.), 3–16.
Copy: Penn.
Second edition:
Title and collation the same, except:

– – – – – Honour. / — / The Second Edition Corrected. / — /
London, / – – – – –

Copy: Nat. Libr. of Scotl. (L.C. 3339.6).

Dublin edition:

Some / Advice / Humbly offer'd to the / Members / Of The /
October Club, / In A / Letter / From A / Person of Honour, / *London*
/ Printed, and Re-printed in *Dublin* by / *C. Carter*. 1713.

[Title within single-lined frame.]
Sm. 8vo (in fours); π⁴, B⁴ — 2 pp. (t. + bl.), 3–16.
Copies: Nat. Libr. of Ireland, and Univ. of Illinois, Urbana.

558. The Fable of Midas.

Sm. folio; 2 pages.
At foot of second page:
Printed for *John Morphew* near Stationers-Hall, 1712.
Published Feb. 14, 1712 (see *Journal to Stella*, under that date).
Copies: Lord Rothschild (this copy has a contemporary MS. note:
N.W. Feb. 16, 1711.), and Harvard.
Another edition:
The same as above, except:

Printed in the Year, 1711.

This is a piracy.

Remarks On The Barrier Treaty

559. Some | Remarks | On The | Barrier Treaty, | Between | Her Majesty | And The | States-General. | — | By the Author of | *The Conduct of the Allies.* | — | To which are added, | The said Barrier-Treaty, | with the Two Separate Articles; | Part of the Counter-Project; The | Sentiments of Prince *Eugene* and | Count *Sinzendorf*, upon the said | Treaty; And a Representation of | the *English* Merchants at *Bruges.* | — | *London,* | Printed for *John Morphew,* near *Stationers-* | *Hall,* 1712. Price 6 *d.*

[Title within double-lined frame.]
8vo (in fours); A–F^4 — 2 pp. (t. + bl.), 2 pp. (The Preface), 5–48.
Published end Feb., 1712 (see *Journal to Stella,* Feb. 20).
Copy: Penn.
Second edition:
Same title and collation, except:

– – – – | with the Two *Separate Articles;* Part of | the *Counter-Project*; The *Sentiments* of | Prince *Eugene* and Count *Sinzendorf,* | upon the said *Treaty*; And a *Represen-* | *tation* of the *English* Merchants at | *Bruges.* | — | The Second Edition. | — | *London,* | ———

Exactly the same printing as the first edition.
Copy: Library Peace Palace, The Hague.

560. *Dublin edition:*
Some | Remarks | On The | Barrier Treaty | Between | Her Majesty | And The | States-General. | — | By the Author of | *The Conduct of the Allies.* | — | To which are added, | The said Barrier-Treaty, | with the Two Separate Articles; | Part of the Counter-Project; The | Sentiments of Prince *Eugene* and | Count *Sinzendorf,* upon the said | Treaty; And a Representation of | the *English* Merchants at *Bruges.* | — | *Dublin,* | Re-Printed for *John Hyde* Bookseller | in *Dames-street.* 1712.

[Title within double-lined frame.]
Sm. 4to; [A]–D^4, E^2 — 2 pp. (t. + 'Preface' on verso), 3–36.
Copy: T.C.D. (RR mm 53.7).

561. *Another Dublin edition:*
Some | Remarks | On The | Barrier Treaty, | Between | Her Majesty | And The | States-General. | — | By the Author of | *The Conduct of the Allies.* | — | To which are added, | The said Barrier-Treaty, | with the Two Separate Articles; Part | of the Counter-Project; The Senti- | ments of Prince *Eugene* and Count *Sin-* | *zendorf,* upon the said Treaty; And | a Representation of the *English* Mer- | chants at *Bruges.* | — | *London,* Printed for *J. Morphew;*

And / Re-printed and Sold by *E. Waters* in / *Essex street*, at the *Corner* of *Sycamore-* / *Alley*, *Dublin*, 1712.

> [Title within double-lined frame.]
> Sm. 8vo (in fours); A–D⁴ — 2 pp. (t. + bl.), 2 pp. (The Preface), 5–32. —
> A 2 wrongly signed A 1.
> Copy: Penn.

1645. *Another Dublin edition or issue* (?):

Some / Remarks / On The / Barrier-Treaty / Between / Her Majesty / And The / States-General / — / By the Author of / *The Conduct of the Allies.* / — / To which are added, / The said Barrier-Treaty, with / the Two separate Articles; Part of the Coun- / ter-Project; The Sentiments of Prince Eu- / gene and Count Zinzendorf, upon the said / Treaty; And a Representation of the English / Merchants at Bruges. / — / Dublin: Re-printed by *E. Waters* at the New / Post Office Printing House in *Essex-street*, at / the Corner of *Sycamore-Alley*.

> [Title within double-lined frame.]
> Sm. 8vo (in fours); π⁴, [four leaves lacking], C–D⁴ — 2 pp. (t. + bl.), 2 pp.
> (Preface), 5–32 (9–16 lacking).
> Copy: Nat. Libr. of Ireland.

562. *Edinburgh edition:*

Some / Remarks / On The / Barrier Treaty, / Between / Her Majesty / And The / States-General. / — / By the Author of / *The Conduct of the Allies.* / — / To which are added, / The said Barrier-Treaty, / with the two Separate Articles; Part of the / Counter-Project; The Sentiments of Prince / *Eugene* and Count *Sinzendorf*, upon the said / Treaty; And a Representation of the *En-* / *glish* Merchants at *Bruges.* / — / *Edinburgh:* / Re-printed by Mr. *Robert Freebairn*, / and sold at his Shop in the *Parliament-Closs*, 1712.

> 8vo (in fours); π⁴, B–D⁴ — 2 pp. (t. + bl.), 1 p. (The Preface), 4–32.
> Copies: Nat. Libr. of Scotland LC 618.2, and Penn.

563. *French translation:*

Remarques / Sur Le Traité / De La Barriere, / Entre Sa Majesté Britanni- / que & les Etats Generaux. / *Par l'Autheur de la Conduite des Alliez,* / Ausquelles est ajoûté ledit Traité De La / Barriere; avec les deux Articles sepa- / rez, partie du Contre-Projet; / *Les Sentimens du Prince Eugene,* & *du* / Comte de Sinzendorf, *sur ledit Traité*; / Et La Representation des Marchands / Anglois à Bruges. / *Traduit de l'Anglois sur la seconde Edition.* / A Londres, chez Jean Morphew, proche la Sal- / le des Imprimeurs. 1712. / [ornament] / A Luxembourg, / Chez André Chevalier. / — / 1712.

> Sm. 8vo; [A]–C⁸ — 2 pp. (t. + bl.), 3–[4] (Preface), 5–48.
> Copy: Kon. Bibl. (pamphlet 16064).

The above also forms part of the collection: *Recueil De Quelques Pieces Nouvelles*, &c. (see No. 552, *ante*).

564. *Another French translation (abridged?):*
Remarques abrégées sur le Traité de la Barrière fait entre Sa Majesté Britannique et les Etats Généraux à la Haye. — No Place, No Date (1712).

[Mentioned by Sybil Goulding, *Swift En France*, 1924, p. 182.]

565. *Dutch translation* (pp. 118–159) *in:*
Tractaat / Tusschen / Hare Brittannische / Majesteit / en de Hoog Mog. Heeren / Staten Generaal, / Om te verzekeren de Successie tot de Kroon / van Groot Brittannien, en te verzorgen / een Barriere voor de Staten Generaal: / *Met de Instructien van de Koninginne aan de Heren / Marlboroug en Townshend, het Tegen Project, / verscheide Extracten van Brieven, en andere / Bewys-stukken dienaangaande: mitsgaders / eenige Aanmerkingen voor en tegen het / voornoemde Tractaat.* / Uit het Engelsch vertaalt. / [ornament] / *T'Amsterdam,* / — / By Christiaan Petzold, in de / Kalverstraat, by de Osjes-sluis, 1712.

Sm. 8vo; [*]⁴, A–N⁸, O⁴ — 2 pp. (t. + bl.), 3 pp. (Korten Inhoud), 3 pp. (Tot Den Lezer), [1]–42 (Tractaat Van Barriere), 43–59 (Tegen-Project), 60–117 (Extract van de Brief van den Lord Townshend), 118–216 (Aanmerkingen Op Het Tractaat Van Barriere En Het Tegen Project Door den Schryver van het Gedrag der Geallieerden).
Copy: Kon. Bibl. (pamphlet 16067).

566. *Spanish translation:*
Breves Reflexiones, / Sobre El Tratado / De La Barrera, / Hecho Entre Su Magestad Britanica, / Y Los Estados Generales, En La Haya, / El Dia 29. De Octvbre De 1709. / *Por El Mismo Avtor / del primer Papel, intitulado:* / La Conducta De Los Aliados. / — / En que vàn insertos, el Tratado de la Barrera; / los dos Articulos secretos; parte del Contra- / Proyecto; los Dictamenes del Principe Eugenio, y / Conde de Cincendorf, sobre este mismo Tratado; / y vltimamente, la Representacion de los / Mercaderes Ingleses de la Ciudad / de Brujas. / — / *Traducido del Inglès à la Lengua Francesa, y de esta / al Idioma Castellano.* / — / Con Licencia: Año de 1712.

[Title within decorated frame.]
4to; [A]–D⁴, E² — 2 pp. (t. + bl.), 2 pp. (Advertisement by the Author), 1–31 + bl.
Copy: B.M. T 1303 (20).
For contemporary criticism, see at the end of *Conduct of the Allies*.

577. A / Proposal / For / *Correcting, Improving* and *Ascertaining* / The / English Tongue; / In A / *Letter* / To the Most Honourable

/ Robert / *Earl of* Oxford *and* Mortimer, / *Lord High Treasurer* / Of / Great Britain. / = / *London:* / Printed for Benj. Tooke, at the / *Middle-Temple-Gate, Fleetstreet.* 1712.

> [Title within double-lined frame.]
> 8vo (in fours); [A]–F⁴ — 2 pp. (h.t. + bl.), 2 pp. (f.t. + bl.), 5–48.
> Text dated: London, Feb. 22, 1711, 12. — Swift's name printed on half-title and at the end.
> Copy: own.
> Published soon after May 17, 1712 (advs. in *The Post Boy*, and in *The London Gazette*).

Second edition:
Same title and collation, except:

– – – Britain. / — / The Second Edition. / — / *London:* / – – –.
> Copy: Penn.

Contemporary criticism

1051. Reflections On Dr. Swift's Letter To The Earl of Oxford, About The English Tongue. London, A. Baldwin.
> 8vo; 4 pp., 1–35 + bl. — [By John Oldmixon].

578. Some / Reasons / *To Prove,* / That no Person is obliged by / his Principles, as a *Whig,* / To Oppose / *Her Majesty* / Or Her / Present Ministry. / = / In a Letter to a Whig-Lord. / = / *London,* / Printed for *John Morphew,* near *Stationers-* / *Hall,* 1712. Price 3*d.*

> [Title within double-lined frame.]
> 8vo (in fours); [A]–C⁴ — 2 pp. (t. + bl.), 3–24.
> Copy: B.M. 104 b 6.
> Monck Mason, 279 n., says that the Whig Lord was Lord Ashburnham.
> Published early June, 1712 (see *Journal to Stella,* May 31 and June 17).

579. *Dublin edition:*
Some / Reasons / To / Prove, / That no Person is obliged by his Principles, / as a *Whig,* to Oppose / Her Majesty / Or Her / Present Ministry. / — / *In a Letter to a Whig-Lord.* / — / [ornament] / — / London. Printed; And Re-Printed in Dublin by *C.* / *Carter* in *Fish-shamble street.* 1712.

> [Title within single-lined frame.]
> Sm. 8vo (in fours); A–B⁴ — 2 pp. (t. + bl.), 3–16.
> Copy: T.C.D. (R.R.m.m. 53.10).

***

580. T – – *l* – – *nd*'s Invitation to *Dismal,* to Dine / with the Calves-Head Club. / — / *Imitated from* Horace, *Epist.* 5. *Lib.* I. / — /

Folio; 1 page.

English verse, in 1 column, dated: *January* 29.; under that, Latin verse, in 2 columns.

Published end of June, 1712 (adv. in the *Examiner*, June 26).

Another edition:

Title and description the same as above, except that there is a comma after *January*. Printed from a different type-setting.

About a dozen variations in spelling, punctuation, capitalization, etc. in the English text.

Copy: Nat. Libr. of Scotl. Pamph. 10 (76).

For a "Representation of the State of the Nation", see Davis, Vol. VI, p. xvi.

581. Peace and Dunkirk; | Being An | *Excellent New Song upon the Surrender of* Dunkirk | *to General* Hill. | To the Tune of, *The King shall enjoy his own again.*

Sm. folio; 1 page.
At foot of page:

London, Printed in the Year, 1712.

Published early July, 1712 (see adv. *Examiner*, July 3–10).

582. A Hue and cry after Dismal; | *Being a full and true Account, how a* Whig L – – d | *was taken at* Dunkirk, *in the Habit of a Chimney-* | *sweeper, and carryed before General* Hill.

Folio; 1 page.
At foot of page:

London, Printed in the Year, 1712.

Published ca. July 17, 1712 (see adv. *Examiner*, July 10–17).

583. *Another edition:*

Dunkirk *to be Let,* Or, *A Town Ready Furnish'd.* | With | A Hue-and-Cry after Dismal: | *Being a full and true Account, how a* Whig *L—d was taken at* Dunkirk, | *in the Habit of a Chimney-Sweeper, and carried before General* Hill. | *To which is added the Copy of a* Paper *that was found in his Pocket.*

Folio; 1 page.
At foot of page:

London, Printed in the Year. M.DCCXII.

Copies of both editions in Bodl. (MSS. Rawl. D. 383.135, and Pamph. 305 (1712) 6.53).

Apart from the title, the second edition differs from the first in having inserted in the middle of the text (as indicated in the title): "It is said, that he had the following Verses found in | his Pocket, which he scatter'd up and down the Town. | *Old* Lewis *thus the Terms of Peace to Burnish,* | *Has lately let out*

Dunkirk *Ready Furnish'd*; | *But whether 't is by* Lease, *or* Coppy-hold, | *Or* Tenure in Capite, *we've not been told:* | *But this we hope, if yet he pulls his Horns in,* | *He'll be oblig'd to give his Tenants Warning."*

Messrs. Quaritch published a facsimile of a copy of the first edition in their possession.

It would seem, both from the title and the additional rhyme of the second edition, that in the meantime a Whig pamphlet had appeared with some such title as the following: "Dunkirk let out ready furnished, on condition of good payment". At least I found a copy of a Dutch translation (Kon. Bibl., pamphlet 16071), entitled: "Duynkerken Gestoffeert verhuurt op voorwaarde van goede Betaling." — 4to; 4 pp.; in which the strange conditions on which Dunkirk has been surrendered are represented as ridiculous, and therefore untrustworthy.

Another 'Dunkirk' piece is: The Description of Dunkirk With Squash's and Dismal's Opinion. &c. Printed in the Year MDCCXII. — Sm. folio; 1 page. — Elr. Ball, *Swift's Verse*, 130, ascribes it to Swift. — Cf. *Poems*, 1097–8.

584. Numb. 33. of *The Examiner*, Vol. II (July 10–17, 1712) has this advertisement: "Just Publish'd, Dunkirk still in the Hands of the French, being a plain and true Discovery of a most notorious Falshood, invented by Jacobites and Tories, that the Town of Dunkirk was lately delivered to the English. Pr. 1 d." — This pamphlet is mentioned by Swift in the *Journal to Stella* (July 17, 1712) under the title: *Argument that Dunkirk is not in our Hands*, as written by him. No copy has as yet been discovered.

585. A Letter from the | Pretender, | *To a Whig-Lord.*

Sm. folio; 1 page.
The letter is dated at top: "*S. Germain, July* 8. 1712", and signed at foot: "James R."
Copy: Lambeth (66 A 8 (4)).
Monck Mason, 279 n., says that the Whig Lord was the Earl of Wharton.
Published July 19, 1712 (see *Journal to Stella*, under that date).
Copy: Lambeth (66A 8 (4)).

585A. A | Letter | Of | Thanks | From My | Lord *W******n | To The | Lord B^p of S. *Asaph,* | In the Name of the | *Kit-Cat-Club.* | — | [ornament] | — | Printed in the Year 1712.

8vo; [A]⁸ — 2 pp. (h.t. + bl.), 2 pp. (f.t. + bl.), 5–14, 1 page adv. (— | *Just Published,* | The Speech of *John Ketch,* Esq; at the | Burning of a late Scandalous and Ma- | licious Preface. *Price* 1 *d.* | —) + blank.
Published July, 1712.
Copies: Texas Univ., Nat. Libr. of Ireland, and Clark Memorial Libr. (Univ. of California).
In some copies the word "Pence" in "Price Two Pence" on the half-title is spelt "Pense".
See Rothschild 2042, and Davis, VI, 147.

Second edition:

586. A | Letter | Of | Thanks | From My | Lord *W*****n | To The | Lord B^p of S. *Asaph,* | In the Name of the | *Kit-Cat-Club.* | — | — | Re-printed in the Year 1712.

8vo; A⁸ — 2 pp. (h.t. + bl.), 2 pp. (f.t. + bl.), 5–13, 3 pp. blank. — A 3 wrongly signed A 2.
Copy: Penn.

Contemporary criticism

1050. The Tryal and Condemnation of Don Prefatio d'Asaven', for Endeavouring to Resist, Subvert, and totally Destroy the Doctrines of Passive-Obedience, Indefeasible Hereditary-Right, and A . . . y Power: With His Speech at the Place of Execution, in which are some Remarks upon Jack Ketch's being lately turn'd Tory, and the Letter pretended to be written by the Lord W . . . . n to the B . . . p of St. A . . . h. 1712.

In his cat. 166 Dr. Barnard says it deals largely with "Mrs. Examiner" (Mary de la Rivière Manley) and the "Plain Dealer"; the latter admits in cross-examination that perhaps his name is Jonathan, adding "Will you give me a Deanery if I tell you?"

587. Mr. *C—ns*'s / Discourse / Of / Free-Thinking, / Put into plain *English*, by way of / Abstract, / For The / Use of the Poor. / — / *By a Friend of the* Author. / — / *London*, / Printed for *John Morphew*, near *Stationers-* / *Hall*, 1713. Price 4*d.*

[Title within double-lined frame.]
8vo (in fours); [A]–D⁴ — 2 pp. (t. + bl.), 3–31 (advs. on verso).
Published Jan. 25, 1713 (adv. in the *Examiner*, Jan. 26).
Copies: B.M. 1114 b 7., and Nat. Libr. of Scotland (916).

589. Part of the / Seventh *Epistle* / Of The / First Book / Of / Horace / Imitated: / And / Address'd to a Noble Peer. / = / *London:* / Printed for *A. Dodd*, at the *Peacock* without / *Temple-Bar.* 1713. Price 3*d.*

[Title within double-lined frame.]
4to; π⁴, B² — 2 pp. (t. + bl.), 3–12.
Published Oct. 23, 1713.
Copy: Penn.

Second edition:
Same title and collation as the first edition, except:

– – – – Peer. / — / The Second Edition. / — / *London:* / – – – –

Third edition:
Same title and collation as the first edition, except:

– – – – – Peer. / — / The Third Edition. / — / *London:* / – – – –

The second and third editions are the same printing as the first edition.
Copy: Penn.

590. *Dublin edition:*
= / The Seventh / Epistle / Of the first Book of / Horace / Imitated. / And Address'd to a Noble Lord.

4to; 1–4.
At foot of p. 4:

Dublin: Reprinted for *John Henly,* Bookseller in | *Castle-sttreet* [*sic*], 1713.

Also in:
Abel Boyer's *Political State Of Great Britain,* Nov. 1713, VI, 340.
Answered by Diaper, who was patronized by Swift.

1083. An Imitation Of The Seventeenth Epistle Of The First Book of Horace. Address'd to Dr. S. – – – – – – ft. By Mr. Diaper. London. John Morphew, 1714. — 4to; 1–16.

591. The | Importance | Of The | Guardian | Considered, in a Second | Letter | To The | Bailiff of *Stockbridge.* | — | By a Friend of Mr. *St – – – le.* | — | — | *London:* | Printed for *John Morphew,* near *Stationers* | *Hall.* 1713. Price 6 *d.*

> [Title within double-lined frame.]
> 8vo (in fours); A–F⁴ — 2 pp. (t. + bl.), 2 pp. (The Preface), 5–46, 2 pp. blank. Ca. Oct. 31, 1713; see Davis, VIII, x–xiii.
> Copy: Penn.

592. A | Preface | To The | B – – – – p of *S – – r – – m*'s | Introduction | To the Third Volume of the | History of the Reformation | Of The | Church of *England.* | — | By *Gregory Misosàrum.* | — | —— *Spargere voces* | *In vulgam ambiguas;* & *quaerere conscius arma.* | — | *London:* | Printed for *John Morphew,* near *Stationers* | *Hall.* 1713. Price 6*d.*

> [Title within double-lined frame.]
> 8vo (in fours); [A]–G⁴ — 2 pp. (t. + bl.), 2 pp. (The Preface), 5–56.
> Copy: B.M. 4106 a 48.
> *Second edition:*
> Same title and collation as the first edition, except:

> – – – *arma.* | — | The Second Edition. | — | *London:* | – – –

> Copies: Bodl., U.L.C., B.M. 698 C 15 (1), and Penn.

593. *Dublin edition:*
A | Preface | To The | B—p of S—r—m's | Introduction | To the Third Volume of the | History of the Reformation | Of The | Church of *England.* | — | By *Gregory Misosarum,* | — | – – – – – *Spargere voces* | *In vulgum ambiguas;* & *quaerere conscius arma.* | — | Dublin, | Printed by *D. Tompson* for *John Henly* at the | *Black-Moor's* Head, in *Castle-Street,* 1714.

> Sm. 8vo (in fours); π⁴, B–F⁴ — 2 pp. (t. + bl.), [I]–II (The Preface), 5–46, 2 pp. blank.
> Copy: Penn.

594. The | First *Ode* | Of The | Second Book | Of | Horace | Paraphras'd: | And | Address'd to *Richard St – – le,* Esq; | — |

En *qui promittit cives, urbem sibi curae,* | *Imperium fore,* & *Italiam,* | & *delubra* | *deorum.* Hor. | — | *London:* | Printed for *A. Dodd,* at the *Peacock* without | *Temple-Bar.* 1713. Price 3 *d.*

[Title within double-lined frame.]
4to; [A]⁴, B² — 2 pp. (t. + bl.), 3–11 + blank.
As to this piece Elr. Ball, *Swift's Verse,* 140, is a little sceptical.
Published Jan. 6 or 7, 1714.
Copy: Bodl. Pamph. 311, 1713. 6.23.
Another state:
　Same title and collation as above, except for the year, which is 1714. The printing is the same, but the catchword 'Thou' at the foot of p. 3 in the 1713 issue is present in some 1714 copies (Nat. Libr. Dublin, Chapin Libr. and Penn), absent in others (Bodl. F. 2.1. Linc. 9).

595. *Dublin edition:*
The | First *Ode* | Of the Second Book of | Horace | Paraphras'd. | And | Address'd to *Richard St – – le,* Esq; | — | En *qui promittit cives, urbem sibi curae,* | *Imperium fore,* & *Italiam,* & *delubra deorum.* Hor. | — |.

4to size; no signatures — [1]–4. — Text begins at once under the title.
At foot of p. 4:

Dublin: | Reprinted for *John Henly,* Bookseller in *Castle-street,* 1714.

Copy: T.C.D. (P.gg.20.4).

***

The Publick Spirit Of The Whigs

596. The | *Publick Spirit* | Of The | Whigs: | Set forth in their Generous | Encouragement of the Author | Of The | *Crisis:* | With Some | Observations | On The | Seasonableness, Candor, Erudition, | and Style of that Treatise. | = | *London:* | Printed for *John Morphew,* near *Stationers-Hall.* | MDCCXIV. | Price One Shilling.

4to; π¹, B–F⁴, G³ — 2 pp. (t. + bl.), 1–45 + bl.
Published Feb. 23, 1714 (adv. in *The Post Boy* of Feb. 20–3).
Copies: Forster and Penn.
There is another (censored) issue. Owing to objections raised by the Scots Lords the passage referring to them was omitted, namely: 5 paragraphs — 102 lines — from p. 21, l. 4 from foot ('After Two and twenty Pages spent' – – – –) to p. 24, l. 8 from foot ('I have only one Thing more to say' – – – – –). This was effected by reprinting sheets D (pp. 17–24) and E (pp. 25–32), with the result that in the re-issue sheet D consists of pp. 17, 18, 19, 20, 21 and 23, sheet E of pp. 24, 26, 27, 28, 29, 30, 31 and 32.
Copy: Forster.
Second edition:
　Title and collation the same as in the first (uncensored) edition, except:

– – – Treatise. | — | The Second Edition. | — | *London:* | – – –

Copy: U.L.C. (U.24.8.25).
There is also another (censored) issue of this edition, as is the case with the first edition.
Copy: Lambeth (110 D 20 (15)).

Third edition:
Title and collation the same as in the first (censored) edition, except:

– – – Treatise. / — / The Third Edition. / — / *London:* / – – –

The Bodl. has two copies of this edition (Fr. 1. Linc. 10 and G. Pamph. 1140. 17.), which are not exactly the same. In pp. 24 and 28 the second copy shows a widening-out of some lines where the text was too close printed in the first copy, resulting in a shifting of words to the next line.
[I have not found an uncensored issue of this edition.]
Copy: Penn.

Fourth edition:
Title and collation the same as in the first (censored) edition, except:

– – – Treatise. / — / The Fourth Edition. / — / *London:* / – – –

Copies: T.C.D. and Penn.
[I have not found an uncensored issue of this edition.]
First, second, and third editions printed from the same type. For a description of the 2nd ed., see Rothschild 2056.

597. *Another edition:*
The / Publick Spirit / Of The / *Whigs,* / Set forth in their generous encouragement, of / the Author of the Crisis. / With some Observations on the seasonableness, Candor, Erudition & Style of that Treatise. / — / *The Fourth Edition.* / Price 1. s. But to Subscribers Half a Crown. / — / [ornament] / — / *London,* / Printed for John Morphew, near / *Stationers-Hall.* 1714.

Sm. 8vo (in fours); π^1, A–K⁴ — 2 pp. (t. + bl.), 1–80.
Copy: T.C.D. Fag. H.11.55(7).
Aitken, *Life Of Steele,* II, 421, mentions a Third Edition, Corrected, 1714, 12mo; but he does not give publisher or place. — I have not seen such an edition.

598. *Another edition:*
The / *Publick Spirit* / Of The / Whigs, / Set forth in their Generous / *Encouragement of the Author* / Of The / *Crisis.* / — / According to the First Original Copy. / — / *London:* / Printed for T. *Cole,* MDCCXIV.

8vo (in fours); A–E⁴ — 2 pp. (t. + bl.), 3–39 + bl. — Uncensored edition.
Copies: B.M. 104 b 34, and Penn.

599. *Dublin edition:*
The / *Publick Spirit* / Of The / Whigs: / Set forth in their Generous / Encouragement of the Author / Of The / *Crisis:* / With

Some / Observations / On The / Seasonableness, Candor, Erudition, and / Style of that Treatise. / — / The Third Edition. / — / Dublin: / Printed for J. Henly, Bookseller in Castle-street, / 1714.

> Sm. 8vo (in fours); A–E⁴ — 2 pp. (t. + bl.), 3–38, 2 pp. blank. — Uncensored edition.
> Copy: Penn.

600. *Another Dublin edition:*
The / Publick Spirit / Of The / Whigs: / Set forth in their Generous / Encouragement of the Author / Of The / Crisis: / With Some / Observations / On Thet / Seasonableness, Candor, Erudition, and Style / of that Treatise. / — / The Fourth Edition. / — / Dublin: Printed in the Year 1714.

> [Title within double-lined frame.]
> Sm. 8vo (in fours); [A]–E⁴ — 2 pp. (t. + bl.), 3–40.
> Copy: Nat. Libr. of Ireland.

601. *French translation:*
L'Esprit / Des / Whigs, / Manifesté, par le genéreux Encou- / ragement qu'ils donnent à l'Au- / teur de la Crise. / Avec / Quelques Remarques / Sur la Publication faite à propos, la Candeur, / l'Erudition & le Stile de cette Pièce. / Traduit de l'Anglois. / [ornament] / A Londres, / Chez Jean Morphew, Libraire. / — / MDCCXIV.

> [Title in red and black.]
> Sm. 8vo; π¹, A–F⁸, G⁵ — 2 pp. (t. + Avertissement du Libraire, on verso), [1]–106. — Uncensored edition.
> Copy: Kon. Bibl. (pamphlet 16209).
> Sybil Goulding, *Swift En France*, 1924, p. 182, mentions an edition of *L'Esprit des Whigs*, Amsterdam [chez David Mortier], 1714, 8vo. — I have not seen it.

602. *Dutch translation:*
De / Publyke Geest / Der / Whigs / Geopenbaard in derzelver eedelmoedige / aanmoediging van den *Autheur* van de / Crisis; / *Met eenige aanmerkingen op de gevoeglykheyd,* / *openhartigheyd,* *geleerdheyd en styl van* / *dat Tractaatje.* / Uyt het Engelsch vertaald / Door / A. G. L. / [ornament] / Gedrukt tot Groningen, / En te bekomen tot Amsterdam by *N. Lobedanius,* / Boekdrukker in de Vergulde A, achter / 't Stadhuys.

> [Title in red and black.]
> Sm. 8vo; π¹, A–D⁸, E³ — 2 pp. (t. + Errata, on verso), 1–69 + bl. — Uncensored edition.
> Copy: Bibl. Maatsch. Ned. Letterk., Leiden.

603. *German translation* (pp. 707–77) *in:*

Curieuses / Bûcher u. Staats- / *Cabinet* / XXV. Eingang. / Vor-
stellend / I Nachricht von dem Grafen / von / Peterborough. /
[*First column:*] II. L'Esprit des Whigs oder / Widerlegung der
Crise / des M. Steele. / III. Vier Piecen von Mr. Stee- / le, als nem-
lich: Grûnde / warum Dûnkirchen vôllig / zu demoliren. / Der
letzte Engelsmann. / [*Second column:*] Die Sache Mr. Steele, oder /
Erzehlung derer wieder ihn / vorgenommenen Procedu- / ren. /
Schreiben an ein Parlaments= / Glied wegen der Bill wider / den
Anwachs des Schisma- / tis. / IV. Gedancken ûber den verân-
derten Zu= / stand von Grosz-Britannien durch die glûckli= / che
Besteigung des Thrones von Grosz-Britan= / nien Sr. Churfl.
Durchl. von Han= / nover. / — / Anno MDCCXIV.

12mo.
Copy: University Library, Leipsic.

Contemporary criticism

1076. The Humble Address Of – – – – – – the Lords – – – To Her Majesty.
With Her Majesties Most Gracious Answer. London, John Baskett &c., 1713.
— Folio; 1–4. — Contains the petition of the Lords to the Queen to discover
the author, the printer, and the publisher of *The Publick Spirit of the Whigs.* —
Copy: Quaritch.

1077. By the Queen, A Proclamation, For Discovering the Author of
– – – – – – The Publick Spirit of the Whigs, &c. London, John Baskett &c.,
$17\frac{13}{14}$. — Very large folio; 1 page. — Copy: Quaritch.

1078. The Scots Nation and Union Vindicated From The Reflections cast
on them In An Infamous Libel Entitl'd The Publick Spirit of the Whigs, &c.
London, A. Bell &c., 1714. — Sm. 4to; 1–28. — Ascribed to Defoe.

1079. The Publick Spirit Of The Tories, Manifested in the Case of the Irish
Dean, And his Man Timothy. London, J. Roberts, 1714. — 4to; 1–12. —
Contains an attack on Swift. — Copy: Nat. Libr. of Scotl.

1080. The Crisis upon Crisis. A Poem. Being an Advertisement Stuck in the
Lion's Mouth at Button's: And Addressed to Doctor S – – – – t. &c. London,
J. Morphew. 1714. — 4to; 2 pp., 1–18. [A MS. note on the title of the B.M. copy
says: "Agt Mr Steele".]

632. A / Rebus / Written by a Lady, On / The Rev. *D* – – – *n*
S – – – *t.* / With His / Answer.

Folio; 2 pages.
The Answer begins three-quarters down the first page and continues on
the second.
Copy: Huntington.
The time of composition and publication seems to be between 1714 and
1720 (see *Poems,* 715).

Also in:
Miscellanea, Vol. II, 1727, pp. 76–8. (See H. Teerink, "Swift's Cadenus and Vanessa", in *Harvard Library Bulletin,* II, No. 2, 1948, 254–7.)
    Also in No. 661 (a).

606. An / Argument / To prove, That / The Abolishing / Of / Christianity / In / *England,* / May, as Things now stand, be attended / with some Inconveniencies, and per- / haps not produce those many Good / Effects propos'd thereby. / — / *London:* / Printed for Timothy Atkins, in / the *Strand.* 1717.

> [Title within double-lined frame.]
> Sm. 8vo (in fours); A–E⁴ — 2 pp. (h.t. + bl.), 2 pp. (f.t. + bl.), 5–38, 2 pp. blank.
> First published in the *Miscellanies,* 1711. Above is the first separate publication.
> Copies: Bodl. G. Pamph. 839(8), and Penn.
> *A retouched version:*
> See No. 78.

607. *French translation* (pp. 251–96) *in:*
Histoire / *De* / Martinus / *Scriblérus,* / De Ses Ouvrages / & de ses Découvertes; / *Traduite de l'Anglois de Monsieur* / Pope. / Quae Regio in terris nostri non plena Laboris? / *Virg. Aen. I.* 464. / [ornament] / A Londres, / Chez Paul Knapton, dans / Ludgate Street. / = / M.DCC.LV.

> 12mo; I–XXII, 1–324.

608. *German translation:*
Einige Grůnde, warum die Abschaffung des christlichen Religion, wie die Sachen nun stehen, doch ůble Folgen haben und nicht alle die guten Wirkungen hervorbringen důrfte, welche man sich davon verspricht.

> [Mentioned by Vera Philippović, *Swift In Deutschland,* 1903, pp. 20–1. It is an adaptation rather than a translation, by Johann Georg Schlosser, in the year 1788.]

609. *Reprinted* (pp. 296–322) *in:*
Religious Pamphlets / Selected And Arranged / By The Rev. Percy Dearmer, M. A. / *With An Introduction And Notes* / [ornament] / London / Kegan Paul, Trench, Trubner & Co. / 1898.

> 8vo; 1–380 (including h.t., before f.t.).
> Copy: Sächsische Landesbibl., Dresden.

610. A Decree for Concluding the Treaty between Dr. Swift and Mrs. Long. This is pp. [1]–4 of the first section in:

Letters, / Poems, / And / Tales: / Amorous, Satyrical, / *and* Gallant. / Which passed between / *Several* Persons *of* Distinction.

/ — / Now first Publish'd from their respective / *Originals*, found in the Cabinet of that / Celebrated *Toast* Mrs. Anne Long, / since her Decease. / — / [ornament] / — / *London:* / Printed for E. Curll in *Fleetstreet*. 1718. / [Price Two Shillings.]

8vo (in fours); π^2, B–M⁴, N²; B–C⁴, D²; A⁴, A⁴ — 2 pp. (t. + bl.), 2 pp. (Contents), [1]–92; [1]–19 (advs. on verso); 8 pp. advs., 8 pp. advs.

Copies: Yale (complete), B.M. (lacking the second four leaves of advs.), Bodl. (lacking the first and second four leaves of advs.), Havard (lacking D 1 of the first section, as well as the first and second four leaves of advs.).

Case, No. 307 says: "This is a made-up miscellany: the second series of signatures, pp. 1–19, is a remainder copy of a pamphlet entitled *An Epistle to the Right Honourable Joseph Addison, Esq.*, from which the title-page and perhaps some other preliminary matter has been removed."

Note: The 1718 volume also contains (p. 26) a letter with some verses annexed, probably written by Swift in 1699 to Lady Mary Chambers, the elder sister of Lady Betty Germaine (cf. *Corresp.* V, 229 n., 457, and Elr. Ball, *Swift's Verse*, 43). — *Poems*, 1069–70, says: doubtful.

Both pieces re-issued (see No. 16); reprinted, and called 2nd ed. on the separate t.p. (see No. 19); reprinted in *Mr. Pope's Literary Correspondence*, Vol. II, 1735, 8vo, p. 66; 12mo, p. 120 (Griffith, Nos. 386, 403).

619. A / Letter / From / A Lay-Patron / To A / Gentleman, / Designing for / Holy Orders. / — / *Quid igitur profuit vidisse te Veritatem quam / nec defensurus esses nec secuturus.* Lactant. / — / *Dublin:* / Printed by *E. Waters* in *Syeamore* [*sic*] - *Alley*, 1720.

Sm. 8vo (in fours); π^1, [A]–C⁴, D² — 2 pp. (t. + bl.), 1–28. Dated at the beginning 'Dated *July* the 9th, 1719–20.', and at the end (January 9th, 1719–20). — 'July' is apparently a misprint for 'January'.

Copy: Marsh Cas. XI 31 (5).

Another edition:

618. A / Letter / To A / Young Gentleman, / Lately enter'd into / Holy Orders. / — / By a Person of Quality. / — / ☞ *It is certainly known, that the following Treatise was / writ in* Ireland *by the Reverend Dr.* Swift, Dean / of *St.* Patrick's *in that Kingdom.* / — / [ornament] / *London:* / Printed for J. Roberts at the *Oxford Arms* in / *Warwick-Lane.* MDCCXXI. Price 6*d.*

8vo (in fours); A–D⁴ — 2 pp. (t. + bl.), 3–31 + bl.

Dated at the beginning 'Dated *January* the 9th, 1719–20.', and at the end 'January 9th, 1719–20.'

Published Jan. 3, 1721 (advs. in *The Daily Courant*, and in *The Post Boy*).

Copy: Penn.

Second edition:

The title and collation are the same, except:

– – – – *Kingdom.* / — / The Second Edition. / — / [ornament] / *London:* / – – – – –

German translation in:

54. Capitain / Samuel Brunts / Reise / nach / Cacklogallinien, / und weiter / in den Mond, / Nebst dem / Leben Harvays, / der weltbekannten / Zauberers in Dublin, / Und einigen andern Moralischen und / Satyrischen Schriften / Herrn D. Swiffts, / aus dem Englischen übersetzt. / = / Leipzig 1735.

Sm. 8vo; π^1 (frontisp.), π^1, a^2, A–R^8, S^4 — 2 pp. (frontisp.), 2 pp. (t. + bl.), 4 pp. (Vorrede), [1]–280.

Contains translations of two genuine pieces of Swift: *A Letter to a Young Gentleman, Lately enter'd into Holy Orders*, and *A Letter to a very Young Lady on her Marriage*. Also of some doubtful ones. For *Cacklogallinien*, see No. 1222, *post*.

Copy: Penn.

Second edition:

Same collation (but not the same printing) and title as the first edition, except:

– – – – übersetzt. / — / Die Zweyte Auflage. / — / Leipzig 1736.

Copy: Penn.

Another edition or issue:

Leipzig, 1751 (frontisp., 280 pages).

I have not seen a copy:

620. *German translation:*

Des Dr. Jonathan Swifts / Schreiben / an einen / jungen Geistlichen. / Aus dem Englischen. / — / Als ein besonders lehrreicher Unterricht für / Prediger. / [ornament] / = / Wien, 1782.

12mo; 1–58.
Copy: University Library, München.

612. A / Proposal / For the universal Use / Of *Irish* Manufacture, / In / Cloaths and Furniture of Houses, *&c.* / Uterly [*sic*] / *Rejecting* and *Renouncing* / Every Thing wearable that comes from / England. / [ornament] / — / *Dublin*: Printed and Sold by *E. Waters*, in *Essex-street*, at / the Corner of *Sycamore-Alley*, 1720.

8vo (in fours); [A]–B^4 — 2 pp. (t. + bl.), [3]–15 + bl.
Published April or May 1720.
Copies: T.C.D. RR pp 57.4, and B.M. C 53 c 14.
The B.M. copy has correct 'Utterly' on the title-page.

613. *Reprinted* (pp. 17–25) *in:*

No. 1.] [*Price 2d.* / The Irish Confederation. / = / Irish Political Economy. / By / Jonathan Swift, Dean Of St. Patrick's / And / George Berkeley, Bishop Of Cloyne. / Edited By / John Mitchel. / Dublin: / Printed For The Irish Confederation, / By William Holden, 10, Abbey-Street. / 1847.

[Title within double-lined frame.]
12mo (in sixes); B–C⁶, E² — 2 pp. (t. + bl.), [III]–VI (Preface), [7]–39 +
printer's name on verso.
Copy: B.M. 8146 aa 55 (1).
Contains: Short View State of Ireland, Proposal Irish Manufactures, and
Extracts from the Querist (by G. Berkeley).

Contemporary criticism:

1661. An / Answer / To The / Proposal / For the / Universal Use /
Of / *Irish* Manufactures, / And utterly rejecting and / renouncing
every Thing / that is wearable that / comes from *England.* / — /
Frangimur si Collidimur. / — / *Dublin:* Printed, 1720.

Sm. 8vo (in fours); π⁴, B⁴ — 1 p. (title), [2]–16.
Copy: R.I.A. (Haliday Vol. 51, No. 2).
Elr. Ball, *Swift's Verse,* 174, note 31, says that it is probably by Swift him-
self; Davis, *Prose Works,* IX, expresses no opinion.

Another edition of An Answer, with a different title:
614. A / Defence / Of / *English* Commodities. / Being an /
Answer to the Proposal / For the Universal Use of / *Irish* Manu-
factures, / And / Utterly rejecting and renouncing every Thing /
that is Wearable that comes from *England.* / — / *Frangimur si
Collidimur.* / — / To which is Annexed, / An Elegy upon the
much lamented Death / of Mr. Demar, the famous Rich Man, who
/ Died at *Dublin* the 6th Day of *July,* 1720. / — / *Written by Dean*
Swift. / — / Printed at *Dublin:* And Reprinted at *London,* by
J. Ro- / berts in *Warwick-Lane.* MDCCXX. Price 6*d.*

8vo (in fours); [A]², B–D⁴, E² — 2 pp. (t. + bl.), 2 pp. (To The Reader),
1–23 + bl., 25–8 (Elegy).
Copies: Bodl. Pamph. 359, and B.M. 8245 b 71.

1598. A / Letter / To the Reverend Dr. Swift Dean of St.
Patrick's Dublin; / Relating to the present State of the Ma- /
nufactures of Ireland.

Sm. 8vo; no signatures — [1]–8. — Text begins at once under the title.
At foot of p. 8:

— / Dublin Printed, by C. Carter, 1721.

Copy: R.I.A. Hal. Pamph. 54(2).

901. An Excellent New Song upon a Seditious Pamphlet. [1720] — Elr.
Ball, *Swift's Verse,* 156, says that in this song Swift took vengeance on the
grand jury that found a true bill against the printer of his *Proposal for the Universal
Use of Irish Manufacture.*
Cf. *Poems,* 236. — Not known to have been printed at the time; at least,
no copy found.

611. An / Elegy / On the much lamented Death of Mr. *Demar*, the Famous / rich Man, who died the *6th* of this Inst. *July*, 1720.

> [Title in black border.]
> Folio; 1 page.
> Copies: B.M. 11602 i 1 (1), and T.C.D. Press A7.5 (211a).
> The last four lines are said to have been written by Stella.

1662. *Another edition:*
An / Elegy / On the much lamented Death of Mr. Joseph Demar, / The Famous rich Man, who died in Dublin the 6th / of this inst. July, 1720.

> [Title in heavy mourning border.]
> Folio; 1 page.
> Copy: Rothschild 2060.

> *Also in:*
> The Weekly Journal: or, British Gazetteer, Sat., July 23, 1720.
> *Also in:*
> A Defence Of English Commodities, &c.
> *Also in:*
> Pinkethman's Jests: Or, Wit Refined. London: 1721, 2nd part, p. 121.

611A. [head-piece] / Run upon the Bankers. / [text follows immediately — 16 stanzas].

> No imprint. — Copy has "1720" in MS. on 1st page.
> No signatures–[1]–3 + bl.
> Copy: J. Barry Brown, Esq.

611B. *The* Run *upon the* Bankers, *and,* The South-Sea *Detected.*

> Folio; one page (two columns).
> At foot of second column:

Cork: Printed by *Samuel Terry* in *Cock-Pit-Lane*: 1721.

> Copy: Lord Rothschild.
> The Run, &c. covers the first column, the South-Sea, &c. (not by Swift) the second.

623. The / Bubble: / A / Poem. / — / [ornament] / — / *London*, / Printed for Benj. Tooke, at the *Middle-Temple-Gate* / in *Fleet-street*; and Sold by J. Roberts, near the / *Oxford-Arms* in *Warwick-Lane*. M.DCC.XXI.

> 8vo (in fours); π^4, B–C^4 — 2 pp. (h.t. + bl.), 2 pp. (f.t. + bl.), 5–23 + bl.
> Contains 55 stanzas.
> Published ca. Jan. 3, 1721.
> Copy: B.M. 993 f 51 (3).

Another edition:

The | Bubble: | A | Poem. | — | [ornament] | — | *London:*
Printed for *Benj. Tooke:* And are to be | Sold at *John Paton*'s Shop in
the *Par-* | *liament-*Closs. 1721. | [*Price Two Pence.*]

> Sm. 4to; [A]⁴, B² — 2 pp. (t. + bl.), 3–12.
> Contains 55 stanzas.
> Copy: Harold Williams.

624. *Another edition:*

The | Bubble: | A Poem. | — | *Apparent rari nantes in gurgite
vasto:* | *Arma virûm, tabulaeque & Troja gaza per undas,* | Virg.
| — | [ornament] | — | *London:* Printed for *Ben. Tooke,* at the
Middle-Temple-Gate in *Fleet-street*; and Sold by *J. Roberts,* near
the *Oxford-* | *Arms* in *Warwick-Lane:* And Re-printed in *Dublin,*
1721.

> Sm. 8vo (in fours); [A]–B⁴ — 2 pp. (t. + Advertisement on verso),
> [3]–15 + bl.
> This edition has 57 stanzas, against the 55 of the London edition.
> *Also in:*
> *The Evening Post* for Jan. 24–6, 1721, which quotes two stanzas, and
> ascribes them to Swift.
> *Also in:*
> *The Bubblers Medley, or a Sketch of the Times Being Europes Memorial for the
> Year 1720;* Printed for Tho: Bowles Print & Map Seller next the Chapter
> House in Sᵗ Paul's Church Yard London. — Broadside. — Prints ten of the
> stanzas, engraved. — Cf. Nichol Smith, *Letters Swift To Ford* (Oxford,
> 1935), p. 185.
> *Also in* Vol. II, pp. 147–58 of:
> A Miscellaneous Collection Of Poems, Songs and Epigrams. By several
> Hands. Publish'd by T. M. Gent. – – – Dublin, Printed by A. Rhames,
> 1721. — 2 vols., 12 mo. — 'T. M.' stands for 'Thomas Mosse'. — 57 stanzas.
> — Cf. Case, Nos. 320 (1) and (2).

Also in:

20. *Miscellaneous* | Poems, | Original and Translated, | By
Several Hands. | *Viz.* | [*First column:*] Dean Swift, | Mr. Parnel, |
Dr. Delany, | Mr. Brown, | [*Second column:*] Mr. Ward, | Mr.
Sterling, | Mr. Concanen, | And Others. | = | Published by Mr.
Concanen. | — | *Sparsa coegi.* | = | *London:* | Printed for J. Peele,
at *Locke's-Head* in | *Pater-noster-Row.* MDCCXXIV.

> [Title within double-lined frame.]
> Large 8vo; π⁸, B–Dd⁸ — 2 pp. (t. + bl.), [III]–VII (Dedication), 1 p.
> blank, 6 pp. (Contents), 2 pp. (bl. + Advertisement, Errata), [1]–416 (415
> misnumbered 399).
> Three pieces (pp. 140, 148, 208) are by Swift: 'Apollo to Dean Swift',
> 'The Bubble', 'An Epilogue spoken by Mr. Griffith.' (see 622a, 623, 625–6).
> Copy: Penn.
> *Also in* (pp. 94–108):
> A New Collection Of Poems On Several Occasions. By Mr. Prior, and
> Others. – – – London: Printed for Tho. Osborne – – – – MDCCXXV.

(Case, Nos. 334 and 334 (b), mentions two variants, with only very slight differences in the title-pages. Pickering & Chatto, cat. 312, item 304, records another edition, also Tho. Osborne, 1725, with a different arrangement of the pieces, and not, as the others, 12mo in sixes, but in twelves.)

Second edition, 1727.

Also in:

Miscellanies, The Last Volume, 1727; new title: 'The South-Sea. 1721.' — 44 stanzas.

Also in:

Faulkner's Vol. II, 1735; new title: 'Upon the South-Sea Project. Written in the Year 1721.' — 55 stanzas.

Also in:

Miscellanies, Volume The Fifth, 1735. — 44 stanzas.

Edinb. ed. 1721 (H.W. in T.L.S. Oct. 20, 1945) — 55 stanzas.

Cf. Nichol Smith, *Letters Swift to Ford,* p. 182 etc.; *Poems,* 248–50.

Delany and Swift

(Jan.–Feb., 1721)

On Jan. 10 Delany wrote two sets of verses on a window in the Deanery, which Swift answered in *Apollo to the Dean.* Delany responded in *News from Parnassus,* to which Swift answered in *Apollo's Edict.*

The first to appear in print was Delany's *News from Parnassus,* in *The Daily Post,* March 22, and in *The Weekly Journal: or; British Gazetteer,* March 25, also as a Broadside (Copy: J. Barry Brown); next *Apollo's Edict.* With the exception of the last they were all reprinted (pp. 137, 138, 140, 215) in *Miscellaneous Poems,* 1724.

Cf. Elr. Ball, *Swift's Verse,* 157–9 + notes; *Poems,* 259–72.

904. [headpiece] / *Apollo's* Edict.

4to size; no signatures, text at once under the title — [1]–4.

Copy: T.C.D. P. gg. 9 (16).

Written by Swift in a playful mood (mind the three triplets), and probably printed for private circulation only.

Also in:

Gulliveriana, 1728 (see No. 32). — With a few very slight corrections.

Also in:

Poems On Several Occasions [by Mrs. Barber], 1734 (see No. 747).

Here are very important corrections betraying the hand of Swift. There are several stylistic emendations for the better, three triplets have been eliminated, the names of four persons known as Swift's friends (Kelly, Eliza, Rochford, and Boyle) have been taken up, their friendship dating from later than 1721.

Faulkner's edition of the *Works,* 1735, does not contain this poem, nor his 1738 edition; it was perhaps overlooked. Hence it was not in the London *Miscellanies,* 1735, either.

Also in:

Vol. IV of the Miscellanies, Fairbrother, 1735 (see No. 33).

Printed, with only a few very slight corrections, from the original 4to pamphlet.

Note: The last twelve lines of the poem, referring to the Countess of Donegal, may have been published separately on her death in 1743. They were reprinted in *The Story of the Injured Lady*, 1746, p. 67 (see No. 79), and in Cogan's *Supplement to the Works of Dr. Swift*, 1752, p. 125 (see No. 81).

1583. The / Present Miserable State of Ireland. / In a Letter / From a Gentleman in Dublin to his Friend in London.

> Folio; 2 pages.
> At foot of second page:
> London Printed: And Re-printed in Dublin by Sarah Harding in Moles-worth's- / Court in Fishamble-Street, 1721.
> The text is signed: J.S.
> Copy: Yale.
> *Also in:*
> Mist's *The Weekly Journal or Saturdays-Post, with freshest Advices Foreign and Domestic,* Sept. 30, 1721.
> In this case the text is dated March 15, 1720/1, and signed: S.T.

Another edition:
749. The / Present Miserable State of / *Ireland.* / In a Letter from a Gen- / tleman in *Dublin*, to his / Friend S. R. *W.* in *London.* / Wherein is briefly stated, the Causes / and Heads of all our Woes. / — — — — — — / *Dublin:* Printed, *&c.*

> Sm. 8vo size; no signatures — 1 p. (title), [2]–8.
> Signed on p. 8: J.S.; under it there is a poor woodcut of Swift.
> Copy: Gilbert Coll., Dublin.

750. *Another edition, or issue* (?):
The / Present Miserable State of / *Ireland.* / In a Letter from a Gen- / tleman in *Dublin*, to his / Friend S. R. *W.* in *London.* / Wherein is briefly stated, the Causes / and Heads of all our Woes. / — / *Dublin:* Printed, in the / Year 1735.

> Sm. 8vo; 1–8.
> Signed on p. 8: J. S., and: Dublin, *May*, 1735.; under it there is a poor woodcut of Swift.
> Copy: Harold Williams.

751. *Another edition* (different title):
The / *Case* / Of the Kingdom of / *Ireland.* / Taken into Con-sideration; in a Let- / ter to a Member of Parliament, in / the Behalf of *Trade*, &c. / — / *Nisi Utile est quod facimus, stulta est Gloria.* / — / — / *Dublin:* Printed, *&c.*

> Sm. 8vo size; no signatures — 8 pages of which only p. 2 is numbered.
> — Text begins on verso of title.
> Copy: Sion Coll. (K. 11 X 7).

625. Epilogue, / To be spoke at the / Theatre-Royal / This present Saturday being *April* the 1st. In the Behalf of the Di- / stressed *Weavers.*

Folio; 1 page.
At foot of page:

Dublin Printed by *J. W.*

626. *Another edition:*
An / Epilogue, / As it was spoke by / Mr. Griffith / At the / Theatre-Royal / On Saturday the First of *April*. In the Behalf of the Distressed / *Weavers*.

> This is on one side of a small folio sheet; on the other there is (by Sheridan): A Prologue, Spoke by Mr. Elrington At the Theatre-Royal On Saturday the First of April. In the Behalf of the Distressed Weavers. [At foot of page:] Dublin Printed by John Harding.

1650. *Another edition:*
The Encouragement of the Ladies of Ireland to the Woollen / Manufactury / and the Downfall of Callicoes. / — / An Epilogue: / Spoke at the Theatre-Royal in Dublin, on the 1st April in the be- / half of the Distressed Weavers; When all the Nobility Appear'd in Stuffs. / Limerick. Printed by Andrew Welsh, at the Sign of the Globe in / Key-Lane, where all manner of Printing work is done, at / Reasonable Rates.

> Folio; 1 page. — The reverse has an unsuccessful pull of the same poem. Copy: Lord Rothschild.
> *Also in:*
> The St. James's Post, April 10–12, 1721.
> *Also in:*
> The Weekly Journal: or, British Gazetteer, April 15, 1721.
> *Also in:*
> The Gentleman's Journal, April 15, 1721.
> *Also in:*
> The Weekly Journal, or Saturday's Post, May 13, 1721.
> There was an *Answer* to it (no separate edition of it known). *Prologue, Epilogue,* and *Answer* reprinted in *Miscellaneous Poems,* 1724.

630. The Bank thrown down. / To an Excellent New Tune.

Folio; 1 page.
At foot of page:

— / Dublin: Printed by *John Harding* in *Molesworth's-Court*.

> Published Dec. 1721.
> Copy: T.C.D. Press A 7.6 (2). — The copy in the B.M. (839 m 23 (93)) and that in the Gilbert Coll. Dublin (Newenham Pamph. 1 (29)) are close-cropped at foot, so that in both the imprint has been cut off.
> Cf. Elr. Ball, *Swift's Verse,* 164.

630A. *Another edition:*
The / Bank thrown down / To an Excellent New Tune.

Folio; 1 page.
At foot of page:

— / Dublin Reprinted in *Mountrath-street* 1721.

Copy: Nat. Libr. of Ireland.

627. The / Journal.

Folio; 1 page (2 columns).
In Curll's *Miscellanea*, Vol. I, 1727, it is called 'The Journal'; in *Miscellanies*, Vol. III, 1732 'The Country Life'; in Faulkner's Vol. II, 1735 'The Part of a Summer, At The House of *George Rochfort*, Esq.; Written in the Year 1723.'
    Elrington Ball, *Swift's Verse,* 163, ascribes it to the autumn of 1721; published 1721-2.

Answered by:
— / A / Description / In Answer to the / Journal.

Folio; 1 page (2 columns).
At foot of page:

— / *Dublin:* Printed in the Year, MDCCXXII.

Copy: B.M. 839 m 23 (26).
Written by Percival, Dean of Emly.

628. *Another edition:*

Dobell's cat. 105, item 99, mentions another edition printed on the recto of a single folio leaf, on the verso of which there is: *A Description In Answer to the Journal.*
Also in:
Baker's News; or, the Whitehall Journal, Jan. 1722-3.
Also in:
The Weekly Journal: or, British Gazetteer, Jan. 19, 1722-3.

629. The last speech and dying words of Ebenezor Elliston, who is to be executed this second day of May, 1722. Publish'd at his desire for the common good.
Dublin: Printed by John Harding in Molesworth's-court in Fish-shamble-street. [1722] 2 pp.

Copy: Harvard.
T.C.D. (Press A. 72 No. 28) has another piece (different text) connected with Elliston:

The Last Farewell / *Of* Ebenezor Elliston / To this / Transitory World.

Folio; one page (two columns).
At foot of page:

— / Dublin: Printed by *John Harding* in *Molesworth's Court* in *Fish-shamble Street* / For *Elizabeth Sadlier* in School-House Lane near High-street.

Cf. *Prose Works,* Vol. IX, 363.

917. The First of April: / A / Poem. / Inscrib'd to Mrs. *E. C.*

Folio; 1 page (2 columns).
Copies: Huntington, and R.I.A. (24. C. 32).
Elr. Ball, *Swift's Verse*, 171, 326–7, dates this 1723, and says that it is a compliment in verse addressed by Swift to Mrs. E. Cope, the wife of his friend Robert Cope, to whose seat Loughgall he had paid a long visit in the summer of 1722. — Cf. *Poems*, 320.

633. Some / Arguments / Against enlarging the / *Power of Bishops,* / In letting of / Leases. / With / *Remarks* on some *Queries* / Lately published. / — / *Mihi credite, major hæreditas venit unicuique ve-* / *strûm in ijsdem bonis à jure & à legibus, quam ab* / *ijs à quibus illa ipsa bona relicta sunt.* / Cicero *pro* A. Caecina. / — / *Dublin:* / Printed for *J. Hyde*, 1723.

8vo (in fours); [A]–C⁴ — 2 pp. (t. + bl.), 3–23 + bl.
Text dated *October* 21, 1723.
Copy: T.C.D. (P. ii. 34.9).

The Drapier's Letters and Verses

During the year 1724, besides several shorter pieces in verse and prose, five Letters appeared. There is a sixth (properly written before the fifth, about Oct. 26, 1724), and a seventh (written in the summer of 1725), both for the first time printed in Vol. IV of Faulkner's edition of the *Works,* 1735.

Here follows a list in chronological order:

(1) Letter I (written in Feb., published in March).
(2) A newspaper article in *Harding's Weekly Impartial News Letter*, April 21, 1724.
(3) Letter II (dated Aug. 4, published Aug. 6).
(4) Another Letter to Mr. Harding the Printer (Aug.).
(5) Letter III — Some Observations (dated Aug. 25, published Sept. 5).
(6) A Full And True Account Of The Solemn Procession To The Gallows, At The Execution of William Wood, Esquire, And Hard-Ware-Man (ca. 15 Sept. — no copy traced).
(7) A Serious Poem Upon William Wood (Sept. 17).
(8) Letter IV (dated Oct. 13, published Oct. 22).
(9) To his Grace the Archbishop of Dublin (end Oct.).
(10) Letter VI (dated Oct. 26; not published at the time).
(11) An Excellent New Song Upon His Grace Our good Lord Archbishop of Dublin (Nov.).
(12) Prometheus (Nov.).
(13) Seasonable Advice (dated Nov. 11, distributed Nov. 14).
(14) An Extract out of a Book (ca. Nov. 23).
(15) The Presentment of the Grand Jury (ca. Nov. 28).
(16) A Letter from a Friend To the Right Honourable (Dec. 1).
(17) Letter V (dated Dec. 14, published Dec. 31).
(18) A Second Letter From A Friend To the Right Honourable (Jan. 4, 1724/5).
(19) Letter VII (summer 1725; not published at the time).

The above are probably all by Swift; moreover there are several doubtful ones; for further details see Herbert Davis, *The Drapier's Letters*, 1935, and Lord Rothschild, "The Publication Of The First Drapier Letter," *The Library*, 4th series, 19 (June 1938), 107–15, who kindly supplied me with information concerning some of his exceptional copies.

635. (I) A / Letter / To The / *Shop-Keepers, Tradesmen, Farmers,* and *Common People* / of *Ireland,* Concerning the *Brass Half-Pence* Coined by Mr. *Woods,* / with a *Design* to have them *Pass* in this Kingdom. / — / By M. B. *Drapier.* / — /

Folio; 4 pages (double columns). — Text begins under the title.
At foot of 4th page:

Dublin: Printed by *John Harding* in *Molesworth's-Court*, 1723–4.

There are three main misprints:
(1) p. 2, col. 2, l. 52, 'Kindom';
(2) p. 2, col. 2, l. 59, 'becau';
(3) p. 2, col. 2, ll. 61–2, 'Sterling Current which is Lawful Money' for 'Sterling which is Lawful Current Money'.
There is no Postscript at the end.
This may be a trial copy.
Copies: Goldsmiths', and Lord Rothschild.

Another edition:

A / Letter / To The / *Shop-keepers, Tradesmen, Farmers,* and *Common* / *People* of *Ireland,* concerning the *Brass* / *Half-Pence* Coined by Mr. *Woods,* with a / *Design* to have them *Pass* in this *Kingdom.* / — / By M-B- *Dreiper.* / —.

4to; A⁴ (double columns) — [1]–7 + bl. — Text begins under the title.
Misprints (1) and (2) corrected; (3) remains.
No Postscript.
There is no imprint. It may be a trial copy, possibly from a secret press in a summer-house in Delany's garden at Delville, or a Limerick edition (the type shows some similarity with that of the Limerick edition of the second Drapier Letter), which would account for the spelling 'Dreiper'.
Copy: Lord Rothschild.

Another edition:

A / Letter / To The / Shop-Keepers, Tradesmen, Farmers, and / Common People / Of / Ireland, / Concerning the / Brass Half-Pence / Coined by / Mr. Woods, / With / A Design to have them Pass in this / Kingdom. / — / By M. B. Drapier. / — / *Dublin:* Printed by *J. Harding* in *Molesworth's-* / Court.

Sm. 8vo; [A]⁸–[1] (title), [2]–16. — Text begins on verso of title.
The third misprint remains. No Postscript.
Copy: Lord Rothschild.

636. *Another edition or issue:*

A / Letter / To The / *Shop-Keepers, Tradesmen, Farmers,* / and *Common-People* of *Ireland,* / Concerning the / Brass Half-Pence /

Coined by / M.ʳ Woods, / With / A Design to have them Pass in this / Kingdom. / Wherein is shewn the Power of the said Patent, / the Value of the Half-Pence, and how far every Person / may be oblig'd to take the same in Payments, and how / to behave in Case such an Attempt shou'd be made by / Woods or any other Person. / [Very Proper to be kept in every Family.] / By M. B. Drapier. / — / *Dublin*: Printed by *J. Harding* in *Molesworth's-Court.*

> [Title within double-lined frame.]
> Sm. 8vo; [A]⁸ — [1] (title), [2]–16. — Text begins on verso of title.
> All the three misprints corrected. Postscripts at the end.
> Copies: U.L.C. (Hib. 8. 724.7 (1)), B.M. (C 58 b 18 (1)), Gilbert Coll. Dublin, Goldsmiths', T.C.D., R.I.A., Yale.
> Facing p. 150 in Birkbeck Hill's *Unpublished Letters Of Dean Swift* (No. 185, *ante*), there is a facsimile title, but it is in single-lined frame, and there is no comma behind the word 'Patent'. I have not seen such a copy.

637A. *Another edition:*

A / Letter / To The / *Shop-Keepers, Tradesmen, Far-* / *mers,* and *Common-People* of / *Ireland,* / Concerning the / Brass Half-pence / Coined by / Mʳ· Woods, / With / A *Design* to have them *Pass* in this / Kingdom. / Wherein is shewn the Power of the said Pa- / Tent, the Value of the Half-Pence, and / how far every Person may be oblig'd to take the / same in Payments, and how to behave in Case / such an Attempt shou'd be made by Woods / or any other Person. / [Very Proper to be kept in every Family.] / — / By M. B. *Drapier.* / — / Dublin: Printed by *J. Harding* / in *Moles-worth's-Court.*

> [Title within double-lined frame.]
> Collation and details the same as preceding copy.
> The name 'Woods' on the title and throughout the text.
> Copy: Lord Rothschild.

637. *Another edition:*
> Title, collation, and details the same as preceding copy.
> The name 'Woods' on the title, but 'Wood' throughout the text.
> Prof. Herbert Davis, *The Drapier's Letters,* 1935, p. LXXXII, says: "In this third edition there are differences of punctuation and spelling on every page, and alterations which indicate that it was carelessly set up. It seems probable that it may have been hurriedly put out as late as August 1724, as a result of Swift's complaint at the end of Letter II that Harding had allowed it to go out of print, in spite of continued demands for it. This suggestion is strengthened by the fact that (except in the title) the name Wood is correctly spelt throughout, instead of Woods, which is the form of spelling used still in Letter II as well as in the first two editions of Letter I, and was probably generally used in Dublin, until the correct form was introduced by the newspaper reports of the recommendations of the Committee of the Privy Council which appeared on August 18, 1724."

637B. Harding's / Weekly Impartial / News Letter [woodcut in the middle] / — / Tuesday April 21, 1724 / —

> Folio; 2 pages (double columns).
> At foot of second page:

— / Dublin: *Printed by* John Hardin [*sic*] *in* Molesworth's-Court *in* Fishamble-Street, wher [*sic*] / *Advertisements* are taken in at reasonable Rates.

> Copy: Gilbert Coll., Dublin.
> On the second page there is a communication, dated 'Dublin, April 21.,' saying that in the *London Postman*, dated April 17, 1724, was published a paragraph, dated 'London April 11.,' announcing that on April 10 a Committee of Council had met at the Cockpit in London to consider the Representations of the Irish Parliament, and that orders had been given for Wood's coins to be tested. After this paragraph (13 lines), a comment on it (49 lines) follows of which Prof. Herbert Davis says that "it can without hesitation be attributed to Swift". (Cf. Prof. Davis, *The Drapier's Letters*, 1935, pp. XXV etc., 209; and Davis's *Prose Works*, Vol. X, pp. XIII, 153, 215.)

638. (II) A / Letter / To / Mr. *Harding* the Printer, / Upon Occasion of a / Paragraph / In His / News-Paper / of *Aug.* Ist. / Relating to Mr. *Woods*'s Half-Pence. / — / By M. B. *Drapier.* / Author of the Letter to the / Shop-Keepers, &c. / — / Dublin: / Printed by *John Harding* in *Moles-* / *worth*'s-Court in *Fishamble-Street.*

> [Title within double-lined frame.]
> Sm. 8vo; [A]⁸ — 1 p. (t.), 2 (misprinted 3)–16. — Text begins on verso of title. — Dated Aug. 4, published Aug. 6, 1724.
> Copies: B.M. 8133 a 10 (3), Goldsmiths', T.C.D., Seligman, Yale, and U.L.C. Hib. 8. 724. 7 (3).

639. *Another edition:*

A / Letter / To / Mr. *Harding* the Printer, / Upon Occasion of a / Paragraph / In His / News-Paper / of *Aug.* 1st. / Relating to Mr. *Wood*'s Half-pence. / — / By M. B. *Drapier.* / Author of the Letter to the / Shop-Keepers, *&c.* / — / Dublin: Printed by *J. Harding* / in *Molesworth*'s-Court.

> [Title within double-lined frame.]
> Sm. 8vo; [A]⁸, [1]–16. — Text begins on verso of title.
> Copies: Quaritch, cat. 432, item 210, Pickering & Chatto, and Harvard. — Facs. in *Prose Works*, VI, 31.
> As to priority, Quaritch cat. 667 (1949), item 617, says that probably the second edition was first published, because the imprint has not the addition 'in Fishamble-Street'. But Prof. Davis seems to be nearer the truth, pointing to the fact that the first edition has the incorrect 'Woods', whereas in the second there is at least an attempt at correction, the title-page, p. 13, and p. 16 having correct 'Wood'. (See the note under 637.)

640. *Another edition:*
An / Answer / To / Mr. *Wood*'s Proposal, / Relating to his / Copper – – Half – – Pence: / In Which / *The* Pernicious, *and* Ruinous / Consequence, *of their being* Re- / ceived, *and* Passing, *in this* / Kingdom, *is clearly Stated.* / — / In a Letter to Mr. *Harding*, Printer / in *Dublin*, upon occasion of a Paragraph, / in his Newspaper, of *Aug.* 1. / — / By *M. B.* Draiper, Author of the *Letter to the* / *Shop-keepers*, &c. / — / [ornament] / *Limerick:* / Printed and Sold by *S. Terry.* Price *One Penny.* / Where may be had the said *Author's Letter* / to the *Shopkeepers*, &c Price 1 *d.*

[Title within double-lined frame.]
Sm. 8vo; [A]⁸ — [1]–16. — Text begins on verso of title.
Published Aug. 15.
Copy: Rothschild, 2083.

640A. Another / Letter / To / Mr. Harding the Printer, / Upon Occasion of the / Report of the Committee / Of The / Lords of His Majesty's most Honourable Privy-Council, / In Relation to / Mr. *Wood*'s Half Pence and Farthings, *Etc.* lately Publish'd.

Folio; 1 page.
At foot of page:

— / Dublin *Printed by* John Harding *in* Molesworth's Court *in* / Fishamble street.

Copy: Forster 8572. The copy in B.M. (8145 h. 16) is mutilated, the lines at foot having been cut off.

641. (III) Some / Observations / Upon a Paper, Call'd, The / Report / Of The / Committee / Of The / Most Honourable the *Privy-Council* / In / England, / Relating to Wood's *Half-pence.* / — / *By* M. B. *Drapier.* / Author of the Letter to the / *Shop-Keepers*, &c. / — / *Dublin*: / Printed by *John Harding* in *Moles-* / *worth*'s-*Court* in *Fishamble. Street.*

[Title within double-lined frame.]
Sm. 8vo; [A]–B⁸ — 1 p. (t.), 2–32. — Text begins on verso of title. — Dated Aug. 25, published Sept. 5, 1724.
Copies: U.L.C. (Hib. 8.724.7 (2)), Goldsmiths', T.C.D., Nat. Libr. Dublin, Seligman, Yale.
Some copies have misprints (p. 12, l. 1, extraordinrry; p. 16, l. 34, consiist), others have them rectified. Correction apparently took place during the press-work. — Pages 27, 28, and part of 29 are in smaller type than the rest.

642. *The Fourth Edition Corrected:*
Exactly the same title as in No. 641, *ante*, except:

– – – – / *Shop-Keepers*, &c. / — / The Fourth Edition Corrected. / — / *Dublin:* – – – – – – –

Sm. 8vo; [A]–B⁸ — 1 p. (t.), 2–32.
Copy: R.I.A. (Haliday Pamphlets Vol. 62 No. 1).

I presume that the second and third editions never existed, and that even this 'Fourth Edition Corrected' is a publisher's trick, for I venture to suppose that it is the same printing as the first edition with alterations effected during the press-work. The misprints on pp. 12 and 16 appear corrected. Page 23, ll. 22–5 has this passage in the first edition: 'The Patentee was obliged to make every Half-penny One hundred and Ten Grains *Troy* weight, whereby 2*s*. 2*d*. only could be coyned out of a Pound of Copper.'; it has been removed from this 'Fourth Edition Corrected'. Pages 27, 28, and part of 29 are in smaller type than the rest. Photostatic reproductions of the two titles prove that, but for the addition 'The Fourth Edition Corrected.', they are absolutely identical. — However, as I have not seen copies side by side, I cannot be sure.

643. *Another 'The Fourth Edition Corrected':*
Some / Observations / Upon a Paper, Call'd, The / Report / Of The / Committee / Of The / Most Honourabe [*sic*] the *Privy-Council* / In / England, / Relating to Wood's *Half-pence*. / — / By M. B. *Drapier*. / Author of the Letter to the / Shop-Keepers, *&c.* / — / The Fourth Edition Corrected. / — / *Dublin:* / Printed by *John Harding* in *Molesworth*'s- / *Court* in *Fishamble-Street*.

[Title within double-lined frame.]
Sm. 8vo; [A]–B⁸ — [1]–32. — Text begins on verso of title.
Copies: R.I.A. (Haliday Tracts, Box 172 Tract 6), Nat. Libr. Dublin, Harvard.

Though this edition agrees with the one recorded in No. 642, *ante*, in having all the 'points' mentioned there, it is a different printing throughout.

However, I have seen a copy in the possession of Messrs. Pickering & Chatto with the misprint 'Honourabe' on the title-page, which does not collate 1–32, but 1–36; and I noted that pp. 17–32 were in larger and cruder type than the rest. This constitutes another issue; probably pp. 1–16 are the same printing as above, and the rest is new.

643A. A Full And True Account Of The Solemn Procession To The Gallows, At The Execution Of William Wood, Esquire, And Hard-Ware-Man.

No contemporary copy traced. First publication known, in Faulkner's *Works,* 1735, Vol. IV, 243–9.

643B. A Serious / Poem / Upon / William Wood, / *Brasier, Tinker, Hard-Ware-Man, Coiner, Counterfeiter,* / *Founder* and *Esquire*.

Folio; 2 pages.
At foot of second page:

— / Dublin: Printed by *John Harding* in *Molesworth*'s-*Court*.

Copies: U.L.C. Hib. 3.730.1 (30), Forster.
Also (abbreviated) *in:*
Abel Boyer's *Political State of Great Britain,* Sept. 1724, XXVIII, 297–9.
Also (abbreviated) *in:*
The British Journal, Oct. 3, 1724; again Oct. 24, 1724.

644. (IV) A | Letter | To The | Whole People | Of | Ireland. | — | *By* M. B. *Drapier.* | Author of the Letter to the | *Shop-Keepers,* &c. | — | *Dublin:* | Printed by *John Harding* in *Moles-* | *worth*'s-*Court* in *Fishamble. Street.*

[Title within double-lined frame.]
Sm. 8vo; π^8, B^4 — 2 pp. (t. + bl.), 3–22, 2 pp. blank. — See also note under next number.
Copies: U.L.C. Hib. 8.724.7 (4), R.I.A., P.R.O. (State Papers 63, Vol. 384), Harvard, Yale.

645. *Second edition* (another issue only), with the same title, except:
– – – – – | *Shop-Keepers,* &c. | — | The Second Edition Corrected. | — | *Dublin:* | – – – – – –

Sm. 8vo; π^8, B^3 — 2 pp. (t. + bl.), 3–22.
Copies: R.I.A., Gilbert Coll., Harvard, Yale, Nat. Libr. Dublin, T.C.D., own.
Notes:
(1) This 'Second Edition Corrected' was printed from the same type as the first edition. It had a leaf B 4 (p. [23] + blank), bearing the following:

Advertisement.

Those who have bought the first Edition, are desir'd to mend the following Errata. Page 14. Line 19. between *Statutes* and *finding,* put *without.* Pag. id. Line 33. between *am* and *far* put *so.* Pag. 17 Line 19. between *Lye* and *for,* instead of *even,* put *merely.* Pag. 20. Line 11. between *and,* and Hirelings, put *His.*

As this leaf can have no use for this 'Second Edition Corrected', because the four corrections have been effected in the type still standing, it was clearly destined for buyers of the first edition. So that in copies of the former this leaf will generally have been cut out, in those of the latter generally pasted in. However, copies of either may appear in which this process has not been carried out.
(2) Prof. Herbert Davis, *The Drapier's Letters,* 1935, pp. LXXXVI–VII, mentions a separate issue of the leaf bearing *Advertisement,* a copy of which he found bound up with *A Defence of the Conduct of the People of Ireland,* 1724 (Nat. Libr. Dublin, P. 641). However, in connection with what has just been said, it is probably not a separate issue, but a stray leaf only.
(3) The Nat. Libr. Dublin has a cross-combination, viz. sheet [A] (pp. [1]–16) of the first ed., sheet B (pp. 17–22, 2 pp.) of the second ed.
(4) T.C.D. has a copy of the second ed. with a blank space between the two rules on the title-page, showing however, an erasure, probably of: The Second Edition Corrected.

1152. To his Grace | The | Arch-Bishop of Dublin, | A | Poem. | — | *Serus in coelum redeas diuq*; | *Laetus intersis Populo* — Hor. | —.

Folio; 1 page.
At foot of page:

— | Dublin: Printed by John Harding in Molesworth's- | Court in Fishamble-Street.

Copy: B.M. 839 m 23 (118).
Letter VI not publ. at the time, *Prose Works*, Vol. X, 95 etc.

1153. An Excellent New / Song / Upon His Grace / Our good Lord Archbishop / Of / Dublin. / — / By honest JO. one of His Grace's Farmers in Fingel: / *To the Tune of* / —.

Folio: 1 page.
At foot of page:

— / Dublin: Printed by *John Harding* in *Molesworth*'s-*Court*, 1724.

Copies: U.L.C., Gilbert Coll., B.M. (mutilated). 839 m 23 (29).

1154. Prometheus, / A / Poem.

Folio; 1 page (2 columns).
At foot of page:

— / Dublin: Printed in the Year, 1724.

Published probably Nov. 1724.
Copies: T.C.D. Press A 7.6 (12), B.M. 839 m 23 (32).
Also in:
Mist's Weekly Journal, or Saturday's Post, Jan. 16, 1724–5, Nº 325, pp. 2022–3.
Also in:
Fraud Detected – – – 1725 (see No. 21).

648. Seasonable Advice. / Since a *Bill* is preparing for the *Grand Jury*, to find against the Printer of the *Drapier*'s *last Letter*, there are / several things maturely to be considered by those Gentlemen, before whom this *Bill* is to come, before they / determine upon it.

Folio; 1 page.
At foot of page:

Novem. 11*th* 1724.

Distributed Nov. 14, 1724.
Copy: Forster (8572).

649. An Extract out of a Book, Entituled, an exact Collection of the De- / bates of the House of Commons held at *Westminster*, *October* 21. / 1680. *Pag.* 150.

Quarter sheet (18 × 12 cm); 1 page.
Distributed ca. Nov. 23, 1724.
Copy: P.R.O. (State Papers 63, Vol. 384).
The U.L.C. copy (Hib. 3.730.1¹⁶) has a different alinement, namely:

An Extract out of a Book, Entituled, an exact Collection of the / Debates of the House of Commons held at *Westminster*, *October* / 21. 1680. *Pag.* 150.

VOYAGES

DE

GULLIVER.

TOME PREMIER.

Seconde Edition, revûë & corrigée.
par le Docteur Swift — Revû par
l'abbé . . . . Desfontaine

A MILDENDO,

Chez les Freres PIGMEOS.

Avec Privilége de l'Empereur de Lilliput.
1 7 2 7.

Voyages de Gulliver (no. 390). A surreptitious printing, though its pre
face is initialed by Hypolite-Louis Guerin, who held the royal privilege
and printed the legitimate editions. (University of Pennsylvania)

A
Short VIEW
OF THE
STATE
OF
IRELAND.

D U B L I N:
Printed by *S. HARDING*, next Door to
the *Crown* in *Copper-Alley,* 1727-8.

A Short View of the State of Ireland (no. 663). A rare copy of Swift's essay
on Irish economic problems, the contents of which were later reprinted
in *The Intelligencer*, xv. The triple fleur-de-lis ornament appears in some
early issues of *The Intelligencer*. (University of Pennsylvania)

And T.C.D. has still another copy:

An Extract out of a Book, Entituled / An exact Collection of
the Debates / of the House of Commons, held / at Westminster,
Oct. 21st. 1680. / Pag. CL.

650. [headpiece] / The / Presentment / Of The / Grand-Jury /
Of The / County of the City / Of / Dublin.

> Folio; 2 pages.
> At foot of second page:

Dublin: Printed by *Pressick Rider* and *Thomas Harbin,* at the
General-Post- / *Office* Printing-House in the *Exchange* on *Cork-Hill,*
1724.

> The date is ca. Nov. 28, 1724.
> Copies: Forster 8572 and T.C.D.

1137. Letter from a Friend To The Right Honourable, etc. Dublin: Printed
in the Year 1724.

> Folio, 2 pages.
> Dated: Dec. the First 1724. (signed N.N.).
> Copy: Forster, T.C.D.

647. A / Letter / To the Right Honourable the / Lord
Viscount *Molesworth.* / — / By *M. B. Drapier,* Author of the Letter
/ to the *Shop-keepers, &c.* / — / They compassed me about also
with Words of / Deceit, and fought against me without a Cause.
/ For my Love they are my Adversaries, but I give / my self unto
Prayer. / And they have rewarded me Evil for Good, and / Hatred
for my Love. *Psalm* 109. *v.* 3, 4, 5. / Seek not to be Judge, being
not able to take / away Iniquity, lest at any Time thou fear the /
Person of the Mighty, and lay a stumbling / Block in the Way of
thy Uprightness. / Offend not against the Multitude of a City,
and / then thou shalt not cast thy self down among / the People.
/ Bind not one Sin upon another, for in One thou / shalt not
be Unpunished. *Ecclus.* Ch. 7. V. 6, / 7, 8. / — / *Non jam prima
peto Mnesttheus, neque vincere certo:* / *Quanquam* O! *Sed superent,
quibus Hoc, Neptune,* / *dedisti.* / — / *Dublin:* / Printed by *John Harding*
in *Moles-* / *worth's Court* in *Fishamble-street.*

> [Title within double-lined frame.]
> Sm. 8vo; π^8, B^8 — 2 pp. (t. + bl.), [III]–VII.
> (Directions To The Printer), 1 p. blank, [1]–22, 2 pp. blank. — Dated
> Dec. 14, published Dec. 31, 1724.
> Copies: U.L.C. Hib. 8.724.7 (12), Goldsmiths', B.M., T.C.D., Nat. Libr.
> of Ireland, R.I.A., Harvard, Yale.

1137A. A / Second Letter / From A Friend / To the Right
Honourable / — / — / *Ubi semel recto dieratum est in Praeceps*

pervenitur — a rectis / in vitia, a vitiis in prava, a pravis in Praeci-pitia. *Vell. Pater.* / Self-Love, is the Love of one's Self, and of every thing else for one's own / Sake: It makes a Man the Idolater of himself, and the Tyrant of others. / *Rochfaucault.*

Folio; 4 pages (double columns). — Signed at the end N.N., and dated Jan. 4. 1724/25.
Copy: B.M. 1250 m 13.
Prose Works, Vol. X, Contents, says: "attributed" to Swift. — There were 'A Third Letter From —— To the ——' and 'A Fourth Letter To the Right Honourable' (both B.M.), but they are not by Swift.
There were also 'The Fifth and Last Letter To the People of Ireland' and 'The Sixth Letter To The Whole People Of Ireland' (both B.M.), but they are not by Swift, and pretend rather to be sequels of Letter IV (No. 644).

Collected editions

21. Fraud Detected: / Or, The / *Hibernian* Patriot. / Containing, / All the *Drapier*'s Letters to the People of *Ireland,* / on *Wood*'s Coinage, &c. Interspers'd with the / following Particulars, / *viz.* / [*First column:*] I. The Addresses of the / Lords and Commons of / *Ireland*, against *Wood*'s / Coin. / II. His Majesty's Answer / to the said Addresses. / III. The Report of his / Majesty's most honou- / rable Privy Council. / IV. Seasonable Advice to / the Grand Jury. / [*Second column:*] V. Extract of the Votes / of the House of Com- / mons of *England*, upon / breaking a Grand Jury. / VI. Consider-ations on / the Attempts, made to / pass *Wood*'s Coin. / VII. Reasons, shewing / the Necessity the Peo- / ple of *Ireland* are un- / der, to refuse *Wood*'s / Coinage. / To which are added, / Prome-theus. A Poem. / Also a new Poem to the *Drapier;* and the Songs Sung / at the *Drapier*'s Club in *Truck Street, Dublin*, never / before printed. With a Preface, explaining / the Usefulness of the Whole. / — / *Dublin:* Re-printed and Sold by *George Faulkner* / in *Pembroke-Court, Castle-street*, 1725.

[Title within double-lined frame.]
8vo (in fours); π⁴, ∗∗⁸, B–Ee⁴ — 2 pp. (t. + bl.), [I]–VI (The Preface), [7]–14, [1]–222, 2 pp. unnumbered.
Copy: Penn.

22. *Another edition* (different title):
The Hibernian Patriot: / Being a Collection of the / *Drapier*'s / Letters / To The / People of Ireland, / Concerning / Mr. *Wood*'s Brass Half-Pence. / Together with / Considerations / On The / Attempts made to pass that Coin. / And / Reasons for the People of *Ireland*'s / refusing it. / To which are added, Poems and Songs / relating to the same Subject. / — / *O thou, whatever Title please thine Ear,* / Dean, Drapier, Bickerstaff, *or* Gulliver? / *Whether*

thou chuse Cervantes' *serious Air,* | *Or laugh and shake in* Rab'lais *easy Chair,* | *Or praise the Court, or magnify Mankind,* | *Or thy griev'd Countrey's* Copper Chains *unbind,* | *From thy* Boeotia *tho' her Pow'r retires,* | Grieve not, my Swift, at ought our Realm acquires. | Dunciad. | — | Printed at *Dublin*. | *London:* | Re-printed and Sold by A. Moor in St. *Paul's Church-yard,* | and the Booksellers of London and *Westminster,* | MDCCXXX.

8vo; π^1, A^3, B–R^8, S^4 — 2 pp. (t. + bl.), 6 pp. (The Preface), [1]–264. Copy: Penn.

634. His Grace's Answer | To | Jonathan.

Folio; one page (two columns).
At foot of page:

Dublin: Printed in [*sic*] Year, 1724.

Copy: Huntington.
This is Swift's answer to:

— | A | Petition | To | His G --- e the *D --- e* of G ------ N. | — | *Non Domus et Fundus* --- Hor. | — | [text in two columns] | — | *Dublin*, Printed in the Year, MDCCXXIV.

Folio; one page (two columns). — Copy: Huntington.
This *Petition* had been addressed, early in 1724, by Jonathan Smedley, Dean of Clogher, to the Duke of Grafton, and contained a request for an addition to a favour already received (namely his promotion from the deanery of Killala to that of Clogher). In the opening lines Smedley mockingly referred to Swift's success in a similar case (see No. 589), which induced Swift to retort in the *Answer*.
For another Answer, see No. 1203.

651. A | Letter | From | D. S—t. to D. S—y. | — | *Quid de quoque Viro, cui dicas, sepe caveto,* | — |

Folio; 1 page (2 columns).
This is Swift's answer to Smedley's:
A Satyr. Canit, ante Victoriam Triumphum. Printed in the Year, MDCCXXV. — Folio; 1 page (2 columns).
For further answers, see Nos. 1202–4, *post*.

653A. — | The | Birth | Of | *Manly Virtue* | From | Callimachus. | — |

Folio; π^6 — 2 pp. (t. + bl.), 2 pp. (Preface), 1–8.
At foot of p. 8:

Dublin: Printed by George Grierson.

Copy: Clark Memorial Library.

Another edition:

653. The / Birth / Of / *Manly Virtue,* / From / Callimachus. / — / *Inter Callimachi sat erit placuisse Libellos,* / *Et cecinisse modis, pure Poeta, tuis.* Propert. / *Gratior & pulchro veniens in corpore virtus.* / Virg. Æn. V. / — / [ornament] / — / *Dublin:* / Printed by and for George Grierson, at the / *Two Bibles* in *Essex-Street.* M,DCC,XXV.

> Very sm. 8vo; no signatures — 2 pp. (t. + bl.), 2 pp. (Preface), [1]–4.
> Copy: Forster 8562.

Also in:

> *Cadenus and Vanessa,* 3rd ed., J. Roberts, 1726.
> Elr. Ball, *Swift's Verse,* 194–5, presumes that Swift, in addressing this piece to Lord Carteret, wished Delany, who was then seeking preferment, to gain the credit of having written it. It gave rise to two other pieces, both in praise of Swift:

1200. To His Excellency The Lord Carteret, Occasion'd by seeing a Poem Intituled, The Birth Of Manly Virtue. Dublin: S. Harding, 1725. — Folio; 4 pages.

1201. A Poem Inscrib'd to the Author Of The Birth of Manly Virtue. &c. Dublin: Printed in the Year MDCCXXV. — Folio; 1 page.

Cadenus And Vanessa

The text of the following editions was printed from two manuscripts, chiefly differing in the absence, or presence, of the ten incriminating lines towards the end of the poem, beginning: "But what Success Vanessa met, Is to the World a Secret yet."

The order of their appearance is probably as follows [a and p indicate absence or presence of the ten lines]:

  (I) *ca.* April 19: Dublin 2726 [*sic*] (a)
      2nd Dublin ed. (p)
  (II) May 19: Roberts (p)
       2nd ed. (a)
       3rd ed. (p)
  (III) May 19: Blandford and Peele (a)
        2nd, 3rd, 4th, 5th, 6th, 7th eds. (all p)
  (IV) early June: Edinb. ed. Roberts and Ramsay (p)
       early June: its re-issue (p)
  (V) early June: *Miscellanea,* Vol. I (p)
      June 13: Warner re-issue (p)

Cf. *Poems,* 683, etc.; H. Teerink, "Swift's *Cadenus and Vanessa*", and "Swift's *Cadenus and Vanessa* again", in *Harvard Library Bulletin,* II, No. 2, 1948, and III, No. 3, 1949.

657. *Cadenus* / And / *Vanessa.* / A / Poem. / — / *From the Original Copy.* / — / [ornament] / = / *Dublin:* / Printed in the Year, 2726. [*sic*]

> 8vo (in fours); [A]–D⁴ — 2 pp. (t. + bl.), 3–32.
> Copies: T.C.D. (R.R. kk 41), and Penn.

Second edition:

Cadenus | And | *Vanessa*. | A | Poem. | — | The Second Edition. | — | [ornament] | = | *Dublin:* | Printed in the Year, 1726.

8vo (in fours); [A]–D⁴ — 2 pp. (t. + bl.), 3–32.
Copy: R.I.A. 175(7).

659. *Another edition:*

Cadenus | And | Vanessa. | A | Poem. | — | [ornament] | — | *London*, | Printed: And Sold by *J*. *Roberts* at the *Oxford-* | *Arms* in *Warwick-Lane*, 1726. Price 6 *d*.

8vo (in fours); [A]–E⁴ — 2 pp. (h.t. + bl.), 2 pp. (f.t. + bl.), [5]–37, 3 pp. blank.
Copies: B.M. (C 71 h 10), and Bodl.
Some copies have the following errata slip pasted in:

Errata.

Pag. 8. lin. 6. for *the* r. *her*. P. 11. l. 1. for *in* r. *from*. l. 14. r. *Prudes*. P. 13. l. 17. r. *computing*. P. 18. l. 18. r. *Purlieus*. P. 27. l. 5. for *head* r. *time*. P. 28. l. 6. for *guilt* r. *grief*. P. 29. l. 12. for *complaisance* r. *consequence*. P. 36. l. 5. r. *reading*.

Second edition:

Cadenus | And | *Vanessa:* | Or, The | Judgment of *Venus*, | A | Poem. | — | *Written by Dr.* Sw—ft, *upon Himself and* | Mrs, Vanh – – – y, *his Favourite Lady*. | — | When Miss delights in her Spinet, | A fidler may her Fortune get. | A Blockhead with melo- dious Voice | In Boarding-Schools can have his Choice; | And oft the Dancing-Masters Art | Climbs from the Toe to reach the Heart. | In Learning let a Nymph delight, | The Pedant gets a Mistress by't. | — | The Second Edition. | — | *London:* | Printed by J. Roberts in *Warwick-lane*, and sold | by the Booksellers in Town and Country. 1726. | (*Price Four-Pence.*)

8vo (in fours); [A]–D⁴ — 2 pp. (t. + bl.), 3–32.
Copy: Harold Williams.
This follows the Dublin 2726 ed. page for page.

Third edition:

Cadenus | And | *Vanessa:* | Or, The | Judgment of *Venus*. | A | Poem. | To which is added, The Birth of | Manly Virtue. | — | Inscrib'd to his *Excellency* the Lord Carteret. | — | *Gratior & pulchro veniens in corpore Virtus*. Virg. Aen. V. | — | The Third Edition. | — | *London:* | Printed for J. Roberts in *Warwick-lane*, and | sold by the Booksellers in Town and Country. | M.DCC.XXVI. | (*Price Four-Pence.*)

8vo (in fours); A–D⁴ — 2 pp. (t. + bl.), [3]–26 (Cadenus and Vanessa), [27]–32 (The Birth of Manly Virtue).
Copy: Penn.

658. *Another edition:*

Cadenus | And | *Vanessa.* | A | Poem. | — | *By Dr.* S—t. | — | [ornament] | = | *London,* | Printed for N. Blandford, at the | *London-Gazette, Charing-Cross;* and sold | by J. Peele, at *Locke's-Head* in *Pater-* | *noster-Row.* 1726. (Price 6 *d.*)

> 8vo (in fours); A–D⁴ — 2 pp. (t. + bl.), [3]–31 + blank.
> Copies: B.M. (922 i 30), U.L.C. (Hib. 7.726.20), and Penn.

Second edition:

> I have not met with a copy of this.

Third edition:

> The same title as that of the first edition, except:

– – – | [ornament] | — | The Third Edition. | — | *London,* | – – –

> 8vo (in fours); A–D⁴ — 2 pp. (t. + bl.), [3]–32.
> Copy: Penn.

Fourth edition:

Cadenus | And | *Vanessa.* | A | Poem. | To which is added, | A True and Faithful Inventory | of the Goods belonging to Dr. S—t, | Vicar of *Lara Cor;* upon lending his | House to the Bishop of ——, till his | own was built. | — | *By Dr.* S—t. | — | The Fourth Edition. | — | *London,* | Printed for N. Blandford, at the | *London-Gazette, Charing-Cross;* and sold | by J. Peele, at *Locke's-Head* in *Pater-* | *noster-Row.* 1726. (Price 6 *d.*)

> 8vo (in fours); A–D⁴ — 2 pp. (t. + bl.), [3]–31 (Cadenus and Vanessa), [32] (A True and Faithful Inventory).
> Copy: Penn.
> This edition was printed from the same type as the third edition; only the type of pages 29, 30, 31 was compressed to admit the six lines of page 32, by which the latter came free for the *Inventory,* here first printed, and written by Sheridan at the end of May 1724. It was also published in a broadside:

931. A Letter Sir There having been some Editions of Dean Swift's Cadenus and Vanessa publish'd before the following little Copy was added to it; you are desired to give it the Publick in a single Paper, that those Gentlemen may be supply'd with it, who have not the last Edition of that excellent Poem. A True and faithful Inventory of the Goods belonging to D. Sw—t, Vicar of Lara Cor; upon lending his House to the Bishop of M—, till his own was Built. — Folio; 1 page. — Copy: T.C.D.

Also in:

> The Dublin Weekly Journal, Numb. LXVI, Sat. July 2, 1726, p. 256.
> For further editions see Autrey Nell Wiley, "Unrecorded Printings of Thomas Sheridan's Inventory Of Dean Swift's Goods At Laracor", in *Notes and Queries,* Feb. 7, 1948, and May 4, 1948. — Cf. Elr. Ball, *Swift's Verse,* 197; *Poems,* 1034–5.

Fifth edition:

> Title and collation the same as those of the fourth edition, except:

— | The Fifth Edition. | —

> Copy: U.L.C. Hib 5. 726.5.

Sixth edition:
Title and collation the same as those of the fourth edition, except:

— / The Sixth Edition. / —

Copy: Penn.

Seventh edition:
Title and collation the same as those of the fourth edition, except:

— / The Seventh Edition. / —

Moreover 'S—t' has been twice printed as: Sw—t.
The last page has an adv. under the *Inventory*.
Copy: Penn.
The fourth, fifth and sixth editions are from the same type; the seventh
has been reset.
In *The London Journal*, July 2 (printed for Peele and Blandford), there is a
large extract from the poem.

658A. *Another edition:*
Cadenus / And / Vanessa. / A / Poem. / — / [ornament] / — /
London, / Printed and Sold by *J. Roberts* in *Warwick-* / *Lane*, and in
Edinburgh by *Allan Ramsay*, / 1726. Price 6 *d.*

8vo (in fours); [A]–D⁴, E² — 2 pp. (t. + bl.), 3–34 (text), [35] ('Advertisement' of books for sale by Ramsay), [36] (blank).
Copies: Harvard, Rothschild.

661. *Another issue:*
Cadenus / And / Vanessa. / A / Poem. / — / [ornament] / — /
Printed in the Year, M.DCC.XXVI.

8vo (in fours); L–O⁴, P² — 2 pp. (t. + bl.), 83–114 (text), [115] ('Advertise-
ment' of books for sale by Ramsay), [116] (blank). —
According to D. F. Foxon, the first 80 pages, A–K⁴, which are lacking,
contain Young's *Universal Passion* & *Love of Fame*.
Copy: B.M. 992 h 7.4.
Printed from the same type-setting as the preceding edition.
See H. Teerink, "Swift's *Cadenus and Vanessa* again", in *Harvard Library
Bulletin* III, No. 3, 1949.

661A. *Another edition:*
Cadenus / And / *Vanessa*, / A / Law Case. / — / *By Dean* Swift.
/ — / [ornament] / — / *London:* / Printed for T. Warner in *Pater-* /
Noster-Row. M.DCC.XXVI.

12mo (in sixes); [A]–C⁶, *² — one leaf lacking (?), 2 pp. (t. + bl.), 5–36
(text), [37] (*Clavis*), [38] (*A Rebus*), [39–40] (*The Answer*).
Copies: Clark Memorial Libr., and Harvard (both lacking A 1).
Another issue:
Miscellanea, Vol. I, 1727, pages 88–119 (see No. 24) is from the same type-
setting as the above 'Warner' edition. See H. Teerink, "Swift's *Cadenus and
Vanessa*", in *Harvard Library Bulletin*, II, No. 2, 1948, 254–7.
For the *Rebus* and *The Answer* see No. 632.

Criticism

1298. One Epistle To Mr. A. Pope, Occasion'd By Two Epistles Lately Published. &c. London: J. Roberts. — 4to; I–VIII, 9–24. — The year is 1730. On p. 20 there are eight lines referring to Swift and Vanessa.
Cf. Elwin and Courthope, *The Works Of Alexander Pope*, V, 228–9.

1358. In his letter of June 20, 1766, to George Montagu, Horace Walpole, speaking of the two new volumes of Swift's correspondence that had then just appeared, says: "There is one [letter] to his Miss Vanhomrigh, from which I think it plain he lay with her, notwithstanding his supposed incapacity, yet not doing much honour to that capacity, for he says he can drink coffee but once a week, and I think you will see very clearly what he means by coffee." (cf. Walpole's Letters, ed. Mrs. Paget Toynbee, 1903 &c., Vol. VII, 7–9).
Walpole's suggestion of an immoral meaning is shared by S. Lane Poole (Fortnightly Review, 1910, p. 331), but other critics are of a different opinion (cf. *Corresp.* III, 57, n. 3).

656. A / Riddle / *By* the Revd. *Doctor D – – – – – y*, inscrib'd to the / Lady *C – – – – – – – – t.*

Halfway there is:

Answered by the Reverend *Dean S – – – – t.*

Folio; 1 page.
At foot of page:

Printed in the Year, MDCCXXVI.

The *Riddle* and the *Answer* begin respectively:
    'I Reach all Things near me, and far off to boot,'
    'With half an Eye Your Riddle I spy.'
Copy: T.C.D. Press A 7.4 (73).
Riddle and *Answer* also in:
Curll's *Miscellanea*, II, 82–4.

Also in:
The Gentleman's Magazine, Aug. 1762, XXXII, 381, and Sept. 1762, XXXII, 441 respectively.
    Cf. *Poems,* 937–9; 911 etc.
About this time Delany wrote more riddles:
A Riddle By the Revd. Doctor D—y, inscrib'd to the Lady C—t. Printed in the Year, MDCCXXVI.
    (beginning: 'Of all inhabitants on earth,' — Copy: T.C.D. Press A 7.4 (50)).
A Third Riddle By the Revd. Doctor D—y. Printed in the Year 1725–6.
    (beginning: 'In Youth exalted high in Air,' — Copies: T.C.D. Press A 7.4 (16), U.L.C. Hib. 3.730.1 (41))
A Fourth Riddle By the Rv. D. D—y. (with a second piece: A Receipt For Cuckolding. By a Female Physician.) Printed by R. Dickson, in Dame-street opposite the Castlemarket, 1726.
    (beginning: 'I am a thing esteem'd by all,' — Copy: B.M. 839 m 23 (144))
    Cf. *Poems,* 914 etc.

Also in:
946. Miscellaneous Poems, By Several Hands: Particularly – – – – – – –
Dean S—, – – – – – – – Publish'd By Mr. Ralph. London: C. Ackers &c.
MDCCXXIX. — 12 mo; 12pp., 1–348. — Contains two riddles (pp. 126–30),
beginning: 'Of all Inhabitants on Earth', &c.; and 'By something form'd, I
nothing am', &c.

> Case, 354 (b) mentions a re-issue of this book.
> Cf. *Poems,* 936, 935.

934. A Letter to the Freemen and Free- / holders of the City of
Dublin, who / are Protestants of the Church of Ire- / land as by
Law Established.

> Folio; 2 pp. (double columns). — No imprint.
> Copy: T.C.D. Press A.7.2.120.
> Published end of Oct. 1727.
> This and the following piece seem to be genuine. They were written in
> support of the candidature of Alderman Stoyte for the membership of the Irish
> House of Commons to represent the City of Dublin. — See Davis, *Drapier's
> Letters,* 325–47, 351, where several other pieces connected with this election-
> eering campaign are mentioned.

935. Advice / To the Electors of the / City Of / Dublin.

> Folio; 2 pp. — No imprint, unless cut off.
> Copy: T.C.D. Press A 7.2.216

663. A / Short View / Of The / State / Of / Ireland. / [ornament]
/ *Dublin:* / Printed by *S. Harding,* next Door to / the *Crown* in
Copper-Alley, 1727–8.

> Sm. 8vo; A⁸ — 2 pp. (t. + bl.); 1, 4–15 (text); 1 p. blank.
> Written late in 1727, published ca. Jan. 28, 1728.
> Copy: Penn.

664. *Another edition:*
A / Short View / Of The / State / Of / Ireland / [ornament] / — /
Printed for, and Sold by *Combra* / *Daniell,* Bookseller, opposite
the Main / Guard.

> [Title within double-lined frame.]
> Sm. 8vo; [A]⁸ — 2 pp. (t. + bl.), 3–15 + bl.
> Copy: U.L.C. Hib. 8.727.4.

Also in:
Mist's Weekly Journal or Saturday's Post.
Reprinted (with an Introduction by Sheridan) *as:*
The Intelligencer, No. XV (see No. 666, *post*).
Also in (pp. 7–16):
The Irish Confederation, &c., 1847 (see No. 613, *ante*).

1283. A / Letter / To the Author of the / Short View / Of The / State of *Ireland*. / — / By the Author of Seasonable Remarks. / [Latin quotation from Horace] / — / — / *Dublin:* / Printed and Sold by S. Powell, in *Copper-* / *Alley,* near *Cork-Hill.* 1728.

> Sm. 8vo; no signatures — 1 p. (t.), 2–8.
> Copy: B.M. 523 c 38 (9).
> This Letter is probably by Sir John Browne.

665. An / Answer / To A / Paper, / Called / A Memorial / Of the Poor *Inhabitants, Tradesmen* and / *Labourers* of the Kingdom of / *Ireland.* / — / By the Author of the Short View of the / State of *Ireland.* / — / [ornament] / = / *Dublin:* / Printed by S. Harding, next Door to the / *Crown* in *Copper-Alley,* 1728.

> Sm. 8vo; [A]⁸ — 1 page (title), 2–16.
> Dated March 25, 1728.
> Copies: B.M. 523 c 38 (21), U.L.C. Hib. 8.724.7 (15), T.C.D. R.R.m.m.65 (16).
> This is Swift's answer to:
> To The R—d Dr. J—n S—t, The Memorial Of the Poor Inhabitants, Tradesmen, and Labourers of the Kingdom of Ireland. Dublin: Printed by Thomas Walsh in Skinner-Row. —
> Sm. 8vo; 1 p. (t.), 2–8.
> Copies: B.M. 523 c 38 (11), and Gilbert Coll. Dublin (mutilated).
> The author of the *Memorial* was Sir John Browne. See Browne's letter to Swift of Apr. 4, 1728 (*Corresp.* IV, 24).

666. The / Intelligencer, / — / Numb. I. / — / Saturday, May 11. *To be Continued Weekly.* / — / [ornament] / = / *Dublin:* / Printed by S. Harding, next Door to / the *Crown* in *Copper-Alley,* 172 [*sic*; 8 dropped away]

> Sm. 8vo size; no signatures — 2 pp. (t. + bl.), 3–7 + bl.
> There are twenty numbers. Most of them have 8 pages, but Nos. IX, XI, XIII, XIV, XV and XIX have 16 pages each. They are dated from May 11, 1728 to Dec. 2, 1728; No. XX (8 pp.) is dated on the title-page 1729, and at the end: May, the 7th, 1729. Moreover, there is another Number XX (2 pp.), dated on the title-page 1728, which is in praise of the *Intelligencer.* The titles are all different, generally with a Latin or English quotation.
> Copies (all 20): Forster (8545).
> R.I.A. has a set in which Nos. XVI, XIX, and the second No. XX are lacking, and a slightly different title in No. I:

The / Intelligencer, / — / Numb. I. / — / For *Saturday* / *May* 11*th,* 1728. to be / continued Weekly. / [ornament, between For / *May* 11*th,* / continued / on the left, *Saturday* / 1728. to be / Weekly. / on the right] / = / *Dublin:* / Printed by S. Harding, next Door / to the *Crown* in *Copper-Alley,* 1728.

The following numbers are by Swift (cf. *Corresp.* IV, 307–8, and T. Sc. IX, 309–31):

Numb. I: Introduction.

Numb. III: A Vindication of Mr. Gay, and the Beggar's Opera.

Numb. V: A Description of what the World calls Discretion.

Numb. VII: The Character of Corusodes and Eugenio.

[In *Miscellanies. The Third Volume,* 1732, pp. 206–21, Numbers V and VII were combined under the title: An Essay On The Fates of Clergymen.]

Numb. VIII: A Dialogue between Mullinix and Timothy (only the verses by Swift).

Numb. IX: The foolish Methods of Education among the Nobility.

Numb. X: Tim and Gay's Fables (only the verses, except the last four lines, by Swift).

Numb. XV: The Services the Drapier has done his Country, and the Steps taken to ruin it (this is a reprint of 'A Short View of the State of Ireland', with a preface by Sheridan).

Numb. XIX: The Hardships of the Irish being deprived of their Silver, and decoyed into America.

Numb. XX: Dean Smedley, gone to seek his Fortune. The Pheasant and the Lark (the first by Swift; the second by Delany, and answered by Swift)—cf. 695.

Cf. *Poems,* 454, 772, 782.

667. *Reprint of Numb. XIX:*

A / Letter / From The / Revd. *J.S.D.S.P.D.* / To A / Country Gentleman / In The / *North* of *Ireland.* / — / [ornament] / = / Printed in the Year, MDCCXXXVI.

8vo size; no signatures — 1 p. (title), [2]–8 (text).

Copies: B.M. 8145 bb 91; R.I.A. Haliday, Vol. 126, No. 10.

Probably this late reprint was elicited by a pamphlet in favour of "the Regulation of the Coin" then in consideration:

A Letter From A Gentleman In The North of Ireland, To His Friend in Dublin, In Relation to the Regulation of the Coin. Dublin: Printed in the Year MDCCXXXVI.

8vo; [A]⁴ — 2 pp. (t. + bl.), [3]–8.

Copies: T.C.D. N.g.52 (17); R.I.A. Haliday, Vol. 126, No. 11.

Cf. No. 754, *post.*

668. *Another reprint of Numb. XIX:*

The / *Hibernian* Patriot: / Or, A / Vindication of Dean *Swift,* in a Letter to / Mr. *G. F.* in *Dublin.* / *Sir, Belfast, Sept.* 15, 1737. / Some malicious Persons among Us have been so ungrateful to that truly / worthy Patriot *J. S.D.S.P.* as to give out, upon the long wish'd for Re- / duction of our Gold Coin, he hung out a black Flag on the highest Pinacle / of St. *Patrick*'s Steeple. / As We of the Linen-Manufacture have particular Obligations to that Gen- / tleman, I hope you'll be so kind to print the following Paper, which will be / a sufficient Vindication of him, and an Obligation to *M. B.* Linen-Draper. / *S—t*'s Works, Vol. IV. *Dublin:* Printed by *G—e F—r,* 1735, p. 339. / *N.B.* In the following Discourse the

Author personates a Country Gentleman / in the North of *Ireland:* / And this Letter is suppos'd as directed to the Drapier. / Having on the 12th of *October* last, received a Letter signed *Andrew Dealer* and / *Patrick Pennyless,* I believe the following Paper, just come to my Hands, will / be a sufficient Answer to it. / *Sic vos, non vobis,* / *vellera fertis oves.* / Written in the Year 1728. / Sir, / [text follows]

> Folio; 2 pages.
> At foot of second page there is: To be continued.
> Copy: Gilbert Coll. Dublin.

Contemporary criticism

1295. The True / Character / Of the / Intelligencer. / — / Written by *Pady Drogheda.* / —

> Broadside.
> At foot:

Printed in the Year 1728.

> Copy: Huntington.
> This is an attack by Delany on Sheridan and Swift, joint writers of the *Intelligencer.* It was answered by Swift in:

683. On *Paddy*'s Character of the / Intelligencer.

> Folio; 1 page.

Also in:

> The Entertainer, consisting of pieces in prose and verse, witty, humorous, or curious. Vol. I (probably all published) — 8vo — Printed for F. Cogan, 1746 (from cat. Dobell, No. 89, item 144).

Collected editions

34. The / Intelligencer. / — / *Omne vafer vitium ridenti Flaccus amico* / *Tangit, & admissus circum praecordia ludit.* / Pers. / — / [ornament] / — / Printed at *Dublin.* / *London* / Reprinted, and sold by *A. Moor* in St. *Paul*'s / Church-yard, and the Booksellers of / *London* and *Westminster.* MDCCXXIX.

> 8vo [A]³, B–O⁸, P⁵ — 2 pp. (t. + bl.), 2 pp. (To The Reader), 2 pp. (Contents), 1–217 + bl. Contains Nos. 1–19.
> Copy: B.M. PP 6177.

35. *Second edition:*

The / Intelligencer. / — / *Omne vafer vitium ridenti Flaccus amico* / *Tangit, & admissus circum praecordia ludit.* / Pers. / — / By the *Author* of *a* Tale *of a* Tub. / — / *The* Second Edition. / — / [ornament] / — / London: / Printed for Francis Cogan, at the / *Middle-Temple-* Gate in *Fleet-street.* / MDCCXXX.

12mo; [A]⁴, B–M¹², N² — 2 pp. (t. + bl.), 3 pp. (to the Reader), 3 pp. (Contents), 1–268. Contains Nos. 1–20.
Copies: B.M. 239 g 10, and Penn.

German imitation

1331. Gespräch zwischen einem Römisch–Catholischen Priester und zweyen Herrenhutern die Frage betreffend: Ob die Protestantische Pfarrer eine der gröszesten Landplagen auf der Welt seyn? Nebst einem Unterricht des berühmten D. Swift, Worinnen denen geistlichen Studenten gewiesen wird, wie sie gar leicht zu einem Pfarrdienste gelangen können; &c. Zum Druck befordert von Traiano Machiavelli. Franckfurth und Leipzig. 1752.

Sm. 8vo; [A]–H⁸, I⁶ — 2 pp. (t. + bl.), 14 pp. (Vorrede), 2 pp. (bastard title + bl.), [3]–124.
Copy: Penn.
Pp. 11–41 pretend to be a translation of a piece by Swift (see the title), but they are an original German satire, the idea being based on Swift's *Intelligencer*, Numb. VII.

The Journal Of A Dublin Lady

669. The / Journal / Of A / *Dublin* Lady; / In a Letter to a Person of / *Quality*.

Sm. 8vo size; no signatures, unless cut off, the copy in R.I.A. being close shaved — pp. [1]–8 (text begins at once under above title).
At foot of eighth page:

— / *Dublin:* Printed by *S. Harding* next Door / to the *Crown* in *Copper-Alley*, where / Gentlemen may be furnished with the / *Intelligencer*, from No 1, to No 19.

Copy: R.I.A. 78/3.
Published early 1729; written by Swift during his first stay with the Achesons at Market Hill, June 1728 till Feb. 1729.

669A. *Another edition:*
The / Journal / Of A / Dublin Lady / In A / Letter / To a Person of / Quality. / — / The Second Edition Carefully Corrected / And Amended, / — / [ornament] / — / *Dublin:* Re-printed by *Nicholas Hussey* on / the *Blind-Key*, 1729.

Sm. 8vo size, no sigs. — 2 pp. (t. + bl.), 3–16.
Copy: Bodl. Vet. A4 f 185 (7).

670. *Another edition:*
The / Journal / Of a Modern Lady / In a Letter to a Person of Quality.

Large folio; 2 pages (3 columns).
On p. 2, under second column:

London Printed by George Gorden;

Copy: B.M. 1872 a 1 (169*).

671. *Another edition:*

The / Journal / Of A / Modern Lady. / In A / Letter / To A / Person of Quality. / — / By the Author of Cadenus and Vanessa. / = / First Printed at *Dublin;* and now Reprinted / at *London;* for J. Wilford, near / *Stationers- |. Hall*, MDCCXXIX. / [Price Four Pence.]

8vo (in fours); [A]–C⁴ — 2 pp. (t. + bl.), [3]–23 (advs. on verso).
Copies: B.M. 11631 e 33, and Bodl. Jessel e 1111.

Also in:
Fog's Weekly Journal, Feb. 15, 1729.
(The last number of Mist's Weekly Journal appeared on Sept. 21, 1728; on Sept. 28, 1728 it was continued by Mist's friends as Fog's Weekly Journal.)

672. *Another edition:*

= / The / Journal / Of A / Gameing Lady of Quality. / A Tale. / In a Letter to a Friend. / — / *By Messieurs* Swift *and* Pope. / —

This is H 4–6, I⁴ = pp. [73]–86 in the *second Part of The Court-Gamester*, entitled:

The / Knowledge / Of / Play, / Written for Public Benefit, and / the *Entertainment* of all *Fair Players.* / Wherein / I. It is demonstrated, that Fortune has not that / *Power* in *Play*, which is commonly ascribed to Her. / II. The *Chances* of the *Games* of Hazard, Pharao, / and Basset, are *calculated* and *determined;* proving, / that in *Games* of *Judgment*, *Skill* will always get / the better of *Chance.* / III. By detecting the *Frauds* in *Play*, that *Eagerness* for / *Gameing* might be suppressed, to the Preservation of / *Estates*, and the *Advancement* of the *Sciences.* / — / Translated from the Latin Original of / John Rizzetti, with Improvements by Richard / Seymour, Esq; Author of *The Court-Gamester*, and / Designed as a *second Part* of that Work. / — / Addressed to the Prince of Wales. / — / London: / Printed for E. Curll, over-against *Catherine-Street* / in the *Strand*. 1729. (Price 2 *s.* Bound.)

Sm. 12mo (in sixes); [A]², B–H⁶, I⁴ — 2 pp. (t. + bl.), 2 pp. (Dedication), [I]–VI, 1–86.
Copy: B.M. 7913 b 48.
This is the first edition of the second Part of *The Court-Gamester*. The 1st, 2nd, and 3rd editions of *The Court-Gamester* (by Richard Seymour = pseud. for John Mottley) had appeared in 1719 (dated 1718), 1720, and 1722. In 1728 the 4th edition was published, to which in 1729, *The Knowledge Of Play* was added as a second Part. In 1732 the two volumes 1728–9 were re-issued with new titles dated 1732:

The / Court Gamester. / — / In Two Parts. / — / Part I. Containing, / — — — — — — / Part II. Containing, / The Knowledge of Play, — — — — — — / To which is added, / The Journal of a Gameing Lady of Quality, a / Tale. In a Letter to a Friend. By Dr. *Swift*.

/ — / *London:* / Printed, and Sold by J. Wilford, behind / the *Chapter-House*, near St. *Paul*'s. 1732. / (Price 2 *s*. 6 *d*. Bound.)

The / Knowledge / Of / Play, / &c. [same title as in 1729] / *London:* / Printed, and Sold by J. Wilford, behind / the *Chapter-House*, near St. *Paul*'s. 1732. / [Price 1 *s*. Stitch'd.]

> 12mo; A–D¹², E⁵ — 2 pp. (t. + bl.), III–VI (Preface), [7]–103, 1 p. unnumbered, 2 pp. (Contents).
> For the second Part see above.
> Copy: B.M. 1041 c 14.

673. *Also* (pp. 27–40) *in:*
The / Metamorphosis / Of The / Town: / Or, A / *View of the Present Fashions.* / A / Tale: / After the Manner of Fontaine. / — / The Second Edition. / — / To which is added, / The Journal of a Modern Lady. / In a Letter to a Person of Quality. By Dr. Swift. / = / *London:* / Printed for J. Wilford, at the *Three Flower-* / *de-Luces* behind the *Chapter-House* in St. / *Paul*'s Church-yard. MDCCXXX. / [Price 6 *d*.]

> 8vo (in fours); [A]–E⁴ — 2 pp. (t. + bl.), [3]–40.
> Copy: B.M. 11631 e 37.

Also (pp. 27–40) *in:*

(2) The / Metamorphoses [*sic*] / Of The / Town: / Or, A / *View of the Present Fashions.* / A / Tale. / After the Manner of / Fontaine. / — / The Third Edition. / — / To which is added, / The Journal of a Modern Lady. / By Dean *Swift.* / — / *London:* / Printed for J. Wilford, at the *Three Flower-de-Luces* / behind the *Chapter-House* in St. *Paul*'s Church-yard. / 1731. Price 6 *d*.

> Same collation as the second edition, but a different printing.
> Copy: B.M. T 1056 (14).

Also (pp. 36–48) *in:*
The / Metamorphoses [*sic*] / Of The / Town: / Or, A / *View of the Present Fashions.* / — / By the late celebrated / Mrs. *Elizabeth Thomas,* / Who has so often obliged the Town, under the Name of / *Corinna.* / — / To which are added, / I. The Female Metamorphosis; or, Ladies trans- / formed into China-Cups. / II. The Journal of a Modern Lady. / III. The Furniture of a Woman's Mind. / IV. An Inventory of a Lady's Dressing-Room. / — / The Fourth Edition. / = / *London:* / Printed for J. Wilford, at the *Three Flower-de-Luces*, in / the *Old Bailey.* MDCCXLIII. / Price One-Shilling.

> 8vo (in fours); [A]–G⁴, H³ — 2 pp. (t. + advs. on verso), [3]–24 (Metamorphoses), [25]–35 (Piece I), [36]–48 (Piece II), [49]–53 (Piece III), [54]–62 (Piece IV).
> Copy: Bodl.

12—J.S.

674. *Another edition:*

The / Journal / Of A / Modern Lady. / — / Written by Dean Swift. / — / [quotation: 8 lines] / — / [ornament] / = / *London:* / Printed and Sold by W. Parker, at the / first House on the Right-Hand in Half- / pav'd-Court, in Salisbury-Court, Fleet- / Street, 1740.

12mo; 1–12.
I saw this copy at a dealer's.

An imitation (?):

The / Journal / Of A / Dublin Beau. / — / Written by a Young Lady. / — / Facit indignatio versum. / — / [ornament] / — / Dublin. / Printed by Nicholas Hussey, Oposite / the Hand and Pen on the Blind-key, 1728–9.

Sm. 8vo; [A]^8 — 2 pp. (t. + bl.), 3–15 + bl.
Copy: R.I.A. Hal. Tracts, Box 181, Tract 10.

***

675. The Substance Of What Was Said By The Dean Of St. Patrick's To The Lord Mayor And Some Of The Aldermen, When His Lordship Came To Present The Said Dean With His Freedom In A Gold Box. (26 Jan., 1729/30).

Advertisement By Dr. Swift, In His Defence Against Joshua, Lord Allen. (18 Feb., 1729/30).

[I have seen neither. *Prose Works*, VII, 168, says that the B.M. has a broadside copy of the former, but for the moment it seems to be lost]. Cf. No. 1293, *post*.

Numb. 5717 The Flying Post; Or, Post-Master. Thursday March 19, 1730. (Contains a letter from Dublin, concerning the presentation of the Freedom of the City to Swift, Jan. 1729.)

1163. Drapier's Hill.

In: Fog's Weekly Journal, Aug. 30, 1729.
Also in: The Dublin Weekly Journal, Saturday Sept. 13, 1729 (here it is entitled 'Drapier's Hall').

Swift's plan of building Drapier's Hill (summer 1729) came to nought (see *Poems,* 873, etc.).

676. A Modest / Proposal / For preventing the / Children / Of / Poor People / From being a / Burthen to their Parents, / Or The / Country, / And / For making them Beneficial to the / Publick. / = / *Dublin:* / Printed by *S. Harding*, opposite the *Hand and* / *Pen* near *Fishamble-Street*, on the *Blind Key.* / MDCCXXIX.

Sm. 8vo; A^8 — 2 pp. (t. + bl.), 3–16.
Published end Oct. 1729 (adv. in Harding's Dublin Intelligence, 8 or 18 Nov.)
Copies: Bodl. Godw. Pamph. 1854 (5), Forster 34 A 25, and Rothschild 2116.

677. *Another edition:*

A Modest / Proposal / For preventing the / Children / Of / Poor People / From being a Burthen to / Their Parents or Country, / And / For making them Beneficial to the / Publick. / — / By Dr. Swift. / — / *Dublin*, Printed by *S. Harding:* / *London*, Re-printed; and sold by *J. Roberts* / in *Warwick-lane*, and the Pamphlet-Shops. / M.DCC,XXIX.

8vo (in fours); π^4, B^4, C^2 — 2 pp. (h.t. + bl.), 2 pp. (f.t. + bl.), [5]–19 (adv. on verso).
Copy: B.M. 1077 2 27 (8).

678. *Another edition:*

A Modest / Proposal / For preventing the / Children / Of / Poor People / From being a Burthen to their Pa- / rents or the Country, / And for making them Beneficial to the / Publick. / — / [ornament] / — / *Dublin:* / Printed: And Reprinted at *London*, for / Weaver Bickerton, in *Devereux-Court* / near the *Middle-Temple*. M.DCC.XXX.

8vo (in fours); π^4, B–C^4 — 2 pp. (h.t. + advs. on verso), 2 pp. (f.t. + bl.), 5–23 + bl.

Second edition:

The same title and collation as those of the first edition, except:

– – – – – / Publick. / — / The Second Edition. / — / [ornament] / *Dublin*, / – – – – – –

Copy: Texas.

Third edition:

The same title and collation as those of the first edition, except:

– – – – – / Publick. / — / The Third Edition. / — / [ornament] / *Dublin*, / – – – – – –

Copy: B.M. 1079 i 26 (4).

Also included in:

A / View / Of The / Present State of Affairs / In the Kingdom of / *Ireland;* / In Three Discourses. / Viz. / I. A List of the Absentees of *Ireland*, and the / *Yearly Value* of their Estates and Incomes spent / abroad. With Observations on the present Trade and / Condition of that Kingdom. / II. The Present State of *Ireland* Consider'd: / Wherein the List of the Absentees of *Ireland* is / occasionally Answer'd. / III. A Modest Proposal for Preventing the / Children of *Poor People* from being a *Burthen* to their / Parents or the Country, and for making them / Beneficial to the Publick. By Dr. *Sw—ft.* / = / Printed at *Dublin:* / Reprinted at *London*, for Weaver Bickerton, / in *Devereux-Court*, near the *Middle-Temple*. / M.DCC.XXX. / — / (Price Two Shillings.)

8vo (in fours); π^4, A–M^4; π^1, B–D^4, C^2; π^4, B–C^4 — 2 pp. (t. + bl.), 2 pp. (title: List Absentees, + bl.), 2 pp. (Dedication to Carteret + bl.), 2 pp. (The Preface), [1]–94, 2 pp. ('Ordered' + bl.); 2 pp. (t. + bl.), 5–32; 2 pp. (h.t. + advs. on verso), 2 pp. (f.t. + bl.), 5–23 + bl.

Copy: B.M. 8145 b 53.

This is a made-up volume, the third part consisting of *The Third Edition* recorded above (same printing).

679. *Also in:*
A Libel On Dr. D—ny, &c. (see No. 36).

680. *French translation* (pp. 369–84) in:
Recueil / De / Pieces Curieuses / Sur Les / Matieres / Les Plus Interessantes. / Par / Albert Radicati, / *Comte de Passeran.* / [ornament] / *A Rotterdam,* / Chez la Veuve Thomas Johnson Et Fils. / M.DCC.XXXVI.

8vo; *^{5}, A–Aa^8 and one leaf inserted between A 7 and A 8 — 2 pp. (title + Contents on verso), III–X (Dedicace), 1–10 (Factum d'Albert), 2 pp. (title: Discours + bl.), 13–14 (Declaration de l'autuer), 2 pp. extra (Table des Matieres), [15]–384.

Copy: Bibl. Nat. Paris (Z 31197).

Contemporary criticism

The Craftsman, Dec. 12, 1730, reflected on Swift's *Modest Proposal.* S.W. wrote an answer, not published at the time (cf. Temple Scott VII, 219; *Works,* Vol. IX, 1772, p. 28).

Delany And Swift

(1729–30)

Towards the end of 1729 Delany, soliciting further preferment, published:

1609. An Epistle To His Excellency John Lord Carteret Lord Lieutenant of Ireland. Dublin: Printed by George Grierson. Where a small Edition of this Poem may be had. — Folio; no signatures — 2 pp. (t. + bl.), 6 unnumbered pages.

Copies: U.L.C. Hib. 3.730.1 (2), Nat. Libr. of Ireland.

1610. *The "small Edition":*
An Epistle To His Excellency John Lord Carteret Lord Lieutenant of Ireland. Dublin: Printed by and for George Grierson, at the Two Bibles in Essex-Street. MDCCXXX. — Sm. 8vo; no signatures — 2 pp. (t. + bl.), 6 unnumbered pages.

Copies: T.C.D. P. pp. 3 (13), Nat. Libr. of Ireland, Forster.

This piece was several times reprinted (see below), also (pp. 157–162) in: The Tribune. Part II. To which is added, An Epistle To His Excellency John Lord Carteret, &c. Printed at Dublin. London: Reprinted, – – – – T. Warner – – – 1729 (a periodical running to 21 numbers, by Delany and Sheridan — originally published in Dublin, by S. Powell, 1729. Copy: Forster; 19 numbers, paged consecutively [1]–152.); also (p. 88) in: The

Flower-Piece: A Collection Of Miscellany Poems. &c. London: J. Walthoe, &c. 1731 (again in 1733).

Delany's *Epistle* elicited several answers (and answers to answers), some of them by Swift, which follow here.

Cf. *Poems*, 486 — my 951, 950, 952, 954, 955.

Elr. Ball, *Swift's Verse*, 247, etc.

684. An / Epistle / Upon An / Epistle / From a certain Doctor / To a certain great Lord: / Being A / *Christmas-Box* for D. D – – –ny. / — / —— *Palatinae Cultor facunde Minervae*, / *Ingenio frueris qui propiore Dei*. / *Nam tibi nascentes* Domini *cognoscere Curas*, / *Et secreta* Ducis *Pectora nôsse licet*. / Mart. Lib. 5. Ep 5. / — / Dublin: Printed in the Year 1730.

    Sm. 8vo size; no signatures — 2 pp. (t. + bl.), [3]–8.
    Copies: T.C.D. (P pp. 3 (11)), and Forster (8562).

Also in:
686. An / *Epistle* / To His Excellency / John *Lord* Carteret / Lord Lieutenant of / *Ireland*. / — / To which is added, an *Epistle*, / upon an *Epistle*; being / A *Christmas-Box* / For / Doctor D – – – – – –ny. / — / *Dublin:* Printed, in the Year 1730.

    Sm. 8vo; no signatures — 1 p. (title), 2–8.
    Copy: Forster 8562. Copy B.M. 11601 ccc 38 (4) is incomplete, having only 3 pages of text.

Also in:
685. Select / Poems / From / *Ireland:* / Being / I. A Satyr in Imitation of Persius; by an *English* / Noblemen. [*sic*] / II. An Extemporary Poem by the Earl of *Ch—d*. / III. A Christmas-Box for Doctor *D—ny*, in / Answer to his Epistle, printed in the second / Part of the Tribunes. / IV. A Reply to the Christmas-Box in Defence of / Doctor *D—ny*. / Printed at Dublin: / *London*, / Reprinted and Sold by T. Warner at the *Black-Boy* / in *Pater-Noster-Row*. MDCCXXX. / Price (6*d*.)

    8vo (in fours); π^1 (probably E 4), B–D⁴, E³ — 2 pp. (t. + bl.), 1–14 (Satyr), 15–16 (Extemp. Poem), 17–24 (Epistle upon an Epistle), 25–30 (Answer).
    Copies: Nat. Libr. of Ireland, and Bodl. 12–1205.
    Piece IV (A Reply) had appeared separately, entitled:
    An Answre [*sic*] To The Christmas-Box. In Defence Of Docter [*sic*] D—n—y. By R—t B—r. &c. Dublin: Printed in the Year, MDCCXXIX. — Sm 8vo size; no signatures (unless cut off?) — 2 pp. (t. + bl.), 3–7 + bl.
    Copy: Forster 8562 (V).
    The title would suggest that this answer was written by Rupert Barber; but the real author was Sheridan (cf. Elr. Ball *Swift's Verse*, 250 + note 30).
    The *Answre* was also printed in:

Numb. 5717 The Flying Post; Or, Post-Master. Thursday March 19. 1730. Sold by J. Roberts, at the Oxford Arms in Warwick-Lane, where Advertisements are taken in. — Folio; 2 pages.

687. A / Libel / On / D - - - - - - - - D - - - - - - - - - / And A / Certain Great *Lord.* / — / [ornament] / — / Printed *Anno* MDCCXXX.

> Sm. 8vo (four leaves); A⁴ — 2 pp. (t. + bl.), 3–8.
> Copy: Penn.

688. *Another edition:*
A / Libel / On / D— D—. / And A / Certain Great Lord. / — / [ornament] / — / Printed in the Year MDCCXXX.

> Sm. 8vo size; no signatures — 1 p. (title), [2]–8.
> Copies: B.M. 11601 ccc 38 (3), Forster, and Rothschild 2118.

690. *Also in:*
The / Censoriad: / A / Poem. / — / Written Originally by Martin Gulliver. / — / Illustrated with sundry Curious Annotations of divers / Learned Commentators, *Scholiasts* and *Criticks.* / — / —— — *Faelicia, tempora, quae te* / *Moribus opponunt!* —— —— Juv. / — / —— Thou Vermin wretched, / As e'er in meazel'd Pork was hatched! / Thou Tail of Worship, that dost grow / On Rump of Justice, as of Cow! / Hudibras. / — / [ornament] / = / *London;* / Re-printed from the *Dublin* Third / Edition, for Weaver Bickerton, in / *Devereux-Court*, near the *Middle-Temple.* / M.DCC.XXX. / (Price Six-Pence.)

> 8vo; 1–23 (*Advertisement* on verso), 25–32. — Pages 25–32 are *A Libel on Dr. D* - - - - - - - - - - - - *y*, &c.

689. *Another edition* (different title):
A / Satire / On / Dr. *D—ny.* / — / By *Dr.* Sw—T. / — / To which is added, / *The* Poem *which occasion'd it.* / = / Printed at *Dublin:* / And Re-printed at *London*, for *A. Moore*, / near St. *Paul*'s. MDCCXXX.

> 8vo (in fours); π², B–D⁴ — 2 pp. (h.t. + bl.), 2 pp. (f.t. + bl.), [5]–17 + bl. (To Dr. D—y = the Satire), 2 pp. (title: Epistle + bl.), [21]–27 + bl. (Epistle).
> Copies: B.M. 11633 cc 2 (12), and Forster.

689A. A / Libel / On / D— D - - - - - -, / And A / Certain Great Lord / — / [ornament] / — / Printed in the Year MDCCXXX.
4to; π⁴, B² — 2 pp. (t. + bl.), [3]–12.
Copy: J. Barry Brown, Esq.

689B. *Another edition:*

A / Libel / On / Dr. D——*ny*, / And a certain Great Lord. / *By*
Dr. Sw—t. / *Occasion'd by a certain* Epistle. / — /. To which is
added, / I. An Epistle to his Excellency *John* Lord / *Carteret*, by
Dr. D——*ny*. / II. An Epistle on an Epistle; or a *Christ-* / *mas-Box*
for Dr. D——*ny*. / = / Printed at *Dublin:* / And Re-printed at
London, for *A. Moore,* / near St. *Paul*'s. M DCC XXX. / (Price 6 *d.*)

8vo (in fours); π^1, B–D^4, E^3 — 2 pp. (t. + bl.), [5]–18 (To Dr. D—ny
[= Libel]), [19]–28 (Epistle to Carteret), [29]–34 (Epistle on Epistle).
Copies: Library of Congress, Chapin Libr., and Texas.
As the text begins on page [5], it would seem at first sight that a leaf (half-
title?) is wanting in front. But as none of the three copies recorded has such
a leaf, it is probable that the original E 4 was used to print the title on, in
which case the book is complete as recorded above.

689C. A / Libel / On / Dr. D—*ny*, / And a certain Great Lord. /
By Dr. Sw—t. / *Occasion'd by a certain* Epistle. / — / To which is
added, / I. An Epistle to his Excellency *John* Lord / *Carteret*, by Dr.
D—*ny*. / II. An Epistle on an Epistle; or a *Christ-* / *mas-Box* for
Dr. D—*ny*. / III. Dr. *Sw—t*'s Proposal for preventing the / Children
of poor People being a Burthen / to their Parents or Country,
and for ma- / king them beneficial to the Public. / — / The Second
Edition. / — / Printed at *Dublin:* / And Re-printed at *London*, for
A. Moore, / near *St. Paul*'s. MDCCXXX. (Price 6 *d.*)

8vo (in fours); A–B^4, C 1, [E]^3 — 2 pp. (t. + bl.), [3]–13 (To Dr. D—ny),
13–18 (Epistle to Carteret), [19]–24 (Epistle on Epistle).
A 2 wrongly signed B 2. — Page [19] which is C 1, is unsigned, but page
21 is correctly signed E 2. — *Finis.* at foot of p. 24.
Copies: Texas and Penn.
In spite of the mention on the title-page, the Texas copy and Penn's lack
Dr. Sw—t's Proposal. But there is a copy with this piece added in the Bodl.
(Godw. Pamphl. 20), which collates:
8vo (in fours); π^4 (the second signed B 2), B–D^4 — 2 pp. (t. + bl.), [3]–13
(To Dr. D—ny), 13–18 (Epistle to Carteret), 19–24 (Epistle on Epistle),
[25]–32 (Modest Proposal).
Finis. at foot of p. 24. — The 'Modest Proposal' is a later addition in
narrower type. — Signature C is signed regularly.
Comparison of the two Texas copies, 1st and 2nd editions, has shown that
E 1–3, paged [29]–34 in the first and [19]–24 in the second, are the same printing, from which it may be concluded that *The Second Edition* was resolved
upon when the type of the first part of the book had already been distributed,
but that of the second part was still standing.

36. *Another edition:*

A / Libel / On / Dr. D—*ny*, / And a certain Great Lord. / By
Dr. Sw—t, / *Occasion'd by a certain* Epistle. / — / To which is Added
/ I. An Epistle to his Excellency *John* Lord / *Carteret*, by Dr. D—*ny* /
II. An Epistle on an Epistle; or a *Christmas* / *Box* for Dr. D—*ny*.

/ III. Dr. *Sw—t*'s Proposal for preventing the / Children of Poor People being a Burthen / to their Parents or Country, and for ma- / king them beneficial to the Public. / — / *Dublin*: Printed, / *London*: Reprinted for *Capt. Gulliver* / near the *Temple*, MDCCXXX. / (Price Sixpence.)

> 8vo (in fours); [A]–C⁴, B⁴ — 2 pp. (t. + bl.), [3]–9 (To Dr. D—ny, occasioned by an Epistle = The Libel), [10]–13 (Epistle), [14]–18 (Epistle on Epistle), [19]–32 (Proposal). ['Finis.' at foot of p. 32, not at foot of p. 18. Catchword at foot of p. 18: A. Mo].
> Copy: U.L.C. D dd 25.113 (3).
> *Also in* No. 38 (copy dated 1733).

Also in:

40. Miscellanies. / Consisting chiefly of / Original Pieces / In / *Prose* and *Verse*. / — / By D - - n S - - - - t. / — / *Never before Published in this Kingdom*. / — / [ornament] / = / *Dublin* Printed. / *London*: Re-printed for A. Moore / in *Fleetstreet*, 1734. / (Price One Shilling.)

> 8vo (in fours); π¹, B–G⁴, H³ — 2 pp. (t. + bl.), [1]–7 (Apology to Lady Carteret), 8–16 (Libel on D— D—), 17–22 (An Epistle upon an Epistle), 23–28 (An Epistle to Lord Carteret), 29–38 (The Drapier Demolished), 39–48 (A Proposal For An Act of Parliament To sell the Bishops Lands), 49–50 omitted in numbering, 51–53 (To the Rt. Honourable Sir Richard Poynes, kt.), 54–5 (A Copy of Verses upon two celebrated Modern Poets), 1 p. blank. — H 4 probably used to print the title on.
> Copy: Penn.
> 'A proposal - - - To sell the Bishops Lands', when first published in 1732, had a different title (see No. 716a).

40A. *Another edition:*

Miscellanies. / Consisting chiefly of / Original Pieces / In / *Prose* and *Verse*. / — / By *D - - n S - - - t*. / — / *Never before published in this Kingdom*. / — / [ornament] / = / *Dublin* Printed. / *London*: Re-printed for A. Moore in / Fleetstreet, 1734.

> 12mo (in sixes); [A]–C⁶ — 2 pp. (t. + bl.), 3–36.
> Copy: Harold Williams.

691. A / Panegyric / On The / Reverend D - - n *S* - - - - *t*. / In / Answer / To The / Libel / On / Dr. *D - - y*, and a certain Great L - - d. / — / [ornament] / — / Printed in the Year 1729–30.

> 16mo size; π¹, A³ — 2 pp. (t. + bl.), 3–8.
> Copies: B.M. 11631 a 63 (8), and Forster.
> Elr. Ball, *Swift's Verse*, 252–3, ascribes it to Swift himself.

692. *Another edition:*

A / Panegyric / On the Reverend / Dean *Swift*. / In Answer to / *A* Libel *on* Dr. Delany, / *and a certain Great* Lord. / — / Never before Printed. / — / *London:* / Printed for J. Roberts in *War-wick-Lane*, / and N. Blandford at the *London-* / *Gazette*, *Charing-Cross*. MDCCXXX. / (Price Six-pence.)

> 4to (in twos); π^1, B 1, B–D^2 — 2 pp. (t. + bl.), [3]–15 + bl.
> Copy: B.M. 11631 e 61.

Also in:

A Vindication of the / Libel / On Dr. *Delany*, / And a certain Great Lord. / Together with A / Panegyric / On Dean Sw—t; / *In Answer to the Libel.* / — / To which is Added / I. The said Libel on Dr. *Delany*, &c. / II. Dr. *Delany*'s Epistle which occasion'd it. / III. An Epistle on an Epistle; or a *Christmas-* / *Box* for Dr. *Delany*. / — / *Dublin:* Printed, *London:* Re-printed for *J. Wilford* / near *Stationers Hall*, M.DCC.XXX. / And sold at the Pamphlet Shops. / (Price Sixpence.)

> 8vo (in fours); [A]–C^4, D^2 — 2 pp. (t. + bl.), [3]–4 (Vindication), [5]–11 (Panegyric), [12]–18 (To Dr. D—ny = the Libel), [19]–22 (Epistle), 23–27 (Epistle on an Epistle), 1 p. blank.
> Copy: Clark Library.
> The 'Vindication' was also published separately:

954. A Vindication of the Libel: Or, A New Ballad; Written by a Shoe-Boy, on an Attorney, who was formerly a Shoe-Boy, &c. Printed in the Year, 1729–30. — Folio; 1 page.
> Cf. Elr. Ball, *Swift's Verse*, 259, note 29, who ascribes it to William Dunkin.

693. To / Doctor *D–L - - - Y,* / On The / Libels / Writ against him. / — / — *Tanti tibi non sit opaci* / *Omnis arena Tagi.* Juv / — / [ornament] / — / *London:* Printed. And, / Dublin Reprinted in the Year MDCCXXX.

> Sm. 8vo; no signatures — 2 pp. (h.t. + bl.), 2 pp. (f.t. + bl.), [5]–16.
> Copies: B.M. 11601 ccc 38 (5), and Forster.

694. *Also in:*

Select / Poems / From / *Ireland:* / — / Part II. / — / Containing, / I. A Letter to Dr. D - - - l - - - y on the Libels writ a- /gainst Him. / II. The *Pheasant* and the *Lark.* A Fable. / III. A friendly Apology for a certain Justice of the / Peace, by Way of Defence of *H - - rtley Hut-* / *ch—n*, Esq; / — / Printed at Dublin: / *London,* / Reprinted and Sold by T. Warner at the *Black-Boy* / in *Pater-Noster-Row.* M.DCC.XXX. / (Price 6*d.*)

> 8vo (in fours); π^2 (probably E 3 and E 4), B–D^4, E^2 — 2 pp. (advs.), 2 pp. (t. + bl.), [1]–12 (Letter), [13]–24 (Fable), [25]–28 (Apology).
> Copy: Nat. Libr. of Ireland. The Bodl. copy 12θ 1205 has no leaf of advs.

695. After the above pieces Delany wrote:
> The Pheasant And The Lark. A Fable. &c. Dublin: Printed in the Year MDCCXXX. — Sm. 8vo size; no signatures — 2 pp. (t. + bl.), [3]–8.
> Copies: B.M. 11601 ccc 38 (10), and Forster.

Also in:
  The *Intelligencer*, Numb. XX, May 7, 1729. (This may be its first appearance in print — cf. *Poems*, 507.)
  The *Daily Post*, April 4, 1730.
  The *Intelligencer*, 2nd ed. 1730 (No. 35).
  Select Poems From Ireland, Part II (No. 694).
  It was answered by Swift in:

An / Answer / To / Dr. *D* – – – – – *y*'s Fable / Of The / Pheasant / And The / Lark. / — / [ornament] / — / Printed in the Year 1730.

  Sm. 8vo; [A]⁴ — 2 pp. (t. + bl.), 3–7 + bl.
  Copies: B.M. 11601 ccc 38 (6), and Forster.

700. Lady A—S—N / Weary of the / Dean.
  Folio; 1 page (2 columns).
  At foot of page:

Printed in the Year MDCCXXX. / — / Just publish'd, / A View of the Irish Bar, in a Character of the Lawyers.

  Written during Swift's first stay with the Achesons at Market Hill, June 1728 till Feb. 1729.
  Published early 1730.
  Copy: U.L.C. Hib. 3.730.1 (5).
  Also in: *The Daily Post Boy*, Apr. 7, 1730.
  Also in: *An Elegy On Dicky and Dolly*, &c. (No. 966, *post*), where it is entitled: The Narrative of *D.S.* when he was in the North of *Ireland*.
  Also in: *The Gentleman's Magazine*, April 1732, II, 717.

696. An / Apology / To The / Lady C—R—T. / On Her Inviting Dean S – – F – – T / To Dinner; He came accordingly, / but, Her Ladyship being Abroad, / went away: At Her Return, She en- / quired for him; and not hearing of / him, sent the next Day to invite him / again: When he came, he went to / make an *Apology*, for his going / away, but my Lady wou'd accept of / none but in Verse. / — / [ornament] / = / Printed in the Year 1730.

  Sm. 8vo size; no signatures — 2 pp. (t. + bl.), 3–8.
  Copy: Forster 8562 (V).
  There is a copy in T.C.D. (P. pp. 3.16), which has a double rule over the ornament, and a single one under it:

– – – – Verse. / = / [ornament] / — / Printed – – – –

Also in:
  The *Whitehall Evening Post*, March 19, 1730.

Also in:
  The *London Journal*, March 21, 1730.
  This piece was probably written in the autumn of 1725 (see *Poems*, 374–5).

697. A / Vindication / Of His / Excellency / The / Lord C – – – – T, / From The / Charge / Of favouring none but / Tories,

High-Churchmen and / Jacobites. / — / By the Reverend Dr.
S—T. / — / *London:* / Printed for T. Warner at the *Black-Boy* / in
Pater-Noster-Row. MDCCXXX. / (Price 6*d.*)

> 8vo (in fours); π^2 (probably E 3 and E 4), B–D^4, E^2 — 2 pp. (h.t. + bl.),
> 2 pp. (f.t. + bl.), 1–27 (advs. on verso). — Page 17 misnumbered 11.
> Published April 1730.
> Copy: Penn.

698. *Another edition:*
A / Vindication / Of His / Ex—y the Lord *C*—, / From / The
Charge of favouring / none but *Toryes, High-Church-* / *men,* and
Jacobites. / — / [ornament] / — / *London:* / Printed, and *Dublin*
Re-printed in the Year / MDCCXXX.

> Sm. 8vo (in fours); [π]^5, B–D^4, E^3 — 2 pp. (h.t. + bl.), 2 pp. (f.t. + bl.),
> [3]–37 + bl. (Probably E 4 used as h.t.).
> Copy: Bodl. Godw. Pamph. 20.

701. An Excellent New / Ballad: / Or, / The true *En* – – – *sh*
D – – – n to be hang'd for a / R – – – – – pe.

> Folio; 2 pages.
> Written during Swift's third stay at Market Hill, June till October 1730.
> The dean meant was Thomas Sawbridge, Dean of Ferns.
> Published summer 1730.
> Copy: U.L.C. Hib. 3.730.1 (53).
> See *Poems*, 516.

705. *Horace* Book I. / Ode XIV. / — / *O navis, referent,* &c.
/ — / Paraphrased and inscribed to *Ir—d.* / — / The Inscription. /
Poor floating Isle, tost on ill Fortune's Waves, / *Ordain'd by* Fate *to be*
the Land of Slaves: / *Shall moving* Delos *now deep-rooted stand,* / *Thou,*
fixt of old, be now the moving Land? / *Altho' the Metaphor be worn and*
stale / *Betwixt a State, and Vessel under Sail;* / *Let me suppose thee for*
a Ship a-while, / *And thus address thee in the Sailor Stile.* / = / Printed
in the Year MDCDXXX. [*sic*]

> Sm. 8vo size; no signatures — 2 pp. (t. + bl.), [3]–7 + bl.
> Published in Dublin, summer 1730.
> Copy: T.C.D. P. pp. 3.9.
> *Reprinted in:*
> *The Daily Post Boy,* No. 6636, Friday, Aug. 14, 1730.
> *Reprinted in:*
> *The Grand Question debated,* &c., Faulkner, 1732 (No. 714, *post*), where it
> covers three leaves (pp. 13–18), preceded, on p. 12, by 'The Publisher to the
> Reader', referring to it.

699. *Traulus.* / — / The first Part. / — / In A / Dialogue /
Between / Tom and Robin. / — / [ornament] / — / Printed in the
Year MDCCXXX.

Sm. 8vo size; no signaures — 2 pp. (t. + bl.), [3]–8.
Published Aug. 21, 1730 (adv. in *The Daily Post Boy*).
Copy: B.M. 11601 ccc 38 (11).

Another issue:
    Poems, 795 mentions another issue "with a few variations in spelling and punctuation, but no verbal differences — save a plural for a singular in l. 68". Cf. Ashley Library Catalogue VI, 32.

Traulus | — | The Second Part. | — | [ornament] | — | Printed in the Year MDCCXXX.

Sm. 8vo size; no signatures — 2 pp. (t. + bl.), [3]–7 + bl.
Copies of both 'Parts' in Nat. Libr., Dublin; and in B.M. 11601 ccc 38 (11).
Only *The First Part* in:
The Daily Post Boy, August 21, 1730.

1611. *Part of the 9th* Ode *of the 4th Book of* Horace, | *address'd to Dr.* William King, *late Lord Arch-Bishop of* Dublin. | *Paulum sepultae*, &c.

This *Ode,* composed by Swift about Sept. 1721, was first printed (p. 49) in:
    Miscellaneous Poems, By Several Hands. Published by D. Lewis. – – – London: Printed by J. Watts. MDCCXXX. (This is Vol. II; Vol. I had appeared in 1726).

Also in:
    Story Injured Lady 1746, p. 63.
    Cf. Case, 337; *Poems*, 241, etc., 1132–3.

702. In the *Preface* of 'Poems On Several Occasions – – – – – – – Dublin: Printed by George Faulkner – – – – MDCCXXX. — 8vo; 2 pp., I–IV, 2 pp. (Preface), 8 pp., 1–4, 1–189', the author, the Rev. M. Pilkington, says that Swift "kindly condescended to peruse the poems, and honoured them with his corrections and remarks."

703. *Another edition:*
Poems On Several Occasions. – – – By Matthew Pilkington, M.A. Revised by the Reverend Dr. Swift. London: Printed for T. Woodward – – – – Charles Davis – – – and W. Bowyer. MDCCXXXI. 8vo; frontisp., I–XIV, 4 pp., 1–184.

Another edition:
704. The Life Of John Carteret Pilkington – – – – Poems on Several Occasions; By the Author's Father. Revised and corrected by the late Dean Swift. – – – London: R. Griffiths, and T. Becket. M.DCC.LXI.
    Two vols; 12mo.
    This would seem to be a reprint of 'The Real Story Of John Carteret Pilkington – – – London, 1760.', 4to, to which the 'Poems On Several Occasions' were added. Mention of Swift's assistance has been removed to the title-page.

The Advertisement to the Reader (pp. 3–8) in the following work is by Swift:

707. Memoirs / Of / Capt. *John Creichton.* / = / Written by Himself. / = / [ornament] / — / Printed in the Year, 1731.

12mo; 1–170.

708. *Another edition:*
The / Memoirs / Of / Capt. John Creichton. / From his own Materials, / Drawn up and digested by / Jonathan Swift, / D.D.D.S.P.D. / First printed in the Year, 1731. / Glasgow: / Printed for R. Urie. MDCCLXVIII.

12mo; I–XII, two blank leaves, 13–227 + bl.
Copy: own.
The Historical Works Of the Reverend Dr. Jonathan Swift, Vol. III, 1769 (No. 105, *ante*) is the same printing, except for the renewed title-page.

709. *Another edition:*
Autobiography. / A Collection / Of The / Most Instructive and Amusing / Lives / Ever Published, / Written by the Parties themselves. / With brief Introductions, and Compendious / Sequels carrying on the Narrative to the / Death of Each Writer. / Volume XI. / J. Creichton. — W. Gifford. — T. Ellwood. / London: / Printed for Hunt and Clarke, / York Street, Covent Garden.

This volume contains:
The / Memoirs / Of / Captain John Creichton, / From his own Materials, / Drawn up and digested by / Jonathan Swift, D.D. D.S.P.D. / First printed in 1731. / London, 1827. / Re-printed for Hunt and Clarke, / York Street, Covent Garden.

12mo (in sixes); π^1 (frontisp.), π^6, B–DD⁶, EE⁴ — 2 pp. (frontisp. portrait of William Gifford), 2 pp. (1st title + printer's name on verso), 2 pp. (2nd title + bl.), [V]–VI (Introduction), [VII]–VIII (Advertisement), [IX]–XII (To The Reader) + bl., [13]–78 (Creichton), 2 pp. blank, 2 pp. (title: Memoir Gifford + bl.), 2 pp. (Introduction + bl.), [5]–34 (Gifford), 2 pp. blank, 2 pp. (title: Life Ellwood + bl.), [I]–II (Introduction), [5]–214 (Ellwood), 2 pp. blank.
Copy: Bodl. 2106 f 32.

709A. *Another issue:*
The / Memoirs / Of / Captain John Creichton, / From His Own Materials, / Drawn Up And Digested By / Jonathan Swift, D.D. D.S.P.D. / First Printed In 1731. / London: / Whittaker, Treacher, And Arnot, / Ave-Maria-Lane. / — / MDCCCXXX.

12mo (in sixes); [A]–F⁶, G⁴ — 2 pp. (h.t. + bl.), 2 pp. (t. + bl.), [V]–VI (Introduction), [VII]–XI (Advertisement), 1 p. blank, [13]–78, 2 pp. blank.

Copy: Am. Antiq. Soc., Worcester (Mass.). This copy lacks half-title, pp. IX–[XII], and the blank leaf at the end.

706. With Favour and Fortune fastidiously blest, &c.

Printed on one side of a quarto sheet, 23.5 × 14.3 cm. The French, in italic print, without any title, covers the upper part of the sheet; the English version below it, is headed:
Imitated in *English*.
Copy: Harold Williams.

These lines consisting of French verses satirizing Cardinal Fleury, followed by an imitation in English directed at and containing a 'character' of Sir Robert Walpole, were sent by Swift (in MS., but not in his own hand), in a letter to the Countess of Suffolk, Oct. 26, 1731 (cf. *Letters To and From Henrietta, Countess Of Suffolk*, 1824, II, 32; Elr. Ball, *Swift's Verse*, 217–8; Shane Leslie, *The Script of Jonathan Swift*, 19–20 + note).

712. Helter Skelter, / Or / The Hue and Cry after the Attornies, / going to ride the Circuit.

Narrow folio; 1 page.
Published probably Nov. 1731 (see Elr. Ball, *Swift's Verse*, 278; *Poems*, 573).
Copy: B.M. 1890 e 5 (4).

Also in:
A Proposal Humbly offer'd (See No. 37).

711. The / Place / Of The / Damn'd: / — / By J.S.D.D.D.S.P. D. / — /

Folio; 1 page.
At foot of page:

Printed in the Year, 1731.

Also in:
No. 37, and *Fog's Weekly Journal*, Dec. 4, 1731.

710. A / Proposal / Humbly offer'd to the / P – – – – – – – – – – – t, / For the more effectual preventing the / further Growth of *Popery*. / With The / Description and Use of the Ecclesiastical / *Thermometer*, very proper for all / Families. / — / *Insani sanus nomen ferat, aequus Iniqui / Ultra quam satis est, virtutem si petat Ipsam*. / Hor. / — / By C—P—, Esq; / = / *Dublin:* / Printed in the Year MDCCXXXI.

Sm. 8vo size; no signatures — 1 p. (title), [2]–16 (text).
Copy: B.M. 8133 a 59.

Another edition:
37. A / Proposal / Humbly offer'd to the / P – – – – – t, / For the more effectual preventing the further / Growth of *Popery*. / With The / Description and Use of the Ecclesiastical / *Thermometer*,

very proper for / all Families. / — / *Insani Sanus nomen ferat, Æquus Iniqui, / Ultra quàm satis est, virtutem si petaet ipsam.* / Hor. / — / By Dr. *S—T.* / — / To which is added, / The Humble Petition of the Weavers / and Venders of Gold and Silver Lace, / Embroiderers, *&c.* / As also two Poems, *viz.* / Helter Skelter, or the Hue and Cry after the / Attornies upon their riding the Circuit. / And / The Place of the Damn'd. / = / *Dublin* Printed. / *London,* Re-printed for *J. Roberts* in *Warwick- / Lane.* MDCCXXXI. Price Six Pence.

8vo (in fours); [A]–D⁴ — 2 pp. (t. + bl.), 3–20 (Proposal), 21–28 (Humble Petition), 29–31 (Helter Skelter), 31–32 (Place of the Damn'd).
Published Dec. 6 or 7, 1731 (*Poems,* 573).
Copies: B.M. 700 g 65, Forster 8562 (34 A 30).
No separate edition of 'The Humble Petition' known.

Second edition:

37A. A / Proposal / Humbly offered to the / *P—t,* / For the more effectual preventing the further / Growth of *Popery.* / With The / Description and Use of the Ecclesiastical / *Thermometer,* very proper for / all Families. / — / *Insani Sanus nomen ferat, Æquus Iniqui, / Ultra quàm satis est, virtutem si petat ipsam.* / Hor. / — / By Dr. *S—T.* / — / To which is added, / The Humble Petition of the Weavers / and Venders of Gold and Silver Lace, / Embroiderers, *&c.* / As also two Poems, *viz.* / Helter Skelter, or the Hue and Cry after the / Attornies upon their riding the Circuit. / And / The Place of the Damn'd. / — / The Second Edition. / — / *Dublin* Printed. / *London,* Re-printed for *J. Roberts* in *Warwick- / Lane.* MDCCXXXII. Price Six Pence.

The same collation as above.
Copy: Penn.

713. (1) A / Soldier / And A / Scholar: / Or The / Lady's Judgment / Upon those two / Characters / In the Persons of / Captain —— and D—n *S—T.* / = / *London:* / Printed for J. Roberts in *Warwick-Lane.* MDCCXXXII. / [Price Six-pence.]

4to (in twos); π², B–E² — 2 pp. (t. + bl.), [3]–19 (advs. on verso).
Published Jan. 22, 1732.
Copy: John Rylands Libr., and Rothschild 2128.
Written by Swift during his second stay with the Achesons at Market Hill, June till Oct., 1729.

(2) *Second edition:*
Same title and collation as those of the first edition, except:

S—T. / — / The Second Edition. / — / *London:* /

Copy: Nat. Libr. of Scotl.
Except for the title-page, the first and second editions are the same printing.

(3) *Third edition:*
Same title and collation as those of the second edition, except:

– – – – – / — / The Third Edition. / — / – – – – –

Copy: Penn.

(4) *Fourth edition:*
Same title and collation as those of the second edition, except:

– – – – - / — / The Fourth Edition. / — / – – – – –

Copy: Penn.
     Except for the title-page, the third and fourth editions are the same printing.

714. *Dublin edition* (different title):

The / Grand Question / debated: / — / Whether / Hamilton's Bawn / Should be turn'd into a / Barrack, / Or A / Malt-House. / — / According to the London Edition, with Notes. / — / [ornament] / — / London printed by A. Moore. And, / Dublin Reprinted by George Faulkner, in *Essex-Street*, / M,DCC,XXXII.

8vo (in fours); π^4, B^4, C^2 — 2 pp. (t. + '*The* Preface *to the* English *Edition.*' on verso), [3]–11 (The Grand Question Debated), [12] (The Publisher to the Reader), [13]–18 (Horace Book I. Ode XIV.), 2 pp. advs.
Published end of Jan. 1732. Cf. Rothschild 2130.
Penn has two copies, one on thick, the other on thin paper.
The London and Dublin editions are from different manuscripts.
For 'Horace Book I. Ode XIV.', see No. 700.
The title-page of this Faulkner edition refers to an edition 'London printed by A. Moore', and its verso has 'The Preface to the English Edition.' No London edition printed by Moore has been traced.
Cf. *Poems*, 863–5; *Review English Studies*, Vol. 15, 1939, p. 328; *Times Literary Supplement*, Oct. 20, 1945.

Also in:
The Gentleman's Magazine, Feb. 1732, II, 624.

715. *Another edition:*

The Grand Question Debated, / Whether / *Hamilton's Bawn* should be turned into a Barrack or a Malt House. / Written in 1729 by Dean Swift, and / Read with great Applause by Mr. Henderson, at *Freemason's-Hall.* / — /

Very large folio; 1 page (4 columns). — A large illustration, dated April 16, 1785, at top of page.
At foot of fourth column:

Printed for J. Wallis, Ludgate Street, London. / (*Entered at Stationer s-Hall.*)

Copy: B.M. (C. 20 f 2 (254)).

Contemporary criticism

1612. An / Answer / To / *Hamilton's* Bawn: / Or, A short Character of Dr. *S—t.*

4to; no signatures — Page [1] (title; text begins under it), verso blank, page 2 (text continued and finished, verso blank).

Copy: R.I.A. Haliday 185 (18).

Written by William Tisdall (?) (see *Poems*, 1123).

716. Considerations / Upon Two / Bills / Sent down from the R—H— the / H— — of L— — / To the H—ble / H— — of C— — — / Relating to the / Clergy / Of / I**.*.*.*.*.*.* D. / — / [ornament] / — / *London.* / Printed for A. Moore, near St. *Paul's*, / and Sold by the Booksellers of *Westminster* / and *Southwark*, 1732.

> Sm. 8vo (in fours); π^4, B–E⁴, F 1 — 2 pp. (t. + bl.), [3]–42, 2 pp. blank.
> Dated at end: *Dublin Feb.* 24, 1731–2.
> Copy: Penn.
> Before publication an extract of this piece, in the shape of five 'Queries humbly offered' was printed by Faulkner in his *Dublin Journal* of Feb. 26, 1731–2 (see Faulkner's Vol. I, 18mo, 1762, p. XII), for which he was ordered into custody by the House of Lords, so that he suffered severely in his private property and his health.
> The two bills were The Bill of Residence, and The Bill of Division.

717. *Another edition:*

Considerations / Upon Two / Bills, / Sent down from the / Rt. Hon. the House of Lords / To The Honourable / House of Commons of *Ireland,* / Relating To The / Clergy / Of That Kingdom. / — / *By the Rev. Dr. Swift, D.S.P.D.* / — / To which is added, / A Proposal for an Act of Parliament, / to pay off the Debt of the Nation, / without taxing the Subject, by which the / Number of Landed Gentry, and substantial / Farmers will be considerably encreas'd, and / no one Person will be the poorer, or contri- / bute one Farthing to the Charge. / — / By A— P—, *Esq*; / — / *Dublin,* Printed; / *London,* Re-printed for J. Roberts at the *Oxford* / *Arms in Warwick-Lane.* 1732. / (Price Six-pence.)

> 8vo (in fours); A–D⁴ — 2 pp. (t. + bl.), 3–22 (Considerations), 23–32 (Proposal).
> Copy: Penn.
> Although the title says that the *Proposal* is "*By* A[lexander] P[ope], *Esq*;", the style and treatment of the subject clearly show that it was written by Swift.

***

Separate edition of the *Proposal*:

717A. A / Proposal / For An / Act of Parliament, / To pay off the / Debt / Of The / Nation, / Without taxing the Subject, by / which the Number of landed Gentry, and sub- / stantial Farmers will be considerably encreased, and / no one Person will be the

poorer, or contribute / one Farthing to the Charge. / — / By
A— P—, Esq; / = / *Dublin:* / Printed in the Year M,DCC,XXXII.

Sm. 8vo; no signatures. — 2 pp. (h.t. + bl.), 2 pp. (f.t. + bl.), [5]–15,
[16] (adv.: Speedily will be publish'd: / An Examination of cer- / tain *Abuses,
Corrup-* / *tions,* and *Enormities* in the / City of *Dublin.*)
Copies: Texas, and T.C.D.
Not to be confounded with 'An Infallible Scheme To pay the Publick Debt
Of This Nation In Six Months, &c. 1731', which was written by Matthew
Pilkington, and strongly repudiated by Swift (see *Corresp.,* IV, 286).

Also in:
Miscellanies, 1734 (see No. 40).

1301. The Reconciler: Or, Some Remarks Upon Two Pamphlets Lately
publish'd, (viz.) A Letter &c. - - - - And Considerations upon Two Bills
sent down from the R— H— the H— of L—, to the H— the H— of C—,
Relating to the Clergy of I—d. &c. Dublin, 1732. — 8vo; 1–30, 1 p. (*Adv.* and
Errata) + bl. — Copy: U.L.C. — Cf. No. 716, *ante.*

718. An / Examination / Of Certain / *Abuses, Corruptions,* /
And / *Enormities* / In The / City of *Dublin.* / — / [ornament] / — /
Dublin: Printed in the Year 1732.

Sm. 8vo (in fours); π⁴, B–C⁴, D² — 2 pp. (t. + bl.), [3]–27 + bl.
Copies: B.M. 115 a 4, and Nat. Libr. of Ireland.

719. *Another edition:*
City Cries, / Instrumental and Vocal: / Or, An / Examination /
Of Certain / Abuses, Corruptions, / And / Enormities, / In / *Lon-
don* and *Dublin.* / — / By the Rev. Dr. Swift, D.S.P.D. / — / *Dublin,*
Printed; / *London,* Re-printed for J. Roberts at the *Oxford* / *Arms*
in *Warwick-Lane.* 1732. / (Price Six-pence.)

8vo (in fours); [A]–D⁴ — 2 pp. (t. + bl.), [3]–30, 2 pp. advs.
Pickering & Chatto, cat. 322, record a copy with a frontisp. engraved by
Van der Gutch. I have not seen such a copy.

966. An / *Elegy* / On / *Dicky* and *Dolly,* / With the / *Virgin:* / A
/ Poem. / To which is Added / The Narrative of *D. S.* / when he
was in the North of *Ireland.* / *Dublin:* / Printed by James Hoey, at
the Pamphlet- / Shop in *Skinner-Row,* opposite to the *Tholsel,* /
MDCCXXXII.

8vo (in fours); [A]⁴ — 2 pp. (t. + bl.), [3]–7, 1 p. advs.
Copy: U.L.C. Hib. 7.732.22.
The *Elegy,* here first printed, refers to the death within four days of each
other in April 1728, of General Gorges and Dorothea Stopford, Countess of
Meath. Another and later title is 'An Epitaph on General G - - - - - s and
Lady M - - th.'
The *Virgin* is not by Swift. The *Narrative* had already appeared in 1730
(see No. 700). — Cf. *Poems,* 429.

1651. *A Poor* Ir-sh *Parson's Prayer.*

In: *The Gentleman's Magazine*, June 1732, II, 821.
In: *Fog's Weekly Journal*, Sept. 15, 1733 (no title).
Another title for this piece is: *On The Irish Bishops 1732*. Other pieces
written on this subject by Swift are: *Judas*; and *On the Bill for the Clergy's
Residing on their Livings* (neither of them separately published at the time);
moreover: *Considerations upon Two Bills* (see No. 716, 717).

720. The / Lady's / Dressing Room, / To which is added, A /
Poem / On / Cutting down the Old Thorn at *Market Hill*. / — /
By the Rev. Dr. *S—T*. / — / *London*, / Printed for J. Roberts at
the *Oxford Arms* in *Warwick Lane*. / MDCCXXXII. / (Price Six
Pence.)

4to; [A]–B⁴, C² — 2 pp. (t. + bl.), [3]–12 (The Lady's Dressing Room),
[13]–19 (A Poem, &c.), [20] (Advice, &c. + An Epigram, &c.).
Published before June 12, 1732 (see Swift's letter to Pope, June 12, 1732).
Copy: B.M. 11630 c 5 (2).
Though dated 1732, both pieces had been written earlier, at Market Hill,
the first in 1730, the second in 1728.
Besides the two pieces mentioned in the title, the book also contains (on
p. [20]) the two other pieces mentioned in the title of the second edition.
Pieces II and III were also printed in *The London Magazine* for June 1732,
p. 147.
Piece II also occurs in *Fog's Weekly Journal*, July 15, 1732.

Second edition:
The / Lady's / Dressing Room. / To which is added, / I. A
Poem on cutting down the Old Thorn at / *Market Hill*. / II. Advice to a Parson. / III. An Epigram on seeing a Worthy Prelate
go out / of Church in the Time of Divine Service to wait on his /
Grace the D. of *D*. / — / By the Rev. Dr. *S—T*. / — / The Second
Edition. / — / We may observe, the finest Flowers, and the most
delicious Fruits, some- / times owe their Nutriment and Increase
to such kind of Matter, as is most / offensive to the Senses, which
themselves have the greatest Power to gratify. / Fiddes. / — /
London, / Printed for J. Roberts at the *Oxford Arms* in *Warwick
Lane*. / MDCCXXXII. / (Price Six Pence.)

The same collation and the same printing as those of the first edition, except
for the title-page and four Errata which have been corrected in the type.
The ornaments on p. [3] are also different.
Copies: B.M. 11631 cc 9, and Penn.

721. *Dublin edition:*
The / Lady's *Dressing-Room*. / A / Poem. / — / By *.*.*.*.*.*.*.*.
/ — / [ornament] / = / *London*, Printed, and *Dublin*, / Reprinted,
in the Year 1732.

8vo size; no signatures — 2 pp. (t. + bl.), 3–8.
Copy: T.C.D. (N. g.52 (7)).

Second edition:
The same title and collection except:

– – – / [ornament] / — / The Second Edition. / — / *London*, – – –

Copy: Forster 8562.
The Dublin edition tones down some of the offensive passages of the
London edition.

722. *Third edition:*
The / Lady's *Dressing-Room*. / A / Poem. / — / By D—n
S – – – – – *t.* / — / From the Original Copy. / — / The Third
Edition. / — / [ornament] / — / *Dublin:* Printed and sold by
George / Faulkner in *Essex-street*, 1732.

Sm. 8vo size; no signatures — 2 pp. (t. + bl.), [3]–8.
Copy: B.M. 11632 aa 43.

722A. *Another edition:*
The Lady's Dressing-Room, / Discover'd; / A / Poem. / — /
By *D – – n S – – t.* / — / — / — / *Corke:* / *Printed and Sold by Andrew* /
Welsh, next Door but one to the Corke- / *Arms, near the Corn-Market,*
1732–3.

Sm. 8vo size; no signatures — 2 pp. (t. + bl.), 3–8.
Copy: Harold Williams.

Third Corke edition:
The same title and collation as the first Corke edition, except:

– – – – *S – – t.* / — / From the Original Copy. / — / The Third
Edition. / — / *Corke:* / – – –

Copy: Harold Williams and Rothschild 2136.
I have not seen or heard of the second Corke edition.

Also in:
Besington's Evening Post, June 17, 1732.
The Gentleman's Magazine, June 1732, II, 819.
The Muse in Good Humour, 1744, p. 76.

Answers and sequels:
1304. The Gentleman's Study In Answer To The Lady's Dressing-Room.
London, Printed, and Dublin, Reprinted, in the Year 1732. — 8vo; [A]⁴ — (2
pp. bl.), 3–8. — Copy: Forster.

961. Chloe Surpriz'd: Or, The Second Part Of The Lady's Dressing-Room.
To which are added, Thoughts upon Reading the Lady's Dressing-Room, and
the Gentleman's Study. The former wrote by D – – – – n S – – – – t, the
latter by Miss W—— London, Printed, and Dublin, Reprinted, in the Year
1732. —
8vo size; no signatures — 2 pp. (t. + bl.), [3]–8.
Copy: Forster.

1310. The Dean's Provocation For Writing the Lady's Dressing-Room. A
Poem. London, T. Cooper, MDCCXXXIV. — Folio; 1–8.

1613. A Modest / Defence / Of A Late / Poem / By an unknown Author, call'd / The Lady's *Dressing-Room*. / — / [ornament] / — / *Dublin:* / Printed by George Faulkner, in *Essex-street*, / opposite to the *Bridge*, MDCCXXXII.

> Small 8vo; no signatures — 2 pp. (t. + bl.), [3]–8 (text).
> Copies: J. Barry Brown, Esq., Naas, Co. Kildare, Ireland.; Nat. Libr. Dublin.

**   *⁎⁎⁎*

1614. A / Poem / On / Cutting down the Old Thorn at *Market Hill*. Advice to a *Parson*. / An *Epigram*.
On seeing a worthy *Prelate* go out of *Church* / in the Time of *Divine Service*, to wait on / his Grace the D – – of D – – –

> These three pieces are B 3–4 and C 1–2 = pp. [13]–[20] in the 1st and 2nd editions of *The Lady's Dressing Room* (No. 720).
> The second and third pieces were reprinted in:
> *The London Magazine*, June 1732, p. 147.
> *Fog's Weekly Journal*, July 15, 1732.

723. The / Advantages / Propos'd By / Repealing / The / Sacramental Test, / Impartially / Considered. / — / [ornament] / — / *Dublin:* / Printed by George Faulkner, in *Essex-* / *street*, opposite to the *Bridge*, MDCCXXXII.

> Sm. 8vo size; no signatures — 2 pp. (t. + bl.), [3]–16.
> Published winter 1732.
> Copy: U.L.C. Hib. 8.732.8.

724. *Another edition:*
The / Advantages / Proposed By / Repealing / The / *Sacramental Test*, / Impartially / Considered. / — / *By the Rev. Dr.* Swift, *Dean of St.* Patrick's. / — / To which is added, / Remarks on a Pamphlet intitled, / *The* Nature *and* Consequences *of the* / *Sacramental Test consider'd.* / With Reasons humbly offer'd for / Repeal of it. / — / *Dublin*, Printed; / *London*, Re-printed for J. Roberts at the *Oxford Arms* / in *Warwick-Lane*. 1732. / (Price Six-pence.)

> 8vo (in fours); A–D⁴ — 2 pp. (t. + bl.), 3–12 (The Advantages), 13–30 (Remarks), 31–2 (Appendix).
> Copy: Penn.
> *Remarks* refers to a pamphlet, containing both 'The Nature and Consequences' and the 'Reasons' (see the title), which is a serious piece on the presbyterian side, and of which a separate edition, Dublin, 1732, 12 mo, seems to exist (see *Prose Works*, IV, 25). But these 'Reasons', in spite of the similarity of the title, have nothing to do with Swift's satirical work: 'Reasons humbly offered to the Parliament of Ireland For Repealing the Sacramental Test, &c. In Favour Of The Catholics', of which no edition, either separate or in combination with other pieces, seems to exist earlier than in *Political Tracts*, 1738, Vol. II, 253 (cf. T. Sc. IV, 87, etc.).

725. *Also in:*

The / Dispute adjusted, / About The / *Proper Time* / Of applying for a / Repeal / Of The / *Corporation* and *Test* Acts: / By Shewing / That *No Time* is proper. / — / By the Right Reverend Father in God, *Edm.* / Lord Bishop of *London.* / — / To which are added, / The Advantages propos'd by Repealing the / *Sacramental Test:* As also, some *Queries* / relating thereto. / — / By the Reverend Dr. *J.S.D.S.P.D.* / — / *Dublin:* / Printed and sold by George Faulkner, in / *Essex-street*, opposite to the *Bridge*, 1733.

> Sm. 8vo (in fours); π^4, B–E⁴ — 2 pp. (t. + bl.), [3]–13 (The Dispute adjusted), 14–27 (The Advantages Propos'd), [28]–37 (Queries), 2 pages, dated: Dublin, November 21, 1733, and announcing the intended publication of Faulkner's 4 vols. of Swift's Works, 1 page blank.
>
> Copy: Penn.
> See also No. 124.

726. Quaeries / Wrote by / Dr. *J. Swift*, in the Year 1732. / Very proper to be read (at this Time) by every / Member of the Established Church.

> Folio; 2 pages (2 columns).
> Also in: *The Dispute adjusted*, &c. (No. 725, *ante*).
> See also No. 124, *ante*.
> Marsh's Library has a broadsheet, entitled: "Some Queries Upon The Demand of the Presbyterians to have the Sacramental Test repealed at this Session of Parliament. Printed in the Year MDCCXXXIII."; which, though not the same version, repeats the ideas of above.

1615. *A New Simile For the Ladies* (by Sheridan), and *An Answer To a Scandalous Poem* (by Swift), were published together in 1733 in an eight-leaf pamphlet. Mr. Harold Williams saw an incomplete copy of it, lacking the first and last leaves. The title of the *Answer* in that copy was:

An / Answer / To a Scandalous / Poem, / Wherein / The Author most audaciously pre- / sumes to cast an Indignity upon / their Highnesses the *Clouds,* / by comparing them to a *Woman.* / — / Written by Dermot O- Nephely, / *Chief Cap. of* Howth. / — / [ornament] / *Dublin:* / Printed in the Year, M,DCC,XXXIII.

The *New Simile* appeared separately:

960. A / *New Simile* / For The / Ladies, / With / *Useful Annotations.* / — / *To make a Writer miss his End,* / *You've nothing else to do but mend.* / — / [ornament] / — / *Dublin:* Printed in the Year 1732.

> Very small 8vo; [A]⁴ — 2 pp. (t. + bl.), 3–8.
> Copy: Forster 8562III.
> I don't know whether the *Answer* was also published separately.
> Cf. *Poems*, 612, 613, 616.
> See also *The Muse in Good Humour*, 1744.

727. The / Life / And / Genuine Character / Of / Doctor *Swift*. / — / Written by Himself. / — / [ornament] / — / *London:* / Printed for J. Roberts in *Warwick-Lane*, and / Sold at the Pamphlet Shops, *&c.* 1733 / (*Price One Shilling.*)

Folio; π^4, C–E² — 2 pp. (h.t. + bl.), 2 pp. (f.t. + bl.), 2 pp. (To the Reader + bl.), 2 pp. (To Alexander Pope, *Esq.*;), [9]–19 + bl.
Published April 1733.
Copies: T.C.D., and Penn.
There are three versions of this poem: [A] Roberts, 1733 (the one just recorded), [B] Bathurst, 1739 (No. 771), and [C] Faulkner, 1739 (No. 774). The [A] version has 202 lines, [B] 381 lines, [C] 484 lines.
In an interesting article in *The Book Collector's Quarterly*, II, March 1931, pp. 57–73, Prof. Herbert Davis says that [A] is to be taken as a seemingly spurious, but really genuine production of Swift's pen, secretly handed by him to the press through the Rev. M. Pilkington, with an intention to show Pope his displeasure at the way in which Pope had edited his [Swift's] works in the *Miscellanies*, Vol. III, 1732. Later on Swift entrusted the [C] version to Dr. William King for publication in London. The latter consulted Pope, and together they effected radical alterations, omitting about 160 lines and all the notes, while inserting over 60 lines from the [A] version, the result being the [B] version. And lastly Swift had the genuine [C] version published by Faulkner in Dublin. In Faulkner's edition of Swift's *Works*, Vol. VIII, 1746, both the [A] and [C] versions were printed.

728. *Another edition:*
The / Life / And / Genuine Character / Of The / Rev. Dr. *S – – t*, D.S.P.D. / — / Written by Himself. / — / [ornament] / *London:* / Printed for J. Roberts in *Warwick-Lane*, / and sold by the Booksellers, *&c.* 1733.

Sm. 8vo (in fours); π^4, B⁴, C² — 2 pp. (t. + bl.), 2 pp. (To the Reader + bl.), 4 pp. (Dedication to A. Pope), 9–20.
Copy: Forster 8562.

729. *Another edition:*
The / Life / And Genuine / Character, / Of The / Rev. Dr. *S – – – – t*, D.S.P.D. / — / Wtitten [*sic*] by Himself. / — / [monogram] / — / London: / Printed, And Re-printed and Sold by *Edward* / *Waters*, on the *Blind Quay*, *Dublin*, 1733.

Sm. 8vo size; no signatures — 1 p. (title), 1 p. (To the Reader), 2 pp. (Dedication to Alexander Pope), 5–12.
Two copies: R.I.A. (Haliday Vol. 110 No. 5 and No. 6).

729A. A Song, *by Dr.* Swift.

In: *The Gentleman's Magazine*, June 1733, III, 320. Reprinted by Faulkner in Vol. II, 1735, p. 430, with the title:

A *Love Song.* / In the *Modern* Taste. / Written in the Year 1733.

1616. *Verses written by* Dr. Swift.

In: *The Gentleman's Magazine*, July 1733, III, 372.

These verses were Swift's acknowledgment of two presents sent to him on his birthday, Nov. 30, 1732, a paper book by Lord Orrery, and a silver standish by Delany, both accompanied by a set of verses. Orrery's and Delany's verses had already appeared in *The Gentleman's Magazine*, Jan. 1733, III, 40.

There was another person (Mrs. Pilkington) who presented a copy of verses, "Sent with a Quill to the Dean of St. Patrick's, upon hearing he had received a Present of Ink and Paper." (*Mrs. Pilkington's Memoirs*, 1748, I, 111; Iris Barry's reprint, 1928, p. 77.)

The verses of Orrery, Delany, and Mrs. Pilkington:

1307. To the Reverend Doctor Swift, Dean of St. Patrick's. With a Present of a Paper-Book, finely bound, on his Birth-Day, November 30, 1732.

Verses left with a Silver Standish, on the Dean of St. Patrick's Desk, on his Birth-Day.

Sent with a Quill to the Dean of St. Patrick's, upon hearing he had received a Present of Ink and Paper.

Dublin, George Faulkner, 1733. — 4to; 4 pages. — Copy: U.L.C.

730. A / Serious and Useful / Scheme, / To make an / Hospital for Incurables, / Of / Universal Benefit to all His Majesty's / Subjects. / Occasioned by a Report, that the Estate of / Richard Norton Esq; was / to be appointed by Parliament / for such an Endowment. / To which is added, / A Petition of the Footmen in and about *Dublin.* / — / By a Celebrated Author in *Ireland.* / — / *Faecunda Culpae Secula!* — Hor. / — / *London:* / Printed for J. Roberts, at the *Oxford Arms* in / *Warwick-Lane.* MDCCXXXIII. / Price 6d.

8vo (in fours); π^1, B–E⁴, F 1 — 2 pp. (t. + bl.), 1–30 (A Serious And Useful Scheme), [31]–34 (A Petition).

The first piece is dated: Aug. 10, 1733; the second, first published here: Dublin 1732.

Published autumn 1733.

Copies: U.L.C. (Hib. 7.733.12), and Penn.

731. *Another edition:*

A / Serious and Useful / Scheme, / To make an / Hospital for Incurables, / Of / Universal Benefit to all His Ma- / jesty's Subjects. / — / Humbly addressed to the Rt. Hon. the Lord *.*.*.*.*, / the Rt. Hon. Sir *.*.*.*, and to the Rt. Hon. / *.*.*.* * *, Esq; / — / *Faecunda Culpae Secula!* — Hor. / — / To which is added, / A Petition of the Footmen in and about *Dublin.* / — / By the Revd. Dr. *J.S.D.S.P.D.* / — / Printed at *London:* And, / *Dublin:* / Printed by *George Faulkner*, in *Essex-Street*, / opposite to the *Bridge*. 1733.

Sm. 8vo (in fours); [A]–D⁴, E² — 2 pp. (t. + bl.), [3]–31, [32]–34, 2 pp. advs.

Copy: Gilbert Coll., Dublin.

732. *Another edition or issue:*

A / Serious and Useful / Scheme, / To make an / Hospital for Incurables, / Of / Universal Benefit to all His Ma- / jesty's Subjects. / — / Humbly addressed to the Rt. Hon. the Lord *****, / the Rt. Hon. Sir *****, and to the Rt. Hon. / ****** *, Esq; / — / To which is added, / A Petition of the Footmen in and about *Dublin*. / — / *Faecunda Culpae Secula!* — Hor. / — / Printed at *London*: And, / *Dublin*: / Printed by *George Faulkner*, and Sold at his Shop / in *Essex-Street*, opposite to the *Bridge*, and by *G.* / *Risk, G. Ewing* and *W. Smith*, Booksellers in *Dame-* / *Street*, 1733.

Sm. 8vo (in fours); π⁴, B–D⁴, E² — 2 pp. (t. + bl.), [3]–31 (Scheme), [32]–33 (Humble Petition), 2 pp. (adv.).
Copy: B.M. 11631 aa 47 (10).

733. *Another edition:*

The same title and collation as those of the preceding copy, except:

— — — — — — / *****, Esq; / — — — — — — — / Printed at *London*: And, / *Dublin*: Re-printed by George Faulkner, in / *Essex-street*, opposite to the *Bridge*, 1734.

Copy: Forster 8562 (34 A 25).

734. The / *Presbyterians* Plea / Of / Merit; / In Order to take off the / Test, / Impartially Examined. / — / [ornament] / — / *Dublin*: / Printed and sold by George Faulkner, in / *Essex-street*, opposite to the *Bridge*, 1733.

Sm. 12mo; 1–22, 2 pp. (advs.).

735. *Another edition:*

The / *Presbyterians* Plea / Of / Merit; / In Order to take off the / Test, (in *Ireland*,) / Impartially Examined. / With an Account of the State of Po- / pery in that Kingdom, and of the / Origin and Principles of the *Dissen-* / ters in General. / To which is added, / *An* Ode to Humphry French, Esq; / Late Lord Mayor of *Dublin*. / = / *London*: / Reprinted from the Dublin Edition, for G. F. and / Sold by A. Dodd, near *Temple-Bar*; and at the / Pamphlet-Shops. [Price Six-Pence.]

8vo (in fours); [A]–D⁴ — 2 pp. (t. + bl.), [3]–28, [29]–32 (Ode).
Copy: Penn.
The *Ode* is very doubtful.

736. *Second edition:*
Same title as preceding copy, except:

– – – – General. / — / The Second Edition. / — / To which is added, / A Narrative of the Attempts the *Dis-* / *senters* in *Ireland* have made for / procuring the *Repeal* of the Test. / = / London: / Reprinted from the Dublin Edition, for G. F. and / Sold by A. Dodd, near *Temple-Bar*; and at the / Pamphlet-Shops. [Price Six-Pence.]

8vo; 1–42.
As the title shows, the *Ode* in the first [London] edition has been replaced by the *Narrative* in this second edition.

Its ascription to Swift is as doubtful as that of the *Ode*. It is a reprint of *The Correspondent*, Nos. III and IV, a periodical 'Printed by James Hoey, in Skinner-Row, 1733', of which only six numbers of four pages each, paged consecutively 1–24, appeared.

(Copy: U.L.C. Hib. 7.733.5), — Cf. Nic. Smith, 161 + n.2.

This second edition is announced as "Just Published (from the fifth Dublin Edition) Price 6 d." in an advertisement which appears at the end of a pamphlet entitled: *A Vindication Of The Protestant Dissenters*, &c. (see No. 968, *post*). The "fifth" Dublin Edition looks like a publisher's trick. The advertisement further says: "N.B. *The Narrative is given* gratis *to those who bought the first Edition*." This means that copies may be found of the *Narrative* separately, or annexed to the first [London] edition.

See also No. 124, *ante*.

Contemporary criticism

968. A Vindication of the Protestant Dissenters, from the Aspersions cast upon them, in a late Pamphlet, intituled, The Presbyterians Plea of Merit, in order to take off the Test, impartially examined. Dublin, 1733. — 12mo. — Copy: Quaritch, cat. 371, item 670.

Another ed.: – – – – – – – London: Reprinted from the Dublin Edition, for G. F. and Sold by A. Dodd, &c. — 8vo; 1–62, 1 p. advs. + bl. — Cf. Nos. 734–6, *ante*.

738. Ten *Reasons* for Repealing the *Test Act*.

Folio; 1 page.
Copy: T.C.D. (Press A 7.3.257).
Not to be confounded with T.C.D.N.g. 52 (14): "Reasons For the Repeal of the Sacramental Test. Number I. Dublin: Printed by S. Powell, in Crane-lane, MDCCXXXIII." — 8vo; 1–16; which is quite different.

For a long list of pamphlets relating to the *Test*, see Monck Mason, *History of St. Patrick's Cathedral*, 1819–20, pp. 387–8 notes; and *Prose Works*, IV, 25–8.

739. Advice / To The / Free-Men of the City of *Dublin*, in the Choice of a Member to / Represent them in Parliament,

Folio; 2 pages (double columns).
At foot of second page:

Printed in the Year 1733.

Copy: R.I.A. (24 C 32).
[Written by Swift in support of Humphry French; see No. 735, *ante*.]

745. An / Epistle / To / A Lady, / Who desired the Author to make / Verses on Her, / In The / *Heroick Stile*. / — / Also / A Poem, / Occasion'd by Reading / Dr. *Young*'s Satires, / Called, / The Universal Passion. / = / *Dublin*, Printed: / And Reprinted at *London* for J. Wilford, at the / *Three Flower-de-Luces* behind the *Chapter-House*, / *St. Paul's Church-Yard*. M.DCC.XXXIV. [Price 1 *s*.]

Folio; π^1, B–E², π^1 — 2 pp. (t. + bl.), [1]–15 (Epistle), [16]–18 (A Poem). — Page 13 misnumbered 16.
Published Nov. 15, 1733.
Addressed to Lady Acheson.
Copies: Forster D2 A 25 and Penn.
No copy of a Dublin edition is known.

Both pieces also in:
39. — / A / New Miscellany / For the Year 1734. / Part I. / Containing / I. An Epistle to a Lady, who desired the / Author to make Verses on her in the Heroick Stile. / II. On reading Dr. *Young*'s Satires called, the *Uni-* / *versal Passion*. / III. On Poetry: A Rapsody. / IV. On the Words, *Brother-Protestants*, and *Fellow-* / *Christians*. / —

8vo; 2 pp., 1–23 + bl.
Part II (8vo; 2 pp., 25–48) contains nothing by Swift.

741. On / Poetry: / A / *Rapsody*. / = / [ornament] / = / Printed at Dublin, and Re-printed at *London:* / And sold by J. Huggonson, next to *Kent*'s Coffee- / House, near *Serjeant*'s-Inn, in *Chancery-Lane*; and / at the Booksellers and Pamphlet-shops, 1733. / [Price One Shilling.]

Folio; π^1, B–G², H¹ — 2 pp. (t. + bl.), [3]–28. — On p. 28 under 'Finis.' there are two lines 'Errata'.
Published Dec. 31, 1733.
Copies: Penn, Rothschild 2147, and Harvard.
Nearly fifty lines were omitted by the printer on political grounds. They are added in the margin of a copy, in the hand of Orrery. — See *Poems*, 639, and *The Times Lit. Suppl.*, Oct. 20, 1945.
No earlier Dublin edition known.

742. *Another edition:*
On / Poetry: / A / *Rapsody*. / — / [ornament] / — / Printed at Dublin, and Re-printed at *London*, / And Sold by J. Huggonson, next to *Kent*'s Cof- / fee-House, near *Serjeants*-Inn in *Chancery-Lane*, / and at the Booksellers and Pamphlet-shops.

8vo (in fours); π^4, A–C⁴ — 2 pp. (t. + bl.), 3–22, 2 pp. blank — Page 20 misnumbered 2.

According to D. F. Foxon, this was printed in Edinburgh by R. Fleming.
Copy: Penn.

743. *Another edition:*

On / Poetry: / A / *Rapsody.* / = / [ornament] / = / *London*
Printed, and / *Dublin* Re-printed, by and for S. Hyde, / Bookseller
in *Dame-Street*, 1734.

Sm. 8vo (in fours); π^4, A–C⁴, D² — 2 pp. (t. + bl.), [3]–26, 2 pp. advs.
Copy: Penn.

Contemporary criticism

1311. A Rap At The Rapsody. &c. London, J. Roberts, MDCCXXXIV. —
Folio; π^2, B² — 2 pp. (t. + bl.), [3]–8.
Copy: B.M. 11633 i 10.

1316. An Essay On Preferment. By the Author of the Rapsody on the Army.
Dublin: Printed in the Year, 1736. — 12mo; 1–16. — Copy: U.L.C.
Another edition: An Epistle On Preferment, Inscribed To The Rev. Dr.
Swift, D. S. P. D. &c. London: Joseph Collyer, &c. D.DCC.XLIV. [*sic*] —
Folio; 2 pp., 1–17 + bl. — Copy: Penn.

1319. An Epistle To Dean Swift. A Poem. &c. By a Gentleman in the Army.
Hereford, MDCCXXXIX. — Folio; 4 pp., 1–16.

747. To the Right Honourable / John, *Earl of* Orrery.

This occurs in:
Poems On Several Occasions. London: Printed for C. Rivington – – – –
M.DCC.XXXIV.
Large 4to; I–XLVIII, 1–283 + bl., 7 pp. + bl. (*Index*). — These *Poems* are
by Mrs. Mary Barber.
Other editions: 8vo, 1735, and 8vo, 1736 (these two are the same printing,
only different title-page).
Copy: Penn.

746. Some / Reasons / Against The / Bill for settling the Tyth
of *Hemp*, / *Flax*, &c. by a *Modus*. / — / [ornament] / = / *Dublin:* /
Printed by George Faulkner in *Essex-Street*, / opposite to the
Bridge. MDCCXXIV. [*sic*]

8vo (in fours); [A]–B⁴, C² — 2 pp. (t. + bl.), [3]–20 (pp. 16–20 are: Some
further Reasons).
The year is apparently a misprint for 1734.
Published winter 1733–4.
Copies: T.C.D. N.g. 52 (11), and Nat. Libr. of Ireland.

746A. Vertiginosus, inops. surdus, male gratus amicis; (4 lines).
Deaf, giddy, helpless, left alone, (8 lines).
In: The Gentleman's Magazine, Nov. 1734, IV, 623.
Also in: Miscellaneous Poems On Several Occasions. By Mr. Dawson, &c.
– – – – To which are added, – – – – A Copy of Verses spoke Extempore by

Dean Swift, upon his Curate's complaint of hard Duty. London: – – – J. Roberts – – – A. Dodd – – – T. Payne – – – J. Fisher – – – 1735.

746B. Verses spoken extempore by Dean Swift on his Curate's complaint of hard Duty.
In: The Gentleman's Magazine, Dec. 1734, IV, 698.
Also in: Miscellaneous Poems On Several Occasions – – – – 1735.
Also in: No. 65.

746C. The Parson's Case.
In: The Gentleman's Magazine, Dec. 1734, IV, 698.
Also in: The Daily Journal, Dec. 12, 1734.

744. A / Beautiful / Young Nymph / Going to Bed. / Written for the Honour of the *Fair Sex*. / — / *Pars minima est ipsa Puella sui.* / Ovid Remed. Amoris. / — / To which are added, / *Strephon and Chloe.* / And / *Cassinus* and *Peter*. / = / *Dublin* printed: / *London* reprinted for J. Roberts in *Warwick-Lane*, / — / MDCCXXXIV. / (Price One Shilling.)

4to; 1–31 (advs. on verso).
All the three pieces belong to the year 1731.
Published Dec. 5, 1734 (adv. in *The Grub Street Journal*).
No copy of a Dublin edition is known.
Nos. 744 and 745 conveyed by Mrs. Barber to Pilkington for publication in London.
All three pieces also in: The Muse in Good Humour, 1744, pp. 70, 29, 54.

1652. *Strephon and Chloe* also in:
D—n Sw—t's / Medley. / Containing, / I. His Scheme for making Religion and the / Clergy useful; [&c.] / II. Reasons against Coition, [&c.] / III. The Natural History of the Arbor Vitae, / or the Tree of Life. [&c.] / — / Together / With several other curious and entertain- / ing Things, not mentioned in the Title. / — / *Dublin* Printed: / *London* Re-printed, and sold by the Book-sellers / in Town and Country. 12mo; 1–120.

Copy: Worc. Coll. Libr., Oxford (L.R. 5.31), Coll. Rothschild 2247.
Contains also: *Phyllis: Or The Progress of Love* (first printed in *Miscellanies, The Last Volume*, 1727, then in Faulkner's Vol. II, 1735, and in *The Muse in Good Humour*, 1744, p. 18).
The London Magazine, XVIII, 532. *The Monthly Catalogue* for Nov. 1749 has:
35. Dean Swift's Medley, pr. 1 *s.* —
This seems to fix the date of this book.

988. *The* Furniture *of a* Woman's / Mind. / *Written by Dr.* Swift.

Quarter-sheet broadside (25 × 20 cm.); no place, date, or printer but imprint may have been cut off. One page (two columns); illustration (in brown-red) of a room at the top.
Copy: B.M. 1871 eg (212). The catalogue says 1750 (?).
Begins:

'A Set of phrases learnt by rote;'

It may be regarded as a study for 'The Journal of a Modern Lady'; see No. 669–74.

Also in: The London Magazine, Feb. 1735, IV, 93, where it is entitled: The Furniture of a Woman's Mind. Written in the Year 1727.

Also in: The Muse in Good Humour, 1744, p. 86.

A verse reply to it appeared in *The London Magazine*, April 1735, IV, 211. Cf. *Poems*, 415.

752. The / Legion Club.

This is C 3–4, D⁴, E 1–2 (recto) = pp. 13–27 in:

S—t *contra omnes*. / An / *Irish* Miscellany. / Containing, / I. Some Proposals for the Regulation and / Improvement of *Quadrille*. / II. The Legion Club. / III. A Curry-Comb of Truth for a certain Dean: / Or, The *Grub-street* Tribunal. / IV. The Scall'd Crow's Nest. A very old Tale. / — / — *Nec pluribus impar*. / — / [ornament] / — / *Dublin* Printed: And *London* Re-printed; and / Sold by R. Amy, over-against *Craggs-Court*, / *Charing-Cross;* Mrs. Dodd, at the *Peacock* / without *Temple-Bar;* and by the Book and / Pamphlet-sellers of *London* and *Westminster*.

> 8vo (in fours); π¹, B–G⁴, H² — 2 pp. (t. + bl.), [1]–12 (A New Proposal), 13–27 (The Legion Club), 28–42 (A Curry-Comb of Truth), [43]–51 (The Scall'd Crow's Nest) + bl. — G 3 signed G 2.
> Copies: Forster 8562, and Penn.
> Only *The Legion Club* is genuine; the other two are doubtful (see Nos. 978, 979, *post*).
> The date of this book must be ca. 1736, as appears from the separate publications of some of the pieces in it. See also the register of books in *The Gentleman's Magazine*, June 1736, VI, 360, where it is listed as sold by Mrs. Dodd.

753. *Also in:*

Poems / On / Various Subjects: / *Viz*. / The Legion Club, by D – – n S—t. / The Gymnasiad. / The Causidicade. / An Epistle to Dr. Thompson. / [ornament] / Glasgow: / Printed by Sawney Mᶜ Pherson. / M.DCC.LVI.

> Sm. 8vo (in fours); π², [B]–M⁴, N² — 2 pp. (h.t. + bl.), 2 pp. (f.t. + bl.), [1]–13 (The Legion Club) + bl., [15]–48 (The Gymnasiad), [49]–72 (The Causidicade), [73]–92 (An Epistle).
> Copies: Bodl. G. Pamph. 1598 (3), B.M. 11631 b 55 (2), and Penn.

Imitations:

1361. The East India Culprits. A Poem. In Imitation Of Swift's "Legion Club". (By an Officer, who was present at the Battle of Plassey.). G. Kearsly, MDCCLXXIII.

> 4to (in twos); π¹, B–E² — 2 pp. (t. + bl.), 1–15 + bl.
> Copy: B.M. 164 n 29 (seems to lack the half-title).

1365. The Legion Club: A Vision. Found Among Dean Swift's Manuscripts.

Large 4to size; no signatures — [1]–7 + bl. — Text begins at once under the title. — Dated at foot of p. 7: Quilca, 1735.

Copy: B.M. 644 k 21 (14). — The catalogue dates it 1783 (?).

***

754. Reasons / Why we should not / Lower the Coins / Now current in this / Kingdom. / Occasioned by a Paper Intituled, / *Remarks on the* Coins current *in this* / Kingdom. / To which is added, / *The Rev.* Dean Swift*'s* / Opinion, / Delivered by him, in an Assembly of above / One hundred and Fifty eminent Merchants / who met at the Guild Hall, on *Saturday* / the 24th of *April*, 1736, in order to draw / up their Petition, and Present it to his Grace / the Lord-Lieutenant against lowering said / Coin. / — / *Dublin:* Printed and sold by *E. Waters* in *Dame-street*.

> Very sm. 8vo; no signatures — 2 pp. (t. + Swift's Reasons, on verso), 3–8.
> On verso of the title there is:
> The Rev. Dean *Swift*'s Reasons against low- / ering the Gold and Silver Coin.
> Copy: Nat. Libr. of Ireland.
> Cf. No. 667; also Wagner, *Irish Economics*, Nos. 158–64, 166, etc.
> For 'Ay and No. A Tale From Dublin. Written in 1737.' (not printed at the time), see *Poems*, 841; also *Corresp.*, VI, 206.

755. A / Proposal / For Giving / Badges / To The / Beggars / In All The / Parishes of *Dublin*. / — / By the Dean of St. Patrick's. / — / [portrait of the Dean, subscribed: *M. B. Drapier*] / = / *Dublin:* / Printed by George Faulkner, Bookseller, in / *Essex-Street*, opposite to the Bridge, / MDCCXXXVII.

> 8vo; [A]⁸, B⁶ — 2 pp. (t. + bl.), [3]–25, 3 pp. advs.
>
> *Another state:*
> The same printing (title, pagination, contents), but a different collation by signatures:
> 8vo; [A]⁸, B⁴, C².
> The difference seems to be in the last four pages only.
> Both are signed 'J. Swift.' and dated '*April* 22, 1737', but the first has a rule under it, the second a printer's ornament. In the first state the adv. at the end reads: *Speedily will be Published*, &c., in the second: *Next Week will be Published*, &c.
> Copies: Rothschild 2156; U.L.C. Hib. 8.737.13 is the second state.

756. *Another edition:*
A / Proposal / For Giving / Badges / To The / Beggars / In All The / Parishes of *Dublin*. / By The / Dean of St. *Patrick*'s / [ornament] / *London,* / Printed for T. Cooper at the *Globe* in *Pater Noster Row.* / MDCCXXXVII. / Price Six Pence.

> 4to; [A]–B⁴ — 2 pp. (t. + bl.), [3]–16.
> Copies: U.L.C. (Hib. 5.737.4), and Rothschild.
> Text dated '*April* 22, 1737.', and signed 'J. Swift'.

757. An / Imitation / Of The / Sixth Satire / Of The / Second Book / Of / Horace. / *Hoc erat in Votis,* &c. / — / The first Part done in the Year 1714, / By Dr. Swift. / The latter Part now first added, / *And never before Printed.* / — / London: / Printed for B. Motte and C. Bathurst / in *Fleet-Street,* and J. and P. Knapton in / *Ludgate-Street,* MDCCXXXVIII. / (Price One Shilling.]

Folio; π⁴, C–G² — 2 pp. (h.t. + bl.), 2 pp. (f.t. + *Advertisement* on verso), [1] (second h.t.), 2–23 + blank (Latin and English on opposite pages).
Partly by Swift (lines 1–132), partly by Pope (lines 133–221).
Swift's part, with the exception of lines 9–28, had been written in July 1714, and first printed in *Miscellanies.*
The Last Volume, 1727, pp. 33–41, there numbered lines 1–112.
In 1738 were added lines 9–28 (by Swift); the rest by Pope.
See *Poems,* 197–8.

758. The / Beasts Confession / To The / Priest, / On / Observing how most Men mistake / their own Talents. / — / Written in the Year 1732. / — / [ornament] / = / *Dublin:* / Printed by George Faulkner. / — / MDCCXXXVIII.

8vo (in fours); [A]–C⁴ — 2 pp. (t. + bl.), I–IV (Preface), 1 p. (Advertisement), 1 p. (blank), 9–22, 2 pp. blank.

Second edition:
Title and collation the same, except:

– – – Year 1732. / — / The Second Edition. / — / [ornament] / = / – – – –

Copy: U.L.C. (lacking the 2 pp. blank at the end).

759. *Another edition:*
The / Beasts Confession / To The / Priest, / On / Observing how most Men mistake / their own Talents. / — / By *J. S.* D. S. P. / — / [ornament: wheel between two cornucopias] / — / *Dublin,* Printed: / *London,* Re-Printed: And Sold by *T. Cooper,* / at the *Globe,* in *Pater-Noster-Row,* 1738.

8vo (in fours); π⁴, B–C⁴ — 2 pp. (h.t. + bl.), 2 pp. (f.t. + bl.), 2 pp. (Advertisement + bl.), [7]–22, 2 pp. blank.
Copy: B.M. 1465 f 42.

Second edition:
Same printing as the preceding edition, except for the title:

– – – – – D.S.P. / — / The Second Edition. / — / [ornament: wheel between two cornucopias] / — / – – – – –

Copies: Nat. Libr. of Scotl. (957), Forster, Eton, and Penn.

760. *Another second edition:*
Same title, except:

– – – / [ornament: two angels] / — / *Dublin*, Printed: / *London*, Re-Printed: And Sold by *T. Coo- / per*, at the Globe, in *Pater-noster-row*, 1738.

8vo; 1–16. — Smaller type and thinner paper.
Copy: Dobell's cat. 105, item 148.

Also in:
769. — / A / Letter / To The / Printer.

This Letter, signed J. Swift, and dated: Deanry-House, *Dec.* 13, 1737, occurs in:
Some Thoughts On The Tillage of Ireland: — To which is Prefixed, A Letter to the Printer, from the Reverend Doctor Swift, Dean of St. Patrick's recommending the following Treatise. Dublin: Printed by and for George Faulkner. M,DCC,XXXVIII.

8vo (in fours); π^4, B–G^4, H^2 — 2 pp. (h.t. + bl.), 2 pp. (f.t. + bl.), 2 pp. (Swift's Letter), 1–54. — It seems that copies should have an errata slip (the U.L.C. copy has not).
[Written by Alexander McAwley.]
Copy: Penn.

770. *Another edition:*
– – – – – London: Printed for T. Cooper – – – – 1737. Price Six Pence.

8vo; 1–32.

A Complete Collection Of Genteel And Ingenious Conversation

763. A / Treatise / On / Polite Conversation. / = / [ornament] / = / *Dublin:* / Printed by and for George Faulkner. / — / M,DCC,XXX,VIII.

8vo; [A]–H^8, I^2 — 2 pp. (t. + slip of *Errata* pasted on verso), I–XXXVI (Introduction), 2 pp. (another title + 'Dramatis Personae', on verso), [1]–94.
Published spring 1738, probably simultaneously with the London edition.
Copy: B.M. 1077 g 50.
The slip of *Errata* reads:

Errata, in the Introduction. / Page XVII. Line 12. *for* Direction, *read* Discretion, / Page XX. Line 11. *for* I have therefore, by the / chief Patterns, *read* Wherein I follow the chief / Patterns.

The type-setting of this volume (with alterations of signatures and pagination) was also used to form part of Vol. VI, 1738 (see No. 42). The above printing was first, because it has the *Errata pasted* on a slip on the verso of the title, whereas Vol. VI has them *printed* on that verso. Another proof is that the printing of Vol. VI was at first concluded with sheet P (two leaves only

= pp. 209–[212]), and that sheet Q (eight leaves = p. [213], etc.) begins the *Treatise*.

761. A Complete / Collection / Of Genteel and Ingenious / Conversation, / According to the Most / Polite Mode and Method / Now Used / At Court, and in the Best / Companies of England. / — / In Three Dialogues. / — / By *Simon Wagstaff*, Esq; / — / *London:* / Printed for B. Motte, and C. Bathurst, at / the *Middle Temple-Gate* in *Fleet-street*. / — / M.DCC.XXXVIII.

8vo; π^2, a–e^8, f^4, B–O^8, P^4 — 2 pp. (bl. + advs.), 2 pp. (t. + bl.), [I]–LXXXVI (Introduction), 2 pp. (title + 'Dramatis Personae' on verso), [1]–215 (adv. on verso).
There are also L. P. copies, on slightly thicker paper.
Published spring 1738.
Copies: B.M. C 58 g 18, New York Public. Libr., and Penn.
They have a picture of Neptune in the centre of the headpiece of page [I].

Another edition:
The same title and collation, but a different printing from the preceding one. It has a bowl of fruit in the centre of the headpiece of page [I]. I have placed it after the other, because it shows widening-out of two full lines. The first edition has on page [I]:
first line: As my Life hath been chiefly
last line: I have so much labour'd, as that
catchword: of
where the second edition has:
first line: As my Life hath been
last line: wherein I have so much labour'd,
catchword: as
Copy: New York Public. Libr.

762. For a 12mo edition see No. 31.

764. *An adaptation:*
Tittle Tattle; / Or, / Taste A-la-Mode. / A New Farce. / Perform'd with Universal Applause by a / Select Company / Of / Belles and Beaux, / At The / Lady *Brilliant's* Withdrawing-Room, / *Pour tuer le Tems.* / — / By *Timothy Fribble*, Esq; / — / *Whoe'er He be, who to a* Taste *aspires,* / *Let him read* This, *and be what he desires:* / In Men *and* Manners vers'd, *from* Life I *write*; / *Not what was* Once, *but what is* Now *polite.* / Man *of* Taste. / — / *London:* / Printed for R. Griffiths, at the *Dunciad*, in / St. *Paul's* Church-Yard. / MDCCXLIX. / (Price One Shilling.)

8vo (in fours); π^4, B–F^4, G^2 — 2 pp. (t. + bl.), [III]–VII (Dedication), 1 p. (Dramatis Personae), 9–52.
Copy: B.M. 1346 e 41.
This is a dramatized version of *Polite Conversation*.

765. *Another edition:*

A Complete / Collection / Of genteel and ingenious / Conversation, / According / To the most polite Mode and Method now / used at Court, and in the best Com- / panies of England. / — / In several Dialogues. / — / A New Edition. / — / By Dr. *Jonathan Swift.* / = / London: / Sold by R. Stanton, P. Atchison, / W. Dickson, and H. Salmon. / MDCCLXXIX.

12mo; A–H¹², I⁶, K⁴ — 2 pp. (t. + bl.), [3]–60 (Introduction), 1 p. (The Men. The Ladies.), 1 p. (The Argument), [63]–212. — Frontisp. (Swift).
Copy: Penn.

766. *Another edition:*

Polite / Conversation, / Consisting Of / Smart, Witty, Droll, / And Whimsical / Sayings, / Collected For His / Amusement, / And Made Into A / Regular Dialogue. / — / By Dr. Jonathan Swift, / Dean of St. Patrick's, Dublin. / — / London: / Printed For Joseph Wenman, / No. 144, Fleet-Street. / M,DCC,LXXXIII.

Sm. 12mo (in twelves and sixes, alternately); A¹² — K⁶, L⁴ — 2 pp. (t. + bl.), 3–33 (Introduction), 1 p. blank, 35–120 (Polite Conversation), [121]–131 (Rules That Concern All Servants In General), [132]–186 (Directions To Servants). — Frontisp.
Pp. 35–6 repeated in numbering.
Copy: Penn.

1617. In an 'Advertisement', inserted into *Faulkner's Dublin Journal*, July 4–8, 1738, Swift expressed his regret that he had never been able to purchase a real estate in lands for the endowment of a hospital for the support of lunatics, idiots, and those they call incurables; and that therefore he was compelled and was now able to lend two thousand pounds at five per cent upon good security, leaving it to his executors to purchase the lands (for the meaning of 'purchase' in this connection, see the N.E.D. purchase, sb., II 10).
Cf. *Corresp.*, VI, 85–7.

***

Verses on the Death of Doctor Swift

For an account of the sequence of the following editions and issues, the details attendant upon publication of the poem, and the relationship of the text to that of the authorized version printed by Faulkner, see under No. 1604, and A. H. Scouten, "The Earliest London Printings of *Verses on the Death of Doctor Swift*," *Studies in Bibliography*, XIII (1961), 243–8; Herbert Davis, "Verses on the Death of Doctor Swift," *Book Collector's Quarterly*, I (1931), 57–73; Sir Harold Williams, *Poems*, II, 551–3; H. Teerink, "Swift's *Verses on the Death of Doctor Swift*," *Studies in Bibliography*, IV (1951), 183–8, VII (1955), 238–9; Maurice Johnson, "Verses on the Death of Doctor Swift," *Notes and Queries*, CXCIX (November, 1954), 473–4; and *Correspondence*, IV, 273, V, 30, VI, 106–16.

771. Verses / On The / Death / Of / Doctor Swift. / Written by Himself: Nov. 1731. / [ornament: cock in medallion] / *London:* /

Printed for C. Bathurst, at the *Middle Temple-Gate* | in *Fleetstreet*.
MDCCXXXIX.

> Folio; π^1, B–E², F 1 — 2 pp. (t. + bl.), [1]–18.
> Published Jan. 19, 1739.
> Copies: Yale (large, untrimmed copy, 14¾ by 9¼), Harvard, Princeton,
> Columbia, Texas, Folger, Logan Square (Philadelphia), Maurice Johnson,
> Sir Harold Williams, Lord Rothschild, and Penn.

1600. *Second edition:*

Verses | On The | Death | Of | Doctor Swift. | Written by Him-
self: Nov. 1731. | The Second Edition. | [ornament: Fame blowing
a trumpet] | *London:* | Printed for C. Bathurst, at the *Middle-
Temple Gate* | in *Fleetstreet*. MDCCXXXIX.

> Folio; π^2, B–E² — 2 pp. (t. + bl.), [1]–18.
> Copies: Harvard, Texas and Penn.

1601. *Another second edition:*

Verses | On The | Death | Of | Doctor Swift. | Written by Him-
self: Nov. 1731. | The Second Edition. | [ornament: bust on
pedestal] | *London:* | Printed for C. Bathurst, at the *Middle-Temple
Gate* | in *Fleetstreet*. MDCCXXXIX.

> Folio; π^2, B–E² — 2 pp. (t. + bl.), [3]–20.
> Copies: Texas and Penn.

1602. *Third edition:*

Verses | On The | Death | Of | Doctor *Swift*. | Written by Him-
self: Nov. 1731. | The Third Edition. | [ornament: urn on base]
| Printed for C. Bathurst, at the *Middle Temple-Gate* | in *Fleetstreet*.
MDCCXXXIX.

> Folio; π^2, B–E², — 2 pp. (t. + bl.), [3]–20.
> From his examination of copies at Harvard, the British Museum, and in
> the possession of Sir Harold Williams, D. F. Foxon states that this printing
> seems to be partly the same setting of type as 1601 and would therefore
> precede 1603.

1603. *Another third edition:*

Verses | On The | Death | Of | Doctor *Swift*. | Written by Him-
self; *November* 1731. | — | The Third Edition. | — | [ornament]
| — | *London*, | Printed for C. Bathurst, at the *Middle-Temple-
Gate* in *Fleet-street*. | MDCCXXXIX.

> Folio; π^2, B–E² — 2 pp. (t. + bl.), [3]–20.
> Copies: Harvard and Penn.

772. *Another edition:*

Verses | On The | Death | Of | Doctor *Swift*. | Written by Him-
self: Nov. 1731. | [ornament] | *London:* | Printed for C. Bathurst,
at the *Middle Temple-Gate* | in *Fleetstreet*. MDCCXXXIX.

8vo (in fours); [A]–C⁴ — 2 pp. (t. + bl.), 3–22, 2 pp. blank.
According to D. F. Foxon, this edition was actually printed by Thomas Ruddiman, Edinburgh, 1739.
Copies: Harvard and Penn.

773. *Another edition:*
Same title and collation as preceding copy, except the year: MDCCXLI.
Copy: Forster 8562 (34 A 31).
According to D. F. Foxon, who examined copies at Forster and Harvard, this was printed by T. Ruddiman, Edinburgh, 1741.
Copy: Forster 8562 (34 A 31).

774. *Faulkner editions:*
Verses / On The / Death / Of / Dr. *S* – – – –, D.S.P.D. / Occasioned / By reading a Maxim in *Rochefoulcault*. / — / *Dans l'adversité de nos meilleurs amis nous trouvons* / *quelque chose, qui ne nous deplaist pas.* / In the Adversity of our best Friends, we find / something that doth not displease us. / — / Written by Himself, *November* 1731. / = / *London* Printed: / *Dublin:* Re-printed by George Faulkner, / — / M,DCC,XXXIX.

8vo (in fours); π⁴, B–F⁴ — 2 pp. (t. + bl.), 2 pp. (The Publisher's Advertisement + bl.), 5–44, 3 pp. (Advertisement. *For the Honour of the Kingdom of Ireland.*), 1 p. book advs.
Copy: Penn.
Second edition:
Title and collation the same as those of the first edition, except:

– – – – / Dr. *Swift*, D.S.P.D. / – – – – – – – 1731. / — / The Second Edition. / = / *London* – – – – –

Copy: Forster 7082, Rothschild 2170.

Third edition:
Title and collation the same as those of the second edition, except:

– – – / — / The Third Edition. / = / – – – – –

Copy: Penn.

Fourth edition:
Title and collation the same as those of the second edition, except:

– – – – / — / The Fourth Edition. / = / – – – – –

Copy: Penn.

Fifth edition:
Title and collation the same as those of the second edition, except:

– – – – / — / The Fifth Edition. / = / – – – –

Copy: Harold Williams.
These five editions are the same printing with alterations in the type setting still standing. The alterations at first concern especially some of the notes, afterwards almost exclusively the punctuation.

Variants occur, owing to the wrong mating of sheets of one edition with those of another.

The sixth edition (see below) is a different printing.

Sixth edition:

Title the same as that of the second edition, except:

– – – we find some- / thing that – – – – – / — / The Sixth Edition. / = / *London* Printed: / *Dublin:* Re-printed by George Faulkner. / — / M,DCC,XLI.

8vo (in fours); π^4, B–F^4 — 2 pp. (t. + bl.), 2 pp. (The Publisher's Advertisement + bl.), 5–41, 4 pp. (Advertisement. *For the Honour of the Kingdom of Ireland.*), 2 pp. book advs. + bl. — P. 40 misnumbered 38.

The following five editions are clandestine printings of 'Verses'. See H. Teerink, *Studies in Bibliography*, IV (1951), 183–8, and VII (1955), 238–9, for evidence — chiefly the presence of the date 1736 on the initial title page of No. 1605 — that these may have preceded the Bathurst editions of 1739.

However, A. H. Scouten, in *Studies in Bibliography*, XIII (1961), 243–8 by a collation of the text in the Bathurst printings and No. 1605, demonstrates the priority of the Bathurst editions and shows that No. 1605 was probably set from No. 1602.

1604. *[Caption-title]:*

[3] / [decorated bar: stencils] / Verses / On The / Death of Dr. Swift. / Occasioned by reading the following Maxim / in *Roachfoucault* / *Dans l'adversite de nos meilleurs amis nous trouvons toujours / quelque chose, qui ne nous deplaist pas.*

12mo (in sixes); A 2–6 — pp. 3–12.
Unfortunately the title-leaf (and possibly a frontispiece) is lacking.
Copy: Nat. Libr. of Ireland.

1605. *An* / Essay / *On* / Man. / With some / Humorous Verses / on the / *Death of Dean Swift,* / Written by Himself. / [ornament] / Dublin: / Printed, & Sold by the Booksellers of / London & Westminster. / — / MDCCXXXVI.

12mo (in sixes); π^2, B–D^6, π^1, E^6 — 2 pp. (frontisp.), 2 pp. (above t. + bl.), [III]–VI (Contents), [1]–36; 2 pp. (frontisp., bust of Dean Swift), 2 pp. (title: Verses + bl.), 3–12.
Copy: U.L.C. Hib. 7.750.31.
The title 'Verses' reads:

Verses / On the Death of / Dr. *Swift.* / Occasioned by reading the following Maxim in / *Rochfoucault.* / *Dans l'adversite de nos mellieurs amis nous trouvons tou- / jours quelque choses, qui ne nous deplaist pas.* / Written by Himself; *Nov.* 1731. / [ornament] / *Dublin,* Printed: / *London:* Re-printed, and sold by the / Booksellers of London and Westmin- / ster.

775. An / Essay / On / Man. / In / Four Epistles to a Friend. / — / Corrected by the Author. / — / The Seventh Edition. / — / [ornament] / — / *London:* / Printed for J. Witford, near the *Chapter-* / *House*, St. *Paul*'s. M.DCC.XXXVI.

12mo (in sixes); [A]–C⁶, D⁵ (D 6, the last leaf of the 'Verses', lacking) — 2 pp. (t. + bl.), [III]–VI (Contents), [7]–38 (*Finis.* at foot); [39]–46 (Verses). — The 'Verses' are D 2–5 (D 2 partly visible on p. [39]).
Copy: Bibliotheque Mazarine, Paris (42481).
The caption-title on p. [39] of the 'Verses' reads:

[decorated headpiece] / Verses / On The / Death of Dr. Swift. / Occasioned by reading the following Maxim / in *Rochfoucalt.* / *Dans l'adversite de nos meilleurs amis nous trouvons toujours* / *quelque* *chose, qui ne nous deplaist pas.* /

This Mazarine volume contains three separately-paged pieces: (1) 'The Hind and Panther' (lacking two leaves in front, and a blank (?) leaf at the end); (2) The 'Essay' and the 'Verses' (as above); (3) 'The Dunciad', London–Dublin, G. Faulkner, &c., 1728 (Griffith No. 206); preceded by a MS. title: "The Hind and Panther an heroic poem wrote by Mʳ Dryden with several other curious poems by the celebrated Mʳ Pope and Swift London printed in the year 1756."
It is impossible to say (1) whether these three pieces (and perhaps more?) were really *published* with a *printed* title dated 1756, or whether the MS. title only represents a *plan* for a made-up miscellany in that year; (2) whether the leaf or leaves (lacking at the end of the *Verses On The Death*) bear the rest of that poem only, or more.

1607. An / Essay / On / Man. / In / Four Epistles to a Friend. / — / Corrected by the Author. / — / A New Edition. / — / [ornament] / — / *London:* / Printed for, and sold by the Booksellers, / in *Town* and *Country.*

Sm. 8vo; [A]⁴, B–D⁸ — 2 pp. (frontisp.), 2 pp. (t. + bl.), [V]–VIII (Contents), [1]–35 + bl. (Essay), [37]–47 + bl. (Verses).
Copy: B.M. 11631 bb 25. (Maynard Mack writes that this is Griffith 412.)
The caption-title on p. [37] reads:

[decorated bar, stencils] / Verses / On The / Death of Dr. Swift. / Occasioned by reading the following Maxim / ['in' omitted] *Rochfoucalt.* / *Dans l'adversite de nos meilleurs amis nous trouvons toujours* / *quelque chose, qui ne nous deplaist pas.*

1608. Verses / On the Death of / Dr. *Swift.* / Occasioned by reading the following Maxim in / *Rochfoucault.* / *Dans l'adversite de* *nos mellienrs amis nous trouvous tou-* / *jours quelque choses, qui ne nous* *deplaist pas.* / Written by Himself; *Nov.* 1731. / [ornament] / *Dublin,* Printed: / *London:* Re-printed, and sold by the / Booksellers of London and Westminster.

Sm. 8vo; π^1, A^4, B^2 — 2 pp. (frontisp., bust of Swift), 2 pp. (title + bl.), 3–12.
Copy: U.L.C. S721.d.73.4.

₊

778. Some / Free Thoughts / Upon The / Present State / Of / Affairs. / — / Written in the Year 1714. / — / [ornament] / = / *Dublin:* / Printed by and for George Faulkner. / M,DCC,XLI.

8vo; 4 pp., 1–32.
This is a separate issue of the last section included in *Letters to and from Dr. J. Swift*, 8vo, 1741 (see No. 44, *ante*). Written at Litcombe 1714, but withheld.

779. *Duodecimo edition:*
The same title as above.
12mo; 4 pp., 1–22.
This is a separate issue of the last section included in *Letters to and from Dr. J. Swift*, 12mo, 1741 (see No. 51, *ante*).

780. *Another edition:*
Some / Free Thoughts / Upon The / Present State / Of / Affairs. / — / By the *Author of* Gulliver's *Travels.* / — / [ornament] / = / *Dublin* Printed: / London, Re-printed for T. Cooper, at the / Globe in *Pater-Noster-Row.* 1741. / [Price Six-Pence.]

8vo (in fours); π^2, B–D^4, E^2 — 2 pp. (t. + bl.), 2 pp. (Advertisement to the Reader + bl.), 1–27 (adv. on verso).
Copies: B.M. 1093 d 77, and Penn.

781. *Another edition:*
Some / Free Thoughts / Upon The / Present State / Of / Affairs. / — / Written in the Year 1714. / — / [ornament] / = / *Dublin,* Printed: / *London,* Reprinted for J. Brindley in / *New-Bond-Street;* and sold by T. Cooper at the / *Globe* in *Pater-Noster-Row.* M,DCC,XLI. / [Price Sixpence.]

8vo (in fours); π^2, B–E^4 — 2 pp. (t. + bl.), 2 pp. (Advertisement + bl.), 1–32.
Copy: U.L.C.

77. 'The Muse in Good Humour: Or, a Collection of Comic Tales, &c. From Chaucer, Prior, Swift, La Fontaine, Dr. King, and other eminent Poets – – – London: Printed for J. Noble, – – – 1744' contains:

(1) (on p. 18) Phillis, Or, the Progress of Love. Written A.D. 1719.
(First printed in: *Miscellanies, The Last Volume,* 1727, p. 236; and in Faulkner's Vol. II, 1735, p. 120.)
(2) (on p. 73) A Pastoral Dialogue.
(First printed in: *Miscellanies, The Third Volume,* 1732, p. 35; and in Faulkner's Vol. II, 1735, p. 220.)
(3) (on p. 86) The Furniture of a Woman's Mind. Written in the Year 1727.

(First printed in: Faulkner's Vol. II, 1735, p. 413; and in *Miscellanies, Volume the Fifth*, 1735, p. 112.)

Reprinted in: *The London Magazine*, Feb. 1735, IV, 93.

Reprinted: The Furniture of a Woman's Mind. Written by Dr. Swift. 4to; one page. (No place, printer, or date. — The B.M. catalogue says: 1750?).

(4) Several 'Riddles' (see *Poems*, 914), of which it is impossible to say, which are genuine.

In 'The Muse in Good Humour – – – –. 6th ed. 1751':

(5) (on p. 171) A quiet Life, and a good Name To &c. Writ A.D. 1719.

(First printed in: Faulkner's Vol. II, 1735, p. 349; and in *Miscellanies, Volume the Fifth*, 1735, p. 59.)

(6) (on p. 321) An Answer To a late scandalous Poem, wherein the Author most audaciously presumes to compare a Cloud to a Woman By Dennis Nephelee, chief Cap. of Howth.

(This is Swift's answer to Sheridan's: 'A New Simile For The Ladies, With Useful Annotations.') — 'A New Simile' appeared as a sm. 8vo pamphlet of 8 pages: Dublin: Printed in the Year 1732.

The 'Answer' did not appear separately at the time, but together they were published as a sm. 8vo pamphlet of 16 pages: Dublin, 1733.

Case, 450 says that The Muse in Good Humour, Part I, 4th ed., 1745, and Part II, 2nd ed., 1745, form a set. Further editions are: also London 1746, sm. 8vo, 2 vols. in one continuous pagination. 6th ed., 1751 (Vol. II, 1757); 7th ed., 1766 (Vol. I only ?); 8th ed., 1785. The B.M. has an edition: Cooper, 1745 (incomplete).

Cf. *Poems*, 221, 879, 415, 914, 219, 612 (etc.).

Directions To Servants

787. Directions / To / Servants. / — / By the Revd. Dr. Swift, D.S.P.D. / — / [monogram] / — / *Dublin:* / Printed by George Faulkner, in *Essex-Street.* / M,D,CC,XLV.

8vo; π^2, B–E^8, F–I^4, K^2 — 2 pp. (t. + bl.), [I]–II (The Publisher's Preface), 1–21 + bl., 1–74, 77–9 + bl. (no break in the text).

Copies: K. I. Forster 8562–34 A 28, and own.

This is a separate issue of the first part of Faulkner's Vol. VIII, 1746 (first issue). See No. 44. — No volume-number at foot of first page of each new sheet, except on p. 77.

The Publisher's Preface, signed G. F. and dated Dublin, Nov. 8, 1745, states that the manuscript may be seen in the Printer's Custody, and that he gives it as it is found in the original. For this reason Mr. P. J. Dobell, in one of his catalogues, says that this edition "can reasonably be claimed as the actual princips".

788. [*Second*] *Dublin edition:*

Directions / To / Servants. / — / By the Revd. Dr. Swift, D.S.P.D. / — / [monogram] / — / *Dublin:* / Printed by and for George Faulkner, / M,DCC,XLVI.

8vo; [A]–F^8, G^4 — 2 pp. (t. + bl.), [I]–II (The Publisher's Preface), 1–12, 17–25 + bl., 1–6, 33–48, 23–77 + bl. (no break in the text.)

Copies: Forster 8562–34 A 22, and own.

This is a separate issue of the first part of Faulkner's Vol. VIII, 1746 (second issue).

See No. 44. — Volume-number (Vol. VIII.) at foot of first page of each new sheet.

In this second edition two paragraphs belonging to 'Directions to the Cook', beginning 'If your Butter' and 'If your Dinner' have been removed to the end of that section (see pp. 57–8 first issue, and cf. pp. 25–6 second issue).

785. Directions / To / Servants / In General; / And in particular to / [*First column:*] The Butler, / Cook, / Footman, / Coachman, / Groom, / House-Steward, / and / Land-Steward, / [*Second column:*] Porter, / Dairy-Maid, / Chamber-Maid, / Nurse, / Laundress, / House-Keeper, / Tutoress, or / Governess. / — / By the Reverend Dr. Swift, D.S.P.D. / — / *I have a Thing in the Press, begun above twenty-eight Years / ago, and almost finish'd: It will make a Four Shilling / Volume; and is such a* Perfection Of Folly, / *that you shall never hear of it, till it is printed, and / then you shall be left to guess. Nay, I have* Another / Of The Same Age, *which will require a long Time / to perfect, and is worse than the former, in which I will / serve you the same Way.* Letters to and from Dr. / Swift, *&c.* Lett. LXI. alluding to Polite Conver- / sation and Directions To Servants. / — / *London:* / Printed for R. Dodsley, in *Pall-Mall*, and / M. Cooper, in *Pater-Noster-Row*, / MDCCXLV. / [Price One Shilling and Six-Pence.]

8vo; π^1, A–E^8, F^7 (F 8 probably used as title-page) — 2 pp. (t. + bl.), 1–93, [94] (The Contents).

786. *Second edition:*
Same title and collation as those of the first edition, except:

– – – – – / And in particular to the / Butler, / – – – – Servants. / — / The Second Edition. / — / *London:* / – – – – – – – – / MDCCXLVI. / – – – – – – –

Comparison of the two copies, first and second editions, in Bodl. (G. Pamph. 884. 1, and Douce D.D. 228.3) would seem to show that they are from the same type, with the exception of the title-pages, while the word 'Contents' on the last page of the first ed. is in larger type than in the second ed.

1653. Directions / to / Servants / in General; / And in particular to the / [*First Column:*] Butler, / Cook, / Footman, / Coachman, / Groom, / House-Steward, / and / Land-Steward, / [*Second Column:*] / Porter, / Dairy-Maid, / Chamber-Maid, / Nurse, / Laundress, / House-keeper, / Tutoress, or / Governess. / [rule] By the Rev. Dr. Swift, D.S.P.D. / [rule] / London, / Printed for C. Hitch, in *Pater-Noster Row;* / C. Davis, against *Gray's Inn Gate, Holborn;* / and R. Dodsly, in *Pall-Mall.* / MDCCXLIX. / [Price One Shilling.]

8vo; B–G⁸, H², B 1ʳ (t.p.), B 1ᵛ ("I have a thing in the Press"), B 2ʳ– H 2ʳ ("Rules"), H 2ᵛ ('Contents').
Copy: Penn.

789. *Another edition:*
Directions To Servants / In General, / And in particular to the / [*First column:*] Butler / Cook / Footman / Groom / Chamber-maid / [*Second column:*] House-keeper / Nurse / Laundress / Children's-maid / Dairy-maid, &c. &c. / By Dr. Jonathan Swift. / Perth: / Printed for and sold by R Morison Bookseller / M,DCC,LXXVIII.

12mo (in sixes); [A]–E⁶, F³ — 2 pp. (t. + bl.), [3]–66.
Copy: B.M. T 461 (6).

790. *Another edition:*
Included in *Polite Conversation*, 1783 (see No. 766, *ante*).

794. *German translation:*
Des / Herrn Dr. Jonathan Swifts / wo nicht unverbesserlicher / doch wohlgemeynter / Unterricht / für alle Arten / unerfahrner Bedienten, / aus / vieljåhriger sorgfåltiger / Aufmerksamkeit u. Erfahrung / zusammengetragen. / — / Aus dem Englischen über-setzt. / — / Frankfurt und Leipzig. / 1748.

Sm. 8vo; [*]⁸, A–G⁸ — 2 pp. (t. + bl.), 14 pp. (Vorbericht), [1]–112.
Copy: Penn.

794A. Ludwig Telpels / ganz / funkel nagel neue / Bauren Moral / mit einem / laecherlichen Woerterbuch / vermehret / und / in das Teutsche uebersetzt / von / Palato. / [woodcut] / — / Kamtschacka 1752.

8vo; A–R⁸ — [1–4], 5–272.
Pp. 59–98 contain an abbreviated German version (the drop-head title on p. 59 reads: Antang. / — / Wohlgemeynter / Unterricht / fuer alle Arten / unerfahrner Bedienten. / — /, consisting only of the 'General Rules'; the 'Kellner', chaps. 1–13; the 'Laguay', chaps. 1–6, 8–20, 22–24, 28–40; the 'Kammermaedgen', chaps. 1, 4, 6–17.
Copy: B.M. 8410 bb 41.
'Kamtschacka' seems to stand for 'Stettin and Ulm'; see E. Weller's, 'Die falshen und fingirten Druckorte'.
Information kindly supplied by Mr. D. F. Foxon, of the B.M.

795. *Another edition:*
Title and collation the same as preceding copy, yet not the same printing (apparent from differences in capitals, head-pieces, misprints, i.a. p. 112, l. 11 'Geruch' in one, and 'Gerruch' in the other edition).
Copy: Penn.

German imitation:
1342. Die Kunst Sinnreich zu quålen in practischen Regeln, &c. Aus dem Englischen der Frau Lenox. Hamburg und Leipzig, bey Georg Christ. Grund und Adam Heinr. Holle. 1754. — 12mo; 1–180. — This is an imitation of

Swift's 'Directions To Servants', teaching ladies and gentlemen how to torment their servants, &c.

797. *German translation:*
Unterricht für alle noch unerfahrene Bediente, aus dem Englischen. Aurich, Luschky, 1764.

[From: Vera Philippović, *Swift In Deutschland*, 1903, p. 19. I have not found a copy.]

798. *German translation:*
Aufklärung der Bedientenwelt. Auch den Herrschaften nützlich zu lesen. Aus dem Englischen des Doctor Swift. Zeitz und Naumburg bey Heinze. 1794.

[From: Vera Philippović, *Swift In Deutschland*, 1903, pp. 21–2. The year is there given as 1764, but the text shows that this is a misprint for 1794. I have not found a copy.]

799. *German translation:*
Swift's / Klugheits-Regeln / für / Befehlende und Dienende. / — / Enthaltend / 1) Unterricht für's Gesinde. / 2) Von der guten Lebensart oder den / feinen Sitten. / Aus dem Englischen. / — / Zeitz, / bey Wilhelm Webel. 1800.

12mo; 2 pp., 1–117 (*Inhalt* on verso).
Copy: Bayerische Staatsbibl., München.

1618. The / Story / Of The / *Injured Lady*. / Written by Herself. / In a Letter to Her Friend, / With his Answer. / Now occasionally re-published, and addressed to all *true Lovers* / of Honour, Truth, Justice and Liberty. / With / A Short Preface. / — / *By* A. Freeman, *Barber and Citizen of* Dublin. / — / [ornament] / = / *Dublin:* / Printed for James Byrn, in *Thomas-Street*, 1749. / (Price Two-pence.)

8vo (in fours); [A]–B⁴ — 2 pp. (t. + bl.), 3–6 (Preface, signed A: Freeman, and dated: Dublin, *Sept. 20th*, 1749.), 7–12 (The Story), [13]–15 (The Answer), 1 p. blank.
Copies: B.M. 8145 aaa 43, and Nat. Libr. of Ireland.
The 'Story' and 'Answer' were probably written early in 1707, but for practical reasons not published at that time. A. Freeman, the writer of the Preface in the 1749 reprint, was possibly Charles Lucas, who was responsible for the publication of the *History of the Four Last Years of the Queen* 1758 (Cf. two articles by Godfrey Davies in the *Huntington Library Quarterly*, Vol. VI, No. 4, Aug. 1943, and Vol. VIII, No. 4, Aug. 1945).
This had already been printed with other pieces in 1746 (No. 79).

806. A True / Copy / Of The Late / Rev. Dr. Jonathan Swift's / Will. / Taken from, and compar'd with, the / Original.

8vo; no signatures — [1]–8. — Text begins at once under above title. No place, year, or printer's name.
Copy: Penn.

805. *Another edition:*

A True / Copy / Of The Late / Rev. Dr. Jonathan Swift's / Will. / Taken from, and compar'd with, / the Original. / — / [ornament] / = / *Dublin.* / Printed by Edward Bate in *Georges-Lane.* / MDCCXLVII.

8vo; no signatures — 2 pp. (t. + bl.), [3]–14 (possibly last blank leaf lacking).
Copy: U.L.C. Hib. 7.747.16.

804. The / Last Will / And / Testament / Of / Jonathan Swift, *D.D.* / Attested by Jo. Wynne, Jo. Rochfort, / and William Dunkin. / Taken out of the Perogative [*sic*] Court of / *Dublin.* / Dublin Printed: / London Reprinted; and sold by M. Cooper / in *Paternoster-row.* / MDCCXLVI.

8vo; 2 pp., 1–25, two unnumbered pages, 26, 27 + bl. — The two unnumbered pages (bl. + h.t.) between 25 and 26 do not belong to one leaf. The first is the verso of D 1, the other the recto of D 2. This is of course a typographical error.
Copy: own.

Obituary notices:
1324. George Faulkner. The Dublin Journal. From Saturday October the 19th, to Tuesday October the 22nd, 1745. — Contains the announcement of Swift's death. The following number contains the resolution of some students of Trinity College, Dublin, to buy a marble bust of Swift. And in the number of March 21–5, 1749, we read: "There is arrived from London a Marble Busto of the late Rev. Dr. Swift, D. D, D. S. P. D. the Workmanship of Mr. Ruvilliac." It was given by "the Class of Senior Sophisters", and verses for its inscription are proposed.

1325. The Dublin Courant. From Saturday, October 19, to Wednesday, October 23, 1745. Dublin: Oli. Nelson. — Contains an obituary notice of Swift, while by way of elegy the "Verses on the Death of the Reverend Doctor Swift, &c. Written by Himself, November 1731." are given.

Parodies:
1327. An Authentic Copy Of the Last Will and Testament Of the Reverend Dr. Swift, &c. Dublin, Printed; London, Reprinted; J. Oldcastle. 8vo (in fours); [B]–D⁴, E 1 — 2 pp. (t. + bl.), [3]–26. This is a parody.
Copy: Forster 8562 (34 A 30).

1330. Sammlung satyrischer Schriften. &c. Leipzig, Im Verlage Johann Gottfried Dycks. 1751. [There are 4 vols., 1751–51–52–55. The author is G. W. Rabener].
Vol. II (8vo; 1–288) contains (pp. 231–70, and 271–6): "Geheime Nachricht von D. Jonathan Swifts letztem Willen", and "Nachricht von einem Schlüssel zu Swifts Codicille". Both are parodies.

913. The Storm. Minerva's Petition.

This is pp. 1–4 in:
Poems On Several Occasions, From Genuine Manuscripts Of Dean
Swift, – – – – London: J. Bromage – – – 1749.
It is here first printed, although Elr. Ball, *Swift's Verse*, 167, 176, maintains
that its first appearance took place as a broadside in the winter of 1722, of
which, however, no copy has been found. It is a bitter attack on Josiah Hort.
For further relations between Swift and Hort, their enmity and reconcilia-
tion, see No. 978 and cf. *Poems*, 301 etc., 822 etc.
8vo (in fours); π^1, B–H^4, I^3 — 2 pp. (t. + bl.), 1–61 + bl.
Pp. 59 and 61 misnumbered 69 and 51.
Copy: B.M. 1346 g 2 (2).

815. Reflexions / On / Courtship / And / Marriage: / In two
Letters to a Friend. / Wherein a practicable Plan is laid down for /
Obtaining and Securing / Conjugal Felicity. / To which is annexed,
/ A Letter to a very young Lady on her / Marriage. By Dr. Swift. /
Philadelphia, Printed. / *Edinburgh*, Reprinted, For William Gray
iunior. / MDCCL. / [Price Eight Pence.]

Sm. 8vo (in fours); π^2, A–F^4, G^2 — 2 pp. (t. + bl.), [III]–IV (Advertise-
ment), [1]–42, [43]–52 (A Letter by Dr. Swift).
Copies: Huntington, and New York Public Libr.
The 'young Lady' was Deborah Staunton, who married John Rochfort
('Nim') on Jan. 19, 1722–3. A manuscript of the *Letter*, a fair copy in Swift's
hand, dated Feb. 11, 1722–3, is in the Huntington Library. The *Letter* was
first printed in the *Miscellanies*, Vol. II, 1727, pp. 319–37. (Cf. Katherine
Hornbeak, *Swift's Letter to a Very Young Lady on her Marriage*, in *The Huntington
Library Quarterly*, Feb. 1944, Vol. VII, No. 2, pp. 193–6).
Two Philadelphia editions, neither containing Swift's *Letter*, had preceded
in 1746 and 1749; a third, containing the *Letter* appeared in 1758. See Joseph
Sabin, *A Dictionary of Books Relating to America*, Nos. 68692, 68693. Sabin
had his references from Hildeburn, *Issues of the Press of Pennsylvania*, 1885.
There was also a Philadelphia–London edition, Charles Corbet, 1750, but
it does not contain Swift's *Letter*.
A German translation of the *Letter* had also been published in 1735 (see
No. 54).

816. *Another edition:*
Reflections / On / Courtship / And / Marriage: / In two Letters
to a Friend. / Wherein a practicable Plan is laid down / for Ob-
taining and Securing / Conjugal Felicity. / To which is annexed, /
A Letter to a very young Lady on / her marriage. By Dr. Swift. /
Together with / Two Essays on Jealousy. / By Mr. Addison. /
London: / Sold by A. Thomson, R. Nicholson, / T. Davidson, W.
Manson, and / P. Newton.

12mo; [A]–C^{12}, D^6, E^4 — 2 pp. (t. + bl.), [III]–VI (Advertisement),
[1]–83, 3 pp. blank. — Frontisp. portrait of Swift.
Swift's *Letter* is pp. 55–67.
Copy: B.M. 8416 de 30. — The catalogue says 1759 (?).
See also Rothschild 2189.

817. *Another edition:*

Instructions / For / A Young Lady, / In every Sphere and Period of Life. / Containing, / [*First column:*] I. A Mother's Ad- / vice to her Daugh- / ters. / II. Two Letters to a / Lady upon the sub- / ject of Religion, / by a Clergyman. / [*Second column:*] III. A Letter to a / Young Lady on her / Marriage. / IV. An Epistle upon / the Cultivation of / Taste. / V. Fables for the / Female-Sex. / = / Edinburgh: / Printed by A. Donaldson, and sold at his / Shop, No. 48, East corner of St. Paul's / Church-yard, London; and at Edinburgh. / = / M.DCC.LXXIII.

12mo; π^2, A–L^{12}, M^8, N^2 — 2 pp. (t. + bl.), 2 pp. (Contents + bl.), [1]–284.

Swift's *Letter* is pp. 164–82.

Copy: B.M. 8415 b 16.

819. *German adaptation:*

Brief / an / Hermione. / — / All other goods by Fortune's hand are giv'n, / A wife is the peculiar gift of Heav'n. / Vain Fortune's favours, never at a stay; / Like empty Shadows, pass and glide away, / One solid comfort, our eternal wife, / Abundantly supplies us all our life: / This blessing lasts (if those who try say true / As long as hearts can wish . . . . and longer too. / Pope. Januar. and May. / — / Breslau, / bey Gottlieb Loewe. 1789.

16mo; 1–76 (including h.t., before f.t.). — The verso of h.t. says that this is "eine Umarbeitung von Swifts Brief an eine Braut in der Wochenschrift: the Rambler, nach den Bedürfnissen unserer Zeit."

Copy: Preuszische Staatsbibl., Berlin.

1619. The Lady's / Pocket Library. / Containing: / 1. Miss More's Essays. / 2. Dr. Gregory's Legacy To His Daughters. / 3. Lady Pennington's Unfortunate Mother's Advice / To Her Daughters. / 4. Marchioness Of Lambert's Advice Of A Mother To / Her Daughter. / 5. Mrs. Chapone's Letter On The Government Of The / Temper. / 6. Swift's Letter To A Young Lady Newly Married. / 7. Moore's Fables For The Female Sex. / [Type ornaments] / Philadelphia: / From The Press Of Mathew Carey, / No. 118, Market-Street. / March 20, M.DCC.XCII. /

12mo; [A]^2, B–Z, Aa–Bb^6, Cc^4; sig. Cc 4 (blank?) wanting in NYPL copy, 1–297 + bl., 2 pp. (blank?).

"*A Letter to a very young Lady on her Marriage.* / *By Dean Swift.*" pp. [225]–235.

Copy: New York Public Libr.

1620. *The* / Lady's / Pocket Library. / Containing, / 1. *Miss More's Essays.* / 2. Dr. Gregory's / Legacy to his Daughters. /

3. Lady Pennington's / Unfortunate Mother's Advice to her Daughters. / 4. Marchioness Of Lambert's / Advice of a Mother to her Daughter. / 5. Mrs. Chapone's / Letter on the Government of the Temper. / 6. Swift's Letter / To a young Lady newly married. / 7. Moore's Fables / *For The Female Sex*. / [Filet] / Philadelphia: / Printed By R. Folwell, / *For Mathew Carey*. / M.DCC.XCIV. /

12mo; [A]², B–Z⁶, Aa–Bb⁶, [C]⁴, 1–293 + bl., 2 pp. *Contents*, 1–4 (advs.).

"*A Letter to a very young Lady on her Marriage.* / *By Dean Swift.*" pp. [222]–232.

Copy: New York Public Libr.

1621. The / Lady's / Pocket Library. / Containing, / 1. Miss More's Essays. / 2. Dr. Gregory's / Legacy To His Daughters. / 3. Lady Pennington's / Unfortunate Mother's Advice to her Daughters. / 4. Rudiments Of Taste, / By The Countess Of Carlisle. / 5. Mrs. Chapone's / Letter on the Government of the Temper. / 6. Swift's Letter / To A Young Lady Newly Married. / 7. Moore's Fables. / For The Female Sex. / — / *Third American Edition, Improved.* / — / Chambersburg: / Printed By Dover & Harper, / *For Mathew Carey,* / Philadelphia. / M,DCC,XCVII.

12mo (in sixes); [A]², B–Dd⁶ — 2 pp. (t. + bl.), 2 pp. (To the Ladies of the United States + bl.), [5]–238, [239]–249 (A Letter by Dean Swift), [250]–312, 312–[314] (Contents), 2 pp. blank.
Copy: Huntington.

1622. Reflections / On / Courtship And Marriage. / In / Two *Letters* To A Friend: / Wherein / A Practicable Plan Is Laid Down For / Obtaining And Securing / *Conjugal Felicity.* / To Which Are Added, A / Letter, / To A Very Young Lady, / On Her Marriage. / By Dean Swift. / And, An / Essay On Jealousy. / In / Two Discourses. / By Joseph Addison, Esq. / [Filet] / Harrisburgh, Pennsylvania: / Printed By Allen And Wyeth. / M,DCC,XCIII. /

12mo; a⁴, A–H⁶; sig. a 1 blank, 4 pp. (bl. leaf and f.t.), III–VI, 1–95 + 1 p. (advt.).

"Letter / To / A Very Young Lady, / On / Her Marriage. / By Dean Swift." / pp. [63]–78.

Copy: New York Publ. Libr.

808. Brotherly Love. / A / Sermon, / Preached In / St. *Patrick*'s Church; / On *December* 1st, 1717. / By / Dr. Jonathan Swift, / Dean of *St. Patrick*'s, Dublin. / Dublin: / Printed by George Faulkner in Essex-street. / MDCCLIV.

8vo (in fours); π^2, B–D^4 — 2 pp. (t. + bl.), 2 pp. (To the Reader + bl.), 5–26, 2 pp. (Advertisement).

Copies: U.L.C. Hib. 7.754.63, Nat. Libr. of Ireland, and own.

The presence of 'Vol. IX.' at the foot of the first page of each new sheet shows that this sermon was also to form the first section of a new volume of Faulkner's edition of Swift's *Works*. However, ultimately it did not appear in Vol. IX (1758), but in Vol. X (1762); not in this original state, but reprinted.

807. Brotherly Love. / A / Sermon, / Preached In / St. *Patrick*'s Church; / On *December* 1st, 1717. / By Dr. Jonathan Swift, / Dean of St. *Patrick*'s, Dublin. / [ornament] / *London:* / Printed for R. and J. Dodsley, in *Pall-mall*; / and sold by M. Cooper in *Paternoster-Row*. / MDCCLIV. / [Price Six-pence.]

4to; π^4, B–C^4 — 2 pp. (t. + bl.), 2 pp. (Advertisement + bl.), [5]–24.

Copies: B.M. 694 e 4 (11) and 225 i 15 (11).

1623.

On Good-Manners And Good-Breeding.

To a Friend who had been much abused in many inveterate Libels.

These two pieces were first printed in Delany's 'Observations Upon Lord Orrery's Remarks – – – – London, – – – MDCCLIV.', pp. [295]–308, 309–10. The second piece seems to belong to 1730.

(Cf. No. 692) For the 2nd piece see *Poems*, 506.

Both first printed as a footnote (pp. 81–9) in 'The Dreamer – – – London: – – – W. Owen – – – – MDCCLIV', an anonymous prose satire (by Dr. William King, Principal of St. Mary Hall, Oxford).

Lines 51–106 of the Answer reprinted in *The Dublin Literary Gazette*, April 24, 1830, p. 271.

Cf. *Poems*, 431.

See Rothschild, p. 591.

1624. A Dialogue between an eminent Lawyer and Dr. Swift, Dean of St. Patrick's, being an allusion to the first Satire of the second book of Horac. [sic] *Sunt quibus in satyra*, &c. Written in the Year 1729.

First printed (pp. 194–6) in: Deane Swift's 'An Essay Upon The Life, Writings, and Character Of Dr. Jonathan Swift – – – London, – – – Charles Bathurst – – – MDCCLV.'

Also in: *The Gentleman's Magazine*, Aug. 1762, XXXII, 380.

Cf. *Poems*, 488. — Belongs to Feb. 1730.

The History Of The Four Last Years Of The Queen

809. The / History / Of The / Four Last Years / Of The / Queen. / — / By the late / Jonathan Swift, / D.D.D.S.P.D. / — / Published from the / Last Manuscript Copy, Corrected and / Enlarged by the Author's Own Hand. / = / London: / Printed for A. Millar, in the Strand. / MDCCLVIII.

8vo; A–Bb^8, Cc^4 — 2 pp. (t. + bl.), III–XVI (Advertisement), [1]–392. — In some copies Z 3 is misprinted Z 2.

Copies: Penn, Rothschild 2186–8.

Published by Charles Lucas (see No. 79).

812. *Another edition:*

The / History / Of The / Four Last Years / Of The / Queen. / — / By the late / Jonathan Swift, / D.D.D.S.P.D. / — / Published from the / Last Manuscript Copy, Corrected and / Enlarged by the Author's Own Hand. / = / London: Printed for A. Millar, in the Strand, / And / Re-printed for George and Alexander Ewing in / *Dame-street, Dublin.* / MDCCLVIII.

> 8vo; A–Q⁸, R⁴ — 2 pp. (t. + bl.), III–XIV (Advertisement), [3]–249 3 pp. blank.
> Copy: Penn.

813. *Another edition:*
> The same title as preceding copy, except:

> – – – – – Ewing / in *Dame-street,* – – – – –

> 12mo; 2 pp. (t. + bl.), III–XIV (Advertisement), [3]–282.
> This is a separate issue of the greater part of Ewing's Vol. IX, 12mo, 1758 (see No. 98, *ante*).

810. *Another edition:*

The / History / Of The / Last Session of Parliament, and of / the Peace of Utrecht. / Written at Windsor in the Year, 1713. / — / By the Rev. Dr. J. Swift, D.S.P.D. / — / [monogram] / = / Dublin: / Printed by George Faulkner in Essex-Street, / — / M,DCC,LVIII.

> 8vo; 2 pp. (t. + bl.), [1]–310.
> This is a separate issue of the greater part of Faulkner's Vol. IX, 8vo, 1758 (see No. 45, *ante*).

811. *Another edition:*

The / History / Of The / Last Session of Parliament, and / of the Peace of Utrecht. / Written at Windsor in the Year, / 1713. / — / By the Rev. Dr. J. Swift, D.S.P.D. / — / [monogram] / = / Dublin: / Printed by George Faulkner in / Essex-Street, M,DCC,LVIII.

> 12mo; 2 pp. (t. + bl.), [1]–234.
> This is a separate issue of the greater part of Faulkner's Vol. IX, 12mo, 1758 (see No. 51, *ante*).

814. *French translation:*

Histoire / Du Regne / De / La Reine Anne / D'Angleterre, / Contenant / *Les Négociations de la paix d'Utrecht,* / *& les démêlés* *qu'elle occasionna* / *en Angleterre.* / Ouvrage posthume du Docteur Jonathan / Swift, Doyen de S. Patrice / en Irlande; / Publié sur un Manuscrit corrigé de la propre main / de l'Auteur, & traduit de l'Anglois par M****. / [ornament] / A Amsterdam, / Chez Marc-Michel Rey, / & Arkstée & Merkus. / = / M.DCC.LXV.

A

LIBEL

ON

D—— D————,

AND A

Certain Great LORD.

Printed in the Year MDCCXXX.

THE
WORKS
OF
J.S, D.D, D.S.P.D.
IN
FOUR VOLUMES.

CONTAINING,

I. The Author's MISCELLANIES in PROSE.

II. His POETICAL WRITINGS.

III. The TRAVELS of Captain *Lemuel Gulliver.*

IV. His Papers relating to *Ireland*, confifting of feveral Treatifes; among which are, The DRAPIER'S LETTERS to the People of *Ireland* againft receiving *Wood*'s Half-pence: Alfo, two Original DRAPIER'S LETTERS, never before publifhed.

In this Edition are great Alterations and Additions; and likewife many Pieces in each Volume, never before publifhed

---

DUBLIN:
Printed by and for GEORGE FAULKNER, Printer and Bookfeller, in ESSEX-STREET, oppofite to the Bridge. MDCCXXXV.

The Works of J.S, D.D, D.S.P.D. (no. 41). Faulkner's four volumes, appearing in March, 1735, constituted the first authoritative edition of Swift's works by themselves. This is the copy of Lady Anne Acheson.
(University of Pennsylvania)

12mo; [a]¹², A–R¹², S⁴ — 2 pp. blank, 2 pp. (h.t. + bl.), 2 pp. (f.t. + bl.),
VII–XXIV (Preface), [1]–416.
   Copy: B.M. 9512 a 20.
   Translation by M. A. Eidous.

Contemporary criticism

1352. A Whig's Remarks On The Tory History Of The Four last Years of
Queen Anne. By Dr. Jonathan Swift, D. S. P. D. &c. London: J. Staples,
MDCCLVIII. — 8vo; I–IV, 1–65 + bl.

1353. An Appeal to the Public. [Text at once under this] — 8vo; 1–8. —
[At foot of p. 8: Essex-street, March 28. 1758.] — Copy in Nat. Libr. Dublin,
which has a type-written leaf in front, saying: "Anonymous pamphlet showing
that G. Faulkner had the sole right to publish Swift's "History of the four last
years of the Queen"."
   An Attempt to Answer Mr. George Faulkner's Extraordinary Appeal to the
Public — This is the Ewings' reply to the 'Appeal'.

1353A. Epigram.
In: The Annual Register, 1759, II, 328.
Cf. *Poems*, 843.

820. An / Essay / Upon The / Civil Wars / Of / France, /
Extracted from curious Manuscripts. / And Also Upon The /
Epick Poetry / Of The / European Nations, / From Homer down
to Milton. / — / By Mr. de Voltaire. / — / To which is Prefixed, /
A short Account of the Author. / — / By J.S.D.D.D.S.P.D. / — /
Dublin: / Printed for William Ross, Bookseller in *Grafton-street*.
/ — / MDCCLX.

   8vo; 1–82, 2 pp. (advs.).
   Swift's *Account* covers one page only, and seems to belong to the year 1728.

820A. A Satirical Elegy On the Death of a late Famous General.
   In: *The Gentleman's Magazine*, May 1764, XXXIV, 244.
   It refers to Marlborough's death, June 16, 1722.

821. On the Day of Judgement. By Dean Swift.
   This is on p. 4 (1st column) of:

The *St. James*'s Chronicle; / Or, *British* Evening-Post. / — /
Price Two-Pence Halfpenny.] From Saturday April 9 to Tuesday
April 12, 1774. No. 2053. / — /

   Large folio; 4 pp. (4 columns on each page).
   At foot of page 4:

— / *London:* Printed for H. Baldwin, at the Britannia Printing-
Office, No. 108, Fleet-Street, where Advertisements are taken in,
and Letters to the Author received.

On p. 4 (1st column) there is:
On the Day of Judgement. By Dean Swift.

822. *Reprinted* (pp. 25–6) *in:*
The / Monthly Review; / Or, / Literary Journal: / From July to December, 1774. / With / An Appendix / Containing the Foreign Literature. / By Several Hands. / — / Volume LI. / — / [ornament] / = / London: / Printed for R. Griffiths: / And Sold by T. Becket, Corner of the Adelphi, in the Strand. / M,DCC,LXXIV.

8vo; I–VIII, 1–568, 8 pp. (*Index*).
Also in: *The Gentleman's Magazine*, Oct. 1775, XLV, 492.
Of this piece Elrington Ball, *Swift's Verse*, p. 277, has said that it is believed to have been written about the year 1731, and that these lines "were evidently guarded jealously by Swift, but in some way they came into the possession of Faulkner, who passed them on to his patron Lord Chesterfield".
In PMLA, XLVIII (1933), 850–5, Prof. S. L. Gulick, Jr., has traced the way in which this poem came into the Swift canon: Chesterfield sent a copy of the poem to Voltaire in a letter, dated Aug. 27, 1752. When Chesterfield's *Letters to his Son* were published on April 7, 1774, this letter was Letter 66 in Vol. II, but the poem was not in it. After having first appeared in the *St. James's Chronicle*, and in the *Monthly Review* (see above), it was printed in the 4th edition of Chesterfield's *Letters to his Son*, which was published Oct. 29, 1774, in one of the eleven notes new to this edition. These eleven notes were also published separately, in 4to to be added to the 1st ed., in 8vo to the 2nd and 3rd eds. — German translation in *Briefe – – – Chesterfield an seinen Sohn*, 6 vols., Leipzig, 1774–7, in Vol. VI, 1777. — French translation in *Lettres – – – Chesterfield a son fils*, 4 vols., Strasbourg & Vienne, 1785, in Vol. III, 1785.
In 1775 Nichols inserted the poem into Swift's *Works*, Vol. IX, Part II, 4to. (No. 87).
For the earliest known text, see William Collins, *Drafts & Fragments* (1956), pp. 41–3.

823. The / Family Chaplain: / Being A Complete / Course of Sermons / Upon The / Festivals And Fasts / (Throughout the Year) / As Prescribed In / The Book Of Common-Prayer. / Selected From / The Celebrated Discourse / Of / [*First column:*] Abp. Tillotson, / Abp. Secker, / Bp. Stillingfleet, / Bp. Atterbury, / Bp. Conybeare, / Bp. Warburton, / Dr. Swift, / [*Second column:*] Dr. Littleton, / Dr. Hole, / Dr. Waterland, / Dr. Clarke, / Dr. Fothergill, / Dr. Brown, / And Others. / The whole intended to explain and vindicate the Christian / Faith; to promote and perfect the pious Design of / Mr. Nelson / In His / Companion For The Festivals And Fasts / Of The Church; / And to render an acceptable Service to the Clergy, by the / Supply of so desireable a Collection. / — / In Two Volumes. / — / Volume II. / = / London, / Printed for L. Davis, in Holborn; and R. Baldwin, / in Pater-Noster Row. 1775.

[Title within double-lined frame.]
Vol. I:
8vo; π^2, A–Hh^8, Ii^4, Kk^2 — 2 pp. (t. + bl.), 2 pp. (Dedication + bl.),
[I]–XI (Preface), 2 pp. (Rules), 1 p. (Contents 1st Vol.), 2 pp. (t. + bl.),
[1]–491 + bl.
Vol. II:
Large 8vo; π^2, B–Kk^8, Ll^6 — 2 pp. (t. + bl.), 2 pp. (Contents 2nd Vol.),
[1]–508, 16 pp. Index.
Copy: B.M. 1455 cc 10.
Pp. 110–23 contain Swift's *Sermon On Trinity Sunday*.

1654. A / Sermon, / On The / *Trinity*. / — / By Jonathan Swift,
D.S.P.D. / — / — / Reprinted at Portland, from the Edinburg
Edition, / By Benjamin Titcomb, jun. / MDCCXCII. / —.

8vo; 4 pp. (h.t. + f.t.), [5]–21 + blank.
Copy: H.E. Huntington Library.

115. A Select / Collection / Of / Poems: / With / Notes, / Bio-
graphical And Historical. / — / The Fourth Volume. / — / London:
/ Printed By And For J. Nichols, / Red Lion Passage, Fleet-Street.
/ MDCCLXXX.

Sm. 8vo; π^2, B–Z^8, Aa^2, π^1, B^4 — 2 pp. (h.t. + bl.), 2 pp. (f.t. + bl.),
1–356, 357*, 358*, 357–64. — Frontisp. portrait of Steele between the titles.
Copy: B.M. 238 e 18.
Contains two genuine Swift pieces: pp. 305–6 *Cantata*, p. 306 *Epigram
Extempore*; and two doubtful ones: p. 50 *When the Cat's Away*, p. 303 *Ode To
King William*.
The whole set consists of 8 vols: I–IV, 1780; V, 1782; VI, 1780; VII,
1781; VIII, 1782.

825. The / European Magazine, / For January 1795.

This contains the first instalment (pp. 37–41) of:

Curious Remarks on "Bishop Burnet's History Of His / Own
Times." / By Dr. Swift, the late Lord Hardwicke, and the late /
Speaker Onslow. (Never before published.)

Continued in the numbers for March, June, Aug., Oct., Nov., Dec., 1795,
and Feb. 1796 (pp. 157–61, 374–6, 88–91, 245–8, 312–15, 392–5, 87–9 respectively).
Reprinted in Barrett's *Essay*, 1808 (see No. 136, *post*), and in later editions
of Burnet's *History*, starting with 1823.

827. The / Churchman Armed / Against The / *Errors Of The
Time*. / — / By "The Society For The Distribution Of / Tracts In
Defence Of The United Church / Of England And Ireland, As By
Law Estab- / lished." / — / In Three Volumes. / Vol. II. / = /
London: / Printed for J. J. Stockdale, No. 41, Pall-Mall, and F. C.
and / J. Rivington, St. Paul's Church Yard. / — / 1814.

Large 8vo; π^2, B–2Q^8, 2R 1 — 2 pp. (t. + printer's name on verso), 2 pp. (Contents), [1]–610.
Copy: B.M. 495 f 15.
Contains (pp. 7–45) Swift's *Sentiments of a Church of England-Man.*

SECTION VI

DOUBTFUL

✦✦✦

1625. Ode to King William, On His Successes In Ireland.
This is p. 13 in: *The Gentleman's Journal: Or the Monthly Miscellany*, July, 1692.
Also in:
A Select Collection of Poems, Vol. IV, 1780, p. 303 (No. 115 — Sep. Works 1780).
This ode (in quatrains) has been thought to be the one written by Swift ca. 1690–1 on King William's Irish successes, but it is more probable that the authentic one (in pindarics) is entitled: "Ode to the King. On his *Irish* Expedition. And *The Success of his Arms in general*. Written in the Year 1691.", first printed in Vol. IV of Fairbrother's *Miscellanies*, 1735 (see No. 33, IV). — Cf. *Poems*, 3–13.

481. *Aenigma.* / By Mr. *S.T.*

The *Aenigma* in the last Mercury explain'd. / By Mr. *S. W.* Followed by another *Aenigma*, by the author of the Explanation. *The Aenigma in the last Mercury explain'd.* By Mr. *F – – – – r.*
They begin respectively:
"From India's burning Clime I'm brought," &c.
"Your House of Hair and Lady's Hand," &c.
"I'm wealthy and poor," &c.
"In Rigging he's rich, tho in Pocket he's Poor." &c.
They occur on pp. 96–7, 116–17, and 145 in:

The / Muses Mercury: / Or, / Monthly Miscellany. / Consisting of / Poems, Prologues, Songs, Sonnets, Translations, / and other Curious Pieces, Never before Printed. / By the Best and most Celebrated Hands. / To which is added, / An Account of the *Stage*, of the New *Opera's* and / *Plays* that have been Acted, or are to be Acted this Season; / And of the New Books relating to *Poesy*, *Criticism*, &c. lately Publish'd. / — / For the Month of *April*. / — / To be continu'd Monthly. / — / [ornament] / — / *Ex Quovis Ligno non fit Mercurius.* / — / *London*, Printed by *J. H.* for Andrew Bell, at the *Cross Keys* / and *Bible* in *Cornhill*, near *Stocks-Market*. 1707.

The Muses Mercury – – – For the Month of *May*. – – – 1707.
The Muses Mercury – – – For the Month of *June*. – – – 1707.
The first and the second were reprinted about 1725 as:

482. A / Riddle / By Dr, S—t, to My Lady Carteret. Answer'd / By Dr. S—g,

Sm. folio; 1 page.
Copy: B.M. 839 m 23 (135).
Cf. Elr. Ball, *Swift's Verse*, 62.

Also reprinted in:
The Gentleman's Magazine, Aug. 1762, XXXII, 381, and Sept. 1762, XXXII, 441.
Cf. *Poems*, 911–13.

503. Jack Frenchman's Lamentation. / An Excellent New Song, / To the Tune of *I'll tell thee Dick*, &c.

Folio; 1 page (2 columns). — 13 stanzas.
At foot of page:

London: Printed, and are to be Sold by *John Morphew*, near *Stationers-Hall*. 1708.

Copy: Quaritch (cat. 432, item 195).
On the authenticity of this piece, see *Notes And Queries*, 12th Series, Vol. VIII (No. 157, April 16, 1921, pp. 301–3: Congreve As A Ballad-Writer, by F. Elrington Ball); *The Review Of English Studies*, Vol. II (1926), pp. 322–8, and Vol. III (1927), pp. 73–4, 212–14 (articles by Harold Williams and Sir Charles H. Firth); Shane Leslie, *The Script of Jonathan Swift*, p. 7.

504. *Another edition:*
Jack Frenchman's Lamentation, / An Excellent New Song. / To the Tune of, *I'll tell the* [sic] *Dick*, &c. Or, *Who can but love a Seaman*, &c.

Small folio; 1 page (2 columns). — 14 stanzas.
Under the title there is a woodcut, showing soldiers marching with drum beating and colours flying.
Copy: B.M. (1876 f 1 (40)).

505. *Another edition:*
Jack French-Man's Defeat: / Being an Excellent New Song, to a Pleasant Tune, / called, *There was a Fair Maid in the* North-Country, / *Came Triping over the Plain*, &c.

Small folio; pp. 1–2 (double columns). — 14 stanzas.
Printed in Black Letter. — Woodcut between title and text.
Copy: B.M. (C. 40 m 10 (103)).

506. *Also in:*
The / Battel of Audenard. / A / Poem, / Occasion'd / By the Glorious Victory ob- / tain'd over the *French* near that Place, / the 11th of *July*, 1708. N.S. by the / Confederate Army under the Com- / mand of his Grace the Duke of *Marl-* / *borough*, Monsieur *D'Auverquerque*, and / Prince *Eugene* of *Savoy*. / With the *Characters* of the Ge- / neral Officers, who were present in the / Engagement. / Also / A New Copy of Verses of *Jack Frenchman's* / Lamentation. / *London*, / Printed and Sold by *H. Hills*, in the *Black-fryars*, near / Water-side, For the Benefit of the Poor. 1708.

8vo; [A]⁸ — 1 p. (title), 2 pp. (Preface), 4–15 (A Poem), 16 (Lamentation).
Copy: Bodl. G. Pamph. 1278 (5).

507. *Another edition:*

Jack Frenchman's Lamentation, | An Excellent New Song, | To the Tune of *I'll tell thee Dick, &c.*

> Folio; 1 page (2 columns). — 13 stanzas.
> Edinburgh? Imprint at foot cut away?
> Copy: B.M. 12350 m 18 (3).

846. A True Narrative Of what pass'd at the Examination Of the Marquis De Guiscard, At The Cock-Pit, The 8th of March, 17$\frac{10}{11}$. &c. London: John Morphew, 1711. — 8vo; 1–43, 1 p. advs. Copy: Penn.

> Another ed.: – – – – – Printed in the Year 1711. [No place; no printer]. — 8vo; 1–23 + bl. — Copy: Penn.
> Dublin ed.: – – – – – London: John Morphew, Re-Printed in Dublin, C. Carter, 1711. — 12mo; 1–16.
> Written by Mrs. Manley, and partly by Swift, who also revised it extensively for the press. — Cf. *Journal to Stella*, April 16 and 28, 1711.
> *The Spectator*, No. 50, Friday, April 27, 1711, and No. 575, Monday, Aug. 2, 1714, contain hints and a paragraph attributed to Swift. — Cf. *Journal to Stella*, March 16 and 28, 1711.

849. The Reasons Which induc'd Her Majesty To Create the Right Honourable Robert Harley, Esq; A Peer of Great-Britain. London: J. Morphew. 1711. — 4to; 1–8 [Pp. 3–5 Latin; pp. 6–8 English; adv. at foot of p. 8]. — Supposed to have been drawn up by Harley himself or Dr. Robert Freind, and revised by Swift. — Early May, 1711.

> Another ed.: Same title. — 4to; 1–7 (advs. on verso). [Latin and English facing each other].

850. The Reasons Which induc'd Her Majesty To Create the Right Honourable Sir Simon Harcourt A Peer of Great-Britain. London: J. Morphew. 1711. &c. — 4to; 1–7 (advs. on verso). [Latin and English facing each other]. — Supposed to have been drawn up by Harley, and revised by Swift. — Early May, 1711.

538. A | *Learned Comment* | Upon | Dr. Hare's Excellent Sermon | Preach'd before the | *D. of* Marlborough, | On the Surrender of | Bouchain. | — | *By an Enemy to Peace.* | — | *Et multis utile Bellum.* | — | *London,* | Printed for *John Morphew*, near *Statio-* | *ners-Hall.* 1711. (Price 2 *d.*)

> [Title within double-lined frame.]
> 8vo; [A]^8 — 2 pp. (t. + bl.), 3–16.
> By Mrs. Manley; hints by Swift. — Cf. *Journal to Stella*, Nov. 3, 1711.
> Copy: Penn.
> There seems to be a second edition, but I have not seen a copy.

858. A True Relation Of the several Facts and Circumstances Of the intended Riot and Tumult On Queen Elizabeth's Birth-day. &c. London, John Morphew. 1711. — 8vo; 1–16. Copy: Penn.

Second ed.: – – – – The Second Edition, Corrected. – – – – 1711. — 8vo; 1–16. — Copies: Bodl., and Penn.

Edinburgh ed.: – – – – London, John Morphew: And Edinburgh Reprinted by James Watson &c., 1711. — 8vo; 1–16.

Another edition:

No place, no year, no imprint. — Sm. 8vo size; no signatures — 1–8. Text begins at once under the title. Copy: Nat. Libr. of Ireland.

By Mrs. Manley; hints by Swift. — Cf. *Journal to Stella,* Nov. 17 and 26, 1711.

847. To The Right Honourable Mr. Harley, on His first Appearing in Publick, after the Wound given Him by Guiscard. London: John Morphew, 1711. — Folio; 2 pages. — Copy: U.L.C.

847A. Reſpectful / Observations / On a late Print, call'd / A / Memorial; / Said to be Publiſh'd by the / Baron de Bothmar, / In the Name of his / Electoral Highneſs of *Hanover.* / *London:* / Printed for John Morphew, near / *Stationer's Hall.* 1712. / *Price 3 d.* / Small 8vo, 23 p.

 Small 8vo. 23 p.
 Cf. J. to St., Dec. 5, 1711.
 Copy: Huntington.

848. A Comment Upon The History Of Tom Thumb. &c. London, J. Morphew. 1711. — 8vo; 1–24. — Written in ridicule of Addison's "Chevy Chase".

Second ed.: – – – – – The Second Edition, corrected. London, J. Morphew, 1711. — 8vo; 1–24. — Copy: Bodl. and Penn.

861. The Story Of The St. Alb—ns Ghost, Or The Apparition Of Mother Haggy. &c. London: Printed in the Year 1712. — 8vo; 1–16. Copy: Penn.

Third, fourth, and fifth eds.: Titles and collations the same as those of the first. I have not seen a copy of the second ed.

Another ed.: – – – – – – London: Printed in the Year MDCXII. [*sic*] —8vo; 1–8.

Dublin ed.: – – – – – London: Printed; And Re-Printed in Dublin, 1712. — 8vo; 1–16.

For 'Keys' to this pamphlet, see No. 1052, *post.*

860. Numb. I. The Plain Dealer. To be Published every Saturday. – – – – – Saturday, April 12, 1712. London: J. Morphew. — Folio; 2 pages. — There were seventeen numbers in all, up to and including Aug. 2, 1712. Copy: Penn.

865. The Representation Of The Loyal Subjects Of Albinia. &c. Printed in the Year 1712. — 8vo; 1–14. Copy: Penn.

Dublin ed.: – – – – – London Printed: And Re-printed and Sold by E. Waters, &c. 1712. — 12mo; 1–14. — Copy: Nat. Libr., Dublin.

Another ed.: A Representation of the Loyal Subjects of Albinia to their Sovereign upon his concluding a Treaty of Peace with his Foes. — 8vo; N.D. [Dobell, cat. 76, item 305].

***

862. A / Fable / Of The / Widow and her Cat.

Folio (half-sheet); 2 pages (single columns; 9 stanzas).
At foot of second page:

Printed for *John Morphew*, near *Stationers-Hall*, 1712.

Copy: Bodl. MS. Eng. poet. c.6 (15).
Published beginning of Jan. 1712.
If Swift's words in the *Journal to Stella*, Jan. 4, 1712, which seem to refer
to this piece, are to be taken as the truth, it is "a ballad made by several
hands": Lord Treasurer, Swift ("I added three stanzas"), and "Dr. Arbuthnot
had the greatest share." It was only much later that it was ascribed to Swift
and Prior. Cf. Sir Charles Firth, *Review of Engl. Studies*, 1925, I, 456; Elr. Ball,
Swift's Verse, 124–5; Poems, 151–2.

Another edition:
Same title as above.
Sm. folio; one page (two columns; 9 stanzas).
At foot of page:

Printed in the Year MDCCXII.

Copy: B.M. G 1390 (9).

Another edition:
Same title as above.
Folio; 2 pages (single columns; 9 stanzas).
At foot of second page:

Printed in the Year 1712.

Copies: U.L.C. Syn. 3.71.4 (6), and Texas.

Another edition:
Same title as above.
Folio; one page (two columns; 9 stanzas).
At foot of page:

London, Printed for *Philpot* near *Charing-Cross*, 1711.

Copy: Bodl. 4 Δ 260 (20).

Another edition:
Same title as above.
Folio; one page (9 stanzas).
At foot of page:

London Printed; *And Re-printed in* (rest, as well as part of the last
stanza, torn off.)

Copy once in the possession of Mr. P. J. Dobell (cat. 105, item 299). May
be a Dublin reprint.
Also in:
Political State of Great Britain, Jan. 1711–12, III, 13.
Answered by:

863. The Fable of the Shepherd and his Dog, In Answer to the Fable of the
Widow and her Cat, London: Printed in the Year, MDCCXII. — Folio; 1 page.
— Publ. Jan. 28, 1712.
Copy: Penn.

1299. When the Cat's away, The Mice may play. A Fable, Humbly inscrib'd to Dr. Sw—t. London: A. Baldwin. — Folio; 4 pages. — Publ. 31 Jan. 1712 (see *Journal to Stella*, under that date, and advs. in *The Spectator* Jan. 31, Feb. 1 and 2, 1712). — Probably by Prior.
Also in:
A Select Collection of Poems, 1780, Vol. IV, p. 50 (my No. 115).

864. A Fable Of The Housewife And Her Cock. London, Printed in the Year 1712, and Sold by the Booksellers. — Sm. folio; 2 pages.

875. Proposals For Printing A very Curious Discourse, in Two Volumes in Quarto, Intitled, Ψευδολογία Πολιτική; Or, A Treatise of the Art Of Political Lying, With An Abstract of the First Volume of the said Treatise. London: John Morphew, 1712. — Sm. 4to; 1–22, 2 pp. advs. —
Published Oct. 1712.
Copy: Penn.
Dublin ed.: – – – John Morphew, Re-printed Edward Waters, Dublin, 1712. — 8vo — Copy: cat. Pickering & Chatto, cat. 345, item 443 (1949).
Edinburgh ed.: 1712.
Edinburgh ed.: – – – – – Edinburgh: Reprinted in the Year MDCCXLVI. — 8vo; 1–20.
German translation in: Geheime Papiere, von Dr. Friedrich Ludwig Lindner. &c. Stuttgart, bei Friedrich Franckh. 1824. — 8vo; I–XVI, 1–311 + bl., 8 pp. [Pp. 281–31] are: Die Kunst politischer Lûgen; nach Swift.] — Copy: Penn.
Reprinted (pp. 105–23) in: Political Pamphlets, &c. London Kegan Paul, &c. 1897.

895. Ars Pun-ica, sive Flos Linguarum: The Art of Punning; Or The Flower of Languages; In Seventy Nine Rules: For The Farther Improvement Of Conversation, And Help of Memory. By the Labour and Industry of Tom Pun-Sibi. &c. Dublin: James Carson, 1719. — Sm. 4to; 16 pp., I–XII, 13–38, 2 pp. — Copy: Gilbert Coll., Dublin and Penn.
By Sheridan, but Swift and others may have contributed something. — See also Nos. 16 and 19, and cf. *Poems*, 1101.
Another ed.: – – – – – – By the Labour and Industry of Tom Pun-Sibi. (i.e.) Jonathan Swift, D.D. &c. The Second Edition. Printed at Dublin in the Year 1719. Reprinted at London for J. Roberts in Warwick-Lane. (Price One Shilling.) — 8vo (in fours);
[A]–F⁴, G³ — 2 pp. (t. + bl.), 3 pp. (Dedication), 5 pp. I–XIII + bl., 1–27, 3 pp. (Another Preface). — Copy: Forster.
There seems to be a first ed. of this Roberts reprint, but I have not seen it.
Third ed.: Same title and collation as preceding copy. — Copy: Bodl.
Fifth ed.: 1746 (cf. Ralph Straus, *The Unspeakable Curll*, 313).
Also in: A Collection Of Scarce, Curious and Valuable Pieces, Both in Verse and Prose; &c. Edinburgh: W. Ruddiman, M,DCC,LXXIII. — 12mo; 8 pp., 1–412. — Another ed.: – – – – Edinburgh, Ruddiman & Co., 1785.

899. The Right Of Precedence Between Phisicians and Civilians Enquir'd into. &c. Dublin: John Hyde, and Robert Owen. 1720. — 8vo; 2 pp. (h.t.), 1–30. [Hitherto considered genuine, but Swift's words in his letter to Ford of April 4, 1720, make it very doubtful whether this piece is by Swift (cf. Nichol Smith, *The Letters Of Swift To Ford*, XLIV 87 and note 3).]
Another ed.: – – – – – Dnblin [*sic*]: Printed: And Reprinted at London, for J. Roberts &c. MDCCXX. — 8vo; 2 pp. (h.t.) 1–30.

Another ed.: – – – – – Written by Dr. Swift. Printed at Dublin in the Year 1720; and Reprinted at London for J. Roberts, &c. — 8vo; 1–32. [Verso of h.t. has a *Letter* saying that this piece is by Swift.] — Copy: Penn.

Second ed.: – – – – – The Second Edition. [For the rest same title and collation as preceding copy.]

Edinburgh ed.: – – – – – Written by Dr. Swift. London Printed, and Edinburgh Re-printed, MDCCXX. — 4to; 1–12. — Copy: Nat. Libr. of Scotl.

900. The Characters Of Two Independent Whigs, Viz. T.G of the North, And Squire T of the West. &c. London: John Morphew. 1720. — 8vo; 1–22 + blank leaf. — Swift speaks rather mysteriously of this piece in his letter to Ford of April 15, 1721 (cf. Nichol Smith, *The Letters Of Swift to Ford*, 90–1, and note 3). — T.G. stands for Thomas Gordon, and T. for [John] Trenchard. They published a paper, called *The Independent Whig* (collected edition: London, J. Peele, 1721.)

621. A / Letter / Of / Advice / To A / Young Poet; / Together / With a Proposal for the / Encouragement of Poetry in / this Kingdom. / — / *Sic honor & nomen divinis vatibus atq*; / *Carminibus venit* —— Hor. / — / [ornament] / — / *Dublin:* / Printed for J. Hyde, in *Dames-street*, 1721.

[Title within double-lined frame.]
8vo (in fours); π^4, B–D^4 — 2 pp. (t. + bl.), 3–32.
Dated December 1, 1720.
Copies: Bodl. (G. Pamph. 785 (16)), B.M. 818 a 16, and Penn.
Of late some doubts have arisen as to the authenticity of this piece — see Herbert Davis, *Essays Prof. Nichol Smith's 75th Birthday*, p. 27; and *Prose Works*, Vol. IX, pp. XXIV–VII.

622. *Another edition:*
A / Letter / Of / Advice / To A / Young Poet: / Together / With a Proposal for the / Encouragement of Poetry in / this Kingdom. / — / *Sic honor & nomen divinis vatibus atq;* / *Carminibus venit* —— Hor. / — / By J. Swift. / — / Printed at *Dublin*, Re-printed at *London*, and / Sold by *W. Boreham* at the *Angel* in *Pater-noster-* / *Row*. 1721. / (Price Six-Pence.)

8vo (in fours); [A]–D^4 — 2 pp. (h.t. + bl.), 3–32.
Copies: U.L.C. Hib. 7.721.14; B.M. 1077 1227 (7).

Second edition:
Same title and collation, and printed from the same type, except:

– – – – J. Swift. / — / The Second Edition. / — / Printed at *Dublin*, Re-printed at *London*, and / Sold by *W. Boreham* at the *Angel* in *Pater-noster-* / *Row*. 1721. (Price Six-Pence.)

Copies: U.L.C. Hib. 5.721.8; and Forster.
The following eight pieces are given with some hesitation by Prof. Herbert Davis (*Prose Works*, Vol. IX, p. VI and Introduction), and are spoken of as "probably written by Swift", and as "attributed to Swift and his friends".

909. Subscribers to the Bank / Plac'd according to / Their Order and Quality. / With / Notes and Queries.

> Folio; two pages.
> At foot of second page:

Dublin: Printed by *John Harding* in *Molesworth's-Court* in / *Fishamble Street.*

> Copies: Marsh, B.M. 1890 e. 5 (161), U.L.C., and Nat. Libr. of Ireland. Published about the middle of Nov. 1721.

> *Reprinted in:*
> The Eyes of Ireland Open. Being, A short View of the Project for Establishing The Intended Bank of Ireland – – – In a Letter from a Lady at Dublin to her Friend in the Country. To which is added – – – Subscribers to the Bank – – – – The Second Edition. London: Printed from the 2d Edition of the Dublin Copies, J. Roberts, 1722. — 8vo (in fours); π^4, B–C^4, D^2 — 2 pp. (t. + bl.), 3–18 (Letter), [19]–28 + bl. (Subscribers) — Page 25 omitted in numbering. — Copy: B.M. 8225 a 26.

631. A / Letter / To The / K – – – – – – – at Arms. / From a Reputed Esquire, / One of The / Subscribers to the Bank.

> Folio; 2 pages.
> At foot of second page:

Dublin: Printed by John Harding in Molesworth's-Court.

> Dated Nov. 18, 1721.
> Copies: T.C.D. Press A7.6 (4), and Yale.

631A. Swearers Bank, / Or, / Parliamentary Security for a new Bank. / *Si Populus vult decipi, decipiatur.*

> Half-sheet; 2 pages (double columns).
> At foot of second page:

Dublin: Printed by *Thomas Hume*, next Door to the *Walsh*'s-Head, in *Smock*-Alley.

> Copy: Yale.

615. The / First Part / Of The / Swearers Bank: / Or, Parliamentary Security / For A / New Bank. / — / Si Populus vult decipi, decipiatur. / — / [ornament] / — / *Dublin:* Printed by *Thomas Hume*, next / Door to the *Walsh's*-Head in *Smock-Alley*, / 1721.

> Sm. 8vo size; no signatures (may have been cut off?) — 1 p. (title), [2]–8. The year 1721 altered with pen into 1720.

The / Second Part / Of The / Swearers Bank, / With New / Reasons / To Encourage that Project. / — / *Non fumum ex fulgore*

sed ex fumo dare lucem, | *Cogitat, ut speciosa dehinc miracula pro-*
mat. | — | *Dublin:* Printed by *Thomas Hume,* next | Door to the
Walsh's-Head in *Smock*-Alley, | 1720.

Sm. 8vo; [A]², B⁴ — 2 pp. (t. + bl.), [3]–12.
Copy (both parts): Gilbert Coll., Dublin.

616. *Another edition:*
The | *Swearer's*-Bank: | Or, | Parliamentary Security | For |
Establishing a new Bank | In | *Ireland.* | Wherein | The Medicinal
Use of Oaths is considered. | (With | The *Best in Christendom.*
A Tale.) | — | *Written by Dean* Swift. | — | *Si Populus vult decipi*
decipiatur. | — | To which is prefixed, | An Essay upon *English*
Bubbles. | *By* Thomas Hope, *Esq;* | — | *Dublin:* | Printed by
Thomas Hume, next Door to the | *Walsh's-Head* in *Smock-Alley.*
1720. Reprinted at | *London* by J. Roberts in *Warwick-Lane.*

8vo (in fours); π², a⁴, B–C⁴, D² — 2 pp. (h.t. + bl.), 2 pp. (f.t. + bl.),
[I]–VIII (Essay Bubbles), 1–14 (The Swearer's Bank), 15 (Postscript),
16 (adv.: Lately Publish'd, Written by Dean Swift), 17–19 (The Best in
Christendom), [20] (blank). — Contains only the 'First Part' of 'The Swearer's
Bank'.
Copies: Yale, B.M. 12316 i 34.
Poems, 1101, says that 'The Best in Christendom' is an afterthought, not
by Swift. Wagner, *Irish Economics*, No. 7, mentions a copy with 15 pages only.
Possibly this is the first issue, without 'The Best in Christendom'.

617. *Another edition:*
The | Swearer's -Bank: | Or, Parliamentary Security | For |
Establishing a New Bank | In | *Ireland.* | Wherein the Medicinal
Use of Oaths | is Considered. | — | *Written by Dean* Swift. | — |
Si Populus vult Decipi Decipiatur. | — | To which is prefix'd, |
An Essay upon *English* Bubbles. | By Thomas Hope Esq; | — |
The Third Edition. | — | *Dublin,* | Printed by Thomas Hume,
next Door to the *Walsh's-* | Head in *Smock-Alley:* Reprinted at
London by | E. Curll in the *Strand.* M.DCC.XXI.

8vo (in fours); [A]–C⁴ — 2 pp. (t. + bl.), 3–23 + bl.
8vo; 1–23 + bl. — Contains only the 'First Part' (pp. 11–23).
Copy: Bodl. (Godw. Pamph. 213 (8)).
Ralph Straus, *The Unspeakable Curll,* 1927, p. 282, mentions a third edition,
1727. [?]

Also in:
The Entertainer, consisting of pieces in prose and verse, witty, humorous,
or curious. Vol. I (probably all published). Printed for F. Cogan, 1746. —
8vo (From cat. Dobell, No. 89, item 144).

910. A Letter from a Lady in Town to her Friend in the Country,
Concerning the Bank. | Or, The List of the Subscribers farther
Explain'd.

Folio; two pages (double columns).
At foot of second page, under the second column:

Dublin: Printed by John Harding.

> Text dated at top: *Dublin, Dec.* 1. 1721.
> Copies: Marsh, and Nat. Libr. of Ireland.
> Reprinted in:
> The Eyes of Ireland Open.

910A. The / Last Speech and dying Words / Of The / Bank of Ireland. / Which was Executed at College-Green, on Saturday the 9th Inst.

> Folio; one page (two columns).
> At foot of page:

— / *Dublin*: Printed by *John Harding* in *Molesworth's Court* in *Fishamble Street.*

> Copies: Harvard, and Nat. Libr. of Ireland.

Answered by:
The Bank's / Ghost / Appearing to the People of Ireland, / Or, / *An Answer* to the last Speech and Dying / *Words* of the Bank. — Folio; one page. — At foot of page: Dublin Printed: 1721. — Copy: Nat. Libr. of Ireland.

906. = / The Wonderful Wonder / Of / Wonders.

> 4to size; no signatures — [1]–4 — Text begins at once under the title.
> Copy: B.M. 1881 c 3 (22).
> Another ed.: The / Wonderful / Wonder of Wonders. / Being An / *Accurate Description* / Of The / Birth, Education, Manner of / Living, Religion, Politicks, / Learning, *&c.* / Of / Mine A – – – – se. / — / *London:* / Printed in the Year MDCCXXII. — Sm. 8vo; 1–14 + bl. (12 omitted in numbering). — Sometimes bound in at the end of Miscellanies, 4th ed., 1722 (No. 19).
> Copy: Forster 8535 (34D6).
> Second ed.: The Wonderfull Wonder of Wonders; Being – – – A—se. By Dr. Sw—ft. With a Preface, and some Notes, Explaining the most difficult Passages – – – – The Second Edition. London: Printed from the Original Copy from Dublin, and Sold by T. Bickerton, at the Crown in Pater-Noster-Row. 1721. Pr. 4d.
> 8vo (in fours); [A]–C⁴ — 2 pp. (h.t. + bl.), 2 pp. (f.t. + bl.), [V]–X (Preface), [3]–16.
> Copies: Forster 8937 (19D13), and Penn.
> Third ed.: Same title and collation as those of the preceding ed. — Copy: Eton.
> Fourth ed.: I have not seen a copy.
> Fifth ed.: The Wonderful Wonder Of Wonders: Or The Hole-History Of The Life and Actions Of Mr. Breech, The Eighth Wonder of the World. Being An Accurate Description of &c. By Dr. S—t. &c. The Fifth Edition. London; A. Moore, M.DCC.XXII. —

8vo (in fours); [A]–C⁴ — 2 pp. (h.t. + bl.), 2 pp. (f.t. + bl.), [V]–X (Preface), [3]–16.

Copy: B.M. 1080 i 72 (h.t. lacking).

Sixth ed.: About the same title as the fifth ed. – – – – – The Sixth Edition. London; Printed from the Original Copy from Dublin, and Sold by A. Moore near St. Paul's. M.DCC.XXII. Price Four-Pence.

8vo (in fours); A–C⁴ — 2 pp. (h.t. + bl.), 2 pp. (f.t. + bl.), V–X (Preface), 11–24.

Copies: B.M. 12331 C 19, Yale, and Penn.

1655. In 1725 Ambrose Philips wrote a poem on Lord Carteret's eldest daughter, which induced several persons in London and Dublin to write imitations and parodies in ridicule of Philips's style of poetry.

(1) Ambrose Philips's Poem (or Ode?) on Miss Carteret.

(2) A Poem sent from London, in imitation, on Miss Hervey of a day old, in Dublin thought to be by Pope (see *Corresp.*, III, 292 n.).

(3) A New Poem Ascrib'd To the Honourable Miss Carteret. Dublin, R. Dickson, and E. Ne[e]dham. N. D. Sm. folio; one page (two columns).

(4) A Lady's Answer to Mr. Ambrose Philips's Poem. Dublin, printed in the year 1725. Folio; π⁴, including half-title. Dobell cat. 105, item 227.

(5) A New Poem (No. 3) and A Lady's Answer (No. 4) printed together on recto and verso of a folio half-sheet. No imprint.

(6) A New Poem ascrib'd to the Lady who wrote An Answer to Mr. Philips's Poem on Miss C—t.

923. (7) Namby Pamby. Or, A Panegyric on the New Versification address'd to A – – – P – – – Esq; &c. By Capt. Gordon, Author of the Apology for Parson Alberony, and the Humourist. — Folio; 1 page (2 columns). — Written, by Henry Carey or Swift, in ridicule of Ambrose Philips's style of poetry. Cf. *Corresp.* III, 292; and Elr. Ball, *Swift's Verse*, 202.

Copy: B.M. 93 gm 23 (186).

Also in: A Learned Dissertation On Dumpling; Its Dignity, Antiquity, and Excellence. &c. The Third Edition. London, J. Roberts, &c. 1726. — 8vo; 4 pp., 1–25, 4 pp. (*Namby Pamby*), 2 pp., 1 p.

Copy: Penn.

[Pudding and Dumpling Burnt to Pot. Or, A Compleat Key To The Dissertation On Dumpling. &c. London: A. Dodd, &c. M.DCCXXVII. — 8vo; 4 pp., I–IX + bl., 11–30, 1 p. *Advertisement to the Curious* + bl. — This *Advertisement* says that the author is hard at work on a treatise, entitled: Truth brought to light, or D—n S—t's Wilsden Prophecy unfolded; being a full Explanation of a Prophetical Poem, called Namby Pamby, which, by most People, is taken for a Banter on an eminent Poet, now in Ireland; when in Fact, it is a true Narrative of the Siege of Gibraltar, the Defeat of the Spaniards, and Success of the British Arms. &c.]

Also in: Pudding and Dumpling Burnt to Pot. &c. The Second Edition. To which is added, D—n S—t's Wilsden Prophecy; vulgarly called Namby Pamby: With an Explanation of the same, proving it to be &c. London: A. Dodd, &c. 1727. — 8vo; 2 pp., I–IX + bl., 11–30, 1 p. (*A Full Explanation Of D— S—s Wilsden Prophecy*), 32–7 (*Namby Pamby*), 1 p. (*The Lara Cor Prophecy*).

(8) Namby Pamby's / Answer to / Captain Gordon. / — / *Goosy Goosy Gander* / Where *shall I Wander*. / —.

Folio; one page (2 columns). — Begins: Nymphlings three, and three, and three,

Copy: B.M. 839 m 23 (185).

(9) Namby Pamby's / Lamentation, / For the Departure of Mr. No. body.

Folio; one page (2 columns). — Begins: Must He then alass depart, Copy: B.M. 839 m 23 (184).

(10) Mocking is Catching, or a Pastoral Lamentation for the Loss of a Man and no Man, in the simple style, by the Author of Namby Pamby. London, printed and Dublin re-printed by George Faulkner, 1726. Folio half-sheet. (cat. Dobell 105, item 229).

(11) A / Satyr / To / The *Author* of *Namby Pamby*, / Address'd to *Amb. P — — p*'s Esq; / — / By a Lady / —.

Folio; one page (2 columns).
At foot of page:

Printed in the Year MCCDXXVI. [*sic*].

Copy: T. C. D. Press A7.6 (21).

924. (12) A Christmas Box for Namby Pamby, Or, A second part to the same Tune. &c. — Narrow folio; 1 page.
Cf. Elr. Ball, *Swift's Verse*, 202.

652. (13) A / Poem / Upon R—r a Lady's Spaniel.

Folio; 1 page (2 columns).
Also in:
Mist's Weekly Journal for Saturday, July 2, 1725.
Note:
'Namby Pamby' was written by Henry Carey or by Swift. The *T.L.S.*, Dec. 7, 1933, contains an article by Mary Segar, who thinks "that there is some reason to suppose the nickname Namby Pamby was invented by Swift".

Elr. Ball (Corresp., III, 292 n.) says that the Poem sent from London (see No. 2 above) cannot be 'Namby Pamby', as hitherto thought, because there is no mention of Miss Hervey in it.

'A Christmas Box for Namby Pamby, Or, A second part to the same Tune', and 'A Poem Upon R—r a Lady's Spaniel' have been ascribed to Swift.

Cf. Elr. Ball, *Swift's Verse*, 202; *Corresp.*, III, 278–9, 281, 292, 294–5, 316; Williams, 270–1 n., 1124–6.

932. A Letter To the Bishop of M. by Dr. Sw—t, being a faithful Inventory of the Furniture of a certain Gentleman in T. C. &c. Dublin: George Faulkner, 1726. — Sm. folio; 2 pages.
[On verso there is: A New Ballad In Praise of the Ancient and Loyal City of Londonderry] — Copy: Penn.

927. A History of Poetry, In a Letter to a Friend. By the Rev[d.] D — — — — S — — — — t. Dublin: E. Waters, 1726. — Folio; 2 pages. — Copy: T. C. D.

938. Considerations On Two Papers Lately Published. The First, called, Seasonable Remarks, &c. And the other, An Essay on Trade in General, and on That of Ireland, in Particular. Dublin: Printed in the Year 1728. — 8vo; 1–16.

The *Seasonable Remarks* and the *Essay* are supposed to have been written by Sir John Browne; they were answered by the *Considerations*, possibly by Swift. To this Sir John Browne replied in *An Appeal*; it was followed by *A Letter* (see No. 939, *post*), possibly by Swift. All five were reprinted together in:
A Collection Of Tracts, Concerning the Present State of Ireland, &c. London: T. Woodward and J. Peele. MDCCXXIX. — 8vo; 4 pp., 1–46, 8 pp., 47–144. (sheets P and Q are wrongly paged 121–8, and 113–20, which should be 113–20, and 121–8).
Copy: Penn.

939. A Letter In Answer To a Paper, intitled, An Appeal To the Reverend Dean Swift. By the Author of Considerations on Two Papers, &c. Dublin: Thomas Hume, 1728. — 8vo; 1–16. — Copy: T. C. D.
Also in: A Collection Of Tracts, &c. (see No. 938, *ante*).
Also in: Reflections Little to the Purpose, On A Paper Less to the Purpose. By the Author of Seasonable Remarks. &c. Dublin: S. Powell, etc., 1729. — 8vo; I–VIII, 1–72.
There was also A Reply To the Observer on Seasonable Remarks (see Wagner No. 93) — unless it is the same as An Appeal, B.M. 8245 b 92 (3).
Cf. Wagner, Nos. 89–95, 102, 117.
Cf. Browne's letter to Swift, *Corresp.*, IV, 24.

944. A Poem By D—S—. On The Scheme Propos'd to the People of Ireland. Humbly Address'd to the Skilfull and Ingenious Mr. Maculla, &c. Dublin: Thomas Walsh. — 12mo; 1–8. — Copy: U. L. C.

953. The Session of the Critics: Or, The Contention For the Nettle. A Poem. To which is added, &c. With the following Miscellanies, viz. I. On a Thanksgiving, which happened just before Lent. By Dean Swift. II. &c. London: Cooper, &c. [ca. 1730]. — Folio.

958. An Infallible Scheme To pay the Publick Debt Of This Nation In Six Months. Humbly offered to the Consideration of the present P——t. &c. Printed in the Year 1731. —
Very sm. 8vo size; no signatures — 2 pp. (t. + bl.), [3]–16.
Copy: Forster 34 A 25.

Another ed.: ——————— By D—n S—t. &c. Dublin, Printed. London, Reprinted for H. Whittridge, &c. MDCCXXXII. —
8vo (in fours); [A]–C⁴ — 2 pp. (t. + bl.), [3]–23 + bl.
Copy: Bodl.
Also in: Schemes From Ireland, For The Benefit of the Body Natural, Ecclesiastical, and Politick. &c. Dublin Printed: London, Reprinted for J. Roberts &c. MDCCXXXII. — 8vo; 1–31 (advs. on verso).

959. A Scheme Humbly offer'd, for making R—n and the C—y useful. &c. Printed in the Year MDCCXXXI. —
Sm. 8vo (in fours); π⁴, B–C⁴ — 2 pp. (t. + bl.), [3]–22, 2 pp. (Advertisement + Errata).
Copy: Forster 34 A 25.
Also in: Schemes From Ireland, &c. (see No. 958, *ante*).
Also in: Reason Against Coition. &c. London: H. Hook, and the Booksellers of London and Westminster. 1732. — 8vo; 1–64.
Also in: D ———— n Sw ———— t's Medley. &c. Dublin Printed: London Re-printed, and sold by the Booksellers in Town and Country. — 12mo; 1–120.

1656. Count Piper's Packet: / Being a Choice and Curious / Collection / Of / Manuscript Papers, / In Prose and Verse; / That were found bundled under a Bench upon *Duke* / *Humphry's Walk* in *St. James's Park*, on *Tuesday* / the First of *August* 1732, by a Pensioner of *Chelsea-* / *Hospital*. / Containing (among many other Valuable Pieces, / never before Published) *viz*. / [14 titles in 2 columns divided by a single line of rule] / = / *London:* / Printed for T. Walton, in *Long-Acre:* And Sold by the Booksellers / and Pamphlet-Shops of *London* and *Westminster*. M.DCC.XXXII. / (Price One Shilling.)

8vo (in fours); π^1, B–H^4, I^3 — 2 pp. (t. + bl.), 1–62.
Copy: Bodl. — Possibly 'Collin's Complaint, Burlesqu'd. By D – – – – S – – – – –', pp. 33–96, is by Swift.
Cf. *Case*, 375.

1306. Milton Restor'd, And Bentley Depos'd. Containing, I. Some Observations on Dr. Bentley's Preface. II. His various Readings and notes on Paradise Lost, – – – III. Paradise Lost, Attempted in Rime, Book I. Addressed to Dr. Bentley, From Dean Swift. – – – Numb. I. – – – London: E. Curll—1732.
8vo; I–VIII, 9–29 (adv. on verso).
Copy: Bodl. G. Pamph. 396 (4).
Probably refers to Bentley's edition of 'Paradise Lost.'

969. The Ladies Lottery: Or, A New Scheme For A Ten Thousand Pound Fortune. Written by Dean Swift. &c. Dublin printed: London Re-printed, and sold by Mrs. Dodd &c. — 8vo; 1–62. A folding leaf between pp. 16–17. — From Dobell's cat. 105, item 255, who says that it is impudently described on the t.p. as "Written by Dean Swift", whereas, in fact, it is the following tract with a new t.p.: A Scheme for a New Lottery, or a Husband and Goad for Forty Shillings, by an Old Sportsman. Printed for T. Dormer, 1732.

973. A Panegyrical Poem on the Horn-Book. With a surprizing Satire upon a very surprizing Lord, Written by Dr. Swift.
[Announced by Curll and others in The Daily Journal of Feb. 24, 1733].

1657. The Christian Poet – – – To which is added, – – – A Birth-Day Poem, by Dean Swift. – – – London: Booksellers in Town and Country. 1735. 'A Birth-Day Poem' is on pp. 43–4.
Cf. *Case*, 339.

975. Ub— Bub— A— Boo: Or, The Irish-Howl. In Heroic Verse. By Dean Swift. London: J. James, and the Booksellers of London and Westminster, MDCCXXXV. — 8vo; 2 pp., 1–39 + bl.
Cf. Elr. Ball, *Swift's Verse*, 298.
Dobell, cat. 16 (1936) mentions another edition, 1735, 8vo, 1–55 + bl. (A to G in fours).

978. A New Proposal For the better Regulation and Improvement of Quadrille. &c. Dublin: Printed by George Faulkner in Essex-street. 1736. — Folio; 2 pages.
Another ed. (4to, a half-sheet): Same title and collation, but no imprint. — Copy: Penn.
Also in: S—t contra omnes. (No. 752, *ante*).

Cf. Wilde, *The Closing Years Of Dean Swift's Life*, 1849, p. 178, note b, and Elr. Ball, *Swift's Verse*, 291–2. This piece was written by Bishop Josiah Hort (see No. 913, *ante*), but it would seem that Swift induced Faulkner to insert two paragraphs in ridicule of Bettesworth, with the intention to annoy both Hort and Bettesworth together.

983. The Humours of the Age: Or, Dean Swift's New Evening-Post. &c. Numb. I. (To be continued Weekly). London: J. Wright &c. — 4to; 1–4 (dated on p. 2: From the Bath, October 15, 1738.).

984. Memoirs Of the Extraordinary Life, Works, And Discoveries Of Martinus Scriblerus. By Mr. Pope, Dublin: George Faulkner. M.DCC.XLI. — 12mo (in sixes); π^1, a⁶, B–P⁶ — 2 pp. (t. + bl.), [1]–12 (Introduction), 1–165, 1 p. Contents, 2 pp. blank. — Contains 17 chapters. — Appeared first in Pope's Works, Vol. II, 1741 (Griffith 529), where we find chapters I–XII, XIV–XVII.
Copy: Nat. Libr. of Ireland.
French translation in: Histoire De Martinus Scriblerus, &c. (No. 607, *ante*).

783. The / History / Of / *Martin.* / Being / A Proper Sequel to *The Tale of a Tub.* / With / A Digression concerning the Nature, / Usefulness, and Necessity of Wars and Quar- / rels. / — / By the Rev. D—n S—t. / — / *Not sparing his own Clergy Cloth,* / *But eats into it like a Moth.* / — / To which is added, / A Dialogue between *A — — — P — — e,* / Esq; and Mr. *C — — — s, C — — — ffe,* Poets, / in St. *James's Park.* / — / *London:* / Printed for T. Taylor, at the *Rose,* in *Exeter-* / *Exchange.* MDCCXLII.

8vo (in fours); π^2, B–C⁴, C² — 2 pp. (h.t. + advs. on verso), 2 pp. (f.t. + bl.), [5]–24.
2 pp. (t. + bl.), 3–8.
Copy: Bodl. (Godw. Pamph. 1911–1).
For the first time printed as an addition to the 1720 ed. of the *Tale* in *Misc. Works, Com. & Div.* (No. 17, *ante*); then also in the 1734 ed. (No. 235, *ante*).

784. *Another issue:*
The / History / Of / Martin. / Giving / An Account of his Departure from Jack, / and their setting up for themselves, on which / Account they were oblig'd to travel and meet / many Disasters, finding no Shelter near Pe- / ter's Habitation: Martin succeeds in the / North, Peter thunders against Martin / for the Loss of the Large Revenue he used to / receive from thence. Harry Huff sent / Martin a Challenge to fight, which he re- / ceiv'd; Peter rewards Harry for the pre- / tended Victory, which encourag'd Harry to / huff Peter also. With many other extraor- / dinary Adventures of the said Martin in se- / veral Places with many considerable Persons. / With / A Digression concerning the Nature, Useful- / ness, and Necessity of Wars and Quar- / rels. / — / By the Rev. D—n S—t. / — / To which is added, / A Dialogue between *A — — — P—e,* Esq; and / Mr. *C—s C—ffe,* Poets, in St.

James's Park. | — | *London:* | Printed for J. Temple, near *St. Dunstans Church, Fleet-* | [rest cut off]

8vo; 2 pp. (t. + bl.), 5–24.

The above is the B.M. copy (1080 i. 25 (6)); the Bodl. copy (Godw. Pamph. 1999 (22)) is even more shaved. Neither has a half-title. Pp. 5–24 are exactly the same printing as pp. 5–24 of the first issue; only the title is new.

985. Etwas vor alle Menschen Oder Allgemeine Druck-Fehler, so in der Welt passiren, und klüglich zu verbessern sind, von D. Swifft. Aus dem Englischen ins Teutsche übersetzt. Gedruckt nach dem Leipziger Exemplar. &c. Franckfurt 1749. — 4to; 1–8. — Copy: Penn. [Spurious].

986. D. Swiffts Schertz- und ernsthaffte Lebens-Regeln, Nach Art seiner Druck-Fehler, Aus dem Englischen ins Teutsche übersetzt. Gedruckt nach dem Leipziger Exemplar. Franckfurt 1749. &c. — 4to; 1–8. — Copy: Penn. [Spurious].

987. Dean Swift's Ghost, To The Citizens of Dublin. Concluding with a Word particularly to the Weavers. Dublin: Printed in the Year 1749. — 8vo; 1–8. [Different from No. 982, *ante*] — Copy: Penn.

991. Some Account Of The Irish. By the late J. S. D. D. D. S. P. D. &c. London: M. Cooper. M.DCC.LIII.

8vo (in fours);   ⁴, B⁴ — 2 pp. (t.t. + Advertisement), 2 pp. (f.t. + bl.), [5]–15 + bl.

1644. Observations on the Religion of Nations, particularly the Religion of England. By Dr. Jonathan Swift, Dean of St. Patrick's, Dublin. Dublin: Printed by George Faulkner. M.DCC.LXVIII.

994. The Progress Of Law and Justice. A Tale. By The Late Dean Swift. &c. Dublin: Printed For The Editor. M.DCC.LXXVI. — 4to; 2 pp. (t. + Adv. on verso), [3]–8. — Copy: Penn.

995. Das Taschenbuch für Kosmopoliten und Denker aus einem alten Manuscript des berühmten Satirikers Swift aus dem Englischen übersezt von einem gewesenen preuszischen Offizier. Halle, 1789. — Sm. 8vo; 2 pp. (t. + bl.), 4 pp. (Nachricht des Uebersetzers), 7–113, 3 pp. (Inhalt). Copy: Penn. [Spurious].

BIOGRAPHY AND CRITICISM, 1709–1895

✠✠

1032. The Ballance Of Power; or, a Comparison of the Strength of the Emperor and the French King. 1709. — 8vo; 15 pp. — Contains references to Swift.

1038. Remarks Upon the Present Negotiations of Peace Begun between Britain and France. — 8vo. — Contains, on p. 23, a bitter attack on Swift. [Dr. Barnard's cat. 166, item 220].

1073. Plot upon Plot: A Ballad. &c. — Folio; 1 page. — This deals with the so-called 'Bandbox Plot' (see *Journal to Stella*, Nov. 15, 1712), and contains an attack on Swift.
Also in: A Pill to purge State-Melancholy, &c. London, 1715. — 12mo; I–XII, 1–164. — The Third Edition, with Additions. London, R. Burleigh, 1716. — 12mo; I–XII, 1–168.
Also in Vol. II of: Political Ballads Of The Seventeenth And Eighteenth Centuries, W. W. Wilkins, 2 vols., London, Longman &c., 1860.

1081. An Hue and Cry After Doctor S – – t; Occasion'd by a True and Exact Copy of Part of his own Diary, found in his Pocket-Book, &c. To which is added a Poem, To Robert Earl of Oxford, &c. London: J. Roberts, 1714. — 8vo; 1–23 + bl. (no h.t.). — Copy: Nat. Libr. of Scotl.
Second ed.: Same title, with the omission of 'To which is added a Poem, &c.'. — Instead of the 'Poem' the text has 'A Copy of Verses fastn'd to the Gate of St. P——'s C——h D——r, on the Day of the I——t of a certain D—n.' [by Smedley] added, but it is not mentioned in the title. — 8vo; 1–23 + bl. (h.t. before f.t.). — Copies: Bodl., and Penn.
Third ed.: Same title as that of the second. — 8vo; 1–23, 1 p. advs. (practically the same printing as that of the second ed.). — Copy: Penn.
Another third ed.: An Hue and Cry After The Examiner Dr. S—t. [rest as in the second ed.] — 8vo; 1–15 + bl. — Copies: Nat. Libr. Dublin, and J. Barry Brown, Esq.
I have not seen copies of the fourth and fifth editions.
Sixth ed.: Same title and collation as those of the [second] third edition. — Copy: T. C. D.
Another edition: An Hue and Cry After The Examiner. Dr. S – – – – – – t. &c. To which is added A Copy of Verses fasten'd to the Gate of St. P—'s C—h D—r, on the Day of I—t of a certain D—n. London: Printed in the Year, 1727. — 8vo; 1–15 + bl. — Copies: B.M., and Penn.

882. I. A / Genuine Epistle / From / *M—w P—r*, Esq; at *Paris,* / To the Reverend / *J—n S—t*, D.D. at *Windsor.* / With A / Letter / To / Sir *Patrick Lawles,* / Late the Pretender's Nuncio. / By an unknown Hand. / — / *Publish'd from the Original Manuscripts,* / *By* Timothy Brocade, / Late Author of the Examiner. / — / [2 lines of Latin] / — / *London:* / Anno Salutis M.DCC.XIV. / *Price* 6 *d.*

At foot of p. 20:

Printed for *A. Boulter*, without *Temple-Bar*.

8vo (in fours); π^4, B^4, C^2 — 2 pp. (t. + bl.), 2 pp. (Advertisement by the Publisher + bl.), 5–20.
Copy: Penn.
Later another pamphlet was added, bearing no individual title, but caption title only:

An / Ode / To The / Pretender. / Inscrib'd to Mr. Lesley and Mr. Pope.

8vo (in fours); B^4, C^4, C^2 — 1–19 + bl.
Copy: Yale (wrongly bound), Penn.
The first part contains *A Genuine Epistle* and *A Letter*, the second *An Ode* and *Mortimer His Fall*.
This is Case, 273b.

II. — / A Farther / Hue and Cry / After Dr. *Sw* – – – – *t*. / Being / A Collection of Curious Pieces / found since his Departure. / — / *Price* 6d.

8vo (in fours); π^1; π^4, B^4, C^2; A^4, B^3 — 2 pp. (above title + bl.); 2 pp (title: A Genuine Epistle + bl.), 2 pp. (Advertisement by the Publisher + bl.), 5–20; 1–13 + bl.
This is the first part of I (same printing), followed by a reprint of the second part of I (again caption title only). The title: 'A Farther Hue and Cry', derived from the earlier title: 'An Hue and Cry', was printed as B 4 of the second part, and placed in front by way of general title.
Copies: Yale, and Penn.

III. A Farther / Hue and Cry / After Dr. *Sw* – – – – *t*. / Being / A Collection of Curious Pieces / found since his Departure. / *Viz.* / I. A Genuine Epistle from *M—w P—r*, Esq; / at *Paris*, to the Rev^d Dr. *J—n Sw—t* at *Windsor:* / II. Smut's Epitaph. / III. A Letter to Sir Patrick Lawless, late / the Pretender's Nuncio. / IV. An Ode to the Pretender, written by / several Hands in *Greenwich* Park. / V. Earl Mortimer's Fall. A Fragment. / *Publish'd from the Original Manuscripts*, / *By* Timothy Brocade, Esq; / Late Author of the Examiner. / — / [2 lines of Latin] / — / The Second Edition. / — / *London:* / Printed for A. Boulter. MDCCXIV. / *Price 6d.*

8vo (in fours); π^1; A^4, B^4; 2 A^4; 2 B^3 — 2 pp. (h.t. + bl.); 2 pp. (above title + bl.), [3]–16; 1–13 + bl.
The half-title reads:

— / A Farther / Hue and Cry / After Dr. *Sw* – – – – – *t*. / Being / A Collection of Curious Pieces / found since his Departure. / — / *Price* 6d.

This is a reprint of the first part of I or II, followed by a reprint of the second part of II. The half-title was printed as B 4. As the general title shows, there is one more poem, *Smut's Epitaph* (for the name of *Smut*, see No. 1086).
Copy: Yale.
This is Case, 273c.

886. Dr. S – – – – – – 's Real Diary; Being A True and Faithful Account of himself, for that Week, wherein he is Traduc'd by the Author of a scandalous and malicious Hue and Cry after him: Containing, His entire Journal, from the Time he left London, to his Settling in Dublin. &c. London, R. Burleigh, 1715. — 8vo; 12 pp., 1–26.

Another issue:
888. Saint Patrick's Purgatory: Or, Dr. S – – – t's Expostulation With his Distressed Friends in the Tower and elsewhere. &c. London, R. Burleigh, MDCCXVI. — 8vo; 12 pp.; 10 pp., 1–26. — The title concerns only the first 12 pages. The rest (10 pp., 1–26) is: Dr. S – – – – – – – 's Real Diary &c., 1715 (see No. 886, *ante*), from which the leaf bearing title has been cut away.

Another issue:
888A. Dr. S—'s Real Diary; &c. London Printed: And Re-printed in Dublin, 1715.
[Title within single-lined frame.]
Sm. 8vo; [A]–C^4, D 1–2 — 2 pp. (t. + bl.), 7 pp. (Dedication), 1–15 (Diary), 15–17 (Verses 'The Fox and the Goat'), 17 (Conclusion).
Copy: J. Barry Brown.

1084. A Prefatory Epistle Concerning some Remarks To be published on Homer's Iliad: Occasioned by The Proposals of Mr. Pope towards a new English Version of that Poem. To the Reverend Dr. Swift, Dean of St. Patrick's. By Richard Fiddes, &c. London, John Wyat &c., 1714. — 16mo; 1–120. — Written to ingratiate himself with Pope and Swift.

1085. A Strange, Unprecedented and Unheard-of Apparition, &c. By Patrick Swift-Sight, D. D. London, R. Burleigh, 1714. — 8vo; 1–19 + bl. — Copy: U.L.C.

1086. The Enigmatical Court, &c. Part I. London, J. Baker, 1714. — 8vo; 4 pp., 3–21 + bl. — Contains a character of Swift under the pseudonym of 'Smut'. — Copy: Penn.

1086A. *Dublin edition:*
– – – – London Printed; And Reprinted in Dublin, for G. Risk, Bookseller at the London in Dames-street, over-against the Horse-Guard, 1714.
Sm. 8vo in fours; [A]–B^4 — 2 pp. (t. + bl.), 3 pp. + bl. (A List, mentioning Swift by name), 5–16.
Copy: J. Barry Brown, Esq.

1087. The Ox roasted And The Bull baited. On the Examiner's Supporters, called Ox and Bull. — Folio; 1 page. — Contains a criticism on Swift.

1088. The Immorality of the Priesthood: being an Historical Account of the Factious and Insolent Behaviour of the Inferior Clergy, Ever since the Reformation. J. Roberts. 1715 — 8vo. — Contains a bitter attack on Swift.

1090. The Ode-Maker. A Burlesque on the Dean of Kil—a's Ode to the Right Honourable the Earl of Ca—n. T. Warner, 1719. — Folio; 8 pp. — Contains an appeal to the Dean of Killala, Jonathan Smedley, to stop his 'Ode'

14*

making, but rather tell the world what Swift is doing, after which six stanzas relating to Swift follow.

Also an 8vo edition: London Printed, and reprinted in Dublin, 1719. Copy: Rothschild, 2216.

1091. The Tickler, No. III, 1719. — Sm. 4to; 20 pages. — Contains: Mr. Lewis of Covent Garden, his letter to Jonathan Swift. — From Dobell's cat. 379, item 619.

894. A Dedication To A Great Man, Concerning Dedications. &c. London: James Roberts, 1718. — 8vo; 1–32. — Copy: Guildhall.

[Wrongly attributed to Swift, who disclaimed it (*Corresp.* III, 116 n 4); the author seems to be Thomas Gordon, writer of 'The Independent Whig.' (See No. 900.)]

Second, third, fourth, sixth and seventh editions: Practically the same titles and collations as those of the first. I have not seen a copy of the fifth ed. From the fourth ed., the year is 1719. — Copy, 6th ed.: Penn.

Dublin ed.: – – – – – – The Sixth Edition Corrected. With a Preface. Dublin: James Carson, for Joseph Leathley, 1719. — 8vo; 1–24.

French translation: Dédicace-Critique Des Dédicaces, &c. Traduite sur la septiéme Edition de l'Anglois, du fameux M. Swifte. Imprimé à Roüen, & se vend A Paris, Chez François Barois, M.DCC.XXVI. — 18mo; 12 pp., 1–70. — Copy: Bibl. Nat. Paris.

Answered by:

1092. A Letter To the Reverend Mr. Dean Swift, Occasion'd by a Satire Said to be written by Him, Entitled, A Dedication to a Great Man, concerning Dedications. &c. London, James Roberts, 1719. — 8vo; 1–22. — Cf. No. 894, *ante.*

1094. The Invitation In Imitation of Horace's Epistle to Torquatus. – – – – – Written by Mr. T. S – – – to D – – – r S – – –. Dublin, 1720. — Folio; 1 page. — This is an invitation to dinner from Sheridan to Swift.

1095. Poems Upon Several Occasions. By the Author of, The Match at Foot-Ball. [i.e. Matthew Concanen] Dublin, A. Rhames, for E. Dobson, 1722. — 8vo. — Contains a poem 'In Vindication of the Modern Poets', in which Swift is mentioned.

1096. A Letter From the Quidnunc's At St. James's Coffee-House and the Mall, London, To their Brethren at Lucas's Coffee-House, in Dublin. &c. — Folio; 2 pages. — Dobell cat. 105, item 217.

1626. A / Letter / From / *A Young* Lady, / To the Rev^d. D – – – – n *S* – – – – *t.* / — / *Presenti tibi matures largimur Honores.* / — / [ornament] / — / Printed in the Year 1724.

8vo; 1–8.
Copy: Nat. Libr. of Ireland, Dublin.

1125. The Present State Of Ireland Consider'd: In a Letter to The Revd. Dean Swift. By a True Patriot. Dulce & decorum est pro Patria mori. Hor. Printed in the Year, 1724. — Sm. 8vo; [A]⁴ — 1 p. (title), [2]–8. — Copy: T.C.D. Pp. 15 (5).

1197. An Express From Parnassus, To the Reverend Dr. Jonathan Swift Dean of St. Patrick's. [1724?] — Folio; 2 pages. — Copy: Forster.

1198. Tom Pun-Sibi Metamorphosed; or, The Giber Gibb'd. &c. Dublin, Printed in the Year 1724. — Folio; 1 page. — Contains an attack on Swift, probably by Smedley.

Answered by:
1628. The Rivals. A Poem. Occasion'd by Tom Punsibi, Metamorphos'd, &c. — Folio; 2 pages (single columns) — Copy: T.C.D. Press A7.6 (26).

1199. The Battle Of The Poets. An Heroick Poem. In Two Canto's. &c. London, J. Roberts, 1725. — Folio; 1–20. — Swift and others are attacked in this poem. The author is Thomas Cooke.

Another edition:
London Printed And Dublin Reprinted and sold by George Faulkner at the Pamphlet-shop in Essex-street opposite to the Bridge 1731.
2 pp. (t. + bl.), 2 pp. (Prologue, Dramatis Personae), [5]–16.
Copy: J. Barry Brown, Esq.
Reprinted, with alterations, in:
Tales, Epistles, Odes, Fables, etc. by Thomas Cooke; T. Green, 1729.

Also in:
Original Poems — by Thomas Cooke; 1742.

1202. Trinity Colledge Vindicated. Or A Short Defence, Of The Reverend Dean Swift. By S. O——s, L. S. Dublin, Printed by G. N. opposite the Bear in Crane-Lane, 1725. — Folio; 1 page. — This is an answer to Smedley's *A Satyr*, &c., by Swift's henchman Samuel Owens, a locksmith (see No. 651, *ante*).

1203. A Scourge For the Author of the Satyr, Gibing on Trinity College, and on the Reverend Dean Swift, Hibernia's Apollo; Presented To the Reverend Dean Smedley, with Remarks on his Petition to the Duke of G—ft—n. Written by S. O. L. S. Printed in the Year, 1725. — Folio; 1 page. — Another answer to Smedley, by Owens (see No. 651, *ante*).

1204. Satyr Satiris'd, An Answer To A Satyr on The Reverend D—n S—t. Infreta &c. — Sm. folio; 1 page. — Another answer to Smedley's *A Satyr*, &c. (see No. 651, *ante*).

1205. Advice from Fair[yland,] An Imitation of our Prese[nt Poets.] Inscrib'd To [The] Poetasters of Dublin. But more Particularly, several Reptiles of T. C. Being K. Oberon's Declaration. Dublin: Printed by G. N. and R. D. in Dame-Street. 1726. — Folio; 1 page. — B.M. copy mutilated. — An answer to the three preceding pieces (Nos. 1202–4, *ante*).

1206. An Essay On Gibing, With a Project for its Improvement. &c. Dublin: Thomas Thornton, 1725. — 8vo; 1–16.
Also in: *Miscellanea*, 1727, Vol. II (No. 24, *ante*).
[This may have something to do with No. 1203, *ante*.]

1207. A Poem To D — — — — — — — — S — — — — — — — Dublin: Printed in the Year 1724–5. — Sm. folio; 1 page.

1208. A Second Poem, To Dr. Jo—n S—t. &c. Dublin: Printed in the Year. MDCCXXV — Folio; 1 page.

1209. A Congratulary [*sic*] Poem To The Reverend Daen [*sic*] Swift. By Robert Ashton. &c. Dublin: Printed 1725. — Folio; 1 page.

1210. A Congratulary [*sic*] Poem On Dean Swift's Return to Town. By a Member of the Club, held at Mr. Taplin's in Truck-street, October, 7th. 1725. &c. Dublin: Printed in the Year, 1725. — Folio; 1 page.

1211. A Poem Delivered to the Reverend Doctor Swift, Dean of St. Patrick's, Dublin; By a Young Nobleman, November 30. 1725. Being the Dean's Birth-Day. — Folio; 2 pages. — The 'Young Nobleman' seems to be Lord Orrery. Copy: Penn.

1212. An Epistle in behalf of our Irish Poets, to the Right Hon. Lady C[arteret]. Dublin, E. Needham, 1726. — Folio. — Swift and Delany are mentioned in it. — Dobell cat. 105, item 233.

1658. The Hotch-Potch Or, Favourite Fricasse'd: With a Ragoust of Spiders, Cow-heels, and Old Hat. Serv'd up in a Dish of Meditation. By Menasseh Ben Mirrash, Cook and Purveyor to the Sons of Parnassus. Printed for A. Moore, 1727.
8vo — Contains reference to Swift and 'Meditation On a Broomstick.' (P. M. Hill's cat. 38, item 226.)

1213. An Account Of The Journey-men Weavers grateful Congratulation of the Rev. Dr. Swift Dean of St. Patrick's safe Arrival, with his kind Answer, and Bounty to their Corporation. Sep. the 5th 1726. J. Gowan, 1726. — Folio; 2 pages (on the second page is: The Catch sung by the Journey-men Weavers, &c.). — Copy: U.L.C.

1214. A Poem On The Dean of St. Patrick's Birth-Day, Nov. 30th being St. Andrew's-Day. J. Gowan, 1726. — Folio; 1 page.

655. A young Lady's Complaint for the Stay of Dean *Swift* / in *England*.

Folio; 1 page.
At foot of page:

Dublin: Printed by George Faulkner in / Pembroke-Court Castle-street. 1726.

Copy: T.C.D. (Press A. 7.4. (86)).
Elr. Ball, *Swift's Verse*, 228, calls it doubtful.

1276. A Poem on the Birth-Day of Her late Majesty Queen Anne of Ever Glorious Memory. Dedicated to the Reverend Dean Swift. Writ by Rob. Ashton. 1726–7. — Taken from Elr. Ball, *Swift's Verse*, 333.

1277. Tom Punsibi's Letter To Dean Swift. Printed in the Year, 1727. — Folio; 1 page (2 columns). — Copy: T.C.D. Press A7.6 (24). — A satire on Sheridan's poverty when inviting Swift to his house.

1278. A Congratulatory Speech, Of the Loyal and Charitable Society of Woollen Broad-Cloath-Weavers, in Honour to the Reverend Doctor Jonathan Swift, Dean of St. Patrick's Dublin, upon his safe Arrival in this Kingdom, Spoken to his Reverence by William Beedem, Clerk of the said Society, the Fourth Day of October, One Thousand Seven Hundred and Twenty-Seven. — Folio; 1 page. — Copy: T.C.D.

1279. Postscript. Just arrived from Twickenham (as I am assured) Mr. Pope's Receipt to make Soup. For the Use of Dean Swift.

[Added to the 'Dedication' in *Atterburyana*, 1727 — see No. 24, *ante*.]

Also in: The Altar of Love, H. Curll, 1727 (3rd ed., 1731).

Also in: Mr. Pope's Literary Correspondence, Volume the Second, London, E. Curll, 1735. — 8vo and 12mo.

Attributed to Gay, and to Pope.

1659. An EPICK / POEM. / On the Renowned and never to be forgotten WILLIAM LEIGH, M.A. and Fellow of / St. *John*'s College in *Cambridge*, Who in the *Anno Christi* 1589. and in the Thirty First Year / of the Reign of the Renowned Lady *Elizabeth*, Queen of *England*, Invented the most Mi- / sterious and most Beneficial Arts of Stocking-Frame-Making, and Stocking-Frame Knitting: / And also in Praise of the Loyal and Charitable Society of Stocking-Frame-Knitters of the City / and County of *Dublin*, Who in Honour to the Immortal Memory of their Founder, and for / the Promotion of Love and Charity, hath a Sermon Preach'd at St *Audeon*'s Church, in *Dublin*, / on Monday being the 30th. of *October*, 1727. / — / By Mr. *William O Brien*, S.M. / — / And most Humbly Dedicated to the Revd. *Jonathan Swift*, D.D. and Dean / of St. *Patrick*'s, Dublin. /

Single sheet, printed on both sides. Double column.
At foot:

/ — / *DUBLIN:* Printed by S. POWELL, in *Copper-Alley*, MDCCXXVII.

Copy: T.C.D. Press A, 7, 4, No. 213.

1280. Some Memoirs Of The Amours and Intrigues Of a Certain Irish Dean, &c. Part I. London, J. Roberts. — 8vo; 8 pp., 1–99 + bl. (at the end, on p. 99, the Second Part is promised).

– – – – – – Part II. London: J. Roberts, 1728. — 8vo; 8 pp., 1–68.

Both 'Parts' in R.I.A. Hal. Pamph. Vol. 79 (1–2). The B.M. has Part I only.

Third edition: Dublin, R. Dickson, MDCCXXX. (The Bodl. copy 270 f 192 has Part I only.)

1281. For 'An Appeal to the Reverend Dean Swift', and 'A Letter in answer to a Paper intitl'd, An Appeal to the Reverend Dean Swift', see Nos. 938 and 939, *ante*.

1282. The Weekly Journal: Or, The British Gazetteer. N° 153 Saturday, April 27, 1728. (B.M. Burney 267*b*.) — Contains a ballad, to the tune of the 'Soldier and the Sailor', in which Swift and others are satirized. (Cf. Elr. Ball, *Swift's Verse*, 215.)

1290. Sawney. An Heroic Poem. &c. London, J. Roberts, 1728. — 8vo; 2 pp., I–XVI, 1–45 + bl. — The author is James Ralph. Swift is abused on p. 20.

8vo (in fours); π^1, A⁴, a⁴, B–F⁴, G³ — 2 pp. (t. + bl.), [I]–XVI, [1]–45 + bl.

Copy: B.M. C116 b 2 (7).

1293. A letter from Dublin concerning the presentation of the Freedom of the City to Swift, Jan. 1729. In Numb. 5717 The Flying Post; Or, Post-Master. Thursday Mar. 19, 1730. Sold by J. Roberts &c. — Folio; 2 pages. Cf. No. 675, *ante.*

1296. The Inspir'd Poet, Or An Epistle To The Young Poets and Authors of the City of Dublin. Inscrib'd to the Reverend Dean Swift. &c. Dublin, 1730. — 16mo; 1–8. — Copy: Forster.

1297. Advice To a Certain Dean. &c. Printed in the Year, 1730. — Folio; 1 page.

1300. An Epistle To a certain Dean, Written Originally in Italian, by Carlo Monte Socio, &c. London: Printed, and Dublin re-printed in the Year 1730. — 12mo; 1–8.

1302. A Specimen Of Thought Upon The Gloomy Region: &c. – – – – By John Thomson. &c. – – – Dublin, M.DCC.XXXII. — 12mo; 2 pp., I–XLIV, 1–30. — Contains a poem (pp. III–IV) and a letter (p. V) to Swift. — Copy: Forster.

1303. The Spleen: A Poem. Humbly inscrib'd to a certain Dean. Printed in the Year, MDCCXXXII. — Folio; 2 pages. — Copy: Dobell cat. 105, item 254.

1308. Letters Concerning The English Nation. By Mr. De Voltaire. Translated from the French by John Lockman. London, C. Davis &c, MDCCXXXIII. — 8vo; 16 pp., 1–253 + bl., 18 pp. (*Index*). — The English version appeared before the French. Swift is mentioned in Letters XXII, XXIII and XXIV.
Further editions:
English: Dublin, Faulkner, 1733. — 12mo.
French: Basle, 1734. — 12mo.
French: Rouen, Jore, 1734.
French: Amsterdam, E. Lucas, 1734.
French: Amsterdam, 1735.
English: 1760. — 12mo. Lond. 1741, 2nd ed. Glasgow, 1752.

1309. The Upper Gallery, a Poem. Inscribed to the Revd. Dr. Swift, D. S. P. D. Dublin, George Faulkner, 1733. — Copy: Dobell cat. 90, item 86.

1629. The St. James's Evening Post. Numb. 3030. March 22–5, 1735, contains the story of a trick played by Dean Swift on some of his friends which ended unfavourably for himself.
(2) *Ibid.*, Numb. 3098. Aug. 28–30, 1735, contains: Dean Swift's Country Post.
(3) *Ibid.*, Numb. 4002. Sept. 6–9, 1735, contains the story of Dean Swift riding on the strand, and being in danger of being thrown from his horse by a clergyman shooting his gun too near him, in spite of Swift's warning.

1312. The Grand Accuser The Greatest of all Criminals. Part I. London: J. Roberts, 1735. — 8vo; 1–80. — Contains a defence of Marlborough, and an attack on the authors of the *Examiner* and the *Craftsman*, both very clever, but very dangerous, whom he considers to be the same person, i.e. Swift.
Copy: Penn.

1314. The Toast. An Heroick Poem In four Books, Written originally in Latin, By Frederick Scheffer: Now done into English, and illustrated with Notes and Observations, By Peregrine O Donald Esq; &c. Dublin: Printed. London: Reprinted in the Year MDCCXXXVI. — 4to; frontisp., I–LXVI, 2 pp.,

1–118, *113–*118, 119–232, 1 p. *music* + bl. — The first edition, entitled: 'The Toast, An Epic Poem In Four Books – – – – Vol. I., Dublin: Printed in the Year, 1732', 8vo, contained two 'Books' only, and no more was published at the time. — The author is Dr. William King, Principal of St. Mary Hall, Oxford. He and Swift probably got acquainted in 1734–5. When in 1736 the book was reprinted (see above), two 'Books' were added, the *Epistola Ad Cadenum* [i.e. Swift] was inserted (pp. III–XI), while references to Swift in the text and notes of Books III and IV (p. 81, &c.) also bore testimony to King's esteem for Swift. In 1747 the 1736 edition was re-issued. The year in the imprint was cleverly and almost invisibly altered by erasure. Leaf M 4 (pp. 87–8) was cancelled, and between pp. 86 and 89 were inserted nine leaves, marked *M (1–4), *N(1–4), and *O, and numbered 87–8, *89–*104. — See: *The Book Collector's Quarterly*, Number IV, Oct. 1931, pp. 29–56; and Harold Williams, *The Toast An Heroick Poem*, 1932 (Ye Sette Of Odd Volumes, No. XCIV).
Copy: Penn.

1315. The Dunciad. An Heroic Poem. To Dr. Jonathan Swift. &c. London, Lawton Gilliver, 1736. — Sm. 8vo; frontisp., 1–263 + bl. — Griffith mentions two variants, Nos. 405 and 406, the difference being in the frontisp. only. The inscription to Swift occurs on the title-page only. Apart from a few lines of praise in the beginning of the work, which had occurred almost from the first, there is nothing of the kind in the book itself.

1317. The Old Woman and her Goose. A Tale. Devised on Account of a certain late Project. Inscrib'd to the Revd. Jonathan Swift, D. D. D. S. P. D. Pa. Pat. &c. Dublin: Printed in the Year MDCCXXXVI. — 8vo; 1–8. — Copy: Penn.

979. A Curry-Comb of Truth for a certain Dean: Or, The Grub-street Tribunal. &c. Dublin: Printed in the Year MDCCXXXVI. — 8vo; no signatures — 1 p. (title), 2–8. (See *Poems*, 1137.)
Copy: Forster.
Also in: S—t contra omnes. (No. 752, *ante*.)

980. A Brush To The Curry-Comb of Truth, &c. Or, The Drapier. An Eclogue in Imitation of Virgil's Silenus. &c. Dublin: Printed in the Year MDCCXXXVI. — 8vo size; [A]⁴ — 2 pp. (t. + bl.), 3–8.
Copy: Forster.

1630. Some Reflections, Concerning the Reduction of Gold Coin in Ireland. Upon the Principles of the Dean of St. Patrick's and Mr. Lock: – – – – Dublin: Printed in the Year M,DCC,XXXVII.
8vo; [A]⁸ — 16 pages. — Copy: T.C.D. RR11.26 (12).
Wagner 177 has this note: "Recalls Swift's remarks in the Intelligencer, No. 19."

1631. The Lord Knows What, By the Lord knows Who.
Folio; 2 pages. — At the end: Meath-Street Printed: By the Lord Knows who, 1737. — Copy: Yale.
Wagner 178 says: "Various references to the Primate, Dean Swift and others. Opposes the reduction of the gold coin, which had just taken place."

982. A Collection Of Welsh Travels, And Memoirs of Wales, Containing I. The Briton Describ'd, or a Journey thro' Wales: Being a pleasant Relation of D—n S—t's Journey to that ancient Kingdom, &c. London: J. Torbuck &c. 1738. — 8vo; frontisp., 4 pp., VII–XV + bl., 1–64, 1–30, 1–15 (advs. on verso).

Another ed.: – – – – – – – London: J. Torbuck &c. (no year, but the titles of Nos. II and V in it, are dated 1742). — 8vo; 2 pp., 3 pp. + bl., III–VII + bl., 1–115 (advs. on verso).

Another ed.: – – – – – – – London: J. Torbuck &c. (no year, but the titles of Nos. II and V in it, are dated 1749). — 12mo; I–VIII, 1–111 + bl.

Another edition of "The Briton Describ'd" (different title): Dean Swift's Ghost. &c. London: J. Wilkinson. MDCCLIII. — 12mo; I–VI, 6 pp., 1–60. (Cf. No. 987.)

[This piece is not by Swift, but by William Richards (1643–1705), who, as a result of a journey into Wales in 1673, wrote: Wallography; Or The Britton Describ'd: Being A Pleasant Relation of A Journey into Wales, &c. London, Obadiah Blagrave, 1682. — 16mo; 14 pp., 1–127 + bl. — I noted a copy with a different imprint: London, Printed for Edward Caudell Bookseller in Bath, 1682.]

1318. Grobianus; Or, The Compleat Booby. An Ironical Poem. In Three Books. Done into English, from the Original Latin of Friderick Dedekindus, By Roger Bull, Esq; &c. London, T. Cooper, MDCCXXXIX. — 8vo; I–XVI, 1–276, 12 pp. (*Contents*). — Copy: Penn. — Contains a dedication to Swift. — The original poem was published at Frankfort in 1549.

1320. The Enthusiasm. A Poem. With a Character of Dr. Jonathan Swift. &c. – – – By Mr. P. H. Author of the Poet. Dublin, James Hoey, 1739. — 12mo; 1–7 + bl. — Copy: U.L.C.

1321. Lobschrifft des Lobes, Worinnen die besondern und höchstmerckwürdigen Begebenheiten und Zufälle des Lobes zu neuern Zeiten umständlich berühret, und die Glückseligkeit unserer Tage, die wir dem Lobe zu dancken, Aus der Neuern Weltweiszheit ausführlich erwiesen und Methodo Swifftiana dargethan wird, Von Apelles Post Tabulam. Franckfurth, Jena, Halle und Leipzig. 1739. — 12mo; 4 pp., 1–52. — Copy: own. — The author treats his subject after the method of Swift.

1322. The Dean And The Country Parson. An Imitation of the First Eclogue of Virgil. By Edward Lonergan. Dublin, E. Waters, 1739. — Sm. 4to; 16 pages (in Latin and English). — Copy: cat. Quaritch.

1323. Epistola Ad Franciscum Bindonem, Arm. Cui Adjiciuntur Quatuor Odae. Dublinii: Typis Georgii Faulkneri; MDCCXL. — 8vo; 1–56. — Copy: Gilbert Coll., Dublin. — Contains, in Latin and English, an Epistle to Bindon occasioned by his painting a picture of Swift, and praise of Swift himself.

Another edition: [same title] Authore Gulielmo Dunkin, A. M. – – – M,DCC,XLI. — 8vo; 1–56. — Copy: Penn.

1326. A Catalogue Of Books, The Library of the late Rev. Dr. Swift, Dean of St. Patrick's, Dublin. To be Sold by Auction. &c. Dublin: George Faulkner, MDCCXLV. — 8vo; 2 pp., 1–29 + bl. — The title does not say that it also contains a list of Dr. Francis Wilson's books (pp. 17–29). — Copies: Scott's library at Abbotsford, and one in possession of Mr. Harold Williams.

Dean Swift's Library With a Facsimile of the Original Sale Catalogue And Some Account of Two Manuscript Lists Of His Books By Harold Williams. Cambridge, 1932. — 8vo; I–VIII, 1–93, 3 pp. blank, 2 pp., 1–16 (350 copies).

1328. The Charter Of His Majesty King George II. For Erecting and Endowing St. Patrick's Hospital. Founded by the Last Will Of The Reverend Doctor Jonathan Swift. &c. Dublin: George Faulkner. M,DCC,XLVI. — 8vo; 1–15 + bl. — Copy: U.L.C.

Another ed.: − − − − − − Dublin: J. Jones. 1798. — 8vo; 1–16. — Copy: U.L.C.

1632. The Memoirs Of Mrs. Laetitia Pilkington, − − − Written by Herself. − − − With Anecdotes of several eminent Persons, Living and Dead. In Two Volumes. Vol. I. − − − Dublin: Printed for the Author, MDCCXLVIII.

8vo; [a]⁴, A–P⁸, Q⁴ — 2 pp. (t. + bl.), 2 pp. (Dedic. to Sir Robert King), V–VII + bl. (Preface), [1]–246, 2 pp. blank. Vol. II. (about the same title, only different quotations).

[A]–U⁸ — 2 pp. (t. + bl.), [III]–VIII (Dedication), [IX]–XVI (Preface), [1]–299, 5 pp. blank.

Copy: Nat. Libr. of Ireland.

1329. Memoirs Of Mrs. Laetitia Pilkington, − − − − − − Written by Herself. − − − − With Anecdotes of − − − − Dean Swift − − − − Dublin Printed; London Reprinted, R. Griffiths and G. Woodfall, 1748. —

8vo; 2 pp. (t. + bl.), 2 pp. (Dedication), V–VIII (Preface), [1]–302, 1 p. adv. concerning Vol. II + bl. — Copies: own, and Nat. Libr. of Ireland (lacking last leaf). — I have not seen Vol. II.

Reprinted: Vols. I–II, 12mo, 1749 (Dublin Printed: London Reprinted: R. Griffiths, 1749).

Re-issued: Vols. I–II, 1751 (The Third Edition. London: R. Griffiths, 1751.) — The same printing as Vols. I–II, 1749.

The Third and last Volume Of The Memoirs Of Mrs. Laetitia Pilkington, Written by Herself. − − − − With the Conclusive Part of the Life of the Inimitable Dean Swift. London: R. Griffiths, 1754. — 12mo; I–XXIII + bl., 1–268.

The Third and Last Volume − − − − − − London: Printed, and Dublin Reprinted in the Year MDCCLIV. Price a British Half Crown.

2 pp. (t. + bl.), [III]–XXIV, [1]–264, 2 pp. blank.

Copy: Nat. Libr. of Ireland.

Reprinted: Vols. I–II–III, 12mo, 1776 (Dublin: Printed By Peter Hoey, at the Mercury No. I, in Skinner-Row. M,DCC,LXX,VI.) —

2 pp. (t. + bl.), 2 pp. (Dedic.), [V]–VI (Preface), [7]–193 + bl.

2 pp. (t. + bl.), [5]–6 (Dedic.), 7–9 (To Sir Robert King), [X]–XIV (Preface), [1]–223 + bl.

2 pp. (t. + bl.), [I]–IV (Dedic.), [V]–XII (Preface), [1]–160.

Copies: Nat. Libr. of Ireland, and own.

For a selection from Mrs. Pilkington's *Memoirs*, see No. 102.

Reprint of Mrs. Pilkington's 3 vols. in 1: Memoirs of Mrs Letitia Pilkington 1712–50 Written by Herself With an Introduction by Iris Barry. George Routledge and Sons, Ltd. London. [1928] (The English Library Edited by J. Isaacs). — 8vo; I–VIII, 1–487 + bl. Frontisp. and 6 plates.

Copy: Penn.

1332. Memoirs Of The Life And Writings Of Jonathan Swift, D. D. Dean of St. Patrick's, Dublin. &c. London: J. Cooper, M,DCC,LII.

12mo (in sixes); π¹, A–K⁶, L⁴ — 2 pp. (t. + bl.), 3–129 (Errata on verso).

Copy: Forster (17 B 47).

1333. Remarks On The Life and Writings Of Dr. Jonathan Swift, Dean of St. Patrick's, Dublin, In a Series of Letters From John Earl of Orrery To his Son, the Honourable Hamilton Boyle. &c. London, A. Millar, MDCCLII. — 8vo; frontisp. portrait of Swift by B. Wilson, 2 pp., 1–339 + bl., 9 pp. (*Index*) + bl. [L 7 cancelled, and a new leaf substituted]. — There are also copies on large and thick paper. Copy: Penn.

Second Edition, Corrected. London: A. Millar, M.DCC.LII. — 12mo; frontisp. portrait of Swift by Ravenet, 2 pp., 1–214, 8 pp. (*Index*).

Third Edition, Corrected. London: A. Millar, M.DCC.LII. — Same collation as second ed., with 2 pp. advs. at the end. — Copies: U.L.C., and own.

Fourth Edition. London, A. Millar, M.DCC.LII. — 8vo; frontisp. portrait of Swift by B. Wilson, 2 pp., 1–321 + bl., 9 pp. (*Index*) + bl. — There are also copies on large and thick paper. — Copies: Forster, T.C.D., and Penn.

Fifth Edition. London, A. Millar, M.DCC.LII. — 12mo; frontisp. portrait of Swift by Ravenet, 2 pp., 1–240, 10 pp. (*Index*). — Copies: Forster, and own.

Dublin editions: Dublin: George Faulkner, MDCCLII. — 8vo; frontisp. portrait of Swift by B. Wilson (different from that in the London ed.), 6 pp. (including h.t. bearing vignette portrait of Orrery, before f.t.), 1–339 + bl., 9 pp. (*Index*) + bl. — There are also Large Paper copies. — Copies: T.C.D., and Penn.

Dublin: George Faulkner, MDCCLII. — 12mo; same title and collation as the 8vo Dublin ed., but no frontisp. portrait of Swift. — This is exactly the same printing as the 8vo ed.; only the signature marks are different. — Copies: T.C.D., and own.

German translation: Des Grafen John von Orrery Väterliche Briefe an seinen zu Oxford studirenden Sohn, &c. Hamburg und Leipzig, Georg Christian Grund &c. 1752. — 12mo; frontisp. portrait of Swift, 12 pp., 1–280. — Copy: own.

French translation: Lettres Historiques Et Philologiques Du Comte D'Orreri, &c. Londres, Et se trouve à Paris, Lambert, M.DCC.LIII. — 12mo; frontisp. portrait of Swift, 8 pp., 1–352. — Copy: own.

1334. A Candid Appeal From the late Dean Swift To The Right Hon. the Earl of O—y. &c. London: W. Owen, MDCCLII. — 4to; 1–9 + bl.

1335. Emendations On An Appeal from the late Dean Swift. Or Right Hon. Earl of Orrery Vindicated. &c. London: M. Cooper, MDCCLII. — 4to; 1–11 + bl.

1336. A Letter To the Right Reverend the Lord Bishop of Clogher, &c. – – – – To which is added, A Letter To the Right Honourable John Earl of Orrery, Occasioned by The Character which his Lordship gives of Dean Swift's Sermon on the Trinity, in his Remarks on the Life and Writings of the Dean. &c. London: J. Noon, MDCCLII.
8vo (in fours); [A]–G⁴, H² — 2 pp. (t. + bl.), 3–59, 1 p. advs.
Copy: B.M. T1764 (7).
The Letter to Orrery is pp. [39]–59 = text, preceded by t. + bl.
Copy: Penn.

1337. A Letter From A Primate To A Pretender Found By A Patriot Stander-by. To which is added, The Oracle of Dagon. And a Letter from Dean Swift to George F – – – k – – r. Isle of Man. Printed in Poultry-Yard, by Benjamin Free, for the Gaff-Maker. — 8vo; 1–15 + bl. — The letter from Swift to Faulkner (pp. 14–15) is meant to reproach the latter with reprinting *Orrery's Remarks*, which are here called a libel on Swift. — Copies: Gilbert Coll., Dublin, and T.C.D.

1338. A Letter From a Gentleman in the Country, to his Son in the College of Dublin. 1751.
Letter II. From a Gentleman &c. Dublin: Oli. Nelson, MDCCLII.
Letter III. From a Gentleman &c. Dublin: Booksellers, MDCCLIII.
Letter IV. From a Gentleman &c.

From *Dublin* foon to *London* fpread,

'Tis told at **Court**, the **Dean** is dead.

And Lady *S----* in the Spleen

Runs laughing up to tell ***.

** fo gracious, mild and good

Cries, " is he gone ! 'tis time he fhou'd.

He's dead you say, why let him rot

"   *   *   *   *   *

I'm glad the Medals were forgot.

"   *   *   *   *

I promis'd it is true, but when ?

"   *   *   *   *

I only was the P- -fs then.

"   *   *   *   *

But now a C- s-t to the

" *   *   *   *

You know, 'tis quite a different thing).

"   *   *   *   *

Now *Chartres*, at --------- Levee,

Tells with a Sneer the Tidings heavy :

                                             Why,

Verses on the Death of Doctor Swift (no. 771b). Sig.C2ᵛ of the first issue of the second edition, where a contemporary hand has inscribed the missing lines. (University of Pennsylvania)

THE

WORKS

Of the REVEREND

Dr. JONATHAN SWIFT,

DEAN of *St. Patrick*'s, DUBLIN.

With an ACCOUNT of his

LIFE and WRITINGS.

AS ALSO,

Hiſtorical and explanatory NOTES, and
a great Number of ORIGINAL PIECES,
in Verſe and Proſe.

The Whole properly digeſted.

In Eleven neat Pocket VOLUMES, printed in a new
beautiful Silver Type.

DUBLIN:

Printed by GEORGE FAULKNER. MDCCLXII.

*To the very worthy, learned,
and ingenious William
Smith, D. D. Provost of
the University of Philadelphia, from his
very much obliged,
most obedient, and
most humble Servant*

*Dublin,
Dec. 29,
1763*

George Faulkner

The Works of the Reverend Dr. Jonathan Swift (no. 53). A presentation copy
to William Smith, first Provost of the University of Pennsylvania, then
Philadelphia, signed by George Faulkner. The 18mo edition of 1762.
(University of Pennsylvania)

8vo; 1–24; 25–50; 51–97; 98–156; 1 p. (*Errata*, and intimation that Letters V and VI will speedily be published, but presumably they never were) + bl. — T.C.D. has Letters I and II only, the Nat. Libr. Dublin has Letters III and IV only. They contain a severe attack upon *Orrery's Remarks*.

1339. Dean Swift For Ever, or Mary the Cook-maid to the Earl of Orrery; to which are added Thoughts on various Subjects, from the Dean's manuscript in Mrs. Mary's possession. J. Robinson, N. D. — Folio. — From an antiq. book cat.

1340. A Dialogue Between Dean Swift and Tho. Prior, Esq; In the Isles of St. Patrick's Church, Dublin, On that memorable Day, October 9th, 1753. &c. Dublin: G. and A. Ewing, 1753. — 8vo; 2 pp., 1–134. — This is a satire on the political state of Ireland.
Copy: Penn.

1341. The Lives Of The Poets Of Great Britain and Ireland, To the Time of Dean Swift. &c. – – – – – By Mr. Cibber. In Four Volumes. London: R. Griffiths, MDCCLIII.
In spite of the title, which says 'In Four Volumes', there is a fifth: – – – – – By Mr. Cibber, and other Hands, Vol. V. London: R. Griffiths, MDCCLIII. — 12mo; 6 pp., 1–354.
Theophilus Cibber (son of Colley Cibber) only revised and improved the work, hence his name on the title-page. But the real author was Robert Shiels (amanuensis of Samuel Johnson), who had died in 1753.
The Life Of Swift (Vol. V, pp. 73–100) is largely based on *Orrery's Remarks*; but Shiels "improves upon his model, for the malice of Shiels is a refinement on lord Orrery's." (Monck Mason, *The History and Antiquities of St. Patrick's*, 1820, p. 440 note).

1343. Observations Upon Lord Orrery's Remarks On The Life and Writings Of Dr. Jonathan Swift, &c. – – – – To which are added, Two Original Pieces – – – – never before publish'd. London, W. Reeve &c., MDCCLIV. — 8vo; 16 pp., 1–310.
Copy: Penn.
Dublin edition: – – – – Dublin: Robert Main, MDCCLIV. — 12mo; 16 pp., 1–211 + bl.
The 'Preface' is signed *J. R.* (i.e. Dr. Delany).

1344. The Life Of The Revd. Jonathan Swift, D. D. Dean of St. Patrick's, Dublin. By John Hawkesworth. &c. London: Printed, And Dublin: Re-printed for S. Cotter, MDCCLV. — 12mo; I–VIII, 1–176. — Copy: own.

1345. An Essay Upon The Life, Writings, and Character, Of Dr. Jonathan Swift. Interspersed with some occasional Animadversions upon the Remarks of a late critical Author, and upon the Observations of an anonymous Writer on those Remarks. &c. – – – By Deane Swift, Esq; &c. – – – London, Charles Bathurst, MDCCLV.
8vo; π^2, B–Aa^8, Bb^4; A–C^8, D^2, π^3 — 2 pp. (h.t. + bl.), 2 pp (f.t. + bl.), [1]–375, [376] (advs.); [1]–52, 2 pp. (Errata + bl.), 4 pp. (Proposals for printing Sam. Butler's Remains). —
Pp. 49–52 (D 1–2) of the second section form a double-leaf; likewise the 4 pp. 'Proposals'; between these two double-leaves, the Errata have been pasted in. Possibly the first copies published ended with p. 52.
Copy: Penn.

Dublin edition: – – – – – London: Printed, Dublin: Re-printed, in the Year MDCCLV. — 8vo; 2 pp., 1–396, I–LII.
Errata on verso of t.p.

1346. A Letter To Dean [i.e. Deane] Swift, Esq; On His Essay upon the Life, Writings, and Character Of Dr. J. Swift. By the Author of the Observations on Lord Orrery's Remarks, &c. London, W. Reeve &c., 1755. — 8vo; 1–31 + bl. [By Dr. Delany.]

1347. Memoirs: Containing the Lives of Several Ladies Of Great Britain. &c. London: John Noon, MDCCLV.
There is a second title: Memoirs Of Several Ladies Of Great Britain, &c. London: John Noon, M.DCC.LV.
8vo; 4 pp. (the two titles), III–XXXI, 9 pp., 1–527 (advs. on verso). In *The History Of These Memoirs* (pp. XIX–XXXI) we are told that this book is only one of eight volumes intended as a *Supplement* to a much larger work. However, this larger work, when almost ready for the press, was unfortunately destroyed by fire, and has therefore to be written anew. At the end (pp. XXVII–XXXI) there is an *N. B.*, which says that "in an Appendix to the Second Volume of this work, the reader will find an account of two very extraordinary persons, *Dean Swift*, and Mrs. *Constantia Grierson* of Dublin"; after which follow three pages on Swift, who is taxed for his pride and his church-views. — However, this Second Volume, or its Appendix, was never written and never published.
This book was written by Thomas Amory, author of *The Life Of John Buncle*. It should not be confounded with *Memoirs Of Several Ladies Of Great Britain*, by George Ballard, Oxford 1752.
Copy: Penn.

1348. The Tell-Tale: Or, Anecdotes Expressive of Characters of Persons Eminent for Rank, Learning, Wit, Or Humour, &c. London: R. Baldwin, 1756. — 2 vols. — 18mo. — Contains some anecdotes relating to Swift.

1350. Anecdotes of Dean Swift and Miss Johnson. By C.M.P.G.N.S.T.N.S. This is pp. 487–91 in:
The Gentleman's Magazine And Historical Chronicle for Nov. 1757, London, D. Henry and R. Cave. — Also pp. 555–60 in: *The Gentleman's and London Magazine and Monthly Chronologer*, Nov. 1757, Dublin, John Exshaw.
Cf. Wilds, *The Closing Years Of Dean Swift's Life*, 1849, 108–14.

1351. Verses Sent To The Dean On His Birth-day, With Pine's Horace Finely Bound. By Dr. J. Sican. [ca. 1733].
Printed in: Dodsley's "Collection Of Poems By Several Hands", 6 vols., 1758 (in Vol. IV, 189–91).
Also in: Bell's "Classical Arrangement Of Fugitive Poetry", Vol. VI, 1789, pp. 29–31.

1354. The Life Of Dr. Jonathan Swift, Dean of Saint Patrick's, Dublin. &c. By W. H. Dilworth, M. A. London: G. Wright. MDCCLVIII. —
12mo; [A]², B–F¹², G⁸, H² — 2 pp. (t. + bl.), III–IV (Preface), [1]–139 + bl.
Copy: B.M. 10855 a 16.
Reprint: – – – – London: H. Woodgate and S. Brooks, M.DCC.LX.
12mo; π², B–F¹², G⁸, H³ — 2 pp. (t. + bl.), [III]–IV (Preface), [1]–137, 5 pp. advs.
Copy: B.M. 633 C2 B.

1355. Conjectures On Original Composition. In A Letter To The Author Of Sir Charles Grandison. &c. London, A. Millar &c., M.DCC.LIX. — 8vo;

4 pp., 1–112. — Contains a severe criticism on Swift (p. 62, &c.). The author is Edward Young.

1356. A New and General Biographical Dictionary; Containing &c. London, T. Osborne &c., MDCCLXI. — 8vo; 12 vols., 1761-7. — Swift is in Vol. XI (pp. 47–65).
Second ed.: 8vo; 15 vols., 1798; edited by W. Tooke. — Swift is in Vol. XIV (pp. 253–68).
Third ed.: 8vo; 32 vols., 1812–17; edited by Alexander Chalmers. — Swift is in Vol. XXIX (pp. 51–68).

1633. *The* | British Plutarch; | *Or,* | Biographical Entertainer. | *Being a Select Collection of* | The Lives at large | Of the most Eminent Men, | *Natives* of *Great Britain* and *Ireland*; | | From the Reign of Henry VIII. to George II. | Both inclusive: | *Whether distinguished as* | [First column] Statesmen, | Patriots, | [Second column] Warriors, | Divines, | [Third column] Poets, | Philosphers. | *Adorned with Copper Plates.* | Vol. XI. | [ornament] | *London*; | Printed by the King's Authority, | For Edward Dilly in the Poultry; | *MDCCLXII.* | J. Ellis sculp. [Engraved title, with flourishes.]

> 12mo; π^1, B–I^{12} — 2 pp. (t. + bl.), [1]–189 + bl., 2 pp. (Contents + bl.), — Five engraved portraits.
> Swift is: portrait + pp. 138–56.
> The whole collection seems to contain 12 vols.
> Copy: Engels.

1357. Biographia Britannica: &c. London, J. Walthoe &c., MDCCLXIII. — Folio. 6 vols. — Swift is in Vol. VI, Part I (pp. 3857–79).
There is a second edition, 1778–93, Vols. I–V, but it is unfinished (only A to Fastolff), and does not contain Swift.

1634. In Faulkner's *Journal*, No. 3816, Nov. 19–22, 1763, Faulkner declares his intention of placing a bust of Swift by Cunningham on the outside of his new house in Essex-street. In 1776 it was given to the chapter of St. Patrick's Cathedral, and then placed over the monumental tablet in the Cathedral, where it is still to be seen.

102. The Celebrated | Mrs. Pilkington's | Jests: | Or The Cabinet Of | Wit and Humour. | To which is now first added, | A Great Variety of Bons Mots, | Witticisms, and Anecdotes | Of the inimitable Dr. Swift, | Dean of St. Patrick's, Dublin. | The whole forming | The most brilliant Collection of quaint Jokes, | facetious Puns, smart Repartees, enter- | taining Tales in Verse and Prose, Epi- | grams, Epitaphs, Conundrums, &c. &c. | now extant. | — | The Second Edition. | — | Punning *is a Talent which no Man affects to despise,* | *but he that is without it.* Swift. | = | London. | Printed for W. Nicoll, at the Paper Mill, in St. | Paul's Church-Yard. MDCCLXIV.

[Title in red and black.]

12mo (in sixes); frontisp., π^2, B–K^6, L^4 — frontisp., 2 pp. (t. + bl.), I–II (Preface), 1–116.

Contains selections from Mrs. Pilkington's *Memoirs* (see No. 1329), and several pieces by and on Swift. — Copy: B.M. 12316 bb 28.

I have not seen the first edition.

1359. Vita Del Dottore Gionata Swift, &c. – – – – Tradotta fedelmente dal l'Inglese Da Francesco Vanneschi, &c. – – Lucca, 1768, Giuseppe Rocchi. — 8vo; frontisp. portrait of Swift, 1–192. — Copy: Forster.

1360. Ragionamento Istorico Sopra Il Dottore Gionata Swift, &c. – – – – Di T. B. Irlandese Per servire di supplimento alla di lui Vita tradotto recentemente in Italiano, &c. – – – – Lucca, 1769, Giuseppe Rocchi. — 12mo; frontisp. portrait of Swift, 2 pp., 1–12, 3–118. — The Bibl. Mazarine copy has in ink "tommaso Barry" on the title-page, which is clearly the interpretation of "T. B.".

1362. Essays. On Poetry and Music, as they affect the Mind. On Laughter, and Ludicrous Composition. On the Utility of Classical Learning. By James Beattie, LL.D. &c. Edinburgh: William Creech &c., MDCCLXXVI. — 8vo; I–VIII, 1–155 + bl. — Swift is mentioned in it.

4to ed.: – – – – – Edinburgh: William Creech, 1776.

Third ed.: 1779.

1363. The Monthly Review, Oct. 1779, p. 356, contains a sound estimate of Swift's character and genius.

1364. Prefaces, Biographical And Critical, To The Works Of The English Poets. By Samuel Johnson. London: J. Nichols &c., MDCCLXXIX. — There are ten volumes in all, sm. 8vo (Vols. I–IV, 1779; Vols. V–X, 1781), belonging to Nichols's ed. of *The Works Of The English Poets* (No. 113, *ante*), and issued separately. — Swift is in Vol. VIII (pp. 1–112). — Vol. I should have a leaf "Directions to the Binder.", and 'Errata' (2 leaves).

Dublin edition: The Lives Of The English Poets; And A Criticism On Their Works. By Samuel Johnson. Dublin: Whitestone &c., M,DCC,LXXIX. — 3 vols., 8vo, 1779–81–81. — Swift is in Vol. II (pp. 439–96).

London edition: – – – – – – – – – London: C. Bathurst &c., MDCCLXXXI. — 4 vols., 8vo, all 1781. — Swift is in Vol. III (pp. 379–451). [Vol. IV originally ended with a page of advs.: (505) + bl., followed by a leaf "Containing extra printed labels for the four volumes as issued in boards." Later on these two leaves were removed, and pp. 505–34 were added, entitled: The Principal Additions and Corrections &c. – – – – (new p. 505)].

A New Edition, Corrected. — 4 vols., 1783.

There are several further editions, i.a. a German translation (edited by C. F. von Blankenburg; Altenburg, 1781–3, 2 vols. 8vo), and an English ed. (Göttingen, 1783).

1366. Lectures On Rhetoric And Belles Lettres. By Hugh Blair, D. D. &c. London: W. Strahan &c., MDCCLXXXIII. — 4to; 2 vols. — Swift's style is discussed in them.

Further editions: 1801 (Basil, 3 vols.), 1803 (3 vols. 8vo), 1806 (3 vols. 8vo), 1811 (3 vols. 8vo), 1812 (12th ed. London, 3 vols. 8vo, portrait), 1834 (1 vol. 8vo).

1367. Englische Miscellen. Eisenach, bei Johann Georg Ernst Wittekindt. 1783. — 12mo; 1–78. — Contains (pp. 3–6): Eine Anekdote von Swift. — Copy: Preuszische Staatsbibl., Berlin.

1368. The Life Of The Rev. Dr. Jonathan Swift, Dean Of St. Patrick's, Dublin. By Thomas Sheridan, A. M. London: C. Bathurst &c. MDCCLXXXIV. — 8vo; frontisp. portrait of Swift, 20 pp., 1–568. Also portrait of Sheridan. [This is the same printing as Vol. I of the *Works*, 1784 (No. 119, *ante*), but the designation 'Vol. I' on the title-page and at the foot of the first page of each new sheet has been removed.]

The Second Edition: – – – – London: J. F. and C. Rivington &c., MDCCLXXXVII. — 8vo; frontisp. portrait of Swift, I–IV, 16 pp., 1–488. Also portrait of Sheridan.

Dublin edition: – – – – – Dublin: Luke White, M.DCC.LXXXV. — 8vo; 20 pp., 1–489 + bl., 2 pp. (advs.).

Copies: Penn.

German translation: Jonathan Swifts Leben, von Thomas Sheridan geschrieben; abgekürzt und aus dem Englischen übersetzt von Philippine, Freyinn Knigge, herausgegeben von ihrem Vater. Hannover, bey Christian Ritscher. 1795. — 12mo; 4 pp., 1–444.

1369. For *An Inquiry Into The Life Of Dean Swift*, contained in *Literary Relics*, 1789 and 1792, see No. 120, *ante*.

1370. L. T. Rede: Anecdotes & Biography. London 1799. — Contains ten anecdotes about Swift (pp. 401–9).

1371. An Account Of The Life Of the Reverend Jonathan Swift, D. D. Dean of S. Patrick's, Dublin. Traduction interlinéaire à laquelle est ajoutée une Traduction Françoise très-exacte, placée en forme, de Notes. &c. – – – – – Mme Montmorency, Albert-Luynes, An VIII, (1800.). — 4to; 1–501 + bl. — Only 25 copies printed. It seems there is also an edition of 25 copies in sm. 8vo.

1372. Hygëia: Or Essays Moral And Medical, On The Causes Affecting The Personal State Of Our Middling And Affluent Classes. By Thomas Beddoes, M. D. Bristol: J. Mills &c., 1802. — 3 vols., 8vo, 1802–02–03. — Swift's disease is dealt with in Vol. III (Essay Ninth, pp. 186–96). Copy: Penn.

1373. Charles Henry Wilson: Swiftiana, London, 1804. — 2 vols. Sm. 8vo:

I: π^1 of thicker paper, a–b^8, B–O^8 — 2 pp. of thicker paper (t. + bl.), [I]–VIII (Preface), [IX]–XXXII (Life of Swift), [1]–208. Facs. of a Swift letter (a folding leaf).

II: π^1, B–P^8, *P^8, *Q^4, Q^8 — 2 pp. (t. + bl.), [1]–224, [*209]–*232 (Appendix), [225]–237 (Index), 3 pp. advs. Ten facsimiles. Vol. I, 66–7, bears 'The Upstart.'

Copy: B.M. 10824 a 17.

My friend, Mr. David Woolley, Doncaster, Vic., Australia, kindly informed me that there is another issue in which Vol. I has the following preliminaries: [I]–VIII (Preface), [IX]–XCI + bl. (Life). He says that "the text is identical to p. XXV, line 6, and thereafter the Life of Swift is summarily disposed of in 7 pages."

1374. A Biographical History Of England, From The Revolution To The End Of George I's Reign; Being A Continuation Of The Rev. J. Granger's Work: Consisting Of &c. – – – – The Materials being supplied by the Manuscripts left by Mr. Granger, and the Collections of the Editor, The Rev. Mark

Noble, &c. – – – – London: W. Richardson &c., 1806. — 3 vols., 8vo. — The article on Swift is in Vol. II, pp. 163–7. — Granger had gone from Egbert the Great to the Revolution (1688). After four editions of his work had appeared (1769–74, 1775, 1779, and 1804), Noble in 1806 published his continuation from 1688–1727 (see above). In the 5th ed. of Granger's work (1824), Noble's continuation is not included. The article on Swift is by Noble, who at the end quotes 'a character of Swift' left by Granger in MS.

1375. Histoire Critique Du Philosophisme Anglois, Depuis Son Origine Jusqu'a Son Introduction En France, Inclusivement. Par M. Tabaraud, &c. Paris, L. Duprat-Duverger, 1806. — 2 vols., 8vo. — Contains some pages on Swift as to religious matters.

1376. Essai Historique Sur Le Docteur Swift, Et Sur Son Influence Dans Le Gouvernement De La Grande Bretagne, Depuis 1710, Jusqu'a La Mort De La Reine Anne, En 1714; &c. Paris. 1808. — 4to; 4 pp., I–XXXI + bl., 1–504. Frontisp. portrait of Swift between the two titles. — The author is Quentin Craufurd, an Englishman by birth, who settled in Paris in 1780. — Copy: Penn.

136. An / Essay / On / The Earlier Part / Of / The Life Of Swift. / By The Rev. John Barrett, D.D. / And Vice-Provost Of Trinity College, Dublin. / To Which Are Subjoined / *Several Pieces Ascribed To Swift;* / Two Of His Original Letters; / And Extracts From / His Remarks On Bishop Burnet's History. / = / *London:* / Printed For J. Johnson; J. Nichols And Son; R. Baldwin; Otridge And Son; / F. C. And J. Rivington; T. Payne; R. Faulder; G. Robinson; Wilkie And / Robinson; R. Lea; J. Nunn; Cuthell And Martin; J. Walker; T. Egerton; / Clarke And Son; Vernor, Hood, And Sharpe; Scatcherd And Letterman; / Lackington, Allen, And Co.; J. Carpenter; Longman, Hurst, Rees, And Orme; / Cadell And Davies; W. Miller; J. And A. Arch; S. Bagster; J. Murray; / J. Harding; R. H. Evans; And J. Mawman. / — / 1808.

8vo; π^4, B 2–8, C–M^8, N^4, O–Q^8 — 2 pp. (h.t. + printer's name, etc. on verso), 2 pp. (f.t. + bl.), V–VI (Advertisement), VII–VIII (Contents), [3]–232.
Most of the pieces ascribed to Swift are not genuine.
For the greater part (pp. 3–144) this *Essay* (same printing) was included in Vol. I of Nichols's edition, 1808 (see No. 131, *ante*), with alteration of page-numbers and signature-marks.
Copy: Penn.

1378. Literary Anecdotes Of The Eighteenth Century, Comprizing Biographical Memoirs Of William Bowyer, Printer, F. S. A. And Many Of His Learned Friends; &c. By John Nichols, F. S. A. In Six Volumes. London: 1812–12–12–12–12–12–. — Vol. VII (Index), 1813; Vol. VIII, 1814; Vol. IX, 1815.
Illustrations Of The Literary History Of The Eighteenth Century. &c. Intended As A Sequel To The Literary Anecdotes. By John Nichols, F. S. A. London: 1817–17–18–22–28–31–48–58 (8 vols.).
Both series contain details about Swift.

1379. The History Of Fiction: Being A Critical Account Of The Most Celebrated Prose Works Of Fiction, From The Earliest Greek Romances To The Novels Of The Present Age. By John Dunlop. Second Edition. Edinburgh: James Ballantyne &c., 1816. — 3 vols., 12mo. — Swift and *Gulliver's Travels* are mentioned in them.

The first edition is 1814, 3 vols., cr. 8vo, (not examined); further editions: 1845, 1876, 1888. German translation: 1851.

1380. Francis Jeffrey: A review of Walter Scott's edition of Swift's Works (and a malicious criticism of Swift), in *The Edinburgh Review*. For Sept. 1816 to Dec. 1816. Vol. XXVII (Nos. LIII–LIV). Edinburgh 1816. Pp. 1–58. For an answer to it, see No. 1382.

Also in: Contributions To The Edinburgh Review. By Francis Jeffrey, &c. London, Longman &c., 1844. — 4 vols., 8vo. — The article on Swift is in Vol. I (pp. 158–226).

Further editions: 1846 (3 vols.), 1848, 1853 ('The Traveller's Library' 36: Swift And Richardson).

1381. William Hazlitt: Lectures On The English Poets. &c. By William Hazlitt. London: Taylor And Hessey, 1818. — 8vo; 8 pp., 1–331 + bl. — Lecture VI (pp. 206–44) is: On Swift, Young, Gray, Collins, &c.

Further editions: 1819, 1841, 1854 (?), 1869, 1870, 1878, 1894, 1908, 1910, 1924, 1929, &c.

1382. Edward Berwick: A Defence Of Dr. Jonathan Swift, Dean Of St. Patrick's, Dublin; In Answer To Certain Observations Passed On His Life And Writings, In The Fifty-Third Number Of The Edinburgh Review. London: John Nichols And Son, 1819. — 8vo; 4 pp., 1–67 (advs. on verso). — Cf. No. 1380, *ante*.

Copy: Penn.

1383. William Monck Mason: Hibernia Antiqua Et Hodierna. Being A Topographical Account Of Ireland, And A History Of All The Establishments In That Kingdom, Ecclesiastical, Civil, And Monastick; Drawn Chiefly From Sources Of Official Record, By William Monck Mason, Esq. &c. Dublin: Printed For The Author. 1819. — [Second title:] The History And Antiquities Of The Collegiate And Cathedral Church Of St. Patrick, Near Dublin, From Its Foundation In 1190, To The Year 1819: Comprising &c. – – – – – And Biographical Memoirs Of Its Deans. &c. – – – – By William Monck Mason, Esq. Dublin: Printed For The Author. 1819. — 4to; frontisp. (St. Patrick's Cathedral), 8 pp. (first title, dedication, second title, 2 pp. *Contents* covering pp. 1–167 only), 1–444, I–XCVII + bl. — Six more engravings. [The section on Swift, preceded by an engraving of Swift, is pp. 225–444.] Copy: Penn.

In front, pasted in, on an 8vo double-leaf (3 pp. + bl.), between the board and the blank fly-leaf, there is an 'Advertisement', saying that this volume is only a specimen of an extensive work (see the first title above), corresponding in scope with the 'Magna Britannia' of Messrs. Lysons, and the 'Caledonia' of Mr. Chalmers; and that "the biographical part terminates, for the present, with the Life of Dean Swift; the memoirs of the subsequent deans will be supplied with the next part [i.e. an account of Christ-Church Cathedral]."

Consequently, in 1820, appeared the *Supplement To The History Of St. Patrick's Cathedral* (so called on a sheet of paper, pasted on the blue paper cover in which it was contained). But the original ambitious plan had apparently been abandoned; for, contrary to the promise made, the account of Christ-Church Cathedral was not given, the only new matter supplied being "the memoirs of the subsequent deans", while the rest consisted of reprints of several sheets of the former volume, necessitated by the deplorable circumstance that these sheets had been printed on paper of smaller dimensions than that on which the other sheets of the original volume had been printed.

The collation of this blue-cover *Supplement* is:

4to; 10 pp. (new title dated 1820, dedication, 5 pp. Contents + bl.), 385–478, 2 pp., LXXI–XCVII + bl., 103–4.

And the complete volume, after cancellation of old sheets and insertion of the new ones, is:

The History And Antiquities Of The Collegiate And Cathedral Church Of St. Patrick, Near Dublin, From Its Foundation In 1190, To The Year 1819: Comprising &c. – – – – And Biographical Memoirs Of Its Deans, &c. – – – – By William Monck Mason, Esq. Dublin: Printed For The Author, By W. Folds, Strand-Street. 1820.

4to; frontisp. (St. Patrick's Cathedral), 10 pp. (new), 1–102 (old), 103–4 (new), 105–384 (old), 385–478 + 2 pp. (new), I–LXX (old), LXXI–XCVII + bl. (new). Six more engravings.

There are also L. P. copies of the complete book. Collation the same as that just given, but only the 10 pp. of prefatory matter and pp. 441–78 + 2 pp. are from the new sheets, all the rest being from the old ones.

All the above copies are at Penn.

1384. Joseph Spence: Anecdotes, Observations, And Characters, Of Books and Men. Collected From The Conversation Of Mr. Pope, And Other Eminent Persons Of His Time. By The Rev. Joseph Spence. Now First Published – – – By Samuel Weller Singer. &c. London: W. H. Carpenter &c. MDCCC.XX. — 8vo; I–XXXIX + bl., 1–501 (*Errata* on verso). Frontisp. and 3 plates. — Also 50 L. P. copies. — Cf. No. 1385, *post*.

Second ed.: 1858.

1385. Joseph Spence: Observations, Anecdotes, And Characters, Of Books And Men: By The Rev. Joseph Spence. Arranged With Notes By The Late Edmund Malone, Esq. London: John Murray. 1820. — 8vo; I–VIII, 1–302. [This is only a selection; it is from a different MS. from the preceding edition, No. 1384, *ante*.]

1386. Ph.E. Chasles: Essai Historique Sur La Poésie Anglaise et sur les poètes anglais vivans (Swift mentioned in it), in *Revue Encyclopedique*. Troisième Année. Tome IX. Paris, Janvier 1821. Pp. 228–40, 446–58.

1387. G. Regis: Bemerkungen uber Swift und Seine Werke, in *Philomathie von Freunden der Wirschenschaft und Kunst*. Dritter Band. Frankfurt am Main, 1822. Pp. 85–160.

1388. Memoirs Of Jonathan Swift, D. D. Dean Of St. Patrick's, Dublin. By Sir Walter Scott. Paris: A. and W. Galignani, MDCCCXXVI. — 12mo; 2 vols. — This is a reprint of Vol. I of Swift's Works, ed. Walter Scott, 1814 (see No. 138, *ante*).

Also included in editions of collected works of Walter Scott, i.a. in Vol. II of "The Miscellaneous Prose Works Of Sir Walter Scott, Bart.", 6 vols. 8vo, Edinburgh, 1827; in Vol. V of "The Prose Works Of Sir Walter Scott", 9 vols. 8vo, Paris, 1827; &c.

Also: Memoirs Of Jonathan Swift, &c. In Three Volumes. Zwickau, Brothers Schumann, 1829. — 16mo — [Nos. 192–4 of: "The Pocket Library Of English Classics"] — Copy: University Library, Leipsic.

1389. The Oxford Encyclopaedia; Or, Dictionary Of Arts, Sciences, And General Literature. — 4to; six volumes (all 1828) and a Supplement (1831). — Vol. VI, pp. 784-6, contains an article on Swift.

1390. The Gallery of Portraits, with Memoirs and Biographies. London, 1833-7. Ch. Knight. 7 vols. large 8vo. — Contains Swift. — From an antiq. book catalogue.

1391. Ph. Chasles: Les Excentriques (Swift mentioned in it), in *Revue Des Deux Mondes*. Tome Troisième. Troisième Série. Paris 1834. Pp. 497-558.
Reprinted in: Le XVIIIᵉ Siècle en Angleterre, Paris, 1846, Tome II, p. 42, &c.

1392. The Skull Of Dean Swift, Recently Disinterred at Dublin. Dr. Houston: On The Authenticity Of The Skulls Of Dean Swift And Stella.
Both in *The Phrenological Journal And Miscellany*, Vol. IX, Sept. 1834–March 1836. Edinburgh 1836. Pp. 466-71, 603-8.

1393. Phrenology In A Quandary (the Dublin physicians who dug up Swift's skull are severely attacked in it), in *The London Medical Gazette*. Vol. XVII. (Vol. I. For The Session 1835-6.) London 1836. Pp. 97-128.

1635. B.: Inedited Letters of Dean Swift, in *The New Monthly Magazine* for 1842. Vol. LXIV. Pp. 116-20.

1394. The Life & Writings Of Jonathan Swift, D. D. D. S. P. D., &c. Dublin: James M'Cormick, 1844. — 18mo; 1-90. — Copy: Nat. Libr., Dublin.

1395. Henry Lord Brougham: A Sketch Of Sir Robert Walpole (containing a venomous attack on Swift), in *Historical Sketches Of Statesmen Who Flourished In The Time of George III*. [original Series: Paris 1839] New Series. Paris 1844. Pp. 192-207 of the 1844 volume.

1396. Dr. Skae: A review of two books on phrenological subjects (one by James Straton, the other by Daniel Noble) — [he gives his own methods of measuring skulls, i.e. those of Swift and Stella], in *The British Quarterly Review*. Aug. and Nov. 1846. Vol. IV. London. Pp. 397-419.

1397. George Combe: On Criticisms Upon Phrenology. A Review Reviewed, in *The Lancet*. In Two Volumes, Annually. Vol. II. 1846, and Vol. I. 1847. London. Pp. 661-3, 8-11. [This is an answer to No. 1396.]

1398. (1) James Straton: Answer to Dr. Skae.
(2) George Combe: Reprint of No. 1397.
(3) Dr. Skae: Answer to No. 1397, with Combe's remarks on this answer added.
All three in *The Phrenological Journal For The Year 1847*, Vol. XX. Or Vol. X. Of the New Series. Edinburgh 1847. Pp. 36-48, 63-80, 273-90.

1399. W. R. Wilde, M.R.I.A.:
Some Particulars respecting Swift and Stella, with Engravings of their Crania; together with some Notice of St. Patrick's Hospital. With Communications from Dr. Mackenzie and Mr. Hamilton, in the *Dublin Quarterly Journal Of Medical Science*. Vol. III. Feb. and May 1847, and Vol. IV. Aug. and Nov. 1847. Dublin 1847. Pp. 384-434, 1-33.
Separate edition: Popular Errors Respecting The Insanity Of Dean Swift: An Essay. With An Appendix, Containing Several Of His Poems Hitherto Unpublished, And Some Remarks On Stella. By W. R. Wilde, M. R. I. A., F. R. C. S. Dublin: Hodges And Smith, MDCCCXLVIII. — 8vo; frontisp.

portrait of Stella, I–IV, 3–164. Illustrations in the text. — This is an extension of the preceding two articles.

Re-issue: The Closing Years Of Dean Swift's Life; With An Appendix, &c. – – – – Dublin: Hodges And Smith &c., 1849. [This is the same printing as the preceding book; only a new title-page.]

Second edition: The Closing Years Of Dean Swift's Life; &c. – – – Second Edition, Revised And Enlarged. Dublin: Hodges And Smith &c., 1849. — 8vo; frontisp. (Stella), I–IX + bl., 1–184. Illustrations in the text. Leaf with "Opinions of the Press on the First Edition" inserted in front, and leaf of advs. pasted on back cover.

Copies: all in Bodl. Copy: Penn — 2nd ed. —

1400. Life of Swift (and his portrait), in *The Cabinet Portrait Gallery Of British Worthies*. Vol. XII. London 1847. Pp. 66–118.

1401. Irish Rivers. The Boyne, in *The Dublin University Magazine*, Vol. XXIX, Jan. to June 1847. Dublin 1847. Pp. 764–83 (pp. 778–9 contain a reference to Swift and Laracor).

1402. William Howitt: Dean Swift (with three illustrations), in *Homes And Haunts Of The Most Eminent British Poets*. London, 1847. Pp. 176–210 in Vol. I.
[Reviewed (pp. 220–1) in: Fraser's Magazine For Town And Country. Vol. XXXV. January To June, 1847. London: G. W. Nickisson &c.]

1403. In 1847 Thomas De Quincey wrote "Schlosser's Literary History Of The Eighteenth Century", which article contains a libellous attack on Swift.
After that, this article must have appeared with others in a collected form (Ticknor, Reed, & Fields, Boston, U. S.); again, ca. 1856; and again in: The Works Of Thomas De Quincey &c. Third Edition. In Sixteen Volumes. Edinburgh. Adam And Charles Black. 1862, &c. (in Vol. VII, 1863, pp. 35–87)

1404. Lady Duff Gordon: Stella And Vanessa. A Romance From The French. London 1850. — 2 vols., 12mo.

1405. The Amours Of Dean Swift, in *The Times*, Thursday, Oct. 3, 1850, p. 3.
Reprinted in: Essays From "The Times". Being A Selection From The Literary Papers Which Have Appeared In That Journal. &c. London: John Murray. 1851. — 12mo; 8 pp., 1–310, 1 p. adv. + bl. ["The Amours Of Dean Swift" is pp. 214–36. — I possess these pages taken from another copy in which the title and headlines are not, as above, "The Amours Of Dean Swift", but simply "Dean Swift".]

1406. Table-Talk. To Which Are Added Imaginary Conversations Of Pope And Swift. By Leigh Hunt. London: Smith, Elder And Co., 1851. — Sm. 8vo; I–XII, 1–251 (adv. on verso), 1–16 (advs.).
Copy: Penn.

1406A. Isaac Butt: A Pilgrimage to Quilca in the year 1852, in The Dublin University Magazine, Vol. XL, 1852. Pp. 509–26.

1407. W. M. Thackeray: Swift, in The English Humourists Of The Eighteenth Century. London 1853. Pp. 1–54.
German translation: Englands Humoristen von W. M. Thackeray. Uebersetzt von A. v. Müller. Hamburg. F. H. Restler und Melle. 1854. — 12mo; 6 pp., 1–319 + bl. — Swift is pp. 1–53.
Other editions, i.a.: 1853, 1858, 1867, 1885 (Halle), 1900, 1906, 1908, 1910, 1911, 1913.

1408. M. Léon De Wailly: Stella Et Vanessa, in *Supplément au Courrier Francais*. Tome Premier. (1854). Pp. 1–54.
Separate edition: Léon De Wailly: *Stella Et Vanessa*. Paris 1855. — 12mo; 4 pp., blank leaf, 1–229, 3 pp. blank.

1409. Prevost-Paradol: De Decani Jonathan Swift Vita Ex Scriptis Disseruit. Parisiis, 1855. — 8vo; 1–57, 3 pp. (two of them blank). French translation: Prevost-Paradol: *Jonathan Swift Sa Vie et ses Oeuvres*. Paris, 1856. — 8vo; 1–62.

1411. David Masson: Swift, in *Essays Biographical And Critical*. Cambridge, 1856. Pp. 140–77.
Copy: Penn.

1412. Versicles. By Thomas Irwin. London: Bosworth & Harrison &c., 1856. — 12mo; 8 pp., 1–240. — Contains a poem on Swift (pp. 86–98). — Copy: Forster.

1415. Reliquiae Hearnianae: &c. Oxford: James Wright. M.DCCC.LVII. — 2 vols., 8vo [Also 50 L. P. copies.] — Contains references to Swift. [Second ed., enlarged: 3 vols., cr. 8vo, 1869.] (Also L. P. copies.)

1413. H. Taine: Jonathan Swift Son Génie Et Ses Oeuvres, in *Revue Des Deux Mondes*. XXVIIIe Année. Séconde Periode. Tome Seizième. Paris 1858. Pp. 869–940.
Also in: Histoire de la litterature anglaise (by H. Taine, 1st ed. 1864. — English translation by H. Van Laun, 1st ed. 1871).

1414. British Novelists And Their Styles: &c. By David Masson, M. A. &c. Cambridge: Macmillan And Co. &c., 1859. — Sm. 8vo; I–IX + bl., 1–308. — In pp. 89–98 Swift's style is discussed.

1416. Biographie De Jonathan Swift Par Hermile Reynald &c. Paris, L. Hachette Et C[ie], 1860. — 8vo; 4 pp., 1–211 + bl.

1417. The Leaders Of Public Opinion In Ireland. &c. London, Saunders, Otley, And Co., 1861. — 12mo; 4 pp., 1–308. — Swift is pp. 1–60. — The author is W. E. H. Lecky.
Further editions, i.a.: 1871, 1873 (German translation, by Dr. H. Jolowicz. Posen. Verlag von Joseph Jolowicz), 1897 (re-written and much amplified in Vol. I of Temple Scott's ed. of *The Prose Works Of Jonathan Swift*, D. D. 1903 (2 vols.), 1912 (2 vols.).

1636. Joseph Spence: Some Account of the Life, Writings, and Character of Dr. Swift, in *Notes and Queries*, 2nd Series, XI (1861). Pp. 1–3, 21–3, 41–3.

1418. For some criticism on Swift see *The Autobiography And Correspondence Of Mary Granville, Mrs. Delany*, 1861–2.

1419. Lives Of Wits And Humourists. Dean Swift [and eleven others]. By John Timbs, &c. In Two Volumes. London: Richard Bentley, 1862. — 8vo — Vol. I contains the life of Swift (pp. 1–121). — Copy: Sächsische Landesbibl., Dresden.

1420. Le Doyen De Saint-Patrick. Drame En Cinq Actes, En Prose De MM. Léon De Wailly Et Louis Ulbach. &c. Paris, E. Dentu &c., 1862. — 8vo; 1–103 + bl.
The *dramatis personae* are Dr Swift, Dr Tisdal, Esther Johnson, Miss Vanhomrigh (nièce de lord Walpole), Rebecca Dingley, Patrick (domestique de

Tisdal, puis de Swift), Villiams (médecin). The first four acts play at Laracor, the last at Dublin.

1421. Richard Gosche: Jonathan Swift, in *Jahrbuch Für Litteraturgeschichte*. Erster Band. Berlin 1865. Pp. 138–74.

1422. Paul De Saint-Victor: Swift, in *Hommes Et Dieux Etudes D'Histoire Et De Littérature*. Paris 1867. Pp. 501–14.
[Reviewed (pp. 438–48) in: Nouveaux Lundis Par C.-A. Sainte-Beuve &c. Tome Dixième. Paris, Michel Lévy Frères &c., 1868.]

1424. Lessing und Swift. Eine Studie über „Nathan der Weise" von Dr. J. Caro, Professor. Jena. Otto Deistung &c., 1869. — 12mo; 1–105 + bl.

1425. Essays on English Writers, by the Author of "The Gentle Life", London, 1869. — Sm. 8vo. — Contains Swift. [From an antiq. book cat.; I have not seen a copy.]

1426. Swift's Disappointed Life (pp. 18–19), and Swift's Three Loves (pp. 31–2), in *Books And Authors*. Edinburgh. Ca. 1870 (as is betrayed by the last adv. on p. 24 at the end of the book).

1427. The Works Of Alexander Pope. New Edition. &c. – – – By The Late Rt. Hon. John Wilson Croker. – – – – – By Rev. Whitwell Elwin. – – – –London: John Murray, 1871. — 8vo. — There are 10 vols. in all. Elwin edited two volumes of Poetry (Vol. I, 1871; and Vol. II, 1871), and three of Letters (Vol. VI, 1871; Vol. VII, 1871; and Vol. VIII, 1872). In 1881 Courthope resumed the task (Vol. III, 1881; Vol. IV, 1882; Vol. IX, 1886; Vol. X, 1886; Vol. V, 1889). — The *Introduction* in Vol. I contains the story of Pope's conduct with regard to the edition of Swift's Letters, 1741; Vol. V contains Pope's Life (with frequent references to Swift); and Vol. VII has their Letters.

1637. Jacob Larwood: The Book Of Clerical Anecdotes. London ca. 1871 (the advs. at the end have that year). — Contains some anecdotes about Swift.

1638. Adolph Stern: Aus dem 18 Jahrhundert; Biographische Bilder and Skizzen. Leipzig 1874. — Contains a biography of Swift.

1428. Jonathan Swift. Eine literar-historische Studie von Albert Schultheisz, &c. Rothenburg o.d. Tauber. Schneider'sche Buchdruckerei. 1875. — 4to; 1–42. — Copy: Bayerische Staatsbibl., München.

1429. The Papers Of A Critic. Selected From The Writings Of The Late Charles Wentworth Dilke. &c. London: John Murray, 1875. — 2 vols., 8vo. — Vol. I contains a good deal about Swift. The several articles originally appeared in the *Athenaeum*, and in *Notes and Queries*.

1430. A Catalogue Of The Printed Books And Manuscripts Bequeathed By The Reverend Alexander Dyce. &c. London: George E. Eyre And William Spottiswoode, &c. MDCCCLXXV. — Two vols. 8vo. — Vol. I (A To K): I–XXIV, 1–462. Frontisp. portrait of Dyce. Vol. II (L To Z): 1–448, 1 p. Corrections + bl. — Contains only a few books by Swift.

1431. The Life Of Jonathan Swift. By John Forster. Volume The First. 1667–1711. London: John Murray, 1875. — 8vo; frontisp. portrait of Swift, I–XVI, 1–477, 3 pp., 1–20 (advs.). Four facsimiles in the text. — No more than Vol. I published.
New York edition: 1876.

1639. John Doran: Swift and Stella, in *Notes and Queries*, 5th Series, V (1876), pp. 401–2.

1432. Catalogue Of The Library Of Books Of John Forster At Palace Gate House, Kensington, Prepared By Henry E. Rawlins. London: R. Marks, 1876. — 8vo; 2 pp., 1–300. — Contains a catalogue of the Swift books in the Forster Collection, in the Victoria and Albert Museum, South Kensington.
Second edition: 1888. — Large 8vo; I–XXVIII, 2 pp., 1–710. Frontisp. portrait of Forster.

1433. Paget: Swift, in *Blackwood's Edinburgh Magazine*, Vol. CXIX, Jan.–June 1876. Edinburgh 1876. Pp. 527–44.

1434. A. W. Ward: Swift's Love-story In German Literature, in *Macmillan's Magazine*, Vol. XXXV, Nov. 1876 to April 1877. London 1877. Pp. 308–17.

1435. J. van Loenen Martinet: De Jongste Levensbeschryving Van Jonathan Swift [i.e. a review of Forster's *Life Of Swift*, 1875 — see No. 1431], in De Gids. Twee En Veertigste Jaargang. Derde Serie. Aestiende Jaargang. 1878. Eerste Deel. Amsterdam 1878. Pp. 25–64.

1436. Swift By Leslie Stephen. London: Macmillan And Co., 1882. — 8vo; I–X, 2 pp., 1–209 + bl. — This is a volume of the "English Men Of Letters" series, edited by John Morley.
Further editions: 1885, 1889, 1899, 1902, 1903 (twice), &c.

1437. Dr. Bucknill, F.R.S.: Dean Swift's Disease, in *Brain: A Journal Of Neurology*, Vol. IV, April 1881 to Jan. 1882. London 1882. Pp. 493–506.

1438. The Life Of Jonathan Swift Dean Of St. Patrick's, Dublin By Henry Craik, M. A. London: John Murray, 1882. — Large 8vo; I–XXXIV, 1–576. Frontisp. portrait of Swift.
Second edition: 1894, 2 vols. sm. 8vo.

1439. John Churton Collins: Jonathan Swift, in *The Quarterly Review*, Vol. 153, Jan.–Apr. 1882. London 1882. Pp. 377–430. *Id.:* Dean Swift in Ireland. *Ibid.*, Vol. 156, July–Oct. 1883. Pp. 1–56.
Separate edition: Jonathan Swift A Biographical And Critical Study By John Churton Collins &c. London, Chatto & Windus, 1893. — 8vo; I–XVI, 1–280, 1–32 (advs.). — This is an extension of the two articles mentioned above.
Second edition: 1902.
Copy: Penn.

1440. Stanley Lane-Poole: Notes For A Bibliography Of Swift, in *The Bibliographer*, Vol. VI, June–Nov. 1884. London 1884. Pp. 160–71.
Separate edition: Notes For A Bibliography Of Swift. By Stanley Lane-Poole. &c. London: Elliot Stock, 1884. — 12mo; 1–36. — Only 25 copies printed (numbered and signed by the author).

1441. Historische Vorträge. Von Carl von Noorden. &c. Leipzig, Duncker & Humblot, 1884. — 8vo; 6 pp., 1–58, 1–277 + bl. Frontisp. — Swift is pp. 89–113.

1442. Jonathan Swift A Novel In Three Volumes. London: Hurst And Blackett, 1884. — 3 vols., 8vo.

1640. Daniel Hipwell: Swiftiana, in *Notes and Queries*, 6th Series, X (1884). Pp. 42–3.

1641. Edward Solly: Swiftiana, in *Notes and Queries*, 6th Series, X (1884). Pp. 111–12.

1443. Succession Of Clergy In The Parishes Of S. Bride, S. Michael le Pole, and S. Stephen, Dublin. &c. Dublin: J. Charles & Son &c., 1884. — 4to; frontisp. map, 2 pp., I–VI, 2 pp., 5–62. — Pp. 55–6 contain: Note on Swift's Birth Place.

1444. Arvède Barine: Swift D'Après Des Travaux Récens (i.e. Forster, Craik, Leslie Stephen), in *Revue Des Deux Mondes* LVᵉ Année Troisième Période Tome Soixante- Neuvième. Paris 1885. Pp. 321–56.

1446. L. S. [i.e. Leslie Stephen]: Swift, in the *Dictionary Of National Biography*. London, 1885. Pp. 204–27 in Vol. LV.
Re-issue: 1908.
India Paper issue: 1917.

1447. Jonathan Swift Son Action Politique En Irlande Par Jacques Flach &c. Paris, L. Larose et Forcel, 1886. — Large 8vo; 1–15 + bl. — The verso of title says: Extrait de la Revue de la Société des Etudes historiques (Mai–Juin 1886).

1448. Jonathan Swift und G. Ch. Lichtenberg. Zwei Satiriker des achtzehnten Jahrhunderts. Von Richard M. Meyer. &c. Berlin. Wilhelm Hertz, 1886. — 8vo; I–X, 1–84.

1449. Lord Carteret A Political Biography 1690–1763 By Archibald Ballantyne. London, Richard Bentley & Son, 1887. — 8vo; I–XII, 2 pp., 1–428. — Swift often mentioned in it.

1451. The Life Of Richard Steele By George A. Aitken. London, Wm. Isbister Limited, 1889. — 2 vols., 8vo. — Swift frequently mentioned in them.

1452. The Lives Of Notable People. Biographical Library Of F. Pavlenkov. D. Swift. His Life and Literary Activity. A Biographical Sketch by V. I. Yakovenko. &c. Petersburg, 1891. — Sm. 8vo; frontisp. portrait of Swift, 1–109, 3 pp. (advs.) [in Russian].

1453. Swift The Mystery Of His Life And Love By James Hay &c. London: Chapman And Hall, Limited, 1891. — 8vo; I–XVI, 1–361 + bl.

1642. Stanley Lane-Poole: Swift and Stella, in *Notes and Queries*, 8th Series, II (1892), Pp. 302–3.

1455. Eighteenth Century Vignettes By Austin Dobson &c. London, Chatto & Windus, 1892. — Second Series, 1894. — Third Series, 1896. — 3 vols., 8vo. [There is also a Large Paper edition (200 copies; with a special series of illustrations).] — The Second Series (pp. 1–21) contains an essay, entitled: The Journal To Stella.
Further editions: 1907, 1923; also editions in America.

1457. En Engelsk Forfattergruppe Litteraturhistorisk Skildring Fra Det Attende Aarhundreds Første Halvdel Af Adolf Hansen. København, Jakob H. Mansas &c., 1892. — 8vo; 8 pp., 1–285 + bl., 2 pp. — Swift discussed in it.

1460. Voltaire's Visit To England 1726–9 By Archibald Ballantyne. London, Smith, Elder, & Co., 1893. — 8vo; 8 pp., 1–338, 6 pp. (advs.). — Contains references to Swift.

1461. P. Max Simon-Swift Etude Psychologique Et Littéraire &c. Paris, J.-B. Baillière Et Fils, 1893. — 16mo; 1–235 + bl. — Swift is pp. 1–160.

1462. Dean Swift And His Writings By Gerald P. Moriarty, &c. London, Seeley And Co. Limited, 1893. — 8vo; I–VIII, 1–341 + bl., 2 pp. (advs.). Frontisp. portrait of Swift, and eight more plates. — There is also a Large Paper issue (150 copies, numbered).
Second edition: 1901.

1463. A Catalogue Of The Paintings, Manuscripts, Autograph Letters, Pamphlets, Etc. Bequeathed By John Forster, Esq., LL.D. With Indexes. London: Eyre And Spottiswoode, 1893. — Large 8vo; 6 pp., 1–261 + bl. — Records two pictures, several manuscripts, and a few books by or on Swift.

1464. The Age Of Pope By John Dennis &c. London, George Bell And Sons, 1894. — 12mo; 8 pp., 1–258. — Swift is pp. 151–75. [Series "Handbooks Of English Literature. Edited By Professor Hales".]
Further editions: 1896, 1899, 1901, 1906, 1908, 1909, 1918, &c.

1465. Essays About Men, Women, And Books. By Augustine Birrell, &c. London: Elliot Stock, 1894. — 12mo; 8 pp., 1–233 + bl. — 'Dean Swift' is pp. 1–15. — These is also a Large Paper issue.
Further editions: 1899 (2 vols.), 1902.

1466. Historical Sketches Of The Reign Of Queen Anne By Mrs. Oliphant. London, Macmillan And Co. &c., 1894. — 8vo; 8 pp., 1–381 + bl. Frontisp. and sixteen illustrations. — Contains a chapter on 'The Dean' (pp. 228–85).

1643. Alexander von Wolfersdorff Leslie: Was Swift Married to Stella?, in *Anglia*, Sept. 1895, pp. 1–55.

For later critical studies, see Louis A. Landa and James E. Tobin, *Jonathan Swift ; A list of critical studies published from 1895 to 1945* (New York, 1945).

INDEX OF TITLES *

* All entries without indication of an author denote books written by or associated with
Jonathan Swift.